WordPerfect®
Office 2000 Bible

WordPerfect®
Office 2000 Bible

Stephen E. Harris with Erwin Zijleman

IDG BOOKS WORLDWIDE

IDG Books Worldwide, Inc.
An International Data Group Company

Foster City, CA ✦ Chicago, IL ✦ Indianapolis, IN ✦ New York, NY

WordPerfect® Office 2000 Bible

Published by
IDG Books Worldwide, Inc.
An International Data Group Company
919 E. Hillsdale Blvd., Suite 400
Foster City, CA 94404
www.idgbooks.com (IDG Books Worldwide Web site)

ISBN: 0-7645-3241-3

Printed in the United States of America

10 9 8 7 6 5 4 3 2 1

1B/RS/QX/ZZ/FC

Distributed in the United States by IDG Books Worldwide, Inc.

Distributed by CDG Books Canada Inc. for Canada; by Transworld Publishers Limited in the United Kingdom; by IDG Norge Books for Norway; by IDG Sweden Books for Sweden; by IDGBA Ltd. for Australia; by IDG Books Australia Publishing Corporation Pty. Ltd for Australia and New Zealand; by TransQuest Publishers Pte Ltd. for Singapore, Malaysia, Thailand, Indonesia, and Hong Kong; by Gotop Information Inc. for Taiwan; by ICG Muse, Inc. for Japan; by Norma Comunicaciones S.A. for Colombia; by Intersoft for South Africa; by Eyrolles for France; by International Thomson Publishing for Germany, Austria and Switzerland; by Distribuidora Cuspide for Argentina; by Livraria Cultura for Brazil; by Ediciones ZETA S.C.R. Ltda. for Peru; by WS Computer Publishing Corporation, Inc., for the Philippines; by Contemporanea de Ediciones for Venezuela; by Express Computer Distributors for the Caribbean and West Indies; by Micronesia Media Distributor, Inc. for Micronesia; by Grupo Editorial Norma S.A. for Guatemala; by Chips Computadoras S.A. de C.V. for Mexico; by Editorial Norma de Panama S.A. for Panama; by American Bookshops for Finland. Authorized Sales Agent: Anthony Rudkin Associates for the Middle East and North Africa.

For general information on IDG Books Worldwide's books in the U.S., please call our Consumer Customer Service department at 800-762-2974. For reseller information, including discounts and premium sales, please call our Reseller Customer Service department at 800-434-3422.

For information on where to purchase IDG Books Worldwide's books outside the U.S., please contact our International Sales department at 317-596-5530 or fax 317-596-5692.

For consumer information on foreign language translations, please contact our Customer Service department at 800-434-3422, fax 317-596-5692, or e-mail rights@idgbooks.com.

For information on licensing foreign or domestic rights, please phone +1-650-655-3109.

For sales inquiries and special prices for bulk quantities, please contact our Sales department at 650-655-3200 or write to the address above.

For information on using IDG Books Worldwide's books in the classroom or for ordering examination copies, please contact our Educational Sales department at 800-434-2086 or fax 317-596-5499.

For press review copies, author interviews, or other publicity information, please contact our Public Relations department at 650-655-3000 or fax 650-655-3299.

For authorization to photocopy items for corporate, personal, or educational use, please contact Copyright Clearance Center, 222 Rosewood Drive, Danvers, MA 01923, or fax 978-750-4470.

Library of Congress Cataloging-in-Publication Data
Harris, Stephen E., [DATE]
    WordPerfect Office 2000 bible / Stephen E. Harris with Erwin Zijleman.
        p.   cm.
    Includes index.
    ISBN 0-7645-3241-3 (alk. paper)
    1. WordPerfect Office 2000.   2. Business--Computer programs.
    I. Zijleman, Erwin, [DATE]. II. Title.
    HF5548.4.W65H37   1999
    650'.0285'5369--dc21   99-29837
                                                                CIP

ABOUT IDG BOOKS WORLDWIDE

Welcome to the world of IDG Books Worldwide.

IDG Books Worldwide, Inc., is a subsidiary of International Data Group, the world's largest publisher of computer-related information and the leading global provider of information services on information technology. IDG was founded more than 30 years ago by Patrick J. McGovern and now employs more than 9,000 people worldwide. IDG publishes more than 290 computer publications in over 75 countries. More than 90 million people read one or more IDG publications each month.

Launched in 1990, IDG Books Worldwide is today the #1 publisher of best-selling computer books in the United States. We are proud to have received eight awards from the Computer Press Association in recognition of editorial excellence and three from Computer Currents' First Annual Readers' Choice Awards. Our best-selling ...For Dummies® series has more than 50 million copies in print with translations in 31 languages. IDG Books Worldwide, through a joint venture with IDG's Hi-Tech Beijing, became the first U.S. publisher to publish a computer book in the People's Republic of China. In record time, IDG Books Worldwide has become the first choice for millions of readers around the world who want to learn how to better manage their businesses.

Our mission is simple: Every one of our books is designed to bring extra value and skill-building instructions to the reader. Our books are written by experts who understand and care about our readers. The knowledge base of our editorial staff comes from years of experience in publishing, education, and journalism — experience we use to produce books to carry us into the new millennium. In short, we care about books, so we attract the best people. We devote special attention to details such as audience, interior design, use of icons, and illustrations. And because we use an efficient process of authoring, editing, and desktop publishing our books electronically, we can spend more time ensuring superior content and less time on the technicalities of making books.

You can count on our commitment to deliver high-quality books at competitive prices on topics you want to read about. At IDG Books Worldwide, we continue in the IDG tradition of delivering quality for more than 30 years. You'll find no better book on a subject than one from IDG Books Worldwide.

John Kilcullen
Chairman and CEO
IDG Books Worldwide, Inc.

Steven Berkowitz
President and Publisher
IDG Books Worldwide, Inc.

VIII
WINNER

Eighth Annual Computer Press Awards ≥1992

IX
WINNER

Ninth Annual Computer Press Awards ≥1993

X
WINNER

Tenth Annual Computer Press Awards ≥1994

XI
WINNER

Eleventh Annual Computer Press Awards ≥1995

Credits

Acquisitions Editor
Andy Cummings

Development Editors
Valerie Perry
Chip Wescott
Kathy Duggan
Colleen Dowling
Kenyon Brown

Technical Editor
Richard Kahane

Copy Editors
Zoe Brymer
Luann Rouff
Michael D. Welch

Production
IDG Books Worldwide Production

Proofreading and Indexing
York Production Services

Cover Design
Murder By Design

About the Authors

Stephen E. Harris is the founder and president of QwkScreen, a software development and consulting firm dedicated to making the computer screen a friendlier place. Author of the best-selling *WordPerfect 7* and *Corel WordPerfect Suite 8 Bible*, Steve's a proud member of the Corel Beta Squad. He lives in the woods of western Massachusetts with his wife Githa, three cats (Tiger, Becky, and Chester), bears, deer, turkeys, and other assorted wildlife. You'll find Steve, plus more WordPerfect solutions and links, at http://www.qwkscreen.com.

Erwin Zijleman started out as a development sociologist, specializing in urban sociology and education in third-world countries, particularly Southeast Asia. He now works as a software scientist, specializing in PC office applications. Erwin has served as a beta tester for Microsoft, Borland, and WP Corporation products. He now tests almost exclusively for Corel. He lives near Amsterdam, in the historic center of Leiden, with his cat, Bagu.

About the Technical Editor

After a government career, during which he lived and worked everywhere from West Africa to Western Europe, **Richard A. (Dick) Kahane** focused his interests on personal computers. Today, Richard is a sysop on CompuServe's TAPCIS Forum, a computer-applications instructor, and a technical editor. He has taught DOS, Windows, Word for Windows, Quattro Pro, and all versions of WordPerfect since 5.0, and he has edited several books on WordPerfect for a variety of major publishers. A graduate of Princeton University, he is the father of two daughters and lives in Northern Virginia.

To Githa!

Foreword

I'm delighted to see that Steve Harris, with expert assistance from Erwin Zijleman, has updated his best-selling WordPerfect guidance to the latest release of our award-winning office solutions. No matter what you want to do — write a letter, crunch numbers, create a chart, set up a schedule, design a corporate database, or publish a slide show on the Web — this book provides 100 percent of what you need to get the job done.

WordPerfect Office 2000 delivers an amazing array of features. Click and Type with the Shadow Cursor. QuickFind with a single click. Check spelling and grammar on the fly. Automate with macros. Format tables in a flash. Create hyperlinks automatically. WordPerfect Office 2000 unleashes your full productivity potential at home, at school, and in the office.

Whether you're new to WordPerfect Office or a seasoned veteran, the *WordPerfect Office 2000 Bible* is an easy-to-use, accessible guide. You'll find extensive coverage of many powerful new features, including RealTime Preview, Office-wide speech support, and the Trellix Web publishing facilities.

Be sure to check out the "Hands On" and "Instant Expert" chapters, that get you up and running in no time at all. Steve and Erwin have packed this book with great tips, clear, step by step instructions, and plenty of illustrations.

Welcome to WordPerfect Office 2000, and welcome to the *WordPerfect Office 2000 Bible* — I highly recommend them both!

Mike Cowpland
President and C.E.O.
Corel Corporation

Preface

Here we are with a suite to close out one millennium and usher in a new, aptly dubbed WordPerfect Office 2000. You can turn to Chapter 1 for "A Quick Look" at everything that's new.

Let's limit the speechifying to a single turgid heading — "A Bible for the New Millennium" — and get straight to business.

A Bible for the New Millennium

There, the heading says it all! One thing's for sure; you're likely to be as busy in the new millennium as you were in the old, so here's how this Bible can help:

+ It covers shared features apart from the individual applications. This not only makes the precise topic easier to find, it also means that you won't be reading the same instructions two or three times!

+ It aims for clear, brief descriptions and gets right into the step by step instructions. (It isn't a novel!)

+ There is no repetition of the obvious, such as every detail each time you drag a mouse or exit a dialog box. (Do you need instructions on tying laces every time you put on shoes?)

+ Exclusive in-line tips help pack more information into every page.

+ Bulleted summaries at the beginning of each chapter, and a concise list of cross-references at the end help you make the most of this book.

If writing computer books isn't an art, we'd at least like to think it's akin to a craft or a science. We've tried to give you about three book's worth of information in one, in an easy-to-use, accessible format.

What's in This Book?

This book provides detailed coverage of all the shared tools, plus the core applications in both the standard and professional suites. Readers of my *Corel WordPerfect Suite 8 Bible* will be pleased to find additional coverage of:

✦ Dragon NaturallySpeaking

✦ Trellix Web publishing

✦ Adding document references

✦ Assembling multipart documents

✦ Doing calculations in WordPerfect

With an office suite this massive, I naturally have to draw the line with some of the advanced features and bonus programs. There simply isn't room to adequately cover such features as publishing to SGML, for instance, or how to build custom solutions with Microsoft Visual Basic for Applications. Likewise, the addition of Dragon and Trellix had to take precedence over the Corel Print Office and Corel Web Server found in some versions of WordPerfect Office 2000.

Here's some of what you will find in this book:

Part I, "Getting Started," gets you up and running, typing and editing from day one. Learn how to copy and move information, proofread on-the-fly, and manage your screen. Discover how easy it is to talk to your computer, and where to go when you're in need of help.

Part II, "Basic Training," shows you how to undo mistakes and safeguard your work. Learn how to manage your files and use the Corel Versions archiving utility. Get creative with clip art and fonts, and learn how to combine information from several sources. Learn how to use the CorelCENTRAL facilities to write memos and manage your calendar, address books, and card files.

Part III, "CorelCENTRAL and the Internet," covers the general printing and faxing facilities, and shows you how to create Web pages in WordPerfect, and publish to PDF or XML. It covers the fabulous new Trellix facilities — a whole new way to put *information* out to the Internet or your intranet.

Part IV, "Writing with WordPerfect," shows you how to become an instant expert by using the many built-in features that tackle complex tasks with ease. Offering complete coverage of the world's most fabulous word processor, including its large document handling facilities.

Part V, "Crunching Numbers with Quattro Pro," has you jump right in, creating a spreadsheet and working with the automated tools. Learn how to enter formulas, then edit, format, and print your work. Discover how to use the latest analysis and mapping features, and find out how to automate your work.

Part VI, "Showing Your Stuff with Presentations," is, well, fun! Create your own slide show with all kinds of multimedia effects: backgrounds, sounds, fades, bouncing bullets, and more. Learn how to print handouts, and create shows that run anywhere, even on the Internet!

Part VII, "Managing Information with Paradox," goes beyond the technical details in using this powerful information-management tool, including the latest usability enhancements. This section gives you the step-by-step guidance you need to successfully plan, design, build, and administer a complex database project.

Part VIII, "Suite Techniques," gives you inside tips on using writing tools and sorting information. Learn advanced graphic techniques, and learn how to create your own art. Discover how to create effective charts and graphs, and automate your applications with the PerfectScript macro facility.

The appendixes show you how to set up WordPerfect Office, and provide quick references to WordPerfect's settings and Dragon speech commands.

Conventions Used in This Book

This book uses a few conventions to distinguish various elements of the instructions and display:

✦ Key1+Key2 (as in Ctrl+V) means that you press and hold the first key, press the second key, then release both keys.

✦ Command 1 ⇨ Command 2 . . . (as with Tools ⇨ QuickCorrect ⇨ SmartQuotes) means to click the items in succession.

✦ Text you type or speak(!) appears in **bold**.

✦ New terms appear in *italic*.

A mouse or other pointing device is a necessity for most Windows programs. These standard mouse actions are used throughout the book:

Action	*What You Do*
Point	Move the mouse to place the pointer on a screen item.
Click	Press and release the left mouse button once.
Double-click	Quickly press and release the left mouse button twice.
Right-click	Press and release the right mouse button. A shortcut menu (QuickMenu) of context-sensitive choices appears.
Drag	Point to what you want to drag, press and hold the left mouse button, move the mouse, then release the button. You can also drag across text to select it.

A "click" becomes a "tap" if you are using a pen device; "left" becomes "right," and vice versa, if you're using the left-handed mouse setup.

Icons Used in This Book

The *WordPerfect Office 2000 Bible* features special text sidebars indicated by various icons:

Marks a shortcut or neat idea.

Provides extra information, such as what to do in special situations.

Highlights new features in the core applications.

Warns you when you can lose data, mess up your document, or damage your setup if you aren't careful. It might also tell you what to do if things get messed up.

For the Latest Updates . . .

Change is constant in this business, so there's sure to be more happening after we go to press. For the latest on updates, fixes, and upgrades, check out my Web site at qwkscreen.com. (You can also get there through the IDG Book Worldwide Web site at idgbooks.com.) You'll find a lot of tips and some bonus material. I also maintain links to discussion groups, fonts, clip art, and many other resources.

Any comments, suggestions, criticisms, corrections, or requests? Please send them through IDG Books Worldwide, or e-mail me at steveh@qwkscreen.com—thanks. I hope you find this book helpful!

Acknowledgments

While any shortcomings are my own, this massive work is necessarily a team product involving publishers, editors, designers, proofreaders, indexers, and typesetters, as well as the people in the promotion and sales departments. This is an exciting business, but it's also a stressful and competitive one. Thankfully, the dedicated professionals I deal with at IDG Books Worldwide temper the demands of deadlines with nurturing and care for us writers. But there are many of you I never meet or hear from, especially since you do your job so well! Since it's impossible to single out each of you, please allow me to extend my heartfelt thanks to everyone in this hardworking group.

Special thanks to Andy Cummings, captain of the ship, for once again steering my book through the turbulent seas of publishing.

To Erwin Zijleman, what can I say? I couldn't have done this massive project without you!

To Dan Alder of Corel Corporation, and Brian Underdahl, thanks for your contributions to the Paradox chapters.

And many, many thanks to my development editors, Valerie Perry, Chip Wescott, Kathy Duggan, Colleen Dowling, and Kenyon Brown. You somehow put the puzzle together, even as the pieces were changing shape!

This project owes much of its success to the generous and constant support from many dedicated folks at Corel. Many thanks in particular to Michelle Murphy-Croteau for her cheerful and generous assistance. I would certainly be remiss if I didn't acknowledge the wonderful work done by the old development team in Orem, Utah, as well as the new team in Ottawa who assumed this herculean task!

As always, I must thank my attorney/agent Joel L. Hecker, Esq., for his wise counsel and support. Finally, a very special acknowledgment to Githa, my wife, who had the pleasure of reading drafts of new chapters and enduring my crazy schedule. Time for a vacation!

Steve Harris

Contents at a Glance

Contents

Part III: CorelCENTRAL and the Internet   227

Chapter 12: Managing Addresses, Card Files, and Memos 229

Part IV: Writing with WordPerfect   333

Chapter 16: Mastering the WordPerfect Interface 335

Chapter 23: Organizing with Bullets and Outlines 495

Chapter 25: Assembling Multipart Documents 555

Chapter 26: Doing Calculations in WordPerfect...................................567

Part VI: Showing Your Stuff with Presentations   871

Chapter 39: A Hands-On Slide Show 873

Part VII: Managing Information with Paradox   925

Getting Started

A Quick Look

In This Chapter

The core applications

What bonus utilities
you can find

What's new in
WordPerfect
Office 2000

In addition to being a huge bargain, WordPerfect Office 2000 itself is downright huge. This chapter provides an overview of what you'll find, highlighting the latest features.

Talking 2000!

As we careen toward the next millennium, are you ready to talk to your computer? If so, plug in your headphones and open up WordPerfect Office 2000!

Not to worry — you don't have to unplug your keyboard. In fact, WordPerfect Office 2000 meets accessibility standards, which includes support of high-contrast mode and keystrokes to all features.

Veteran users will be pleased with the continued file compatibility with earlier releases, as well as with improved handling of the Microsoft Office formats. You'll also be in for a number of happy surprises, such as Trellix Web publishing, RealTime Preview, Install-As-You-Go, document Navigation Buttons, and a much improved CorelCENTRAL.

What's in WordPerfect Office 2000?

The applications in WordPerfect Office 2000 share a common set of core utilities for such things as handling files, drawing, charting, grammar-checking, managing contacts, and editing toolbars. The applications themselves cover an enormous range of home and business office needs.

Table 1-1 describes the core applications you'll find in the various editions of WordPerfect Office 2000.

Table 1-1
Core Applications in WordPerfect Office 2000

Application	Description	Academic	Standard	Standard with Dragon	Professional and Legal
WordPerfect 9	Word processing and desktop desktop publishing	√	√	√	√
Quattro Pro 9	Spreadsheets and number-crunching	√	√	√	√
Presentations 9	Charts and slide shows	√	√	√	√
CorelCENTRAL 9	Calendar, scheduling, Address Book, card files	√	√	√	√
Paradox 9	Database creation and management				√

Note Users of WordPerfect Suite 8 will notice that Netscape Communicator is no longer included. You can now download Communicator for free from Netscape's Netcenter (http://home.netscape.com); and CorelCENTRAL is designed to integrate with any standard e-mail facility, including Microsoft's Outlook or Outlook Express.

Table 1-2 describes the bonus applications, tools, utilities, and other goodies you'll find in various editions of WordPerfect Office 2000.

Table 1-2
Bonus Applications and Utilities in WordPerfect Office 2000

Application	Description	Academic	Standard	Standard with Dragon	Professional and Legal
Trellix 2.1	User-friendly Web publishing		√	√	√
Dragon NaturallySpeaking 3.0	Speech entry of text and data		√	√	√
NetPerfect	Corporate Web publishing through a central server				√
Corel Print Office	Design layout and image editing			√	√

Application	Description	Academic	Standard	Standard with Dragon	Professional and Legal
PerfectScript	Automate applications with macros	√	√	√	√
Visual Basic for Applications (VBA)	Build cross-product business solutions		√	√	√
Adobe Acrobat Reader	View portable Acrobat docs	√	√	√	√
Bitstream Font Navigator 3.0.1	Font installer and manager	√	√	√	√
Reference Center	Viewable program guides	√	√	√	√
Desktop Application Director (DAD)	Manage applications from the Windows taskbar	√	√	√	√
SDK	Tools for software developers	√	√	√	√
SGML	Create standardized SGML docs	√	√	√	√
Paradox Web Form Designer	Create platform-independent Web forms				√
Application Management Tools	Edit Registry settings and manage network installations	√	√	√	√
Scrapbook	More than 12,000 clip art images and symbols	√	√	√	√
Fonts	More than 1,000 TrueType and Type 1 fonts	√	√	√	√
Photos	More than 200 photos	√	√	√	√

That covers most of it! You'll find many details throughout this book. For installation options and instructions, see Appendix A, "Setting Up WordPerfect Office 2000."

So What Else Is New?

WordPerfect Office 2000 looks familiar, but it's also full of surprises! Speech, of course is a spectacular addition, but you'll encounter a lot of other fun features and subtle improvements.

Office-wide improvements

Both corporate and individual users will appreciate a number of office-wide enhancements (see Table 1-3) that, while individually subtle, add up to a major boost in performance and compatibility:

Table 1-3 Office-Wide Enhancements	
Feature	**Description**
Office Integration	Better integration throughout the WordPerfect Office, including customization, setup, and Bitmap editing.
Third-Party Integration	Enhanced ODMA support lets WordPerfect Office 2000 work better with Document Management Systems such as PC DOCS, Imanage, Worldox, GroupWise, and SoftSolutions. Corel also works closely with Systemanalyse and Programmentwicklung (SAP), the world's largest supplier of business application software, and PeopleSoft, Inc., the market leader in human resources software, to ensure a symbiotic harmony with corporate applications.
Performance	Speedier program engine and user interface.
Compatibility	Import and export to Microsoft Office formats, plus compatible toolbars and setup options. MS Office 97 conversion filters alert the user to differences.
Accessibility	Support of High-Contrast mode, keystroke access to all features, and standard interface controls for use with third-party accessibility tools.
Install-As-You-Go	Saves disk space by not installing certain features until you use them.

Product Enhancements

In addition to the long list of features covered in Table 1-4, you'll also find lots of little surprises throughout WordPerfect Office 2000. In WordPerfect, for example, you'll find that the current page number appears as you drag the box on the vertical scroll bar; you can play with underline line styles and colors; and a scroll bar appears in the style listing when there are too many styles to display. Look for the New Feature icons throughout this book.

Feature	WordPerfect	Quattro Pro	Presentations	CorelCENTRAL	Paradox	Description	Chapter
Publish to PDF	√		√			Publish documents and slide shows to PDF (Portable Document Format), so they can be viewed by anyone who has the free Adobe Acrobat reader.	14
Active X Controls	√	√			√	Insert radio buttons, push buttons, entry fields, and other controls in an online form or document.	14
Enhanced Shapes	√	√	√			Over 100 new shapes for flow-charting, callouts, arrows, stars, and banners.	9
Font Embedding	√					TrueDoc font embedding lets others view the fonts in your documents, even if they're not installed on their system.	8
Printing	√		√	√		Enhanced creation of banners, posters, booklets, and handouts.	13
RealTime Preview	√	√	√			Preview toolbar formatting selections.	3
XML/SGML delivers rich, structured Web data in a standard, consistent way.	√	√				XML (eXtensible Markup Language)	14
Document Navigation	√					Retrace insertion point moves and autoscroll with any mouse.	16
New Document Compare	√					Enhanced document compare facility, with an easy-to-use Author Review mode.	18
Block Make It Fit	√					Size a selected portion of a document to the number of pages you specify.	17
Skewed Table Headers	√					Skew the first row or column of a table to save space and give the table a 3-D look.	22

Table 1-4
Product Enhancements

Continued

Table 1-4 (continued)

Feature	WordPerfect	Quattro Pro	Presentations	CorelCENTRAL	Paradox	Description	Chapter
New Workgroup Features		√				Lets multiple users work on a notebook simultaneously.	33
Formula Markers		√				Quickly find formula cells.	31
New Patterns and Fills		√				More pattern and fill selections, many compatible with MS Excel	34
Page Break Preview		√				Alternative notebook view based on page breaks.	33
Improved Text Parsing		√				QuickColumns enhancements for importing delimited text files.	22
Enhanced Paste Special		√				Select what to want to copy and other options when copying spreadsheet selections.	33
Achive Cross Tabs Tabs		√				Create cross-tabs reports that can be pivoted on demand.	35
Bigger notebooks/ Smaller files		√				Store up to a million rows and 18,000 columns or sheets in compressed format.	30
Edit Everywhere			√			Edit slides in the Editor, Sorter, or Outliner.	39
Color Schemes			√			Coordinated color schemes for your charts, shapes, and lists. Switch schemes to change the look of your entire presentation.	41
Layouts			√			Select from 27 new layouts for your show.	41
Address Book				√		New Address Book database sports a Tree view that makes it easy to manage multiple address listings.	12
Application Bar				√		Auto-hide bar with quick, convenient access to events, tasks, address books, calendars, card files and memos.	11

Feature	WordPerfect	Quattro Pro	Presentations	CorelCENTRAL	Paradox	Description	Chapter
Events & To Dos				√		Embed multiple To Do's within an Event, such as things you must do in preparation for a meeting.	11
Timers				√		Set timers with alarms, independent of events.	11
Vertical Market Templates					√	Database templates tailored to particular markets and industries.	
WordPerfect/ RTF Output					√	Publish Paradox reports to Word-Perfect or to the RTF file format for viewing in WordPerfect, Quattro Pro, and other applications.	
New Database Modeler					√	New, visual way to create and link tables includes drag-and-drop to make it easier than ever to build a database application.	
BDE 4.5					√	Enhanced Borland Database Engine	
Enhanced Copy/Paste					√	Copy and paste from Paradox tables to Quattro Pro.	
JPEG Support					√	Store files in JPEG format in Paradox tables.	
New Experts					√	Experts for creating queries and finding duplicates.	
Spell Checking					√	Spell-check data in tables and forms	

For More Information . . .

On	See
Installing WordPerfect Office 2000	Appendix A
Printing and sending information	Chapter 13
Mastering the WordPerfect interface	Chapter 16

✦   ✦   ✦

Essential Typing and Editing

The best way to get to know WordPerfect Office 2000 is to start using it! In this chapter, you'll get comfortable working with text in WordPerfect as you learn how to perform a multitude of tasks.

For all the fancy charts, graphics, spreadsheets, and shows you can create with WordPerfect Office 2000, writing is still the foundation of communication. Many of the WordPerfect text techniques you'll learn here can also be used when you create a spreadsheet or slide show.

A Quick Tour of WordPerfect's Screen

So, without further ado, start WordPerfect and take a look at the writing screen:

1. Start Windows.

2. Click the WordPerfect icon on the Windows Taskbar (or click Start ➪ Programs ➪ WordPerfect Office 2000 ➪ WordPerfect 9).

This brings you to the WordPerfect document window. Unless you've changed WordPerfect's default settings, your screen should look like the one shown in Figure 2-1.

Chapter 3, "Looking at a Suite Face," goes into the screen particulars. For now, the best way to learn WordPerfect is to jump right in and start typing. Mind you, it's not like learning to drive a car. You're not about to careen off the monitor in a fiery crash, into the depths of your computer's hard disk or central processing unit.

Menubar Toolbar   Property bar   Margin guideline   Scroll bar

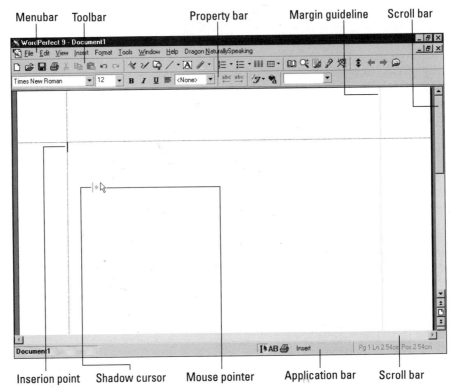

Inserion point   Shadow cursor   Mouse pointer   Application bar   Scroll bar

Figure 2-1: WordPerfect's document window.

 Tip Switching from WordPerfect for DOS? If so, you can use your familiar DOS keystrokes. Click Tools ➪ Settings ➪ Customize ➪ Keyboards, and then click the WPDOS 6.1 Keyboard and click Select ➪ Close. (Wherever WordPerfect's DOS-compatible keystrokes differ from the Windows ones, this book shows them in parentheses.)

Writing a Letter

Now the fun begins. Yes, WordPerfect does so much for you, typing can actually be fun (especially compared to a manual typewriter or a basic text editor).

On the blank document screen, create your letter:

1. Type **Dear George**, and then press Enter to end the line.

2. Press Enter again to skip a line, and then type **WordPerfect is a delite . . .** (including the wrong spellings) and the remainder of the paragraph, as shown in Figure 2-2.

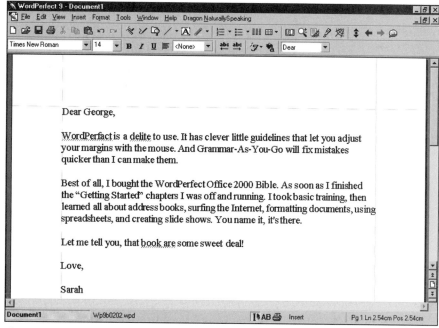

Figure 2-2: Writing a letter.

3. Press Enter two more times, and then type two paragraphs of praise for the *WordPerfect Bible* (just kidding), followed by a closing.

As you type, note how text automatically *wraps* to the next line. Press Enter only when you want to end a paragraph or force the beginning of a new line. Notice, too, that your misspelled words are underlined with hatched red lines. (Questionable grammar may be underlined in blue, as you'll see shortly.)

Correcting Mistakes

The advantages of a word processor quickly become apparent when it comes to correcting mistakes.

Fixing typos

To erase the character you just typed (the one to the left of the insertion point), press Backspace. Pressing the Delete key erases the character to the right of the insertion point.

If you followed directions, you typed "WordPerfact" instead of "WordPerfect" in the second line of the letter. Click the mouse or use the arrow keys to position the insertion point in front of the "a." Press Delete; then type **e**. Note how the red crosshatching disappears, indicating that the spelling is now correct.

Backing out changes with Undo

Use *Undo* when you want to reverse your last editing action. What's an editing action? It can be the words you just typed or the characters you deleted. Almost anything that changes the format of your document counts, such as when you change the line spacing, put a phrase in italics, set tabs, center a line, or move a margin guideline. Undo puts you back to where you were before. (Scrolling or saving your document can't be undone, as no editing has taken place.)

To reverse editing actions by using Undo:

1. Click the undo button on the toolbar or press Ctrl+Z. You can also click Edit ➪ Undo.

2. Repeat Undo to backtrack your editing session, one action at a time, for as many Undos as needed in your document.

WordPerfect allows up to 300 levels of Undo (see Chapter 6, "Working Without Worries"). Presentations allows 10, and Quattro Pro allows 200.

Redoing Undo

To reverse your Undos with *Redo*, click the Redo icon on the toolbar. (You can also click Edit ➪ Redo, or press Ctrl+Shift+Z on a Windows keyboard, or Ctrl+Shift+R on a DOS keyboard.) When there are no more Redos, the Redo arrow on the toolbar appears dim.

Proofreading-As-You-Go

WordPerfect comes with a powerful set of instant proofreading tools, including Grammar-As-You-Go, and automatic typo correction. You can turn any automatic feature on or off from the Tools menu.

Spell-As-You-Go

When you typed "WordPerfect," you probably noticed that its red underlining immediately appeared. That's Spell-As-You-Go in action, a great WordPerfect feature (not in Presentations or Quattro Pro) that highlights possible mistakes as you type them. You can right-click a marked word (such as "delite"), and then click one of the suggested replacements. When there are more than six suggestions, you can point to More, and pick from the remainder of the list (see Figure 2-3).

Prompt-As-You-Go

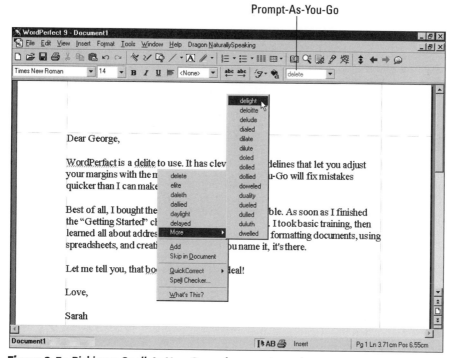

Figure 2-3: Picking a Spell-As-You-Go replacement word.

The Spell-As-You-Go QuickMenu, which appears when you right-click a misspelled word, gives you other options:

✦ *Add* places the word in the user word list, so it won't be flagged as an error again. Your "skip words" can include the names of friends and places, or technical terms not in the WordPerfect Office word list.

✦ *Skip in Document* has the same effect as Add, but only for this document.

✦ *QuickCorrect* puts the word, with its replacement, in your user word list, to correct future errors instantly (see "QuickCorrect" later in this section).

✦ *Spell Checker* takes you to the Spell Checker, where more options are available.

If you want to turn off Spell-As-You-Go, click Tools ⇨ Proofread ⇨ Off.

Cross-Reference   For details on the Spell Checker and word lists, see Chapter 52, "Writers' Lib."

Prompt-As-You-Go and the Instant Thesaurus

You can also correct the word or phrase at the insertion point by selecting from the Prompt-As-You-Go replacements on the property bar. Possible spelling corrections appear in red. Blue text is used for possible grammar fixes. When there's no problem, and the word appears in black, Prompt-As-You-Go turns into an Instant Thesaurus. Simply click a replacement synonym from the list (see Figure 2-4).

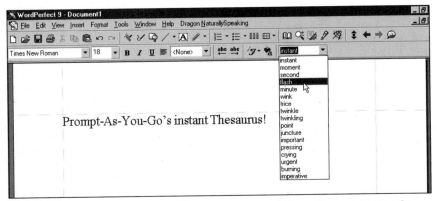

Figure 2-4: When there's no spelling or grammar problem, Prompt-As-You-Go turns into an Instant Thesaurus.

Prompt-As-You-Go checks your grammar and spelling, even when Grammar-As-You-Go and Spell-As-You-Go are off. To turn off Prompt-As-You-Go, click Tools ➪ Proofread ➪ Prompt-As-You-Go, and uncheck Prompt-As-You-Go.

Tip   Turning off this feature may speed up your display.

Automatic typo correction

WordPerfect can *automatically* correct your misspelled or mistyped word, so long as there is only one close replacement. For example, if you type "informtion" leaving out the "a," the program can be pretty certain of what you meant. Likewise, when you transpose two characters, as with "transpsoe," the program can usually correct your mistake.

This automatic correction is off by default, so it won't take you by surprise. To turn it on, click Tools ➪ QuickCorrect, and check "Correct other mis-typed words, when possible."

QuickCorrect

QuickCorrect is the original form of instant correction. There's no guesswork, because the word you type, with its replacement, must be in your user word list.

Try typing **adn**, **alot**, or **july**, and, of course, **potatoe**, to see your mistakes corrected before your eyes. Note that the correction does not appear until you type a space, or tab (or press Enter), indicating that you have completed the word.

If nothing happens when you type these words, make sure that QuickCorrect is turned on. To do so, click Tools ➪ QuickCorrect, and then click "Replace words as you type." Remove the check to turn QuickCorrect off.

QuickCorrect comes with a starting list of replacement words. The real beauty of the feature is that you can add your own common personal mistakes to the list as you make them, together with the correct spelling, so the next time around they'll be instantly corrected. QuickCorrect is also great for shorthand abbreviations, and it can liberate you from the Shift and apostrophe (') keys. See Chapter 52, "Writers' Lib," for details.

Grammar-As-You-Go

Grammar-As-You-Go is another great proofreading tool (WordPerfect only). To turn it on, click Tools ➪ Proofread ➪ Grammar-As-You-Go. (Spell-As-You-Go will be on as well.)

Now when you type **That book are some suite deal!**, "book are" should be under-lined in blue. A right-click shows that there's a problem with subject-verb agreement. You can select either "books are" or "book is" to correct the situation.

Tip   You can also select replacements from the Prompt-As-You-Go list on the prop-erty bar.

No grammar checker is perfect, however, so treat the flags as *possible* errors. Don't feel that you have to get rid of every underline!

More instant correction options

Click Tools ➪ QuickCorrect to take a look at all the instant correction options under the various tabs:

   ✦ *QuickCorrect* (see Figure 2-5) enables you to manually add misspellings or abbreviations, along with their replacements, to the QuickCorrect list.

✦ *QuickWords* are abbreviations that expand as you type. They're more work to set up than QuickCorrect entries, but you can include formatting and graphics (such as for a company letterhead).

✦ *QuickLinks* instantly transform entries into hypertext links that you can click to jump to an Internet address. For example, type **@Corel** to create an instant link to Corel's home page at http://www.corel.com.

✦ *Format-As-You-Go* provides automatic sentence corrections, instant bullets, and other conveniences. For example, the start of a sentence in WordPerfect or Presentations is normally capitalized automatically.

✦ *SmartQuotes* turns straight quotation marks into printers'curly ones.

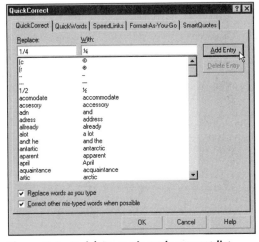

Figure 2-5: QuickCorrect's replacement list.

Cross-Reference For more on Format-As-You-Go and SmartQuotes, see Chapter 17, "Becoming an Instant WordPerfect Expert." You'll find in-depth coverage of QuickCorrect and QuickWords in Chapter 52, "Writers' Lib."

Getting Around the Screen

By now you've probably noticed that there are two basic ways to move around the screen:

✦ By using the arrow (directional) keys

✦ By using the mouse

Most keyboards have four arrow keys—often grouped in an inverted "T"—for moving up, down, left, and right. The arrow keys on the numeric keypad (if you have one) can also be used, provided the Num Lock light is off. As you press the arrow keys, the insertion point (the blinking vertical bar, also known as the *cursor*), moves around the screen.

Using the shadow cursor to click and type

Now, move the mouse and notice how WordPerfect's shadow cursor lets you click anywhere in the screen and start typing (see Figure 2-6). Try moving the mouse around and clicking to get the hang of the shadow cursor. When the shadow cursor is set to appear in text, it disappears after you stop moving the mouse.

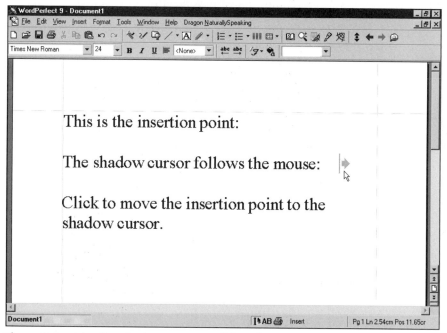

Figure 2-6: Using the shadow cursor to click and type.

Tip   Normally the shadow cursor appears only in your document's white space, not in the text. You can have it snap to margins, tabs, an indent, or spaces. You can also change its color and shape.

The shadow cursor can do a lot of clever things, as you'll see in Chapter 16, "Mastering the WordPerfect Interface," but it takes a while to get the hang of it. For now, you might want to turn it off by clicking the Shadow Cursor button on the application bar at the bottom of your screen.

Caution If you click the left mouse button when the pointer is in the left margin, WordPerfect selects (highlights) the nearest sentence. If this happens, remove the highlighting by clicking in the text area.

Autoscrolling your document

 New Feature To autoscroll your document, click the Autoscroll button on the toolbar and nudge the mouse up or down. Click where you want to stop.

If you have a Microsoft Intellimouse or a similar rodent, you can scroll by turning the wheel. You can also click the wheel and nudge the mouse to autoscroll in any direction, or hold Ctrl down and rotate the wheel to zoom in and out.

Inserting Text Versus Typeover

As you type, you're normally in *insert* mode — words spread out and wrap around to the next line as you type. To see how this works as you edit your letter, go back to the first line of the letter and place the insertion point immediately after "WordPerfect." Press the spacebar, and then type the words **for Windows**. Notice that, as you type, the text after the insertion point is pushed to the right and down. That's what word processing is all about.

At times, you might want to correct your document or add to it by typing over the existing text. Suppose you'd rather "change" the margins than "adjust" them. Go back and position the insertion point in front of the "a" in "adjust." Now, press the Insert key several times and observe how the Insert status on the application bar at the bottom of your screen toggles between Insert and Typeover.

 Tip You can also click the Insert/Typeover button on the application bar to switch modes.

Leave it at Typeover for the moment and type **change**, over "adjust." Notice how the text doesn't move in typeover mode. Toggle back to Insert mode.

Inserting the Date and Time

So far, you've been so busy typing and editing your letter that you haven't put in the date. Click where you want the date to appear, and then click Insert ⇨ Date/Time ⇨ Insert (see Figure 2-7).

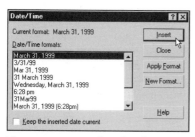

Figure 2-7: Inserting the date.

If you check "Keep the inserted date current," the same date appears, but there's a difference. A *date code* is inserted that refreshes the date each time you open or print your document. This is a handy way to ensure that your letter reflects the current date if you plan to send it later. However, if you want a record of when the letter was sent, leave this option unchecked. Otherwise, the date will change every time you look at the letter.

If none of the available date or time formats is to your liking, click New Format to design a custom one. Click the tabs to display various selections for the Year, Month, Day, and Time (see Figure 2-8). Click Insert to place each code in the "Edit date/time format" box. Add any punctuation, spaces, or text, and then click OK to apply your custom format to any date you insert from that point on.

Tip To change the date format for all your documents, edit the Document Style, as explained in Chapter 21, "Formatting Your Document."

Click the tabs to display various formats

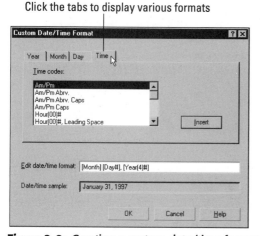

Figure 2-8: Creating a custom date/time format.

Selecting Text

One of the most powerful and flexible features of your WordPerfect Office 2000 programs is their capability to perform operations on selected (blocked) text and graphics. You can move, copy, or delete highlighted information, or change the format of your text. You can even save your block as a file of its own, or copy it to another file.

You have almost as many ways to select information as you have things to do with it. Try these two basic selection techniques:

> ✦ *Using the mouse.* Drag the mouse across the information you want to select, as shown in Figure 2-9, and then release the mouse button. (If you start dragging near a margin guideline, make sure the pointer is still an arrow or I-bar, or you'll drag the guideline instead.) As you drag across words, the selection switches from character-by-character to word-by-word if WordPerfect's "Automatically select whole words" option is checked (Tools ➪ Settings ➪ Environment ➪ General). To override this feature, hold down the Alt key while you drag.

Selected text

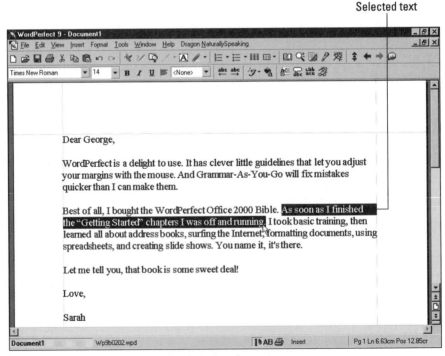

Figure 2-9: You can select text by dragging the mouse.

✦ *Using the keyboard.* Place the insertion point where you want to start your selection, and then press F8. (Press F12 if you're using the DOS-compatible keyboard.) Use the arrow keys to select text one character or line at a time. Press the spacebar (in WordPerfect) to extend the selection word by word, or press any character to extend to the next occurrence of that character.

Tip   For many operations on a single word (such as making it bold or italic), simply place the insertion point anywhere in the word. You don't need to select it.

To remove a selection, click anywhere in the document (except for the left margin), or press F8 (F12 for the DOS-compatible keyboard).

Moving and Copying Text

Now that you know how to select text, you can move it around to rearrange your ideas, or copy it to avoid typing it again. Essentially, you have two ways to move and copy:

✦ *Cut* or *copy* the selected information (text or graphics) to the Windows Clipboard, and then paste it to the new location

✦ *Drag* the information with the mouse and drop it into place

Moving and copying via the Clipboard

The Windows *Clipboard* is a holding area (or buffer) to which you can cut, copy, or append information, and then paste it to another location in the current file, in another file, or even another file in another application.

To move or copy via the Clipboard:

1. Select the information.

2. Place the selection in the Clipboard in either of two ways:

• To move the information, click the Cut button on the toolbar. (You can also press Ctrl+X or click Edit ⇨ Cut.)

• To copy the information, click the Copy button on the toolbar. (You can also press Ctrl+C or click Edit ⇨ Copy.)

3. Move the insertion point to where you want to put the information.

4. Click the Paste button on the toolbar. (You can also press Ctrl+V or click Edit ⇨ Paste.)

When information is in the Clipboard, the Paste button on the toolbar is highlighted, and you can paste it in as many places as you want. Your selection stays in the Clipboard until it's replaced by your next cut or copy operation, or until you exit Windows.

Using paste simple

Normally, the pasting part of the move or copy process pastes your text at the new location with the same font size, style, color, and other attributes from whence it came. For example, if you paste the word "**bold**" in between the words "*large italic*," the result looks like this: *large* **bold** *italic*.

Press Ctrl+Shift+V to paste simple a copy of the text that looks the same as the text at the insertion point, like this: *large bold italic*. You can also right-click your document, and click "Paste without Font/Attributes."

When you use paste simple on a blank line, the text takes on the default font size, style, and color.

Unlike cut, copy, and paste, paste simple does not appear on either the default menu bar or the toolbar (Paste Special on the Edit menu is something different). To add paste simple to either of these places, turn to the customizing instructions in Chapter 57, "Customizing Toolbars, Menus, and Keyboards."

Appending to information in the Clipboard

Instead of replacing the Clipboard's contents each time you copy, you can append to it, and then paste both the old and the new:

1. Select some text, and then click Edit ➪ Append. (Select the necessary blank space or line to separate your clipboard items.)

2. Move the insertion point to where you want to copy the Clipboard's contents.

3. Click the Paste button. (You can also press Ctrl+V or click Edit ➪ Paste.)

This time, your last two selections are copied. You can append to the Clipboard as many times as you want. The entire contents of the Clipboard are always pasted. There's no history according to which you can go back and append only the Clipboard information from, for example, two selections ago.

Using the mouse to drag and drop

For nearby moving or copying, try using the mouse to drag and drop:

1. Drag to make your selection, and then release the left mouse button.

2. Click the selected information, and then drag the pointer to the new location.

3. To move the information, release the mouse button. To copy the information while leaving the original intact, hold down the Ctrl key while you release the mouse button (see Figure 2-10).

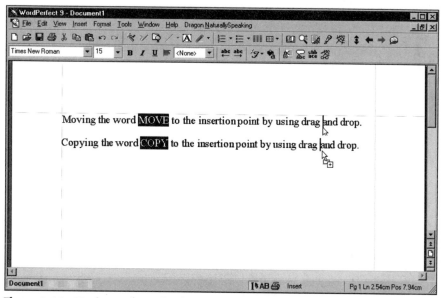

Figure 2-10: Moving and copying by using drag and drop.

If you click and drag by using the right mouse button as described in Step 2, a QuickMenu appears at the new location that lets you choose between move and copy. It even offers you move simple and copy simple (without font attributes).

Making a Bold Impression

Writing is about expression; and while the words themselves have primacy, the manner in which they are visually displayed can add (or detract) from their impact. With a word processor (and its associated printer) you no longer have to use the crude underlining method required with a typewriter to emphasize a point or identify a title. To use bold and italic instead:

1. Click the Bold or Italic button on the property bar (you can also press Ctrl+B or Ctrl+I).

2. Type your text, and then repeat Step 1 to turn off the effect.

To make text you already typed bold or italic, first select the text, or place the insertion point anywhere on a single word.

Note how the bold or italic button is recessed when its attribute is active at the insertion point. You can click the recessed button to remove bold or italic.

 Cross-Reference The full range of text effects (including font, size, color, and other attributes) is described in Chapter 8, "Fonts Fantastic."

Changing Line Spacing

Line spacing is another great word processing convenience. To change your line spacing:

1. Place the insertion point anywhere in the paragraph where you want the change to begin, or select the paragraphs you want to change.

2. Click Format ➪ Line ➪ Spacing.

3. Type the line spacing you want (see Figure 2-11). You can also click the little arrows, or press the up and down arrows on your keyboard.

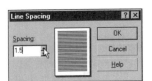

Figure 2-11: Changing line spacing.

 Tip If you work with line spacing a lot, you can add the line spacing button to the text property bar (see Chapter 57, "Customizing Toolbars, Menus, and Keyboards").

Saving and Naming Your Document

Your letter is finished and corrected, so it's time you saved it as a file on your hard disk. (Normally you'll want to save your document before it's finished, in case of a power outage or other unforeseen event.)

The title bar at the top of your screen should read "Corel WordPerfect - Document1." This means that you are in the first document window (you can have nine documents open at once), and that you have yet to save your letter and give it a name.

To name and save a new document:

1. Click the Save button on the toolbar. You can also click File ⇨ Save, or press Ctrl+S (Windows keyboard only).

2. Type a name for your document in the "File name" box (see Figure 2-12), and then click Save.

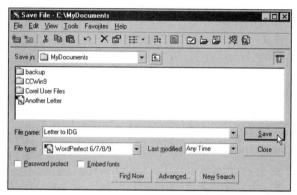

Figure 2-12: Naming and saving a document.

Tip

You can give your documents descriptive names of any length, with spaces between words. Keep them reasonably short for display purposes, and don't use any of the following characters: * + = [ ] : ; . " < > ? / \ |. The program appends the default extension of .WPD to the name you type to indicate that it's a WordPerfect document. (To override the default extension, put the entire filename, including the filename extension, inside quotation marks.)

Cross-Reference

For information on placing your files into particular folders, see Chapter 7, "Managing Your Files."

Printing Your Document

Now that your letter is saved to disk, it's ready to print:

1. Click the Print button on the toolbar. You can also click File ⇨ Print, or press Ctrl+P (Windows keyboard only).

2. Click Print (see Figure 2-13).

Cross-Reference

Various printing options are covered in Chapter 13, "Printing and Faxing Information."

Closing Your Document

Now that your letter is finished, you can close the document window:

1. Click File ➪ Close.

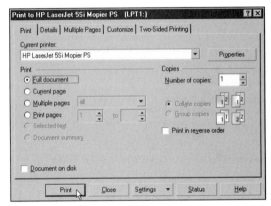

Figure 2-13: Printing your document.

2. If you have changed your document since it was last saved, the "Save changes to . . . ?" prompt appears (see Figure 2-14). To save the latest changes, click Yes. To discard the latest changes, click No. To continue editing your document, click Cancel.

Figure 2-14: You're prompted to save the latest changes when closing the document window.

Exiting WordPerfect

You've covered a lot of word-processing territory! Why not leave the program and take a break before examining the screen details.

To exit WordPerfect:

1. Click File ➪ Exit.

2. If any of your screen documents has changed since it was last saved, answer the "Save changes to . . . ?" prompt as described above.

For More Information . . .

On	See
Understanding screen features	Chapter 3
Using Undo and Redo	Chapter 6
Using the Spell Checker and word lists	Chapter 52
Checking your grammar	Chapter 52
Using QuickCorrect and QuickWords	Chapter 52
Using Format-As-You-Go and SmartQuotes	Chapter 17
Using the shadow cursor	Chapter 18
Customizing toolbars and menus	Chapter 57
Working with fonts	Chapter 8
Organizing files in folders	Chapter 7
Printing and sending information	Chapter 13
Mastering the WordPerfect interface	Chapter 16

✦   ✦   ✦

Looking at a Suite Face

The WordPerfect Office interface is more powerful and intuitive than ever before. Here you'll get a look at its features, including the clever innovations in version 9. You'll also get some great configuration tips.

As you saw in the Chapter 2, "Essential Typing and Editing," it doesn't take much to get up and running, typing and editing text. Now it's time to get acquainted with a number of friendly screen features (and tricks) that will turn your work into a pleasurable cruise. This chapter focuses on the WordPerfect screen, but because WordPerfect is part of a suite of programs, you'll find that much of what you see here applies to the other applications as well.

Hi, DAD!

If you did a typical or custom install of WordPerfect Office 2000, a shortcut to the Corel Desktop Application Director (DAD) is normally placed in your Startup folder. This, in turn, places a clever little DAD control center in the notification area of your taskbar each time you start Windows. To launch a program, simply click its icon (see Figure 3-1).

Tip   Point to an icon for a second or two to reveal the name of its associated program.

You can add and remove programs to and from the DAD display, including your favorite non-Office utilities.

Figure 3-1: To launch a program, click its icon.

Getting Around the Screen

Click the WordPerfect icon on the taskbar (or click Start ➪ Programs ➪ WordPerfect Office 2000 ➪ WordPerfect 9) to display the WordPerfect screen shown in Figure 3-2. From here, you can explore some of the common screen features in WordPerfect Office 2000.

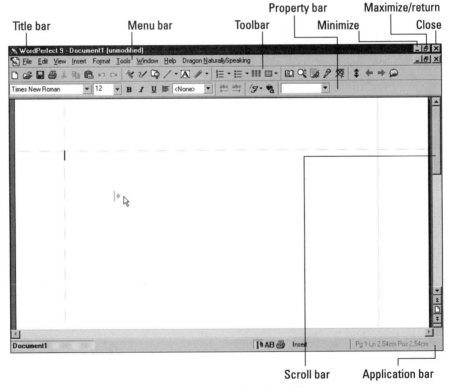

Figure 3-2: Common screen features in WordPerfect Office 2000.

The Windows Taskbar

Windows is a multitasking environment, meaning that it allows several programs to be active at a time, sharing your computer's resources according to each program's needs. You can click taskbar buttons to switch among the active programs.

Outside Feature

The *Windows Taskbar* is where it all begins. You can click the Start button to launch programs, get help with Windows, change settings, and perform other Windows tasks (including shutting down your system). Icons for various utilities (including the WordPerfect Office DAD icons) display in the notification area at the right of the taskbar. You may also see a printer for controlling your print job or a speaker for adjusting sound volume.

You can right-click taskbar buttons (and some icons) to display context-sensitive selections, such as to close a program.

Tip

Double-click the time to adjust your computer's date and time.

What are those little buttons for?

Outside Feature

Several little Windows buttons display in the upper corners of the screen. The top set of buttons on the title bar control the application, while the ones underneath on the menu bar control the application window for the document, spreadsheet, or show. Table 3-1 explains what each button does.

Table 3-1	
Little Buttons at the Top of Your Screen	
Click This Button	**To Do This**
Minimize	Shrink (minimize) your application to a button on the taskbar, or shrink the document to a button placed at the bottom left of the application window
Maximize	Enlarge (maximize) the program to fill the entire screen, or enlarge the document, spreadsheet, or show to fill the program window
Return	Return a maximized window to its previous size
Close	Exit the program or close the window
Application control	Display a menu of application options, such as exiting or changing the window size
Document control	Display a menu of window options, such as closing the document or switching to the next

When you shrink a window, a border appears around it, as shown in Figure 3-3. Position the pointer over a side or corner of the border so that it changes into a double-arrow. Then drag the border to stretch or shrink the window. Each shrunken window has its own title bar, separate from the application title bar at the top of the screen. You can drag the title bar to move a shrunken window to another location.

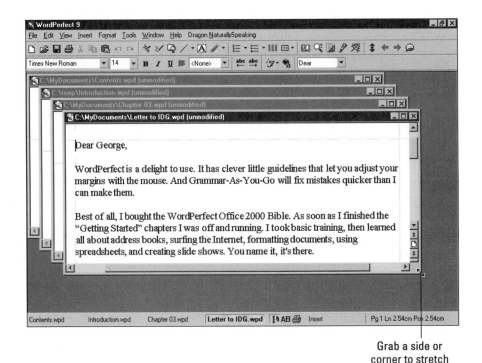

Grab a side or
corner to stretch
or shrink the window

Figure 3-3: You can shrink WordPerfect application windows.

The title bar

The application *title bar* displays the name of the program, along with the name of the document, notebook, show, or other file you're currently working on.

The menu bar

Nearly every program command and feature can be accessed by clicking items on the *menu bar*. Selections are logically arranged under categories. Many menu selections lead to submenus (Edit ➪ Select) or dialog boxes (Edit ➪ Find and Replace). These selections are indicated by right-pointing triangles for submenus or ellipses (...) for dialogs.

To navigate menus and select items with the mouse:

1. Click the menu bar.
2. Scroll the menus by moving the mouse (point to the menu bar to move from menu to menu).
3. Click to select an item.

To navigate menus and select items with the keyboard:

1. Select a menu by pressing the Alt key plus the underlined letter (or press the Alt key alone to go to the left of the menu bar).
2. Scroll the menus by using the arrow keys.
3. Press Enter to select the highlighted item.

To exit a menu without making a selection, click on the document, or press Esc until you return to your document.

Toolbars

Toolbars provide quick mouse access to frequently used features. You can even put the icon for another program (such as a calculator) on a toolbar to launch it right from your screen (see Chapter 57, "Customizing Toolbars, Menus, and Keyboards").

A little downward-pointing triangle to a button's right (as for Highlight, Bullets, or Table QuickCreate) indicates a list or palette from which to make your selection.

You can select various custom toolbars (such as Format, Graphics, or Outline Tools) for particular tasks, or create a custom toolbar of your own. Right-click anywhere on the toolbar to switch to another toolbar at any time.

A toolbar can be displayed at the top, bottom, or either side of the screen, or as a floating palette (see Figure 3-4). Point to a blank spot or edge of the toolbar so that the pointer becomes a four-pointed arrow, and then drag the toolbar to the location you want, waiting until it "snaps" into place before releasing the mouse button.

In WordPerfect you can display a scroll bar on the toolbar when there are more buttons than can fit on the display. To display the scroll bar, right-click anywhere on the toolbar, click Settings ⇨ Options, and then check "Show scroll bar." In Quattro Pro or WordPerfect, you can click View ⇨ Toolbars to display two or more toolbars at a time (but they'll take up a lot of screen real estate). Here's another toolbar trick: When you display the toolbar as a floating palette, drag a side or corner to stretch or shrink it to a different shape (see Figure 3-5).

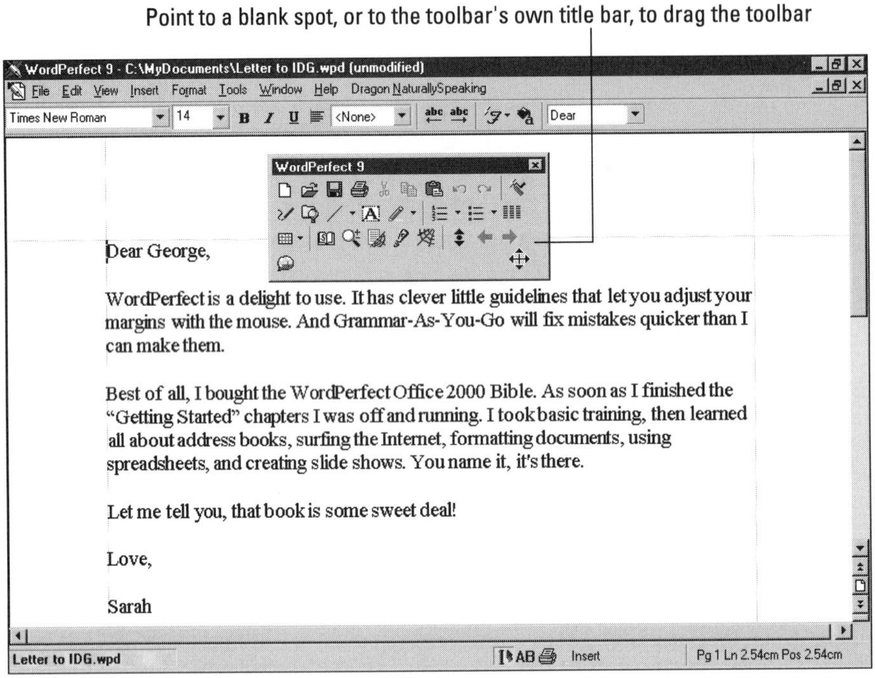

Point to a blank spot, or to the toolbar's own title bar, to drag the toolbar

Figure 3-4: Toolbar displayed as a floating palette.

Figure 3-5: Reshaping the floating toolbar.

The property bar

The *property bar* is a Corel-wide chameleon-like toolbar that offers a different set of features, depending on the current task (such as drawing, tables, or outlining). As with other toolbars, you can customize the buttons of a property bar, or drag it around the screen.

So, what's the difference between a toolbar and a property bar? Essentially, toolbars are for more general features; they tend to stay put, and you can manually switch them whenever you want. The program always selects the appropriate property bar, based on what you're doing at the moment. Select some text, and note how the property bar changes, while the toolbar items remain the same.

Scroll bars

The *scroll bars* along the right side and bottom of the screen enable you to move quickly through long documents. Because you normally scroll WordPerfect documents up and down (not from left to right) you may want to remove the horizontal scroll bar to free up some screen space (click Tools ⇨ Settings ⇨ Display and uncheck Horizontal). The scroll bars shown in Figure 3-6 have the following features:

✦ *Scroll boxes*. As you move through your document, the scroll boxes move along the scroll bars, indicating your relative position. (The length of the scroll box indicates the proportion of the document on display.) Drag a scroll box to quickly scroll to another location.

✦ *Page up* and *page down buttons*. To scroll one page at a time, click the page up or page down button.(Click a blank spot above or below the scroll box to scroll one screen at a time.)

✦ *Scroll arrows*. Click the up or down arrow to scroll line by line or row by row. Hold a button down to scroll continuously.

✦ *Reveal Codes handle* (WordPerfect). Click the Reveal Codes handle to display the hidden formatting codes surrounding the visible text and graphics. Drag the handle to adjust the size of the display. (You'll learn about Reveal Codes in Chapter 16, "Mastering the WordPerfect Interface.")

Browse by button. Click this button multiple times to change the page buttons to table, box, footnote, endnote, position, or comment up and down.

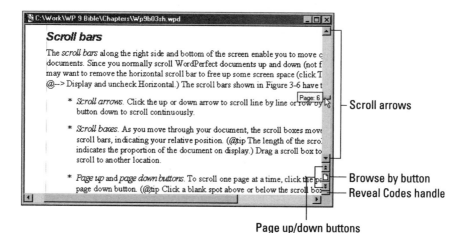

Figure 3-6: Scroll bars, buttons, and handles.

Tip Because simply scrolling does not move the insertion point, you must click the screen to move the insertion point and make your scrolling stick. Otherwise, you'll jump back to your original screen location the moment you press a key.

The application bar

For each document, spreadsheet, or show you open, a button appears on the *application bar* at the bottom of your screen, much like the application buttons on the Windows taskbar (the active window's button appears in bold). You can click these buttons to switch among your open documents, or drag selected information to a button to move or copy it to the document represented by that button (see Chapter 10, "Working Together and Sharing Data"). You can also customize application bar selections and displays (see Chapter 57, "Customizing Toolbars, Menus, and Keyboards").

You'll also find useful features and information on the application bar, such as the page number and location of the insertion point. Quattro Pro has a QuickCell feature that lets you drag a cell to the application bar, to see its updated value when you're working in another location.

Quick Tips and double-clicks

Resting the pointer on a menu, toolbar, property bar, or application bar selection for a second or two pops up a descriptive *Quick Tip*. Menu Quick Tips include any function key shortcuts.

You can double-click some buttons (such as QuickFonts or Table QuickCreate) to call up related dialog boxes. However, the trend is away from double-clicking, toward a more intuitive interface.

Using dialog boxes and QuickMenus

Working with applications these days involves a continuous series of selections. Dialog boxes and QuickMenus present two handy ways to communicate your wishes.

Dialog boxes

Dialog boxes, also known as *dialogs*, can present options in a variety of ways. You can drag a dialog box around the screen by the title bar, or press Esc to dismiss the dialog box without making a selection.

The Print dialog box shown in Figure 3-7 illustrates several dialog box characteristics and features. The "Selected text" item is dimmed (not available) because no text is currently selected. What appears also depends on the selections you make, as when you specify more than one print copy and click Group or Collate. Don't worry if a particular screen's dialog box doesn't exactly match the illustration in the book.

Tab   Drop-down list   What's This? help

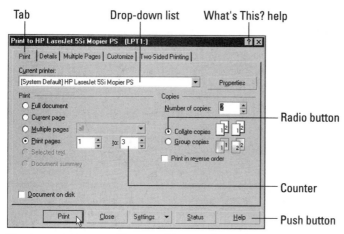

Figure 3-7: Features illustrated by WordPerfect's Print dialog box.

Table 3-2 lists dialog box features illustrated by the Print dialog box (see Figure 3-7) and Font panel of the Font Properties dialog box (see Figure 3-8).

Click + to expand, – to collapse list items

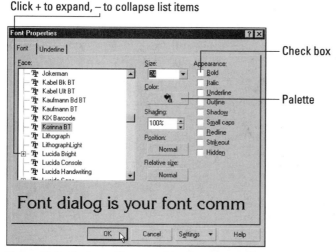

Figure 3-8: Features illustrated by Font Properties dialog box.

Table 3-2
Common Dialog Box Items

Item	How To Use It
What's This?	Click, and then click a button or area to see a What's This? description of the item. You can also right-click the item without clicking the button.
Tabs	Click to display the group of options you want.
Drop-down list	Click the arrow to display the list of options, and then click the option you want.
Counter	Type a number or click the arrows to change the value (also known as a *spin box*).
Push button	Click to perform an immediate action. These buttons — also called *command buttons* — can chain to lower-level dialog boxes.
Radio buttons	Click the option you want. You can only select one.
Check boxes	Click to check the option(s) you want. You can select more than one.
List box	Click the arrows to scroll the list, and then click your selection.
Palette	Click to pop up a visual display of colors or tools from which to choose.
Preview area	View the effect of your selections before they're applied.
Text box	(Not shown, but the Name box in the Save File dialog box is one.) Type your entry or selection.

Some dialog boxes, such as that for WordPerfect's display settings, have an Apply button that lets you try out changes without closing the dialog box.

You can use the following keystrokes in a dialog box:

✦ Tab to go to the next part

✦ Shift+Tab to go to the previous part

✦ Arrow keys to switch among buttons or scroll a list

✦ Enter to activate the highlighted button

QuickMenus

As you work, the program keeps track of where you are and what you're doing. The *QuickMenu*, like the property bar, goes a step further by anticipating what you want to do next. To see how this works, type a few words, and then right-click anywhere in the typing area to display the normal text QuickMenu (see Figure 3-9).

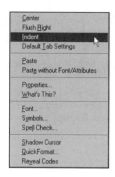

Figure 3-9: Normal text QuickMenu.

Point and click to select a QuickMenu item. To dismiss the QuickMenu, press Esc, or click the left mouse button anywhere outside the menu.

Now, select some text, and right-click your selection. This time you'll see that the formatting selections are replaced by Cut, Copy, and Delete—things you are likely to do with selected text (see Figure 3-10). Right-click in the left margin for a QuickMenu to do such things as select a sentence or adjust your margins.

Figure 3-10: Selected text QuickMenu.

Cascading and Tiling Windows

If you have several windows open within WordPerfect, Presentations, or Quattro Pro, you can click the Window menu, and then click selections to do the following:

✦ *Cascade* the windows as shown previously in Figure 3-3. The active window has a highlighted menu bar. Click anywhere on an inactive window to bring it to the foreground. You can then maximize the window.

✦ *Tile* your windows as shown in Figure 3-11. (Four windows display in a matrix.) This is especially useful to compare two documents. You can tile documents top to bottom, or side by side, and drag text from one document to another (see Figure 3-12).

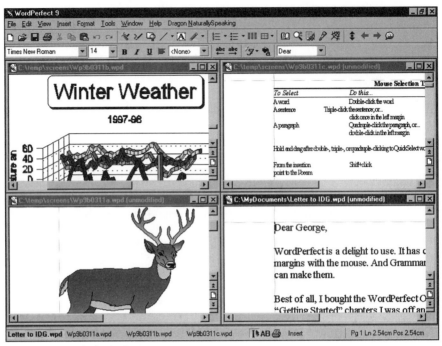

Figure 3-11: Tiled windows.

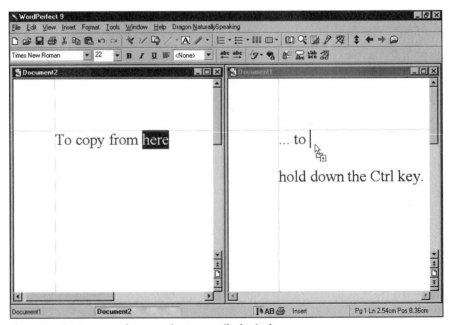

Figure 3-12: You can drag text between tiled windows.

Setting Up Your Windows Screen

Two Windows display options—your taskbar display and your screen resolution—have a major impact on the display of your WordPerfect Office.

Hiding the taskbar

Outside Feature

You don't need the taskbar as you're working in a particular application, so why not tuck it away to give yourself some visual breathing room? Right-click on a blank spot on the taskbar, click Properties, check "Always on top" and "Auto hide," and then click OK (see Figure 3-13). Presto, it's gone! It's still there when you need it, though. Simply point to the bottom of the screen to pop the taskbar into view.

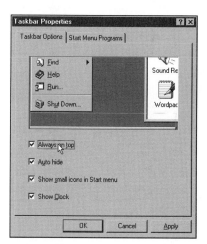

Figure 3-13: Hiding the taskbar.

Resolving screen resolution

Outside Feature

With more 17-inch, 19-inch, and larger monitors around, the selected *resolution*, or amount of information displayed on the screen, is increasingly a matter of choice. Depending on your monitor and graphics card, you may be able to choose anywhere from the minimal 640 × 480 pixels per inch (see Figure 3-14) to 1,024 × 768 pixels (see Figure 3-15), or higher. WordPerfect Office 2000 seems to be most comfortable at 800 × 600 pixels, the resolution used for the figures in this book.

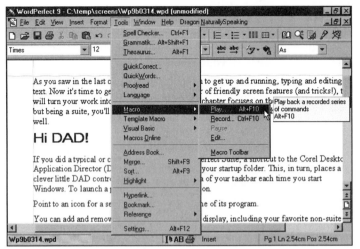

Figure 3-14: Working in 640 × 480 screen resolution.

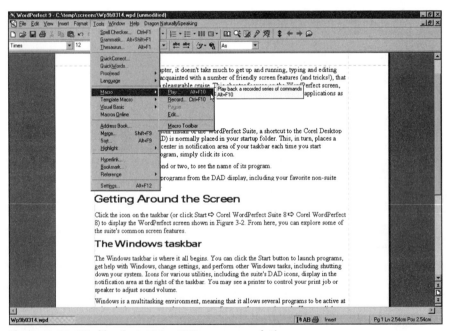

Figure 3-15: Working in 1,024 × 768 screen resolution.

To switch resolutions, exit or minimize your applications, and then right-click on your Windows desktop and click Properties. Click the Settings tab, and then slide the "Desktop area" bar to the left or right to select a lower or higher resolution (see Figure 3-16). Click OK and follow the prompts to change your setting.

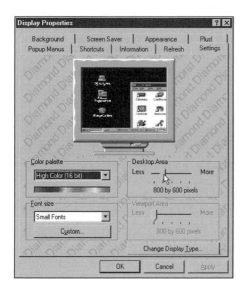

Figure 3-16: Switching your screen resolution.

For More Information . . .

On	See
Customizing DAD	Appendix A
Performing shadow cursor tricks	Chapter 18
Customizing WordPerfect's display	Chapter 31
Using Reveal Codes	Chapter 18
Dragging to the application bar	Chapter 10
Moving and copying information	Chapter 7
Customizing toolbars, menus, and keyboards	Chapter 57

✦   ✦   ✦

Hello Hal!

Speech is our primary, most efficient mode of inter-personal communication. So wouldn't it be nice if we could talk our text, instead of typing it? This chapter explains how NaturallySpeaking works and then shows you how to do some pretty amazing things without a keyboard or mouse. No more worries about carpal tunnel syndrome!

How NaturallySpeaking Works

Talking to the computer, already? What exactly should you say? Well, no need to worry about that. Thanks to increasingly sophisticated software and huge increases in the power of everyday machines, speech recognition is coming of age in the personal computer. This may be no consolation if you bought your machine a couple of years ago, but Dragon's recommendation of a 200MHz processor plus 64MB of RAM is entry-level by today's standards.

The NaturallySpeaking software that comes with WordPerfect Office 2000 inputs text and performs other operations by using your most natural and efficient form of communication, speech. You speak to the computer, instead of using the keyboard or mouse.

Using continuous speech

With earlier *discreet speech* products "you ... had ... to ... pause ... between ... each ... word." No longer! NaturallySpeaking is a *continuous speech* program that actually works better when you talk to your computer like you talk to humans. Learn how to:

- ✦ Correct errors and revise text
- ✦ Control speech features and functions by voice

How does Dragon recognize what you say? Well, it first filters out the background noise and converts your speech into a set

of *phonemes*—the units of sound in a language that serve to distinguish one word from another. Dragon then assembles a list of possible words from the sounds, based on the way you speak, from the 35,000 words in its *active vocabulary*—the most frequently used words out of the total vocabulary of 230,000 words. It then uses your *language model* (how frequently words are used alone and in combination with one another) to assemble your words into the most likely phrase or sentence.

Are the results 100% accurate? No, but consider how often you ask, "What did you say?" or "Huh?" In any case, the more you train Dragon to recognize the words you use and the way you speak, the better your results. Stick with Dragon for a few days and watch how it adapts to your voice and vocabulary. It will even pick up on your accent!

Using Natural Language Commands

Thanks to the *Natural Language Command* feature, you can edit and format documents by speaking commands in a natural way. Instead of memorizing a specific command, such as "italicize that," you can say whatever comes naturally to you, such as "Put that in italics," "Italicize the last paragraph," or "Set font italic." These phrases, and thousands of others, will all accomplish the same task. Just say what comes naturally.

What's in your speech files?

Each user's *speech files* consist of three types of information:

✦ A *voice file* with acoustic information on how you speak

✦ *Vocabulary words*, including your *active vocabulary* loaded in computer memory

✦ A *language model* with personal information on your word frequency and patterns

Your initial speech files are personalized through audio setup and initial training. This chapter shows you how to tweak your files to improve recognition accuracy as time goes on—through error correction, additional training, and vocabulary building.

Using Dragon NaturallySpeaking

The instructions in this chapter focus on how to use Dragon NaturallySpeaking within WordPerfect, but you can also run the program on its own, or from within Quattro Pro and Paradox.

How Dragon works with WordPerfect

When you install Dragon NaturallySpeaking with the WordPerfect suite (see Appendix A), a special Compatibility Module is installed that lets you dictate directly into the WordPerfect screen. NaturallySpeaking user, tools, and help functions are added to the WordPerfect menus, and a button appears on your WordPerfect toolbar to launch the speech module. After you launch Dragon, this button is replaced by others to perform such operations as turning the microphone on and off.

Using Dragon in Quattro Pro and Paradox

Once Dragon is installed, you can launch it from the Tools menu in Quattro Pro and Paradox.

In Quattro Pro you can use Dragon to enter, select, and edit data, apply numeric formats, navigate your notebook, and much more. One especially nice feature is the ability to say menu commands, such as "File New," "File Close," or "Go to Draft View." (Menu commands don't work in WordPerfect.)

Use Dragon in Paradox to navigate tables, records and cells, enter and edit data, and more.

See Appendix C, "NaturallySpeaking Quick Reference," for specific Quattro Pro and Paradox speech commands.

There is no Dragon support in Presentations or CorelCENTRAL.

Using Dragon on its own

Sometimes you may want to run Dragon on its own, outside of any of the WordPerfect Office applications. One reason in particular is if you need to restore your speech files, something that can't be done from any of the WordPerfect Office applications.

To run Dragon on it own, click Start ⇨ Programs ⇨ Dragon NaturallySpeaking Personal for WordPerfect ⇨ NaturallySpeaking Personal for WordPerfect.

Setting Up Dragon to Use for the First Time

When you install the speech module, as described in Appendix A, "Setting Up Your Suite," you can opt to take a 15-minute audio-visual tour of how NaturallySpeaking works (Figure 4-1).

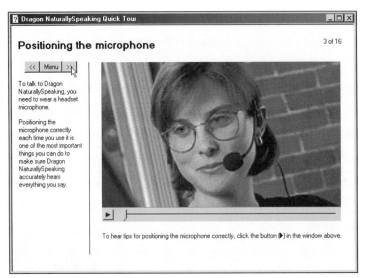

Figure 4-1: Taking the NaturallySpeaking Quick Tour.

The installation sets up a default "Customer" user, which lets you dictate into WordPerfect right out of the box — but what appears on the screen may only remotely correspond to what you say!

Positioning your microphone

Before you get started, position your microphone so that your words are clearly understood and your audio system can be accurately calibrated:

1. Squeeze the foam rubber muffler to feel the flat sides of the microphone.

2. Make sure the face of your microphone (often marked with a small dot) points toward your mouth.

3. Position the microphone a thumb's-width from either corner of your mouth. (The element should be close to your mouth, but not touching.)

 Tip   If extra small words such as "and," "in," or "the" appear in your document when you pause, NaturallySpeaking may be interpreting the sound of your breath as speech. Try moving the microphone slightly farther away from your mouth and to the side.

Give yourself time to get used to wearing the microphone, and position it the same way every time you use it.

Personalizing your speech files

To use speech effectively, you must first personalize your speech files. This is a three-step process:

✦ Create personal user files

✦ Follow the steps of the Audio Setup Wizard

✦ Train NaturallySpeaking to understand the way you speak

Creating personal user files

By creating personal user files, you will personalize the "Customer" speech files to your audio setup and way of speaking:

1. Click the Dragon button. (If the speech module is already loaded, click Dragon NaturallySpeaking ➪ Users ➪ Open.)

2. Select the "Customer" user, and then click Rename to personalize your user name (Figure 4-2).

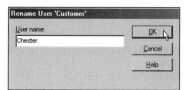

Figure 4-2: Personalizing your user name.

3. Follow the prompts to configure your audio setup and train NaturallySpeaking, as described in the following sections.

Dragon supports multiple users who can each personalize their vocabulary. Click Dragon NaturallySpeaking ➪ Users ➪ New to set up additional users.

When multiple users are set up, you're asked to select your personal profile when Dragon is launched.

Configuring your audio setup

When you personalize the "Customer" user (or set up a new user), the Audio Setup Wizard tests your microphone and sound card, and adjusts them to the proper volume (Figure 4-3). Click the Complete option for a first-time setup, and then click Next and follow the step-by-step instructions.

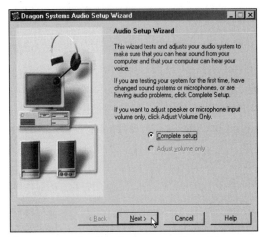

Figure 4-3: Configuring your audio setup.

Audio options, such as the input sound system and microphone boost, depend on your particular hardware. At the end of the setup when the audio summary is presented (Figure 4-4), click Finish to accept the results or click Back to try to improve the results by adjusting your microphone or selecting new options.

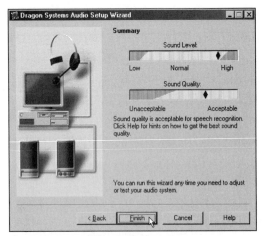

Figure 4-4: Audio configuration summary.

You can run the Audio Setup Wizard at any time to readjust the volume (Dragon NaturallySpeaking ⇨ Tools ⇨ Audio Setup Wizard). You should also run it whenever you change your sound card or microphone.

Completing your initial training

Once your audio is set up, you'll be asked to click Continue and go on to the first stage of training, where you'll read a few brief passages while minor adjustments are made (Figure 4-5).

Figure 4-5: First stage of training.

Next, you'll be asked to complete the second stage of training by reading aloud to the computer for about 30 minutes:

1. Select the text you want to train on (Figure 4-6), and then click Train Now.

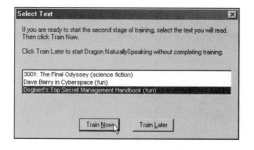

Figure 4-6: Selecting the text for your second stage of training.

2. Read the paragraphs as they appear on the screen. You can pause, back up, or skip words at any time (Figure 4-7). A yellow arrow may sometimes point to text that Dragon wants you to repeat.

3. After you've read the required passages, click Finish to save the training session.

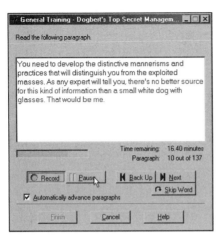

Figure 4-7: Reading to the machine.

You can read additional text at any time, to improve recognition performance (see "Doing supplemental training" later in this chapter).

 Tip   Do supplemental training when you move to an environment that's noisier, quieter, or has different background sounds.

Starting Dragon

The Dragon speech module does not load automatically when WordPerfect starts. Click the Dragon button on the toolbar when you want to start dictating.

The speech module automatically closes when you exit WordPerfect, and prompts you to save changes to your speech files.

Dictating Text in WordPerfect

Now that your training is finished, and Dragon is loaded, you can start talking!

Turning the microphone on and off

When you load the speech module, the microphone on the toolbar (and on the Windows Taskbar) is in the off position. To turn your microphone on or off, click the icon or press the + key on your numeric keypad.

You can also turn the microphone off by saying "Microphone Off."

Pausing the microphone

To pause the microphone when you want it to stop typing your speech, say **"Go to sleep."** To release the pause, say **"Wake up."**

The microphone still listens to what you say in pause mode, but the "Wake Up" command is the only phrase it will recognize. In the meantime, if you clear your throat or answer the phone, words won't appear on the screen.

> **Tip**
>
> When you go back to typing for any length of time, turn the microphone off instead of putting it to sleep for better typing performance.

Talking to WordPerfect

Now turn on your microphone, click where you want your text to appear, and start talking. As you speak, your words magically appear (Figure 4-8)! Your words and commands appear in the small, yellow *Results box* while they're being interpreted.

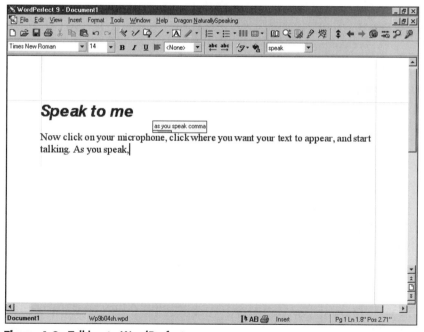

Figure 4-8: Talking to WordPerfect.

> **Tip**
>
> Notice how the words in the Results box often change before they're entered into the document. Just like a human listener, Dragon understands better when you speak in phrases, rather than one word at a time.

For best results when talking to WordPerfect:

✦ Relax and speak naturally, pausing as you normally do

✦ Sit up straight and breathe from your abdomen

✦ Speak without stress, at your normal speed, tone, and volume

✦ Speak in phrases, to give your words context

✦ Pronounce each word clearly, but don't over-enunciate

✦ Take breaks to loosen up, stretch, clear your throat, and have a sip of water

Above all, don't worry. NaturallySpeaking is designed so that speech accuracy is automatically enhanced as you correct the results, but it's not likely to be degraded by your mistakes.

 Caution   You don't have to worry about carpal tunnel syndrome while dictating, but watch out for vocal strain and don't dictate for too long a period.

Doing a practice exercise

Now try a practice exercise. Turn on the microphone and dictate the following text:

> Hello, computer. I feel kind of funny talking to you, especially since I don't even know your name.
>
> I can't believe this, someone actually listens to what I say! It will take a while to get used to this, but I think I'm going to really enjoy this talk-typing.

As you're speaking, do the following:

1. Say **comma**, **period**, **question mark**, and **dash** (in "talk-typing") to add punctuation.

2. Say **New Paragraph**, at the start the second paragraph.

3. When you've finished dictating, say **Go to Sleep**.

Now try editing your passage:

1. Say **Wake Up**.

2. To replace "really enjoy" with "have a good time" say **Select really enjoy**, then say **have a good time**.

3. Say **Move Left 2 Words**, then say **very** to insert "very" between "a" and "good."

4. Say **Undo That** to remove the "very."

5. Say **Select especially**, then say **Italicize That**.

6. Say **Go to Bottom** ⇨ **New Paragraph** ⇨ **Cool!** (**exclamation point**).

7. Say **Microphone Off**.

Speaking text and commands

Everything you say is interpreted either as text or as a *command*, such as "Undo That," that tells Dragon something to do.

To force the recognition of commands, hold down the Ctrl key. To force the interpretation of commands as text, hold down the Shift key.

Adding punctuation, tabs, lines, and paragraphs

As you speak, you must say each punctuation mark, such as "Comma," "Question Mark," "Exclamation Point/Mark," or "Period." For a complete list of punctuation marks, see the NaturallySpeaking Quick Reference (Appendix C).

Say **Tab Key** to insert a tab.

Say **New Line** to start a new line (a single hard return) and **New Paragraph** to start a new paragraph (two hard returns).

Of course, you can still enter and edit your text via the keyboard whenever you like.

Specifying caps and spaces

Use the following commands to specify caps and spaces:

Say	*To*
Caps *word*	Capitalize the first letter of a word
All Caps *word*	Capitalize all the letters in the word
Caps On/Off	Start/stop initial capitalization of all words
All Caps On/Off	Start/stop capitalizing all letters of all words
No Caps On/Off	Start/stop dictating words with no capitalization
Space Bar	Enter a space
No Space *word*	Prevent a space before the word
No Space On/Off	Start/stop no spacing between a series of words

Dictating particular words and symbols

Here's how to dictate particular words and symbols:

To enter	Say
A name	The name, such as "Mark Twain." Many are already in the vocabulary
A hyphenated word	The word, such as "all-knowing." Say "hyphen" between the words if the words aren't normally hyphenated.
An abbreviation	The abbreviation, such as "HTML."
@	at sign
$	dollar sign
#	pound sign
%	percent sign
+	plus sign
_	minus sign
^	caret
&	ampersand
_	underscore
*	asterisk
:-)	smiley face
:-(	frowny face
;-)	winking face

To add new words or symbols to your vocabulary, see "Adding to Your Vocabulary," later in this chapter. For more on special characters and symbols, see Chapter 7, "Managing Your Files."

Dictating numbers

You can dictate numbers as described in the following examples:

To enter	Say
Numeral 1–9	One–nine
4	four
No. 4	Number four
46	Forty-six
253	Two fifty-three
13,684	Thirteen comma six eight four, or thirteen thousand six hundred eighty-four
June 21, 1999	June twenty-one comma nineteen ninety-nine
August 19, 2004	August nineteen comma two thousand four
876-5432	Eight seven six five four three two
$63.29	Dollar sign sixty-three point twenty-nine, or sixty-three dollars and twenty-nine cents.

For more number examples, see Appendix C.

Spelling out a word

To spell out a word or abbreviation, say the letters in quick succession. Spelling is especially handy with name variations. For example, to spell "Shafer" say **s h a f e r**. If a name is not in the vocabulary, you have to say **Cap S**.

Saying e-mail and Web

You can use the No Caps On and No Space commands to dictate an e-mail or Web address that will automatically turn into a link in WordPerfect. A colon and two slashes are automatically inserted after "http."

For example, to enter "http://www.corel.com/sales,"say **No Caps On http No Space www dot corel dot com slash sales No Caps Off**.

If the option to automatically format Web and e-mail address is on (see "Changing miscellaneous and dictation settings" later in this chapter) all you have to say is **http www dot corel dot com slash sales**.

For an e-mail address you can say Chester at myweb dot com.

Yes, there is an easier way to create links.

1. Create a QuickLink (see Chapter 17, "Becoming an Instant WordPerfect Expert.") That way, you can either type or say the link. (You also will display the link name, not the link itself, in your document.)

2. Click Dragon NaturallySpeaking ⇨ Tools ⇨ Vocabulary Editor to enter the QuickLink and its spoken form (see "Creating QuickSpeak," later in this chapter.)

For example, the Web address "http://www.corel.com" might have a QuickLink and a spoken form of "Corel Web link."

Correcting Mistakes and Revising Text

While there's nothing to stop you from correcting mistakes or revising text via the keyboard and mouse, correcting mistakes via the Dragon is the most direct way to improve recognition accuracy.

Correcting mistakes

Until NaturallySpeaking gets to know you well, what appears on the screen may often differ from what you say. To correct the latest phrase:

1. Say **Correct That** to display the list of possible corrections (Figure 4-9). (You can also press the - key on the numeric keypad.)

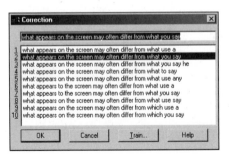

Figure 4-9: Correcting mistakes.

2. Correct the text or select a replacement phrase from the list. You can also say **Choose** and the number from 1–10 (or **Select**, the number, and **Click OK**.)

Once you're talking at a regular clip, you'll often be two or three phrases down the road before you spot an error you want to correct. To correct a previous passage, say **Correct** and then the word or words you want to change, as they appear on the screen.

Another way to immediately correct a recognition error is to say **Spell That**, followed quickly and continuously by the first four to six correct letters of the word or words.

Selecting and revising text

To select words you've dictated (before the insertion point), say **Select**, followed by the word or phrase you want to change, as they appear on the screen. You can then edit your selection with the keyboard or issue any of the following commands:

Say	*In Order To*
Delete/Scratch That	Delete your selection
Spell That	Spell out your revision by saying the letters, numbers, and punctuation
Correct That	Call up the Correction dialog
Bold That	Bold your selection
Italicize That	Italicize your selection
Cap That	Make your selection initial caps
All Caps/No Caps That	Make your selection all/no caps
Center That	Center your selection
Left/Right Align That	Left/right align your selection

Caution When text is selected, NaturallySpeaking may interpret the sound of your breath or other noises as speech and replace the selection with new text. If this happens, say **Undo That** (Ctrl+Z) to restore your original text.

Say **Select Again** to select the next previous occurrence of the same text. Once the top of your document is reached, you can continue to search from the bottom up.

Tip   To remove the selection without doing anything, issue any move command, such as **Move right one word** or **Move to end of line**.

Changing fonts

To change a limited set of fonts or font attributes, say **Set Font** (for the word at the insertion point or the insertion point on), or **Format That** (for selected text), followed by any combination of the following commands:

Face	Size	Style
Arial	4–20	Bold
Courier		Italics
Courier New		Plain
Times		Plain Text
Times New Roman		Regular
		Underline

You can also say **Set Size** or **Format That Size**. For more on fonts, see Chapter 8, "Fonts Fantastic."

Deleting text

To delete a selection, say **Scratch That** or **Delete That**.

To delete the last phrase you said, say **Scratch That**. You can repeat Scratch That up to 10 times.

When no text is selected, saying **Delete That** is the same as pressing the Delete key in WordPerfect.

Cutting, copying, and pasting

You can cut, copy and paste your selections by saying **Cut That**, **Copy That**, and **Paste That**.

To copy your entire document to the Clipboard, say **Copy All to Clipboard**.

For more on using cut, copy, and paste, see Chapter 2.

Undoing editing actions

When you're dictating in WordPerfect, your most recent editing actions are stored in your document's Undo history (see Chapter 5). Saying **Undo That** is the same as pressing Ctrl+Z in WordPerfect.

There's no verbal Redo command for WordPerfect, so to redo your undos, you must click the Redo button on the toolbar or press Ctrl+Shft+Z.

Note When using NaturallySpeaking on its own, there's just one Undo, so the second "Undo That" redoes the Undo.

You can say **Scratch That** to undo a dictation command, such as New Line or Caps On.

Moving Around

You can move the insertion point with the following commands:

Say	Then Say		
Move to/Go to	Top/Bottom (of document)		
Move to/Go to	Top/Start/Beginning/ Bottom/End	of	Selection/Line/ Paragraph/ Document
Move	Left/Back/Right/Forward	1–20 (characters)	
Move	Up/Down	1–20 (lines)	
Move	Left/Back/Right/Forward	a	Word
Move	Left/Back/Right/Forward	1–20	Word(s)
Move	Up/Back/Down/Forward	a	Paragraph
Move	Up/Back/Down/Forward	1–20	Paragraph(s)

Asking for Help

You can ask Dragon for help by voice, and navigate the basic Help topics with voice commands:

1. Say **Give Me Help**
2. When the Help dialog box appears (Figure 4-10), you can navigate topics with the mouse or say any of the following:

Say	*To*
Click Contents/Index/Find	Select the Contents, Index, or Find tabs in the Help dialog
Move Up/Down 1–10	Move up or down in the help contents
Open/Close	Open and close help topics
Click Display	Display a selected help topic
Click *button*	Activate any of the buttons in online help, such as Help Topics, Display, Back, Print, Cancel, or Close
Switch to Previous/ Next Window	Switch among Help, WordPerfect, and other applications.

Figure 4-10: Asking for help.

For help with particular speech commands, say **What Can I Say**, then type a relevant word and say **Click Display** (Figure 4-11).

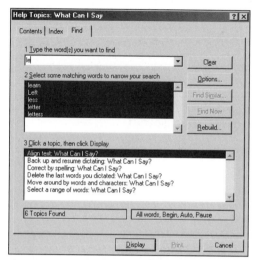

Figure 4-11: Getting "What Can I Say?" help on a particular speech command.

Note

> The *dynamic commands* to control menus and dialog boxes do not work within WordPerfect, other than in the NaturallySpeaking dialog boxes.

Improving Recognition Accuracy

You refine your speech files and improve performance whenever you

- ✦ Correct a recognition error
- ✦ Train words, phrases, or commands
- ✦ Read a passage during supplemental training
- ✦ Add words and phrases to your vocabulary
- ✦ Add words and rebuild your language model via the Vocabulary Builder

You already saw how to correct a recognition error (see "Correcting mistakes," earlier in this chapter.) This section covers the other possibilities.

Training individual words, phrases, or commands

If correcting the recognition of particular words, phrases, or commands doesn't do the trick, you can train NaturallySpeaking to understand your precise pronunciation:

1. Select Dragon NaturallySpeaking ⇨ Tools ⇨ Train Words.

2. Type the word, phrase, or command, then click OK (Figure 4-12).

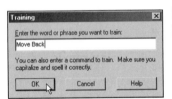

Figure 4-12: Training individual words, phrases, or commands.

3. Click Record, say the displayed text, then click Done.

Commands must be typed with the capitalization that appears on the screen, as with "Go to Sleep."

Training effectively edits the recognition of vocabulary items, but does not add new ones. (You also train new words you add via Find New Words, Vocabulary Editor, and Vocabulary Builder.)

Caution   When running the Training dialog box on its own, a new word or phrase doesn't get added to your vocabulary, even though you're prompted to record it.

Doing supplemental training

Once you've gotten over the initial trauma of talking to your computer, some supplemental training will better attune NaturallySpeaking to your accustomed dictating style:

1. Click Dragon NaturallySpeaking ⇨ Tools ⇨ General Training.

2. Select the text you'd like to read, (Figure 4-13), and then follow the General Training instructions.

Adding to your vocabulary

As you dictate, chances are good you'll come across particular terms, names, and phrases that are not in NaturallySpeaking's 230,000 word vocabulary. You can add words and phrases to your user vocabulary (other user vocabularies are not affected). New words are also placed in your active word list.

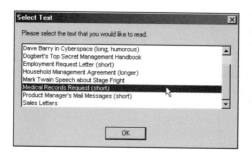

Figure 4-13: Selecting a supplemental training text.

Adding words or phrases

To add a word or phrase to your active vocabulary, you can do any one of the following:

✦ Click Dragon NaturallySpeaking ⇨ Tools ⇨ Vocabulary Editor and type the word or phrase. (See "Creating QuickSpeak," later in this chapter.)

✦ Dictate the new word or phrase, say **Correct That,** and type it in the Correction dialog box. (See "Correcting mistakes," earlier in this chapter.)

✦ Find new words in the current document.

To find new words in the current document:

1. Select Dragon NaturallySpeaking ⇨ Tools ⇨ Find New Words.

2. Check any words you want to add to your active vocabulary (Figure 4-14). (You can double-click a word to edit it.)

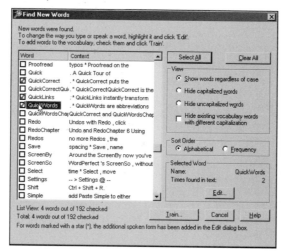

Figure 4-14: Selecting words from your document to add to your vocabulary.

3. Click Train to record how you say the words and add them to your vocabulary (Figure 14-15).

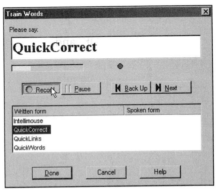

Figure 4-15: Training new vocabulary words.

Deleting a word or phrase

To delete a word or phrase from your vocabulary, click Dragon NaturallySpeaking ➪ Tools ➪ Vocabulary Editor, then type the word or phrase and click Delete. (Check "Show custom words only" to display only the words you've added.)

Rebuilding your language model

Use the Vocabulary Builder to add to your vocabulary and update your active language model based on your word usage and patterns in a collection of documents. This will improve recognition accuracy of the words you commonly use, especially if you write in a specialized area, such as sports, law, engineering, or medicine.

Vocabulary Builder scans your documents to identify new words, moves words from the backup dictionary into the active vocabulary, and modifies your language model based on how often you use particular words and language patterns.

Tip   For best results, add phrases you often use, such as "veterinary clinic," "shadow cursor," or "property bar," before using the Vocabulary Builder.

To rebuild your language model:

1. Pick out representative WordPerfect documents, or documents in Text (.txt), Rich Text (.rtf) or MS Word (.doc) format (if you also have MS Word installed). (You'll get a more accurate language model with documents that are free of spelling mistakes and symbols.)

Tip Scan documents with about 20,000 total words. (In any case, Vocabulary Builder will stop scanning once it has identified 25,000 unique words.) Click Save List to keep a list of your scanned documents for another user or to re-scan at a later date.

2. Click Dragon NaturallySpeaking ⇨ Tools ⇨ Vocabulary Builder.

3. Click Add, select documents for processing, click OK, and then click Begin (Figure 4-16).

4. Check any words you want to add to your active vocabulary. (You can double-click a word to edit it.)

5. Click Train and Build to record selected words, add them to your vocabulary, and rebuild your language model. You can also click Build if no words are selected.

Your changes won't be permanent until you save your speech files.

 Caution Running Vocabulary Builder replaces the current language model with one more attuned to the documents you're scanning. Be sure you want to do this.

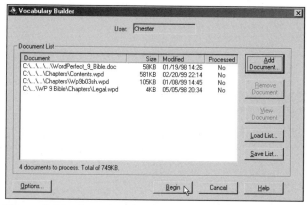

Figure 4-16: Scanning the documents with Vocabulary Builder.

Saving Your Speech Files

By saving your speech files, you update information about your particular speech patterns, and vocabulary words, (and language model information, if you've run Vocabulary Builder.)

By saving changes to your speech files, your recognition accuracy is continuously improved. When you exit WordPerfect, click Yes, when prompted, if you want to save the updates. You can also click Dragon NaturallySpeaking ➪ Users ➪ Save Speech Files at any time.

Your speech files are backed up after every fifth save, or at the interval you specify. Click Dragon NaturallySpeaking ➪ Tools ➪ Options ➪ Miscellaneous to set the interval between backups (Figure 4-17).

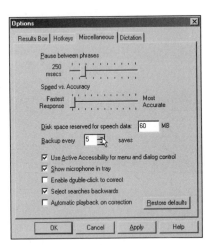

Figure 4-17: Setting the speech file backup interval.

Restoring Your Speech Files

If you find that your recognition accuracy degrades for any reason (such as from the documents you scanned into Vocabulary Builder), you can restore your speech files to a previous state:

1. Click Start on the Windows taskbar, and then click Programs ➪ Dragon NaturallySpeaking Personal for WordPerfect ➪ NaturallySpeaking Personal for WordPerfect.

2. Click User ➪ Restore from the Dragon NaturallySpeaking menu to restore the current user's speech files from their last backup.

Speech Tips and Techniques

To get the most out of NaturallySpeaking, try the tips and techniques in the following sections.

Using hot keys

Dragon's hot keys are especially helpful:

Press	*To*
+ (on the numeric keypad)	Turn the microphone on and off
- (on the numeric keypad)	Call up the correction dialog box
Ctrl (as you speak)	Force words to be recognized as commands
Shift (as you speak)	Force commands to be recognized as words

To customize your hot keys, click Dragon NaturallySpeaking ➪ Tools ➪ Options ➪ Hotkeys.

Creating QuickSpeak

Dragon NaturallySpeaking assumes that you pronounce words the way they're spelled. To dictate words or phrases with different written and spoken forms, use the Vocabulary Editor. This is a great way to create spoken abbreviations, or "QuickSpeak."

1. Click Dragon NaturallySpeaking ➪ Tools ➪ Vocabulary Editor.

2. Type the word, phrase, or command (or select an existing vocabulary entry from the list).

3. Type the spoken form, if you want it to be different from the written form (Figure 4-18).

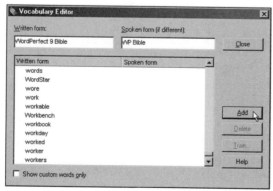

Figure 4-18: Creating Quickspeak.

4. Click Add if it's a new word or phrase.

5. Click Train to dictate the spoken form.

Speaking QuickWords and QuickCorrect entries

You can train NaturallySpeaking to recognize the QuickWords and QuickCorrect entries you've already created, such as a "bizzhead" QuickWord to insert a formatted business letterhead.

When you say "bizzhead," however, Dragon will probably think you're saying "his head," "the said," or something of that order. Once you add "bizzhead" to your vocabulary, Dragon will recognize it.

Saying apostrophe s

To dictate a word with an apostrophe s, say the singular word followed by the apostrophe s as with **Car apostrophe ess**.

If the word already has an s and you want to insert an apostrophe:

1. Say **Select cars**.

2. Say **car apostrophe ess**.

Controlling the Results box

Normally the little, yellow Results box scrolls along with your text as you dictate. To anchor it at another location:

1. Drag the box to the location you want.

2. Right-click the box and click Anchor.

You can also right-click the Results box to select whether it will auto-hide after its set delay.

To specify the Results box auto-hide delay and volume meter height, click Dragon NaturallySpeaking ⇨ Tools ⇨ Options ⇨ Results Box.

Changing miscellaneous and dictation settings

In addition to hot keys and the Results box, you can also change several miscellaneous and dictation settings:

1. Click Dragon NaturallySpeaking ▷ Tools ▷ Options.

2. Click the Miscellaneous tab (Figure 4-19) or the Dictation tab to specify any of the settings described in Table 4-1.

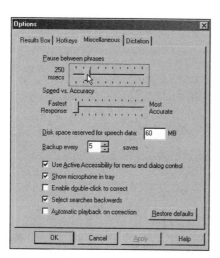

Figure 4-19: Changing NaturallySpeaking's settings.

Table 4-1
Dragon's Miscellaneous and Dictation Settings

Set	Lets You
Miscellaneous Settings	
Pause between phrases	Adjust the length of the pause (normally 250 milliseconds or one-forth of a second) used to distinguish between continuous speech and speech commands. (Too brief a pause will cause commands to be interpreted as text.)
Speed vs. Accuracy	Adjust how long Dragon has to figure out what you're saying. The longer the better, but response depends on the power of your computer and what other programs are competing for system resources.
Disk space reserved for speech data	Set how big your speech files can grow if disk space is limited.

Continued

Table 4-1 *(continued)*

Set	*Lets You*
Miscellaneous Settings	
Backup every *x* saves	Set the automatic backup interval to prevent the loss of speech training.
Use Active Accessibility for menu and dialog control	Use Dragon to control certain menus and dialog boxes in Windows 98.
Show microphone in tray	Display the microphone in the Windows taskbar.
Enable double-click to correct	Lets you double click text when editing with mouse and keyboard.
Select searches backwards	Look though previously spoken text, starting from the most recent, when using the Select and Select Again commands.
Dictation Settings	
Two spaces after period	Place two spaces instead of the standard single space between sentences. (This overrides WordPerfect's Format-As-You-Go setting.)
Format numbers, telephone numbers, currency and times automatically	Have Dragon recognize and format everyday numbers as you normally say them. (This feature uses the Regional Settings from your Windows Control Panel.)
Format Web and E-mail addresses automatically	Dictate e-mail and Web addresses in a natural manner (*e.g.*, **chester at myweb dot com** or **http www dot corel dot com**). It concatenates names in Web and e-mail addresses and recognizes the word "at" as the @ sign. (This option only works when the "Format numbers" setting is checked.)
Allow pauses while speaking numbers and addresses	Pause while speaking a number. (This option only works when the "Format numbers" setting is checked.)

For More Information . . .

On	See
Special characters and symbols	Chapter 7
Using Undo and Redo	Chapter 6
Changing fonts	Chapter 8
Using cut, copy, and paste	Chapter 2
Installing Dragon NaturallySpeaking	Appendix A
Dictating numbers	Appendix C
NaturallySpeaking Quick Reference	Appendix C

✦   ✦   ✦

How to Get Help

No matter how intuitive and powerful your software, it's only as good as the support it provides. With fierce price competition in the software industry, the days of toll-free, unlimited telephone support are over. There is, however, more readily available, easy-to-use support for WordPerfect Office than ever before, including the PerfectExpert, independent journals, and a vibrant user community. Whether you're a beginner looking to format a letterhead, or an expert user researching technical minutiae, answers to your questions are close at hand.

Getting Help Within WordPerfect Office 2000

In most cases, the quickest way to an answer is by way of the extensive online Help facilities:

✦ Help topics on all aspects of the application you're in

✦ Context-sensitive PerfectExpert help with the task at hand

✦ Predesigned PerfectExpert projects with step-by-step guidance

✦ Troubleshooting help

✦ Upgrading help to ease your transition from an earlier version of the program, or a competing program from another vendor

Outside Feature For general Help on using Windows, click Start ➪ Help on the Windows taskbar.

Exploring the Help Topics

Most online Help is found under the Help Topics dialog box. Press F1 or click
Help ➪ Help Topics, and then click the tab for the Help you need:

> ✦ *Index* is usually the quickest and surest way to find a Help topic. Type the first
> few letters of the topic (see Figure 5-1), and then double-click the entry you
> want, or highlight the entry and click Display.

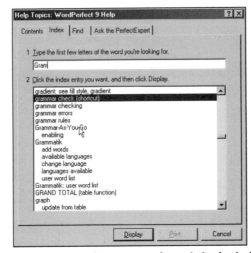

Figure 5-1: Looking up a Help topic in the index.

> ✦ *Find* locates all references to words and phrases you type within online Help.
> You can select matching words to narrow your search, as shown in Figure 5-2.
> Click Options to specify how you want to search on your typed entries; or
> Rebuild to customize the construction of the word search database.

> ✦ *Contents* organizes Help into clickable books of related tasks (see Figure 5-3).
> Double-click through a book until you arrive at the topic you want. Double-
> click open books to close them.

> ✦ *Ask the PerfectExpert* enables you to query the online Help in your own words,
> like "How do I check my grammar?" (see Figure 5-4). Your expert friend then
> lists possible answers, from the most relevant to the least.

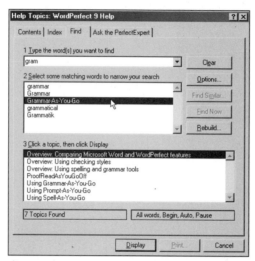

Figure 5-2: Finding Help topics containing specified words.

Figure 5-3: Using the Help contents.

Tip

Click the list when you type your questions to select a recent query.

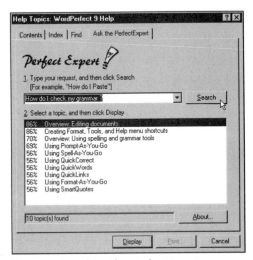

Figure 5-4: Asking the PerfectExpert.

Help on using Help

When a Help topic is displayed, you can click the icons in the Help window for further help on specific tasks or related concepts (see Figure 5-5). You can also click Back to return to the previous topic or Help Topics to look up another topic.

Click to display your note

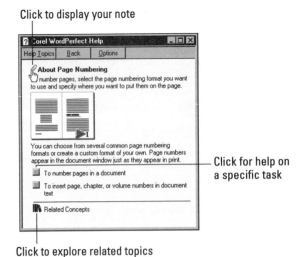

Click for help on a specific task

Click to explore related topics

Figure 5-5: Using Help.

Click Options from the Help display to perform other useful operations, including the following:

✦ *Print Topic,* to get a hard copy.

✦ *Keep Help on Top* ➪ *On Top*, to keep Help in view as you work. (You can change Help's size and shape or drag it out of the way.)

✦ *Annotate,* to add a personal note to a Help topic. When you return to the topic, you can click the paper clip that appears to read, edit, or delete the note.

✦ *Define a Bookmark,* to make it easy to come back to the topic later.

Getting PerfectExpert help as you work

For advice and assistance as you go about your tasks, click the PerfectExpert button (Help ➪ PerfectExpert).

This displays the context-sensitive PerfectExpert Help panel, with helpful tips, relevant Help selections, and buttons to call up features to complete your work (see Figure 5-6). Panel selections vary depending on whether you're editing text, inserting bullets, creating a table, and so on. PerfectExpert Help follows in whatever direction you want to go.

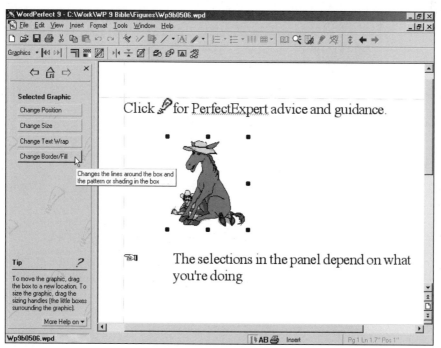

Figure 5-6: Getting PerfectExpert help as you work.

You can point near the edge of the panel to drag it to either side of the screen, or even to float it at another location. Click the Perfect Expert button again to close the panel, or click the Close button in the upper-right corner of the panel.

Getting a jump start with a PerfectExpert project

If you want more than context-sensitive Help, you can get off to a flying start with any of the hundreds of PerfectExpert projects that come with WordPerfect Office 2000:

1. Click the PerfectExpert icon on the taskbar, or click File ⇨ New from Project within an Office application. (The first time you run PerfectExpert, it goes through a long configuration process.)

2. Click the Create New tab and click the list at the top to display projects by application, in brackets or by subject.

3. Select the project you want and click Create (see Figure 5-7).

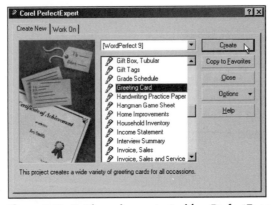

Figure 5-7: Getting a jump start with a PerfectExpert project.

4. Fill in the text, data, graphics, and other items for your project, with help from the PerfectExpert panel (see Figure 5-8).

Adding PerfectExpert categories and projects

From the PerfectExpert dialog box, click Copy to Favorites to add a project to the [Favorites] category. You can also create your own categories, add projects, and more. Click Help in the dialog box for details.

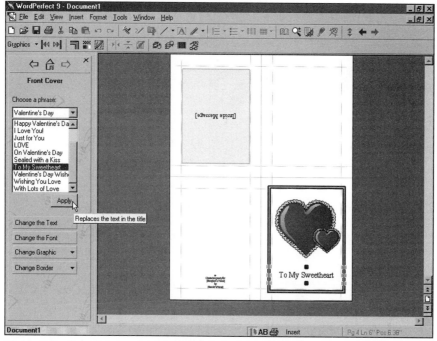

Figure 5-8: Complete your project with help from the PerfectExpert panel.

Getting other context-sensitive help

You have four other ways to get context-sensitive help:

✦ Hold the mouse pointer over a screen selection to display its QuickTip.

✦ For information on an item in a dialog box, click the What's This? button, and then click the item.

✦ For general information on a dialog box or highlighted menu selection, press F1, or click the dialog box's Help button.

✦ Press Shift+F1 (with a Windows keyboard), noting the change in the mouse pointer, and then click an item or use keystrokes.

Using the Reference Center

You can also go to the Corel Reference Center, shown in Figure 5-9, to read the application manuals on your WordPerfect Office CD. Insert the CD into your CD-ROM drive and click Reference Center. If the CD is already in the drive, or if the manuals are installed on a network or other drive, click Start on the Windows taskbar, and then click Programs ➪ WordPerfect Office 2000 ➪ Setup & Notes ➪ Corel Reference Center.

Figure 5-9: Using the Reference Center.

Click the picture of the guide you want to display in the Adobe Acrobat Reader. Then browse the guide or select topics from the contents or index (see Figure 5-10). Click Help ⇨ Reader Online Guide for help in using the Acrobat Reader.

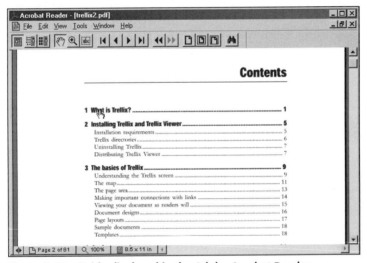

Figure 5-10: Guide displayed in the Adobe Acrobat Reader.

Getting Internet and Other Help

Now that you can buy the entire WordPerfect Office for a fraction of the former price for WordPerfect alone, providing "free" telephone support to every user would be prohibitively expensive. Does this mean that you can no longer get first class support? Positively not! In fact, the Web is turning out to be a fabulous place for getting (and sharing) expert advice and other help — and it really is free!

Joining newsgroup discussions

For the absolutely greatest, liveliest, and friendliest support, join in the various newsgroup discussions at `cnews.corel.com`. Don't be afraid to ask any question, from the "dumbest" to the most obscure and complex. More often than not, you'll get several alternative expert solutions, and as you become more proficient you'll contribute your own!

Web links from WordPerfect Office

You'll find that your WordPerfect Office applications are fully Web-enabled when it comes to getting outside help (see Figure 5-11):

✦ Click Help ➪ Corel Web Site to go to the main support page for WordPerfect Office. From there you can find all kinds of articles, news, discussions, links, services, tools and more.

✦ Click Help ➪ Corel on the Web for links to technical support, tips and tricks, learning and certification, and approved service bureaus.

✦ Click the PerfectExpert button, and then click the Web button in the PerfectExpert panel for Internet help.

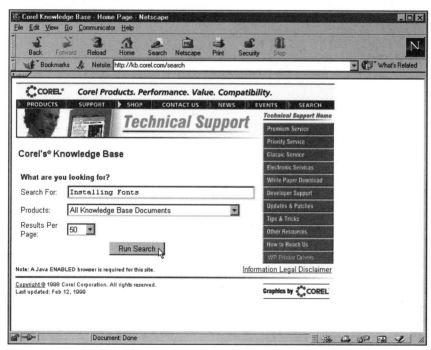

Figure 5-11: Corel's Web support.

From WordPerfect's menus, you'll also find links to printing information and fonts on the Web.

Getting other outside help

Other help outside of the program includes the following:

✦ Various Corel support services. Click Help ➪ Help Topics ➪ Contents and double-click the Corel Support and Services book for details.

✦ CompuServe Forums.

✦ The QwkScreen Web site at `http://www.qwkscreen.com`, where you'll find tips, tricks, and links to other resources and newsgroups.

For More Information . . .

On	See
Using WordPerfect projects and templates	Chapter 28
Using Quattro Pro projects	Chapter 31

✦   ✦   ✦

Basic Training

Working Without Worries

WordPerfect Office 2000 not only does more, it does more for you. Its automated features enable even beginning users to accomplish complex tasks quickly. However, as anyone experienced with computers knows, you can lose work even faster than you create it. That's why this chapter shows you how to work safely, as well as quickly.

Safeguarding Your Work

None of the sophisticated, time-saving tools will do you any good if your work is lost for any reason, whether because of an editing mistake or a hard disk crash. You can't recover what you don't save. This simple logic often escapes many computer users, even though saves and backups are easy to perform. See the next two sections, "QuickSaving your work" and "Making timed backups," for details.

WordPerfect Office 2000 provides automatic backup and undo features that you can configure to your needs. It also sports Corel Versions, a full-fledged archiving utility for tracking and safeguarding multiple file revisions.

You should make safety a regular part of your working habits. For example, a final save before a drastic editing action can be done with the click of a button or the press of a key. As for daily backups, they should be as regular a habit as bathing or brushing your teeth.

You can lose all or part of your work in several ways. Fortunately, you also have several ways to protect your work. Table 6-1 shows what can go wrong, the safeguards you can take, and how to recover when an accident occurs.

Table 6-1
Safeguarding Your Work

What Can Go Wrong	Safeguards	How to Recover
A recent deletion or editing change was a mistake.	Automatic.	Use Undo to reverse your editing actions (1 to 300 in WordPerfect; 10 in Presentations; 200 in Quattro Pro).
Your work gets messed up, so you want to go back to where it was five minutes ago.	Automatic timed backups, plus regular saves that you make.	Close your screen file without saving changes; then reopen the file or backup.
You get kicked out of the application, or your computer freezes, and you must reboot.	Timed backups.	Rename or open the timed backup file when you restart the application.
You change your mind about the changes you just saved and want to go back to the save before that.	Turn on the original document backup feature in WordPerfect or Presentations.	Replace the current document with the .BK! copy.
Today's edits made a mess of your file, so you want to start over.	Daily backups to disk or tape.	Restore yesterday's copy.
You need a file from several or weeks ago, which you since deleted or changed.	Keep backups going back several days, weeks, or months.	Restore the appropriate day's backup copy.
Your computer and backups are lost because of fire, flood, or theft.	Archive a copy of your full backup off-site on a regular schedule.	Restore to another computer from your archived copy.

QuickSaving your work

You can think of the save feature as QuickSave: simply click the Save button on the toolbar, or press a Ctrl+S on the keyboard (Ctrl+F12 for the WP DOS keyboard).

If you get into the habit of QuickSaving your document every few paragraphs, you won't have to worry about losing your work in most situations. The only drawback is that your options for restoring recent changes are reduced, because you're constantly replacing your backups.

Making timed backups

For everyday hazards, timed document backup is a critical line of defense. At the interval you specify, the application automatically makes a backup copy of every window that has changed since the last save.

Timed backups are automatically deleted when you exit the program normally, but if your system locks up, a power failure occurs, or you get kicked out of the program for some reason, your backups are preserved. You'll be able to recover your documents from the timed backups when you restart WordPerfect, so you'll never lose more than a few minutes' work. To make timed backups:

✦ In WordPerfect, click Tools ⇨ Settings ⇨ Files

✦ In Quattro Pro, click Tools ⇨ Settings ⇨ File Options

✦ In Presentations, click Tools ⇨ Settings ⇨ Files ⇨ Backup

Quattro Pro and Presentations backups have a .TMP extension. WordPerfect's automatic backups are named WP{WP}.BK*X*, where X is the number of the document screen from 1 to 9. For more on setting WordPerfect's backups, see Chapter 29, "Customizing WordPerfect."

Making original document backups

WordPerfect and Presentations also have an *original document backup* safeguard that (if you turn it on) makes a copy of your original disk document each time you save your screen changes to disk. The backup goes into the same folder as the original file, using the same name and a .BK! extension.

If original document backup provides another level of protection, why is it off by default? Well, it offers no additional crash protection, and the backups clutter your folders. (They aren't deleted when you exit the application, as are your timed backups.) The feature is only useful when you save a document and then decide you want to revert to the previous version instead.

Backing up your hard drive

Don't expect WordPerfect Office 2000 to take care of all your disaster-prevention and recovery needs. It can deal with things that go on within its programs and get back most of your work when the lights go out, but it can't do anything if your hard disk goes "belly-up" because of a computer virus or mechanical failure. Or, what if your machine is stolen? Unlikely, perhaps, but why chance losing weeks, months, even years, of work and records?

Forget about losing your hard disk. What happens if you discover two days after the fact that you deleted the wrong file? Or, suppose you rewrite a section of your term paper or report and decide after a couple days that the old version was better?

There's only one way to protect your work in these situations. You must back up your hard drive!

If you have copies of your work, you're fine. If you don't, you're helpless. If nothing else, at the end of the day, go to the folder where you keep your important documents and copy them onto floppies. See Chapter 7, "Managing Your Files," for details on copying files.

Note
If your work is on a network drive, it's likely that your files are backed up and archived on a regular schedule. See your network administrator for details.

If you have many files to back up, it's good to have a tape drive, recordable CD, or other removable storage device. You can then use the backup in the Windows System Tools (or a third-party backup program) to do the following:

✦ Copy numerous files from different folders in one operation

✦ Store your backups in a highly compressed format

✦ Automatically run your backups at the time you designate

✦ Save your file settings and other options (such as to back up only the files you have changed since the last backup)

What to back up

Back up anything you don't want to lose. Include folders for your documents, spreadsheets, slide shows, and so on. Other backup candidates are your Windows registry, and the Corel Office 2000 files in Table 6-2.

Table 6-2		
System Files to Back Up		
File	*Description*	*Location*
System.dat	Windows registry	Windows folder
User.dat	Windows registry	Windows folder
CorelCENTRAL files	Addresses, calendars, card files, and memos	Normally in \My Documents\ CCWin9
wp9US.wpt	Default template (US)	\Program Files\Corel\WordPerfect Office 2000\template\Custom WP Templates
qw9EN.wpt	QuickWords	\Program Files\Corel\WordPerfect Office 2000\template\Custom WP Templates

File	Description	Location
wt9us.uwl and wt9us.hst (US English)	QuickCorrect changes, Spell-checker additions, QuickLinks, and end-of-sentence punctuation exceptions	Normally in \My Documents\Corel User Files
template.wb3	Default Quattro Pro template	\Program Files\Corel\WordPerfect Office 2000\template\Custom QP Templates
*.cfg, *.ini, *.inf	QP and PR configuration and setup files	\Program Files\Corel\WordPerfect Office 2000\programs

When to back up

You never know when an accident will occur, or how far back in time you'll want to go. Consider keeping backups by the month, by the week for the last four weeks, and by the day for the current week. With ten sets of backups, you can keep records for the whole quarter:

Backup Group	Backup Set Names
Daily	Monday, Tuesday, Wednesday, Thursday
Weekly	First Week, Second Week, Third Week
Monthly	First Month, Second Month, Third Month

To provide a comprehensive three-month backup:

1. Perform a full backup every Friday evening.
2. Perform an incremental backup (of additions or changes since Friday) on Monday, Tuesday, Wednesday, and Thursday.
3. On the last Friday of every month, perform an additional full backup.

If you're making tape or CD backups, you probably can save tapes or CDs by appending multiple backups on a single tape or CD—especially the incremental daily backups.

As another precaution against fire, flood, theft, or some other unforeseen disaster, you can make an additional backup copy every Friday to archive at a separate location.

Recovering Your Work

Suppose that you lost (or messed up) a file. Because you took the proper precautions, you're not going to break into a cold sweat. The first thing to do is nothing; don't even close the document! Take a minute to size up what happened; then select the appropriate recovery procedures from those discussed in the following sections.

Using Undo as your first line of defense

If something goes wrong with your document, spreadsheet, drawing, or show, consider Undo as your first line of defense. The Undo history maintained with your file enables you to reverse your most recent editing changes (such as deletions, insertions, new font sizes, moving graphics, or copying text).

In WordPerfect, you can click Edit ➪ Undo/Redo History to undo or restore any number of selected actions at once (see Figure 6-1).

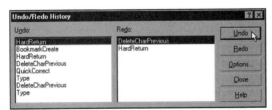

Figure 6-1: Use WordPerfect's Undo/Redo history feature to restore your work.

You can also click Options in the Undo/Redo History dialog to specify how many Undos to retain (1 to 300), and whether they should be saved with your document (see Figure 6-2). Saving your Undos with the document enables you to retrace your steps later, but it makes your files bigger and may enable someone else to see what you've changed.

Figure 6-2: Specifying WordPerfect's Undo/ Redo options.

WordPerfect also has an Undelete feature (assigned to Ctrl+Shift+Z on the DOS keyboard) that enables you to restore, at the insertion point, any of the last three deletions.

Going back to your disk document

As an alternative to undoing actions step by step when your screen document gets messed up, you can discard your screen changes, and then restore the file from your last save to disk:

1. Click File ⇨ Close.

2. When asked to save changes to your document, click No to clear the screen without saving your changes to disk.

3. Open your document as you normally do.

Restoring from a timed document backup

If both your screen and disk documents are messed up in WordPerfect, you might be able to make a reasonably graceful recovery from the automatic timed document backup. To restore from a timed document backup:

1. Close the screen document.

2. Go into the backup folder specified in Tools ⇨ Settings ⇨ Files, and look for WP{WP}.BK*X*, where *X* is the number of the document window you were using.

3. Open the document in WordPerfect, and make sure it's all right.

4. Click File ⇨ Save As.

5. Locate and highlight the original document, and then click Save.

6. Answer Yes to the "Replace this name?" prompt.

If the last timed backup occurred after the document got messed up, then this procedure will be of little benefit. However, it's worth a try.

Recovering from a crash

If an application kicks you out of the system, or your computer crashes and you must reboot, you can recover your work from the timed backup files. To recover from a crash:

1. Restart the application.

2. As you reenter the program, you are asked if you want to open, rename, or delete your timed backups (see Figure 6-3).

3. Click Open to retrieve your backup, and then continue with Step 4. You can also click Rename to preserve your backup in case you find that you need to restore it later. Click Delete only if you're sure that you won't need the backup.

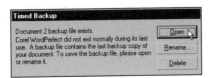

Figure 6-3: You can recover from a timed backup file upon reentering WordPerfect.

4. If the backup you opened is more recent and complete than the original on disk, you can click File ➪ Save As to save the backup document to the original filename.

Tip

If you open or rename your backup files upon reentering WordPerfect, you can click File ➪ Document ➪ Compare to compare the backup to the file on disk (see Chapter 18, "Editing and Reviewing Techniques"), and then decide which one to use.

Going back to the save before last

If original document backup is turned on (WordPerfect or Presentations), you can undo both the current and last sets of changes by restoring the save before last:

1. Click File ➪ Close to exit the screen document. (Answer "No" to any "Save Changes?" prompts.)

2. Click File ➪ Open, and then go to the document's folder (*not* the backup folder), and open the associated .BK! file.

3. If you're sure it's the version you want, click File ➪ Save As, click the document you are replacing, and then click Save.

Restoring from a periodic backup

To recover from a daily, weekly, or monthly backup, perform either of the following tasks:

✦ If you backed up files by using the Open File dialog box, use the same procedure to copy the file(s) back from the backup disk to the folder.

✦ If you used a backup program, follow the program's restore procedures.

Repairing a Damaged Document

Sometimes a WordPerfect document will become damaged in such a way that you can't open it, or it crashes WordPerfect when you edit or save it. When this happens, try running the Restore utility, which was originally designed to fix problems with password-protected files, but turned out to be a great tool for repairing various other document problems, such as corrupted files. This utility works with documents created in WordPerfect 6.x and newer, and can be downloaded from Corel's FTP-site at ftp://ftp.corel.com/pub/WordPerfect/wpwin/8/wp8rest.exe.

Once you've downloaded the utility, here's how to run it:

1. Click Start on the Windows taskbar, click Run ⇨ Browse, and select the program where you downloaded it on your hard drive.

2. Click OK, specify the file to repair and the name of the repaired document (New File), and then click Repair Document.

 You can add the repair utility to your Desktop Application Director display (see Appendix A, "Setting Up WordPerfect Office 2000") or to a toolbar (see Chapter 57, "Customizing Toolbars, Menus, and Keyboards").

Tracking Changes with Corel Versions

Corel Versions acts like a super Undo, by storing multiple updates to your files in one backup, as they evolve toward their final form. Its facilities for annotating revisions and identifying authors are especially useful when you're working on the same documents as a team.

You can track revisions to any type of file, including graphics. You can specify the number of revisions to keep, store them in a highly compressed form, and compare versions side by side. To use Corel Versions, however, it must be selected during a custom install (see Appendix A, "Setting Up WordPerfect Office 2000").

Saving versions of a file

To start an archive of the current file onscreen:

1. Click File ⇨ Version Control ⇨ Save Current.

2. Specify any of the following (see Figure 6-4):

   • *Make first version permanent*, to keep the original from being replaced when the maximum number of temporary versions is reached.

   • *Use compression*, to save disk space. For example, a 50K document may take 15K in compressed form.

   • *Save version to a single location*, to store the versions in the default Versions folder. When you remove the check, versions are saved in the same folder as the original file.

   • *Maximum number of temporary versions*, to specify the number of temporary versions to keep, before they start getting replaced by newer versions.

Figure 6-4: Starting a Versions archive.

To save subsequent versions of the file:

1. Click File ➪ Version Control ➪ Save Current.

2. Check Permanent to make this a permanent copy that doesn't count toward the number of temporary copies (see Figure 6-5).

Figure 6-5: Adding a version to your archive.

3. Add any descriptive comments, such as "Technical review incorporated," or "Includes Maria's comments." (To type multi-line comment, keep typing without pressing Enter. Otherwise, you'll submit the version with what you've typed so far.)

Retrieving a previous version of a file

To retrieve a previous version of a file:

1. Click File ➪ Version Control ➪ Retrieve Current.

2. Select the version you want and click Retrieve (see Figure 6-6).

3. Choose whether you want to replace your screen document with the retrieved version. If you choose No, a new file is created with the name of *OldFilename1.wpd*, *OldFilename2.wpd*, and so on.

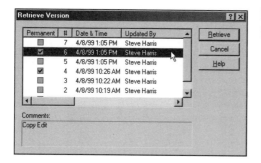

Figure 6-6: Retrieving a previous version of a file.

Setting archive defaults

Corel Versions is a separate application that can be accessed through the Windows Control Panel. To set archive defaults, including where the versions are stored and the number of versions:

1. Click Start on the Windows taskbar, click Settings ⇨ Control Panel, and double-click the Corel Versions icon.

2. Enable or disable version control, and specify the default options, including the archive location and file types to exclude (see Figure 6-7).

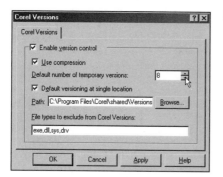

Figure 6-7: Setting archive defaults.

Managing a file's archive

You can view and compare archived versions from the File menu, as described in the following two sections. For the full range of archive management options:

1. Go to the file's folder (not the archive folder) using Windows Explorer or any Corel file-management dialog box.

2. Right-click the file, and then click Corel Versions ⇨ History.

3. You can then change the maximum number of temporary versions; delete, copy, view, or compare (View Multiple) versions; or print a version history (see Figure 6-8).

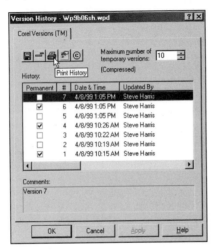

Figure 6-8: Managing a file's archive.

Tip   Select a version and click View Multiple to compare it to the current version.

Viewing an archived version

To view an archived version of the current file:

1. Click File ⇨ Version Control ⇨ Retrieve Current.

2. Click the version and click View.

3. You can right-click in the viewer to select various view, size, display, and print options.

Comparing two versions of a file

To compare two archived versions of the current file:

1. Click File ⇨ Version Control ⇨ Retrieve Current.

2. Hold the Ctrl key and click the two versions you want to compare.

3. Click View Multiple and scroll the versions side by side.

Unfortunately, you'll find no markings indicating what was added, changed, or deleted, to help you with the compare.

Backing up your archives

By backing up your Versions file, you automatically get a backup of the file's entire version history. If you store your archives in the default Versions folder, simply back up the folder to make a copy of the history for all your archives at once.

Moving or deleting an archive

Each file's archive is stored in a special .CV file, that you can't edit directly in WordPerfect (see Figure 6-9). The archive file's name includes the abbreviated name and path of the original file, with dollar signs ($) to indicate the colon (:) and slashes (\). For example, versions of the file "Research Proposal.wpd" in the folder C:\My Documents\Business\Proposals will be stored in the archive C$$MYDOCU~1$BUSINESS$PROPOS~1$RESEAR~1$WPD.cv.

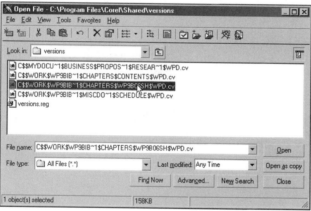

Figure 6-9: Moving or deleting an archive.

Corel Versions can find a file's archive as long as it's in either the file's folder or the default Versions folder. You can, therefore, move an archive freely between the two folders. For example, if your workgroup shares a common default Versions folder, you might move an archive to the shared folder so that others can use it, moving it back after everyone is finished.

To remove a file's archive, delete the .CV file. You can also delete the entire archive folder, but be sure that's what you want to do.

Recycle Bin Diving

Outside Feature

If you follow the measures described in this chapter, you'll have excellent computer accident insurance. Even if you weren't especially careful and all seems lost, it might not be. When a file is deleted on your hard drive, it's tossed into the Windows recycle bin.

As long as the file remains in the bin, you can go to the bin and fish it out. Click the Open button and go to the root folder of your hard drive (see Chapter 7, "Managing Your Files"). You can also double-click the Recycle Bin icon on your desktop, select the files you want to retrieve, and then click File ⇨ Restore.

For More Information . . .

On	See
Setting WordPerfect's backups	Chapter 29
Managing files	Chapter 7
Comparing documents	Chapter 18
Backing up to removable media	Online Help for the Windows or third-party backup program
Recovering files on a network drive	Your network administrator

✦   ✦   ✦

Managing Your Files

A nice thing about computers is that all your documents, spreadsheets, slide shows, and other files are always within easy reach . . . if you can find them. With the help of the suite's file-management tools, you can organize your work so that you'll never lose track of a letter or report. Or, if you do, you can locate it in short order.

The WordPerfect Office Open File dialog box is your control center. As you play around with it for a while, you'll discover many things you can do (such as find, view, open, save, name, move, copy, rename, delete, and print). You can create folders, print file listings, or add items to your Favorites folder. You can perform QuickFinder searches to find the paper your dog ate, even track down a location on the Internet (see Chapter 14, "Web Writing and Publishing").

Note This chapter refers to the Open File dialog box for convenience, but all the suite's file-management dialog boxes (such as Save As or Play Macro) work basically the same way.

Organizing Your Files

The first step in managing your files is to get them organized. The programs, documents, graphics, and other files on each drive are stored in *folders*. Folders can also contain *subfolders*, so files can be organized in a logical hierarchy (or tree), much as you organize the drawers, sections, and folders of a filing cabinet (see Figure 7-1).

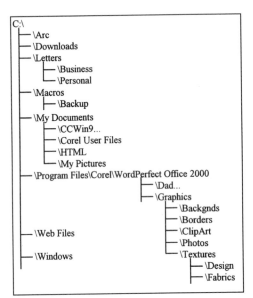

Figure 7-1: Partial illustration of a folder tree.

The tree helps you to see the path to your document's folder. At the top of your WordPerfect screen you'll see the likes of "C:\Letters\Personal\LoveLetter 3.wpd," where "C:\Letters\Personal" is the path to your folder and "LoveLetter 3.wpd" is the particular file. It's the path plus the filename that gives a file its unique identity. That's why you can have two files with the same name in different folders.

Click the Open button (or File ➪ Open), and then click the Open File Tree View button (View ➪ Tree View) to see how your folders are organized (see Figure 7-2). Double-click a folder to open it, or highlight a folder and then press Enter (or click Open). The name and path of the selected folder are shown in the title bar of the Open File dialog box.

Outside Feature   If you don't see the folder's path and name (and want to), you'll have to change your Windows settings. Right-click the Start button on your Windows taskbar, click Explore ➪ View ➪ Options, and then check "Display the full MS-DOS path in the title bar."

Setting Up Your File-Management Display

Click File ➪ Open and click the Open File Toggle Menu button, if necessary, to display the menu bar (refer to Figure 7-2). Then click the View menu, and take a look at the file-management display options described in Table 7-1. You can also click Open File Views button on the Open File toolbar to switch between the large icons, small icons, list, and details views.

Current folder   Path

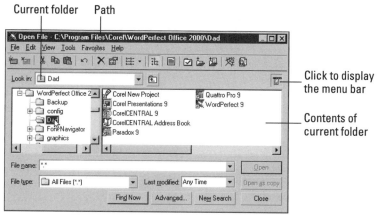

Click to display
the menu bar

Contents of
current folder

Figure 7-2: The Open File dialog box, showing tree view
and folder contents.

Table 7-1
File-Management Display Options

Option	Lets You
Toolbar	Display the toolbar for one-click access to basic features.
Status Bar	See useful information about the current selection, such as the number of objects in a folder, the number and size of selected files, or the descriptive name of a document, spreadsheet, or macro.
Tree View	See how your files are organized.
Preview	Look at your files before opening them. (See "Previewing Files," later in this chapter.)
Large Icons	Display large icons for folders and files. The text size stays the same.
Small Icons	Display small icons for folders and files. You'll see more files.
List	Display folders and files in horizontal columns with small icons. This is the quickest way to browse large folders.
Details	Display folders and files as a scrollable list that includes the size, type, and date last modified. Click the column labels to sort the list; click again to invert the sort (see Figure 7-3). Drag labels to rearrange or resize them.

Tip

Click File ⇨ Properties in WordPerfect to use descriptive names instead of long filenames that hog your file display.

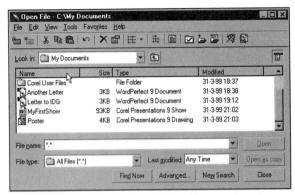

Figure 7-3: Click the column labels to sort the file details list.

Changes to one file-management dialog box affect all others of a similar type.

Adjusting the display size

To adjust the size of your file-management display, drag a side or corner of the Open File dialog box. You can also drag the borders between the windows within the dialog box.

Opening Files

To open a file, select the file and click Open, or double-click the file. To keep the original intact, click "Open as copy" and save the copy to a different name.

You can click the drop-down arrow at the right of the "File name" box to select from the last nine documents you opened (see Figure 7-4).

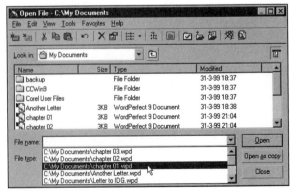

Figure 7-4: Selecting from the last nine files opened.

Navigating folders

Use the scroll bar to navigate the open folder. You can also click in the file listing, and then type the first letter of the filename or scroll with the arrow keys.

To jump to a subfolder, double-click its icon in the right window, or single-click it in the Tree view (when displayed) in the left window. Click the Open File Up One Level button to view the current folder's parent.

 Tip Press the Backspace key to make your way up the folder chain.

Another handy navigational trick is to click the "Look in" drop-down list, and then scroll the list and click the folder or drive you want (see Figure 7-5).

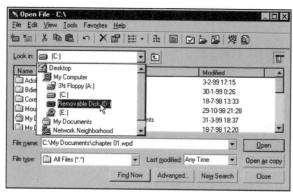

Figure 7-5: Using the "Look in" list.

Narrowing your selections

You can click the "File type" list to display all files (*.*) or only those of a particular type (see Figure 7-6).

If you have an idea of when the file you're looking for was last updated, click the "Last modified" list to narrow the time frame (see Figure 7-7).

Searching for Files

If you don't know where your file is, you can use QuickFinder to search for files by name or content. For example, you can track down every letter that mentions a particular person or company. For superfast searches by content, see "Building Fast Search Indexes" later in this chapter.

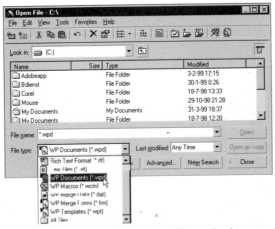

Figure 7-6: Selecting the type of file to display.

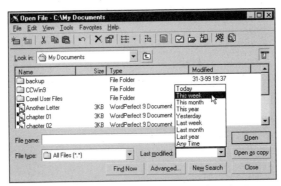

Figure 7-7: Locating a file based on when it was last modified.

The two methods of QuickFinder searching are as follows:

✦ *Basic* searches for all matches on filename or content

✦ *Advanced* searches based on the criteria and options you specify

An advanced search provides visual tools for constructing your search, and it enables you to do the following:

✦ Search by filename only or contents only

✦ Match content on word forms, partial words, and case

✦ Search custom indexes

You can switch back and forth between the two search methods.

Doing a basic search

To do a basic file search by name and content:

1. Click File ⇨ Open and specify the "Look in" folder and subfolders to search.

Tip   Display the Open File status bar (View ⇨ Status Bar) so you can see the progress of your search.

2. Type the filename or contents you're looking for in the "File name" box. When describing the contents, you can use any of the text search operators shown in Table 7-2.

3. Specify the "File type" and "Last modified" range, if possible, to narrow your search.

4. Click Find Now to start your search and build the QuickFinder Search Results list (see Figure 7-8).

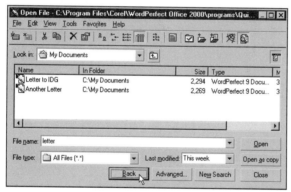

Figure 7-8: QuickFinder search results.

Tip   As soon as your file is found, click Stop Find to terminate the search.

5. Select your file (or files) from the list, or click Back to return to your original folder.

Tip   If you're not sure which file in the search results list is the one you want, click the Open File Preview button to preview the files.

Table 7-2
Text Search Operators for Basic Searches

Search Operator	Sample Query	Selects
(none)	swimming	Files that contain "swimming"
(none)	swimming beach	Files that contain "swimming" and "beach"
& or "and"	swimming & beach	Files that contain "swimming" and "beach"
quotes	"beach ball"	Files containing the phrase "beach ball"
| or "or"	swimming | "beach ball"	Files that contain "swimming" or the phrase "beach ball"
!	! swimming	Files that don't contain "swimming"
..	beach .. umbrella	Files that contain "beach" and an "umbrella" sometime after the first "beach"
( )	! (beach and umbrella)	Files that don't contain both "beach" and "umbrella"
/page	/page watermelon cantaloupe	Files with "watermelon" and "cantaloupe" on the same page
/paragraph	/paragraph watermelon	Files with "watermelon" and "cantaloupe" in the same paragraph
/sentence	/sentence watermelon	Files with "watermelon" and "cantaloupe" in the same sentence
/line	/line watermelon cantaloupe	Files with "watermelon" and "cantaloupe" in the same line
/subject	/subject recipe	Files with "recipe" in the Subject field of their file description
/descriptive_name	/descriptive_name lasagne	Files with "lasagne" in the Descriptive Name field of their file description

Tip   If you get a long list of matching files, try narrowing your search criteria and running another search.

Basic searches match on partial filenames, but only on whole words in their contents. For example, a search on "list" matches on "Booklist.wpd," as well as on any document containing the word "list." However, the word "enlisted" in a document's contents will not match. (See "Doing an advanced search" for more content search options.)

Searching with wildcards

Use the "*" (zero or more characters) or "?" (one character) wildcard in the "File name" box if you're not sure of the exact name or contents. For example, "Te*.wpd" matches on all WordPerfect documents starting with "Te." A search on "wild*d" finds all files containing "wildcard" or "wildcatted."

To search on particular fields in the file description, create a QuickFinder index by using the "Full document with document summary separation" option. For fast page, paragraph, or sentence searches, index down to the respective level. See "Setting QuickFinder indexing options" later in this chapter.

Doing an advanced search

To do an advanced file search by name and/or content:

1. Click File ⇨ Open.

2. You can optionally specify the "Look in" folder to search (other than a custom index), type the filename or contents you're looking for in the "File name" box, or select the "File type" and "Last modified" range.

3. Click Advanced, and then specify any of the following:

   • *Look in,* to select a folder or a Custom Index (at the top of the list)

   • *Search subfolders,* to include lower-level folders

   • *Allow document summary fields in search criteria,* to select summary fields when defining search properties (see "Adding File Descriptions" later in this chapter)

   • *Content Search Criteria,* to match on word forms, partial words, and case (see Chapter 18, "Editing and Reviewing Techniques," for more on text search criteria).

4. To specify a filename or extension, double-click the "Filename contains word(s)" item, and then specify the text (see Figure 7-9).

5. Click the QuickFinder Advanced Find Add button or double-click Insert a New Property to define additional search criteria. Set the And/Or condition, select what you want to search by (see Figure 7-10), and then select a "contains" option and type a search word or phrase.

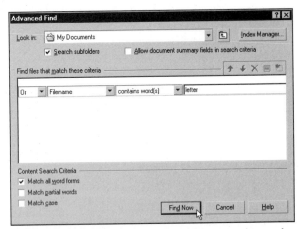

Figure 7-9: Specifying file properties for an advanced search.

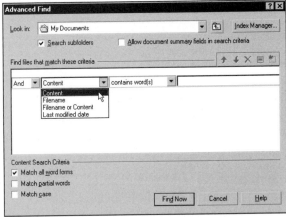

Figure 7-10: Specifying additional search criteria.

6. You can click the arrow buttons to rearrange your search criteria, click the QuickFinder Advanced Find Edit button to edit an item, or click the QuickFinder Advanced Find Delete button to delete an item.

7. Click Find Now to start your search and build the QuickFinder Search Results list.

8. Select your file (or files) from the list, or click Back to return to your original folder.

Going to Your Favorite Locations

Chances are, 90 percent of your work is stored in five or six folders. So why search all over the place for what you need?

Using shortcuts

By placing shortcuts in the Windows Favorites folder, you can go straight to the folders and documents you regularly use. The shortcut is a pointer with a little arrow at the lower-left. Double-click a shortcut to open the actual folder or document. You can also have shortcuts to programs, drives, printers, and other resources. (Renaming or deleting a shortcut has no effect on the object of your shortcut.)

Click the Open File Favorites button in the Open File dialog box to open your Favorites folder. Better yet, click Favorites on the main menu and select where you want to go (see Figure 7-11).

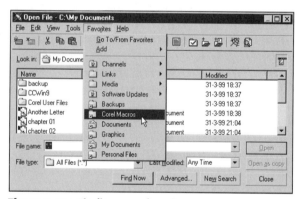

Figure 7-11: Finding your favorites.

Adding a shortcut

Click the Open File Add Folder to Favorites button to add the current folder to your Favorites, or click Open File Add Item to Favorites button to add the selected item(s). (You can also click Favorites ⇨ Add to add a Favorites folder or item.)

Tip

Only keep shortcuts you regularly use. You may also want to deactivate the "Update Favorites with changes" feature under WordPerfect's File settings to keep the folder uncluttered (see Chapter 29, "Customizing WordPerfect").

To delete a shortcut in your Favorites folder, click the Open File Delete button, or right-click it and click Delete.

Performing File Operations

You can perform any file operation from within any file-management dialog box. Many operations (including opening and printing) can be performed on groups of selected files or folders.

Selecting multiple files

To select a consecutive group of files, click the first file, and then hold the Shift key and click the last file.

To select two or more nonconsecutive files, hold the Ctrl key as you click each file. To select all the items in a folder (including subfolders), click Edit ➪ SelectAll (Ctrl+A).

To deselect selected files, click anywhere in the window other than on the selected file(s).

Copying files or folders to another folder

Open File provides an easy-to-follow way to copy selected files or folders (with their contents) to another folder. To copy files or folders to another folder:

1. Select the files or folders to be copied.
2. Click File ➪ Copy to Folder.
3. Click the target folder and click Copy.

To copy files and folders the standard Windows way:

1. Select the files or folders to be copied.
2. Click Edit ➪ Copy (Ctrl+C).
3. Switch to the folder to which you're copying and click Edit ➪ Paste (Ctrl+V).

You can also copy a selected file or group of files by holding down the Ctrl key as you drag to another folder.

Making copies of files or folders in the same folder

To make a copy of selected files or folders within the same folder, click File ➪ Copy to Folder ➪ Copy.

You'll see that copies of your files of folders appear with names in the form of "Copy of *original name*."

Moving files or folders

To move selected files or folders:

1. Click File ➪ Move to Folder.

2. Click the target folder and click Move.

To move selected files and folders the standard Windows way:

1. Click Edit ➪ Cut (Ctrl+X).

2. Switch to the folder to which you're copying, and click Edit ➪ Paste. You can also move a selected file or group of files by dragging them to another folder.

Sending files or folders

To send selected files or folders to another location:

1. Click File ➪ Send To.

2. Select the "send to" location:

   • *3.5" Floppy,* to copy the files or folders to a floppy

   • *Desktop Shortcut,* to put a shortcut icon on the Windows desktop

   • *Mail Recipient,* to e-mail selected files

   • *My Briefcase,* to copy files to another computer, work on them there, and then automatically update the original files

   • *Mail*, to send as an e-mail attachment

   • *HTML*, to publish to an HTML source file or server (see Chapter 16)

   • *Fax*, to fax a document

Your possible "send to" locations depend on your Windows installation.

Renaming a file or folder

To rename a selected file or folder:

1. Click File ➪ Rename (or wait a second or two after you select it, and then click the name).

2. Type the new name; then press Enter or click elsewhere.

Deleting files or folders

Click the Open File Delete button to delete selected files or folders. (You can also click File ⇨ Delete, or press the Delete key.)

Changing file attributes

Every file has four attributes, which are either on (checked) or off (unchecked):

File Attribute	Meaning When Checked
Archive	The file has changed since the last time it was backed up.
Read-only	The file can't be edited or deleted.
Hidden	The file is hidden from listings and searches.
System	This is a vital system file that's off-limits to most programs.

Ordinarily, you don't have to worry about file attributes. (The archive attribute is cleared by your backup program.) You can set a completed file to read-only, as an added measure of protection.

To change attributes of selected files:

1. Click the Open File Properties button, or click File ⇨ Properties.

2. Check or uncheck the attributes you want to change (see Figure 7-12).

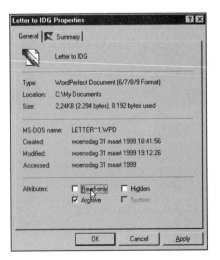

Figure 7-12: Changing file attributes.

Printing files

To print selected files directly from the Open File dialog box, click File ⇨ Print.

Creating or deleting a folder

To create a folder:

1. Go to the drive or folder where you want to create a new folder.
2. Click File ⇨ New ⇨ Folder.
3. Type a name for the folder (the default is New Folder), and then press Enter.

To delete a folder and its contents, click the folder and press the Delete key.

Creating a shortcut

You can create a shortcut to a file, folder, or other resource, and use it like a Favorites shortcut. To create a shortcut:

1. Select the folder where you want to place the shortcut.
2. Click File ⇨ New ⇨ Shortcut, and follow the onscreen instructions.

Printing file lists

You can print a list of the files in a folder, or a partial list of selected files. To print a file list:

1. Click File ⇨ Print File List.
2. Select whether you want to print the list (see Figure 7-13), display it in WordPad, or copy it to the Windows Clipboard.

Figure 7-13: Printing a file list.

Tip   In WordPad, you can edit the list, print it, or save it to a file.

3. Check whether you want to print the selected entries or the entire list.

4. Check if you want to include folders in the listing (if you're printing the entire list).

Mapping network drives

On a network, you can click Open File Map Network Drive button (Tools ➪ Map Network Drive) to designate a network folder as a drive on your machine. (You may be prompted for a password.) Click Tools ➪ Disconnect Network Drive to remove the designation.

Using other file-management tools

Other tools in file-management dialog boxes include the Viewer and QuickFinder described next. You can also access other Windows file-management tools you may have installed, such as Corel Versions, a Zip utility, or Quick View Plus. The options appear on the File menu, or when you right-click selected files.

Previewing Files

When you're not sure which file is the one you want, use the file-management viewer to take a peek at various documents. Otherwise you'll have to open and close each file until you find the one you want. To preview documents:

1. Click the Open File Preview button (View ➪ Preview ➪ No Preview) and browse your documents by selecting them one-by-one.

2. Right-click the preview window (see Figure 7-14) to select the options described in Table 7-3. (Options depend on the type of file and your current view mode.)

3. Click the Open File preview button (View ➪ Preview ➪ No Preview) to close the preview window.

Caution   If you leave the Previewer open, it will be open in every file-management dialog box, even ones such as Save As and Play Macro.

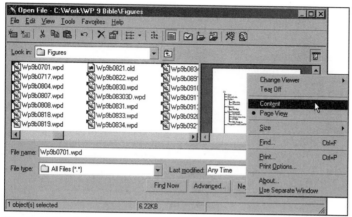

Figure 7-14: Selecting preview options.

Table 7-3
Preview Options

Selection	Lets You
Change Viewer	Switch between the Outside In and WordPerfect viewers.
Tear Off	Tear off a copy of preview window that you can enlarge, but won't update when you click another file. (Click File ➪ Exit to return.)
Content	Wrap text to fit in the preview window. You can further select a Normal display of actual fonts and graphics, or a Draft display with bold and italic attributes, but with only one font type and size, and empty boxes for graphics.
Page View	See the file as it will print, more or less. You can choose a size of Window Width; Window Size (the smallest); and Original Size.
Find (Ctrl+F)	Locate the next or previous occurrence of the text you enter. Check "Match case" to search for text exactly as typed.
Print (Ctrl+P)	Print a draft of the entire document or selected content, with the resolution and number of copies you specify.
Print Options	Change the font and margins of your printed output. You can also select how graphics print, and whether to print spreadsheet headings and database field names.

Continued

Table 7-3 (continued)

Selection	Lets You
About	See the Viewer file formats available.
Use Separate Window	Remove the preview window from the file-management dialog box to use on its own (Figure 7-15). (Right-click and click Use Separate Window to return.)
Font	Change the font type and font size when using the Content view with Draft display. (You may want to use the Tear Off or separate viewer instead.)
Copy (Ctrl+C)	Copy a selection to the Clipboard.

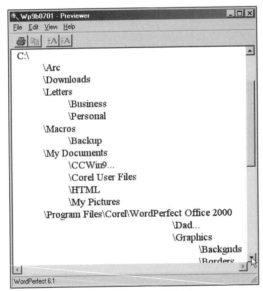

Figure 7-15: Using a separate preview window.

Tip

Instead of fussing with a separate viewer, you will see more of the previewed document if you click the Open File maximize button (the middle one at the top right) so the dialog fills the entire screen. Click the button again to return the Open File dialog to its normal size.

Password-Protecting Your Files

Password protection is one feature that's easy to miss. Perhaps that's how it should be, because then you won't password-protect a document and forget your password.

Sometimes, however, you might have a reason to prevent others from searching, viewing, altering, or printing a document. A password-protected file can still be moved, copied, or deleted without using the password.

You can select enhanced password protection to provide greater security and case-sensitive passwords. If your document has a password of "TigeR," for example, it cannot be opened with "tiger" or "Tiger." Note that Presentations does not offer password protection. And Quattro Pro passwords are *always* case-sensitive.

The password-protect feature is found only in the Save As dialog box. To password-protect a file:

1. Click File ➪ Save As.

2. If you're saving a new file, or want to rename your file, type the filename and path.

3. Check "Password protect," and then click Save.

4. Select either Enhanced or Original password protection (see Figure 7-16).

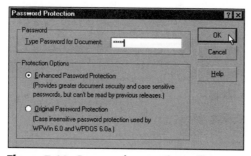

Figure 7-16: Password-protecting a file.

5. Type your password (only asterisks appear), and then click OK.

6. Retype the password to confirm it, and then click OK again.

From this point on, anyone trying to view, open, or print your document is prompted for your password. Remember the password!

To remove password protection from a file, open the file, click File ➪ Save As, and remove the "Password protect" checkmark.

Adding File Descriptions

You can attach a descriptive summary to your current document, show, or workbook, to categorize, annotate, and locate your work. The summaries help you to locate your work more quickly because they appear in file dialogs, and you can also search on them. To add a summary to your current document, workbook, or show, click File ➪ Properties and fill in the fields on the Summary tab (see Figure 7-17).

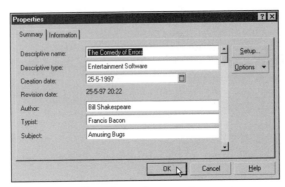

Figure 7-17: Changing a document summary.

Ten fields are included in WordPerfect's default document summary configuration. But if you don't see what you need, you can customize your summaries with more than 50 fields, from Abstract to Version Number:

1. Click File ➪ Properties ➪ Setup, and select or deselect any of the available fields.

2. Drag the names of selected fields to delete or rearrange the fields in the box (see Figure 7-18).

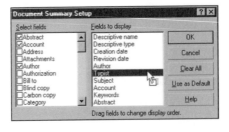

Figure 7-18: Customizing document summaries.

3. To use the new configuration for your new documents, click Use as Default.

Building Fast Search Indexes

Normal searches by content can be painfully slow, but you can create highly compressed Fast Search indexes of every word in every file for the folders you specify. Instead of reading a collection of files from top to bottom, QuickFinder automatically searches your index in a second or two!

Choosing the type of index to create

You can create two types of Fast Search indexes:

✦ *Standard,* to include a single folder or drive, with all of its subfolders. When you do a QuickFinder search in an indexed folder, a Standard Fast Search is automatically performed. You can create as many standard search indexes as you want.

✦ *Custom,* to include multiple folders on different drives, with or without their subfolders. You can select a custom index during an advanced search, instead of searching a particular folder.

Create the type of indexes best-suited to the way your files are organized, and where you normally search. For basic searches in particular folders, Standard Fast Search indexes are simple and automatic. If you need to search folders all over the place at once, Custom Fast Search indexes are a quick and convenient solution. Either way, try to group together the files you search most often, rather than create a single index for an entire hard drive. You can set up both standard and custom search indexes.

Note

Indexes cost you some hard disk space. The size of an index depends on several factors, but figure about 1/50 the size of the original files. If you are indexing 100MB of files, for example, the index might take 2MB of hard disk space.

Creating a Standard Fast Search index

You can index any combination of files or folders. To create a Standard Fast Search index:

1. Click Start on the Windows taskbar, and then click Programs ⇨ WordPerfect Office 2000 ⇨ Utilities ⇨ Corel QuickFinder 9 Manager.

2. Click Create and specify the folder to index (see Figure 7-19).

3. Specify whether you want the index to be manually updated or automatically updated at the interval you specify.

4. Click Options to override any of the general indexing settings. (See "Setting QuickFinder indexing options.")

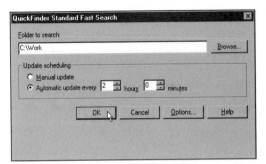

Figure 7-19: Creating a Standard Fast Search index.

A standard index for a folder always includes its subfolders. Create additional indexes for other folders you regularly search.

Creating a Custom Fast Search index

To create a Custom Fast Search index:

1. Click Start on the Windows taskbar, and then click Programs ⇨ WordPerfect Office 2000 ⇨ Utilities ⇨ Corel QuickFinder 9 Manager.

Tip   You can also click Advanced in any file-management dialog box, and then click Index Manager.

2. Click the Custom Fast Search Setup tab, and then click Create and give your index a name (see Figure 7-20).

3. Specify whether you want the index to be manually updated or automatically updated at the interval you specify.

4. Specify a folder to index, check "Include subfolders" if you want to index that folder's lower-level folders, and then click Add. Repeat the process for each folder you want to include.

Note   You can select a folder in the search list to remove it, or click the "Include Subfolders?" list button to toggle subfolder inclusion on or off.

5. Click Options to override any of the general indexing settings, described below.

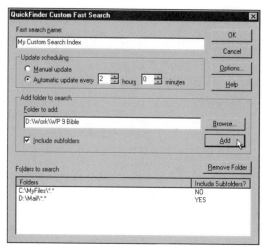

Figure 7-20: Creating a Custom Fast Search index.

Setting QuickFinder indexing options

Click Settings in the QuickFinder Manager to specify various Fast Search indexing options (see Figure 7-21), described in Table 7-4.

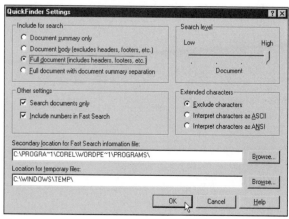

Figure 7-21: Setting Fast Search indexing options.

Table 7-4
Fast Search Indexing Options

Option	Lets You	Suggested Setting
Include for search	Specify the document elements included in the index	Leave at "Full document" or select "Document body" to exclude summary fields, headers, footers, footnotes, endnotes, and so on. Select "Full document with document summary separation" if you want to do separate searches on summaries alone.
Search documents only	Exclude all files except documents	Leave checked to keep the index small, unless you regularly search the contents of executable files.
Include numbers in Fast Search	Index numbers as well as words	Excluding numbers may speed up your searches a bit.
Search level	Index words down to the page, paragraph, or sentence they're in	Leave at Document (High) to keep index size down, unless you need to search on lower-level elements.
Extended characters	Tell the indexer how to treat nonletter or number characters	Leave at Exclude unless you must search on them. Otherwise, interpret them as ANSI for Windows documents, or ASCII for DOS documents.
Location for Fast Search information file	Tell QuickFinder where to put Custom Fast Search indexes (standard indexes are placed in the folders they index)	Normally set once and left unchanged.
Location for temporary files	Tell QuickFinder where to put temporary files used during index creation	Normally leave default setting.

Editing or updating a fast search index

To edit or update a Fast Search index:

1. Click Start on the Windows taskbar, and then click Programs ➪ WordPerfect Office 2000 ➪ Utilities ➪ Corel QuickFinder 9 Manager.

2. Select the index to edit or update, and then click any of the following options:

- *Update* manually updates the index to include the latest files in your search.

- *Rebuild* re-creates the index from scratch.

- *Edit* changes how or when the index is updated, or other options.

- *Delete* deletes the index.

Normally, it's much faster to update an index than to rebuild it. Your updates, however, tend to get large and slow over time, as more documents are added or revised. When that happens, rebuild the index.

Configuring QuickFinder

To configure QuickFinder's visibility in the Windows environment, or to enable/disable automatic index updates:

1. Click Start on the Windows taskbar, and then click Programs ⇨ WordPerfect Office 2000 ⇨ Utilities ⇨ Corel QuickFinder 9 Manager.

2. Click the QuickFinder Configuration tab, and then specify where you want QuickFinder to appear, and whether you want to enable automatic index updates (see Figure 7-22).

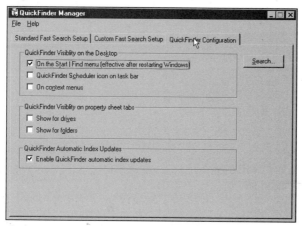

Figure 7-22: Configuring QuickFinder.

For More Information . . .

On	See
Automatically updating your Favorites folder	Chapter 29
Specifying text search criteria	Chapter 18
Publishing to HTML	Chapter 14

✦   ✦   ✦

Fonts Fantastic

The personal computer has prompted a revolution in the everyday uses of fonts. In this chapter, you'll see how WordPerfect Office 2000 offers you more ways than ever to display words.

For all its fancy charts, graphics, and shows, writing is the foundation of communication in WordPerfect Office 2000. While the keyboard may be more impersonal than the pen, easy-to-use font technology gives you new ways to enhance your flyers, invitations, newsletters, and other desktop publications.

Welcome to the Font Family

The terms *typeface* and *font* are used interchangeably to refer to a group of letters, numbers, and other characters that share a distinctive design. A set of related fonts is often referred to as a *font family*. For example, your suite's Futura Medium font family has members for medium, medium italic, bold, and bold italic.

> **Tip** Generally stick to one or two font families in a document, perhaps one for text and one for headings. Too many fonts make your work look cluttered and unprofessional.

Related families can make up an *extended font family*. Using the Futura example, you'll find related families of light, book, heavy, extra black, light condensed, medium condensed, bold condensed, and extra black condensed fonts. Other extended font families can include thin, roman (upright), engraved, oblique, demibold, extra bold, and ultra bold fonts.

Characters stand upon an invisible *baseline*, and the size of the type is measured in *points* (of which there are 72 to the inch) for a single-spaced line (see Figure 8-1). The spacing between the lines of type, known as *leading* (and pronounced *ledding*), was literally fixed by strips of lead in the days of metal type.

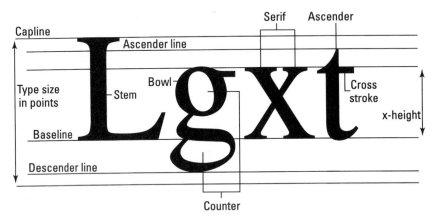

Figure 8-1: Elements of fonts or typefaces.

Another font characteristic is its *x-height*, or the height of a font's lowercase letters, exclusive of their ascenders and descenders. Two fonts can measure the same in points, yet have a different x-height:

Book Antiqua Arial

Other elements to look for are the *bowl* (curved or semicircular line of a letter such as a, b, or d) *stem* (main stroke of a letter like L), and the *cross stroke* in an f or t. Also look at the *counters*, or spaces enclosed in various letters like a, b, d, e, and g.

Classifying Fonts

Fonts can be classified in many ways, and this chapter makes no attempt to cover them all. The purpose here is to provide you with a working knowledge of how different types of fonts can be used to enhance your message.

Fixed and proportional fonts

Fixed, or *monospaced,* fonts are similar to typewriter text. Every character has the same width. A "W" takes up the same amount of space as an "I."

Tip Fixed fonts are handy when you must line up numbers or other characters in columns of text.

Proportional fonts allocate spacing according to each letter's shape and size. Notice how the narrow characters of the fixed Courier font are fleshed out with exaggerated serifs and cross strokes:

Courier with fixed spacing.
CG Times with proportional spacing.

Scalable and nonscalable fonts

A *scalable* font can be enlarged or reduced to almost any point size, depending on the capabilities of your printer. Times New Roman can be scaled to 14.6 points, for example. With *nonscalable* fonts, you must select one of the predetermined sizes that come with the font.

All laser, inkjet, and dot-matrix printers support both scalable and nonscalable fonts. Typewriters and the older daisy-wheel printers support only nonscalable fonts.

Built-in and downloadable fonts

You can also distinguish between fonts that are *built in* (*internal*) to your printer and *downloadable* (*soft*) fonts stored in your computer. Printer fonts have distinctive icons in your font lists (see Figure 8-2).

Printer font   TrueType font

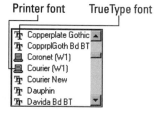

Figure 8-2: You can identify printer fonts by their icons.

Soft fonts are also called *graphical* fonts. The TrueType and Type 1 fonts that come with WordPerfect Office 2000 are soft fonts, as are the TrueType fonts that come with Windows. Type 1 fonts are also known as *Postscript* or *Adobe Type Manager* (*ATM*) fonts. Type 1 fonts are usually high-quality and often are preferred by professional typesetters, but there are excellent TrueType fonts as well.

Soft fonts take longer to print than built-in fonts. But with today's sophisticated printers and faster machines, the difference in speed is usually negligible.

Distinguishing Font Styles

The font classifications discussed so far have had more to do with their technical characteristics than their style. Although it's good to have this technical background, you'll normally be working with scalable fonts and focusing more on matters of style.

Serif and sans serif fonts

A basic stylistic distinction is made between fonts with *serifs,* which finish off the tops and bottoms of letters; and those that are *sans serif* (without serifs). Either style works well in larger sizes, as for a headline:

Headlines can be Serif
...or Sans-serif

In smaller sizes, serifs improve the readability of type by leading your eyes through the text. That's why almost every book, newspaper, or magazine you read is composed in serif fonts.

Other style distinctions

Beyond serif and sans serif, type styles can be classified in myriad ways. In his *Collier's Rules for Desktop Design and Typography,* David Collier identifies seven useful categories, as shown in Table 8-1.

Table 8-1 Collier's Seven Classes of Type		
Class	**Description**	**Example**
Old Style	Resembles handwriting, with inclined curves and contrasting thickness in strokes	Garamond, Bembo Caslon
Transitional	Less analogous to handwriting	Schoolbook, Baskerville
Modern	Marked by an abrupt contrast between thick and thin strokes, and thin horizontal serifs	Bodoni, Normande
Geometric	Sans serif; geometric shapes, with little stroke contrast and circular bowls	Futura, Avant Garde
Humanist	After Roman inscriptions, with contrasting stroke thickness or slightly fluted stems	Gill Sans, Optima
Slab Serif	Heavy square serifs, with or without brackets	Lotus Line Dr., Courier New
Digital	New fonts that appear computer-generated, rather than drawn by hand	Orbit, Amelia

You can also classify fonts according to usage. Here, fonts often are divided into four categories:

✦ *Text fonts* are easy to read and work well in a wide range of sizes. Times Roman, Courier, and Goudy Old Style are good examples of text fonts.

✦ *Display fonts* create good, solid headlines. Display fonts don't work for normal text. Arial Black, CG Poster Bodoni, and Swiss 721 Black Extended are good examples of display fonts.

✦ *Decorative fonts* can add a flourish or set a festive mood. Shelley Volante can create an elegant invitation. Blackletter 686, Caslon Openface, and Engravers' Gothic are other examples of decorative fonts.

✦ *Specialty fonts* include those Wingdings and symbols that you can use to add bullets, check boxes, typewriter keys, and other special touches to your documents.

Recognizing font subtleties

As you work with fonts, you'll find that subtle differences in design can convey quite different impressions. The *HP LaserJet Journal* points out, for example, that its Albertus, Antique Olive, and Univers fonts appear similar, yet have distinct "personalities" (see Figure 8-3).

Ideas, Ltd.

The Albertus headline is showy and distinctive – good for an ad agency's letterhead.

Hilda's Housecleaning

The Antique Olive headline has a casual look – good for friendly neighborhood services.

Death Valley Savings & Loan

The Univers headline is serious and trustworthy – good for a bank.

Figure 8-3: Similar fonts that convey different impressions.

Note   Because font names can be trademarked even though font styles cannot, you may run into similar fonts with different names. Examples include Architect/BluePrint, Futura/ Modern Industrial/Torino, Swiss/Arial/Helvetica, and Univers/Zurich.

Changing Font Appearances

Font possibilities don't end when you select a font. WordPerfect provides various ways you can emphasize text or otherwise change its appearance (see Figure 8-4). You can also emphasize text by varying its size (see Figure 8-5), or by using capitals (see Figure 8-6).

Put words in bold to make them **stand out** from the rest of the pack.

Add more subtle *emphasis* with italics. Use italics for titles of books and journals cited in reports.

Avoid underlining, it's a <u>messy holdover</u> from the typewriter days.

Don't overuse bold and italics, *or they will quickly lose their effectiveness*.

For extra emphasis, see how to reverse text in Chapter 8.

Standard Roman fonts can be altered by the program to produce italic or bold type, but for the most accurate results install the carefully crafted variations as specific fonts. For example, the Geometric Slabserif 703 group from Bitstream has individual fonts for:

> Light
> *Light Italic*
> Medium
> *Medium Italic*
> Medium Condensed
> **Bold**
> ***Bold Italic***
> **Bold Condensed**
> **Extra Bold**
> ***Extra Bold Italic***
> **Extra Bold Condensed**.

Figure 8-4: Varying font appearances.

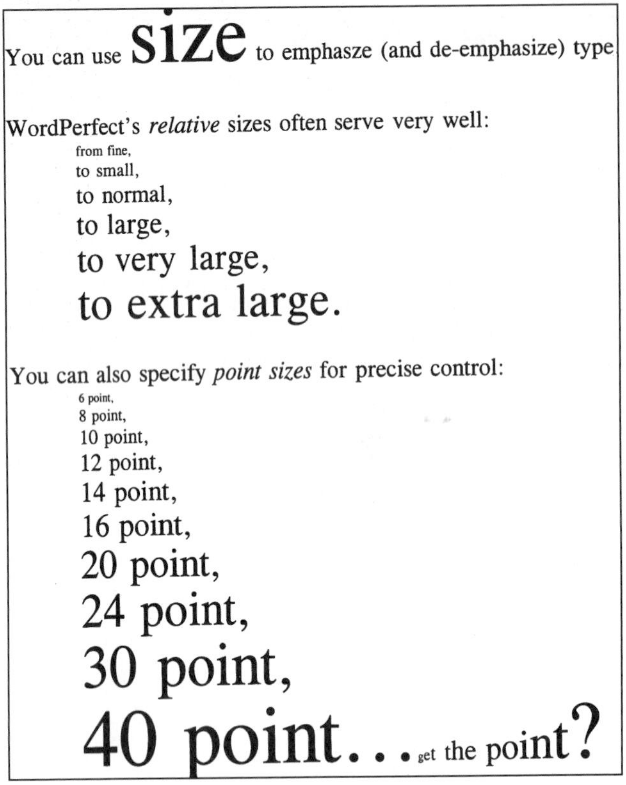

You can use size to emphasze (and de-emphasize) type

WordPerfect's *relative* sizes often serve very well:

from fine,
to small,
to normal,
to large,
to very large,
to extra large.

You can also specify *point sizes* for precise control:

6 point,
8 point,
10 point,
12 point,
14 point,
16 point,
20 point,
24 point,
30 point,
40 point... get the point?

Figure 8-5: Varying font size.

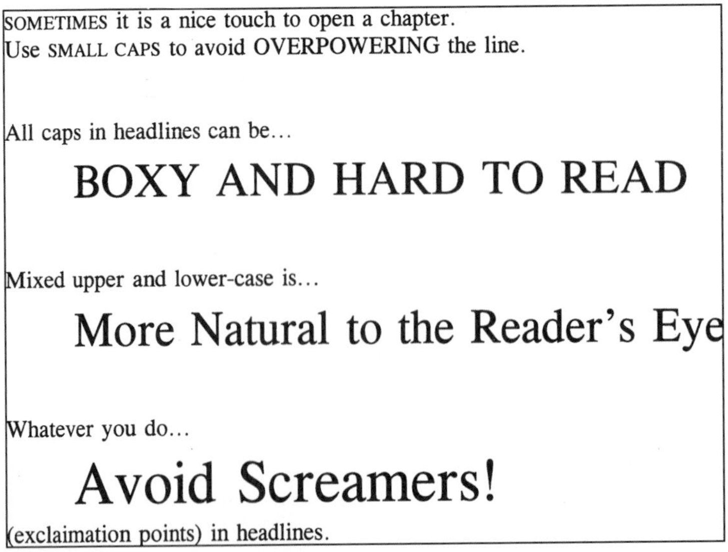

SOMETIMES it is a nice touch to open a chapter.
Use SMALL CAPS to avoid OVERPOWERING the line.

All caps in headlines can be...

BOXY AND HARD TO READ

Mixed upper and lower-case is...

More Natural to the Reader's Eye

Whatever you do...

Avoid Screamers!

(exclamation points) in headlines.

Figure 8-6: Varying capitalization.

WordPerfect has other appearance attributes you can use to create special effects:

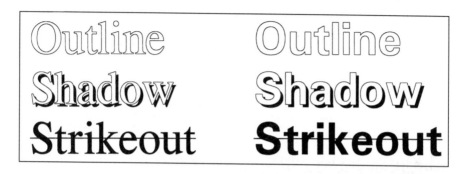

You can use double-underlines for totals in calculations:

$$
\begin{array}{r}
13 \\
\underline{\text{x } 4} \\
{=}52
\end{array}
$$

In Presentations, you can embellish fonts with custom borders and fills, as described in Chapter 41, "Mastering Presentations Techniques."

QuickChanging fonts from the property bar

New
Feature

The quickest way to change the font face or size is from the drop-down lists on the property bar. Simply click and scroll a listing, and then preview and click your selection (see Figure 8-7). Click the Font Color button on the property bar to select another color from the palette.

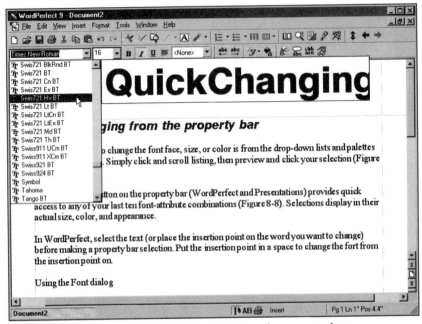

Figure 8-7: Previewing and changing a font from the property bar.

The QuickFonts button on the property bar (WordPerfect and Presentations) lets you quickly apply any of your last ten font-attribute combinations to selected text (see Figure 8-8). QuickFont selections display in their actual size, color, and appearance.

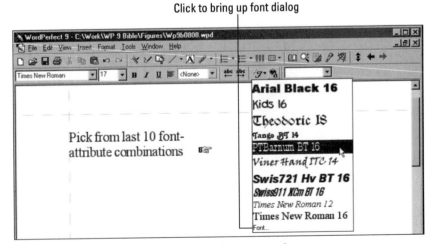

Figure 8-8: Selecting a QuickFont from the property bar.

Using the Font dialog box

The Font dialog box is your font command center (see Figure 8-9). You can get to it in several ways:

✦ Click Format ⇨ Font.

✦ Right-click in your text, and then click Font.

✦ Click the QuickFonts button, and then click Font.

✦ Press F9 (Ctrl+F8 on a DOS-compatible keyboard).

✦ Double-click a font code in WordPerfect's Reveal Codes.

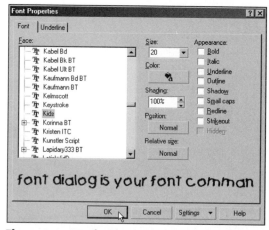

Figure 8-9: WordPerfect's Font dialog box.

The font options you pick are applied to your selected text. If no selection was made, your changes apply from the insertion point on, or to a single word when the insertion point is in a word.

Selecting a font face, size, and style

When you open the Font dialog box, the font characteristics at the insertion point are displayed at the bottom of the dialog box. You can select the font face and size, and you can click the "+" icon to select from various styles for a particular face. You can type a custom font size, such as 12.6, for TrueType and other scalable fonts.

Changing the color or shading of your text

If your printer supports color, click the Color button, and then pick a color from the palette using the arrow keys or the mouse. You can also vary the shading from 1 to 100 percent.

Tip   You can also pick a font color from the property bar.

Changing font position

Click the button for the Position list to create smaller superscript or subscript characters:

$$E = mc^2$$

$$H_2O$$

Changing the font's relative size

Click the button for the Relative Size list to select from six relative sizes ranging from fine to extra large, computed as percentages of your normal document font.

Selecting the font's appearance

You can check (and preview) one or more of the Appearance attributes to apply to your text.

Selecting underline options

When underlining text in WordPerfect, you can click the Underline tab in the font dialog box to specify whether you want to underline All, Text Only, Text & Spaces (the default), or Text & Tabs. Your selection stays in effect until you change it.

New Feature   You can customize the style and color of your underlining, to create cool effects for brochures, fliers, and other documents (see Figure 8-10).

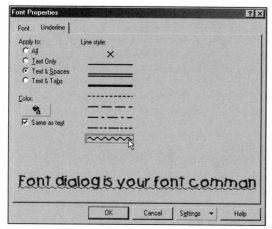

Figure 8-10: Customizing the underline style.

Embedding Fonts

The fonts displayed in the Font dialog box are those supported by your current system and printer. If you move the document to another system or printer, a particular font might no longer be available. In that case, the system substitutes its best guess as to the closest match, which can be a distant match indeed.

New Feature

You can now embed the font characteristics in a WordPerfect document so they'll display and print on another machine with WP 9, even if the fonts are not installed. Click File ➪ Save As, check "Embed fonts" and save the document. (The embedding information increases the size of your file.)

Understanding the Font-Selection Hierarchy

When you're working with fonts in WordPerfect, it helps to understand the font-selection hierarchy, from low to high:

✦ The printer default font

✦ The document default font

✦ The last font used in your document

When you open a new document, you start with the *printer default font* for the currently selected printer. It has the lowest priority.

The *document default font* is the same as the printer default font, unless you change it for the current document. Finally, the last font selection you make while working in your document (inserting a font code) overrides both the printer default font and the document default font.

To change your font defaults:

1. Click Format ➪ Font, and select the font face and size.

2. Click Settings, and then click

   - *Set as default for this document,* to change the document default

   - *Set as default for all documents,* to change the font for all new documents using the current printer

A Font Feast

With the proliferation of inexpensive, high-quality fonts, your creative possibilities are endless. The CD-ROM for WordPerfect Office 2000 comes with more than 1,000 fonts (you can install approximately 1,000 fonts in Windows 95/98). See your product documentation for a listing of the available fonts.

You may have many more fonts from which to choose, including those that are built into your printer, those that you have installed with another Windows program, or others that you have collected on your own.

The Internet is a great source for fonts, including many exotic creations and free samples from commercial foundries that now work with digits instead of molten lead. You can go to the font resources at http://www.qwkscreen.com to start your search for the fonts shown in Figure 8-11 and thousands of others, including additional Windows fonts from Microsoft.

Theodoric Regular – David F. Nalle

A font based on 14th Century calligraphy from Northern England..

GoodCityModern – Andrew S. Meit

This font is based on the original type for the Gutenberg Bible.

TENDERLEAF CAPS – David Rakowski

This display font of rough capital letters resembles twisted branches with leaves.

Figure 8-11: Three of the many fonts available on the Internet.

Managing Your Fonts

With so many fonts available from so many sources, how can you possibly manage them all? Fortunately, the Bitstream Font Navigator that comes with your suite makes it easy to

✦ Find and catalog all your fonts

✦ View and print font samples

✦ Install and uninstall fonts

✦ Organize your fonts into convenient groups

Cross-Reference For information on installing Font Navigator, see Appendix A, "Setting Up Your Suite."

Running Font Navigator

To run Font Navigator, click Start on the Windows taskbar, and then click WordPerfect Office 2000 ➪ Utilities ➪ Bitstream Font Navigator 3.0.1. (For quick access, add Font Navigator to DAD, as described in Appendix A, "Setting Up Your Suite.")

The first time you run the program, the Font Navigator Wizard lets you select the drives or folders that Font Navigator searches for fonts, including your CD-ROM (see "Finding fonts" below). It then sets up and displays a master catalog of all the fonts from all the locations you searched.

The Font Catalog list in the upper-left displays all the available font families. Scroll the list or type the first letters of the font you're looking for. Click a family to view samples of the family members (see Figure 8-12).

Font catalog   Font sample   Installed fonts

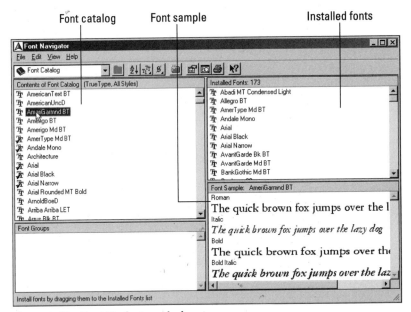

Figure 8-12: Font Navigator windows.

Finding fonts

You can update (rebuild) your catalog of available fonts at any time:

1. Click File ⇨ Find Fonts.

2. Check the drives you want to search. You can include the floppy or CD-ROM (see Figure 8-13). Click the "+" buttons to select particular folders to search.

3. Check "Include subfolders" to search all subfolders of the selected drives or folders.

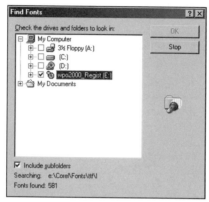

Figure 8-13: Finding fonts to add to your catalog.

Installing fonts

Now that your font catalog is set up, installing fonts is a breeze:

1. Select the fonts you want to install from the Font Catalog list.

2. Drag the selected fonts to the Installed Fonts list window (see Figure 8-14).

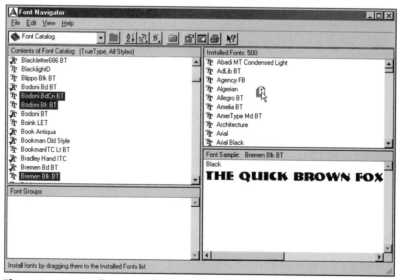

Figure 8-14: Installing fonts by dragging them from the Font Catalog list.

Installed fonts appear checked in the Font Catalog list.

TrueType fonts you install with Font Navigator are *not* copied to the Windows Fonts folder, as this takes up disk space without improving system performance.

Note   To install and view Type 1 Postscript fonts, the Adobe Type Manager must be installed on your system.

Uninstalling fonts

To uninstall unused fonts that clutter up your listing:

1. Select them from the Installed Fonts list.

2. Press Delete or drag them to the Font Catalog list.

Removing fonts from the Installed listing uninstalls the fonts, but does not remove them from the catalog or from your hard drive. To both uninstall fonts and remove them from the catalog:

1. Select the fonts in the Font Catalog list.

2. Press Delete, and then click Yes to remove them from the disk as well, or No to keep them on the disk for possible re-cataloging (see Figure 8-15).

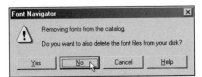

Figure 8-15: Selecting whether to keep your fonts on the hard drive when removing them from the catalog.

Viewing the catalog listing

To display particular types of fonts in the Font Catalog list, click

✦ Font Navigator View All Fonts icon (View ➪ All Fonts) to view all the fonts

✦ Font Navigator View Fonts by Format icon (View ➪ Fonts by Format) to view only TrueType or Type 1 fonts

✦ Font Navigator View Fonts by Style icon (View ➪ Fonts by Style) to view only decorative, monospaced, sans serif, script, serif, or symbol fonts

Tip   Click View ⇨ Customize View, to customize your catalog display by format, style, vendor, character set, embedding, and name.

Viewing particular fonts

Click on any font in the listings to display a sample in the lower-right pane. You can also click

✦ Font Navigator View Font Properties icon (View ⇨ Font Properties) to view a font's family, format, character chart, analog names, location, and other properties (see Figure 8-16)

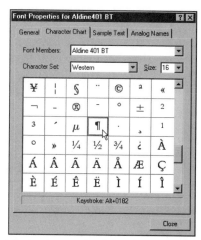

Figure 8-16: Viewing a font's properties.

✦ Font Navigator Explore Font icon (View ⇨ Explore Font) to view various font samples and capabilities (see Figure 8-17)

Tip   To compare two fonts, make sure the "Use single window" option is not checked, and then click another font and click the Font Navigator Explore Font icon.

Working with font groups

You can organize your fonts into convenient *groups,* to quickly install or uninstall all the fonts in the group without having to locate and select each family:

1. Click the Font Navigator New Font Group icon (File ⇨ New Font Group) and type a name for the group.

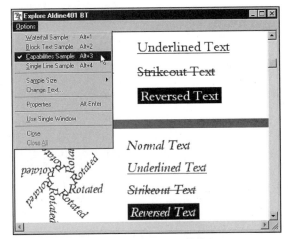

Figure 8-17: Viewing a font's capabilities.

2. Select the fonts to include in the group from the Font Catalog list or Installed Fonts list, and then drag them to the group folder (see Figure 8-18).

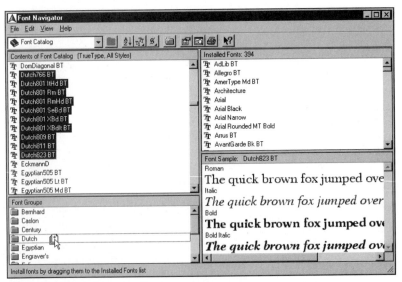

Figure 8-18: Setting up a font group.

You can group your fonts by extended family (Arrus, Dutch, Goudy, Swiss721), or by project ("Annual Report," "Newsletter").

To install a group, drag the font group folder to the Installed Fonts list. To display the fonts in the group, double-click the font group folder.

To uninstall a group, drag its folder from the Installed list to the Font Catalog list.

You can even associate font groups with particular applications or documents, and then create a shortcut to launch the font group with the application. See Font Navigator's Help for details.

Removing duplicate fonts

If you've done numerous font installations in the past, you may have duplicate fonts on your system, wasting valuable disk space. Click File ➪ Settings ➪ Duplicate Fonts to display any duplicates. You can then check the copy you want to use and delete the duplicates. Naturally, you can't remove fonts from your CD-ROM.

Using Special Characters and Symbols

The WordPerfect suite installs special TrueType fonts that provide more than 2,300 special characters and symbols from which to choose.

Some special characters are used for the familiar bullets, em dashes, decimal-align characters, and dot leaders. You can insert many others (such as Greek letters and trademarks) into regular text or use them for other purposes (such as custom bullets or attention-getters). Figure 8-19 displays some uses of special characters.

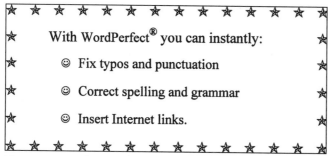

Figure 8-19: A few of the thousands of characters and symbols you can use.

The WordPerfect characters are grouped in 14 sets, numbered from 1 through 14 (set 0 is the ASCII characters and symbols on your keyboard). Figure 8-20 lists the sets with examples.

WordPerfect's Character Sets

Set	Type	# Chars	Examples
0	ASCII	126	A a B b C c @ # $ ^ & * ([
1	Multinational	241	Á á Â â Ä ä À à Å å Æ æ
2	Phonetic	144	ɑ ɒ ɓ ʙ ɔ ɕ ʗ ' " ˘ : ˙ ˋ
3	Box Drawing	87	▌ ■ - │ ┐ ┤ ┴ ┼ = ‖╔
4	Typographic	101	● • ¶ ¿ £ ½ ® ℞ ff ▶
5	Iconic	254	♡ ♂ ♀ ♬ 📧 ✎ ✔ ✪ 🐾
6	Math/Scientific	237	± ≥ ∝ ∑ ∞ → ↓ ▸ ∏
7	Math/Sc. Ext.	228	⌈ ∏ ‖ { ∪ ⟡ ⌐
8	Greek	218	A α B β Β ϐ Γ γ
9	Hebrew	122	א ב ג ד ה ו ז ח
10	Cyrillic	249	А а Б б В в Г г
11	Japanese	62	ヲ オ キ ツ テ ホ モ ン
12	Cur. Font Symbols		(reserved)
13	Arabic	195	٢ ٤ ج خ ز ش ط ع ل ئ ؤ لإ
14	Arabic Script	219	٢ ٣ پ ٹ چ ژ ڈ گ

Figure 8-20: Sampling of WordPerfect characters.

Inserting special characters and symbols

To insert a special character or symbol:

1. Place the insertion point where you want the character to appear, and then press Ctrl+W or click Insert ⇨ Symbol. (Click the Symbols button in WP or QP.)

2. Click the "Character Set" pop-up list and click the character set you want (see Figure 8-21).

3. Click the character you want, and then click Insert, or Insert and Close.

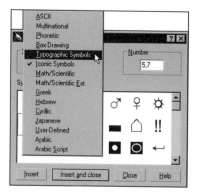

Figure 8-21: Selecting a character set.

Special character tips and tricks

You can perform a number of tricks when inserting special characters or symbols:

✦ Stretch the dialog box to put more characters on display.

✦ Highlight the "Character Set" pop-up list, and then scroll through the character sets by using the up and down arrow keys.

✦ Double-click a character to insert it.

✦ Keep the dialog box open and click the screen where you want to insert the next character.

✦ Type a character's two-digit pair of numbers in the Number box. For example, type 4,12 to insert the Japanese yen symbol (¥) — the twelfth character in the fourth set.

You can also type shortcut key combinations in the Number box to select various special characters. Here are just a few examples; experiment to see if you can find more:

✦ m- (or —) and n- for the em dash and en dash

✦ *., **, *o, and *O for small, large, solid, and hollow bullets

✦ co, sm, tm, and ro for copyright, service mark, trademark, and registered symbols

✦ ?? and !! for inverted punctuation marks; << and > for pointed brackets

✦ v (the letter) or a punctuation mark (', ,, ., -, or ;), in combination with various other letters (lowercase and uppercase) for accents and cedillas

✦ ae, oe, ij (lowercase and uppercase), and ss for combined characters

✦ /2 and /4 for 1/2 and 1/4

✦ +-, <=, >=, =/, ==, and ~~ for common math symbols

✦ c/, f-, L-, ox, and Y= for ¢, *f*, ⅀, ¤, and ¥ (type in case shown)

✦ rx and P| for the prescription and paragraph symbols.

The order in which you type the characters doesn't matter. For example, either rx or xr will get you the prescription symbol.

Tip Create QuickCorrect abbreviations for special characters you regularly use (see Chapter 52, "Writers' Lib"), and then all you'll have to do is type the abbreviation. You can also assign characters to particular keystrokes (see Chapter 57, "Customizing Toolbars, Menus, and Keyboards").

Discovering characters and symbols in other fonts

Other Windows fonts may offer additional characters and symbols. Examples include Fences, MS Line Draw, MT Extra, Symbol, and Wingdings. When you type lowercase or uppercase characters in these fonts, special characters come out instead.

Creating Mathematical and Scientific Equations

Special characters and symbols are also used by the WordPerfect Office Equation Editor. The Equation Editor builds mathematical or scientific equations and formulas for textbooks, papers, and other documents (see Figure 8-22). It doesn't solve the equations or test their validity.

"My tenure for some $H_2O!$," cried the scientist in the Sahara.

$$x = \frac{-b \pm \sqrt{b^2 - 4ac}}{2a}$$

$$\begin{pmatrix} a_1 a_2 & \cdots & a_r \\ b_1 b_2 & \cdots & b_r \\ c_1 c_2 & \cdots & c_r \end{pmatrix}$$

$$NH_4NCO \xrightarrow{\text{Heat}} H_2N - \overset{\overset{O}{\Updownarrow}}{C} - NH_2$$

Figure 8-22: Mathematical and scientific equations

WordPerfect's Legacy Equation Editor

WordPerfect also comes with the legacy text-based Equation Editor used prior to release 8. Documentation on its use is included in the WordPerfect guide in the Reference Center.

The old editor is automatically invoked when you edit an equation created by it, or when you insert a custom graphics box by using the Equation or Inline Equation styles (see Chapter 9, "Working with Graphics").

To default to the old Equation Editor, click Tools ⇨ Settings ⇨ Environment, and then click the Graphics tab and click WordPerfect 5.1 to 7 Equation Editor. To use both Equation Editors, check "Show the 'Select Equation Editor' dialog whenever I create an equation."

How the Equation Editor works

The Equation Editor lets you:

✦ Fill in the empty *slots* (dashed rectangles) with numbers and characters, or with more than 150 mathematical symbols from the first three rows of palettes (see Figure 8-23)

✦ Select various formatting *templates* from the last three rows of palettes, including brackets, braces, fractions, radicals, and sums

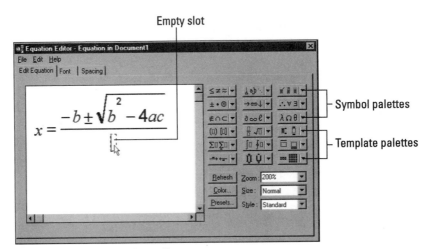

Figure 8-23: The Equation Editor.

You can also insert templates into the empty slots in other templates, to quickly assemble complex equations.

Your default *equation style* is math, with characters in italics, but you can select other styles and fonts to suit your needs.

Creating an equation

To create an equation in WordPerfect or Presentations:

1. Click where you want the equation to appear. (Click with the shadow cursor in WP to position the equation in a blank line.)

2. Click Insert ⇨ Equation to display the Equation Editor window with a single empty slot.

3. If necessary, change your zoom setting to see your equation better, and select the style for the type of character or symbol you're creating.

4. Type text, and select symbols and templates from the palettes to construct your formula.

5. Press the Tab key to move out of a slot or into the next slot (Shift+Tab to move in reverse).

6. To start a new line press Enter.

7. Do either of the following:

- Press F3 (File ➪ Update) to update the equation in your document.
- Click the Close button (File ➪ "Exit and Return to document") to update the equation and exit.

The equations you create are Windows metafile graphics, placed in a character-anchor graphics box at the insertion point in your line of text. You can resize the graphics box, change its anchor type, and so on, as with any other graphics box (see Chapter 9, "Working with Graphics").

Creating the equation examples

Now try your hand at creating the equation examples shown in Figure 8-22, following the general instructions in the earlier section "Creating an equation."

To Create	Do This
The first example	Type H, select the subscript template (see Figure 8-24), type 2, press tab, and then type O!.
The second example	Type x=, select the fraction template (see Figure 8-25), type -b, select the "plus or minus" symbol, select the square root template, type b, select the superscript template, type 2, press tab, type -4ac, and then click the slot for the denominator (or press Tab) and type 2a.
The third example	Select the parentheses template, select the 3×3 matrix template, type **a**, select the subscript template, type **1,** press Tab, type **a**, select the subscript template, type **2**, press Tab twice, select the ellipsis symbol (on the middle palette in top row), press Tab, type **a**, select the subscript template, and type **r**. Now, press Tab twice, and continue filling in the last two rows of the matrix.
The fourth example	Go to the Spacing tab in the Equation Editor and set Line Spacing to 100%. Type **O**, press enter, select the double-arrow up and down symbol, press Enter, type **NH**, select the subscript template, type **4**, press Tab, type **NCO**, select the right-arrow with upper text slot template, type **Heat**, press Tab, type **H**, select the subscript template, type **2**, press Tab, type **N-C-NH,** select the subscript template, and type **2**. Select the double-arrow in the second row, and then nudge it into position by holding down the Ctrl key as you press the arrow keys. Do the same with the "O" in the top row.

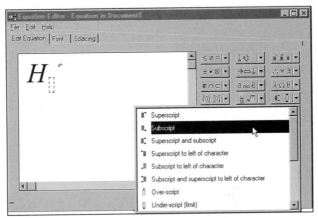

Figure 8-24: Selecting the subscript template.

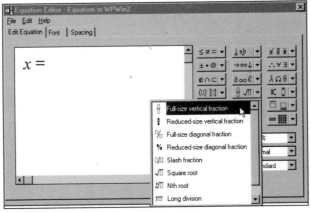

Figure 8-25: Selecting the fraction template.

Editing an equation

Double-click an equation to edit it. Click the equation to apply a border or fill to its box (see Chapter 54, "Adding Graphic Lines, Borders, and Fills").

Deleting an equation

When it comes to deleting an equation, the equation is no different than any other graphics box in your document. To delete an equation, click its graphics box to select it and press Delete.

Typing nonmathematical phrases

Normally, the math style is used in the Equation Editor, with italic characters and automatic spacing (the spacebar is disabled.) To type and space normal text, click Style ➪ Text. (Also see the section "Spacing characters," and the Style Keyboard Shortcuts in Table 8-5.)

Selecting items in an equation

You can select an entire equation, or any characters or symbols, including template symbols, using the various methods described in Table 8-2. Once selected, items can be deleted, or you can change their style or size from the menu bar.

Table 8-2 Selecting Items in an Equation	
To Select	**Do This**
The entire equation	Press Ctrl+A
Any part of the equation	Drag with the mouse
Characters to the left or right of the insertion point	Hold down the Shift key and press the arrow key
A template to the left of the insertion point	Press Backspace (Press Backspace again to delete it.)
A template symbol, such as a character embellishment or a summation sign	Hold down the Ctrl key and click

Tip You can apply templates to selected characters and symbols. For example, you can enter the text and symbols shown in Figure 8-23, and then apply the square root template and vertical divider to selected items.

Using cut, copy, and paste

You can cut, copy, and paste characters in the Equation Editor as you would with any other application (see Chapter 2, "Essential Typing and Editing").

Using Undo

Press Ctrl+Z (Edit ➪ Undo) to erase the last characters you typed.

Erasing the blackboard

If the Equation Editor screen gets smudgy, click the Refresh button to clean it up.

Spacing characters

To change the spacing between characters, or to remove spacing entirely, select the various standard mathematical spaces from the second symbols palette.

Nudging characters

To nudge a character in small increments in any direction, select the character and hold down the Ctrl key as you press the arrow keys. (The nudge increment varies from a one-fourth point at 400% zoom to one point at 100% zoom.)

Aligning a stack of equations

To align a stack of equations or expressions, select the stack, click Format, and select the alignment (including alignment on decimals or equal signs).

You can also use the alignment symbol to line up rows at any position. Place the insertion point where you want to align the row, and then select the Equation Editor Alignment Symbol from the second palette (see Figure 8-26).

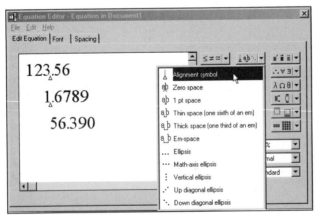

Figure 8-26: Aligning a stack by using the alignment symbol.

Using keyboard commands

The Equation Editor characters are automatically spaced, so the spacebar is turned off unless you're in the text style. To adjust spacing between characters, use any of the keystrokes in Table 8-3.

Table 8-3 **Keyboard Spacing Commands**	
To Insert	*Press*
Zero space	Shift+Spacebar
One point space	Ctrl+Alt+Spacebar
Thin space (one-sixth of an em)	Ctrl+Spacebar
Thick space (one-third of an em)	Ctrl+Shift+Spacebar

For shortcuts to View and Style menu commands, use the keystrokes in Tables 8-4 and 8-5.

Table 8-4 **View Keyboard Shortcuts**	
View Selection	*Press*
100%	Ctrl+1
200%	Ctrl+2
400%	Ctrl+4
Redraw	Ctrl+D

Table 8-5 **Style Keyboard Shortcuts**	
Style Selection	*Press*
Math	Ctrl+Shift+=
Text	Ctrl+Shift+E
Function	Ctrl+Shift+F
Variable	Ctrl+Shift+I
Greek	Ctrl+Shift+G
Matrix-Vector	Ctrl+Shift+B

Check the Equation Editor's online Help for keyboard shortcuts to symbols (such as Ctrl+I for infinity) and templates (such as Ctrl+H for superscript), and embellishments (such as Ctrl+Alt+Hyphen for a vector arrow).

Changing equation spacing and other settings

You can change settings for spacing, style, and size for the equations you create.

To change the space settings, click the Spacing tab, and then scroll the list to enter any new settings for line spacing, matrix row spacing, and so on (see Figure 8-27).

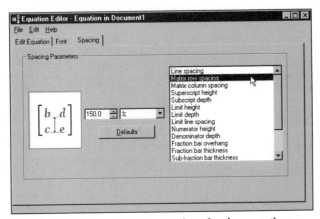

Figure 8-27: Changing space settings for the equations you create.

To change the font sizes for characters, subscripts, symbols, and so on, click the Font tab and specify the sizes in your unit of measure (see Figure 8-28). You can also change the fonts for Greek letters and symbols.

Using preloaded equations

The equation editor comes with several preloaded equations, such as for Bernoulli's equation and Euler's formula. Click the Presets button, select a formula from the list, and click OK (see Figure 8-29).

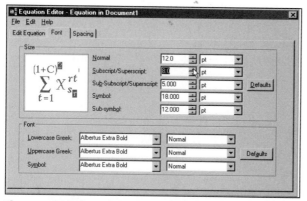

Figure 8-28: Changing font sizes for characters, subscripts, and symbols. Click the Default buttons to restore your fonts to the system defaults.

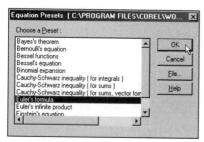

Figure 8-29: Using a preloaded equation.

Creating Fantastic Font Effects with TextArt

For really fantastic 2-D or 3-D font effects, use TextArt to outline, fill, shadow, color, twist, size, and rotate text in any number of ways. TextArt is great for creating a company logo or letterhead, giving a headline a twist, designing a newsletter heading, or just having fun.

Adding a TextArt image to your document

To try out TextArt in a document, spreadsheet, or show:

1. Select your text, or place the insertion point where you want the TextArt image to appear.

2. Click Insert ➪ Graphics ➪ TextArt.

3. Edit your text or replace the "Text" in the text window with as many characters on as many lines as you want. Click Insert Symbol to select any character from the font you're using.

4. Click More to select a text shape from the palette (see Figure 8-30).

Click a shape

Figure 8-30: Selecting a shape for your TextArt image.

5. Pick a font and font style. (Headline-type fonts tend to work best. This is a good place to experiment!)

6. Select a text justification and degree of smoothness. (Smoothness is most noticeable with large, ornate characters.)

7. Apply any of the 2-D options described in the next section, or check "3D Mode" to apply 3-D effects instead.

8. When you're finished, click Close or click anywhere outside the TextArt image.

Applying TextArt's 2-D options

Click the 2D Options tab (and leave "3D Mode" unchecked) to apply any of the options described in Table 8-6.

Table 8-6
TextArt's 2-D Options

Option	Lets You
Text color	Pick a color for the text. You can also do this when you select Pattern, Shadow, or Outline. (The color doesn't show when you select "No Fill.")
Pattern	Click to select a pattern or fill. Pick "None" for a plain, solid color. Pick "No Fill" to show only the outline and shadow. You can select a different color for the pattern or fill.
Shadow	Select the direction and extent of the drop shadow (see Figure 8-31). Click the center of the palette for no shadow. You can pick a color for the shadow as well.
Outline	Select the width and color of the outline surrounding the characters.
Rotation	Click to display the rotation handles (refer to Figure 8-30), and then drag a handle to rotate your text. Double-click to specify a counterclockwise rotation from 0 to 359 degrees (see Figure 8-32).
Preset	Click to select from a palette of TextArt examples.

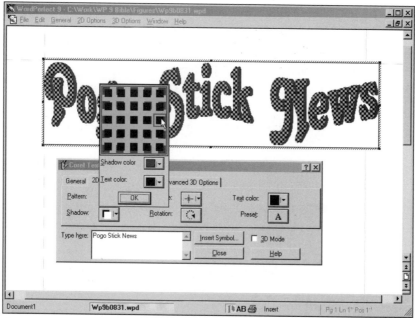

Figure 8-31: Selecting the direction and extent of the shadow.

Figure 8-32: Specifying the degree of rotation.

TextArt can create 2-D images with lots of depth and bounce, and they're more suited to Web pages, because they're smaller than 3-D and take less time to load.

Applying 3-D TextArt effects

To take TextArt to a third dimension, check "3D Mode," and then click the 3D tabs to apply any of the fantastic effects described in Table 8-7.

Table 8-7 TextArt's 3-D Options	
Option	**Lets You**
Lighting 1	Pick a primary text color and the angle from which it shines on your text (see Figure 8-30).
Lighting 2	Pick a secondary text color and lighting angle.
Bevel	Select from a palette of shapes to carve the sides of your text.
Depth	Adjust the thickness of the 3-D effect.
Rotation	Select from a palette of rotation angles.
Free Rotate	Display a global grid (see Figure 8-33) that you can drag to rotate your text in any direction. (Unless you have superfast graphics, give your computer time to catch up between moves.)
Preset	Click to select from a palette of 3-D examples.
Textures	Apply textures to the front, back, and bevel of your text (Figure 8-34).
Texture size	Adjust the size of the texture pattern.
Texture lighting	Adjust the brightness of the textures.
Quality	Select from 4-bit black-and-white or 8- or 16-bit color at various resolutions.

Tip

Don't pick a higher quality than you need—going from 8-bit to 16-bit color doubles the size of your image file, and the size grows by the square of the resolution!

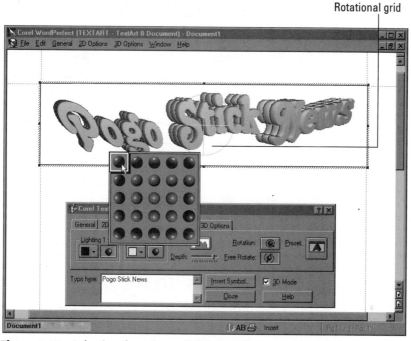

Figure 8-33: Selecting the primary lighting angle (note the global rotational grid).

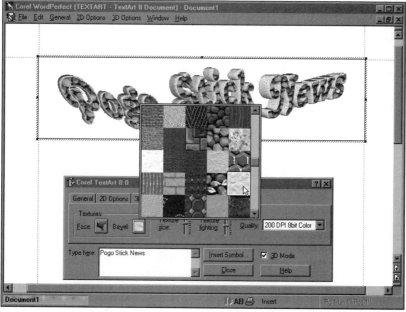

Figure 8-34: Applying a texture.

Changing the size or position of a TextArt image

You can move or resize a TextArt image just like any other graphic, or put a border around it. For example, you can right-click an equation, click Border/Fill, then apply a single line border with rounded corners and a drop shadow (see Chapter 54, "Adding Graphic Lines, Borders, and Fills").

Saving and copying TextArt images

TextArt images are normally saved with the documents in which they are placed, not as separate TextArt files.

If you plan to use TextArt images in multiple documents, you can save them as otherwise empty documents in their own folder. That way, you can easily find and insert your TextArt letterheads, logos, and other images when you need them.

Once you have edited a TextArt image to your satisfaction, save it as you would any other WordPerfect document by choosing Save or Save As from the File menu.

To save the TextArt image alone as a WordPerfect (.WPG) graphic that can be inserted in other documents or presentations:

1. Click the TextArt image to select it. (You don't have to be in TextArt.)

2. Click File ➪ Save As ➪ Selected Image ➪ OK (see Figure 8-35).

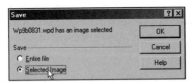

Figure 8-35: Saving a selected image as a WordPerfect graphic.

3. Save the image to a location and name it, using the .WPG filename extension.

You can also copy a selected TextArt image to another Windows application via the Clipboard (see Chapter 10, "Working Together and Sharing Data").

Editing a TextArt image

To edit a TextArt image, double-click it to return to TextArt. You can also right-click the image and then click Corel TextArt 9 Document Object ➪ Edit.

For More Information . . .

On	See
Installing Bitstream Font Navigator	Appendix A
Creating QuickCorrect abbreviations	Chapter 52
Assigning characters to keystrokes	Chapter 57
Working with graphics boxes	Chapter 9
Using cut, copy, and paste	Chapter 2
Adding borders to graphics	Chapter 54
Fitting text to a curve	Chapter 55
Using the Clipboard	Chapter 10

✦   ✦   ✦

Working with Graphics

Graphic images can make all the difference between a dull document or slide, and snappy, professional letterheads, newsletters, fliers, brochures, and shows. Working with graphics is a dream in WordPerfect Office 2000. You get thousands of clip art images (plus slide backgrounds, photos, borders, and textures) that you can use to liven up your newsletters, fliers, reports, cards, or any other kind of document or show. WordPerfect Office 2000 has the unprecedented ability to handle practically every graphic format around, giving you the freedom to assemble and use graphics from a myriad of sources.

The examples in this chapter focus on WordPerfect because of its wide variety of graphics boxes and the special ways you can use graphics in relation to document text.

 Note　In order for the WordPerfect procedures to work as described in this chapter, click Tools ⇨ Settings ⇨ Environment ⇨ Graphics, and make sure that "Drag to create new graphics boxes" is *not* checked.

Distinguishing Types of Graphics

When using graphics in desktop publishing, it helps to be aware that they fall roughly into three categories:

✦ *Bitmap (raster)* images, composed of thousands of *pixels* (tiny squares), created by scanners and paint programs. The resolution (sharpness) of a bitmap depends on the size of its pixels, which is often expressed in dots per inch (dpi). For example, a 600 dpi image will appear sharper when enlarged than a 300 dpi one. The 600 dpi file will also be four times as big.

✦ *Vector* graphics, created by drawing, charting, and CAD programs. They form pictures out of mathematical lines and curves, and don't lose their sharpness as you change their size or shape.

✦ *Metafile* graphics are a hybrid of bitmap and vector components.

Bitmaps are good for fine art and photographs with subtle shadings and vivid detail, though they often have ragged edges ("raggies") when enlarged. Vectors and metafiles are best for line art and drawings (such as clip art). Their file size usually is much smaller than comparable bitmaps, which can gobble up disk space by the megabyte.

WordPerfect Office 2000 lets you import graphics in any of the formats listed in Table 9-1.

Table 9-1
Graphic Formats the WordPerfect Suite Can Import

Graphic Format	Filename Extension	Graphics Type
Adobe Photo Shop	.PSD	Bitmap
AutoCAD	.DFX	Vector
Bitmap	.BMP, .DIB	Bitmap
CALS Compressed	.CAL	Bitmap
CompuServe GIF	.GIF	Bitmap
Computer Graphics Metafile	.CGM, CMF	Vector
Corel PHOTO-PAINT	.CPT	Bitmap
CorelDRAW	.CDR, .CDT, .PAT, .CMX	Bitmap
Encapsutated PostScript	.EPS	Vector
Enhanced Windows Metafile	.EMF	Metafile
FAX (TIFF)	.TIF	Bitmap
GEM Paint	.IMG	Bitmap
H-P Plotter (HPGL)	.HPG, .HP, .PLT	Vector
JPEG	.JPG, .JPE	Bitmap
Kodak Photo CD	.PCD	Bitmap
Lotus PIC	.PIC	Vector
Macintosh PICT	.PCT	Metafile
MacPaint	.MAC	Bitmap

Graphic Format	Filename Extension	Graphics Type
Micrografx Graphic	.MGX	Metafile
Micrografx Picture Publisher 4	.PP4	Bitmap
OS/2 Bitmap	.BMP	Bitmap
PC Paintbrush	.PCX	Bitmap
Portable Network Graphic	.PNG, .GIF	Bitmap
Scitex CT Bitmap	.SCT	Bitmap
Tagged Image Format File	.TIF	Bitmap
TruevisionTarga	.TGA	Bitmap
Windows Cursor/Icon	.CUR, .ICO	Bitmap
Windows, Wavelet Compressed Bitmap	.WI, .WVL	Bitmap
Windows Metafile	.WMF	Metafile
WordPerfect (versions 5-9) Graphic	.WPG	Metafile
WP Works 2.0 Paint	.WPW	Bitmap

What's just as impressive is that you can preview any of these image types in any file management dialog box. To see the conversions installed on your system click Insert ⇨ Graphics ⇨ and then click From File the "File type" list.

What You Can Do with a Graphics Box

When you add a chart, clip art, picture, or other graphic object to a document, slide, or spreadsheet, it's placed into a container, or frame, known as a *graphics box*. You can think of the graphics box as a super picture frame that enables you to

- ✦ Move the graphic around
- ✦ Stretch or shrink the contents
- ✦ Group or layer multiple graphics
- ✦ Set off the graphic with borders and fills
- ✦ Control the flow of text around the graphic
- ✦ Add descriptive captions

You'll see how to perform graphics box operations in short order. But first, you must understand when a graphics box *isn't* a "graphics" box:

- ✦ When it contains text (including a button box or Sticky Note)
- ✦ When it contains a table

You put text or a table in a graphics box so that you can drag it around, add borders, and do all the other things you can do with a graphics box. The only thing you can't do is enlarge or shrink the table or text, just the box. (An equation in a box is different, because its text is treated as a graphical object.)

What's a graphics box style?

Click Insert ➪ Graphics ➪ Custom Box, and take a look at the graphics box styles you can choose from (see Figure 9-1). These styles are simply prepackaged combinations of graphics box attributes (anchor, border, fill, caption, and so on), suited to various types of graphics and text. For example, when you compare the standard text box to the Sticky Note box, you'll see that the standard box is wide, it sets off the text with a thin border, and it's positioned to the side of your text. The Sticky Note is narrow and borderless, has a yellow fill, and sits on top of your document text.

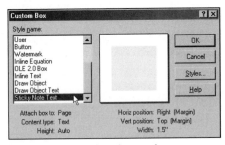

Figure 9-1: Graphics box styles.

Rather than examine each style in detail now, later in this chapter you'll see how the attributes for all graphics boxes work.

Adding Graphics

You have several ways to add graphics to your work:

- ✦ Draw, paint, or scan your own art (see Chapter 55, "Creating Your Own Art")
- ✦ In WordPerfect, insert watermarks (see Chapter 21, "Formatting Your Document") and tables-in-a-box (see Chapter 22, "Formatting with Columns and Tables")
- ✦ Change your slide show background (see Chapter 39, "A Hands-on Slide Show")
- ✦ Create TextArt (see Chapter 8, "Fonts Fantastic"), equations (see Chapter 8), and charts (see Chapter 56, "Charting Data")

✦ Insert clip art from the Scrapbook

✦ Create text boxes

✦ Insert other graphic objects, such as an image that you capture from the Internet (see Chapter 14, "Web Writing and Publishing")

This chapter covers clip art, text boxes, and other graphics, but graphics box operations apply to all the types.

Inserting clip art from the Scrapbook

Your Scrapbook facility displays thumbnails of the more than 12,000 clip art images that come with WordPerfect Office 2000, together with photos, sound clips, and movies. A few images are installed on your hard drive, but most remain on the CD.

To insert a clip art image by using the Scrapbook in WordPerfect, Presentations, or Quattro Pro:

1. Click the Insert Clipart button (Insert ➪ Graphics ➪ Clipart).

2. Browse the thumbnails in any of the image categories.

3. Click Find if you want to search the Scrapbook's index, based on keywords attached to items or text in the filenames (see Figure 9-2). (Select from the drop-down lists to repeat recent searches.)

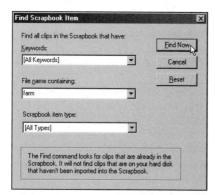

Figure 9-2: Searching the Scrapbook's index.

4. Double-click the clip art you want. You can also drag it from the Scrapbook, or click Insert (see Figure 9-3). (Right-click to copy an image to the Clipboard, or find another image with a keyword search.)

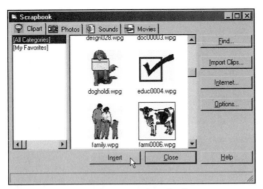

Figure 9-3: Inserting Scrapbook clip art.

5. Click Close, if necessary, to dismiss the Scrapbook, and then drag the image to where you want and click outside the box to deselect it.

Adding to your Scrapbook collection

Your Scrapbook database is a catalog of thumbnails and descriptions to help you locate media files stored elsewhere on your hard drive, on a server drive, or on your WordPerfect Office CD. To add any accessible items to your scrapbook:

1. Click the Insert Clipart button (Insert ➪ Graphics ➪ Clipart).

2. Click the Scrapbook tab and select the category to which you want to add the items. (Click Options ➪ "Create category" to add a new category to the list.)

3. Do any of the following:

   • Drag an item from a document or presentation to the Scrapbook thumbnail window, and then type any search keywords and select display categories (see Figure 9-4). (If the item, such as an object you drew, doesn't have a name, it's given the temporary name of Scrap*X*, where X is an incremental number.

   • Click Import Clips, and then browse and select the items to add, using the file selection techniques discussed in Chapter 7, "Managing Your Files." (The file types searched for depend on the Scrapbook tab you selected.) You'll have the option to define the keywords and categories for individual items.

   • Click Internet to get items from the Scrapbook Web page, and then follow the onscreen directions.

To delete items from the Scrapbook, right-click each item and click Delete. You can also hold down the Shift key and click to select multiple items, and then press Delete.

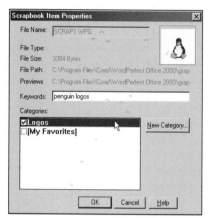

Figure 9-4: Adding an item to the Scrapbook.

Adding, renaming, and removing categories

Right-click in the category list to create (add) a new category under any of the tabs. Select a category and right-click to rename or remove a category.

Tip

Removing a category does not delete the thumbnail images from the Scrapbook database.

Selecting Scrapbook display and update options

You can click the Options button in the Scrapbook to select the following display and update options:

✦ *Large icons,* to display large thumbnails. Remove the check if you want to see more (but smaller) thumbnails.

✦ *Filename,* to display the filename of the item with it's thumbnail.

✦ *Keywords,* to display each item's search keywords.

✦ *Display all thumbnails,* to display thumbnails for all items in the Scrapbook, including ones that aren't currently available (for example, those on your WordPerfect Office CD when it's not in the drive). Items currently not available are marked with a red X.

✦ *Update all thumbnails,* to update the names and paths for all your thumbnails after images have been moved or renamed. Those not found are marked with an X. This process can take a long time.

✦ *Update the selected thumbnail,* to check the name and path of the selected thumbnail's item .

Inserting graphics from a file

To insert any other graphic you have on file:

1. Click Insert ⇨ Graphics ⇨ From File.

2. Select the file and click Insert.

3. Drag the graphic to where you want it, and then click outside the box to deselect it.

Drawing graphics boxes with the shadow cursor

WordPerfect's shadow cursor makes it a cinch to insert graphics. To draw a graphics box with the shadow cursor:

1. Click the Shadow Cursor button on the application bar, if necessary, to turn on the shadow cursor.

2. Drag anywhere in your document's white space (not in a line of text) to draw a box.

3. Release the mouse, and then select the type of box you want (see Figure 9-5).

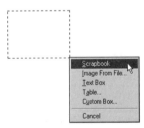

Figure 9-5: Drawing a graphics box with the shadow cursor.

Creating a floating text box

By enclosing text in a graphics box, you can float (position) the text anywhere on the page, independently from the rest of your document text. This is especially useful for creating a pull-quote of an excerpted line or phrase, in a larger or display typeface, to draw the reader's attention to an article or story. You can also apply other graphics box treatments to your text box, such as a shadow, border, or fill.

To create a floating text box in WordPerfect:

1. Click Insert ⇨ Text Box (or drag the shadow cursor and click Text Box).

2. Type your text, using any fonts or formatting you please (see Figure 9-6). (Click the shadow cursor in the appropriate area of the box to center or right-align your text.)

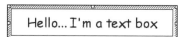

Figure 9-6: Creating a floating text box.

To create a floating text box in Presentations, click Insert ➪ Text Box, drag to create the box, and then type and format your text.

Creating an in-line text box

An in-line text box enables you to apply special treatment to selected text, just as with a floating text box, except the box stays put within the part of a line of text. To put part of a line of text in a box in WordPerfect:

1. Type your line of text.

2. Select the words you want to put in a box and then click the Text Box icon (Insert ➪ Text Box.)

Creating a Sticky Note

A Sticky Note box sits on top of your document; you use it to write notes to yourself. To create a Sticky Note in WordPerfect:

1. Drag a box with your shadow cursor.

2. Click Custom Box and select the Sticky Note Text box.

3. Type and format your Sticky Note text, and then click outside of the box when you're done.

Creating reversed text

When text is in a box, you can reverse it (making the text white in a colored background instead of dark on a white background). To create reversed text:

1. Click the edge of the box to select it.

2. Click the Graphic Fill button and select a solid fill of the color you want.

3. Click in the text box, select the text, and then click the Font Color button to preview and select white or another contrasting color for your text.

Selecting Graphics and Text Boxes

Many graphics box operations (including moving and deleting) begin by selecting the box. Click anywhere in a standard graphics box to select it and display the sizing handles (see Figure 9-7). To select multiple boxes, hold down the Shift key as you click each box.

Figure 9-7: Sizing handles appear around selected boxes.

When you click in a text box (including a Sticky Note or button), a border of slashes appears around the box to indicate that you're in Text Edit mode (refer to Figure 9-6). You can move or size a text box in Edit mode, but sometimes you'll need to select the box alone (to delete it, for example) by pointing to the border and clicking (see Figure 9-8).

Tip You can also right-click a text box and click Select Box.

> Point to the border and click to select a text box.

Figure 9-8: Point to the border and click to select a text box.

If you're editing the text within the box and want to select the box instead, first click outside the box, and then click the border.

Displaying and Hiding Graphics

When you're editing text on a slower machine, you can click View ⇨ Graphics to toggle the graphics display to empty boxes and speed up scrolling. The graphics will still print.

Mastering Graphics Box Techniques

You can right-click a graphics box to edit it, or select the box and select items from the property bar. When you have multiple graphics in a document, you can click the Previous or Next button on the property bar to go from graphic to graphic.

Try the following WordPerfect exercise to get a hang of the basic graphics box techniques:

1. Open a blank new document, click Insert ⇨ Graphics ⇨ Clipart, and drag a clip art item from the Scrapbook; then

   • Click outside the graphics box to deselect it. (Click the box to select it again.)

   • Click anywhere within the box to drag it to another location. (Hold down the Ctrl key to make a copy.)

   • Drag a corner handle to size the image proportionally (see Figure 9-9).

   • Drag a side handle to stretch or squeeze the image (see Figure 9-10).

   • Press Delete to remove the box.

Figure 9-9: Drag a corner handle to size an image proportionally.

Figure 9-10: Drag a side handle to stretch or squeeze the image.

2. Click Insert ⇨ Text Box, and then do any of the following:

   • Click the middle of the box with the shadow cursor to center the line.

   • Type and format some text, just as you would in a document. (You can even use Reveal Codes in a text box.)

   • Click outside the box to deselect it, and then point to the border and click to select just the box.

- Position the pointer anywhere along the border, and then drag the box (see Figure 9-11).
- Drag a handle to stretch or shrink the amount of text that displays. Note how the size of the text doesn't change.

Figure 9-11: Click the border to drag a text box.

One more thing: When you double-click a graphic image, you'll end up editing the image itself in Presentations, or whatever application it is assigned to.

Layering Graphics Boxes

WordPerfect's *drawing layer* lets you arrange a stack of overlapping graphics boxes. It also enables Sticky Notes (which lie on top of your text) and watermarks (which go behind it). In the following exercise, you'll practice layering different kinds of graphics boxes.

1. Type a few lines of text.

2. Click in your text, click Insert ➪ Graphics ➪ Custom Box, and click Custom Box.

3. Select the Sticky Note Text box, put some text in it, and then click outside the note.

4. Right-click the box and click Select Box, and then hold down the Ctrl key and drag the note to create a copy.

5. Click Behind Text to put the second note behind the text (see Figure 9-12).

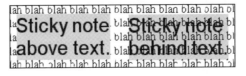

Figure 9-12: Sticky Notes above and behind text.

6. Drag three graphics from the Scrapbook and place them in a stack by dragging them on top of one another.

7. Select a graphic and then click the Graphic Up and Graphic Down button to move it up and down in the stack (see Figure 9-13). Click Graphics ➪ To Front and Graphics ➪ To Back to move it to the top or bottom of the stack.

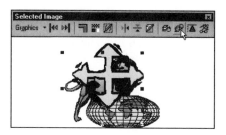

Figure 9-13: Moving graphics up and down the stack.

8. Click the Previous or Next button to select different graphics in the stack.

For more on layering graphics, see Chapter 55, "Creating Your Own Art."

Grouping Graphics Boxes

You can group objects within a graphics box in Presentations (see Chapter 55, "Creating Your Own Art"). In WordPerfect or Presentations, you can also group graphics boxes themselves and then drag them around as one. This feature is especially handy for superimposing text on graphics.

Try the following exercise in grouping graphics boxes:

1. Open the Scrapbook and then drag the cow and the callout (speech balloon) onto your document.

2. With the callout selected, click Flip to flip it from left to right, and then drag it over to the cow and click outside of the box to deselect it.

3. Click Insert ⇨ Text Box, and type what the cow is saying.

4. Drag the handles to shrink the box around your text, and then drag the box to position it over the callout. (You'll also want to remove the border, as described later.)

5. While holding down the Shift key, click the cow, and then the text box, and then the callout. Notice how handles appear around the group as you click (see Figure 9-14).

Figure 9-14: Hold down the Shift key as you click each graphic to select a group.

6. Click Graphics ➪ Group to lock the graphics together.

You can now drag the graphics around and position them in relation to text as a group. Editing changes (such as to the border or fill) apply to every individual graphic, not the rectangle around the group.

To separate the boxes in a group, right-click one of the graphics and click Separate.

Editing the Appearance of a Graphics Box

You can change the appearance of a graphics box in your document by changing its style, border, or fill.

Changing the style of a graphics box

To change the style of a graphics box (such as from Image to Figure), select the box and click Graphics ➪ Style, or right-click the box and click Style.

Changing the border or fill of a graphics box

To change the border or fill of a graphics box, select the box and click the Graphic Flip Vertical or Graphic Fill button, and then select a border or fill from the palette (see Figure 9-15).

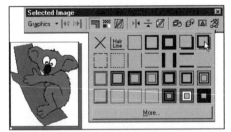

Figure 9-15: Changing the border of a graphics box.

To access the full range of border and fill customization options, click More on either the Border or Fill palette, or right-click the graphic and click Border/Fill (see Figure 9-16).

See Chapter 54, "Adding Graphic Lines, Borders, and Fills," for more information on customizing borders and fills.

Changing the Size, Position, and Spacing of a Graphics Box

Once you add a graphics box to a WordPerfect document, you'll probably want to change its size or position. You may also want to change its inside or outside spacing.

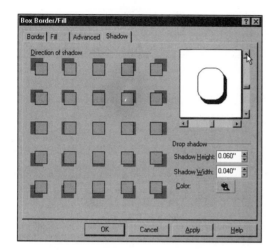

Figure 9-16: Accessing all the border and fill options.

Specifying a precise graphics box size

While the mouse is the quickest tool for resizing a graphics box, you can also give it a precise size:

1. Select the graphic and click Graphics ⇨ Size.

2. Specify one of the following width and height options (see Figure 9-17):

   • *Set*, to specify a particular width or height

   • *Full*, to fill the width of the column, cell, or page, or the height of the page

   • *Maintain proportions*, to keep the original image proportions as you adjust one dimension, or to reset a distorted image

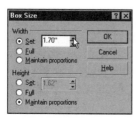

Figure 9-17: Specifying a precise graphics box size.

Changing the anchor type and position

Every graphics box in WordPerfect has one of the following anchors to position it in relation to text:

✦ *Page* (Image, Sticky Note, Table, Watermark) lets you attach the graphics box to the entire page (watermark), or to a particular location on the page, so it doesn't shift about as you add or delete text.

✦ *Paragraph* (Figure, Text) keeps the graphics box attached to a particular paragraph as you edit text, even when the paragraph shifts to another page.

✦ *Character* (Button, Inline Text) treats your graphics box as a single character that shifts along the line as you edit your text.

To change a graphic's anchor type and position:

1. Select the graphic and click Graphics ⇨ Position.

2. Select an anchor from the "Attach box to" list (see Figure 9-18).

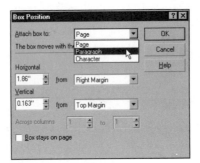

Figure 9-18: Changing the anchor type.

3. Specify the positioning options for the type of anchor you selected.

Tip   To use a graphic of your scanned signature in e-mail or a fax, set the anchor to character or paragraph to keep it attached to the closing phrase.

Adjusting the inside or outside spacing of a graphics box

To adjust the space between the contents and border of a graphics box in WordPerfect, or the space between the border and the text surrounding the box:

1. Select the box and then click the Graphic Border button (or the Graphic Fill button) ⇨ More ⇨ Advanced.

2. Click the Inside and Outside spacing palettes to specify the spacing you want (see Figure 9-19).

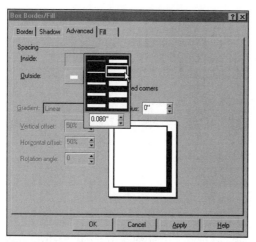

Figure 9-19: Adjusting the inside or outside spacing of a graphics box.

Creating and Editing Captions

You can add captions to your WordPerfect images with either identifying text or automatic numbering (such as Figure 1, Figure 2, and so on) used for document references. You can employ several positioning, appearance, and numbering style options in customizing captions.

Adding a caption to a graphics box

To add a caption to a graphics box:

1. Click the box and click Caption.

2. Type the caption text you want (see Figure 9-20).

Figure 9-20: Default caption for the second cow.

Tip   Use the property bar selections to change the font face, color, and other attributes.

Editing a caption

To edit a caption, select the graphic and click Caption (or right-click the graphic and click Edit Caption).

Deleting a caption

To delete a caption, right-click the graphic and then click Caption ⇨ Reset. Reset not only deletes the caption, but also returns the caption style (if it has been altered) to the default for that type of graphics box.

Changing the position of a caption

The default caption position for most graphics box styles is outside of the border, at the bottom left. To change the caption's position, right-click the graphic, click Caption, and then specify a different position, either inside or outside of the border (see Figure 9-21).

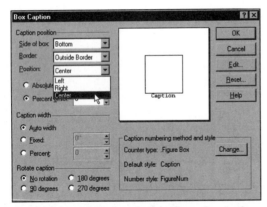

Figure 9-21: Changing the position of a caption.

Rotating a caption

You can rotate a caption in 90-degree increments, as shown in Figure 9-22. This is especially handy when you want to print a caption along the side of a graphics box, rather than across the top or bottom.

To rotate a caption, right-click the graphic, click Caption, and select a rotation of 90, 180, or 270 counterclockwise degrees.

Send E-mail and spare a tree

Figure 9-22: Caption rotated 90 degrees.

Adjusting the caption width

You can adjust the width of a caption to the layout of your graphics and text. This is especially handy if you are printing a caption on the side of a graphic (see Figure 9-23), or if you are rotating a caption printed at the top or bottom.

To adjust the width of a caption, right-click the graphic, click Caption, and specify either a fixed width or a percentage of the box's width.

Controlling the Flow of Text Around a Graphic

The impact of a graphic comes primarily from its relation to the textual elements. Earlier in this chapter, you learned how to layer graphics above and behind text. In many cases, however, you'll want your text to flow around a graphic. Figure 9-24 illustrates a few of the possibilities.

Figure 9-23: Adjusting the caption width (before and after).

To change the flow of text around a graphic:

1. Select the graphic and click the Wrap Text button (or right-click the graphic and click Wrap).

2. Select the wrap you want (see Figure 9-25):

   • *Neither side*, to have the graphics box stand alone, with no text on either side of it.

   • *Square*, to align text with the sides of the box.

   • *Contour*, to wrap text around the image within the box, when there's no border. (Text also contours to a border with rounded corners.)

   • *Behind Text/In Front of Text*, to place the graphic behind or in front of the text.

With a square or contour wrap, you also specify the side it wraps around. The Largest Side option causes the text to flow around the side of the box with the most white space.

Creating a Custom Graphics Box Style

You can create a custom graphics box style for all your documents, with the particular border, fill, anchor, content, spacing, caption, wrap, and other options you want:

Figure 9-24: Flowing text around graphics.

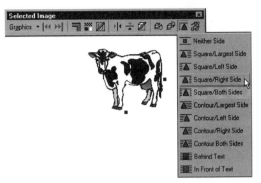

Figure 9-25: Changing the flow of text around a graphic.

1. Click Format ➪ Graphics Styles ➪ Box ➪ Create.
2. Give your style a name, and specify the options you want (see Figure 9-26).

Figure 9-26: Creating a custom graphics box style.

To insert your custom graphics box, click Insert ➪ Graphics ➪ Custom Box and select your style from the list.

Changing the Properties of a Graphic Image

In addition to moving or sizing a graphics box, you can change the properties of the image within it. Use the image tools to crop, rotate, scale, or flip an image, or adjust such attributes as its brightness, contrast, color, and fill:

1. Select the graphic and click the Graphic Image Tools button to display the Image Tools palette shown in Figure 9-27.

Figure 9-27: Image Tools palette.

2. Use any of the tools shown in Table 9-2 to change the properties of your image.

Table 9-2 Image Tools	
Image Tool	**Lets You**
Rotate	Rotate the image around a selected point (see Figure 9-28).
Move	Move the image within the box.
Flip Vertical	Flip the image left to right.
Flip Horizontal	Flip the image top to bottom.
Zoom	Zoom the entire image in or out, or zoom (crop) a selected part of the image. You can also reset an image to its original size.
BW Threshold	Display a color image in black and white, and select a dividing line (threshold) between black and white (see Figure 9-29).
Contrast	Adjust the contrast of the image.
Brightness	Adjust the brightness of the image.
Fill	Select normal fill, no fill (transparent image with background showing through), or white fill (the image displays in outline with white fill).
Invert Colors	Switch the colors of the image to their complements.
Edit Contents	Edit the image in its drawing program.
Edit Attributes	Access all the image-editing tools from one dialog box and specify precise numeric settings (see Figure 9-30). You can also specify the image print parameters.
Reset Attributes	Reset the image display to its original state.

Figure 9-28: Rotating an image.

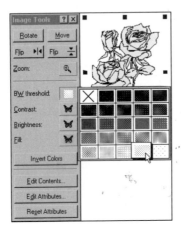

Figure 9-29: Selecting a threshold when converting a color image to black and white.

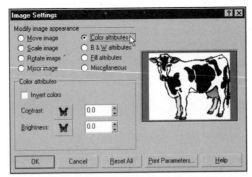

Figure 9-30: Setting all the image attributes at once.

To reposition the Image Tools palette, drag its title bar. Click on your document to dismiss the palette.

For More Information . . .

On	See
Inserting watermarks	Chapter 21
Drawing, painting, and scanning art	Chapter 55
Changing slide show backgrounds	Chapter 39
Creating TextArt	Chapter 8
Creating equations	Chapter 8
Charting data	Chapter 56
Adding Web graphics	Chapter 14
Layering and grouping graphic objects	Chapter 55
Adding graphic borders and fills	Chapter 54
Generating caption lists	Chapter 24

✦   ✦   ✦

Working Together and Sharing Data

WordPerfect Office 2000 is at its seamless best when it comes to sharing or transferring text, charts, spreadsheets, graphics, and other information. This chapter explains when to copy, link, embed, and convert information.

Let's say you're writing the annual report for Cyclops Software, Inc., with charts created in Presentations using data from a Quattro Pro spreadsheet or Paradox database. The financial data is only preliminary, and will be revised several times over the next three weeks. Does that mean you must keep checking which figures have changed, and then type the revisions to your WordPerfect charts? No way! Every time you open the document, dynamic links to the accounting data automatically update the charts (see Figure 10-1).

That takes care of your charts. Now suppose that you must gather text for your report from a variety of word processing sources. Will this take hours of manual conversion or transcribing? Not likely. WordPerfect can convert text to and from other word processors with aplomb.

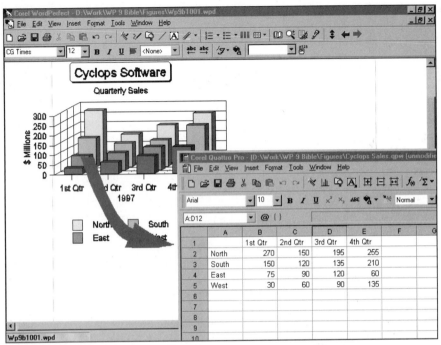

Figure 10-1: WordPerfect chart linked to Quattro Pro spreadsheet.

How Applications Work Together

WordPerfect Office 2000 fully supports Object Linking and Embedding (OLE) 2.0, the most advanced system for sharing information in the Windows environment. It also supports the older technology of Dynamic Data Exchange (DDE) for sharing information with pre-Windows 95 programs that aren't OLE-enabled.

With OLE 2.0, you can create an object of information shared between two programs (such as a table of information in WordPerfect taken from a Quattro Pro spreadsheet). Double-clicking the table object in WordPerfect takes you directly to Quattro Pro, where you can edit the data and then click outside the object's frame to return to your WordPerfect document. Editing a graphic or TextArt object in Presentations works the same way. The process is so seamless (because of the common interface among the WordPerfect Office 2000 programs) that you hardly notice which application you're in.

Your application can be either a *client* on the receiving end of information created elsewhere, or a *server* sending its data to a client. A word processor normally acts as a client (or *container*) of information created by spreadsheet, database, graphics, and other server (or *source*) applications.

If this terminology is a bit circular and confusing, don't worry about the machinations behind the scene. The important thing to know is that you can double-click a spreadsheet graph or clip art image in your WordPerfect document to edit it, and then click back on your document to return to WordPerfect. It is, however, helpful to understand the distinction between linking and embedding information.

Linking information

When you *link* data (such as a graphic or spreadsheet), you maintain a connection with the originating program. If Presentations is on the client (receiving) end of the link, a code is inserted in your Presentations slide that points to the originating file and application. Your slide is smaller, because the data itself is not copied. As long as the link is not broken (that is, when the server data can be found), you can keep the copy up-to-date.

Information linked by using OLE 2.0 can be updated automatically, whereas DDE links usually must be updated manually. Whatever the type of link, you can always do manual updates, or break the link to keep the copy from changing.

You can also link objects within an application, such as from one Presentations slide to another.

Embedding information

When you use OLE to *embed* a copy of another program's information into a slide, you can double-click the information to edit it in the original program. (DDE does not allow embedding.) The changes you make in Presentations don't affect the original data. On the other hand, when the original information is updated, the information in your document will no longer be current. You can embed spreadsheets, graphics, sound, video, and other types of objects.

To copy, link, or embed?

In Chapter 2, "Essential Typing and Editing," you learned how to copy and paste information by using the Windows Clipboard. With the addition of data sharing, you have three ways to incorporate information created by one application into another:

✦ Paste or import a copy

✦ Link to the object

✦ Embed the object

Table 10-1 summarizes the differences between the three methods.

Table 10-1
Choosing to Copy and Paste, Link, or Embed

Method	What It Does	How Information Is Updated
Paste or import	Copies the object from another application.	Manually. Delete the copy and repeat the process.
Link	Establishes a connection in the source that lets you view information in the client application.	Can be updated manually or automatically, as long as the link is maintained (that is, the server object can be found).
Embed	A "snapshot" copy of the server object is placed in the client.	No automatic update, but you can double-click the object to edit it in the source application.

Embedding and Linking Objects

WordPerfect Office 2000 provides three ways to embed or link objects:

✦ By using the Windows Clipboard

✦ By using the Insert Object and other dialog boxes

✦ By dragging-and-dropping objects between programs (linking only)

Objects can include text, graphics, spreadsheet data, sound clips, and so on.

 Tip   Various PerfectExpert projects delivered with WordPerfect Office 2000 automate the process of embedding and linking between applications.

Pasting or linking via the Clipboard

To embed or link information by using the Clipboard:

1. Open the file in the application that has the information you want to embed or link. (To link to a file, it must be saved and named.)

2. Select all or part of the information, and then click the Copy button (Edit ➪ Copy) to place it on the Windows Clipboard. (Don't exit the application if you want to create a link.)

3. Open the receiving application and click where you want the information to appear.

4. Click the Paste button (Edit ➪ Paste) to embed a copy of the information, or click Edit ➪ Paste Special ➪ Paste Link to paste a picture of the information with a link to the original file (see Figure 10-2).

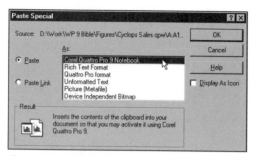

Figure 10-2: Using Paste Special to embed or link via the Clipboard.

5. Click OK to return to your document. If you're asked if you want to update linked information, click Yes.

Using Insert Object to embed or link

To embed or link information by using the Insert Object dialog box, click Insert ⇨ Object, and then click one of the following (Figure 10-3):

✦ *Create New* (to create the object now). Specify the object type (such as Bitmap Image or Video Clip) and click OK. This opens the application associated with the data. Create the data within the bounding box that appears. (You can resize the box to make it larger or smaller.) When you are finished, click outside the bounding box.

✦ *Create from File* (the object's already created and saved). Specify the path and filename. Check Link if you want to insert a link to the data, rather than the data itself.

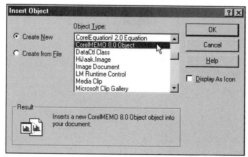

Figure 10-3: Using Insert Object to embed or link.

Dragging and dropping objects

You can drag-and-drop to embed an object

- ✦ Between tiled applications
- ✦ Via the Windows taskbar
- ✦ From an icon or scrap on the desktop
- ✦ From the Windows Explorer

To drag objects between tiled applications:

1. Launch WordPerfect and Presentations to create a new WordPerfect document and a new drawing or slide show.

2. In Presentations, select a shape from the tool palette, and then drag to create the shape.

3. Right-click the Windows taskbar, and then click Tile Horizontally or Tile Vertically.

4. Drag the shape to WordPerfect. Hold down the Ctrl key if you want to copy it (see Figure 10-4).

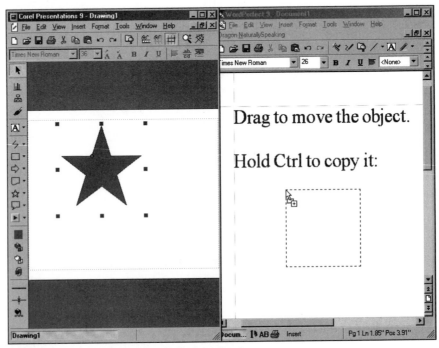

Figure 10-4: Dragging between tiled applications.

To drag objects via the Windows taskbar:

1. Launch the programs and create the shape as described in Steps 1 and 2 of the previous example.

2. From Presentations, drag the shape (hold down the Ctrl key to copy) to the WordPerfect button on the Windows taskbar (not to the DAD icon), but don't let go of the mouse button or Ctrl key. The WordPerfect window will open automatically.

3. Drag the shape into your WordPerfect document.

To drag-and-drop reusable scraps via the desktop:

1. Right-click the Windows taskbar and click Cascade.

2. Select the information and drag it to the desktop. This creates a scrap icon that you can drag to another application to embed it as an OLE 2.0 object.

To drag-and-drop a file, such as a graphic or document, via the Windows Explorer:

1. Right-click the Start button on the Windows taskbar and click Explore.

2. Locate the file and drag it to the application window or onto the desktop.

Editing embedded objects

OLE makes it easy to modify an embedded object. To edit an embedded object:

1. Double-click the object. (This activates the application used to create the data.)

2. Return by clicking anywhere outside the bounding box for the data.

Editing information in linked objects

Linked data doesn't actually reside in your client file, such as a WordPerfect document. Rather, the data is contained in another file created by the source program. Depending on how the applications interact, you can modify linked data in one of two ways:

✦ Double-click the linked data in the client file. With some OLE-compliant applications, this activates the application and loads the data for editing.

✦ Open the server application and retrieve the data file. Modify the data file and save it. Open the client file and then double-click the object containing the linked data to update it.

Changing, updating, or breaking a link

To change, update, or break a link:

1. Click Edit ➪ Links and select the link (see Figure 10-5).

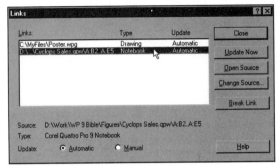

Figure 10-5: Changing, updating, or breaking a link.

2. Click any of the following:

   • *Update Now,* to reflect the latest source information

   • *Open Source,* to edit the information in the source application

   • *Change Source,* to keep the link but change the file it's linked to

   • *Break Link,* to keep the information but leave it unchanged when the source file is edited

An OLE link is also broken when the data object in the client application is deleted.

Converting Information

Many file formats are used in personal computing. As each word processing, spreadsheet, database, and graphics developer added tricks and features to the various programs, a diversity of formats emerged, much as the diversity of human cultures evolved a variety of languages. Programs (such as Adobe Acrobat) have been devised to publish information from many programs in their original appearance and fonts across Windows and other platforms. However, these don't provide cross-application access to the data itself, which is an especially severe limitation when you're creating a new document from assembled materials.

As products mature, a few common formatting languages may emerge, as with HTML for Web pages. Until that time, however, you may frequently need to convert text, graphics, and data in and out of your WordPerfect applications. Fortunately, WordPerfect Office 2000 is an accomplished translator.

This section covers text conversions. Graphic conversions are covered in Chapter 9, "Working with Graphics." Spreadsheet conversions are explained in Chapter 35, "Analyzing Data," and database conversions are discussed in Chapter 51, "Paradox Tricks and Techniques."

Converting text in WordPerfect

WordPerfect provides conversion filters for many common and not-so-common document formats. Not every filter is automatically installed, so if the format you are bringing in isn't recognized, you can run the Corel setup program to install additional filters.

WordPerfect (including WordPerfect 5.*x*) documents are automatically converted when opened into WordPerfect 9.

New Feature WordPerfect 6, 7, 8, and 9 share a common standard document format. WP automatically detects and converts text from many formats, including ASCII, ANSI, WP 5.*x*, Word Pro, and MS Word 6.0/7.0, and 97.

When WP isn't sure of what type of document you're opening, the converter displays its best guess, but lets you make the final choice (see Figure 10-6).

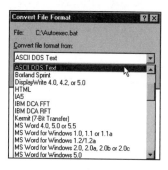

Figure 10-6: Specifying the format of the file you're opening.

When you open or insert a document created in another word processor, a few formatting and other features may get lost or changed along the way. Depending on the nature of the conversion, you might find it necessary to delete spaces and perform other edits to format the document the way you want it to appear in WordPerfect. The Reveal Codes window is especially suited to this task.

Tip When opening ANSI or ASCII text files that you intend to save in WordPerfect format, you might want to select a "CR/LF to SRt" conversion. This converts single carriage returns and line feeds to soft returns (instead of hard returns) so your text needs less manual formatting.

When you save a converted document you edited, you are given the choice to save it as a WordPerfect document or convert it back to the original format (see Figure 10-7).

You can also select Other, and then select the appropriate filename extension from the "As type" list, and give the document a name.

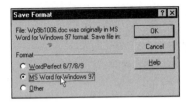

Figure 10-7: Saving converted text after it has been edited.

 To automatically save a document back to its native format, click Tools ➪ Settings ➪ Files, and check "On save, keep document's original file format."

You can use Save As to export a WordPerfect document to the WordPerfect 5.*x* format, or to that of another word processor.

As a general rule, the less formatting involved, the better text converts. Try to avoid such complexities as tables, columns, headers, footers, page numbering, bullets, styles, graphics, sound clips, and hypertext. Often Rich Text Format (RTF) can be used as an intermediary between two word processing programs (see the next section, "Converting text via the Clipboard"). RTF uses text codes to preserve basic type and formatting elements. Unformatted ASCII and ANSI files offer the lowest common denominator for text transfers.

Converting text via the Clipboard

The Clipboard stores information in multiple formats to facilitate the transfer of text and graphics between programs. When you copy information between WordPerfect documents via the Clipboard, the native WordPerfect formatting is conveyed. When you copy and paste between applications, the most detailed common Clipboard format (usually RTF) is automatically used in translating the original information to the WordPerfect format.

You can use Paste Special (Edit ➪ Paste Special) to override the default conversion. For example, Figure 10-8 displays the available options when pasting from WordPad to WordPerfect. Formats dependent on the source application no longer display once that application is closed.

To view the contents of the Clipboard (see Figure 10-9), click the Start button on the Windows taskbar, and then click Programs ➪ Accessories ➪ Clipboard Viewer.

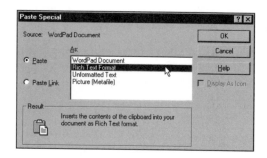

Figure 10-8: Using Paste Special to select a Clipboard format.

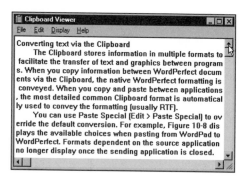

Figure 10-9: Viewing the Clipboard's contents.

The Viewer's Display menu lists the formats available for the particular information on the Clipboard. (Formats that cannot be viewed on the Clipboard appear dimmed.) Check Auto to return to the original format.

You can often preserve many of the basic text formatting features (as well as tables and graphics) when transferring via the Clipboard. You may be able to transfer text and graphics simultaneously, but you'll often get better results transferring them separately.

When cutting and pasting between word processors (such as Word and WordPerfect), you can paste unformatted text to remove all text formatting. To cut and paste unformatted text between word processors:

1. Select the text and then click the Copy button (Edit ⇨ Copy) to copy it to the Clipboard.

2. Switch to the receiving application and click where you want to paste the text.

3. Click Edit ⇨ Paste Special, and select Unformatted Text.

Changing your default file save format

New Feature

Normally you'll want save your documents to the WordPerfect 6/7/8/9 format, as it provides a powerful feature set and widespread compatibility. To change your default file save format, click Tools ➭ Settings ➭ Files, and select from the list of supported document types (see Figure 10-10).

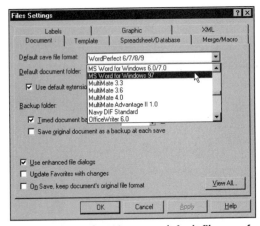

Figure 10-10: Changing your default file save format.

Selecting the WordPerfect 5.1/5.2 format ensures even wider compatibility, but with the sacrifice of some advanced formatting. You can also select a Microsoft Word format if your document is going to a recipient who uses that standard.

For More Information . . .

On	See
Inserting sound and video	Chapters 14, 39, 41
Inserting bookmarks in documents	Chapter 18
Linking to Web pages	Chapter 14
Using the Windows Clipboard	Chapter 2

✦   ✦   ✦

Organizing Your Life

The CorelCENTRAL personal information manager (PIM) can help you organize your life and coordinate your activities with the outside world. CorelCENTRAL provides an easy-to-use set of tools to manage your time, tasks, appointments, contacts, and other personal information. This chapter introduces CorelCENTRAL and shows you how to schedule events and tasks. In Chapter 12, "Managing Addresses, Memos, and Card Files" you'll learn how to use the remaining facilities.

What's CorelCENTRAL?

CorelCENTRAL is a mini-suite of applications known as a Personal Information Manager (PIM), which helps bring order to your personal life and your complex interactions with the outside world. You can think of CorelCENTRAL as a software Swiss army knife, with the following interconnected components:

+ A *Day Planner* control center that pops into view, to show you today's agenda and launch the other CorelCENTRAL mini-applications

+ A *Calendar* that lets you schedule tasks and events far into the future

+ *Alarms* to remind you to do the things you said you would

+ *Memos* to jot down the particulars associated with tasks and events

+ A flexible *Card File* for storing all types of information, such as insurance policies, gift lists, and family history

+ An Office-wide *Address Book* for keeping all your contact names, addresses, phone numbers, and so on, on earth and in cyberspace

Tip   The Day Planner and Calendar display the same events and tasks. You enter items once in either view.

What If I Already Have a PIM?

If you're already using a PIM, such as Outlook, Sidekick, GroupWise, or InfoCentral, there's no need to copy your Address Book or card file information by hand to use in CorelCENTRAL.

The next chapter describes how CorelCENTRAL can import and export information from and to a number of different formats, including HotSync coordination with the 3Com PalmPilot.

Using the Day Planner

New Feature   The Day Planner provides a handy view of the day's events and unfinished tasks (see Figure 11-1). It also has buttons to access the full Calendar, as well as the Address Book, Card Files, and Memos.

Launching the Day Planner

Your WordPerfect Office installation gives you the option to place a shortcut in your Windows Startup folder to launch the Day Planner when you start Windows. Without a shortcut, you can launch the Day Planner in either of two ways:

✦ Click the CorelCENTRAL icon on the Windows taskbar if the Desktop Application Director is running

✦ Click the Start button, and then click WordPerfect Office 2000 ⇨ CorelCENTRAL 9

Viewing the Day Planner

The default location for your Day Planner is on the right side of your screen. It slides discreetly out of view as soon as you click on another Windows application. Whenever you want to see the Day Planner, rest your mouse pointer on the edge of the screen where it is located. You can also click the Day Planner button on the Windows taskbar to alternately display and hide the Day Planner.

Tip   If you don't want the Day Planner button to appear on your taskbar, see "Changing the Day Planner's settings."

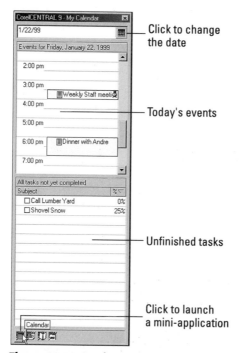

Figure 11-1: CorelCENTRAL Day Planner, showing the day's activities and buttons to launch other mini-applications.

Changing the size of the day planner

To widen your Day Planner display and bring more information into view, drag the side with your mouse (see Figure 11-2). Drag the side back if you want to make it smaller.

Viewing dates and times

The Day Planner displays events and tasks for the current date, based on your computer's date and time. Scroll the event listing to see earlier or later events. To see events and tasks for a different date, click the CorelCENTRAL MiniCalendar button at the upper-right, then select a different date (see Figure 11-3).

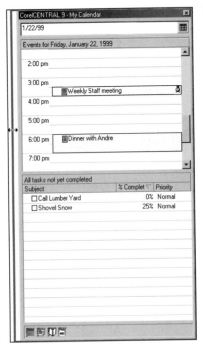

Figure 11-2: Changing the size of your Day Planner.

Figure 11-3: Selecting another date to display.

Changing the Day Planner's settings

To change the Day Planner's settings (see Figure 11-4), right-click on its title bar, click Settings, and then specify any of the settings described in Table 11-1.

Tip

The default is zero, but set it to one or two seconds if you find that it accidentally pops up a lot.

Figure 11-4: Changing the Day Planner's settings.

Table 11-1
Day Planner Settings

Setting	Lets You
Always on top	Keep the Day Planner from being hidden by any other active applications.
Autohide	Have the Day Planner slide out of view when you're not pointing at it.
Location	Display the Day Planner on the left or right. (Drag the title bar to move it to the other side.)
Run on startup	Place a shortcut in the Windows Startup folder to launch the Day Planner when you start Windows. Remove the check to delete the shortcut.
Show in Taskbar	Place an application button on the Windows taskbar that you can click to display or hide the Day Planner.
Day Planner	Delay Set the number of seconds it takes the Day Planner to appear when you point to the side of the screen.

Displaying the Calendar

To display the full Calendar, click the Day Planner Display Calendar button at the bottom of the Day Planner, or click Start ➪ WordPerfect Office 2000 ➪ Utilities ➪ CorelCENTRAL Calendar (see Figure 11-5).

Click the toolbar buttons to switch among the Day, Week, and Month views. The scroll bar in the middle of the Calendar lets you scroll by the month, or click the arrows to switch among the months and years.

To go to a particular date, click the CorelCENTRAL Go To Specific Date button (Calendar ➪ Go To Specific Date). To return to today's tasks and events, click the CorelCENTRAL Go To Today button (Calendar ➪ Go To Today).

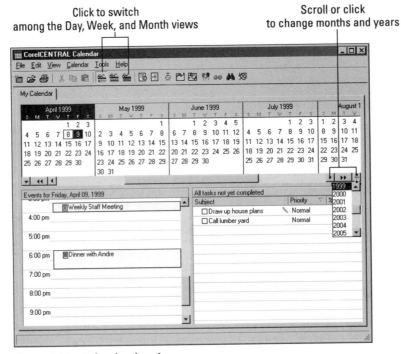

Figure 11-5: Calendar day view.

Scheduling Events

CorelCENTRAL's Day Planner and Calendar can bring a little order to your life by keeping track of luncheons, meetings, appointments, conferences, vacations, birthdays, and other events. Events you schedule in the Day Planner automatically appear in the Calendar, and vice versa.

Scheduling an event

To quickly schedule an event for a particular day:

1. Display the Day Planner or Calendar and switch, if necessary, to the particular day.

   To switch dates in the Calendar, click the CorelCENTRAL Go To Today button (Calendar ⇨ Go To Today) or the CorelCENTRAL Go To Today button (Calendar ⇨ Go To Specific Date).

2. Click the line in the Events list nearest to the time for the event, type a description, and press Enter.

Tip Double-click a time to access all the options in the New Event dialog box, described in the next section.

Events you enter this way default to a duration of one hour, with no alarm (see Figure 11-6).

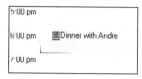

Figure 11-6: Events default to one hour's duration, with no alarm.

Tip Drag an event's borders to lengthen or shorten its duration.

Using the New Event dialog box

For the full range of event options, use the New Event dialog box:

1. In the Daily Planner or Calendar, double-click on a time, or right-click in the Events list and click Add Event. In the Calendar, you can also click the CorelCENTRAL New Event button (Calendar ➪ New Event).

2. Type the event's subject (see Figure 11-7).

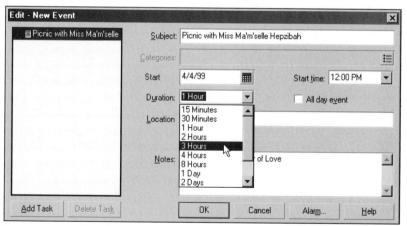

Figure 11-7: Using the New Event dialog box.

3. Specify the start date and time, duration, and optional location. You can type a time (e.g., 12:10 P.M.) or duration (e.g., 7 Hours) that isn't in the drop-down list. (For all day events, see "Scheduling an event over one or more days.")

4. Click the Alarm button to set an alarm for the event.

5. Type any free-form comments or notes, and then click OK to save the event.

Tip   Press Ctrl+Enter to start a new note line.

Scheduling an event over one or more days

Most events (such as a meeting, test, or dinner) have a duration of hours or minutes. Some events (such as a conference or final exams) can take place over one or more days.

To schedule a multi-day event:

1. Create an event as previously described in "Using the New Event dialog box."

2. Check the "All day event" box, and set the duration to the desired number of days.

Your multi-day events appear at the top of the Events list in the Daily Planner and your Calendar's Day view, and as a descriptive bar across the dates in the Week and Month views.

Editing, moving, copying, or deleting an event

To edit an event in the Day Planner or Calendar, do any of the following:

✦ Double-click the event.

✦ Right-click the event to set the alarm, or to edit or delete the event.

✦ Drag the event to another starting time (see Figure 11-8). (Hold down the Ctrl key to copy it.)

Figure 11-8: Dragging an event to another starting time.

✦ Drag the top or bottom border of the event box to change its starting or ending time.

You can also click an event and then press Delete to remove it.

To change an event's description, click the description, and then click again and type the new description.

Responding to an event's alarm

As the time for an event approaches, an alarm sounds and a reminder appears (see Figure 11-9). You can either click OK to dismiss the reminder permanently, or click Snooze to be reminded again at the end of the snooze interval.

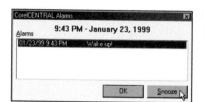

Figure 11-9: Responding to an event's alarm.

Changing an event's alarm settings

By default, an event's alarm is set to sound 10 minutes before the event, with a "snooze" option to repeat the alarm every 5 minutes until you turn it off.

To change the alarm settings for a particular event:

1. Click the event and click the CorelCENTRAL Alarm button (Calendar ⇨ Set Alarm), or double-click its alarm icon.

2. Specify the Remind Me Before Event and Set Snooze Interval times (see Figure 11-10).

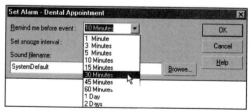

Figure 11-10: Changing an event's alarm settings.

3. Select the .WAV file you want to use for the alarm.

You can change alarm settings by clicking the Alarm button in the Event dialog box when creating or editing an event.

Setting Quick Alarms

If you just need a "wake up" reminder after putting the bread in the oven, use the Quick Alarm mini-application. Click the CorelCENTRAL Quick Alarm button on the Windows taskbar, type a subject, and set the timer (see Figure 11-11). You can type a precise number of minutes. Click the Advanced button to select a date, snooze interval, or sound.

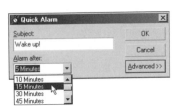

Figure 11-11: Setting a Quick Alarm.

To view, change, add to, or delete pending Quick Alarms, right-click the Quick Alarm icon and click Edit Quick Alarm.

Scheduling Tasks

You schedule tasks in much the way that you schedule events. The main distinction between an event and a task is that an event occurs at a particular time, whereas a task must be completed by a certain date. Thus, an event has an alarm, while a task is assigned a priority and percentage completed.

Uncompleted tasks carry over to the following days. They don't go away until checked 100% complete.

Scheduling a task

To quickly schedule a task for a particular day:

1. Display the Day Planner or Calendar and switch, if necessary, to the particular day.

2. Click in the task list, type a description, and press Enter.

Tasks you enter this way show a Normal priority and 0% complete, and have a completion date of that day.

Using the New Task dialog box

For the full range of task options, including a completion date, use the New Task dialog box:

1. In the Daily Planner, right-click in the Tasks list and click Add Task. In the Calendar, click the CorelCENTRAL New Task button (Calendar ➪ New Task).

2. Type the subject for the task, and then type a category or click the CorelCENTRAL Event Category button to select one or more categories (see Figure 11-12). (You can add or delete categories from the dialog box.)

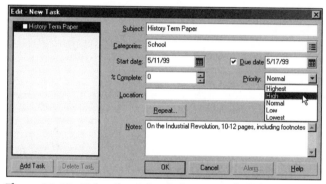

Figure 11-12: Using the Calendar's New Task dialog box.

3. Specify the start date and, if applicable, check Due Date and specify the date.

4. You may specify the percent complete, priority, and location.

5. Type any comments or notes in the Notes window, and then click OK to save the task.

Completing a task

To mark a task as 100% complete, simply click its check box. Removing the check sets the completion percentage back to zero.

Right-click the task to set a partial completion percentage.

Editing or deleting a task

To edit a task in the Day Planner or Calendar, do either of the following:

✦ Double-click the task.

✦ Right-click the event to set the priority or percent complete, or to edit or delete the task.

You can also click a task and then press Delete to remove it.

To change a task's description, click the description, and then click again and type the new description.

Changing the task list display

To select the columns to appear in the task display of your Day Planner or Calendar, right-click the column headings and check the items you want (see Figure 11-13).

Figure 11-13: Selecting the columns to appear in your task list.

To sort your tasks by subject, priority, or percent complete, simply click the applicable button at the top of the task list. Click the button a second time to reverse the sort order.

Tip   An up or down triangle on the button shows which column you've sorted on.

Drag the lines between buttons to adjust the column widths.

To filter the task display by category, completion status, or time period:

1. Click the Status button at the very top of the task list.

2. Select the category, status, and time period you want to display (see Figure 11-14).

Figure 11-14: Selecting the category, status, and time period for your task list display.

Adding Subtasks to Events and Tasks

You can add subtasks to events and tasks, such as a phone call to arrange a dinner or research you have to do for a term paper:

1. Right-click the event or task, and click Add Subtask.

2. Fill in the subject, date, priority, and other information, as described earlier in "Using the New Task dialog box."

You can also add subtasks to subtasks, down to as many as six levels.

To add subtasks while creating an event or task, click the Add Task button.

A plus sign (+) next to an event or task indicates that subordinate subtasks are hidden; a minus sign (-) indicates that all the subtasks are showing (see Figure 11-15).

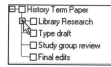

Figure 11-15: Displaying subtasks.

Adding Links to Events and Tasks

By adding links to events and tasks, you can go anywhere and do anything with a click of the mouse:

1. Click the event or task to which you want to add a link.

2. Click Tools ⇨ Link To, and select the type of link:

   • *Memos*, to jump to the memo you select

   • *Card File*, to jump to the card file record you specify

   • *File/Application*, to launch the program you specify

   • *Folder*, to go to a folder to open a document

   • *E-mail*, to compose and send a message to the designated address

   • *Web Site*, to go to a designated Internet address

When you add the link, a Link icon appears in the event or task. Click the Link icon to activate the link.

You can specify the contents for most types of links (such as a phone number) either before you create the link or as you create it.

You can also right-click an event or task to create, edit, or delete a link.

Tricks with Subtasks, Events, and Tasks

To move a subtask to another event, task, or subtask, drag the subtask to the task, event, or subtask to which you want to attach it. Hold down the Ctrl key to copy the subtask.

When moving or copying to another subtask, make sure the target subtask is displayed.

Tip   To "demote" an event or task to subtask status, drag it to another event, task, or subtask. To promote a subtask to full event or task status, drag it to a blank line in the event or task list.

To change an event to a task, drag it to the task list. To change a task to an event, drag it to the event list.

When in the Calendar, you can cut, copy, and paste tasks and events:

1. Click the task or event. (Hold down the Ctrl key to select multiple items.)

2. Click the Cut (Edit ⇨ Cut) or Copy button (Edit ⇨ Copy).

3. To paste the items, click the new event or task list location and click the Paste button (Edit ⇨ Paste).

Cross-Reference   For more information on cut, copy, and paste, see Chapter 2, "Essential Typing and Editing."

Repeating an Event or Task

While most events or task items are one-shot deals, some occur on a regular basis (such as a weekly meeting, a biweekly paycheck, periodic checkups, or annual birthdays, anniversaries, and holidays).

To repeat an event or task:

1. Double-click the event or task, and then click the Repeat button.

2. Click the appropriate tab according to how you want to repeat the event: Weeks of Month, Days of Month, Weeks, or Days (see Figure 11-16).

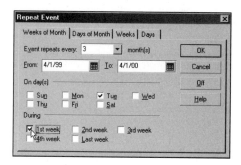

Figure 11-16: Repeating an event or task.

3. Specify the Event Repeats Every interval.

4. Specify the From and To dates over which you want the event to repeat.

5. Select, when applicable, the days on which you want to repeat the task or event; and the weeks during which it should be repeated.

Note

When you edit or delete a single instance of a repeating event or task, you will be asked if you want to change or delete all other instances or just the current one.

Scheduling Holidays

To schedule annual national or religious holidays in the Calendar:

1. Click the CorelCENTRAL Holiday button (Calendar ➪ Holidays).

2. Check the nations and religions for which you want the holidays to appear (see Figure 11-17).

Figure 11-17: Adding holidays to the Calendar.

To remove holidays, click Calendar ➪ Holidays and remove the check from the nations or religions for which you want to remove the holidays.

Creating Multiple Calendars

You can create multiple Calendars to schedule different tasks and events. For example, you can have one Calendar for personal use and another for work, or various members of your family can have their own Calendars.

To create a Calendar, click File ⇨ New, and specify the new calendar's name and path (see Figure 11-18).

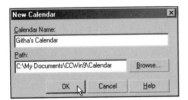

Figure 11-18: Creating a Calendar.

To switch among your calendars in the Calendar display, click the tabs below the toolbar (see Figure 11-19).

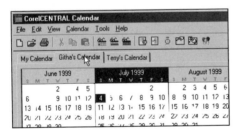

Figure 11-19: Click the tabs to switch among various Calendars.

To rename the current Calendar, click File ⇨ Rename. Click File ⇨ Delete to delete it.

Importing a Calendar

To import a Calendar from CorelCENTRAL 8, click File ⇨ Import, select the Calendar file type, and then browse to select the Calendar. (CorelCENTRAL 8 Calendars can be found in your Planner's Calendar folder.)

Printing Your Calendar

To print from your Calendar:

1. Click the Print button (File ⇨ Print), and then specify the view you want, the starting date, and the number of days, weeks, or months (see Figure 11-20).

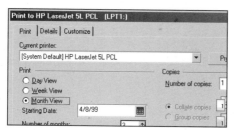

Figure 11-20: Printing your Calendar.

2. Click the Page Setup tab to specify the page size, margins, and other formatting.

3. Click the Layout tab, check the items to include, and then click Print.

 For more details on printing, see Chapter 13, "Printing and Faxing information."

Publishing Your Calendar to HTML

You can publish your Calendars to HTML, for posting on the Internet or corporate intranet:

1. Click File ⇨ Publish to HTML, and then specify the items you want to include and the range of dates you want to publish (see Figure 11-21).

2. Click the Banner/Signature tab to type the banner to show at the top of the page, and identifying information for the signature block at the bottom.

3. Click the Location tab to specify the location and filename prefix (the beginning characters of the filename), whether you want to be warned when overwriting an existing file, and whether you want to view the file in your browser immediately.

 For more information on publishing to HTML, see Chapter 14, "Web Writing and Publishing."

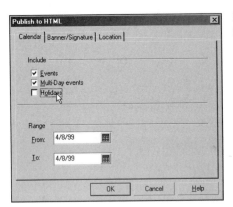

Figure 11-21: Publishing your Calendar to HTML.

Keeping Your Calendar in Working Order

Your Calendar file is maintained in a sorted database with pointers or links among the records. If the events or tasks displayed in your Calendar appear scrambled or lost, the database may be corrupted. If that happens, try rebuilding the indexes that coordinate how information is sorted, linked, and displayed:

1. Click File, Maintenance, and then click one of the following (see Figure 11-22):

   • *Rebuild Indexes,* to fix any index errors

   • *Clean up Calendar and rebuild indexes,* to purge deleted information and fix errors

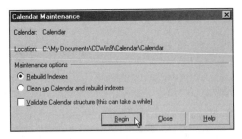

Figure 11-22: Keeping your Calendar in working order.

2. Click Begin.

If you still have problems after rebuilding the indexes, you may also need to check "Validate Calendar file structure (this can take a while)."

Purging deleted information also makes your Calendar database smaller and more efficient.

For More Information . . .

On	See
Managing addresses, card files, and memos	Chapter 12
Understanding databases	Chapter 43
Adjusting your screen display	Chapter 3
Using cut, copy, and paste	Chapter 2
Printing and faxing information	Chapter 13
Creating Web pages	Chapter 14

✦   ✦   ✦

CorelCENTRAL and the Internet

◆ ◆ ◆ ◆

Managing Addresses, Card Files, and Memos

T he previous chapter showed you how to use
CorelCENTRAL to organize your activities. Here you'll
learn about the rest of the CorelCENTRAL mini-applications:
the Address Book, Card Files, and Memos.

Using the Address Book

CorelCENTRAL's Address Book is a super phone book in which
you can store names and addresses, e-mail addresses, phone
numbers, Web addresses, and other information about your
personal and business contacts.

You can create multiple Address Books for different needs. For
example, you can have one Address Book for personal use and
another for work, or various members of your family can have
their own Address Books.

You can also open or import Address Books you may already
have, or export your CorelCENTRAL Address Books for use in
other applications.

Using MAPI and directory server Address Books

**New
Feature**

The Messaging Application Programming Interface (MAPI)
maintained by Microsoft is an industry-wide standard for
messaging applications (such as Address Books and e-mail
programs).Your CorelCENTRAL Address Book automatically
includes any other MAPI-compliant address books in its
display.

Because CorelCENTRAL is MAPI-compliant, it automatically searches for MAPI-compliant Address Books on your computer, from such programs as Microsoft Outlook or Novell GroupWise, and lists them under the MAPI book in the tree view.

Likewise, your CorelCENTRAL Address Book can be accessed by other programs that use MAPI.

You can also connect to directory server Address Books, which will appear in the tree view.

How address books are organized

Address Books are collections of records, like any other data file or database:

✦ Although there is only one Address Book application, each book shown in the tree view is referred to as an "Address Book."

✦ Each record includes individual fields for the first name, last name, phone number, and so on.

✦ Records in a CorelCENTRAL Address Book can be organized into convenient *groups*, letting you display the entire Address Book or just a particular group.

Understanding types of address entries

You can add four types of entries to a CorelCENTRAL Address Book:

✦ *Person,* to enter an individual's details

✦ *Organization,* to enter the address and contact information of an organization

✦ *Resource,* to enter the name, type, and owner of that resource

✦ *Group,* to enter the names of a group and its members

Add your organizations first; then you can select the organization from the Company list when you create a person's entry. When you add or edit a group, you can select the persons to be members of that group.

Tip   A person can be a member of more than one group.

Opening your CorelCENTRAL Address Book

You can open your Address Book application in any of the following ways:

✦ Click the Address Book taskbar icon on the Windows taskbar if the Desktop Application Director is running

✦ Click the Day Planner Display Address Book icon at the bottom of the CorelCENTRAL Day Planner

✦ Click the Start button; then click Programs ⇨ WordPerfect Office 2000 ⇨ Utilities ⇨ CorelCENTRAL Address Book

✦ In WordPerfect, click Tools ⇨ Address Book.

Viewing Address Books

To view an Address Book's entries, click the book in Tree view (see Figure 12-1).

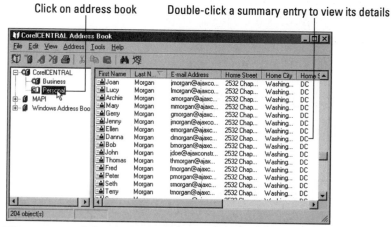

Figure 12-1: Click an Address Book to view its entries.

Note how your CorelCENTRAL Address Book also lets you see and use other MAPI, LDAP, and Windows Address Books that may be available to you.

Opening individual Address Books

You can open an Address Book to add it to the Tree view.

To open a CorelCENTRAL Address Book, click File ⇨ Open and select from the previously opened books (see Figure 12-2).

To open a MAPI-compliant address book that does not appear in Tree view, click File ⇨ Open ⇨ Other and select the book.

Your CorelCENTRAL Address Book automatically searches for all MAPI-compliant Address Books on your computer.

Figure 12-2: Opening a CorelCENTRAL Address Book.

Opening other CorelCENTRAL Address Books

To open a CorelCENTRAL 9 Address Book that doesn't appear among your previously opened books:

1. Click File ⇨ Open and click the CorelCENTRAL button.

2. Click Browse to locate and select the Address Book folder.

3. Select from the list of available Address Books.

Connecting to a directory server Address Book

Your CorelCENTRAL Address Book can connect to, and display, a network Address Book employing the standard Lightweight Directory Access Protocol (LDAP):

1. Click File ⇨ New, and then select Directory Servers and click OK.

2. Type a name for the Address Book, and its Server URL (see Figure 12-3).

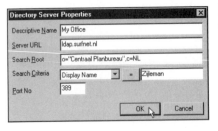

Figure 12-3: Connecting to a directory server Address Book.

3. Type one or more search roots in the Search Root box. (To search multiple roots, separate them using commas, with no spaces.)

   LDAP databases contain lots of data. By using search roots, you can limit the search to certain parts of the database. Common search roots are "c" for Country and "o" for Organization. In Figure 12-3, the search is limited to an address in The Netherlands for a particular organization.

4. Select a field from the Search Criteria list.

5. Click the button next to the Search Criteria box to select "= Equal To" or "[ ] Contains."

6. Type your search text and port number.

Closing individual Address Books

To close an Address Book, click on the book in Tree view, and then click File ⇨ Close.

Viewing and editing entries

Double-click an entry in the summary listing to view or edit its details (see Figure 12-4). You can also click an entry and click the Edit Address button (Address ⇨ Edit), or right-click an entry and click edit.

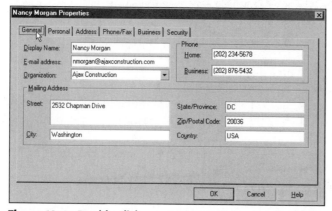

Figure 12-4: Double-click a summary entry to view its details.

Click the tabs to view and edit various items in the entry.

Adding and deleting entries

To add an entry to your Address Book:

1. Click the New Address button (Address ⇨ New Entry). You can also right-click in the detail listing and click New Entry.

2. Select the type of entry you want to add, and then click the tabs to add various items (see Figure 12-5).

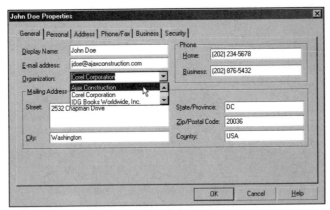

Figure 12-5: Adding a personal Address Book entry.

To delete an entry, click the entry and click CorelCENTRAL Address Book Delete Address button (Address ⇨ Delete), or press the Delete key. You can also right-click an entry and click Delete.

Moving or copying entries

To move an address entry to another Address Book, drag the entry to the Address Book in Tree view. Hold the Ctrl key down to copy the entry instead of moving it.

You can also drag entries to various address groups that appear in Tree view.

Tip   Drag address groups in the tree listing to copy them to other books. You can even drag a group to another group to cascade the group listing.

Cutting, copying, and pasting entries

To cut, copy, and paste address entries:

1. Click the address entry.

Tip   Hold Ctrl to select multiple entries.

2. Click the toolbar Cut button (Edit ⇨ Cut) or the toolbar Copy button (Edit ⇨ Copy).

3. To paste the entries, click an Address Book or group it Tree view, and then click the toolbar Paste button (Edit ⇨ Paste).

Cross-Reference   For more on cut, copy, and paste, see Chapter 2, "Essential Typing and Editing."

Customizing an Address Book's display

You can customize an Address Book's display by selecting and arranging columns, and by sorting and filtering entries.

Selecting and arranging columns

To select the columns to appear in an Address Book's summary display, click View ➪ Columns (or right-click on the column headings) and check the items you want (see Figure 12-6).

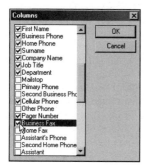

Figure 12-6: Selecting the columns to appear in your Address Book's summary display.

Drag the lines between buttons to adjust the column widths. You can drag the buttons to rearrange your listing, although your settings won't be retained from session to session.

Sorting address entries

To sort your address entries by name, company, city, or any other item on display, click the applicable button at the top of the listing. Click the button a second time to reverse the sort order. (An up or down triangle shows which button you've sorted on.)

Filtering your address listing

To filter your Address Book's listing on various items:

1. Click View ➪ Filter and select an item to filter on.

2. Click the = button to select a filter operator, and then specify the filter text (see Figure 12-7).

Tip

Partial matches work, so you can just type "Ajax" when looking for employees of the Ajax Corporation.

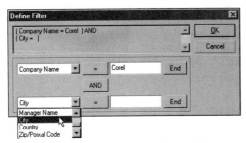

Figure 12-7: Filtering your address listing.

3. Click End and Insert Row to specify additional filter conditions, or click OK to filter the records.

Filter conditions are similar to the extraction statements used when sorting records in WordPerfect (see Chapter 53, "Sorting Information").

To redisplay all your address records, click View ⇨ Remove Filter. (If your address records don't reappear, try clicking View ⇨ Refresh.)

Creating new Address Books

To create a new Address Book for business, personal, or other use:

1. Click the New Address Book button (File ⇨ New), and select the type of book you want to create (see Figure 12-8):

- *CorelCENTRAL,* to create a new CorelCENTRAL Address Book
- *Directory Servers,* to connect to a directory server Address Book
- *MAPI,* to create a MAPI-compliant Address Book that can be used in other applications (CorelCENTRAL Address Books are also MAPI-compliant)

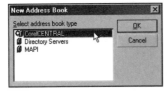

Figure 12-8: Creating a new Address Book.

2. Click OK and type a name for the book.

Renaming or deleting an Address Book

To rename the Address Book currently displayed, click File ➪ Rename.

Click File ➪ Delete to delete the current Address Book.

Securing an Address Book

You can secure an Address Book (other than the default "Addresses" book) to prevent others from seeing or altering it. Security is especially useful when you're sharing Address Books on a network.

To change an Address Book's security:

1. Click the Address Book in Tree view, and then click File ➪ Rename.

2. Click the Security tab (see Figure 12-9), and then check the attributes you want:

    • *Hidden,* to prevent others from seeing the Address Book

    • *Read-only,* to let others view your Address Book, but not alter or delete it

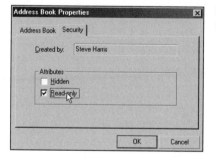

Figure 12-9: Changing an Address Book's security.

Importing and exporting Address Books

If you export an Address Book as ASCII text from another application, such as Microsoft Outlook, you can import it into CorelCENTRAL:

1. Click File ➪ Import, locate the exported address book, and click Open.

2. If necessary, specify the group and record delimiters (see Figure 12-10). (Open the text file in WordPerfect to see what separates the fields and records.)

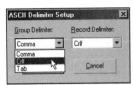

Figure 12-10: Specifying group and record delimiters.

3. Select the imported fields one at a time and map them to their corresponding fields in the CorelCENTRAL Address Book (see Figure 12-11).

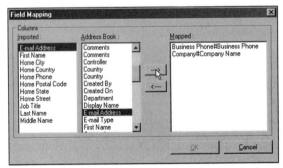

Figure 12-11: Mapping imported fields to corresponding fields in your Address Book.

4. When there are no more fields to map, click OK.

To export an Address Book as an ASCII text file, select the book and click File ➪ Export.

Printing an Address Book

To print an Address Book:

1. Click the toolbar Print button (File ➪ Print), and specify the records you want to print and whether to print them as a table or list (see Figure 12-12).

2. Click the Page Setup tab to specify the page size, margins, and orientation.

Tip

The landscape orientation permits more fields across the page.

Cross-Reference

For more on printing, see Chapter 13, "Printing and Faxing Information."

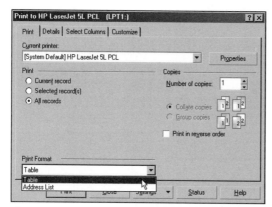

Figure 12-12: Printing an Address Book.

Publishing an Address Book to HTML

You can publish your Address Books to HTML, for posting on the Internet or corporate intranet:

1. Click File ⇨ Publish to HTML, and then specify the layout and the range of entries you want to publish (see Figure 12-13).

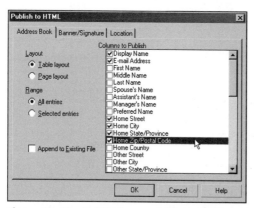

Figure 12-13: Publishing an Address Book to HTML.

2. Click the Location tab to specify the location and filename prefix, whether you want to be warned when overwriting an existing file, and whether you want to immediately view the file in your browser.

Cross-Reference

For more information about publishing to HTML, see Chapter 14, "Web Writing and Publishing."

Using Card Files

CorelCENTRAL's card files provide a handy way to keep track of all sorts of information (such as a book catalog, gardening records, or a car maintenance file). You can organize the cards in each file into *groups* analogous to file subfolders. For example, a recipe file might be divided into groups for breads, fish, vegetables, desserts, and so on (see Figure 12-14).

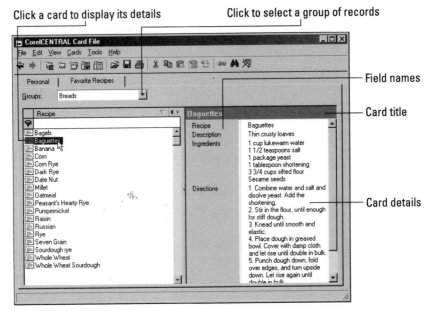

Figure 12-14: A recipe card file.

Each *card* on the left is comprised of individual *fields* for storing particular types of information, such as recipe name, ingredients, cooking instructions, and so on.

A tab appears for each open card file. As with any other office application, you can click the buttons in the upper-right to maximize and minimize your display, or drag a side or corner to adjust its size (see Chapter 3, "Looking at a Suite Face").

The left panel lists all cards. Click the button at the right of the Groups box to display all the records or just a particular group. The right panel is a scrollable display of the individual fields and their contents.

Opening your card file mini-application

You can open your card file mini-application in either of the following ways:

✦ Click the CorelCENTRAL Day Planner Display Card File icon at the bottom of the CorelCENTRAL Day Planner

✦ Click the Start button, and then click Programs ➪ WordPerfect Office 2000 ➪ Utilities ➪ CorelCENTRAL Card File

Tip Add your card file mini-application to your Desktop Application Director to display its icon on the Windows taskbar. See Appendix A, "Setting Up WordPerfect Office 2000."

Adjusting the card file display

To adjust the card file display:

✦ Drag between the buttons in the card listing to adjust their widths (see Figure 12-15).

Drag to adjust the width of a field name column   Drag to adjust the panel divider

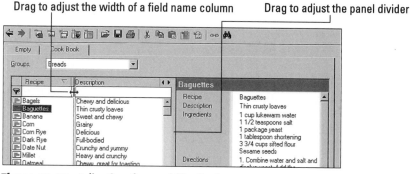

Figure 12-15: Adjusting the card file display.

✦ Drag the divider bar between the card listing and card details to adjust their relative sizes.

✦ In the card details, drag the divider between the field name and field data columns to adjust their widths.

Creating, opening, and closing card files

To create a new card file:

1. Click the CorelCENTRAL New Card File button (File ➪ New), and then type the name to appear on the card file's tab (see Figure 12-16).

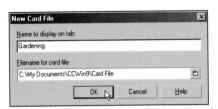

Figure 12-16: Creating a card file.

2. Specify the card file's location.

Tip

Let the filename default to the tab name to avoid confusion.

To open a card file:

1. Click File ⇨ Open and locate your card file folder.

2. Select the card file (*.ccf) you want to open.

To close the selected card file, click File ⇨ Close.

Cross-
Reference

For more information about working with folders and files, see Chapter 7, "Managing Your Files."

Copying a card file

To copy the current card file, with all its fields and records, to a file with another name, click File ⇨ Save As, and then specify the "tab" name for the card file, and the actual filename and location.

Renaming a card file

To rename a card file, click File ⇨ Rename, and type a new name.

Reordering your card file tabs

To change the order of the tabs in your card file display, click View ⇨ Reorder Card Files, and then select a file and click Move Up or Move Down (see Figure 12-17).

Figure 12-17: Reordering your card file tabs.

Deleting a card file

To delete a card file:

1. Click File ⇨ Delete.

2. Select the card file you want to delete and click OK.

Understanding global and local fields

Particular fields in a card file group can either be *global* (key fields that appear in every card in the group) or *local* (fields for a particular card or address).

Tip   When a card is assigned to more than one group, a field can be global in one group and local in another.

Adding, deleting, and duplicating card files

To add a card file:

1. Click the CorelCENTRAL Card File New Card button (Cards ⇨ New Card).

2. Type information in the various fields.

To delete a card file, click the card in the list of cards and press Delete (Cards ⇨ Delete Card).

To duplicate a card file, click the card in the list and click Cards ⇨ Duplicate Card.

Adding fields

Before you can add records to a card file, you have to create fields to hold their information!

To add a global field:

1. Click any card in a group, and click above the global/local divider line in the list of field names.
2. Click the CorelCENTRAL Card File New Field button (Cards ⇨ New Field) and type a name for the field.
3. Click in the card details to fill in or edit the field.

The new field will be inserted beneath the field you selected.

To add a local field to the card file on display:

1. Click the CorelCENTRAL Card File New Field button (Cards ⇨ New Field), or simply click the field name listing.
2. Type a name for the field.
3. Click in the detail panel to fill in or edit the field.

Undoing changes to fields and cards

To undo changes you've made to the current field, click the CorelCENTRAL Card File Undo Field button (Edit ⇨ Undo Field Changes).

To undo all the changes you've made to the current card, click the CorelCENTRAL Card File Undo All button (Edit ⇨ Undo Card Changes).

Cutting, copying, and pasting card files

To cut, copy, and paste card files:

1. Click the card in the listing. (Hold down the Ctrl key to select multiple cards.)
2. Click the toolbar Cut button (Edit ⇨ Cut) or Copy button (Edit ⇨ Copy).
3. To paste the cards, click the card file and select the group, if necessary, and click the toolbar Paste button (Edit ⇨ Paste).

Cross-Reference   For more on cut, copy, and paste, see Chapter 2, "Essential Typing and Editing."

Creating a new group

To add a new group to a card file:

1. Select a group to use as a template for the new group's global fields.

2. If you want to copy some (but not all) of the cards in the current group to the new group, hold down the Ctrl key as you click to select the cards.

3. Click the CorelCENTRAL Card File New Group button (Cards ➪ New Group), and then click one of the following (see Figure 12-18):

   • *Empty*, to create a group with one empty card

   • *Include selected cards*, to copy the cards you selected to the new group

   • *Include all cards from (groupname)*, to copy all the cards from the current group to the new group

Figure 12-18: Creating a new group.

4. To include the global fields in a new card file group, check "Include fields from *groupname*." (Global fields are automatically added to a new Address Book group.)

Deleting or renaming a group

To delete or rename a group, display the group, right-click in the list pane, and click Rename Group or Delete Group.

Caution

Deleting a group deletes its records as well.

Customizing fields

When you first add a field to a card file, you can leave it blank or fill it with any number of alphanumeric characters (text or numbers).

To customize a field's type (such as to currency or e-mail address), or attributes (such as to restrict the number of characters):

1. Right-click on the field name or contents, and then click Field Properties.

2. Click the "Field type" list to specify the type of entry you want the field to contain (see Figure 12-19).

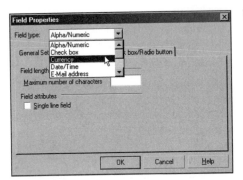

Figure 12-19: Specifying a field's type.

3. For several of the field types, you can specify a maximum number of characters and limit the field to one line.

4. For several of the field types, you can click the Contents tab and type the initial field contents. (Use the initial contents for instructions.)

5. To add a separator between groups of fields, select Separator in the "Field type" list.

6. To create a check box or radio button selection field, select Check box or Radio button in the "Field type" list, and enter the number of items you want. Click the item you want to be the default selection.

Deleting or renaming a field

To delete a field:

1. Click Cards ⇨ Delete Field, or right-click the field and click Delete Field.

2. If you're asked, click Yes to delete the field.

To rename a field, click the field and type a new name.

Duplicating a field

To duplicate a field, click the field in the listing and click Cards ⇨ Duplicate Field.

Adding comment fields

You can attach one or more comment fields to any field in a particular Address Book or card file record:

1. Right-click a field, and then click New Comment Field.

2. Type a name for your comment, and then click to the right of the vertical divider line and type the comment.

Click the plus (+) box to the left of a field to display a field's comment; click the minus (–) box to hide it.

To delete a comment, right-click the comment and click Delete Comment.

A special type of comment is automatically attached to a link field (such as for a phone number or Web address). By editing the comment, you can change the link without activating it.

Changing a field's position or global/local type

To change a field's position in the display order, drag its name up or down within the detail listing (see Figure 12-20). It's a tricky business, so you may need to give it a couple of tries. (Be sure to click and hold the mouse button.)

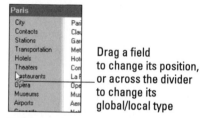

Drag a field
to change its position,
or across the divider
to change its
global/local type

Figure 12-20: Rearranging global and local fields.

You can drag a field across the horizontal dividing line to change it from global (above) to local (below) or from local to global.

Tip   The global/local change applies to the entire group, not just the particular card.

Adding or removing fields from the list display

You can display any number of global fields in the card listing on the left, but only in the order in which they appear in the detail listing. You can add or remove fields from the display in the list panel in one of two ways:

✦ Click the arrows to the right of the field name buttons to display more or fewer fields. (Maximize the display and adjust the field buttons and panel divider to display more fields.)

✦ Right-click any of the field buttons and uncheck the fields you don't want to display (see Figure 12-21).

Figure 12-21: Removing fields from the list display.

Unfortunately, your display changes aren't retained from session to session. The fields will reappear in the next session.

Sorting lists and locating cards

To sort your card file listing on a global field quickly, click the field's button at the top of the list display. Click the button again to reverse the sort. (An up or down triangle shows which button you've sorted on.)

You can type text in the search boxes at the top of the card list in the card file to quickly locate the card by typing the first letters or numbers. Click the button to the left of the search boxes to toggle between Search (the Card File Search button), to highlight the first matching card and those that follow; and Filter (the Card File Filter button), to display only the matching cards.

Viewing several cards at once

You can double-click cards in the listing to view the details of several cards at once in separate windows (see Figure 12-22).

Figure 12-22: Card displayed in a separate window.

Adding links to cards

By adding links to a card file, you can go anywhere and do anything with a click of the mouse:

1. Right-click the field to which you want to add a link (or click the field and click the CorelCENTRAL Link button).

2. Click Link To, and select the type of link:

    • *Memos*, to jump to a CorelCENTRAL memo you've created

    • *Card File*, to jump to the card file record you specify

    • *File/Application*, to launch the program you specify

    • *Folder*, to go to a folder to open a document

    • *E-mail*, to compose and send a message to the designated address

    • *Web Site*, to go to a designated Internet address

3. Make any selections and complete any entries for the type of link you designated.

You can specify the contents for most types of links (such as an e-mail address) either before you create the link or as you create it.

You can also right-click a field, or click the CorelCENTRAL Link button on the toolbar to create a link.

Navigating card file links

Your card file application forward (the CorelCENTRAL Forward button) and back (the CorelCENTRAL Back button) buttons take you to the previous or next view in the session. These work the same way as the Forward and Back buttons on your Internet browser, and are especially handy for returning from a link.

Printing or publishing a card file

To print a card file, follow the instructions in "Printing an Address Book," earlier in this chapter.

To publish a card file to HTML, follow the instructions in "Publishing Your Calendar to HTML," in Chapter 11, "Organizing Your Life."

Keeping your card files in working order

Your card files are maintained in a sorted database with pointers or links among the records. If the cards or entries displayed in your card file appear scrambled or lost, or if you want to clean up after deleting a lot of cards, perform maintenance following the instructions in "Keeping Your Calendar in Working Order," in Chapter 11, "Organizing Your Life."

Creating Memos

The memo mini-application lets you write memos to remind you of appointments, special dates, or things to do.

You can create different memo categories — for home, school, office, and other purposes.

Opening the memo mini-application

You can open your memo mini-application in either of the following ways:

✦ Click the CorelCENTRAL Day Planner Memo iron at the bottom of the CorelCENTRAL Day Planner

✦ Click the Start button, and then click Programs ➪ WordPerfect Office 2000 ➪ Utilities ➪ CorelCENTRAL Memos

Tip   Add your memo mini-application to your Desktop Application Director to display its icon on the Windows taskbar. (See Appendix A, "Setting Up WordPerfect Office 2000.")

Creating a memo

To create a memo:

1. Click the New Memo button (File ➪ New).

2. Type a name for your memo and press Enter (see Figure 12-23).

3. Type the memo's text in the panel on the right (see Figure 12-23).

Renaming a memo

To rename the current memo, click the CorelCENTRAL Rename Memo button (File ➪ Rename), and then type the new name and press Enter.

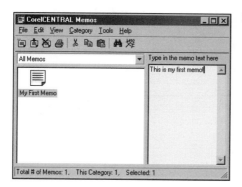

Figure 12-23: Creating a memo.

Deleting a memo

To delete the current memo, click the CorelCENTRAL Delete Memo button (File ➪ Delete).

Cutting, copying, and pasting memo text

You can cut, copy, and paste memo text, as you do in any other Windows application. For details, see Chapter 2, "Essential Typing and Editing."

Finding memo text

To find memo text, click the Search button (Edit ➪ Find), type the text, and click Find Now.

Creating a memo category

To create a memo category, click Category ➪ Add, and type the category name.

Viewing a memo category

You can display all your memos or select a particular category to view from the drop-down list (see Figure 12-24).

Moving memos to a category

If you create memos when all categories are displayed, they won't be assigned to a particular category. You can also move memos from one category to another.

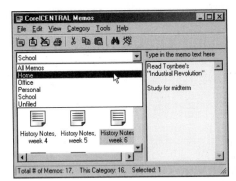

Figure 12-24: Viewing a memo category.

To move a memo to a category (or from one category to another):

1. Click the memo, or hold down the Ctrl key and click more than one memo.

2. Click Category (or right-click) and click Move to Category.

3. Select the category to move to (see Figure 12-25).

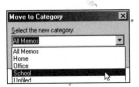

Figure 12-25: Moving memos to a category.

The Memos status bar (View ⇨ Status Bar) displays useful information about the total number of memos and the number in the current category.

Changing your memo list display

Click the View menu to display your memo listing as large icons, small icons, or listings, as you can with any other file-management dialog box (see Figure 12-26).

In Detail view, you can click the Subject bar at the top of the list to sort memos in alphabetic order. Click the bar again to reverse the sort order.

Printing or publishing memos

To print your memos, follow the instructions in "Printing an Address Book," earlier in this chapter.

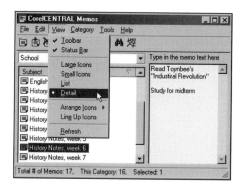

Figure 12-26: Changing your memo list display.

To publish your memos to HTML, follow the instructions in "Publishing Your Calendar to HTML," in Chapter 11, "Organizing Your Life."

For More Information . . .

On	See
Understanding databases	Chapter 43
Sorting information	Chapter 53
Printing and faxing information	Chapter 13
Adjusting your screen display	Chapter 3
Web writing and publishing	Chapter 14
Managing files	Chapter 7
Publishing calendars to HTML	Chapter 11
Cutting, copying, and pasting information	Chapter 2

✦   ✦   ✦

Printing and Faxing Information

Once upon a time, you'd physically distribute a hand-written document (this is true) or, if you worked in a modern office, type it and send it on its way. Only formal publications were typeset. For multiple copies of letters and reports, you had carbon paper, and mimeographed stencils for larger quantities. Then along came that great slayer of forests, the copying machine, making it easier than ever to create multiple copies.

Computer-based word processing turned everyone into a publisher by, in effect, combining the typewriter with the copying machine. With the widespread adoption of electronic information transfer, new forms of publication are emerging.

Where does WordPerfect Office 2000 stand in all this? On the cutting edge, or in the thick of things, depending on how you look at it. Table 13-1 summarizes the diverse ways by which you can print and send information from within the programs.

XML Publishing

XML is a simplified, yet powerful, version of SGML, based on an open international standard issued by the World Wide Web Consortium (W3C).

This chapter covers the generic aspects of printing and faxing information from WordPerfect, Presentations, and Quattro Pro. Chapter 14, "Web Writing and Publishing," covers HTML and Publishing to PDF. You'll also find publishing particulars in the coverage of various applications.

Table 13-1
Ways to Print and Send Information

Printing or Sending Method	Description
Print	The standard publication method, supported by sophisticated formatting, font-handling, and graphics capabilities.
Fax	A simple, quick way of taking and sending a "snapshot" of your formatted document. Some detail is lost in conversion and transmission.
E-mail	A fast, inexpensive way to send text messages anywhere in the world. Files with formatting can be attached.
Publish to HTML	Create interactive documents in the universal standard for viewing on the Internet. Text oriented, with increasingly sophisticated formatting.
Publish to PDF	Send documents in electronic form with formatting and fonts intact. Output can be viewed, annotated, and printed (but not edited) on a variety of machines.
SGML Publishing	WordPerfect installation option to enable the publication of standardized documents, using the enabling technology behind HTML. Used mainly by government and industry.

Preparing to Print

Various technologies for printing to paper are still the mainstay of desktop publishing. You can save paper and toner or ink (and spare some trees) by ensuring that your work is in polished form before you print it. Check spelling and grammar, and then zoom to a full-page view to see that it has a pleasing format.

Also, be sure that the printer you want is displayed on the application bar (in WordPerfect) and ready to go. If not, see the section "Selecting a Printer," later in this chapter.

Printing Basics

To print the current document, spreadsheet, or show:

1. Click the Print button on the toolbar, or click File ⇨ Print.

2. Select the options you want (such as what to print and the number of copies), and then click Print (see Figure 13-1).

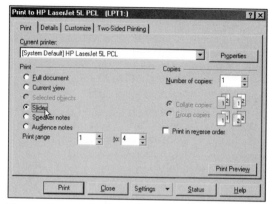

Figure 13-1: Selecting what to print in Presentations.

Controlling the Progress of Your Print Jobs

Suppose you launch the printing of a 72-page report, only to say "Uh-oh, I didn't mean to do that." What do you do? You can cancel your print job if you can catch it, but your software is likely to process your print job so quickly that you continue working with hardly a pause. You may have to head straight for the printer.

Catching up with your print job

When you print your document, the *printer driver* first puts the information into a format that your printer understands and stores it in a temporary file. While this temporary print file is being created, the familiar "Preparing document for printing" message appears.

If it's a large print job, or if your job is queued up behind others on your desktop or network printer, you might be able to catch up with it by double-clicking the printer icon that temporarily appears on the Windows taskbar, next to the clock. You can also click File ➪ Print ➪ Status. If the job is still active, it will appear at or near the top of the Print Status and History List (see Figure 13-2). To stop the process, click Document (from the dialog box menu), and then click Pause Printing or Cancel Printing. To resume a paused job, click Document ➪ Pause Printing.

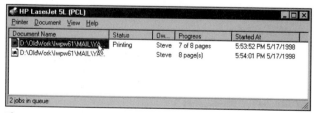

Figure 13-2: Catching up with your print job.

Stopping a job that's printing

Chances are good, however, that the job is already feeding into your printer's memory and pages are spewing out of your printer. Your printer might have a reset button to clear out what's in its memory. However, if the job is more than a couple of pages long, more pages will be sent from your computer to the printer.

So, what's the quickest and surest way to bring printing to a halt? Lift the paper out of your printer's input bin or pull out the paper tray. (Don't try to stop a page that's already feeding through.) You can then cancel what remains of the job in the queue and reset your printer, or turn it off and back on after a few seconds to clear its memory. These are general suggestions. Consult your printer manual for the best way to stop your printer.

Selecting a Printer

In WordPerfect Office you can add, select, and maintain printers via the Print dialog boxes, without having to go to the Windows Control Panel.

You can change your current printer selection or designate an application default printer:

1. Click File ➪ Print, and then click the "Current printer" drop-down list and select the printer you want to use (see Figure 13-3).

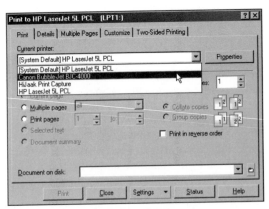

Figure 13-3: Selecting a printer.

2. To designate the printer as your default WordPerfect or Presentations printer, click Settings ➪ Application Default ➪ Replace ➪ OK.

Adding a Printer

To add a printer to your system:

1. Click File ⇨ Print, and then click the Details tab.
2. Click Add Printer and follow the prompts of the Add Printer Wizard.

Setting a Printer as the System Default

To designate a printer as the default for all Windows applications:

1. Click File ⇨ Print, and then click the Details tab.
2. Click System Printers, and then right-click a printer icon and check Set as Default (see Figure 13-4).

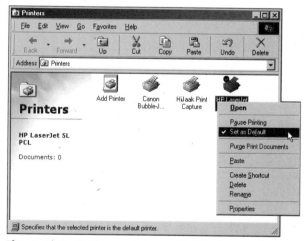

Figure 13-4: Setting a printer as the Windows default.

Faxing Documents

You must switch "printers" when you fax a document, but otherwise the process is the same. Your output is automatically directed to your fax software for transmission.

Setting up to fax

To fax documents from within WordPerfect Office 2000, you must have a fax modem and a Windows fax program installed, either on your machine or on your network server. After the fax program is installed, a *fax driver* (similar to a printer driver) appears in the list of available printers.

The fax program is independent of your WordPerfect Office 2000 and has its own installation and setup procedures. You will, for example, be asked to specify the type of modem you have, and you can add phone book entries that you can select when you send a fax.

Just as a printer driver translates your document into code that your printer understands, a fax driver *rasterizes* your document for transmission over the phone line. It will be put back into a readable form by a fax machine (or a modem and fax program) on the receiving end.

Sending a fax

To send a fax:

1. Click File ⇨ Print, and then select the fax driver from the list of available printers.
2. Specify what you want to fax and click Print.

Monitoring and canceling a fax

Once your work is sent to the fax, the fax program takes over and prompts you as to what to do. To monitor or cancel your fax, switch to the fax program by way of the Windows taskbar.

Printing to a File

One odd-sounding option you'll find under the print details is "Print to file." If your document already is a file, why would you want to print it to another file? Here's the situation: The printer you want to use is not connected to your system or network, and your document won't be printed by the application you're using.

Suppose you want to send the newsletter you created to a service bureau to print on their color PostScript printer. Set up and select the PostScript printer, compose and edit the newsletter, print to a file on your hard drive or removable storage, and then send this file (physically or electronically) to the service bureau.

To print to a file:

1. Click File ➪ Print, and then select the destination printer from the list.

2. Click the Details tab, and then click "Print to file."

3. Specify a filename other than that of your original file document, and then click Print.

To resume printing to your printer rather than to a filename, select your normal printer and set the "Where" under the Details tab back to its normal port (such as LPT1).

The file you print to is no longer a WordPerfect, Presentations, or Quattro Pro document. It's in a printer format that can be fed to the printer on the receiving end. You can print it by using the following DOS Print command (include the path if you're not in the file's folder):

```
Print C:\My Documents\Printfiles\Outdoc01.prn.
```

For More Information . . .

On	See
Setting up printers	Windows online Help
Publishing to HTML and PDF	Chapter 14
Printing in WordPerfect	Chapter 19
Creating custom print settings	Chapter 19
Customizing WordPerfect pages	Chapter 21
Printing spreadsheets	Chapter 37
Printing and publishing in Presentations	Chapter 42

✦   ✦   ✦

Web Writing and Publishing

◆ ◆ ◆ ◆

In This Chapter

Switch between Page and Web view

Publish documents in HTML

Create your own home page

Insert graphics in Web pages

Add headings, lines, tables, and lists

Change color schemes and wallpaper

Create a Web form

Organize your Web pages and graphics

Learn about building XML documents

Publish to PDF

◆ ◆ ◆ ◆

Web writing is here to stay. You may not need to publish to the Web yourself, but if you do, WordPerfect Office offers you all the tools you need.

Understanding Web Terms

Before you plunge into Web writing, you might want to take a quick look at Table 14-1, which defines some of the Web terms you will encounter along the way.

What's a Web Document?

A Web document is material written in HyperText Markup Language (HTML), so it can be viewed in Netscape Navigator, Microsoft's Internet Explorer, and other browsers across the Internet, or within your company's intranet.

Table 14-1
Essential Web Terms

Term	Description
Client	Program on a network (such as Netscape) that makes requests to the server program on another computer (such as a Web server).
Flame	Incendiary newsgroup posting that provides more heat than light. Self-extinguishing when ignored.
Home page	First page that you come to when you launch your browser or visit a Web site.
HTML	Codes or "tags" for text, titles, formatting, backgrounds, graphics, links, and other Web page features.
Hypertext	A special type of database system in which text, pictures, and other objects can be creatively linked, so that information can be accessed through a variety of nonsequential paths.
Internet	A global "network of networks" connecting millions of computers and hundreds of millions of users who exchange data, mail, news, and opinions. The operators of each independent *host* computer decide which Internet services to use and which local services to provide to the global Internet. The terms "Web" and "Internet" are used interchangeably, although there are technical distinctions between the two.
Intranet	In-house network in which members of an organization publish information and interact with one another much as they do on the global Internet. While intranet users can get out to the Internet, access from the Internet to the intranet is usually restricted by a security *firewall*.
Internet Service Provider (ISP)	Commercial vendor or organization that hosts Web sites and provides dial-up access to the Internet.
Newsgroup	Online discussion group or *forum*, in which you can view and post messages.
Online service	Commercial vendor (such as America Online) with in-house forums and Web access.
Portal	Web page, such as Yahoo.com, which serves as a "door" to diverse services and information.
Search engine	Program that searches for Web documents or newsgroup postings containing specified keywords or text.
Spam	Junk e-mail or newsgroup postings. Whatever you do, don't respond to it!

Term	Description
Surfing (pull)	Going into the Internet in search of information; using a browser or search engine.
Thread	Related messages in a newsgroup.
URL	The Uniform Resource Locator (or Web address) is the Internet equivalent of a pathname used by the Web browser to contact a site or locate a file. The URL for Corel's product support, for example, is `http://www.corel.com/support/index.htm`. The http indicates the Web protocol (Hypertext Transport Protocol) used to send and receive messages; www (which is common but not required) indicates that it's a Web address; corel.com tells you who runs the server computer (.com is company; .gov is government; .edu is educational institution; .net is network; .org is organization); and support is the server folder where the page "index.htm" is found. Another protocol you're likely to encounter is ftp, or File Transfer Protocol.
Web browsing (pull)	Searching the Web with browser software (such as Netscape Navigator or Microsoft Internet Explorer).
Web	The World Wide Web, a system of Internet servers that support HTML documents, so that one can jump from one document to another simply by clicking the hot spots. (Not all Internet servers are part of the World Wide Web.)
Web, or internet publisher	Tools for creating HTML documents.
Web editor	Editing screen of your internet publisher.
Web link	A hypertext link attached to highlighted words or an image containing the URL (address) of a Web document. Click the links to jump from page to page on the Internet.
Web pages	Scrollable hypertext documents with HTML formatting codes that you see on the Web.
Web site	Web location for document that belongs to an organization or individual, identified by the URL.
Web server	Computer where Web sites reside. One service provider (such as a university) can support many sites on its Web server, but you can set up a Web site on a personal computer as well (see Chapter 15).
Webcasting (push)	Web broadcasting. The channels you subscribe to that automatically deliver the latest information (or junk news and commercials) to your desktop.

What does HTML look like?

HTML is a collection of styles, indicated by tags, to enhance the appearance of plain (ASCII) text documents when viewed in a Web browser. For example, the heading "So what, exactly, is HTML?," looks something like the following in HTML:

```
<H2><STRONG><FONT FACE="Arial">So what, exactly, is
HTML?</FONT></STRONG></H2>
```

Notice how the text is surrounded by the following four pairs of on/off tags to "mark up" its format and appearance:

- ✦ <H2> to apply the Heading 2 style
- ✦ <STRONG> and </STRONG> to put it in boldface
- ✦ <FONT FACE="Arial"> and </FONT> to change the font

Wait a second . . . doesn't this look familiar? Change the paragraph codes to hard returns, "strong" to "bold," "H2" to "very large," and you'll see that HTML tags are essentially the same as the WordPerfect markups you see in Reveal Codes.

If you're getting the idea that WordPerfect is a markup language too, you have the right idea. And, just as you don't have to type or see the codes in WordPerfect, you won't have to type HTML tags in any of the WordPerfect Office Web writing facilities.

Why reinvent the wheel?

So, why not use WordPerfect in the first place, instead of bothering with HTML? The reason is because HTML was originally designed so that scientific documents, sent over the Internet, would display in roughly the same way on any machine, using any output device, from monitors to Braille readers. The resulting specification of tags described a basic document, employing just a few fonts and styles, that could link to other documents on the Web.

What HTML doesn't do

Because HTML documents are designed to scroll on the screen and jump via links, they don't have page numbers, margins, headers, footers, or watermarks. Nor will you see fill, footnotes, or vertical lines.

HTML is (and was meant to be) much less sophisticated than WordPerfect, precisely because its purpose is to transmit ideas, not to publish complex formats. That's also why you get the warning "You may lose some formatting permanently!" when switching from Page view to Web Page view in WordPerfect.

Because HTML documents are plain text files, you also can't embed graphics, sound, and other multimedia elements in them, as you can with a WordPerfect document, Quattro Pro spreadsheet, or Presentations slide. These objects must be stored separately, and referenced by HTML tags.

Multimedia additions to HTML

Well, that was the idea . . . before the Web's explosive growth and commercialization compelled HTML to incorporate textured backgrounds, tables, flashing text, sound clips, and other multimedia frills and thrills.

Thus, HTML is a rapidly evolving specification. Some vendors have added their own extensions (proprietary additions) so that a document created to one vendor's specifications may not display in its full glory when viewed in another vendor's browser. While you can type any tag you want, the tools in WordPerfect Office generally support only the latest approved HTML standard.

When you visit some Web sites, you'll see rotating 3-D graphics, video, and other advanced features. These are not HTML code or extensions, but behind-the-scenes programs (or applets) created in Java, Shockwave, and other languages that can be transferred over the Internet. (The HTML code simply defines how applets are activated.) You may have to download and install (often free) plug-ins (extensions) to Netscape or Internet Explorer to experience various animation, audio, and video thrills.

Tip For the latest information on the evolving HTML standards, visit the home page of the World Wide Web Consortium at http://www.w3.org. You'll find links to this and other Web publishing sources at QwkScreen's Web site: http://www.qwkscreen.com.

How do you create Web pages?

With so many purposes, and with standards changing so fast, it should come as no surprise that WordPerfect Office offers several Web-publishing alternatives:

✦ WordPerfect provides a Web Page view, which lets you directly compose and edit HTML documents.

✦ You can export your document to Trellix to put it in a structured, user-friendly format, and then publish to HTML from Trellix (see Chapter 15).

✦ You can publish a copy of your WordPerfect document, Presentations slide show or drawing, Quattro Pro spreadsheet, or Paradox table or report to HTML.

✦ Use Show It! to put a Presentations slide show on the Web with animation, sound, video, and transitions.

✦ Use [NetDocs, code name] drag-and-drop interface to create Web pages (Professional edition only).

Office alternatives to HTML

If those options aren't enough, WordPerfect Office offers three other means of Web publishing that transcend the limitations of HTML:

✦ *Publish to PDF (Portable Document Format)* lets you publish, from any core application, documents in the format, fonts, and colors of the original (Professional edition only). These are not actually Web pages (HTML documents), but they can be viewed by anyone who has the widely available and freely distributable Adobe Acrobat Reader. (PDF replaces Envoy publishing in previous versions of the WordPerfect suite.)

✦ *Trellix publishing*, described in Chapter 15, "Publishing to the Web with Trellix," gives you the option of delivering highly structured documents in the proprietary Trellix file format (with the accompanying freely distributable Trellix Viewer), as well as publishing them to HTML.

✦ *XML document building*, briefly described at the end of this chapter, adds a sophisticated tagging facility to provide intelligent functions not available in HTML.

Creating Web Documents in WordPerfect

Because WordPerfect's Internet Publisher is the most generic facility for creating Web pages, that's where this chapter's focus will be. General information, such as using document names and Web links, applies to all applications. Other application-specific features are covered in the appropriate chapters. (See "For More Information . . ." at the end of this chapter.)

Creating a Web document

To create a Web (HTML) document:

1. Open an existing document you want to publish to HTML, or open a new blank document.

2. Click the Switch between Web and Page View button (View ➪ Web Page) to switch to the Web editing (Internet Publisher) environment. (You can also click File ➪ Internet Publisher ➪ Format as Web Document.)

3. Unless the document is blank, you'll receive the warning message that you can lose any formatting that isn't HTML-compatible. Check the box at the bottom if you don't want to see the warning the next time you choose Web View (see Figure 14-1).

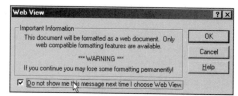

Figure 14-1: Disabling the Web View warning.

4. Upon entering the Web editor (see Figure 14-2), create and format text, tables, hyperlinks, graphics, and so on.

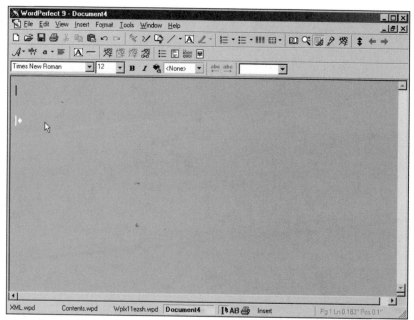

Figure 14-2: Web editing (Internet Publisher) environment, with slate-colored background and custom tools.

5. Click the View in Web Browser button (View ⇨ View in Web Browser) to see how the page will look in your browser.

6. Click the Publish to HTML button (File ⇨ Internet Publisher ⇨ Publish to HTML), and then specify the filename and location for your HTML source (see Figure 14-3).

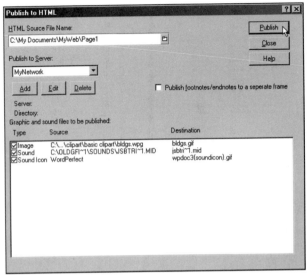

Figure 14-3: Specifying the HTML filename and graphics folder.

7. Select a server to publish to. Click the appropriate buttons to add, edit, or delete a server.

8. Select any graphics and multimedia files to be published along with your HTML.

Specifying names for Web documents

Give careful consideration to how you name your Web documents. In particular, find out from your Web administrator what naming conventions you should follow. If you're putting up a new site, your home page (the page where folks land when they pay a visit), may require a specific name (such as INDEX.HTML).

Note that Web pages can have either of two extensions: .HTM or .HTML. You may have to use the full .HTML extension if your page is going up on a UNIX server, particularly for your home page. Again, check with your Web administrator.

Specifying locations for documents and graphics

You also have to give some thought to file locations, for the following three reasons:

✦ You generally must copy your files to the server location after you create them.

✦ Graphics, sound clips, Java applets, and so on, can be stored separately from your documents.

✦ Hypertext links among your documents must specify precise locations.

You've probably come across plenty of "Location Not Found" messages while browsing the Web, or little icons to indicate missing graphics. You don't want that to happen with your stuff.

Say, for example, the eventual location for your Web documents is *http://webserver/mysite*. To keep things neat, you may want to store your graphics and sound clips in a separate subfolder: *http://webserver/mysite/graphics*. Therefore, if the local folder for your Web documents is *C:\MyFiles\MyWeb*, set up a corresponding graphics folder of *C:\MyFiles\MyWeb\Graphics*. That way, your graphics and documents maintain their relative addresses when moved. The same principles apply if you're creating a more complex structure, such as one with separate document subfolders.

 Tip You can also specify a base Uniform Resource Locator, or URL (File ⇨ Properties ⇨ Advanced), for graphics, sound clips, and so on, in order for documents to locate them. However, that tends to make things still more complicated.

Working in the Web editor

When you work in the Web editor, you'll notice that your menus and dialog boxes are restricted to the HTML possibilities, not the full set of WordPerfect features. The Format menu, for example, has just a few options, compared to the vast array of features available when you create a normal WordPerfect document. You'll also discover a few features that aren't normally available (such as creating a Web form or Java applet).

Click Insert ⇨ Table for an example of what's different in HTML (see Figure 14-4). You'll notice that there are fewer options for such things as table borders and fills (background color); table lines appear raised; and dimensions are in terms of percent or pixels, because objects are designed for browser display.

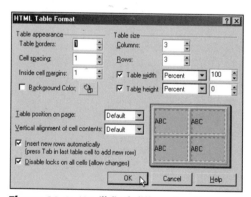

Figure 14-4: You'll find different options when defining a Web table.

You'll be happy to see that Spell-As-You-Go and other proofreading tools are still available. Text is text, no matter where you put it.

Giving your Web page a title

To give your Web document a title (the one that displays in the title bar of the Web browser), click File ➪ Properties ➪ Title, and then click Custom Title and type the title you want. If you don't specify a title, the first occurrence of the highest level heading in your document appears instead.

Applying Web styles

When formatting HTML text for titles, headings, bulleted lists, and so on, there are only 12 paragraph styles from which to choose. These fall into two categories:

✦ Those that change text size, appearance, or format

✦ Those for creating outlines and lists

Click the Web Styles button (Format ➪ Font) to apply the various styles (see Figure 14-5), described in Table 14-2.

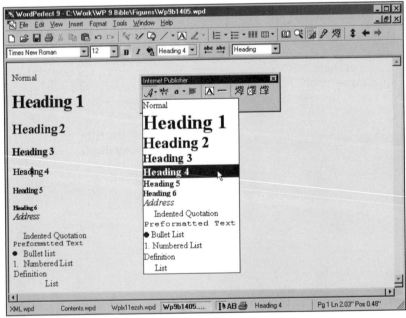

Figure 14-5: Applying Web styles.

Table 14-2 Web Document Styles	
Style	**Description**
Heading 1	Largest heading
Headings 2–6	Headings of decreasing importance, marked for the Table of Contents
Address	Italic text
Indented Quotation	Adjusts the margins for indented quotes (has a special outline type)
Preformatted Text	Monospaced font
Bullet List	Creates a bulleted list (contains paragraph numbers and an outline code set to Bullets)
Numbered List	Creates a numbered list (contains paragraph numbers and an outline code set to Numbers)
Definition List	Creates list of definitions (contains an outline code set to Definitions)

Changing font appearances

For the purpose of universal display, there's generally very little you can do with fonts in HTML. Even font colors don't show up in all browsers. As for the font face, it's best to stick to basics. A fancy headline font may look just fine in your browser preview, but when most people view it on the Web, it'll show up as plain old Times New Roman.

Click Format ➪ Font to apply the font face, size, color, and attributes you want (see Figure 14-6). Just remember: A special font you select may display as a standard font in the browser of a visitor to your Web page.

Creating a Home Page

Now for some fun. In the next few sections, you'll create the home page shown in Figure 14-7.

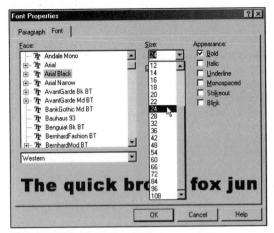

Figure 14-6: Changing font appearances.

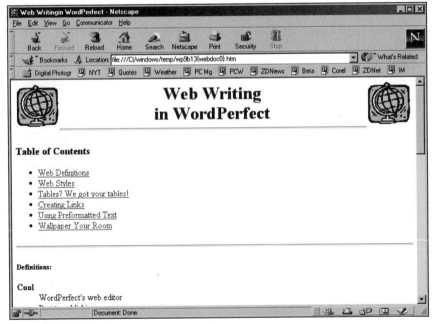

Figure 14-7: Home page you're about to create.

Note that the Table of Contents in Figure 14-7 has underlined hyperlinks to other sections. You'll begin by creating the sections, and then create the Table of Contents at the top.

Starting from a blank screen, first create a "Web Styles" section:

1. In the Web view, type **Web Styles**, and then click the Web Styles button and apply the Heading 2 style to the text.

2. Click the Web Horizontal Line button (Insert ➪ Horizontal Line) to underline your heading (see Figure 14-8).

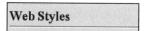 **Figure 14-8:** Heading with horizontal underline.

Web Styles

3. Type the text underneath the heading, like that in Figure 14-5, and apply the various Web styles to create a gallery of samples.

 Tip To change the length, thickness, or justification of a horizontal line, right-click the line and click Edit Horizontal Line.

Previewing your creations

The Web editor provides a good representation of what your page will look like in a browser, but it's still a WordPerfect document, not an HTML one.

To see how your creation looks, click the View in Web Browser button (View ➪ View in Web Browser). This creates a temporary HTML copy and opens Netscape Navigator (or whatever your browser is) to display it there.

 Tip To see your actual HTML code in Navigator, click View ➪ Source.

When you're finished admiring your work, exit Navigator and return to the Web editor. Better yet, leave Navigator up and click the WordPerfect button on the Windows taskbar to return.

Using justification and line breaks

Are you ready to create the fancy stuff at the top of the home page? Go to the beginning of your document and press Enter a few times if you need to make some room at the top.

1. Click the Justification button on the property bar and center the title line.

2. Type **Web Writing**, and then click Insert ➪ Line Break. The line break takes you to the next line without ending the paragraph, so the two lines of your title don't get separated.

3. Type **WordPerfect** and press Enter.

4. Click the Justification button and then click Left.

5. Select the title and apply the Heading 1 style.

Adding graphics

You add graphics to Web documents much as you do in WordPerfect (see Chapter 9, "Working with Graphics"). There are fewer options, of course. There's no drawing layer, and you can anchor to the character or paragraph, but not the page. You can position left, right, or center within the paragraph.

1. Click the Insert Clipart button (Insert ➪ Graphics ➪ Clipart) and then drag an image from the Scrapbook and close the Scrapbook.

2. Right-click the graphic, click Position, click the "Attach box to" list, and click Paragraph.

3. Drag the graphic to the upper-left corner, and then drag a corner handle to adjust it to a reasonable size.

4. Hold down the Ctrl key and drag a copy of the image to the upper-right corner.

5. Click the end of your title and insert a horizontal line.

When you preview or publish your Web pages, you'll get a "Conversion In Progress" message for each graphic that converts to either the GIF (default) or JPEG format for viewing on the Web.

Adding symbols

The general rule for using Ctrl+W symbols in your Web documents is this: don't. Other than the trademark and copyright symbols, accented characters, and various dashes and smart quotes, symbols aren't supported by HTML.

Creating bulleted lists

Next, you'll want to create the bulleted list for your table of contents:

1. Select the Heading 3 style, and then type **Table of Contents** and press Enter.

2. Click the Web Bullets button (Insert ➪ Outline/Bullets & Numbering), click OK, type **Web Definitions**, press Enter, type **Web Styles**, and press Enter again.

3. Add more bulleted entries for other topics you want to include. (Include one for "Wallpaper Your Room," because that will be the topic for your secondary Web page you will link to.)

4. Press Enter ➪ Backspace to end the list.

If you click Insert ⇨ Outline/Bullets & Numbering, you'll see that there are only three bulleted list options in the Web editor: Bulleted, Numbered, and Definition list (see Figure 14-9). The actual appearance of bullets is determined by the browser.

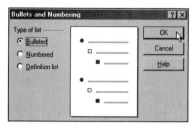

Figure 14-9: Bullets and numbering selections in the Web editor.

The lists in the Web editor are outline styles, so you can press Tab or Shift+Tab to change the levels, just as you change outline levels in an ordinary WordPerfect document.

Although you can tab eight levels, there are only three types of bullets, and all the levels in a numbered list are in standard Arabic numbers. The definition list provides a hanging indent form in HTML. To end a definition list, press Enter ⇨ Backspace in Reveal Codes, or select the Normal style from the property bar.

Formatting with tables

To create a table in the Web editor, click Insert ⇨ Table for all the options, or click and drag on the toolbar as you normally do in WordPerfect.

You can insert graphics, TextArt, and other elements in HTML tables just as you do in WordPerfect tables.

HTML purists may not approve, but tables are a handy way to get around Web formatting limitations when arranging text and graphics on your Web page. Set the width of the table lines to zero if you don't want them to appear. (Table borders in HTML are the same as table lines, not borders, in WordPerfect.)

All the table editing conveniences found in WordPerfect are still available. You can join cells, size columns to fit, and perform any other operations described in Chapter 20, "Controlling Text and Numbering Pages." Because you're still in WordPerfect, you can specify numeric formats, define formulas, lock cells, and perform calculations just as you normally do.

You can add a table-creation section to your Web document (such as the one shown in Figure 14-10).

Figure 14-10: Web table example.

Formatting with columns

To create columns in the Web editor, click the Columns button, or click Format ➪ Columns (see Figure 14-11). You can specify the number of columns, their total width in percent or pixels, and the number of pixels between columns.

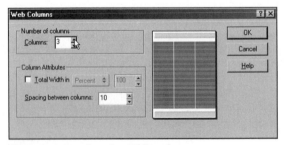

Figure 14-11: Creating Web columns.

Caution   Columns are not yet a Web standard, so things are likely to get messed up in non-Netscape browsers. For now, it's better to use borderless tables instead.

Adding preformatted and monospaced text

The text in your Web document may not display precisely the same after you convert it to HTML and view it in your Web browser. The browser puts as many characters as possible on a line, based on the font style and screen resolution of each user's display.

If you want everyone's browser to show the spaces and line breaks of the original (for example, to display program code or figures in an annual report), use the preformatted style:

1. Place the insertion point where you want to begin typing preformatted text (or select the text you want to preformat).

2. Select the Preformatted Text style from the property bar and type your text.

3. Press Enter and select the Normal style to resume normal text.

Preformatted text uses a monospaced Courier font, with each character taking up the same amount of space. You can also click the Monospace button on the property bar to apply the Courier font. What's the difference? Unlike with preformatted text, the monospaced text's format can vary from browser to browser, as each browser fits as many characters as it can on a line before wrapping to the next.

Wallpapering your room

Formatting text may be a boring subject, but it can't be avoided. Back to the fun stuff. You'll now create a colorful secondary page, and, after that, you'll link your pages together. You'll be amazed at how easy it is to exhibit your artistry.

To get something to work with, create a new Web document, such as the one shown in Figure 14-12, but with whatever title, text, table, or graphics you want.

Now, customize your Web page's color scheme:

Right-click the page, click Properties, and then click the Text/Background Colors tab (see Figure 14-13).

Select colors from the various palettes:

✦ *Normal text*, for any text that's not part of a hypertext link. (You'll still be able to change the color for particular selections of text.)

✦ *Hypertext link*, for a link before it's clicked.

✦ *Visited link*, for the link after it's been clicked, to show that you've already been there.

✦ *Active link*, for the color that flashes momentarily when you click the link.

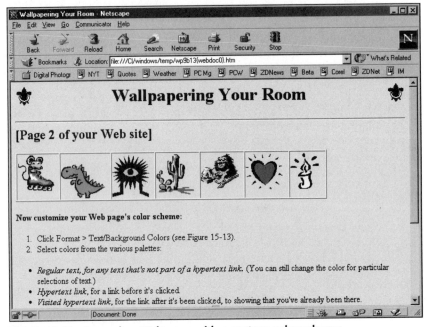

Figure 14-12: Secondary Web page with a custom color scheme.

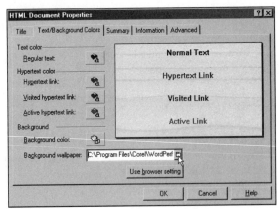

Figure 14-13: Customizing your Web page's color scheme.

✦ *Background color*, for the color of your Web page. (White makes your text and graphics stand out.)

✦ *Background wallpaper*, to wallpaper your room instead of painting it. Click the List button to select from the textured backgrounds that come with WordPerfect Office, but any supported graphic can be used. Be aware, however, that wallpaper doesn't show behind graphics (except where a GIF has a transparent color) and it can make text difficult to read.

Tip   Preview the textures in the file-management dialog box.

Click "Use browser setting" if you want to use the settings specified by the browser instead.

Another way to customize your Web page is to click the Web Color Properties button (Format ⇨ Text Colors/Wallpaper), and then make various selections under the Wallpaper and Text Colors tabs (see Figure 14-14). Note that you can't set a background color this way or use the browser defaults.

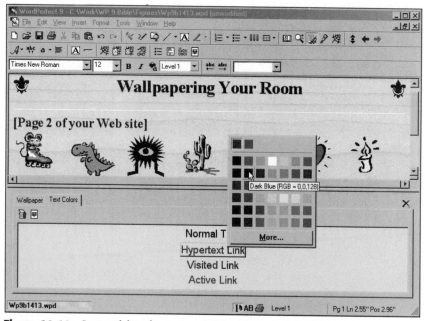

Figure 14-14: Customizing the text and link colors of your Web page.

Creating a Web Form

If you're familiar with the Internet, you're familiar with Web forms. *Web forms* are HTML documents with interactive elements such as radio buttons, check boxes, text boxes, and selection lists. They're a real-time equivalent of the paper form, used to gather information (such as customer names and addresses) and provide feedback.

In WordPerfect's Web view you can add radio buttons, check boxes, selection lists, text boxes and text lines, password fields, submit buttons and submit images, reset buttons, and hidden fields.

Use your browser to save a Web form to disk, and then open it in WordPerfect's Web view, where you can then customize it to your needs.

Note You can set up a Web form in WordPerfect, but WordPerfect doesn't provide the server-side gateway program, such as a CGI script, to gather and process the information entered in the form. See your Internet Service Provider or system administrator for help in getting the form to work.

To add a form field to your Web page:

1. In WordPerfect's Web view, click the Insert Web Form button (Insert ⇨ Create Form) to insert a pair of markers for the form field.

2. Click the appropriate property bar button to select any of the fields described in Table 14-3. (You can also click Insert ⇨ Form Items to select various items from the menu.)

Table 14-3
Form Fields You Can Add to a Web Page

Field	Description
Radio button	Circle with text. Select one item from a group of two or more. (All the radio buttons within a given set must be within the same form field.)
Check box	Square box with text. Select an item on its own.
Selection list	Scrollable list of items from which to make one selection.
Text line	Single line for typing information.
Text box	Sizable block of space for typing information.
Password field	Text line that doesn't display typed text (or displays it as asterisks).
Submit button or submit image	Clicking the button or image sends all the form information to the server-side gateway program for processing.
Reset button	Clears data in the form fields when clicked.
Hidden field	Provides information without direct user input.

3. Click the Web Form Properties button (right-click the form field and click Properties) to specify information applicable to that field type (see Figure 14-15).

Figure 14-15: Specifying a form field's properties.

Tip

Use your browser to save a Web form to disk, and then open it in WordPerfect's Web view, where you can then customize it to your needs.

Adding Hyperlinks

You're now in the final stages of your Web publishing enterprise. You have a home page and a secondary page, both still in WordPerfect format. It's time to add some hyperlinks.

Your hyperlinks (hypertext links) let the viewer jump within the current document to a document on your computer or network, or to a Web page anywhere in the world. Just click the link and off you go! That's what the Web is all about.

Types of links and how they display

You can use a hyperlink to jump to

✦ A bookmark in the current document

✦ The beginning of another document, or a bookmark within it

✦ Any other Internet address

Note

For non-Web documents, you can also create a link to play a WordPerfect macro.

You also have three ways to display a link (see Figure 14-16):

✦ As underlined, colored text

✦ As a text button

✦ As any graphic turned into a button

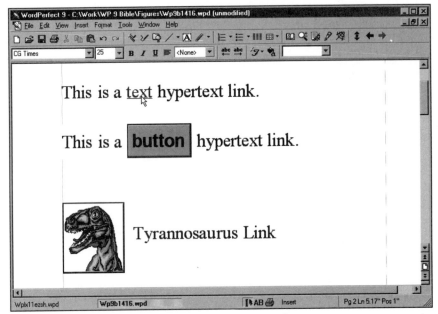

Figure 14-16: Hyperlinks and the Hyperlink property bar.

You can use the Hyperlink property bar (shown in Figure 14-16) to perform any of the operations described in Table 14-4.

	Table 14-4
	Hyperlink Property Bar Buttons

Button	Lets You
Hyperlink Perform	Jump from the link at the insertion point, even when hyperlinks aren't active.
Previous	Go to the previous link in the document.
Next	Go to the next link in the document.
Hyperlink Remove	Remove the current link, leaving the text intact.
Hyperlink Edit	Edit the properties of the current link.
Hyperlink Activate/deactivate	Activate or deactivate all hyperlinks.
Hyperlink Style	Edit the style of text links (WordPerfect only, not for Web documents).

Creating links within a document

Return to your home page in the Web editor to create its internal hyperlinks. Under the Table of Contents of your home page, you should have a bulleted list of topics in your document to which the visitor can jump, as well as the "Wallpaper Your Room" item to jump to the other page.

First, create the bookmarks you want to jump to:

1. Go to the top of your first location, such as the "Web Definitions" heading. (In a Web browser, unlike WordPerfect, the hypertext link positions at the top of the screen.)

2. Click the Web Hyperlink button ⇨ Insert Bookmark (Tools ⇨ Bookmark ⇨ Create), and name the bookmark (see Figure 14-17).

Figure 14-17: Creating a bookmark to link to.

3. Create additional bookmarks for the remaining links.

4. Select the text in your Table of Contents for the first link, click the Web Hyperlink button ⇨ Create Link (Tools ⇨ Hyperlink), and then select the destination bookmark (see Figure 14-18).

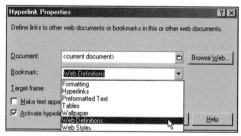

Figure 14-18: Selecting the bookmark to link to.

5. If you want to create a hyperlink button, check "Make text appear as a button."

6. Create links for the remaining items within the document.

Linking to another page

Next on the agenda is creating links between the home page and any secondary pages. To link to another page:

1. Select the text or graphic for the link to the secondary page.

2. Click Tools ⇨ Hyperlink, and then click Document and specify the filename. Specify a filename extension of .HTM (or .HTML), because that's what it will be after the secondary page is published. (Leave out the path if you will be putting both pages in the same folder on the server.)

3. Specify a particular bookmark if you want to link to somewhere other than the top of the document. For WordPerfect documents, the list of bookmarks automatically appears.

Providing a way back

While Web browsers have Back buttons to let you trace back through the pages you've visited, it's advisable to place specific links from a secondary page back to the home page. A Back button at the end of a document that takes the viewer back up to the top is also helpful.

Creating Web links

Normally, you'll want to provide Web links to other sites of interest to your visitor. To create Web links:

1. If you're currently online, go to the location you want to link to.

2. Select the text or graphic to use for the link.

3. Click Tools ⇨ Hyperlink, type the full URL (such as `http://www.corel.com`), or click Browse Web to locate the Web page, and then return to WordPerfect.

4. Click OK, and then point to the link to verify the address (see Figure 14-19), or click the link to test it out.

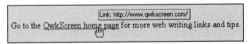

Figure 14-19: Checking out your Web link.

Tip

Web links work in any WordPerfect document, not just ones that are published to HTML.

Adding e-mail links

To create an e-mail link (so visitors can leave a message to you or another person):

1. Select the text or graphic to use for the link.

2. Click Tools ⇨ Hyperlink.

3. In the Document box, type **mailto**:, followed by (without any spaces) the e-mail address (for example, "mailto:JDoe@anywhere.net").

It's customary for links showing Web or e-mail addresses to be in italics. That's what the Address style is for.

Tip   If you don't want the whole paragraph to be in italics, use the italic font attribute instead of the Address style.

Inserting SpeedLinks as you type

When you type text beginning with "www," "ftp," "http," or "mailto," WordPerfect's SpeedLinks feature automatically turns it into a hyperlink.

You can also have any other word or phrase automatically turn into a hyperlink. To have a word or phrase automatically turned into a hyperlink:

1. Click Tools ⇨ QuickCorrect ⇨ SpeedLinks.

2. Type the link word or phrase, and the location to link to (see Figure 14-20).

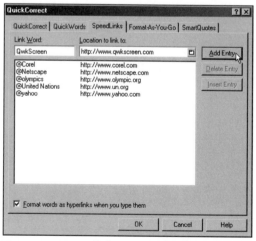

Figure 14-20: Defining a SpeedLink word.

3. To turn SpeedLinks on (or off), check "Format words as hyperlinks when you type them."

Your SpeedLink entry is automatically given the "@" prefix, to distinguish it from an actual name. The prefix is removed from your text as it converts to a link.

Tip   When SpeedLinks is off, you can select a SpeedLink entry in the QuickCorrect dialog box and click Insert Entry to create a link.

Editing a hyperlink's properties

To edit a hyperlink's properties, position the insertion point on the link with the arrow keys (don't click), and click the Hyperlink Edit button. (You can also right-click the link and click Edit Hyperlink.)

Editing a hyperlink's text

To edit a hyperlink's text, position the insertion point on the link (don't click), and edit the text.

Deactivating a hyperlink

To deactivate a text hyperlink (without deleting the text), position the insertion point on the link (don't click), and click the Hyperlink Remove button.

You can also go into Reveal Codes and delete one of the hypertext codes.

Roll the Press!

Your Web pages are finished — in WordPerfect, that is. Now, all you have to do is publish them to HTML, following the instructions in "Creating Web Documents in WordPerfect," earlier in this chapter.

Your Web site is now complete. Put it up with the help of your site supervisor or network administrator, and you're in business!

Building SGML and XML Documents

You can use WordPerfect 9 to create, edit, retrieve, validate, and save documents created with the Standard Generalized Markup Language (SGML) or eXtensible Markup Language (XML).

What is SGML?

SGML is an open international standard (used extensively in business and government) for defining document architecture and markup. Because SGML isolates document formatting from document content, you can transfer documents across platforms and use them in different applications. Once the structure of a document is defined, such as a book's title page, contents, and chapters, the document can be published in different ways (such as to paper and HTML) without affecting the document's content.

What is XML?

XML is a simplified version of SGML, designed especially for Web documents. It enables designers to create their own customized *tags* to provide functionality not available with HTML. For example, XML supports links that point to multiple documents, as opposed to HTML links, which can reference just one destination each. Like SGML, XML is based on an open international standard.

Imagine that you're Web-shopping for a 19-inch computer monitor. Rather than having to check out the Web sites of dozens of vendors, you could use a search engine to quickly find who has the best price, provided that each site outputs data to a standard XML format. With an XML-enabled browser, you would be able to retrieve all the data on monitor X, and then sort the data on price and availability, all in a single inquiry.

One real-world XML example is OFX, the Open Financial Exchange format that banks use to talk to personal-finance software. By agreeing on a standard description of financial data, banks don't have to output data into a different format for every personal-finance package. The creators of personal-finance packages benefit by having the ability to read every bank's transactions with a single module.

While WordPerfect's XML facilities are very much on the cutting edge, XML is a medium of the future that is not directly supported by current Web browsers. Thus, you can't post an XML document on your Web site and expect many more than a handful of viewers to be able to read it.

How are SGML and XML different from HTML?

Both SGML and XML provide the power and flexibility that comes from creating your own Document Type Definition (DTD), or use existing DTDs to structure information for specific purposes.

Compared to XML, HTML is a relatively simple subset of SGML, providing a fixed markup language employing a standard DTD. When you publish to HTML, you know that millions of users employing a standardized browser will be able to read your document.

Creating XML and SGML documents

WordPerfect provides the following facilities to create, edit, retrieve, and save SGML or XML documents:

✦ You create, edit, retrieve, and save SGML or XML documents by using the familiar WordPerfect editing environment.

✦ You create a WordPerfect template (.WPT) from your DTD, by using the DTD Compiler.

✦ You format SGML or XML elements for your documents in the XML Project Designer.

Learning more about XML and SGML

You can learn all about building XML and SGML documents in the SGML & XML Guide in the WordPerfect Office 2000 Reference Center, as well as in the extensive online Help facilities.

For a hands-on experience in creating and working with XML documents, try out the WordPerfect XML Tutorial:

1. Click Start ➪ WordPerfect Office 2000 ➪ Utilities ➪ WordPerfect XML Project Designer.

2. Click Help ➪ XML Tutorial, and then follow the six-part lesson (see Figure 14-21).

Publishing to PDF

You can publish your WordPerfect documents and Presentations slide shows to PDF (Portable Document Format), so they can be viewed and printed by anyone who has the free Adobe Acrobat reader.

To publish your current WordPerfect document to PDF:

1. Click File ➪ Publish to PDF and specify the name and location for the published file (Figure 14-22).

2. Select from the following publishing options:

   • *Full document* to publish the entire file

   • *Current page* to publish the page at the insertion point

   • *Print pages* to specify and publish a range of pages

   • *Selected text* to publish highlighted text

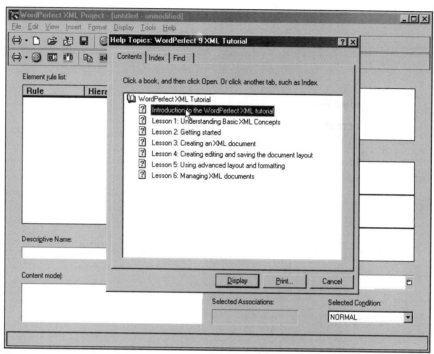

Figure 14-21: Using the tutorial in the WordPerfect XML Project Designer.

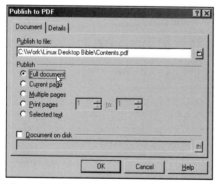

Figure 14-22: Publishing a document to PDF.

Note

Check "Document on disk" to specify a document other than the one you're editing.

3. Click the Details tab (Figure 14-23) to specify any of the following:

- Bitmap compression to reduce the size of your published graphics.

- Advanced to include the document summary, and to publish objects as CMYK, RGB, or Gray to ensure accurate color reproduction.

- Text and Fonts to publish text only, and to specify how you want to handle text. If you publish text as graphics, unusual fonts may display better and the file size may be reduced, since the fonts won't be included. Compressing text streams can also reduce the size of the resulting file, while turning off TrueType to Type 1 conversion may enlarge or reduce the size of the PDF file, depending on the number of fonts.

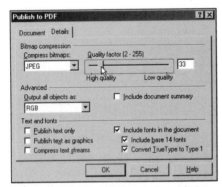

Figure 14-23: Specifying PDF publishing details.

If the recipient doesn't already have it, you can attach a copy of the freely distributable Adobe Acrobat Reader. You can download the latest version from `http://www.adobe.com`.

For More Information . . .

On	See
Publishing to the Web with Trellix	Chapter 15
Web publishing in Presentations	Chapter 42
Web publishing in Paradox	Chapter 51
Adding clip art and pictures	Chapter 9
Formatting and editing tables	Chapter 22
Inserting bookmarks	Chapter 18

✦   ✦   ✦

Publishing to the Web with Trellix

Looking for an excuse to upgrade to WordPerfect Office 2000? The Trellix addition should fit the bill. If you want to put information on the Internet or your corporate intranet, you won't find a better solution — anywhere.

Why Trellix?

With a forest of Web publishers out there, why take notice when a new seedling like Trellix sprouts? Because this one was planted by Dan Bricklin, co-developer of the first electronic spreadsheet.

Trellix is a whole new way of Web publishing. While everyone else is focusing on the latest graphical gimmicks, Trellix is working on new ways to put *information* on the Internet or your intranet. Isn't that what the Web should be about?

What's different about Trellix?

If you have a page or two to publish to HTML, WordPerfect's Web Publisher is the simplest route (see Chapter 14, "Web Writing and Publishing"). But suppose you have a long, complex report, complete with a table of contents, chapters, footnotes, and an index? You can undertake the massive manual job of slicing and dicing your report for viewing in a browser, converting pages to HTML, and then painstakingly inserting the links to stitch the pieces together.

Or you can give the job to Trellix to

✦ Convert your WordPerfect documents to manageable HTML pages

   ✦ Organize information with easy-to-create links, embedded graphics, and spreadsheets

   ✦ Provide a powerful map to easily navigate documents of many pages

The reader gains instant access to your information, in a form that's simple to read (see Figure 15-1).

Page border with list of links   Click page icons in the map   Page body

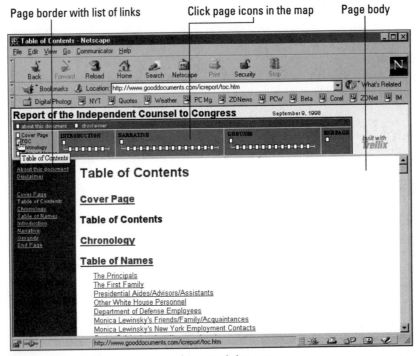

Figure 15-1: Trellix report, viewed in a Web browser.

Note the three components of the Trellix document shown:

   ✦ The *page body* displays the contents of the selected page.

   ✦ An interactive *map* provides a graphical overview of the document, with page icons showing where you are and where you've been.

   ✦ A *border* on the left with links to document parts.

Links in the map and outline, as well as the page body, make navigating complex documents a breeze.

Here you'll learn how to customize these components to best present a particular document.

Working with pages in Trellix

You can put an entire long document in a single Trellix page. But for clear organization and easy navigation, you'll want to break up your document into pages. Each Trellix page contains a single topic or "chunk" of information.

Trellix can automatically slice up your WordPerfect document, based on your original page breaks, heading styles, or fonts (see "Sending a Document to Trellix," in this chapter).

Trellix also has a special type of page called a *container page*, used to present information from somewhere else. See "Adding Container Pages," later in this chapter.

How Trellix works with WordPerfect

Thanks to the integration of Trellix and WordPerfect, you can deliver your reports, legal briefs, articles, or even a book, to everyone's Web browser. You simply create the document in WordPerfect, and then publish it to Trellix in an easy-to-read format.

You can also create a Web document from scratch in Trellix, but the WordPerfect-Trellix combination provides the best way of creating documents, together with the best way to publish them.

Using Trellix files and the Trellix viewer

Trellix documents are in a compact, proprietary file format, with all the fonts, color, formatting, and links intact. They can only be edited in the Trellix program.

If the recipient of the Trellix file doesn't have Trellix, you can attach a copy of the freely distributable Trellix viewer (ViewerSetup.exe), available from the Trellix Web site: `www.trellix.com`. The viewer lets you browse Trellix documents in all their glory — you just can't edit them.

For more universal distribution, you can publish your Trellix document to HTML, complete with the map and other Trellix navigation aides. You'll probably lose some formatting niceties, such as styles, fonts, tab settings, and indents, but anyone with a browser will be able to view it.

Sending a Document to Trellix

To send a WordPerfect document to Trellix:

> **1.** Do either of the following:

- Click Start ➪ WordPerfect Office 2000 ➪ Trellix 2.0, and then click File ➪ Import WordPerfect File.

- Open your document in WordPerfect, and then click File ➪ Publish to Trellix.

2. Choose how Trellix should divide your document into pages:

- *Put all the text into a single Trellix page* puts all your text in a single document.

- *Create a new Trellix page when Trellix finds* breaks up your document using your document's page breaks, heading styles, or large fonts (see Figure 15-2). (Heading styles used for breaks must be named Heading 1, Heading 2, and so on.)

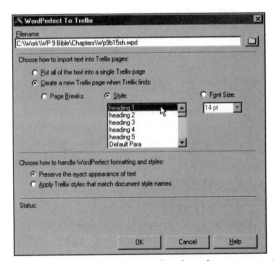

Figure 15-2: Sending a WordPerfect document to Trellix.

3. Tell Trellix how to handle your WordPerfect formats and styles:

- *Preserve the exact appearance of text* removes all styles and uses local formatting to override the default Trellix styles, ensuring that your text appears exactly as it did in WordPerfect.

- *Apply Trellix styles that match document style names* matches your WordPerfect styles with those in Trellix, discarding those that don't match. (This is the preferred approach for working with the Trellix layouts and document designs.)

A copy of your document is then converted to the proprietary Trellix format and given a .tlx filename extension. If you started from WordPerfect, the Trellix application is automatically launched and your document displayed.

Tip

If you're working with a multipart master document in WordPerfect, expand the master before you send it to Trellix.

A Look at the Trellix Screen

The Trellix screen shown in Figure 15-3 looks a lot like WordPerfect's, as described in Chapter 3, "Looking at a Suite Face." This section describes the Trellix particulars.

History toolbar   Formatting toolbar   Standard toolbar   Map toolbar

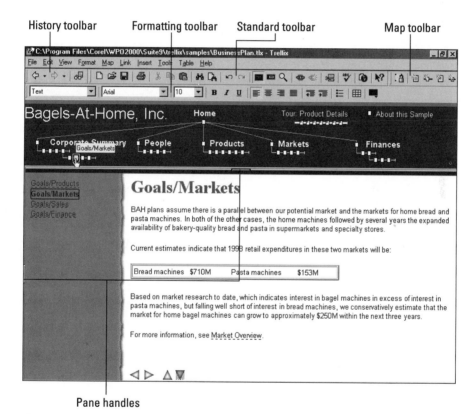

Pane handles

Figure 15-3: Trellix screen.

Toolbars

You'll find four toolbars at the top of your screen:

✦ A *History* toolbar to navigate among pages you've viewed, see how your document appears in the Trellix Viewer, and navigate the current page

✦ A *Standard* toolbar to perform common file and editing operations, toggle the map display, create links, and publish to HTML

✦ A *map* toolbar to add items to the map and lock its background

✦ A *formatting* toolbar to apply styles, fonts, and formatting, and change the colors of fonts and shapes

Click the View menu to select the toolbars you want to display.

Tip   Drag the left side of a toolbar to expand, shrink, or rearrange it, so the buttons you use most are in view.

Menus

Use the menus to access the complete set of Trellix features.

The status bar

The status bar at the bottom of the screen displays helpful system messages about what you're currently doing, such as the column width in pixels when you're resizing a table.

The document map

After sending your document to Trellix, you'll see a map above your document that displays the title of your document, and an icon for each page in a linear sequence. Point to an icon to display the page's title (see Figure 15-4). The current page is in yellow; selected pages appear with a dotted outline.

Click the Trellix View Map button to alternately display and hide the document map. (Drag the border between the page and the map to resize the map area.)

You can click Map ⇨ Main for other map viewing options:

✦ *Float,* to float the map so that it can be moved about and resized (see Figure 15-5)

✦ *200%,* to view a portion of the map in greater detail

There's also an *OverAll* map (Map ⇨ OverAll ⇨ Show) that lets you see the map for a large complex document in its entirety.

You'll learn how to use sequences to arrange your pages and provide alternative paths to traverse your documents later in this chapter (see "Working with Map Sequences").

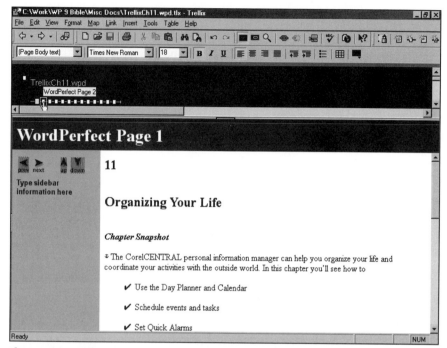

Figure 15-4: Point to an icon in the map to display a page's title.

Figure 15-5: Floating map.

Splitting the page area into two panes

You can split the page area into two panes, to view a different page in each pane (or two parts of the same page). Grab and pull a pane handle to split the area horizontally or vertically (refer to Figure 15-3). To restore the page, pull the handle back.

Displaying the document outline

To display the contents of the map in outline, click View ➪ Outline ➪ Show.

You can insert pages and rearrange sequences, in either the outline or the map. (Point to a page in the outline and see how the map selection follows.)

The outline can also be displayed as a flat list or as a floating box (see Figure 15-6).

Figure 15-6: Outline displayed in a floating box.

An outline can't be published to HTML.

Editing Your Trellix Document

You can add, edit, format, and align text in Trellix much as you would in a WordPerfect document. Select various formatting options from the menus or the formatting toolbar.

Inserting tables

Click anywhere in the page and then click the Trellix Insert Table button (Insert ➪ Table) to insert a table. You can insert columns and rows, add text, graphics, or links, and change background and border properties. Click the table and then click the Table menu to view the options.

You can also resize tables, columns, and rows by dragging borders with your mouse.

The features in Trellix tables are designed to be compatible with HTML.

Changing default fonts in your page layout

To change the default fonts in your page layout, click Format ➪ Edit Page Layouts, and change the fonts for the particular areas.

Working with styles

Trellix provides a number of built-in styles, for headings, bullets, titles, and so on, that are especially suited to HTML publishing.

The text in the page body and each border area has its own *default style*, suitable for the information they're expected to contain. For example, the left border is likely to be used for a list of links, while the top border usually contains the page title.

Applying a style

To apply a style to the current paragraph or selected text:

1. Click Format ⇨ Style, and select a style to apply (see Figure 15-7).

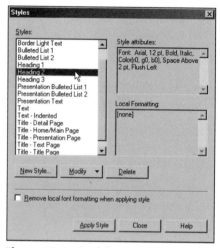

Figure 15-7: Applying a Trellix style.

2. Check if you want to "remove local font formatting when applying style," leaving the pure Trellix style.

You can also apply Trellix styles from the drop-down list on the left of the formatting toolbar. You can't remove local formatting this way.

For information on working with WordPerfect's styles, see Chapter 28, "Working Quickly with Templates, Projects, and Styles."

Modifying a style

To modify a style in your document, click Format ⇨ Style, select the file, click Modify, and change the style's font, format, and other attributes.

Creating a new style

To create a new style for use in your document:

1. Click Format ⇨ Style ⇨ New Style.

2. Give your style a name and select whether to base the style on your current text or on an existing style that you select from the list (see Figure 15-8).

Figure 15-8: Creating a new style.

Deleting a style

To delete a style in your document, click Format ➪ Style, select the file, and click Delete.

Spell-checking your document

To spell-check your document, click Tools ➪ Spelling and specify the part of the document you want to check.

Formatting Your Trellix Document

Trellix provides various standard formatting templates, designs, layouts, and tools that let you publish your documents to the Internet or an intranet, without knowing a thing about HTML. As you work with Trellix, you'll see how easy it is to quickly and consistently apply custom formatting to suit your aesthetic tastes and needs.

Changing the page body and borders

The *page area* beneath the map is made up of the page body and up to four optional borders at the top, bottom, left, and right. Borders usually contain titles, navigation buttons, lists, and explanatory text.

When you send your WordPerfect document to Trellix, you'll initially see a title border at the top and a sidebar on the left with four navigation buttons. (You'll see how these buttons work in "Adding navigation links," later in this chapter.)

Borders can include titles, logos, links, and other information and navigation aides.

To display or change a page border:

1. Click Format ⇨ Page Area, and select the page border.

2. Check whether you want to display the border, and specify its margins and size (see Figure 15-9).

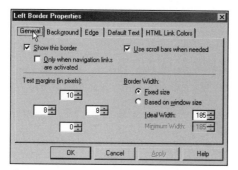

Figure 15-9: Displaying or changing a page border.

3. Click the Background tab to change the color or use an image. (Tile an image both vertically and horizontally to fill the border.)

4. Click the Edge tab to specify the color and width of the edges.

5. Click the Default Text tab to change the default text, paragraph format, tabs, and bullets.

6. Click the HTML Link Colors tab to change the colors for links and visited links.

Cross-Reference

For information on links, see Chapter 14, "Web Writing and Publishing."

To change the page area, click Format ⇨ Page Area ⇨ Page Body. The page body isn't optional, but other than that, the options are the same as those for a page border.

Tip

You can also right-click a page area to change its format and other properties.

Changing your document's design

Each Trellix document employs a *document design*, a collection of styles that give your pages a consistent look when applied to various areas of your screen.

To change your document's design, click Format ⇨ Change Document Design, and select a design from the list (see Figure 15-10).

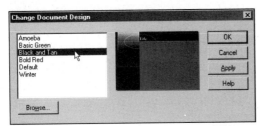

Figure 15-10: Changing your document's design.

Tip

Download the latest designs from the Trellix Web site at www.trellix.com.

Changing page layouts

Each document design includes *page layouts*, for title pages, text, slide presentations, and so on.

To change the page layout:

1. Click Format ➪ Page Layout, and select a layout (see Figure 15-11).

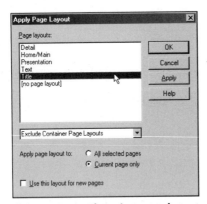

Figure 15-11: Changing page layouts.

2. Select whether to apply the layout to all your pages or just the current one.

3. Check if you want to use the layout for any new pages you create.

Creating a new page layout based on the existing page

Suppose that you've modified the colors, size, and background of your current page layout, and added a company logo. You can save your changes to a new page layout to apply to other pages:

1. Click Format ⇨ Define Page Layout, give the layout a name, and click OK (see Figure 15-12).

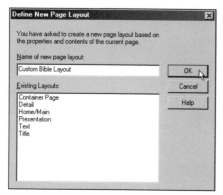

Figure 15-12: Creating a new page layout based on the existing page.

You'll be told that objects will be converted to images, and text will be converted to *static text* that is applied to the beginning of every page employing the layout. When working in pages employing your style, you have to unlock static text (Format ⇨ Unlock Static Text) to edit or remove it. If this is OK, proceed to the next step.

Tip If you don't want to include static text, design your layout from a blank page (Insert ⇨ Page).

2. Make any changes you want in the Page Layout Editor (see Figure 15-13).

3. When you're satisfied with your layout, click Finished.

You can now apply your new layout to other pages.

Selecting multiple pages

To apply formatting to, or perform other operations on, several pages at once, first select them in any of the following ways:

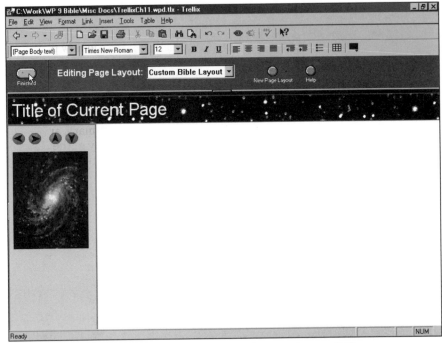

Figure 15-13: Cleaning up your new layout in the Page Layout Editor.

✦ Hold down the Ctrl key while you click multiple icons in the map.

✦ Drag a box around the icons (see Figure 15-14).

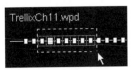

Figure 15-14: Selecting multiple pages by dragging a box around their icons.

✦ Click the sequence line to select all the pages in the sequence.

Dividing a page

To divide (break) the current page:

1. Click in the page area where you want to break the page.

2. Click Edit ➪ Break Page, and then click one of the following:

   • *Create New Page,* to create a new page containing the text following the cursor

- *Create Linked Page,* to beak the page, placing a "more" link from the end of the first page to the beginning of the second

- *Add to Sequence,* to break the page, placing the new page next in the sequence

Specifying a page's identifying fields

Each page has six identifying fields: title, short title, summary, author, keywords, and comments. To change the default title, or to fill in any of the other fields, right-click anywhere in the page, click Properties ⇨ Page, and then enter or change the fields (see Figure 15-15).

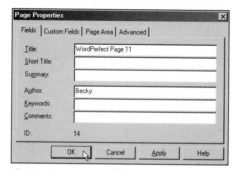

Figure 15-15: Specifying a page's identifying fields.

You can also click the Custom Fields tab and then type information in any of the three custom fields.

Note The page ID is a unique internal number assigned by Trellix that can't be changed.

Creating a new document design

New page layouts, or modifications to existing design, normally apply to the current document only. To apply your custom layouts and styles to other documents, save your changes to the existing document design, or create a new design:

1. Click File ⇨ Save As, and open the DocumentDesigns folder.

2. Select "Trellix Document Design Files" in the "Save as type" listing.

3. Select the design you want to modify or type the name for a new design (see Figure 15-16). The .tld filename extension is automatically appended.

Figure 15-16: Creating a new document design.

Working with templates

To get a head start when creating a Trellix document from scratch, you can select from several *template files* with pages and sequences designed for a specific purpose, and then add your own content (see Figure 15-17).

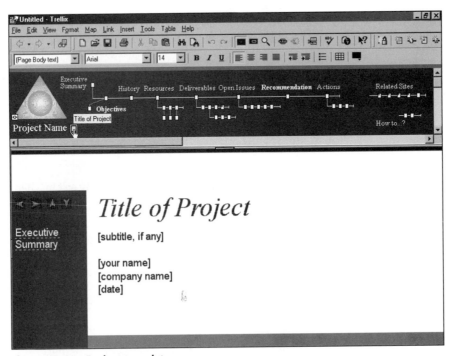

Figure 15-17: Project template.

Templates have preconfigured pages, structures, and map elements, plus examples of Web links, images, tables, and fields. You'll also find "How to...?" pages with helpful suggestions.

You can create your own templates with custom layouts and designs, for your own use or to distribute to others. Most Trellix settings are saved with a template, such as map properties, scroll bars, lists of links, and tour sequences.

Tip   Download the latest templates from the Trellix Web site at `www.trellix.com`.

Creating a new document using a template

To create a new document using a template:

1. Click File ⇨ New, and select from the available templates (see Figure 15-18).

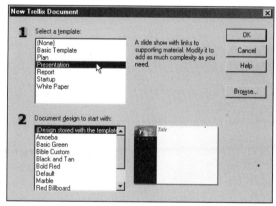

Figure 15-18: Selecting a template.

2. If you prefer, select a different document design to apply to the template structure. (Designs are independent of templates.)
3. Click OK, and then click the Save button (File ⇨ Save) to save and name your file.
4. Fill in your own content, add pages, and adjust the document's structure to suit your needs.

Saving a document as a template

To save the current document as a template:

1. Click File ⇨ Save As, and open the DocumentDesigns folder.
2. Select "Trellix Template Files" in the "Save as type" listing.

3. Select the template you want to modify, or type the name for a new template (see Figure 15-19). The .tlt filename extension is automatically appended.

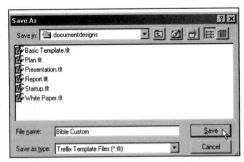

Figure 15-19: Saving the current document as a template.

 Tip   Copy the "How-to...?" pages from a delivered template and customize them with your instructions.

Adding Images

You can add graphic images to any part of the Trellix page or map.

Adding an image to a page

To add an image to a page:

1. Right-click where you want to insert the image and click Insert ➪ Image.

2. Check "Preview image," and then browse to select the image (see Figure 15-20).

Adjusting an image's properties

After you insert the image, chances are good it will be too big or too small. You may also want to crop the image to show only a portion of it, or set a transparent color for the background to show through:

1. Right-click the image and click Properties ➪ Image.

2. Do any of the following:

   • Type a descriptive name for the image.

   • Click the Crop tab and specify the number of pixels you want to crop from each side (see Figure 15-21).

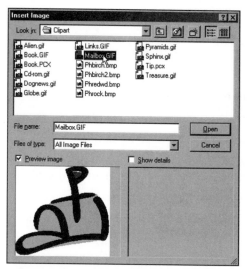

Figure 15-20: Adding an image to a page.

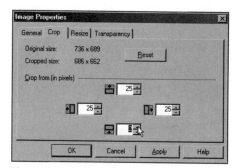

Figure 15-21: Cropping an image.

- Click the Resize tab to enlarge or shrink the image. (Check "Maintain proportions" to avoid distorting the image.)
- Click the Transparency tab to set or change the transparent color that lets the background show through. (Click the eyedropper, and then click the image to pick a color.)

To use an image for your page background, see "Changing the page body and borders," earlier in this chapter.

To add images to the map, see "Adding visual clues to your map," later in this chapter. For more information on working with graphic images, see Chapter 55, "Creating Your Own Art."

Adding Container Pages

You can add *container* pages, to present the reader with information from somewhere else, including a "tour" copy of a page in the current document:

1. Right-click a blank spot in the map and click Insert Container Page.

2. Select the type of contents you want to put in the page body (see Figure 15-22):

   - *None,* to create a blank container page for later use
   - *Trellix Page,* to display a read-only copy of a page in your current Trellix document (see "Creating a tour sequence," later in this chapter)
   - *URL,* to display a "live" page from an intranet or Web site
   - *File,* to present a file from any of your applications, including another Trellix file
   - *Captured Resource,* to present captured HTML images (see "Containing a captured HTML page").

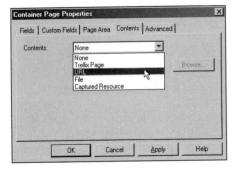

Figure 15-22: Specifying the type of contents for your container page.

3. If you're displaying a file or URL, type or browse to enter its location. (Your Web browser is launched when you browse for a URL.)

4. If you're displaying a Trellix page, select it from the list and then choose whether to display both the page body and borders, or just the page body.

Caution   When you distribute a Trellix document with container pages that reference outside sources, such Web sites or files, you must be sure that the reader has access to those sources at the new location. A file must be in the same path.

Container pages default to the "Container Page" layout with a narration border on the right for explanatory text. You can customize the borders as with any other page.

Container page icons appear in the map with a red dot.

Creating a container page by dragging

To create a container page by dragging a URL's location marker:

1. Display the Web page in Internet Explorer or Netscape, and then click the Screen Restore button in the upper left to shrink the browser window and float it over the Trellix window.

2. Drag and drop the location marker to the Trellix map (see Figure 15-23).

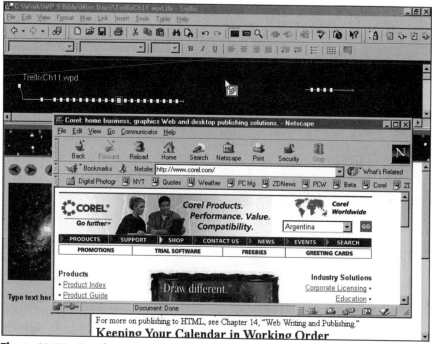

Figure 15-23: Creating a container page by dragging a URL's location marker.

Tip   Use the Forward and Back buttons on the Trellix toolbar to navigate within the Web container page.

To create a container page by dragging a file, right-click the Start button on the Windows taskbar, click Explore, and then locate the file and drag its icon to the map.

Containing a captured HTML page

You can capture and contain HTML pages locally, instead of containing a live Web link. The page will stay as captured, and won't change or disappear along with its Web counterpart. However, if you're displaying anything more than the text and formatting of a single page, it's likely you'll have to edit the HTML source.

To capture and contain an HTML page:

1. Using your Web browser, locate and save HTML pages to disk. Also save any graphics or wallpaper they contain.

2. In Trellix, right-click a blank spot in the map, click Insert Container Page, and then select Captured Resource from the Contents list.

3. Click Insert ➪ From Disk, locate and select your captured images, and then click Open (see Figure 15-24).

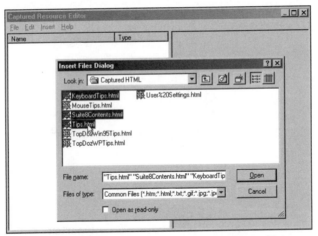

Figure 15-24: Locating and selecting your captured images.

4. Select the name of the "home page" that you want to initially display in the container page, as shown in Figure 15-25. Then click Edit ➪ Set Default (a hand points to the page you chose).

5. Edit the HTML source code to eliminate any paths to graphics, wallpaper, or links among the pages you're saving.

6. Click File ➪ Save & Exit, and then click OK.

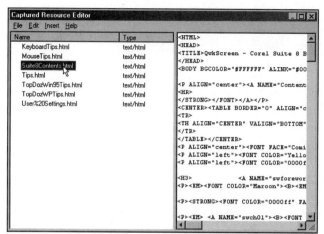

Figure 15-25: Selecting the default "home page" for the container page.

Trellix pulls the specified resources into a new container page.

Caution   If you're saving multiple pages to one container page, they'll have to be internally linked in order for the reader to navigate them.

Cross-Reference   For more on editing HTML source code and paths, see Chapter 14, "Web Writing and Publishing."

Adding Hyperlinks

A key to a successful Trellix document is its *hyperlinks* (hypertext links) to provide convenient navigation to the reader. Hyperlinks are described in Chapter 14, "Web Writing and Publishing," but Trellix offers a number of tricks that you'll learn about here.

You already saw how Trellix automatically puts hyperlinked icons in the document map that take you to the top of a document's pages. You can create several types of links, described in Table 15-1.

Table 15-1 **Types of Trellix Links**	
Type of Link	*Lets You*
Basic	Use text in the current page to describe where the link goes
Field	View current text from a page's properties, such as the title or summary, and go to that page
Anchor	Go to a particular place in a page
Navigation	Go forward or back in a page sequence, or up or down a hierarchy
Top of page	Return you to the top of the page
Up level	Navigate between introductory or overview pages and detail pages
To external file or URL	View another file or Web page
Trellix	Go to a page in another Trellix document on your system
E-mail	Create and send an e-mail message

You can have multiple links to a particular page or anchor, allowing for a variety of navigation routes.

Links can be attached to any text or images in the page, borders, or map.

Creating a basic link

To create a basic link:

1. Select the text or image for your link anywhere in the page body or in a page border.

2. Click the Trellix Create Link button (Link ⇨ Link to a Page Using ⇨ Selection) and then click the icon for the page you're linking to.

Tip   When the outline is displayed, you can click a page title in the outline to create a link.

Using links as you're working in Trellix

When you're working in Trellix, links (other than those in the map) are turned off so that you don't jump around as you edit your pages. Hold down the Ctrl key and click to test out a link.

To see how your links will behave when published, click the Trellix Viewer Preview button (File ➪ Viewer Preview). Click again to return to Edit mode.

Creating a field link

To create a field link that displays the text of a page's identifying fields:

1. Right-click in the page text or border where you want the link to appear (or click the page and click the Link menu).

2. Click Link to Page Using, followed by:

   - *Title Field* to show the page's title in the link

   - *Title & Summary Fields* to show both the page title and summary in the link

   - *Other Fields* to select another field to display in the link (Figure 15-26)

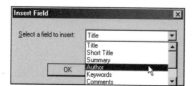

Figure 15-26: Creating a field link.

3. Click the map icon of the page you're linking to.

Creating an anchor link

To create an anchor link:

1. Right-click the spot in the page you want to link to. (If you're going to publish your document to HTML, right-click in a blank line or a spot where the anchor symbol won't be noticed.)

2. Click Insert ➪ Anchor, and give the anchor a name (see Figure 15-27). (Use a descriptive name if you're going to display the name in your link.)

Figure 15-27: Creating an anchor to link to.

3. Move to the location you're linking from (on the current page or another page), and then do either of the following:

- Select the link text and right-click

- Right-click to use the anchor name

4. Click Link ⇨ "Link to an anchor on," and then do either of the following:

- Click Current Page

- Click Another Page, and then click the icon for the page

5. Select the anchor from the list (see Figure 15-28).

Figure 15-28: Selecting the anchor to link to.

Adding navigation links

Most Trellix page layouts already have navigation links for previous, next, up, and down (refer to Figure 15-4). They're placed in the page layout so they can be applied to various pages, and won't scroll off the screen.

The previous and next buttons activate as soon as you have a linear sequence of pages in your document map. The up and down buttons activate when you have up level links to or from the current page.

Tip   Hold down the Ctrl key, or click the Trellix Viewer Preview button, to test out your navigation links.

To add a navigation link to your page's layout:

1. Click Format ⇨ Edit Page Layouts, and click where you want to add the link.

2. Click Link ⇨ Create Navigation Link, and select the direction of your link (see Figure 15-29). (Use "Parent" for up and "First child" for down.)

3. Select one of the link descriptions:

- *Image,* to insert the selected button image

- *Field,* to display one or two of the page's identifying fields, such as the title of the next page

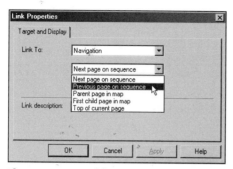

Figure 15-29: Adding a navigation link.

- *Text,* to display the specified text, such as "Up Level"

4. When you've added all your navigation links, click Finished to save the links in your layout.

Adding a top of page link

As a convenience to readers, add to the body of your page a navigation link that takes users back to the top:

1. Click in the page where you want to add the link.

2. Click Link ➪ Create Navigation Link, and select "Top of page" for the direction.

3. Specify the link description as described in Step 3 of "Adding navigation links."

Creating an up level link

Now that you see how to create navigation links, try creating an up level link to a title or contents page, so you can navigate with the up and down buttons:

1. In the map, right-click the page (or right-click the sequence line to select all the pages).

2. Click Choose Up Level, and then click the page to which you want to create the up level link.

In the map, Trellix draws a line from the page (or the left edge of the sequence) to the page you're linking to. When you're on the upper page, the down navigation link becomes active. When you're on a page in the sequence, the up navigation link becomes active.

Linking to an external file or URL

To link to an external file or URL (Web address):

1. Click where you want to insert the link, and then click Link ⇨ Create Link to URL or File.

2. Select whether you want to link to an external file or URL (see Figure 15-30).

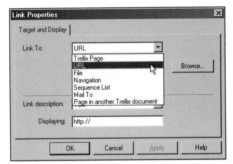

Figure 15-30: Linking to an external file or URL.

3. Type or browse to enter the filename and path or URL. (Your Web browser is launched when you browse for a URL.)

Tip   Click your Trellix page and drag the location marker from Internet Explorer or Netscape to instantly create a URL link. You can then edit the link text.

Linking to a page in another Trellix document

To link to a page in another Trellix document:

1. Click where you want to insert the link, and then click Link ⇨ Create Link to URL or File.

2. From the Link To list, select "Page in another Trellix document."

3. Click Browse to locate the Trellix document, and then click Browse to select the particular page (see Figure 15-31). You can specify a particular anchor if the page has one.

4. Edit the link text to give it a meaningful description.

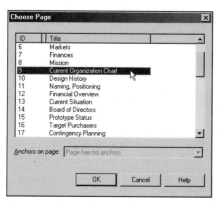

Figure 15-31: Linking to a page in another Trellix document.

Creating an e-mail link

To create an e-mail link:

1. Click where you want to insert the link, and then click Link ➪ Create Link to URL or File.

2. Select "Mail To" from the Link To list.

3. Type the e-mail address and edit the link text to give it a meaningful description (see Figure 15-32).

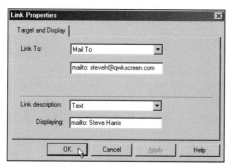

Figure 15-32: Creating an e-mail link.

Editing a link's text

To edit the text of a basic, navigation, or mail to link, click the text in your document and retype it.

To edit a field link's text:

1. Click the link's text (it will turn light gray).

2. Edit the text, and then click outside the link.

When you change the text in the field link, the actual text for that field in the page you're linking to is changed. Your change will be reflected throughout the document.

Breaking a link

To break (remove) a link, select the entire text (or the graphic with the link), and then click the Trellix Unlink button (Link ➪ Break).

The link text will no longer appear underlined.

To break an up level link, right-click the icon for the subordinate page on which the up level link is active, and click Unlink Up Level.

Working with Map Sequences

The interactive document map is an ingenious Trellix invention that lets you easily create, modify, navigate, and understand the contents and structure of documents.

By creating and arranging map sequences, you help the reader to quickly locate topics of interest and navigate their pages.

Creating a sequence

To create a sequence:

1. Right-click a blank area in the map and click Insert Sequence.

2. Drag-and-drop existing pages to the sequence line (see Figure 15-33).

 Figure 15-33: Creating a sequence.

 Tip You can hold down the Ctrl key to copy the page you're dragging as a new page on the sequence line. To place a read-only copy of a page in an alternate sequence, create a tour sequence instead.

The sequence line expands to accommodate the number of pages it contains.

To reposition a sequence, click and drag the sequence line.

To lengthen or shorten a sequence line, click the line and then drag the right border of the surrounding box.

To name a sequence, right-click the sequence line, click Properties, and enter the title.

Tip   The title appears in the outline, not in the map.

Inserting and arranging pages

To insert a new page in a sequence, click the page icon where you want to insert the page, and then click the Trellix Insert Page button (Insert ➪ Page).

To rearrange pages, drag-and-drop their icons on the sequence line. To move a group of pages, first drag around their icons to select them (or hold down the Ctrl key as you click the icons).

Creating a list of pages in a sequence

By creating a list of pages in a sequence, the reader can click on a title to go instantly to that page:

1. Right-click in the page where you want to insert the list, and then click Create List from ➪ Current Page's Sequence.

2. Select one or two fields to use in the list, and the format for the list (see Figure 15-34).

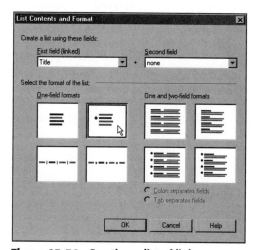

Figure 15-34: Creating a list of links.

To add lists of links to other pages, repeat the preceding procedure.

If you reorder the pages in the sequence, the list is automatically updated.

To create a list of pages in another sequence, right-click and click Create List from ➪ Another Sequence, specify the field(s) and format, and then click the sequence.

To link a sequence to another page, right-click the sequence line, and then click Choose Up Level and click the page.

Creating a tour sequence

You can create *tour sequences* to provide alternative paths through pages in your document:

1. Right-click a blank area in the map and click Insert Tour Sequence. The tour sequence appears as a thick horizontal line.

2. To add a page to the tour sequence, right-click the page and click Add Page to Tour. (If you have more than one tour sequence, first click the sequence you want to add a page to.)

Tour sequence pages are containers (note the red dots) holding read-only copies of the original page.

You can customize the narration border of the container page with tour-specific information—without affecting the text of the original page.

Deleting a sequence or tour sequence

To delete a sequence or tour sequence, click the sequence line and then press Delete or click Edit ➪ Delete.

Caution   Deleting a sequence deletes any associated pages. If you don't want to delete the pages, drag them off the sequence line first.

Click the Undo button (Edit ➪ Undo Delete) if you want to restore a sequence you just deleted.

Dressing Up the Map

Now that you've connected your pages and created tour sequences, you can customize your map display to enhance its visual guidance to the reader.

Changing the map's properties

To change the map's background and other properties, right-click a blank spot on the map, click properties, and then do any of the following:

✦ Pick a color for the background. (Click the eyedropper to select a color from an image.)

✦ Adjust the size of the map, as needed, from the default 160×45 page icon widths. (The default map space at 800×600 resolution is about 66×8 icons.)

✦ Check "Always scroll page into view" to automatically scroll the map, if necessary, to bring the current page's icon into view.

✦ Check "Display labels on pages when zoomed 200%" to see the pages' short titles (or truncated titles when the short title is blank) when the map is zoomed.

✦ Check "Turn grid snapping on" to automatically line up icons, labels, and shapes.

Adding visual clues to your map

You can add background shapes, labels, and images to enliven and simplify the map.

To add a shape:

1. Right-click the map, click Insert Shape, and then click Rectangle, Oval, or Line.

2. Drag the shape to move it. Drag the handles to reshape it (see Figure 15-35).

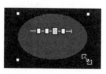

Figure 15-35: Drag a handle to reshape the shape.

3. Right-click the shape and click properties to add an edge or change its color (see Figure 15-36). (You can also link from the shape to a file, page, or URL.)

To add an explanatory label:

1. Right-click in the map and click Insert Label.

2. Use the toolbar to change the label's font, font size, or font color. (The changes don't appear while you're editing.)

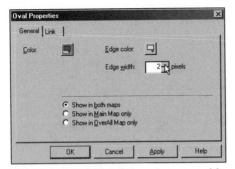

Figure 15-36: Right-click a shape to add an edge or change its color.

3. Type your label text and press Enter.

4. Drag the label to position it.

Double-click a label to edit it.

To add an image to the map, right-click the map, click Insert Image, and then browse to select the image. To adjust properties of the image, right-click the image, click Properties, then click the Properties button and adjust any of the image attributes.

Aligning map elements

To align map elements in relation to one another:

1. Hold down the Ctrl key and click the elements you want to align.

2. Click Map ⇨ Alignment, and click the alignment you want.

You can align any selectable element, including icons, sequences, images, shapes, and labels.

Arranging a stack of images and shapes

If you have overlapping images and shapes in the map, you can change the order in which they appear:

1. Right-click the image or shape you want to move up or down the stack.

2. Click Priority, and then click one of the following:

   • Bring to front

   • Send to back

- Bring forward one
- Send backward one

Locking images and shapes

You can lock map images and shapes into place so that you don't accidentally move them as you rearrange page icons, sequences, and labels. Click the Trellix Lock Map Background button, or right-click a blank area in the map and click Lock Background.

To unlock the images and shapes, click the Trellix Lock Map Background button again, or right-click the map and click Unlock Background.

Distributing Your Document

Your document is all finished? Now what do you do so others can read it? This section shows you the options:

✦ Publish to HTML, the near-universal medium for intranets and Web pages.

✦ Send a Trelligram, an executable HTML package that can be opened in Windows.

✦ Distribute your Trellix document in its original form.

✦ Print your pages the old-fashioned way.

Publishing a document to HTML

In publishing your Trellix document to HTML you may lose some formatting niceties, but you'll ensure near-universal viewing in anyone's Web browser. When you publish to HTML, you can then either open your default browser and view the HTML, or send the HTML files directly to a Web server:

1. Open the document you want to publish. Select the icons or series if you only want to publish certain pages.

2. Click either File ⇨ Publish to HTML ⇨ Export & Preview, or File ⇨ Publish to HTML ⇨ Post to Web.

3. Specify the location and subdirectory for the exported .HTM files, and whether you want to include the Trellix map (see Figure 15-37). (Each document needs its own subdirectory to keep its collection of files separate.)

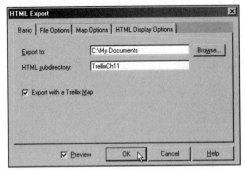

Figure 15-37: Specifying the location and subdirectory for your exported HTML files.

4. Click the File Options tab to set the following:

   • The identifying field, such as the Page ID, title, or short title on which HTML filenames should be based. (The default Page ID, though unique, is not meaningful. You can also use one of the custom identifying fields to specify your filenames.)

   • The filename to be used for the home page, normally "default.htm" or "index.htm." (Check with your system administrator for your installation's standards.)

   • Whether to export the selected pages or the entire document

5. If you're exporting the map, click the Map Options tab to specify

   • Whether your exported map dynamically highlights the link that's clicked

   • Whether readers can bookmark individual pages

   • Whether readers can scroll the map

6. Click the HTML Display Options tab to specify

   • Whether your pages adjust to fit the browser window if the reader resizes the browser

   • Whether your readers will be using only Netscape 4 browsers, or if Trellix should produce more generic HTML that can be viewed in other browsers as well

   • Whether your readers' browsers will be able to use JavaScript. (Deselecting this option slightly reduces the size of the exported files.)

7. Click "Preview" if you want to preview your files as soon as they are exported.

Depending on your choices and your system configuration, Trellix either opens your browser so you can preview the HTML files or opens a local version of Microsoft's Web Publishing Wizard. Use the wizard if you have permission to post to a Web server location.

View the Windows online Help for more information on setting up and using the Web Publishing Wizard.

Mailing a Trelligram

Instead of posting your HMTL pages to an intranet or Web site, you can wrap them in an executable "Trelligram" package that your readers can read using most browsers running under Windows:

1. Click File ⇨ Send Trelligram.

2. Specify your HTML export options as previously described in "Publishing a document to HTML."

   Trellix creates all the necessary HTML elements and associated image files, and then wraps them all in a single executable file (named after the document, with an .exe extension), which it places in the export directory.

3. After Trellix creates the Trelligram, you are presented with three options:

   • *Send*, to open your mail program to a new message with the Trelligram attached

   • *Preview,* to display the HTML output in your default browser (when you return to Trellix after previewing, you can then click Send or Done)

   • *Done,* to close the dialog box

Distributing a Trellix document in its original form

You can distribute a Trellix document in its compact, proprietary file format, with all the fonts, color, formatting, and links intact. It can only be edited in the Trellix program, but you can distribute the free viewer with the document. See "Using Trellix files and the Trellix Viewer," earlier in this chapter.

Printing your Trellix document

Although your Trellix document has many special features for viewing online, you can print it if you must:

1. To print part of your document, click the page or select the pages in the map.

2. Click File ⇨ Page Setup, to specify the page size, orientation, margins, headings, and other options for the printed page.

3. Click the Print button (File ⇨ Print), and select from the following (see Figure 15-38):

   • All pages or selected pages (the maps don't print with the pages)

   • The map at 100% or 200%

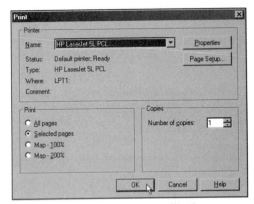

Figure 15-38: Printing your Trellix document.

Adjusting Trellix Session Options

To adjust settings that affect the Trellix session, click Tools ➪ Options, and then specify any of the following (see Figure 15-39):

✦ Whether the "Quick Tour" and the "Start Using Trellix" dialog boxes appear when Trellix starts

✦ Which normally hidden characters, such as anchors, should display in Author mode

✦ Whether to disable the automatic display of Web content within container pages

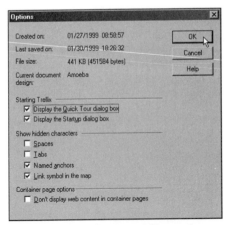

Figure 15-39: Adjusting Trellix session options.

For More Information . . .

On	See
Web writing and publishing	Chapter 14
Using the WordPerfect screen	Chapter 3
Working with graphic images	Chapter 55
Creating hypertext links	Chapter 14
Working with styles	Chapter 24
Adding clip art and pictures	Chapter 9
Formatting and editing tables	Chapter 22
Working with HTML source	Chapter 14

✦   ✦   ✦

Writing with WordPerfect

Mastering the WordPerfect Interface

You already learned the essentials for typing and editing WordPerfect documents in Chapter 2, "Essential Typing and Editing." Chapter 3, "Looking at a Suite Face," introduced you to the office-wide elements of the WordPerfect interface. This part of the *WordPerfect Bible* is devoted to WordPerfect-specific features, starting with screen and keyboard features that make WordPerfect a joy to use. The remaining chapters cover many powerful facilities for enhancing your WordPerfect documents.

WordPerfect presents a lively, flexible working environment, where you'll often find two, three, or even four ways to accomplish the same task. Play around with all the options to find what's most natural for you. If you're an old hand at WordPerfect, take a look at what's new. Whatever you do, have fun!

Taking Visual Shortcuts

WordPerfect presents a lively, even playful, working environment. In addition to such office-wide features as toolbars and QuickMenus, you'll find several visual tools especially designed for a text environment.

New Feature Veteran users should be especially delighted with three new usability enhancements: RealTime Preview, navigation buttons, and Autoscrolling with any mouse.

RealTime Preview

RealTime Preview lets you see how formatting selections, such as columns, fonts, and styles, will appear in your document before make them (see Figure 16-1). This takes the guesswork out of toolbar changes, and saves you the time and headache of applying and removing formats until you find the one that's right.

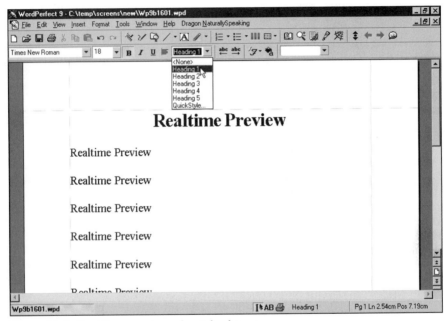

Figure 16-1: RealTime preview of a style change.

Jumping back to where you were

Click the Back button to jump the insertion point back through the previous five positions. Click Forward to redo back a step at a time.

Autoscrolling with any mouse

Click the Autoscroll button, and then move your mouse up or down to automatically scroll your document at whatever speed you want. Click in your document to stop.

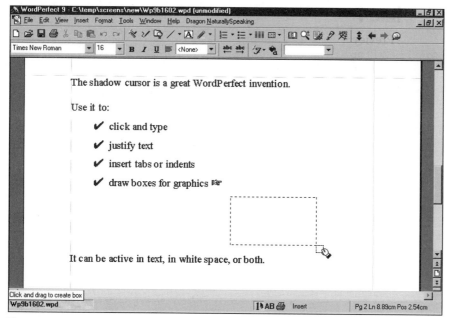

Figure 16-2: Inserting a graphic by dragging the shadow cursor.

Performing shadow cursor tricks

WordPerfect's shadow cursor has emerged as a full-fledged formatting tool. It's also something of a paradox: an intuitive, time-saving feature that can be more annoying than helpful at first use. Before you decide that it's driving you nuts, try out the following tricks.

Configuring your shadow cursor

While you're likely to be content with most features (such as toolbars) as they come out of the box, the shadow cursor is one for which it pays to know about your options. To configure your shadow cursor:

✦ Click Tools ➪ Settings, and then double-click the Display icon.

✦ Click the Color palette to change the color of your shadow cursor.

✦ Click the Shape palette to pick a different shape for when you're pointing to text (see Figure 16-3).

✦ Pick whether you want the shadow cursor to snap to (and insert formatting codes for) margins, tabs, indents, or spaces.

✦ You can have it appear when your pointer is in text (active in text), in white space, or both.

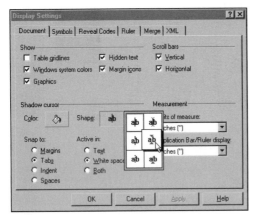

Figure 16-3: Changing the shape of the text shadow cursor.

 Tip
The shadow cursor disappears from text when you stop moving the mouse, so it won't distract you as you type.

Recommended settings

 Tip
If you're not in the mood to experiment, try the following shadow cursor settings: a shape for text of two little triangles, snap to margins (text justification without inadvertent tabs and spaces), and active in both. And don't forget how easy it is to turn the shadow cursor on or off.

Dragging guidelines

One of the most clever features of the WordPerfect screen is the dotted *guidelines* that you can drag to adjust your side, top, and bottom margins. Other guidelines enable you to adjust page headers and footers, or column margins and spacing. Even tables sport guidelines around cells without lines.

As you drag a guideline, a floating *status box* shows you what the new setting will be (see Figure 16-4). Normally, the line will snap to an interval on an invisible grid, as explained in Chapter29, "Customizing WordPerfect."

 Tip
If you mess up your margins, press Ctrl+Z to restore them.

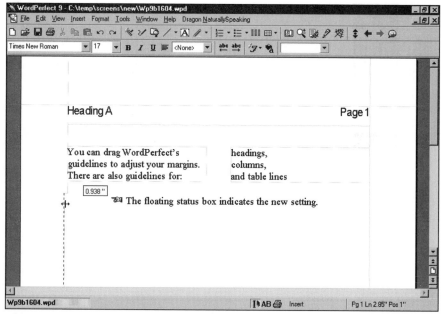

Figure 16-4: Adjusting a margin by dragging its guideline.

To select which guidelines you want to see, click View ➪ Guidelines, and then check the ones you want. You can also remove the check from "Drag to move guidelines" to turn off the drag feature.

Displaying the ruler

WordPerfect's ruler, shown in Figure 16-5, is handy for viewing and adjusting margins, tabs, and columns. Click View ➪ Ruler to display or remove the ruler. See Chapter 21, "Formatting Your Document," for tips on its use.

Figure 16-5: WordPerfect's ruler.

Setting tabs on the fly

You can also change your tab settings on the fly, without displaying the ruler bar. Wherever tabs are set, a tab icon displays in the left margin. When you work in Draft view (described in "Choosing how your document appears," later in this chapter), you must temporarily switch to Page view to see the icons.

To set tabs on the fly:

1. Right-click the paragraph in which you want to change your tabs; then click Default Tab Settings.

2. Click the tab icon to display the tab bar.

3. Drag the markers to remove or adjust the settings (see Figure 16-6).

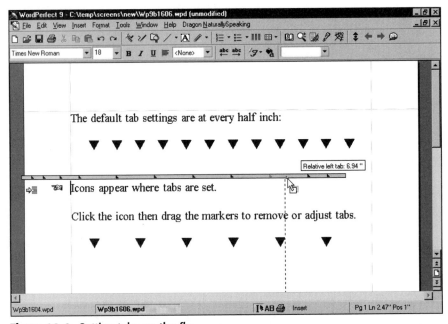

Figure 16-6: Setting tabs on the fly.

4. Click your document when you're finished. The tab bar disappears and your new settings take effect from that point on.

For complete information on using and setting tabs, turn to Chapter 21, "Formatting Your Document."

Tip Tab bar adjustments always start from the default tab settings. To modify a custom tab setting, use the ruler instead.

Fine-Tuning Your WordPerfect Display

With earlier DOS versions of WordPerfect, you could see that the word processor evolved from the typewriter. The screen was analogous to a plain sheet of paper, and all the features could be accessed with shortcut keys.

Many WordPerfect users (including fans of the earlier DOS versions) don't realize that WordPerfect for Windows gives you almost total control over which screen features appear and how documents display. Aside from the title bar and the menu bar, all screen gadgets are optional. Even those two bars can be hidden from view, temporarily giving you a completely blank screen on which to work.

Selecting screen features to display

The View menu gives you control over which screen features display (other than the scroll bars.)

To select the toolbars to display or hide, click View ➪ Toolbars, and check the bars you want (see Figure 16-7). For information on customizing toolbars, see Chapter 57, "Customizing Toolbars, Menus, and Keyboards."

Figure 16-7: Selecting the toolbars to display.

To change your scroll bar display, click Tools ➪ Settings ➪ Display. Then check or uncheck the vertical and horizontal scroll bars.

To quickly clear everything off your screen, click View ➪ Hide Bars. If you are more keystroke-oriented than mouse-driven, or if you are suffering from a temporary visual overload, give this feature a try. You can still call up the menus by using the Alt+letter keystrokes (once you get one menu, you can scroll the rest by using the arrow keys.) To restore your visual gadgets, simply press Esc. This one's for you, DOS fans.

Tip   Assign hide bars to a keystroke!

Choosing how your document appears

The View menu gives you four document display modes from which to choose:

✦ *Draft* lets you see the substance of what you're typing without the distraction of top and bottom margins, page headers, footers, or footnotes. Pages are separated by thin horizontal lines, so you don't "jump" from page to page.

✦ *Page* shows your document as it will look when printed — complete with margins, headers, footers, and footnotes. Information that doesn't print (such as a document comment) is represented by an icon.

✦ *Two Pages* is useful when laying out pages, or when previewing pages for print. You can edit in this view, but the Reveal Codes and Zoom features won't work.

✦ *Web Page* automatically converts your document to a Web page and puts you in the HTML editor (see Chapter 14, "Web Writing and Publishing"). Watch out though; HTML's formatting is not as sophisticated as WordPerfect's, so you can lose WordPerfect formatting when you switch back and forth.

New Feature Your latest view and zoom selections remain in effect for all your documents until you change them again. The manual settings found in previous releases have been removed.

Zooming your display

Zoom lets you shrink or expand your display of text and graphics anywhere from 25 to 400 percent. Zoom won't affect how your document prints.

To zoom your document, click View ⇨ Zoom, or click the Zoom button on the toolbar. Select a set zoom factor, or specify any percentage (using Other on Zoom list) from 25 to 400 (see Figure 16-8).

Figure 16-8: Specifying a zoom percentage.

Zoom also offers the following display options:

✦ *Margin width* displays your text the full width of the window, with minimal white space outside of the margins. Characters usually display larger, but you'll see fewer lines at one time.

✦ *Page width* displays the full left and right margins (the text usually appears smaller).

✦ *Full page* displays your entire page at once (minus top and bottom margins in Draft view). This view is handy for print preview and page layout, but not for editing.

Other viewing options

The View menu offers four other options not covered so far:

✦ *Graphics*, when turned off (unchecked), displays images as blank rectangles. This speeds up your display and doesn't affect how the graphics print.

✦ *Table Gridlines*, when checked, displays table lines as dimmed, dotted lines, and no graphic fills appear. This speeds up your display and doesn't affect printing.

✦ *Hidden Text* turns the display of hidden text on (so it can be seen and printed) or off. (Hidden text and comments are explained in Chapter 18, "Editing and Reviewing Techniques.")

✦ *Show* paragraph symbol, when checked, displays various nonprinting symbols onscreen for every space, hard return, tab, or indent, center, flush right, soft hyphen, advance, and center .

Tip Click Tools ⇨ Settings ⇨ Display ⇨ Symbols to select which symbols display.

✦ *Reveal Codes* displays your document's formatting codes. (See "Revealing the Hidden Formatting Codes," later in this chapter.)

Discovering the "Keys" to Success

If you're looking for tricks and shortcuts, don't forget the keyboard. To erase from the insertion point to the end of the line, for example, simply press Ctrl+Delete (Ctrl+End on the DOS-compatible keyboard). When it comes to speed, there is often no contest between the keyboard and the mouse. Compare clicking the page down box on the scroll bar to clicking the screen to move the insertion point, to simply pressing the PgDn key.

Keyboard features

The typewriter keyboard was an excellent device for entering text. The computer keyboard, in the now-standard "enhanced" version shown in Figure 16-9, includes the features described in Table 16-1, which turn it into a powerful, versatile tool.

Keyboard definitions

Various WordPerfect functions can be assigned to particular keys or key combinations. A set of key assignments constitutes a keyboard definition.

WordPerfect comes with a special Equation Editor keyboard (for the older, nongraphical Equation Editor) and two standard keyboards:

✦ *WPWin Keyboards*, also known as the CUA (Common User Access) keyboards, use standard Windows key assignments. The Home key, for example, takes you to the beginning of a line, while the End key takes you to the end. Print is F5. Ctrl+F4 closes a document window. Alt+F4 exits the application.

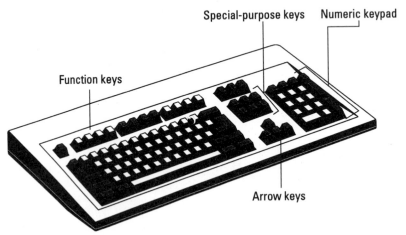

Figure 16-9: Enhanced keyboard.

Table 16-1 Keyboard Features	
Feature	*Description*
Numeric keypad	Found on most full-sized keyboards, it's handy for performing calculations and entering numbers (when Num Lock is on).
Function keys	The pre-mouse standard for performing specific program operations. The best-known function key is F1, for Help.
Shift	Enables all keys, including the function keys, to perform two operations.
Ctrl and Alt	Enable the other keys to do multiple functions, just as the Shift key does. When used in combination with Shift, these keys provide more possibilities than you'd care to remember. Alt+characters open menus. Ctrl turns character keys into easy-to-remember function keys, such as Ctrl+B for bold type or Ctrl+Shift+B to insert a bullet.
Arrow keys	Enable you to move around the screen quickly. Like most other keys, they repeat when you hold them down.
Special-purpose keys	Insert, Delete, Home, End, PgUp, and PgDn are special-purpose keys. They can be especially handy when used in conjunction with other keys (such as Ctrl, Alt, and the arrow keys).
Esc	A quick way out of dialog boxes, menus, and other places.

✦ *WPDOS 6.1* keyboards enable those who cut their teeth on a DOS version of WordPerfect to feel right at home. F12 selects text, instead of F8. Print is Shift+F7. F7 closes a document.

In Chapter 57, "Customizing Toolbars, Menus, and Keyboards," you'll learn how to customize a keyboard definition to your liking.

Using Navigational Keystrokes

You have seen how to go to another location by using the scroll bars. You will find, however, that the arrow keys and other keyboard shortcuts shown in Table 16-2 are usually the quickest way to get around a document. Keyboard shortcuts also move the insertion point as they change your location.

Table 16-2
Navigational Keystrokes

To Move the Insertion Point	CUA Keystroke	DOS Keystroke
One character left/right	←/→	←/→
One word left/right	Ctrl+←/→	Ctrl+←/→
One line up/down	↑/↓	↑/↓
One paragraph up/down	Ctrl+↑/↓	Ctrl+↑/↓
To the end of the line	End	End
To the beginning of the line	Home	Home, Home, ←
To the beginning of the line (before codes)	Home, Home	Home, Home, Home, ←
Up one screen	PgUp	Home, ↑
Down one screen	PgDn	Home, ↓
Up one page	Alt+PgUp	PgUp
Down one page	Alt+PgDn	PgDn
To the beginning of the document	Ctrl+Home	Home, Home, ↑
To the beginning of the document (before codes)	Ctrl+Home, Ctrl+Home	Home, Home, Home, ↑
To the end of the document	Ctrl+End	Home, Home, ↓

For heavy-duty moving within your document, click Edit ⇨ Go To (or press Ctrl+G) to display the Go To dialog box shown in Figure 16-10.

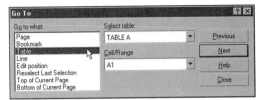

Figure 16-10: Using Go To to move around a document.

When several documents are open, you can click the buttons on the application bar to switch among them, or use the following function key shortcuts:

To Switch To	CUA Keystrokes	DOS Keystrokes
Next open document	Ctrl+F6	F3
Previous open document	Ctrl+Shift+F6	Shift+F3

Using Other Keystrokes

Other keyboard shortcuts to WordPerfect features include the insertion keystrokes, the deletion keystrokes, and the control-alpha shortcut keys.

Insertion keystrokes

The following keystrokes insert various formatting codes in your text:

To Insert	CUA Keystrokes	DOS Keystrokes
Back Tab (Margin Release)	Shift+Tab	Shift+Tab
Hard Page or Column Break	Ctrl+Enter	Ctrl+Enter
Hard Space	Ctrl+spacebar	Ctrl+ spacebar or Home, spacebar
Hard Hyphen	Ctrl+-	Home+-
Soft Hyphen	Ctrl+Shift+-	Ctrl+-

Deletion keystrokes

The following list describes deletion keystrokes you can use:

To Delete	CUA Keystrokes	DOS Keystrokes
Selected text	Delete	Delete
Current character	Delete	Delete
Character to the left	Backspace	Backspace
Word	Ctrl+Backspace	Ctrl+Backspace or Ctrl+Delete
Rest of the line	Ctrl+Delete	Ctrl+End
Rest of the page	Ctrl+Shift+Delete	Ctrl+PgDn

Control+alpha shortcut keys

The nice thing about most of the control-alpha shortcuts in Table 16-3 and Table 16-4 is that they're easy to remember (such as Ctrl+B for bold and Ctrl+I for italics). The control+alpha combinations from V to Z are well worth memorizing. Ctrl+Z can undo all the others in this section!

Table 16-3
Control+Alpha Shortcut Keys

Ctrl+Function	CUA Character	DOS Character
Select All	A	
Expand QuickWords		A
Turn on/off bold	B	B
Copy selection to the Clipboard	C	C
Insert date text	D	
Justify center	E	
Find QuickMark	Q	F
Find and replace text	F	
Go to	G	G
Turn on/off italic	I	I
Justify full	J	
Toggle case of selected text	K	
Justify left	L	L

Continued

Table 16-3 (continued)

Ctrl+Function	CUA Character	DOS Character
Create new document	N	
Resume normal font		N
Open existing document	O	
Print	P	
Insert page number		P
Set QuickMark		Q
Justify right	R	
Repeat the next action		R
Save	S	
Sound clips		S
Outline body text	H	T
Create document based on template	T	
Turn on/off underline	U	U
Paste Clipboard contents	V	V
Insert WordPerfect characters	W	W
Cut selection to Clipboard	X	X
Undo	Z	Z

Table 16-4
Ctrl+Shift Alpha Shortcut Keys

Ctrl+Shift+Function	CUA Character	DOS Character
QuickWords Insert	A	
Select all		A
Insert bullet	B	B
Drop cap	C	C
Insert date code	D	
Find next	F	
Print history	H	
Line break	L	L

Ctrl+Shift+Function	CUA Character	DOS Character
Create document based on template	N	N
Outline define	O	
Print document	P	
Set QuickMark	Q	
Redo	Z	R
Save All	S	
Paste Clipboard contents without formatting	V	V
Undelete		Z

Tip None of the WordPerfect keystrokes are chiseled in stone, especially the control-alpha key combinations. If you're using a DOS-compatible keyboard, for example, you might want to change Ctrl+S from Insert Sound Clip to Save. (See Chapter 57, "Customizing Toolbars, Menus, and Keyboards.")

Revealing the Hidden Formatting Codes

No discussion of WordPerfect's interface is complete without a reference to the hidden formatting codes that govern appearances. Your ability to work with the codes behind the scenes can make all the difference between the program controlling you and you controlling the program. The formatting codes manage every aspect of document display and print — from page margins and font type and size to using bold and italics, inserting graphics, and centering text.

You can reveal (or hide) the formatting codes in the following ways:

✦ Press Alt+F3 (with the DOS-compatible keyboard, you can also press F11).

✦ Right-click in the text area and click Reveal Codes.

✦ Click the Reveal Codes handle at the bottom of the vertical scroll bar.

✦ Click View ➪ Reveal Codes.

When you view the formatting codes, as shown in Figure 16-11, your screen is split into text and code windows. You can drag the divider line to enlarge or shrink the Reveal Codes window, or close the window entirely.

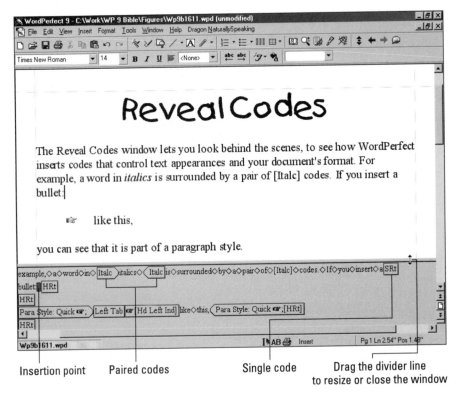

Insertion point   Paired codes   Single code   Drag the divider line
to resize or close the window

Figure 16-11: Use the Reveal Codes window to view formatting codes.

Notice that spaces in Reveal Codes are represented as diamond-shaped bullets, and formatting codes appear as sculptured boxes. The small (red) rectangle in the bottom part of the screen corresponds to the normal insertion point in the text window above.

You'll see two types of formatting codes in the Reveal Codes window:

✦ *Single* (or open) codes that appear as square icons, such as HRt for hard return

✦ *Paired codes* that point toward each other. When you put a word in italics, for example, it has an italic code on either side to turn the feature on and off. Deleting either one of the codes deletes the pair.

Note

Each new document begins with a document style code (which cannot be deleted), based on the Document Style in your default template (see Chapter 21, "Formatting Your Document").

Reveal Codes has the following handy editing features:

✦ A Quick Tip description appears when you point to a code icon.

✦ You can delete a code by dragging it up or down out of the Reveal Codes window and dropping it. As usual, you can undo such a deletion with Ctrl+Z.

✦ An associated dialog box appears when you double-click a code. You can then change your font from Times to Courier, for example; or change your spacing from double to single. (This technique only works with single codes, not paired on/off codes.)

The more you use Reveal Codes, the more you'll appreciate how it helps you to understand and control your document's format. If you never want to look at the codes, fine. But if your document is behaving strangely — for example, you delete a paragraph and your screen suddenly fills with large, bold type — an accidental or leftover formatting code probably is the culprit. Place the insertion point where the problem begins, open the Reveal Codes window, and delete or modify the offending code.

For More Information . . .

On	See
Basic typing and editing	Chapter 2
Office-wide screen features	Chapter 3
Setting display preferences	Chapter 29
Using the ruler bar and setting tabs	Chapter 21
HTML editing	Chapter 14
Customizing menus and keyboards	Chapter 57
Using hidden text and comments	Chapter 18
Setting the default document style	Chapter 21
Customizing your Reveal Codes display	Chapter 29

✦　　✦　　✦

Becoming an Instant WordPerfect Expert

Now that you've learned the basics, you probably think, this is great so far, but I guess it'll take another year to learn the sophisticated stuff, like fine-tuning font sizes and line spacing, drop caps, heading styles, and fancy tables. No way! You're going to try out these features right now. Plus, this chapter will point the way to other easy-to-use (yet powerful) WordPerfect features you'll find in chapters to come.

QuickFinding with a Single Click

If you're looking for the previous or next occurrence of the current word or selection, searching doesn't get quicker than this: click the QuickFind Previous button or the QuickFind Next button on the property bar.

The QuickFind buttons match on whole words only. For example, if you select the "quick" in "quicker" and click a button, you'll match only on the word "quick," not "QuickFinder." You can learn all the finding tricks in Chapter 18, "Editing and Reviewing Techniques."

Format-As-You-Go

Chapter 2, "Essential Typing and Editing," discussed how WordPerfect fixes your spelling, typos, and grammar on the fly. Now click Tools ➪ QuickCorrect ➪ Format-As-You-Go, and take a look at the instant sentence corrections and formatting (see Figure 17-1).

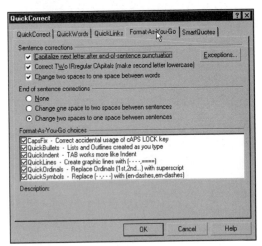

Figure 17-1: Format-As-You-Go.

Instant sentence corrections

The sentence correction options make typing a lot easier:

✦ *Capitalize next letter after end-of-sentence punctuation* means that you don't have to bother with the Shift key when you start most sentences. (You still have to use Shift after headings without punctuation.)

✦ *Correct TWo IRregular CApitals (make second letter lowercase)* gets rid of this annoying typo.

✦ *Change two spaces to one space between words* is great in these days of proportional fonts, when it's hard to tell how many spaces there are.

You'll probably want to select an end of sentence correction, either to turn one space between sentences to two, or two to one.

Tip

When using a proportional font, one space is the standard punctuation for books, newsletters, and most other publications.

Dealing with exceptions

Most sentences end with a period. So do most abbreviations, which is why, if you click the Exceptions button, you'll see a list of words (see Figure 17-2) that don't signal the end of a sentence (such as "corp." or "inc."). Of course, if your sentence ends with an exception, it's back to the Shift key.

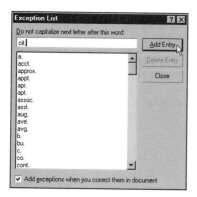

Figure 17-2: Dealing with exceptions.

As you can see from the list, all single letters with a period are ignored (as with "a.m.," "i.e.," or "P.O."). You can manually add other abbreviations to the list, such as op. cit. (two entries).

To add exception words automatically, check "Add exceptions when you correct them in document." Then, when you backspace over the capitalized letter and correct it (before ending the word), the preceding abbreviation gets added to the list.

Other Format-As-You-Go options

Other options for Format-As-You-Go include the following:

✦ *CapsFix* reverses iRREGULAR cAPITALIZATION when Caps Lock is on, and turns off the Caps Lock.

✦ *QuickBullets* begins a bulleted list when you type **o**, *****, **O**, **^**, **>**, **+**, **or -** as the first character on a line, followed by a tab or indent. You can also type a number (for a numbered list), **i** or **I** (for Roman numerals), or a letter (for an alphabetical list), followed by .,), or -, and then a tab or indent. To end the list, press Enter ➪ Backspace.

✦ *QuickIndent* creates a hanging indent paragraph (one that begins with an indent, followed by a back tab) when you press Tab at the beginning of any paragraph line except the first. If the first line already starts with a tab, you end up with a regular indented paragraph instead. You can also press Tab anywhere in the first line to indent the remainder of the paragraph from that tab stop.

✦ *QuickLines* converts four or more hyphens (-) at the start of a line into a horizontal line. (Type four or more hyphens, and then press Enter.) Four or more equal signs (=) insert a double line.

✦ *QuickOrdinals* changes the "st," "nd," or "rd" of ordinal numbers to superscript (1st, 2nd, 3rd).

✦ *QuickSymbols* changes — (two hyphens) to an en dash; or — (three hyphens) to an em dash.

Inserting SmartQuotes

The SmartQuotes options (Tools ➪ QuickCorrect ➪ SmartQuotes) let you substitute the curly printer's quotes in place of the straight-up-and-down variety. You even get different styles to choose from (see Figure 17-3).

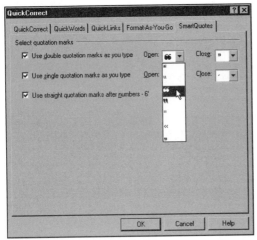

Figure 17-3: Changing the SmartQuote character.

Be sure that "Use straight quotation marks after numbers" is checked when you use SmartQuotes.

Making It Fit

Have you ever tried writing a one-page résumé, but even after taking out every redundant or superfluous word, some text still manages to squiggle over to the next page? You need Make It Fit!

Are you a student about to turn in an eleven-page paper, but your professor set a page limit of ten? You need Make It Fit!

Are you a desktop publisher creating a six-page flier, but your text and graphics take up only five and one-half? You too need Make It Fit!

Sizing a document to fit

To size your entire document to fit:

1. Click Format ➪ Make It Fit, and specify the number of pages you want (see Figure 17-4).

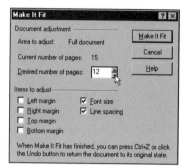

Figure 17-4: Using Make It Fit.

2. Check the items that you are willing to allow WordPerfect to adjust, and click Make It Fit.

WordPerfect then makes several passes of your document to figure out the best combination of adjustments to make, and voilà! It fits! If you don't like the results, press Ctrl+Z to undo it.

If you make further changes to your document, you can run Make It Fit again.

Tip
Use Make It Fit even when the current and desired number of pages are the same. If your flier is five and one-half pages long, Make It Fit expands it to a full six.

The Make It Fit feature shrinks or expands your document up to 50 percent. Unlike most other formatting features, it places these codes in your Document Style (see Chapter 21, "Formatting Your Document"), rather than in the text.

Sizing a block to fit

New Feature
To size a selected block to fit, follow the same procedure as in "Sizing a document to fit," above. The block expands or shrinks *from the starting position of the block on*, to fit the specified number of pages. (To fit a block to pages from top to bottom, place a page break before the block.)

When you size a block to fit, formatting codes are placed before and after the block.

Dressing Up with Drop Caps

Suffering from "drop cap envy"? WordPerfect has the cure! No experience is required to start off your flier, newsletter, article, or chapter with this traditional flourish. Not only can you use drop caps, but also raised caps and many other font effects (see Figure 17-5).

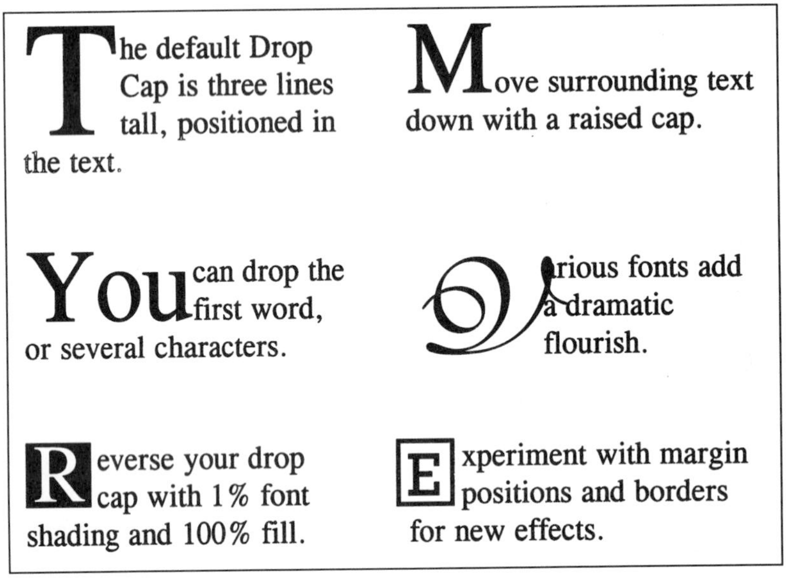

T he default Drop Cap is three lines tall, positioned in the text.

M ove surrounding text down with a raised cap.

You can drop the first word, or several characters.

rious fonts add a dramatic flourish.

R everse your drop cap with 1% font shading and 100% fill.

E xperiment with margin positions and borders for new effects.

Figure 17-5: Drop cap sampler.

Even though the drop cap displays as a fancy graphic, the spell-checker and other writing tools treat it as regular text. To create your own drop cap:

1. Place the insertion point in an existing paragraph, or where you want to begin a new paragraph.

2. Click Format ➪ Paragraph ➪ Drop Cap. The first character of your paragraph, or the first character you type, is given the default drop cap treatment.

3. Place the insertion point before the drop cap, and click the Drop Cap Style button to pick another style (see Figure 17-6). Then customize your drop cap by using any of the options described in Steps 4–8.

Tip Pick the "XA" style in the lower-right corner to turn off a drop cap, or press Ctrl+Z to undo any changes you make.

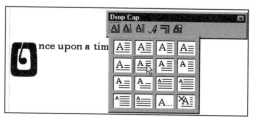

Figure 17-6: Picking a drop cap style.

4. Click the Drop Cap Size button to select a height from two to nine lines. You can even select Other from the list to specify a precise in-between height.

5. Click the Drop Cap Position button to select In Text (the default) or In Margin (100 percent in the margin). Click Other to specify exactly how much you want to move the surrounding text down, or how far you want to move the drop cap into the margin (see Figure 17-7).

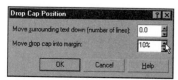

Figure 17-7: Specifying a precise drop cap position.

6. Click the Drop Cap Font button to specify a special font face, style, appearance, color, or shading for your drop cap. (Try a plain or decorative font for contrast.)

7. Click the Drop Cap Border button to specify any kind of border or fill. (See Chapter 54, "Adding Graphic Lines, Borders, and Fills," for complete details.)

8. Click the Drop Cap Options button to include any number of characters or the entire first word in the drop cap (see Figure 17-8).

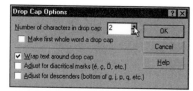

Figure 17-8: Specifying drop cap options.

You can also check any of the following:

✦ *Wrap text around drop cap* (the default) keeps paragraph text from printing over the drop cap.

✦ *Adjust for diacritical marks* moves down slightly drop characters that have diacritical marks.

✦ *Adjust for descenders* wraps paragraph text around parts of drop characters that extend below the baseline on which the characters sit.

Putting on the QuickStyle

Suppose that you just created some nice formats for paragraphs and headings you would like to use in future documents. You might, for example, publish a regular sales brochure or newsletter that you want to give a consistent, professional appearance. By using *QuickStyles*, you can save the format, fonts, and attributes as styles that you can use over and over again.

To create a custom style with QuickStyle:

1. Format the text of an existing paragraph (for a heading, body text, and so on) the way you want all paragraphs of that type to look.

2. Click the paragraph, click the Select Style list on the property bar, and click QuickStyle (Format ⇨ Styles ⇨ QuickStyle).

3. Give the style a name and description (see Figure 17-9).

Figure 17-9: Creating a custom style by using QuickStyle.

4. Click the "Paragraph with automatic update" style type, and then click OK. The style you just created will now appear with your other Document Styles (see Figure 17-10).

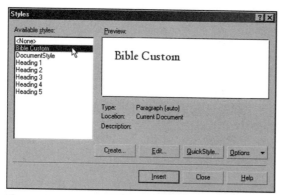

Figure 17-10: Your style now appears with your other Document Styles.

5. If you think you might want to apply the style to other documents, click Options ⇨ Copy ⇨ "Default template" ⇨ OK.

By saving your custom paragraph style to the default template, you can use it in new documents you create. (For more information on templates and styles, see Chapter 28, "Working Quickly with Templates, Projects, and Styles.")

QuickFormat Your Headings

QuickFormat is even quicker than QuickStyles, because you don't even have to give your style a name. QuickFormat is great for applying the same style to all the headings in a document. To use QuickFormat:

1. Click in your formatted heading or paragraph and click the QuickFormat button. (You can also click Format ⇨ QuickFormat, or right-click your document and click QuickFormat.)

2. Click OK to transfer the heading's format paragraph-by-paragraph, or click "Selected characters" first to apply only the current font and attributes to other text, character-by-character, without saving them to a style (see Figure 17-11).

3. Your pointer turns into a paint roller that you can click on other headings to transfer the style, or a paintbrush if you're applying only the character attributes (see Figure 17-12).

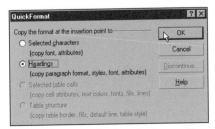

Figure 17-11: Selecting the formatting features to transfer.

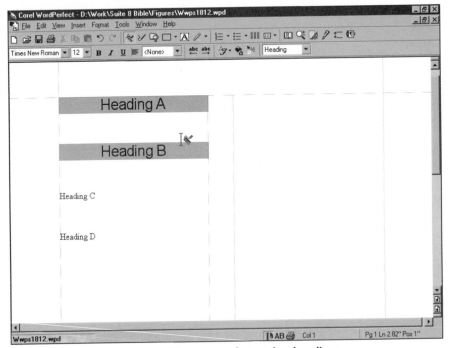

Figure 17-12: Applying the QuickFormat style to other headings.

4. When you're finished painting other text, click the QuickFormat button to turn it off.

You'll find that the styles of all your headings are linked together, to maintain consistency throughout your document. If you make the text of one heading blue, for example, they all turn blue.

To turn off automatic updating:

1. Right-click a QuickFormat (or QuickStyle) heading and click QuickFormat ⇨ Discontinue.

2. Click "Current heading" to turn off the automatic update for just that heading, or "All associated headings" to discontinue automatic updating of all headings with the associated style (see Figure 17-13).

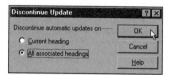

Figure 17-13: Discontinuing QuickFormat's auto-update.

Fancy Tables in No Time

With WordPerfect, you can create tables in no time. Simply click where you want the table to appear, click the Tables button, and then drag to create the size table you want.

Create a 6×7 table, as shown in Figure 17-14, which you'll be using shortly.

Figure 17-14: Creating a table.

QuickFormatting a table

You may be surprised to learn that you can QuickFormat tables, just like paragraphs. Figure 17-15 shows how QuickFormat applies one cell's attributes to other cells in the same or another table. The first table's structure (the border in this case) was instantly applied to the table in the middle.

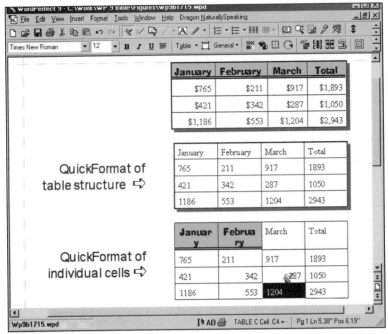

Figure 17-15: QuickFormatting a table's structure or cells.

To QuickFormat tables:

1. Click in the format you want to copy, and then click the QuickFormat button.

2. Select whether to copy the "Selected table cells," or the "Table structure" (see Figure 17-16).

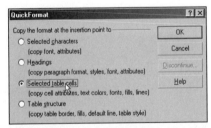

Figure 17-16: Selecting which QuickFormat elements to apply to other cells or tables.

3. Apply the formatting with the roller to other cells or tables, and then click the QuickFormat button again when you're finished.

For complete details on creating and formatting tables, see Chapter 22, "Formatting with Columns and Tables."

SpeedFormatting a table

If QuickFormatting a table sounds great, how about instantly applying a professional-looking style like the one shown in Figure 17-17 to your entire table?

Cyclops Software Sales					
	1st Quarter	2nd Quarter	3rd Quarter	4th Quarter	Total
1997					
1998					
1999					
2000					
2001					

Figure 17-17: Professional-looking table style you can instantly apply.

Try this with the 6×7 table you just created:

1. Type **Cyclops Software Sales** in the upper-left cell, and then type **1997**, **1998**, **1st Quarter**, and **Total** in the cells shown in Figure 17-18.

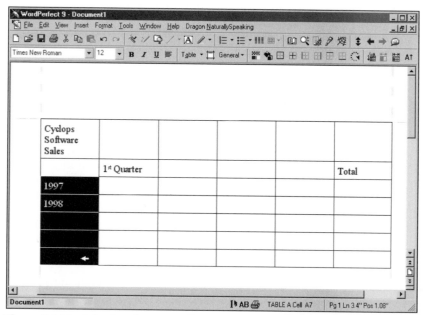

Figure 17-18: Selecting the year cells.

2. Point to the top of the "1997" cell, and then drag to select all of the year cells, as shown in the figure.

3. Click the QuickFill icon to QuickFill in the dates for the remaining years.

4. Drag to select the "1st Quarter" cell and the three cells to its right. Click the QuickFill icon.

5. All the text should now be filled in. Now right-click anywhere in the table and click SpeedFormat. Highlight the Header Fill Double style (or any other style you like), and click Apply (see Figure 17-19).

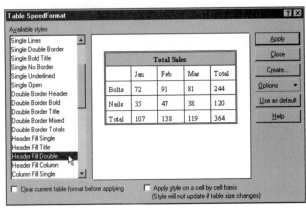

Figure 17-19: Applying a SpeedFormat style to your table.

You'll even learn how to create custom SpeedFormat styles in Chapter 22, "Formatting with Columns and Tables."

In Praise of the QuickMark

Bookmarks are great for keeping your place when you're reading a book. WordPerfect has invented the electronic equivalent, called the QuickMark.

To set the QuickMark, just press Ctrl+Shift+Q. To move the insertion point to it, press Ctrl+Q. (The DOS keystrokes are Ctrl+Q and Ctrl+F, respectively.)

You're allowed one QuickMark per document. Each time you set it, it moves to the new location, just like moving a paper bookmark. (You can see the QuickMark in Reveal Codes.)

Click Tools ➪ Bookmark for options to set a QuickMark at the current location every time you save a document, and to return to the QuickMark the next time you open it.

There's also a Save Workspace setting to insert QuickMarks in your open documents automatically when you exit, and then re-open your documents and return to where you left off when you restart WordPerfect (see Chapter 29, "Customizing WordPerfect"). Regular bookmarks are described in Chapter 18, "Editing and Reviewing Techniques."

Finding Other Cool Stuff

Format-As-You-Go, Make It Fit, drop caps, Table SpeedFormat, QuickStyles, QuickFormat, the QuickMark—these are but a few of the handy, powerful features WordPerfect provides. Table 17-1 provides a sampling of other goodies covered in the chapters to come.

Table 17-1	
Cool Features in Other Chapters	
Feature	*Chapter*
Spell-As-You-Go and Grammar-As-You-Go	2
Correcting typos	2
DAD control center	3
Windows setup tricks	3
Internet goodies and help	5
Automatic backup and recovery	6
Keeping multiple versions in one file	6
Going to your Favorite folders	7
QuickFinder searches	7
Creating 3-D TextArt	8
Grouping graphics boxes	9
Linking information	10
Realtime preview	16
Shadow cursor tricks	16
Margin guidelines	21
Selection tricks	18
Finding and replacing text	18

Continued

Table 17-1 (*continued*)	
Feature	*Chapter*
Printing booklets	19
X of Y page numbering	20
Inserting Watermarks	21
Instant columns	22
Splitting table columns and rows	22
Instant bullets and outlines	23
Creating QuickWord abbreviations	52
Simple sorts	53
Dressing up with borders and fills	54
Recording macros	58

Well, you get the idea. There isn't enough room to list all the quick, powerful, easy-to-use features.

Using Boilerplate

"Enough already! With so many easy-to-use features, it'll take half my life to learn them all, and by that time they'll have invented a bunch more."

OK . . . relax. They're there if you want them, and no one uses them all. Want an opinion of the top five? Here they are:

- ✦ *QuickCorrect.* The best thing that ever happened to typing got even better by automatically fixing typos.
- ✦ *Spell-As-You-Go.* You'll wonder how you lived without it. Grammar-As-You-Go makes a good thing great.
- ✦ *Automatic backup and recovery.* Use it, unless you like living dangerously.
- ✦ *Find and Replace.* An essential and versatile tool.

You're right; that's only four. Thought you'd never ask. You'll never find number five in any glossy full-page ads. In fact, number five isn't a feature at all, just a basic technique you can employ with any word processor: boilerplate. Boilerplate is simply a preformatted document or section (such as a letterhead, résumé, or cover sheet) that you can use over and over again. It's not a style, or a quick-anything, but a reusable copy of work that you did before.

To start with a boilerplate document:

1. Click File ➪ Open, select the file, and then click Open as Copy.
2. Click File ➪ Save, give the copy a name, and then click Save. To insert boilerplate in the document you're working on, click Insert ➪ File, select your boilerplate, and click Insert.

Just like that, you have a proven format; and perhaps much of the text as well!

For More Information . . .

On	See
Tricks with Find and Replace	Chapter 20
Fixing spelling, typos, and grammar on the fly	Chapter 2
Changing the Document Style	Chapter 21
Applying borders and fills	Chapter 54
Using templates and styles	Chapter 28
Creating and formatting tables	Chapter 22
Saving your workspace	Chapter 29
Using bookmarks	Chapter 18

✦   ✦   ✦

Editing and Reviewing Techniques

For all its incredible features, WordPerfect is, at heart, a better way to enter and edit text. In this chapter, you'll get all the text-selection tricks, and turn on the power of Find and Replace. You'll also learn how to insert bookmarks, review and edit comment documents as a group, make comparisons, and insert comments. As for hidden text—just wait and see!

Selecting (Blocking) Text

Selecting text is usually the first step in editing it. To italicize the title of a book, for example, go back and select the title, and then put your selected text in italics. In Chapter 2, "Essential Typing and Editing," you saw the basic ways to select text by using the keyboard or dragging the mouse. Here you'll find a selection technique to suit every taste.

Mastering mouse selection tricks

Normally, you select text with the mouse by dragging. Here are a few more mouse selection tricks:

To Select	Do This
A word	Double-click the word
A sentence	Triple-click the sentence, or click once in the left margin
A paragraph	Quadruple-click the paragraph or double-click in the left margin
From the insertion point to the shadow cursor (or I-beam)	Shift+click

To select multiple words, hold down the mouse button on the second click, and drag the mouse to select word-by-word. Single or double-click in the left margin, and then hold and drag to select sentence-by-sentence, or paragraph-by-paragraph.

Adjusting a selection with the mouse

To adjust the selection with a mouse, hold down the Shift key and do one of the following:

✦ Click to extend the selection to the pointer

✦ Drag to expand or shrink the selection

Using the Edit menu or QuickMenu to select text

Another way to select text at the insertion point is to click Edit ➪ Select, and then click what you want to select. An easier way is to right-click in the left margin and select from the QuickMenu (see Figure 18-1).

Using keystroke selection tricks

To select your entire document in a hurry (for example, to copy it to the Clipboard), press Ctrl+A (Ctrl+Shift+A with a DOS keyboard).

For lesser amounts of text, you can press F8 (F12 on a DOS keyboard) and use the arrow keys to select the text you want. Press any key, including the spacebar, to extend your selection through the next occurrence of that key.

You can also press F8 (F12 for DOS) or hold Shift, and use one of the keystroke selection tricks shown in Table 18-1.

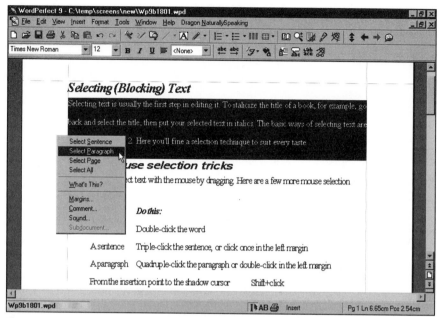

Figure 18-1: Right-click in the left margin to select text.

Selecting from the insertion point to a character

To select from the insertion point to a character, press F8 (F12 on a DOS keyboard), and then type the character to select through (it can be a lowercase or uppercase character, a space, or a tab). Pressing the key again extends the selection to the next occurrence of that character.

> **Tip** Press a period to extend your keyboard selection to the next period, or press Enter to extend it to the hard return at the end of the paragraph.

Selecting text in columns and rectangles

Wait! You're not finished. What about selecting text in tabular columns, or even rectangles of screen text?

To select a tabular column with the mouse, point to a corner of the text, hold down the Shift key, and then hold down the *right* mouse button and drag to select the text (see Figure 18-2).

Table 18-1
Keystroke Selection Tricks

CUA Keystrokes	DOS Keystrokes	To Select (with Select On or While Holding Shift)
Left arrow/Right arrow	Left arrow/Right arrow	One character to the left/right
Ctrl+Left arrow/Right arrow	Ctrl+Left arrow/Right arrow	One word to the left/right
Up arrow/Down arrow	Up arrow/Down arrow	One line up or down
Ctrl+Up arrow/Down arrow	Ctrl+Up arrow/Down arrow	One paragraph up or down
End	End	To the end of the line
Home	Home, Home, Left arrow	To the beginning of the line
Home, Home	Home, Home, Home, Left arrow	To the beginning of the line (before codes)
PgUp	Home, Up arrow (not with Shift)	To the top of the screen
PgDn	Home, Down arrow	To the bottom of the screen
Alt+PgUp	PgUp	To the first line of the previous page
Alt+PgDn	PgDn	To the first line of the next page
Ctrl+Home	Home, Home, Up arrow	To the beginning of the document
Ctrl+Home, Ctrl+Home	Home, Home, Home, Down arrow	To the beginning of the document (before codes)
Ctrl+End	Home, Home, Down arrow	To the end of the document

After the column is selected, you can cut or copy it, and then paste it in a new location. You can also drag it to a new location.

 Caution Save your document before performing columnar surgery. Not all operations are successful!

You can select any rectangle of text, whether or not it is lined up with tabs or indents. However, it's not likely to format neatly if you move or copy it to another location.

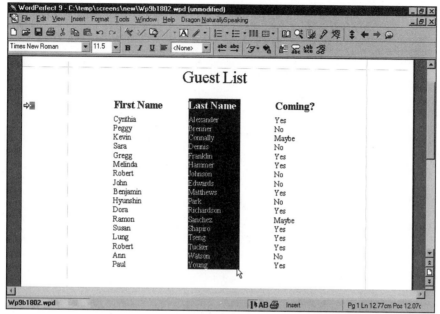

Figure 18-2: Selecting a tabular column by right-button dragging.

To select tabular columns or a rectangular block via the Edit menu:

1. Select from the first character of the column you want to the last character of the last column, such as the beginning to end of the Last Name column in Figure 18-3.

2. Click Edit ➪ Select ➪ Tabular Column. The Last Name column is now the only text selected (see Figure 18-4). Had you chosen Rectangle instead of Tabular Column, the beginning and end of your selection would be opposite corners of the final rectangular selection.

Cross-Reference

For more on columns, see Chapter 22, "Formatting with Columns and Tables."

Finding and Replacing

The more you use Find and Replace, the more you'll find it to be a powerful and versatile editing tool. Selectable find actions and other options discussed in the following sections remain in effect for the duration of the current WordPerfect session.

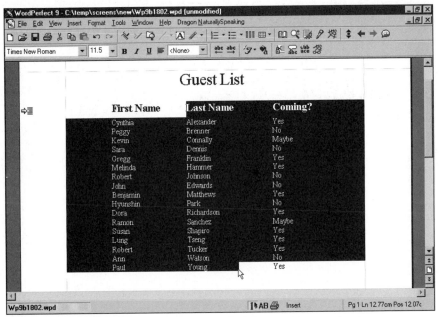

Figure 18-3: Selecting the beginning to end of the Last Name column.

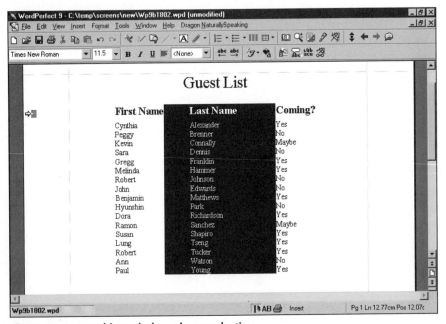

Figure 18-4: Resulting tabular column selection.

Finding a word or phrase

There's no need to strain your eyeballs when searching for a word or phrase:

1. Press F2 (Edit ➪ Find and Replace).
2. Type the word or phrase in the Find box.

Tip   Press Ctrl+W to find a symbol.

3. Click Find Next or Find Prev (see Figure 18-5).

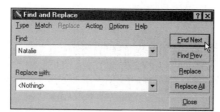

Figure 18-5: Finding a word or phrase.

Find Next searches down from the insertion point, while Find Previous searches up from the insertion point.

QuickFinding the next occurrence

Use the QuickFind buttons on the property bar to find the next or previous occurrence of desired text quickly. Click the word (or select the text) and then click QuickFind Next button or QuickFind Previous button.

QuickFind matches on whole words only.

Selecting Find actions

The normal Find and Replace action is *Select Match* (see Figure 18-6), which lets you see and edit the found text.

Figure 18-6: Selecting Find actions.

Position Before or *Position After* on the Action menu puts the insertion point in front of or after the text, without selecting it. It will be hard to see where your found text is, however, because it isn't highlighted, and you won't even see the insertion point until you exit Find and Replace.

Extend Selection lets you extend the current selection to the specified word, phrase, or code.

Finding and replacing text or codes

You can automatically replace the text (or codes) you find. For example, if you were updating instructions you wrote for WordPerfect 8, you could change all occurrences of "WordPerfect 8" to "WordPerfect 9."

To find and replace text:

1. Press F2 (Edit ⇨ Find and Replace).

2. Type the search word or phrase, or click the drop-down list to select from the last ten entries.

 Tip   Select text, or a code in Reveal Codes, before starting your search to have it automatically appear in the field.

3. Type your replacement text in the "Replace with" box (see Figure 18-7).

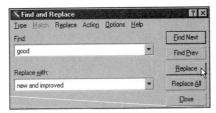

Figure 18-7: Finding and replacing text.

4. Select any options you want to change from the Find and Replace menu bar. (See "More Find and Replace tricks," later in this chapter.)

5. Click the following buttons, as needed:

 Tip   To use a "[?(One Char)]" or "[*(Many Char)]" (zero or more characters) wildcard code in your text searches, click Match ⇨ Codes, and then double-click the code to insert it (typed codes won't work). For example, a search on "wild[*(Many Char)]d" finds "wildcard," or "wildcatted." (You can't start a Find word with the "[*(Many Char)]" code.)

Click	In Order To
Find Next	Find the next occurrence of what you're looking for, with the option of replacing it or not
Find Prev	Find the previous occurrence
Replace	Replace the found item and search for the next. (to delete found text, leave the "Replace with" box empty or showing <Nothing>)
Replace All	Replace all found items without stopping

Finding and replacing all the forms of a word

To find and replace all the forms of a word, click Type ➪ Word Forms. You can then type **fly** in the Find box, for example, to find "fly," "flew," and "flying" in one search. If you also type **drive** in the "Replace with" box, you can replace the various forms of "fly" with "drive," "drove," and "driving" (see Figure 18-8).

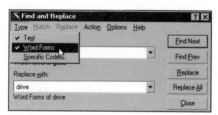

Figure 18-8: Finding and replacing all the forms of a word.

Finding and replacing specific codes

Click Type ➪ Specific Codes to find particular codes for margins, justification, fonts, and so on (see Figure 18-9).

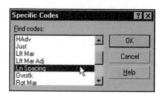

Figure 18-9: Finding and replacing specific codes.

Select the code type you want and then click OK, whereupon the appropriate Find and Replace code selections appear. You can, for example, search for a line spacing of 2 and replace it with a line spacing of 1.5, as shown in Figure 18-10. You can replace a font size of 15 with one of 18. To delete a code instead of replacing it, check "Replace with Nothing."

Tip   To see the codes you find, you must be in Reveal Codes.

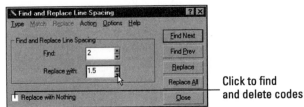

Click to find
and delete codes

Figure 18-10: Changing line spacing by using Find and Replace.

More Find and Replace tricks

Find and Replace offers can perform every trick you can think of. We explore them all in the next sections, going through each menu in the Find and Replace dialog box.

The Match menu

The Match menu, shown in Figure 18-11, presents the following options:

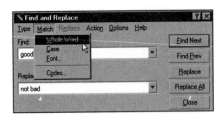

Figure 18-11: Find Match options.

✦ *Whole Word* matches only on separate words. For example, find the three-letter word "tip," but not "tipsy" or "multiple." When replacing, for example, "dog" with "cat," only a pedigree dog is replaced — you won't end up with "catmatic" or an "undercat."

✦ *Case* matches on the exact capitalization. When you type Help in the Find box, you get a match for "Help" or "Helps," but not for "help." Case is especially useful when you are searching for a product name such as "Windows" or a personal name such as "Gates."

✦ *Font* lets you search for text of a specific size, font, or other attribute (see Figure 18-12). You can, for example, limit your search to those occurrences of "Windows" that are in large type, as in a heading.

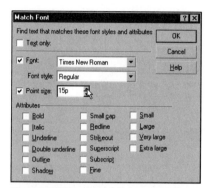

Figure 18-12: Matching text with a specific font and size.

✦ *Codes* lets you search for a code regardless of its value (see Figure 18-13). You can, for example, search for a [Graph Line] code to find and edit a graphics line. Check "Display merge codes only" to select merge codes instead of WordPerfect codes.

The Replace menu

The Replace menu presents the following options:

✦ *Case* replaces text exactly as entered in the "Replace with" box, not with the case of the text found in your document.

✦ *Font* specifies the font, size, and appearance of the replacement text.

✦ *Codes* specifies codes as described earlier in "Finding and replacing specific codes."

Tip

Enter the same text in both the "Find" and "Replace with" boxes to change only its characteristics, such as font or font size.

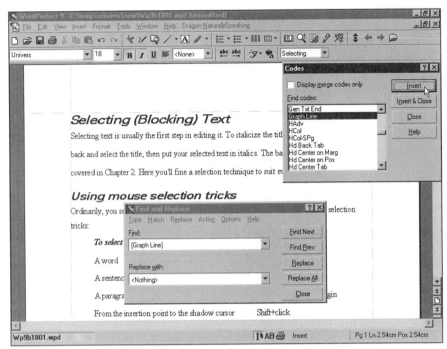

Figure 18-13: Finding a [Graph Line] code.

The Options menu

Normally, you search in all parts of your document, starting from the insertion point, going to the end of the document, and stopping there. Click Options to select from other search possibilities (see Figure 18-14), as shown in Table 18-2.

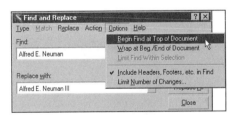

Figure 18-14: Search options.

When you don't specify an automatic wrap search, WordPerfect asks if you want to continue searching when it reaches the beginning or end of your document.

Table 18-2 Search Options	
Option	**Lets You**
Begin Find at Top of Document	Start each search from the beginning, no matter where you are.
Wrap at Beg./End of Document	Search the entire document, starting and ending at the insertion point.
Limit Find Within Selection	Search only selected text (automatic when a text block has been selected).
Include Headers, Footers, etc. in Find	Search all parts of your document, not just the body of your text (default).
Limit Number of Changes	Specify how many items can be replaced.

Inserting and Finding Bookmarks

You saw how to use the "stick-it-in-the-page-to-keep-your-place" QuickMark in Chapter 17, "Becoming an Instant WordPerfect Expert." Bookmarks are similar to the QuickMark, except that you can place as many as you want in a single document, and it takes three quick steps to access the marked place, instead of one. Bookmarks are especially useful for creating hypertext links for jumping from place to place.

Creating a bookmark

To create a bookmark:

1. Click where you want the bookmark.
2. Click Tools ⇨ Bookmark ⇨ Create.
3. Change the text that's automatically picked up to whatever name you like (see Figure 18-15).

Marking selected text with a bookmark

You can drag to select the text for your bookmark name before creating the bookmark. Selected text also gets surrounded by a pair of bookmark codes (unless you remove the Selected Bookmark check). You can automatically select the text again when you find the bookmark.

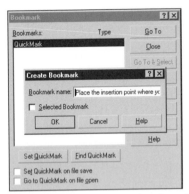

Figure 18-15: Creating a bookmark.

Finding a bookmark

To find a bookmark, click Tools ➪ Bookmark, and then select the bookmark and click Go To (or Go To & Select for a bookmark around selected text).

Moving a bookmark

To move a bookmark (such as when you must change the place of a hypertext link):

1. Click (or select the text) where you want to move the bookmark.

2. Click Tools ➪ Bookmark.

3. Select the bookmark; then click Move.

Note

When you move a selected text bookmark, only the bookmark is moved, not the text.

Renaming or deleting a bookmark

To rename or delete a bookmark, click Tools ➪ Bookmark, select the bookmark, and then click Rename or Delete.

Performing a Team Review

You can write memos and reports, and then send them to others to review as a team. Each person's changes and comments appear in a different color, with deletions showing as strikeout. Upon the document's return, the author can accept or reject the changes individually or as a group. The document can also be displayed without the markings, to see how it will appear if the changes are accepted.

The document under review can be routed manually from person to person, or automatically on a network. The identity of each reviewer is taken from environment settings (Tools ➪ Settings ➪ Environment).

Note

While the instructions here assume that the document has one author, and one or more reviewers, anyone who handles the document can act as an author, a reviewer, or both.

Adding changes as a reviewer

When a document is sent to you for review, the editing changes you make appear in the color you select. You will also see the editing changes made by previous reviewers.

To review the document you received:

1. Open the document, and then click File ➪ Document ➪ Review ➪ Reviewer. (Enter your name and initials, if prompted.)

2. Click the "Set color" button if you want to change your review color (see Figure 18-16).

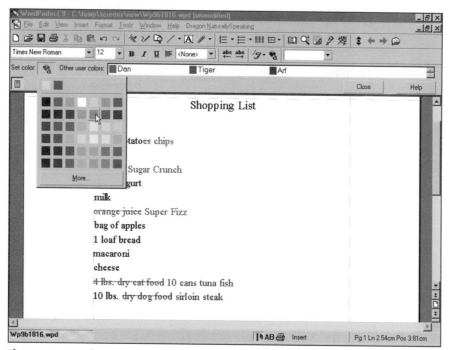

Figure 18-16: Changing the review color.

3. Edit the document:

- Use any editing feature other than sort, such as changing the margins or inserting a graphic (only text changes are marked in your color).

- Edit additions made by others (you can't undo deletions).

- Click the Review Document button to toggle the display of colored markings and deleted (strikeout) text off and on.

4. Click File ⇨ Save to save your changes.

Incorporating changes as the author

To accept or reject changes made by the reviewers:

1. Open the document, and then click File ⇨ Document ⇨ Review ⇨ Author.

2. As you review the document, click any of the buttons (see Figure 18-17), shown in Table 18-3.

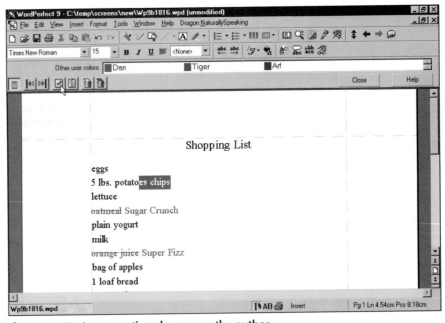

Figure 18-17: Incorporating changes as the author.

3. Click File ⇨ Save to save your changes.

Table 18-3
Review Options

Button	Lets You
▤	Toggle the display of colored markings and deleted (strikeout) text off and on
▸▸❙	Jump to the next revision
❙◂◂	Jump to the previous revision
☑	Accept the current revision
☑	Accept all the revisions, other than those you already rejected
🗑	Reject the current revision (that is, keep the text as you wrote it)
🗑	Reject all the revisions, other than those you already accepted

Tip Once you accept or reject a revision, you can't reverse your decision with Undo. Instead, close the document without saving your changes, and then reopen the document and review it again.

Comparing Two Versions of a Document

Sometimes you want to compare the current screen document with an earlier version on disk. Suppose you're editing a paper, and you realize that some of the old wording may be better than the new. With document compare, you can compare versions , and keep the best from each.

New Feature You have the option to view your comparisons in Author Review mode, where it's easy to accept or reject document revisions. You can compare with any document that WordPerfect can read, including those in Microsoft Word.

Document Compare looks at two versions of a document (either two author versions, or one version by the author and another by the reviewer), and then creates a third document showing the differences between the two.

Note Corel Versions provides a workgroup-oriented system for maintaining and comparing document versions (see Chapter 6, "Working Without Worries").

Comparing document versions in Author Review mode

To compare the current screen document with one on disk in Author Review mode:

1. Click File ⇨ Document ⇨ Compare.
2. Specify the disk document you're comparing with (see Figure 18-18).

Figure 18-18: Comparing document versions.

3. Click whether to show the markings in a new document or the current one.
4. Click Settings ⇨ Compare Then Review to change any of the first three options described in Table 18-4.

Table 18-4 Document Markup Settings	
Setting	**Lets You**
Options	
Marking precision	Choose to mark your changes by the word or character-by-character.
Characters to enclose text to skip in comparison	Specify characters (such as "{}") to surround a passage you want to exclude.
Include in comparison	Include headers, footers, comments, and expanded master documents in your comparison.
Summary of comparison	Display a summary of the document revisions (refer to Figure 18-21).
List of changes	Display a listing of the particular changes, with or without the surrounding context.

Setting	Lets You
Insertions	
Appearance	Select the style for inserted text.
Color	Select the text color for inserted text.
Enclose text with	Surround inserted text with brackets, braces, or other symbol pairs.
Deletions	
Appearance	Select the style for deleted text.
Color	Select the color for deleted text.
Enclose text with	Surround deleted text with brackets, braces, or other symbol pairs.
Show deleted text as	Show deleted text in full, abbreviated, as a symbol, or not at all.
Moves	
Show moves at	Show moves at both locations, just the new location, or not at all.
Color	Select the color for moved text.
Redline Method	
Method	Set the redline method for print insertions to your printer's default (usually a shaded background), marks in the left margin, right margin, or alternating margins (left margin of even pages and the right margin of odd pages).
Redline character	Specify a different redline indicator (a vertical bar with the printer default). Press Ctrl+W to change the symbol.

5. Click Compare/Review, and then review the document changes (see Figure 18-19), just as you would in performing a team review, as described in "Incorporating changes as the author," earlier in this chapter.

6. Click the Save button (File ➪ Save), if you want to keep the results of your review.

Comparing two document versions in Markup mode

To compare the current screen document with one on disk in Markup mode:

1. Follow Steps 1–3 in "Comparing document versions in Author Review mode" above.

2. Click Settings ➪ Compare Only to change any of the settings described in Table 18-4 (see Figure 18-20).

Deleted
(strikeout)

Moved
(Delete/add)   Added

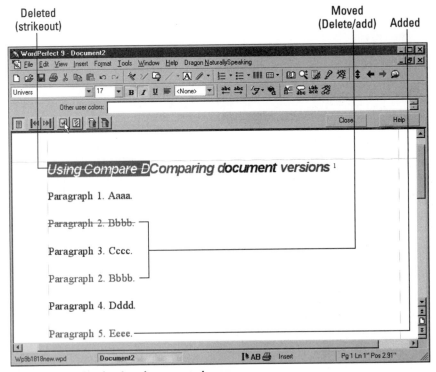

Figure 18-19: Reviewing document changes.

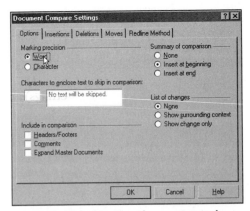

Figure 18-20: Changing document markup settings.

3. Click Compare Only to generate the comparison, with a summary of the changes on top, and markings to show what text has been inserted, deleted, or moved (see Figure 18-21).

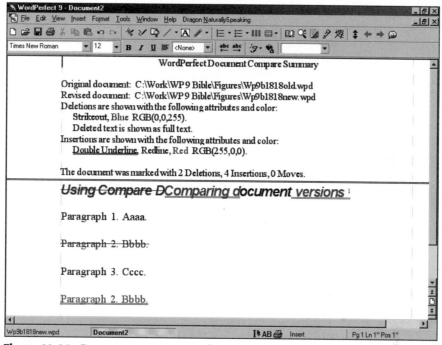

Figure 18-21: Document compare markup.

4. Review your document changes, and then click File ⇨ Document ⇨ Remove Markings and select one of the following (see Figure 18-22):

- *Remove redline markings and strikeout text* removes markings from inserted text and removes deleted text (depending on the document markup settings).

- *Remove strikeout text only* removes deleted text but keeps insertion markings (depending on the document markup settings).

- *Remove document compare deletions only* removes deletions but keeps the compare summary and insertion markings.

- *Remove all document compare markings* returns your document to its original condition.

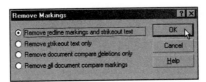

Figure 18-22: Removing comparison markings.

5. Click the Save button (File ➪ Save) if you want to keep the results of your review.

Tip   This feature lets you exclude additions to your new document that you don't want to mark, or passages in the old document that you've deleted.

Inserting Nonprinting Comments

A reviewer can insert comments in a document, with the reviewer's name, initials, and color, rather than perform a document review. Comments can also serve as personal reminders or notes. They neither print nor affect page numbering.

Creating comments

To add one or more comments to a line of text:

1. Click where you want the comment, and then click Insert ➪ Comment ➪ Create. This opens a blank comment screen that looks like a new document screen.

2. Click to insert your initials, your name, the date, or the time. (Click Tools ➪ Settings ➪ Environment to change your name, initials, or comment color.)

3. Type the comment, which can include tables, graphics, and other document elements (see Figure 18-23).

4. Click the Next or Previous button to see or edit other comments, or click the Close button to return to your document.

Converting document text to a comment

If you want to print or distribute an unfinished document, you can convert rough notes or other unfinished text to a comment. As a comment, it won't print until you've edited it into its finished form, and converted it back to text:

1. Select the text.

2. Click the Comment button (Insert ➪ Comment ➪ Create).

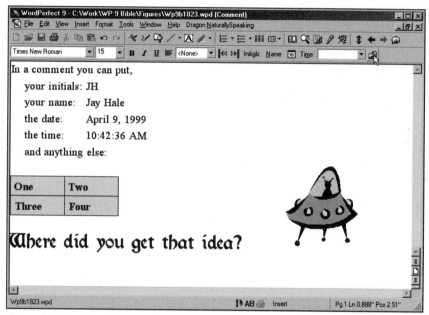

Figure 18-23: Creating a comment.

Viewing and hiding comments

Comments display as shaded text in Draft view. In Page or Two Page view, click the icon (the author's initials or a miniature text bubble) to display a comment (see Figure 18-24). Click outside the comment to hide it again.

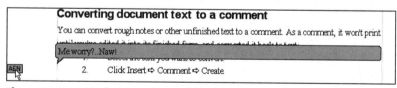

Figure 18-24: Displaying a comment in Page view.

If there is more than one comment on a line in Page view, click the multiple-comment icon, and then click the icon for the particular comment you want to view.

Editing or deleting a comment

To edit a comment, such as to expand a note into full-blown text:

1. Double-click the comment icon (or the comment in Draft view).

2. Edit the comment, and then click the close button.

You can also right-click a comment (or comment icon) to cut, copy, delete, or edit the comment.

Converting a comment to text

Once you edit and expand your comment notes, you can convert them into regular document text. Afterward, you might need to edit the punctuation and format to blend the notes into the existing content.

Tip   To print a comment without converting it to text, click File ➪ Print while editing the comment. The Full Document print selection prints only the comment.

To convert a displayed comment to text and make it a full part of the document, right-click the comment, and then click Convert to Text. (In Draft view, click the comment, and then right-click the bubble.)

Moving or copying a comment

To move or copy a comment, right-click the comment icon (or the comment in Draft view), and then click Cut (to move it) or Copy (to copy it), and paste it in the new location.

Tip   To delete all comments from the insertion point on, click Edit ➪ Find and Replace, click Match ➪ Codes, and then double-click the Comment code. Leave the "Replace with" box empty, and click Replace All.

Printing a comment

To print a comment, double-click the icon (or the comment in Draft view), and then click File ➪ Print, then click Print.

Using Hidden Text

You can think of hidden text as an "invisible ink" font attribute. Like a comment, it can either be hidden or displayed. However, you wouldn't use hidden text for group reviewing or to post notes to yourself, because it affects page numbering and prints when it's not hidden. Use it to include questions, notes, or comments in your document that you can alternately hide or display and print. For example, you might use hidden text to hide the answers to a quiz on the copy you print and give to students.

Hidden text is indistinguishable from regular text when displayed, so it can be printed without conversion. Hidden text expands into view when you want to see it (it even affects page numbers) and shrinks to nothing when you don't. In its normal hidden state, hidden text doesn't even leave an icon behind, as a comment does.

Tip   Open Reveal Codes and place the insertion point at the right of a Hidden code to view its text.

Creating hidden text

To create hidden text:

1. Click the View menu and make sure that Hidden Text is checked (so that you see the text as you create it).

2. Place the insertion point where you want to create the hidden text (or select the text you want to hide).

3. Click Format ⇨ Font, and then check Hidden in the Appearance group.

4. To resume typing normal text, press the right-arrow key to jump past the Hidden code, or repeat Step 3, removing the check.

At this point, your hidden text is still displayed. To hide it, click the View menu and remove the check from Hidden Text.

Tip   To include hidden text in Spell Checker, Grammar Checker, Find, and other operations, including page counts, be sure that Hidden Text is checked in the View menu.

Converting and deleting hidden text

When hidden text is displayed (checked on the View menu) you can edit it and delete it, just as you would ordinary text. You can convert it to regular text by going into Reveal Codes and deleting one of the surrounding Hidden codes.

When hidden text is not displayed, deleting a Hidden code deletes the text as well, so be careful (see Figure 18-25).

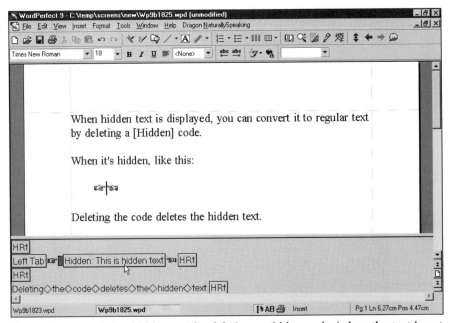

Figure 18-25: Deleting hidden text by deleting a Hidden code (when the text is not displayed).

For More Information . . .

✦   ✦   ✦

Printing Documents, Booklets, and Envelopes

✦   ✦   ✦   ✦

In This Chapter

Use all the print selection tricks

Print multiple pages and copies

Print posters and thumbnails

Do two-sided printing

Add a binding offset

Create custom print settings

Publish booklets

Print envelopes

✦   ✦   ✦   ✦

WordPerfect's printing facilities do everything from finding the mailing address for an envelope to creating booklets ready to be stapled down the middle. You can customize every aspect of printing and create custom settings for different situations.

This chapter covers WordPerfect-specific printing options. Office-wide printing techniques and printer selection are covered in Chapter 13, "Printing and Faxing Information." Publishing to PDF is covered in Chapter 14, "Web Writing and Publishing."

Printing All or Part of a Document

To print all or part of a WordPerfect document:

1. Click the Print button on the toolbar, or click File ⇨ Print. (You can also press Ctrl+P or F5 on a Windows keyboard; Shift+F7 on a DOS keyboard.)

2. Specify what you want to print (see Figure 19-1):

   - *Full document* or *Current page* to print the entire document, or the page at the insertion point.

   - *Multiple Pages* to print particular pages, secondary pages, chapters, or volumes (see "Printing multiple pages," later in this chapter).

• *Print pages* to specify a from-to range of consecutive pages.

• *Selected text* to print text you select.

Tip

Selected text prints in the same page position as it appears onscreen. To have it start printing at the top of the page, enter a hard page break (Ctrl+Enter) just before your passage. Press Ctrl+Z to remove the break after your passage prints.

• *Document summary* to print only the document summary.

Tip

Click the Details tab and check "Include document summary" to print the text and summary.

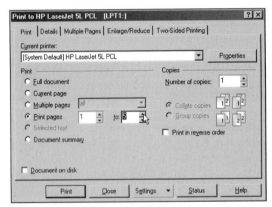

Figure 19-1: Specifying a range of consecutive pages to print.

3. Specify any of the copy, resolution, color, and other options discussed in the sections to follow.

4. Click Print.

Tip

Press Ctrl+Shift+P on a Windows keyboard to print your entire document.

Printing multiple pages

Click File ➪ Print ➪ Multiple Pages to print particular pages, secondary pages, chapters, or volumes, as shown in the examples (see Figure 19-2).

You can click a list button to select any of the last ten multiples you specified.

The volumes you specify take precedence over other settings, followed by chapters, secondary pages, and pages. For example, if you type 3 in the Chapter(s) box, only pages from Chapter 3 will print, even if pages from other chapters are specified in the Page(s)/label(s) box.

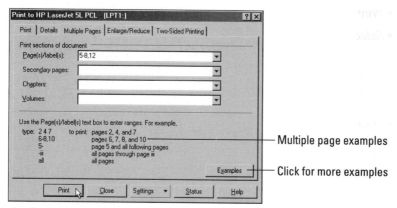

Figure 19-2: Printing multiple pages.

If your document has multiple sections (that is, you have reset the page numbers along the way), you can designate the section, followed by a colon (:), in the Page(s)/label(s) box. For example, if you specify 3:2–5, pages 2–5 in the third section will print. Click Examples for more information.

To print only odd or even pages, see "Two-sided printing," later in this chapter.

Cross-Reference For more on numbering pages, see Chapter 20, "Controlling Text and Numbering Pages."

Printing a document on disk

You don't have to open a document in order to print it. To print a document on disk:

1. Click File ⇨ Print, check "Document on disk," and specify the file you want to print.

2. Specify the pages, copies, and other options, just as you do for a screen document.

Tip You can also print documents from the Open File dialog box (see Chapter 7, "Managing Your Files").

Printing multiple copies

To print multiple copies of your document:

1. Click File ⇨ Print, specify what you want to print, and then specify the number of copies you want (see Figure 19-3).

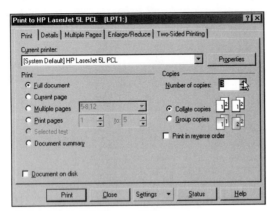

Figure 19-3: Printing multiple copies.

2. Click Collate to print each copy of the entire document before starting on the next copy. Click Group to print all the copies of page 1, then all the copies of page 2, and so on.

3. Click Print.

Caution

The number of copies (like other print settings) stays set for the remainder of the current session, unless you set it back.

Specifying resolution and graphics

To print a document in a hurry (or to save on ink or toner), you can print your text and graphics at less than the highest quality. You can also choose not to print graphics at all—perhaps to proofread text without the distraction of graphics:

1. Click File ⇨ Print. Specify what you want to print, and then click the Details tab and specify High, Medium, or Low in the Resolution drop-down list (see Figure 19-4). Print quality options vary from printer to printer.

2. To print your document without graphics, check "Print text only."

Choosing color or black-and-white

If your printer supports color, you can print colors in black and white by deselecting "Print in color" on the Details tab.

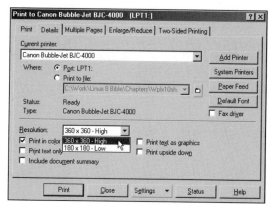

Figure 19-4: Specifying resolution and graphics.

Printing posters and thumbnails

You can enlarge or reduce the printed image to produce multipage posters, thumbnail prints, or anything in between. Click File Í Print Í Customize, and then click any of the following:

✦ Poster, to select a multiple page size from 2 × 2 (four pages) to 6 × 6 (36 pages!) You'll have to trim the pages to put the poster together.

✦ Enlarge/Reduce, to adjust the size of the image from 10 to 600% (6 × 6 pages).

✦ Scale to fit output page, to fit each current document page to the output page size you specify.

✦ Print thumbnails, to put up to 64 miniature pages on a single sheet, with options for page order, numbers, and borders (see Figure 19-5).

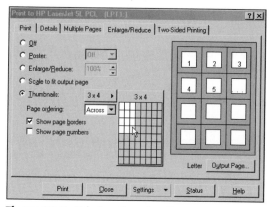

Figure 19-5: Printing thumbnails.

Two-sided printing

Few desktop printers support double-sided printing (duplexing), but you can usually print pages on one side and then turn them over and print on the other. Because there are always at least as many odd pages as even ones, consider printing the even pages first. That way you'll never have a page left in the paper tray after printing the reverse side.

The following method works on many printers:

1. Click File ➪ Print, specify what you want to print, and then check "Print in reverse order."

2. Click the Two-Sided Printing tab, click "Step 2: print even pages," and then click Print (see Figure 19-6).

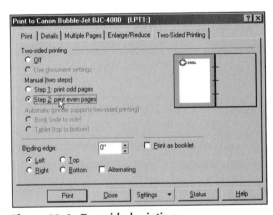

Figure 19-6: Two-sided printing.

3. When the even pages are printed, turn the pages the opposite way and reload them.

4. Repeat Steps 1 and 2, but this time uncheck "Print in reverse order" and print the odd pages.

Various printers handle pages differently, so experiment on a small scale to find the two-sided printing method that works for you.

Caution   Your printer manual might warn you that paper jams can result if you try to print on both sides of the page with your printer. Better-quality, long-grain paper is less likely to jam.

Adding a binding offset

When you create a document that is to be printed and bound, you can add an offset to keep text from disappearing into the bound margin. You can use two types of binding offset:

✦ One that *enlarges* the inside (bound) margin (for single-sided printing, simply adjust the left margin)

✦ One that *shifts* the printed image away from the binding (widens one margin and narrows the other)

It's best to enlarge the bound margin, although you may need to readjust text and graphics when you apply it to an existing document. The image offset is best used for an existing document that you want to shift outward but otherwise leave unaltered.

To apply an offset that enlarges the bound margin:

1. Place the insertion point on the page where you want the offset to begin.
2. Click File ➪ Page Setup ➪ Margins/Layout.
3. Click "Book" or "Tablet," depending on how your document is to be bound (see Figure 19-7).

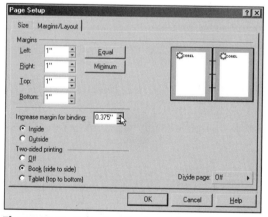

Figure 19-7: Enlarging the bound margin.

4. Click "Inside" or "Outside" and specify the amount to add to the margin.

Preview your binding offset in Two-Page view (see Figure 19-8).

Binding offset

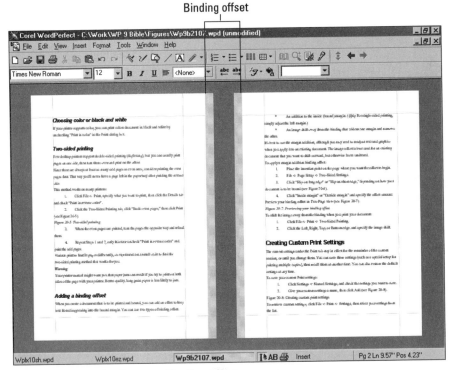

Figure 19-8: Previewing your binding offset.

To shift the image away from the binding when you print your document:

1. Click File ➪ Print ➪ Two-Sided Printing.
2. Click the Left, Right, Top, or Bottom edge, and specify the image shift.
3. Check Alternating to alternate between left and right or top and bottom shifting.

Creating Custom Print Settings

The current settings under the Print tab stay in effect for the remainder of the current session, or until you change them. You can save these settings (such as a special setup for printing multiple copies), and then recall them at another time. You can also restore the default settings at any time.

To save your current Print settings:

1. Click Settings ⇨ Named Settings, and check the settings you want to save.

2. Give your custom settings a name; then click Add (see Figure 19-9).

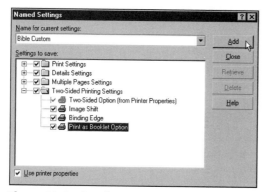

Figure 19-9: Creating custom print settings.

To retrieve custom settings, click File ⇨ Print ⇨ Settings, and then select your settings from the bottom of the list.

To update custom settings, retrieve them, change any of your print options, click Settings ⇨ Named Settings, select the name of the settings from the list, and click Replace.

To save your current settings as the application default, Click File ⇨ Print ⇨ Settings ⇨ Application Default ⇨ Replace ⇨ OK.

To retrieve your default settings, click File ⇨ Print ⇨ Settings ⇨ Application Default ⇨ Retrieve.

To restore your printer properties for such items as resolution, printing of graphics, and number of copies, click File ⇨ Print ⇨ Settings ⇨ Retrieve Properties.

To view or change your printer's properties, click File ⇨ Print ⇨ Properties. Refer to your printer manual and online Help for more information on setting your printer's properties.

Printing Booklets

Booklet printing is a simple and ingenious way to print small phone directories, instructions, menus, and other booklets.

The secret of booklet printing is to first subdivide each physical page of your document into two logical pages. When you print your document as a booklet, your printed pages come out in proper sequence, ready to staple and fold as a booklet.

The page can be divided either horizontally or vertically. (If you subdivide the page into more than two logical pages, you get an error message when you try to print them as a booklet.)

To print your document as a booklet:

1. Place the insertion point at the beginning of the file, and then click File ⇨ Page Setup ⇨ Size.

2. To change to a landscape page layout, click Landscape.

Tip   Landscape orientation on letter-size paper makes a handy booklet when folded in half lengthwise. In its normal (portrait) orientation, letter-size paper makes an attractive menu or brochure.

3. To subdivide your pages, click the Margins/Layout tab, click the Divide page button, and then specify 2 columns and 1 row (see Figure 19-10).

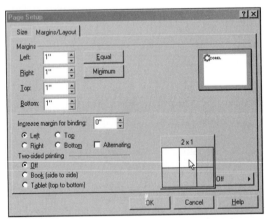

Figure 19-10: Subdividing landscape page layout to create a booklet.

4. While on the Margins/Layout tab, you may want to specify smaller margins, such as 0.5″ in proportion with your smaller pages.

Tip   A smaller font can be helpful too.

5. It helps to set up page numbering (Format ⇨ Page ⇨ Numbering) to arrange your pages after they're printed.

6. Make any editing or formatting changes to your document. (If you want to get fancy, create a title page.) Use Make It Fit (see Chapter 17) to adjust to the number of pages you want. To preview how your pages will print, click the Zoom button on the toolbar to switch to Full Page zoom (see Figure 19-11).

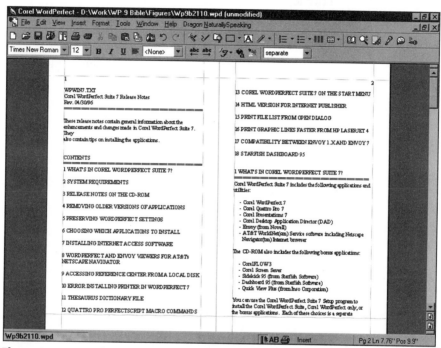

Figure 19-11: Previewing your booklet by zooming to Full Page.

7. Now print your booklet. Click File ➪ Print ➪ Two-Sided Printing, check "Print as booklet," and then click Print. Four booklet pages print on each physical page (two on each side). A 14-page booklet, for example, prints on four pages.

8. Follow the prompts to re-insert your pages, one page at a time, removing any printer pauses (see Figure 19-12).

Figure 19-12: Re-insert pages one at a time.

9. Assemble the pages in the proper order and then fold them. Your booklet is finished!

Creating and Printing Envelopes

New Feature When you produce an envelope in WordPerfect, an envelope page is added to the end of your document, which you can format and print. WordPerfect can automatically pick up the mailing address from your letter and create a bar code out of the zip code.

To create and print an envelope:

1. Select the address, if you don't think WordPerfect will find it.

2. Click Format ➪ Envelope. The last return address you used is displayed (see Figure 19-13). The mailing address also appears if WordPerfect found it, or you selected it.

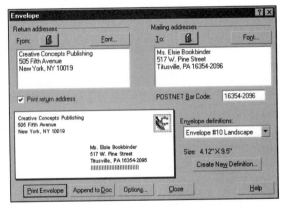

Figure 19-13: Creating and printing an envelope.

3. Click the Envelope Return Address button to select from the last ten return addresses used, or to select one from the Address Book. You can also type the return address. Click the Envelope Mailing Address button to do the same with the mailing address.

4. Select any fonts or formatting from the property bar or menus.

5. Click the Envelope Bar Code button to choose whether to print a USPS bar code and where (Figure 19-14).

Figure 19-14: Selecting bar code options.

6. Drag the guidelines or click the Envelope Position button to change the positions of the return and mailing addresses (Figure 19-15). The adjustments you make apply to all envelopes you print by using that envelope definition.

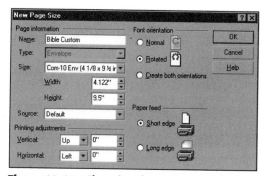

Figure 19-15: Changing the positions of the mailing and return addresses.

7. Click the Envelope Size button if you want to select another envelope size.

8. The envelope will print when you print your document, and the printer will pause for you to insert the envelope. To print the envelope on its own, click File ➪ Print, then select "Current page" and click Print.

To print envelopes with mailing lists and form letters, see Chapter 27, "Mass-Producing with Labels and Merge."

Creating a new envelope definition

If the envelope you're using isn't among the listed sizes, you can create a new definition for it:

1. Click Format ➪ Envelope, then click the Envelope Size button and click Page Setup.

2. Click Options ➪ New and give your envelope a name.

3. Select an envelope size or specify a custom width and height.

4. Specify the paper source, printing adjustments, font orientation, and whether to show the envelope for all printers or just the current one. For more on creating a custom page definition, see Chapter 21, "Formatting Your Document."

Deleting an envelope definition

To delete an envelope definition you no longer want, click File ⇨ Page Setup ⇨ Size, select the envelope definition you want to delete, and then click Delete.

For More Information . . .

On	*See*
Office-wide printing techniques	Chapter 13
Numbering pages	Chapter 20
Printing from the Open dialog box	Chapter 7
Using Make It Fit	Chapter 17
Creating mailing lists and form letters	Chapter 27
Creating a custom page definition	Chapter 21
Printer selection	Chapter 13
Faxing	Chapter 13
Publishing to PDF	Chapter 14

✦   ✦   ✦

Controlling Text and Numbering Pages

Using a word processor can be akin to riding a wild stallion — exhilarating power and speed, with an unnerving lack of control. How do you rein in automatic hyphenation for a particular word, or keep a paragraph from breaking across two pages? You certainly don't want to number pages by hand, but what do you do when the automatic page number gets in the way of an illustration or chart? If you're writing a book, how do you ensure that every chapter starts on an odd-numbered page?

Avoid the crude approach. That's when, for example, you want a particular paragraph to start at the top of the next page, so you push it there by inserting blank lines. You're left with a gaping hole on your screen that you must shrink or enlarge if you change your font, use a different printer, or go back to edit your text. This chapter shows you neater and simpler ways to position text, break it apart, or keep it together.

Using Hyphenation

Hyphenation divides words at the right margin when the whole word can't fit on the line. Hyphenation can be turned on or off (the default). When it's on, WordPerfect handles hyphenation in one of three ways — depending on the hyphenation prompt option you specify. (See "Selecting the hyphenation prompt option," later in this chapter.)

Understanding hyphens, dashes, and hyphenation codes

Automatic hyphenation requires several types of hyphens, dashes, and hyphenation codes to handle possible situations. When WordPerfect hyphenates a word, it inserts an [Auto Hyphen EOL] code, instead of the hyphen character. That way, the hyphen automatically disappears should you edit your text so that the hyphenated word is no longer at the end of the line.

Sometimes the program can prompt you to tell it where to place the hyphen. When that happens, a [- Soft Hyphen] code normally is permanently inserted, so you won't be prompted again as the word moves back and forth from the margin.

Soft hyphens are but one of the types of hyphens, dashes, and hyphen codes you can use, as shown in Table 20-1.

Table 20-1		
Hyphens, Dashes, and Hyphen Codes		
Typed	*Code Display*	*What It Does*
Typed Hyphen	[-Hyphen]	Connects two words, as in "good-looking."
Hyphen character or "hard" hyphen	[-]	Like the typed hyphen, except a word with this character will not break across lines when hyphenation is on; the entire word will wrap to the next line.
Automatic hyphenation code	[Auto Hyphen EOL]	Inserted by automatic hyphenation. Disappears when it's no longer needed.
Soft Hyphen	[-Soft Hyphen]	Normally, inserted by hyphenation prompt. You can also insert it without being prompted to specify where a word hyphenates. A soft hyphen becomes visible and prints only when it divides the word.
Hyphenation Soft Return	[HyphSRt]	Like the soft hyphen, specifies where a word divides if it must be hyphenated, but without inserting a hyphen or space. Useful for words separated by slashes (such as Page Up/Page Down).
Em dash (WP character 4,34)	[:4,34]	Joins two related phrases with a long dash (—). Does not divide text at the right margin when hyphenation is on.

Typed	Code Display	What It Does
En dash (WP character 4,33)	[:4,33]	Indicates a range of numbers (as with page numbers), or separates parts of a phone number. Shorter than an em dash, but longer than a hyphen. Does not divide text at the right margin when hyphenation is on.
Hyphenation Ignore Word	[Cancel Hyph]	Keeps a word (such as a person's name) from being hyphenated. Instead of dividing at the right margin, the entire word wraps to the next line.

Turning on hyphenation

By "hyphenation," WordPerfect means automatic, end-of-the-line hyphenation. You can always split words with a hyphen character, em dash, or en dash, whether hyphenation is on or off. To turn on hyphenation:

1. Click in the paragraph where you want hyphenation to begin.

2. Click Tools ⇨ Language ⇨ Hyphenation.

3. Check "Turn hyphenation on" (see Figure 20-1).

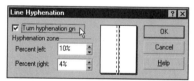

Figure 20-1: Turning on hyphenation.

Follow the same procedure, removing the check, to turn hyphenation off later in your document. To eliminate hyphenation from the document entirely, you can go into Reveal Codes and delete the [Hyph: On] code.

> **Tip**
>
> Hyphenation is off by default. To turn hyphenation on every time you open a new document, add the [Hyph: On] code to the Document Style in your default template (see Chapter 21, "Formatting Your Document").

Selecting the hyphenation prompt option

You can specify the way WordPerfect prompts you when hyphenation is on:

✦ *Always*, to ask you to position the hyphen every time a word can be hyphenated. This is for when you need total control over hyphenation, as in creating advertising copy.

✦ *Never*, to hyphenate words at the right margin without prompting. If the word is not in the main word list, the program uses built-in rules to determine where the hyphen goes.

✦ *When Required* (the default), to position the hyphenation manually only when the program doesn't recognize the word and can't figure out a syllable break.

To change the type of hyphenation prompt, click Tools ⇨ Settings ⇨ Environment, and then click the Prompts tab and select the option you want from the hyphenation prompt list (see Figure 20-2).

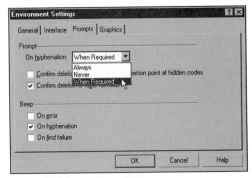

Figure 20-2: Setting the hyphenation prompt option.

Answering the hyphenation prompt

When hyphenation is on, WordPerfect tries to hyphenate a word if it spans both boundaries of the hyphenation zone at the right margin. The *hyphenation zone* is a percentage of the line width — the wider the zone, the fewer words hyphenated. When the line is narrow, as in tables or columns, more words are hyphenated. You can adjust the size of this zone by selecting Tools ⇨ Language ⇨ Hyphenation.

If WordPerfect can't find an appropriate hyphenation location, it normally prompts you for assistance (see Figure 20-3). If you set the hyphenation prompt option to Never, WordPerfect wraps the entire word to the next line without prompting.

Position the hyphen

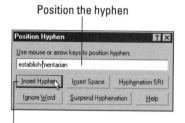

Figure 20-3: Answering the hyphenation prompt.

Click the hyphenation option

When you answer the hyphenation prompt:

1. Position the hyphen within the displayed word by using the arrow keys or by clicking the mouse.

2. Click the hyphenation option you want:

   • *Insert Hyphen*, to use a soft hyphen to divide the word.

   • *Insert Space*, to use a space to divide the word.

   • *Hyphenation SRt*, to divide the word without using a hyphen or space.

   • *Ignore Word*, to wrap the entire word to the next line by inserting a [Cancel Hyph] code.

   • *Suspend Hyphenation*, to temporarily turn off hyphenation during a spell-check or a scrolling command. The word wraps to the next line, but no code is inserted, so you'll be prompted again the next time around.

Manually inserting hyphens

To insert various hyphens and hyphenation codes manually, click Format ➪ Line ➪ Other Codes, and select the code to insert. You can also use keystrokes to insert several types of hyphens and hyphenation codes, as shown in Table 20-2.

Tip When manually hyphenating a word at the end of a line, use a soft hyphen. That way, the hyphen will disappear if it's no longer needed.

Table 20-2
Keystrokes for Hyphens and Hyphenation Codes

Type of Hyphen or Code	CUA Keystrokes	DOS Keystrokes
Hyphen	-	-
Hyphen character or hard hyphen	Ctrl+-	Home, -
Soft hyphen	Ctrl+Shift+-	Ctrl+-
Hyphenation soft return	(Click Format ⇨ Line ⇨ Other Codes)	Home, Enter
Cancel hyphenation of word (immediately before hyphenated word)	Ctrl+/	Ctrl+/

Inserting an em dash or an en dash

You can use em dashes and en dashes (the width of "M" and "N" characters, respectively) to give your documents the professional look of published books and articles. The long em dash (—) indicates a sudden break in thought that causes an abrupt change in sentence structure, or sets off a parenthetical phrase. The en dash (which is one-half the length of the em dash, but longer than the hyphen) is primarily used to indicate continuing numbers or dates, as in pp. 33–42, 1995–98, or Jan–Mar 1998.

When QuickCorrect or the Format-As-You-Go QuickSymbols is on, a triple-hyphen (---) automatically changes to an em dash, and a double-hyphen (--) becomes an en dash. When these features are off, you can press Ctrl+W, and then type **m**- or **n**-.

Breaking Text Apart and Keeping It Together

Arranging text on pages is similar to arranging words in lines—just on a larger scale. For example, if the introduction to your paper takes up less than a page, you may want to end the page there and start the main body of your text at the top of page two. Or, what if you want to make sure that a table or list stays on a single page? The following topics show you how to make sections of text behave.

Inserting page breaks

Normally, when you reach the bottom of a page, WordPerfect inserts a soft page break. That way, the page break will move when you go back and enter more text. But you can also specify precise page breaks in several ways.

Inserting hard page breaks

Sometimes, as with the start of a new chapter, you want to set where a page break should fall. In such cases, press Ctrl+Enter to insert a hard page break (you can also click Insert ➪ New Page). No matter how much text you add or delete, the page will always break at the point you set.

The page break appears as a Hard Page code ([HPg]) in Reveal Codes. You can tell where a hard page break is in Draft view mode by the double solid line across the page. In Page view, a thick black line appears between the pages.

To remove a Hard Page code, place the insertion point just before the page break and press Delete. You can also go into Reveal Codes to delete the [HPg] code.

Forcing a new page

A variation on the hard page break is forcing a new page. Use it when you want to ensure that a particular paragraph always appears at the top of a page. When you force a new page, a [Force: New] code is inserted at the beginning of the current paragraph. As you edit your document, the code stays attached to the paragraph.

To force a new page:

1. Place the insertion point in the paragraph where you want to force a new page.
2. Click Format ➪ Page ➪ Force Page ➪ Start new page (see Figure 20-4).

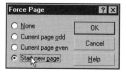 **Figure 20-4:** Forcing a new page.

To remove a Force New Page code, go into Reveal Codes and delete the [Force: New] code.

Keeping paragraphs and lines together

Up to this point you've used "page surgery" to break the current page apart or start a new page. Now you'll see how to keep lines and paragraphs together on the same page.

Keeping a block of text together

You can block protect a selection of text to keep it from splitting across two pages. To keep a block of text together:

1. Select the text. (To keep table rows together, select all the rows.)

2. Click the Block Protect icon. (You can also right-click the block and click Block Protect, or click Format ⇨ Keep Text Together, and check "Block protect.")

The protected block might expand or shrink as you edit it, but the program always tries to keep it together on one page. If the protected block is about to spill over to the next page, the program inserts a soft page break at the beginning of the protected block to move it to the top of the next page.

To remove block protect, open the Reveal Codes window and delete one of the surrounding [Block Pro] codes.

Keeping a number of lines together

You can keep a specified number of lines together with "conditional end of page." Use it to prevent a single-line heading from getting stranded, alone, at the bottom of a page. To keep a number of lines together:

1. Place the insertion point on the first of the lines you want to keep together.

2. Click Format ⇨ Keep Text Together, and check "Number of lines to keep together" (see Figure 20-5).

Figure 20-5: Keeping a number of lines together.

3. Specify the number of lines to keep together (including blank lines).

This feature inserts a single [Condl EOP: #] code. You can go into Reveal Codes to remove it.

Tip   Add conditional end of page to your heading styles, to apply to your headings automatically.

Caring for widows and orphans

Widow/orphan protection prevents one line of a paragraph from getting stranded, alone, at the bottom or top of a page. To enable widow/orphan protection in all or part of your document:

1. Click on the page where you want widow/orphan protection to begin.

2. Click Format ➪ Keep Text Together, and then check "Prevent the first and last lines of paragraphs from being separated across pages" (refer to Figure 20-5).

This places a single [Wid/Orph] code, which can be deleted in Reveal Codes.

Tip To protect every new document, include widow/orphan protection in the Document Style of your default template (see Chapter 21, "Formatting Your Document").

Numbering Pages

Page numbering can be as simple as putting a number at the top of the page, or as sophisticated as including chapter and volume numbers, starting each section on an odd page, or designing a custom numbering format.

Numbering pages in a standard position and format

WordPerfect makes it easy to insert automatic page numbering in standard positions and various formats. To number pages in standard position and format:

1. Place the insertion point on the page where you want the numbering to begin.

2. Click Format ➪ Page ➪ Numbering.

3. Click the Position list and select a page numbering location (see Figure 20-6).

Tip Use the alternating selections for facing pages, as in a book.

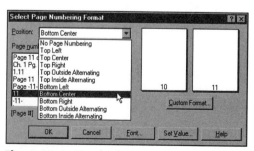

Figure 20-6: Numbering pages in a standard position.

4. Select a page numbering format (see Figure 20-7). (Click "Page *x* of *y*" to display both the current page number "x" and the total number of pages "y".)

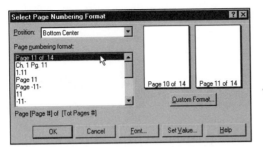

Figure 20-7: Choosing a page numbering format.

Inserting a page number anywhere in your document's text

If you don't want to use a standard page numbering position on a particular page (such as one with a graphic or chart), you can insert an automatic page number anywhere in your document's text:

1. Click where you want the page number to appear.

2. Click Format ⇨ Page ⇨ Insert Page Number.

3. Select the type of page number you want, and then click Insert.

4. Click Format ⇨ Page ⇨ Suppress to suspend any standard numbering for the current page.

Tip To insert page numbers in headers or footers, click the Page Numbering button on the property bar (see Chapter 21, "Formatting Your Document").

Changing the appearance of page numbers

Page numbers normally appear in your document's default font. To change the font or appearance of your page numbers:

1. Place the insertion point on the page where you want the change in the font or appearance of the page numbers to begin.

2. Click Format ⇨ Page ⇨ Numbering.

3. Click Font to select the font face, style, size, color, and shading you want.

Creating custom page numbering formats

Although the standard page numbering formats will take care of nearly all of your page numbering needs, you can create custom numbering formats for practically any conceivable situation. Believe it or not, you can choose from five kinds of page numbers, and these can be displayed in any of five ways, together with any explanatory text. A numbering scheme of "Page iv of 127 in Part C" is not out of the question.

The five kinds of page numbers are as follows:

✦ *Page numbers* increment automatically with each new page. In most situations, this is the only type you'll need.

✦ *Total Pages* is the "y" of a "page x of y" format. The *y* refers to the last numbered page of the document, not necessarily the number of physical pages. For example, if a 30-page document is numbered i–x for the first 10 pages, and 1–20 for the last 20, the Total Pages value will be 20, not 30.

✦ *Chapter numbers* and *volume numbers* can identify the location of text in a large work. Use them for any document division, such as Book 3 or Part IV, not just chapters or volumes. These numbers are normally static, so you must adjust them manually when you get to a new division. For example, if the last page of Chapter 3 is "Chapter 3, Page 78," the first page of Chapter 4 will be "Chapter 3, Page 79," unless you change it.

✦ *Secondary page numbers*, which also increment with each page, are rarer than Elvis sightings. You might use them, for example, if you add 20 pages to the middle of a new edition of a scholarly text, and keep old page numbers along with the new, as in "page 332, old page 312."

Next, you have a choice of ways to display page numbers:

✦ Standard *Arabic numbers* (1,2,3).

✦ Lowercase or uppercase *Roman numerals* (i, ii, iii or I, II, III)

✦ Lowercase or uppercase *letters* (a, b, c or A, B, C)

You can mix and match the number types and displays, and then add any text to accommodate the most esoteric of page numbering schemes.

To create a custom page numbering format:

1. Place the insertion point on the page where you want to insert the custom format.

2. Click Format ⇨ Page ⇨ Numbering ⇨ Custom Format.

3. Type any accompanying text, such as "Volume" or "Page," in the "Custom page numbering format" box.

4. Select the display method for the kind of number you want, and then click "Insert in format" to insert the code (see Figure 20-8).

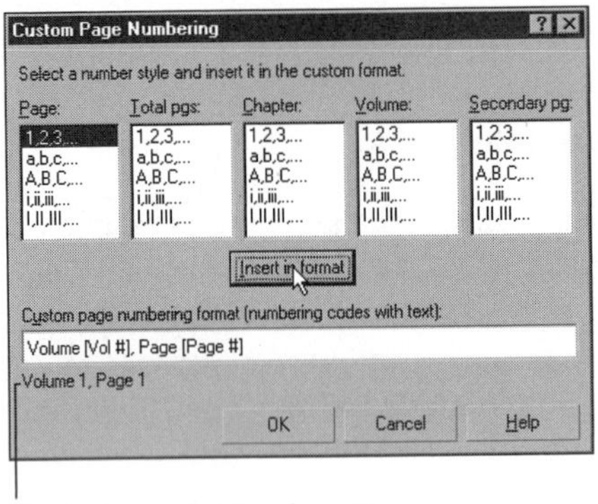

Preview your custom format

Figure 20-8: Creating a custom page numbering format.

5. Repeat Steps 3 and 4 for additional codes and text, such as "Volume II, Chapter 6, Page 342." Be sure to include punctuation and spaces. Preview your custom format just below the edit box.

Your last five custom numbering formats are added to the list of selectable formats. To remove one of your formats from the list, select it and press Delete.

Changing a page number's value and display

You can reset any type of page number (other than total pages) at any point in your document. If you are using chapter or volume numbers, for example, you'll need to manually change the number at the beginning of each chapter or volume.

You might want to change the number display at the same time that you change the number. For example, if you are numbering the Preface or Introduction to a work in lowercase Roman, you'll probably want to switch to regular Arabic numbers at the beginning of Chapter 1, and reset the page number to 1.

To change a page number's value and display:

1. Place the insertion point on the page where you want the change to begin.

2. Click Format ➪ Page ➪ Numbering ➪ Set Value.

3. Click the tab for the type of page number you want to change.

4. Set the page number to the value you want (see Figure 20-9).

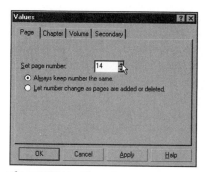

Figure 20-9: Changing a page number's value.

5. Click "Always keep number the same" to keep the number from changing as pages before it are added or deleted (as with "Page 1" for the beginning of Chapter 1). Click "Let number change . . ." to allow the number to increase or decrease in tandem with the number on the preceding page.

6. Click OK, and then select a new page numbering format if you also want to change the number display (as from Roman to Arabic).

Forcing an odd, even, or new page

At times, you might want to be sure that a certain page has an odd or even page number. Or you might want a table of contents, chapter, glossary, or index always to begin on a new page. If your publication is to have facing pages (as in a book), you might want the first page of each section to begin on a new page, and have an odd page number.

To force an odd, even, or new page:

1. Place the insertion point in the paragraph where you want to force an odd, even, or new page.

2. Click Format ➪ Page ➪ Force Page.

3. Click "Current page odd," "Current page even," or "Start new page" (see Figure 20-10).

Figure 20-10: Forcing an odd, even, or new page.

Note   When you force a page, a [Force: Odd], [Force: Even], or [Force: New] code is inserted at the beginning of the current paragraph at the insertion point. If you force an odd or even page, the program inserts a page break only if it needs to.

Suppressing page numbers

You may want to suppress page numbering on certain pages (such as the table of contents, chapter title pages, or on a page where a graph appears).

To suppress the page numbering on a particular page, click Format ⇨ Page ⇨ Suppress, and then check "Page numbering" or check "All" to suppress headers, footers, and watermarks as well (see Figure 20-11).

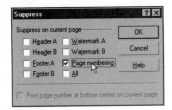

Figure 20-11: Suppressing a page number.

You can also check "Print page number at bottom center on current page," instead of suppressing it, so that it won't interfere with a title or heading.

For More Information . . .

On	See
Setting the default Document Style	Chapter 21
Understanding word lists	Chapter 52
Placing page numbers in headers and footers	Chapter 21

✦   ✦   ✦

Formatting Your Document

For all the fancy graphs, charts, images, sounds, and other special effects you can employ, most communication is still centered around the written word, packaged by the page.

This chapter takes you on a basic formatting tour, covering the line, paragraph, and page. Other formatting elements (such as columns and tables) are covered in subsequent chapters. Borders and fills are discussed in Chapter 54, "Adding Graphic Lines, Borders, and Fills."

Understanding Your Default Document Settings

Every document uses two default settings you can change:

+ A *Document Style* at the beginning of the document
+ The *default font* for the printer you've selected

When the Document Style is empty, it means you're starting with the default format for the language version you've installed. For the U.S. version of WordPerfect, this means a paper size of 8½ × 11 inches, one-inch margins all around, tabs every half inch, single-line spacing, left justification, and so on.

Any changes that you make while working in your document (such as to margins or tabs) take precedence over the default settings.

 Note When you insert another document into the one onscreen, the inserted text is stripped of its original Document Style.

Changing the Document Style

You can't delete the Document Style, but you can edit it to include your personal settings for tabs, margins, justification, and other formatting. You can apply these settings to all new documents you create, by saving them to the Document Style in your default template.

Note   Every document you create takes its initial formatting from either the default template or a selected special template for reports, memos, newsletters, and so on (see Chapter 28, "Working Quickly with Templates, Projects, and Styles").

To change the Document Style:

1. Click File ➪ Document ➪ Current Document Style.

2. Make sure that "Reveal codes" is checked in the Styles Editor dialog box so that you can see the codes you insert (see Figure 21-1).

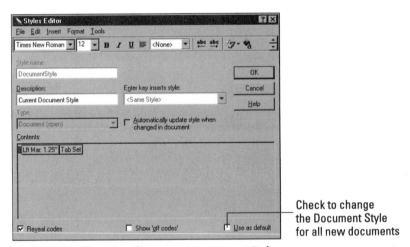

Check to change
the Document Style
for all new documents

Figure 21-1: Changing the current Document Style.

3. Select the formatting items you want to change from the Styles Editor menus, just as you would when working in your document.

4. To change the Document Style for all your new documents, check "Use as default."

Changing the default font

When you open a new document, the default font specified is that for the currently selected printer. To change the default font for all new documents:

1. Click File ⇨ Document ⇨ Default Font.

2. Select the font face, size, and style you want.

3. To change the default font for all new documents using the current printer, check "Set as default for all documents" (see Figure 21-2).

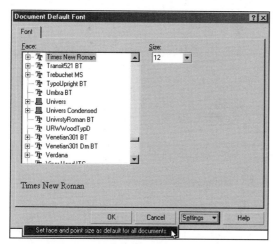

Figure 21-2: Changing the default font for all new documents.

Fine-Tuning Word and Letter Spacing

WordPerfect lets you customize the formatting of everything from the spacing between two letters to the size of your page. This chapter starts from the small end of the scale and works its way up. You'll start by learning how to adjust the space between particular pairs of letters and by refining the word and letter spacing throughout your document.

Adjusting the space between letter pairs

When text is printed, unwanted gaps may appear between certain letter pairs. These gaps are especially apparent between large characters found in advertisements or headlines.

You can use *automatic kerning* to adjust the space between all occurrences of certain letter pairs using instructions built into certain fonts. Use *manual kerning* to adjust the spacing between individual letter pairs, such as to tuck a lowercase "i" under an uppercase "T."

To set automatic kerning:

1. Place the insertion point where you want kerning to begin, or select the text that you want to kern.

2. Click Format ➪ Typesetting ➪ Word/Letter Spacing.

3. Check "Automatic kerning."

To adjust the kerning between a specific pair of characters manually:

1. Place the insertion point between the two characters you want to kern.

2. Click Format ➪ Typesetting ➪ Manual Kerning.

3. Adjust the amount of space between the characters (see Figure 21-3).

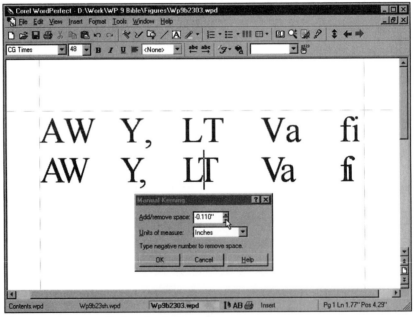

Figure 21-3: Manually kerning letter pairs.

Manual kerning inserts an [Hadv] code, as described in "Advancing text," later in this chapter.

Inserting an em space, en space, or small space

You may occasionally need to insert an em space, en space, or small space between characters. While there are no "space" characters in WordPerfect, you can use the following technique:

1. Type an em dash for an em space, a number for an en space, or period for a small space.

2. Select the em dash, number, or period, and then click the font color button on the toolbar (Format ➪ Font ➪ Color) and select the background color (normally white) to make the character invisible.

As an added convenience, you can create QuickWord entries of your whited-out characters (see Chapter 52, "Writers' Lib"), though you'll have to go back and remove the extra space preceding the QuickWords when you use them.

Adjusting word spacing, letter spacing, and justification limits

As you type, the spacing between letters and words is normally determined by WordPerfect, based on your current printer and font. While these settings will normally produce excellent results, you can use the program's sophisticated typesetting features if you need to adjust these settings manually or use the settings determined by the font manufacturer:

1. Place the insertion point where you want the new word spacing, letter spacing, or justification limits to begin, or select the text you want to adjust.

2. Click Format ➪ Typesetting ➪ Word/Letter Spacing.

3. Specify the "Word spacing" and "Letterspacing" settings (see Figure 21-4):

   • *Normal* (not the default) uses the font manufacturer's specifications.

   • *Percent of optimal* enables you to adjust WordPerfect's settings to increase or decrease the spacing between words or letters. You can set the pitch (characters per inch) instead of adjusting the percentage—the greater the pitch, the tighter the spacing.

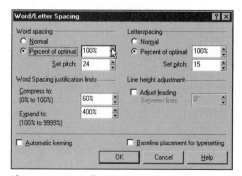

Figure 21-4: Adjusting word spacing, letter spacing, and justification limits.

4. Specify word spacing justification limits (for fully justified text):

- *Compress to* specifies how much the spacing between words can be squeezed to fit the words within the margins.

- *Expand to* specifies how much the spacing between words can be stretched to fill out the space between the margins.

Note   WordPerfect first tries to fit fully justified text to the margins by compressing or expanding the spaces between words, up to the percentage limits. If that isn't enough, the spacing between letters is adjusted as well.

Formatting Lines

You can specify several aspects of the document line, including tab settings, spacing, height, and justification. You can even have numbered lines.

Positioning text with tabs

A *tab* moves the insertion point and text to a specific location on the line. Press the Tab key to insert a [Left Tab] code and move to the next tab setting. Press Shift+Tab to insert a [Hd Back Tab] code and move left to the previous tab setting. (If you're in Typeover mode instead of Insert mode, pressing Tab or Shift+Tab only moves the insertion point through existing text. A tab code is inserted only if there is no text.)

Tip   If you press Tab and the insertion point doesn't move, you've probably reached the last tab setting before the margin.

By default, WordPerfect sets tabs every half inch relative to the left margin. (Moving the left margin normally shifts the tabs as well.) You can remove and reset tabs to position text exactly where you want it. For example, you can remove all but two tabs to set up two tabular columns.

Tip   You can also use columns or labels to line up your text. In particular, see the discussion of various types of columns (including tabular columns) in Chapter 22, "Formatting with Columns and Tables."

Understanding tab types

WordPerfect provides eight types of tabs to align your text. Left tabs are the default, which is why a [Left Tab] code is normally inserted when you press Tab.

Tab types are best shown by illustration, because it's easy to get confused by their names. A *left tab* stays to the left of your text, so the text you type moves to the right of the tab, as shown in Figure 21-5. A *right tab* stays to the right of your text, so the text you type moves to the left. Text centers around a *center tab*, and a *decimal tab* lines up your text on the decimal point (or another character you designate).

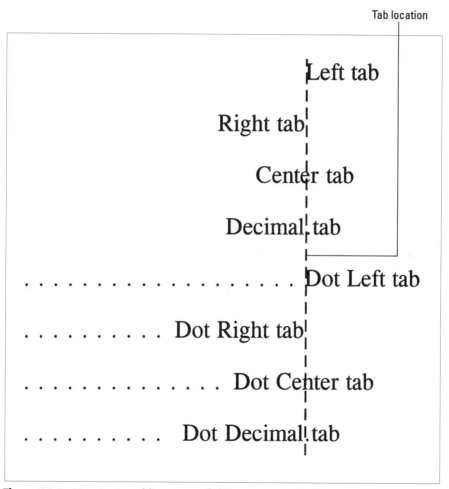

Figure 21-5: How text positions around different types of tabs.

When you use a *dot leader tab*, a row of dots (or whatever character you specify) appears from the insertion point to your tab-aligned text.

When you change the tab type, existing tab codes that follow your settings are converted (other than hard tabs, discussed later).

Setting Tabs

You can change tab settings from the current paragraph on through a document, or just in a block of selected text. Tabs can be set on the ruler, a tab bar, or in the Tab Set dialog box.

Setting tabs with the ruler

The ruler is a handy tool for setting tabs, because you can visualize the tabs as you set them. Click View ➪ Ruler to display the ruler (or press Alt+Shift+F3). The tab settings for the paragraph at the insertion point appear as various shaped triangles on the ruler.

You can click a tab marker and then drag it to a new position, or drag it down off the ruler to remove it (see Figure 21-6). To set a new tab, click the bottom of the ruler where you want it to appear.

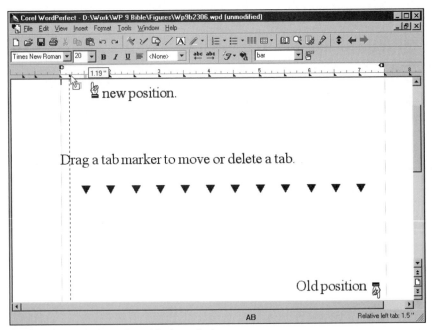

Figure 21-6: Setting tabs with the ruler.

Normally, when you set a tab using the ruler, it will snap to the nearest invisible grid line, located every $1/16$ of an inch, or every millimeter. You can turn off the ruler grid to drag a tab to any location. (Right-click the ruler, click Settings, and then uncheck "Tabs snap to Ruler grid.")

Changing the new tab type

When you click the bottom of the ruler to set a new (additional) tab, the tab is of the default type, normally a left tab. To change the new tab type, right-click anywhere along the lower edge of the ruler and select the type of tab you want (see Figure 21-7). To change an existing tab to the new type, click its icon on the ruler.

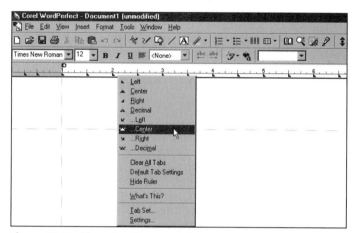

Figure 21-7: Changing the new tab type.

Tab settings affect text from the paragraph at the insertion point on.

Other ruler tricks

To clear all existing tabs, click in the paragraph where you want to clear the tabs, right-click the lower edge of the ruler, and then click Clear All Tabs. Click Default Tab Settings to return to the defaults instead.

To select several tab markers at once, hold down the Shift key and drag across the markers. You can then drag the selected markers to a new location, or delete them by dragging them down off the ruler. To copy the selected group of markers, hold down the Ctrl key as you drag them to a new location.

Using the tab bar

The tab bar, described in Chapter 16, "Mastering the WordPerfect Interface," looks and works exactly like the bottom of the ruler. The tab bar displays at the paragraph where the changes apply, rather than at the top of the screen.

Another subtle but significant point: The first time you display a tab bar in a particular paragraph, the default tab settings are automatically applied.

Using the Tab Set dialog box

For heavy-duty tab setting with all the options, place the insertion point where you want to change the settings, and then click Format ⇨ Line ⇨ Tab Set to call up the Tab Set dialog shown in Figure 21-8. (You can also right-click the ruler or tab bar and click Tab Set.)

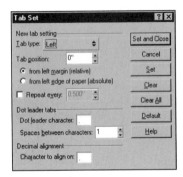

Figure 21-8: Tab Set dialog box.

Specifying a tab's type and position

Select the type of tab you want from the "Tab type" list in the Tab Set dialog box. Specify where you want to place each tab in the "Tab position" box. (You can type decimals or fractions.)

Normally, tabs position "from left margin (relative)." You can click "from left edge of paper (absolute)" to specify tabs that stay put as you adjust the left margin.

You must click the Set button for each setting you specify. (The new tab appears on the ruler.)

To place tabs at regular intervals, click Clear All, and then check "Repeat every," specifying an interval, and click Set.

Clearing tabs and restoring tab settings

The Clear button in the Tab Set dialog box lets you delete individual tabs, although the ruler and tab bar are better suited to that purpose. You can clear all the tabs, and then specify your settings, or click Default to return to the default tab settings.

Changing dot leaders and the align character

You can change the character used for dot leader tabs in the "Dot leader character" box. To create the line of scissors shown in Figure 21-9, press Ctrl+W to insert the iconic symbol 5,33. You can also specify the number of spaces between dot leader characters.

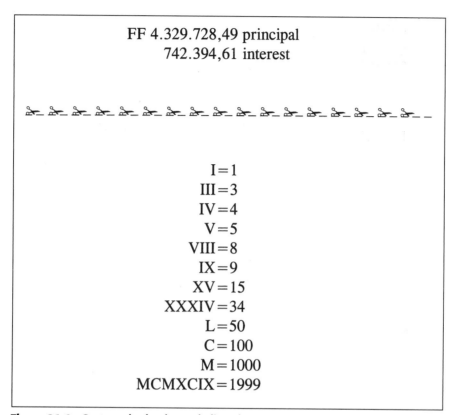

Figure 21-9: Custom dot leader and align characters.

When you use a decimal or dot decimal tab, your entries normally align on the decimal point for U.S. English. You can change this alignment character as well. Figure 21-9 illustrates decimal tabs aligned on commas (above the line of scissors) and equal signs (below the scissors).

Inserting hard tabs

Suppose you want to use a right tab or a decimal tab, instead of a left tab, in a particular line of text, without changing the tab type for the remainder of your document. Insert a *hard tab* of the type you want for one-time use. Hard tabs stay as the type you specify, even if you change the tab type in the rest of your document.

To place a hard tab, click Format ➪ Line ➪ Other Codes, and then click the type of tab you want and click Insert. (To insert a hard back tab, press Shift+Tab, or click Format ➪ Paragraph ➪ Back Tab.)

Indenting

Tabs shift text on a single line. To move all the lines in a paragraph to the next tab setting, use an indent instead of tabbing each line.

The easiest way to indent your text is to press F7 (F4 for a DOS-compatible keyboard). You can also right-click and click Indent, or click Format ⇨ Paragraph ⇨ Indent. The text that you type (until you press Enter) indents to the next tab stop.

When you indent existing text, all text from the insertion point to the end of the paragraph is indented to the next tab stop.

When you click Format ⇨ Paragraph, you have a choice of indent styles:

✦ *Indent* moves all lines of a paragraph one tab stop to the right.

✦ *Double Indent* moves text one tab stop inward from both margins.

✦ *Back Tab* moves the first line of a paragraph one tab stop to the left.

✦ *Hanging Indent* (sometimes called an *Outdent*) moves all lines except the first line one tab stop to the right.

Normally, you'll want to indent from the beginning of a paragraph, not from the middle of a line. Figure 21-10 illustrates the indent types.

TAB indents the first line of a paragraph. To indent the first line of all your paragraphs, click Format ⇨ Paragraph ⇨ Format and specify the amount of your first line indent.

INDENT moves all the lines of a paragraph one tab stop to the right.

DOUBLE INDENT moves text one tab stop inward from both margins.

BACK TAB moves the first line of a paragraph one tab stop to the left.

HANGING INDENT moves all lines except the first line one tab stop to the right.

Figure 21-10: Various ways to indent a paragraph.

For more on formatting paragraphs, see "Customizing the Paragraph," later in this chapter.

Centering a line of text

You can *center* a single line of text (or even part of a line) between the left and right margins (such as for a title or heading). To center a line of text:

1. In an existing line of text, right-click at the beginning of the text you want to center, and then click Center (or click the location and click Format ➪ Line ➪ Center).

2. To create a new line of centered text, click Format ➪ Line ➪ Center, type your text, and then press Enter.

Tip   You can also click the center of your screen with the shadow cursor.

You can center text in columns just as you do with ordinary lines.

When you center two or more lines of selected text, the block gets center-justified, rather than centering each individual line.

Using flush right

Use *flush right* to align a single line of text—or a part of a line—with the right margin. You can also use it to insert dot leaders all the way to the right margin:

1. In an existing line of text, right-click the location where you want the right alignment to begin, and then click Flush Right (or click the location and click Format ➪ Line ➪ Flush Right).

2. For a new line of text, click Format ➪ Line ➪ Flush Right, type your text, and then Press Enter. (You can also click the right margin with your shadow cursor.)

When you use Flush Right on two or more lines of selected text, they get right-justified instead.

Using justification

To *justify* (align) lines of text:

1. Select the lines of text, or click the paragraph where you want justification to begin.

2. Click the toolbar justification button (Format ➪ Justification), and then choose Left, Right, Center, Full, or All to create the various types of justification shown in Figure 21-11. The All option fully justifies all the lines of text, including short lines at the ends of paragraphs that normally aren't spread across the page with full justification.

Tip   Use All to space the characters in a title across the page, as in a circus poster.

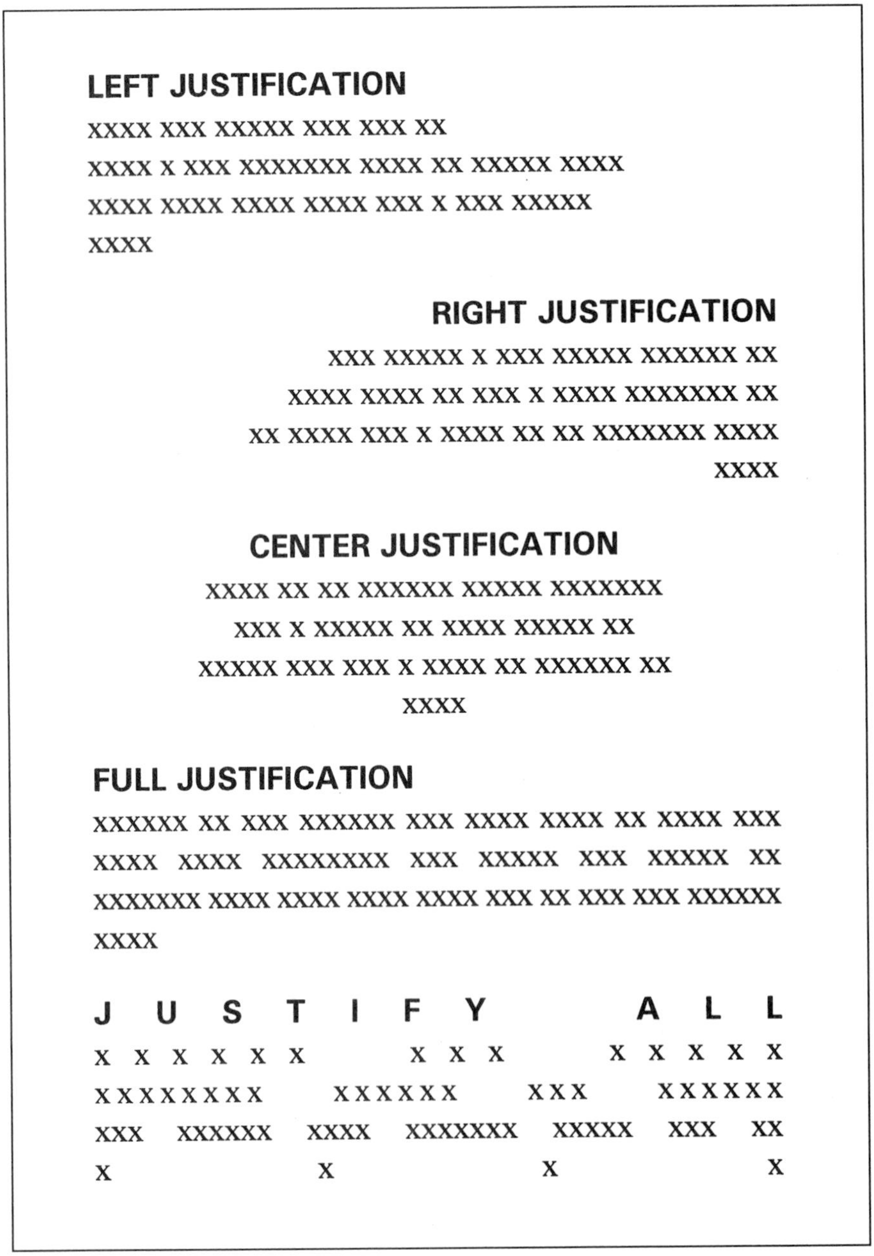

LEFT JUSTIFICATION

XXXX XXX XXXXX XXX XXX XX
XXXX X XXX XXXXXXX XXXX XX XXXXX XXXX
XXXX XXXX XXXX XXXX XXX X XXX XXXXX
XXXX

RIGHT JUSTIFICATION

XXX XXXXX X XXX XXXXX XXXXXX XX
XXXX XXXX XX XXX X XXXX XXXXXXX XX
XX XXXX XXX X XXXX XX XX XXXXXXX XXXX
XXXX

CENTER JUSTIFICATION

XXXX XX XX XXXXXX XXXXX XXXXXXX
XXX X XXXXX XX XXXX XXXXX XX
XXXXX XXX XXX X XXXX XX XXXXXX XX
XXXX

FULL JUSTIFICATION

XXXXXX XX XXX XXXXXX XXX XXXX XXXX XX XXXX XXX
XXXX XXXX XXXXXXXX XXX XXXXX XXX XXXXX XX
XXXXXXX XXXX XXXX XXXX XXXX XXX XX XXX XXX XXXXXX
XXXX

J   U   S   T   I   F   Y   A   L   L

X X X X X X   X X X   X X X X X
X XXXXXXX   XXXXX   XXX   XXXXXX
XXX   XXXXXX   XXXX   XXXXXXX   XXXXX   XXX   XX
X   X   X   X

Figure 21-11: Types of justification.

Justification is always performed paragraph-by-paragraph, not line-by-line. The Justification button on the property bar indicates the justification type used at the insertion point.

Advancing text

To position text precisely, as when you're designing a letterhead or filling out a preprinted form, click Format ➪ Typesetting ➪ Advance, and then specify the distance and direction you want to advance your text, either from the insertion point, the left edge of the page, or the top of the page (see Figure 21-12). An Advance code is placed at the insertion point to move your text.

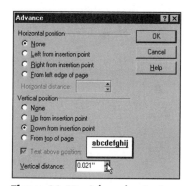

Figure 21-12: Advancing text.

To place the text *below* a vertical position from the top of the page, rather than above it, click "From top of page," and then click "Text above position" to remove the check. To delete an Advance code, drag it out of the Reveal Codes area.

Adjusting line spacing, line height, and leading

Line height, line spacing, and leading are interrelated terms used in controlling the distance between lines of text.

✦ *Line height* is the distance between the top of one (single-spaced) line of text and the top of the next, which includes some white space above the print, as shown in Figure 21-13.

✦ *Line spacing* specifies the number of line heights from one printed line to the next — such as double-spacing or one-and-a-half spacing.

✦ *Leading* (pronounced "ledding") is the white space placed between lines of text.

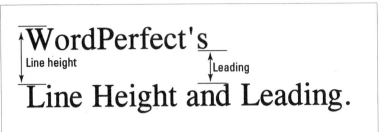

Figure 21-13: WordPerfect's line height and leading.

 Double-spacing actually more than doubles the white space between lines, because you're doubling the total line height, not just the leading.

When you change the font face or size, WordPerfect automatically adjusts the line height to accommodate the change.

Changing line spacing

To change line spacing:

1. Click where you want the new line spacing to begin, or select a block of text.

2. Click Format ➪ Line ➪ Spacing, and then specify the spacing you want (see Figure 21-14).

Figure 21-14: Changing line spacing.

 To change the line spacing between paragraphs (instead of between all lines), see "Changing the paragraph format," later in this chapter.

Adjusting line height

To adjust line height:

1. Click the paragraph in which you want the line height to change, or select the paragraphs you want to change.

2. Click Format ⇨ Line ⇨ Height, and then click

- *Automatic*, to use the default height for the font you're using

- *Fixed*, to specify the exact line height you want (see Figure 21-15)

- *At Least*, to specify a minimum height, no matter what font you're using

Figure 21-15: Adjusting line height.

Adjusting line leading

The leading adjustment specifies the amount of space to add or subtract from the total line height. Leading is an exact adjustment, in inches, points, or some other unit of measurement.

Tip

To adjust spacing by a percentage, rather than by a fixed amount, adjust the line spacing instead.

To adjust line leading:

1. Click the paragraph in which you want the new setting to begin, or select the lines of text that you want to adjust.

2. Click Format ⇨ Typesetting ⇨ Word/Letter Spacing.

3. Check "Adjust leading Between lines" (see Figure 21-16), and then specify the amount of space you want to add between the lines. (You can type your entry in points, such as 3p.)

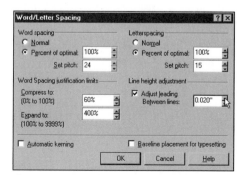

Figure 21-16: Adjusting the leading between lines.

You can specify a negative leading adjustment to close up your lines, but beware of entangling lowercase character *descenders* (like the bottom half of a p) which extend below the baseline, with the characters in the line below.

Numbering lines

Some documents (such as legal documents, contracts, and instructions), use line numbers for reference. To number the lines in your document:

1. Click the paragraph in which you want the line numbering to begin, or select the paragraphs you want to line number.

2. Click Format ⇨ Line ⇨ Numbering.

3. Specify the line numbering options you want, as described in Table 21-1.

4. Check "Turn line numbering on" (see Figure 21-17), and click OK.

Figure 21-17: Numbering lines.

Table 21-1	
Line Numbering Options	
Line Numbering Option	**_Lets You_**
Numbering method	Specify numbers, letters, or Roman numerals
Starting line number	Specify the number assigned to the first line
First printed line number	Specify the first line number to print
Numbering interval	Specify how often to print line numbers
From left edge of page	Position the numbers a specified distance from the edge of the page (or from the center of the space between columns)

Line Numbering Option	Lets You
Outside left margin	Position numbers a specified distance outside the left margin
Restart numbering on each page	Begin with the starting line number at the top of each page
Count blank lines	Include blank lines in your line count
Number all newspaper columns	Number lines in every column
Font	Specify a particular font face, style, size, color, or other attribute for the line numbers

Footnotes, endnotes, headers, and footers are not included when numbering lines. When numbering newspaper columns, click "Outside left margin" to specify where the line numbers will appear in each column. Keep the distance small enough to fit the numbers within the left margins.

To change your line numbering options, click anywhere in the line where you want your new options to begin, and then click Format ➪ Line ➪ Numbering.

To turn off line numbering, click the first paragraph you don't want to be numbered, and then click Format ➪ Line ➪ Numbering and remove the check from "Turn line numbering on."

You can turn line numbering back on later in your document, to start a new line numbering sequence, beginning with the number you specify.

Customizing the Paragraph

As you write, you express your thoughts in sentences and arrange groups of thoughts in paragraphs. Long paragraphs can overwhelm the reader, while very short paragraphs can make your text choppy and hard to follow. The length of your paragraphs may vary, depending on content and audience. For example, paragraphs in a two-page memo or a children's story are normally shorter than those in a scientific paper.

The format of your paragraphs is a major part of your document's appearance. This section shows you several ways to custom-tailor your paragraphs. You can also number your paragraphs (see Chapter 23, "Organizing with Bullets and Outlines") or dress them up with borders and fills (see Chapter 54, "Adding Graphic Lines, Borders, and Fills").

What's a paragraph?

First, how does WordPerfect identify a paragraph? You signal the end of a paragraph every time you press Enter. This places a hard return code in your document and takes you to the next line, to start a new paragraph. A hard page break (Ctrl+Enter) also signals the end of a paragraph.

Changing the paragraph format

To change your paragraph spacing, margins, indent, and other formatting:

1. Click where you want the new paragraph format to begin, or select the paragraphs you want to change.

2. Click Format ⇨ Paragraph ⇨ Format, and then specify the settings that you want to change (see Figure 21-18):

   - *First line indent* automatically indents the first paragraph line a specified amount.

   - *Left margin adjustment* adjust the left paragraph margin relative to the current page margin. A negative amount outdents the paragraph.

   - *Right margin adjustment* adjusts the right paragraph margin relative to the current page margin.

   - *Spacing between paragraphs* adjusts the spacing between paragraphs, in lines or points. (Try this instead of pressing Enter twice.)

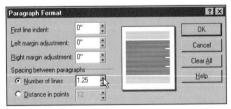

Figure 21-18: Changing the paragraph format.

Tip When adjusting the number of lines, the number is a multiple of the line spacing. If line spacing is 2 and paragraph spacing is 1.5 lines, you'll end up with triple spacing between paragraphs (2 × 1.5).

Returning to the default paragraph format settings

Changes to the paragraph format (unless you applied them to selected paragraphs) remain in effect until you set them back again. To return to the default paragraph indent, spacing, and margin settings:

1. Click the paragraph for which you want to return the default settings.

2. Click Format ⇨ Paragraph ⇨ Format ⇨ Clear All.

Deleting paragraph settings

If you don't like your new paragraph settings, you can go into Reveal Codes and delete the offending code. (There are separate codes for first-line indent, paragraph spacing, left margin adjustment, and right margin adjustment.)

Reusing paragraph attributes and styles

Suppose you just created a nice paragraph format that you would like to use in future documents. You might want, for example, to regularly publish a sales brochure or issue standard invoices or reports that have a consistent, professional appearance. You can do this by saving the format, fonts, and attributes of existing paragraphs, including headings, as styles that you can use over and over again.

Cross-Reference

Chapter 17, "Becoming an Instant WordPerfect Expert," shows you how easy it is to save and apply paragraph styles by using the QuickFormat and QuickStyle features.

Customizing Your Pages

Page appearance can be critical in getting your message across. You can adjust margins, add headers or footers, display a watermark, number the pages, and add borders. You can even create a custom paper size.

You don't have to use the same page format throughout your document. You can create a title page using a large, decorative font with a border, and then use a more subdued format for the body of the document.

The following sections show you many ways in which you can customize your page. Also see Chapter 54, "Adding Graphic Lines, Borders, and Fills." Page numbering options are described in Chapter 20, "Controlling Text and Numbering Pages."

Adjusting page margins

Page margins are the white spaces to the right of, left of, above, and below the text on the printed page. The default U.S. settings are one inch all around.

When you adjust the left and right margin settings, you affect the current paragraph and all subsequent paragraphs. When you adjust the top and bottom margins, you affect the current page and all subsequent pages. The settings remain in effect until you change them again.

To adjust your page margins:

1. Click the paragraph (for left or right margins) or page (for top or bottom margins) where you want the margin change to begin.

2. Click Format ⇨ Margins, and specify your new settings (see Figure 21-19).

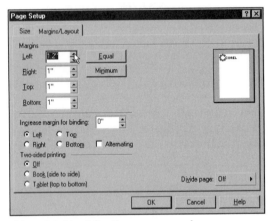

Figure 21-19: Adjusting page margins.

Tip   Click Equal to adjust all margins at once, or click Minimum to set your margins to the smallest values your printer can handle. For the smallest possible equal margins, first click Minimum, and then click Equal.

Adjusting a margin using the mouse

To adjust a margin using the mouse, drag its guideline, as described in Chapter 16, "Mastering the WordPerfect Interface."

Deleting page margin settings

If you don't like your new page margins, you can immediately reverse your changes by pressing Ctrl+Z (Undo). Later on you can go into Reveal Codes and delete the individual margin codes.

Changing your default page margins

To change the page margins for all your new documents, choose page margin options while editing the Document Style. See "Changing the Document Style," earlier in this chapter.

Centering text on the page

Although you can center any line or paragraph horizontally between the left and right margins, you must center the page to have the text centered vertically from the top to the bottom. Figure 21-20 shows a book title page with the text centered on the page. The graphics box with the horse was added after the text was typed.

How to Stay Alive Around Thoroughbreds

by

Ima Goode Jumper

Figure 21-20: Text centered vertically on the page.

To center text on the page:

1. Click the page you want centered, or the page where you want centering to begin.

2. Click Format ➪ Page ➪ Center.

3. Click to center the "Current page," or "Current and subsequent pages" (see Figure 21-21).

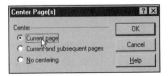

Figure 21-21: Centering text on the page.

Click File ➪ Print Preview to see how your centered text will print.

To turn off page centering, click the page where you want centering to end, and then click Format ➪ Page ➪ Center ➪ No centering.

Selecting a page size and orientation

The page size in your document should match the paper you're printing it on. WordPerfect supplies standard page definitions from which to choose, but you can create your own for any size paper your printer can handle.

The default page size for the U.S. version of WordPerfect is $8\frac{1}{2} \times 11$ inches. The default orientation is *portrait*, with lines of text across the width of the paper (like this page). The other orientation is *landscape*, which prints the text along the length of the paper.

To select another page size or orientation:

1. Click where you want the new page setting to begin.

2. Click File ➪ Page Setup, or Format ➪ Page ➪ Page Setup.

3. Select the page size definition and orientation you want.

4. To change just the current page and revert to the same or a different format for subsequent pages, check "Following pages different from current page" and specify, if necessary, new settings for the following pages (see Figure 21-22).

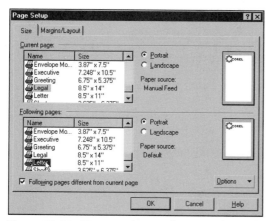

Figure 21-22: You can change the page size and orientation for both the current page and following pages.

Creating a custom page definition

If the paper size you want is not on the list of predefined sizes for your printer, create a custom paper definition:

1. Click File ⇨ Page Setup ⇨ Options ⇨ New, and give your definition a name (see Figure 21-23).

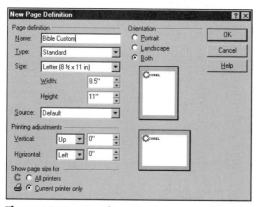

Figure 21-23: Creating a custom page definition.

2. Select a page type (such as standard, letterhead, labels, or envelope).

3. Select a page size or specify a custom width and height.

4. Select the page source. Most desktop printers have only one source, so the setting should normally be left as Default. Select Manual Feed if you're defining an envelope or special form that must be fed one sheet at a time.

5. Select an orientation of Portrait, Landscape, or Both.

Tip

Most printers rotate the font, rather than the paper, to print in landscape orientation, so select Both to permit both portrait and landscape printing.

6. Specify printing adjustments to shift your text away from the unprintable zone on your printer—either up, down, left, or right. (Normally, it makes more sense to adjust your document's text, if needed, rather than the page definition.)

7. Click whether you want to show the page size for all printers, or just the current one.

To use your custom page definition as the default for all your new documents, select your page definition while editing the Document Style. See "Changing the Document Style," earlier in this chapter.

Editing or deleting a page definition

To edit or delete a page definition, click File ➪ Page Setup, select the definition, click Options, and then click Edit or Delete.

Regenerating page definitions

You can *regenerate* your printer's page definitions, either to update the listed sizes for definitions you've edited or to restore edited and deleted definitions to their original state. Click File ➪ Page Setup ➪ Regenerate, and then choose All Sizes From Printer, or New Sizes Only.

Creating Headers, Footers, and Watermarks

Headers and *footers* print at the top or bottom of every page, or on alternate odd or even pages. In a book, they usually include the page number, along with the book title, or the name of the chapter or section. In papers or reports, they're a handy place for such information as the revision date, author, company name, or filename (Insert ➪ Other ➪ Filename).

Watermarks are shaded graphics or text images that appear behind your document text. They can add a customized elegance to your printed page, or display an arresting element such as "TOP SECRET." A watermark can consist of a company logo, text (usually a decorative font in a large size) or any other graphic. (The watermark shown in Figure 21-24 uses a clip art image.) Like headers and footers, you can place watermarks on every page, or on alternating odd or even pages.

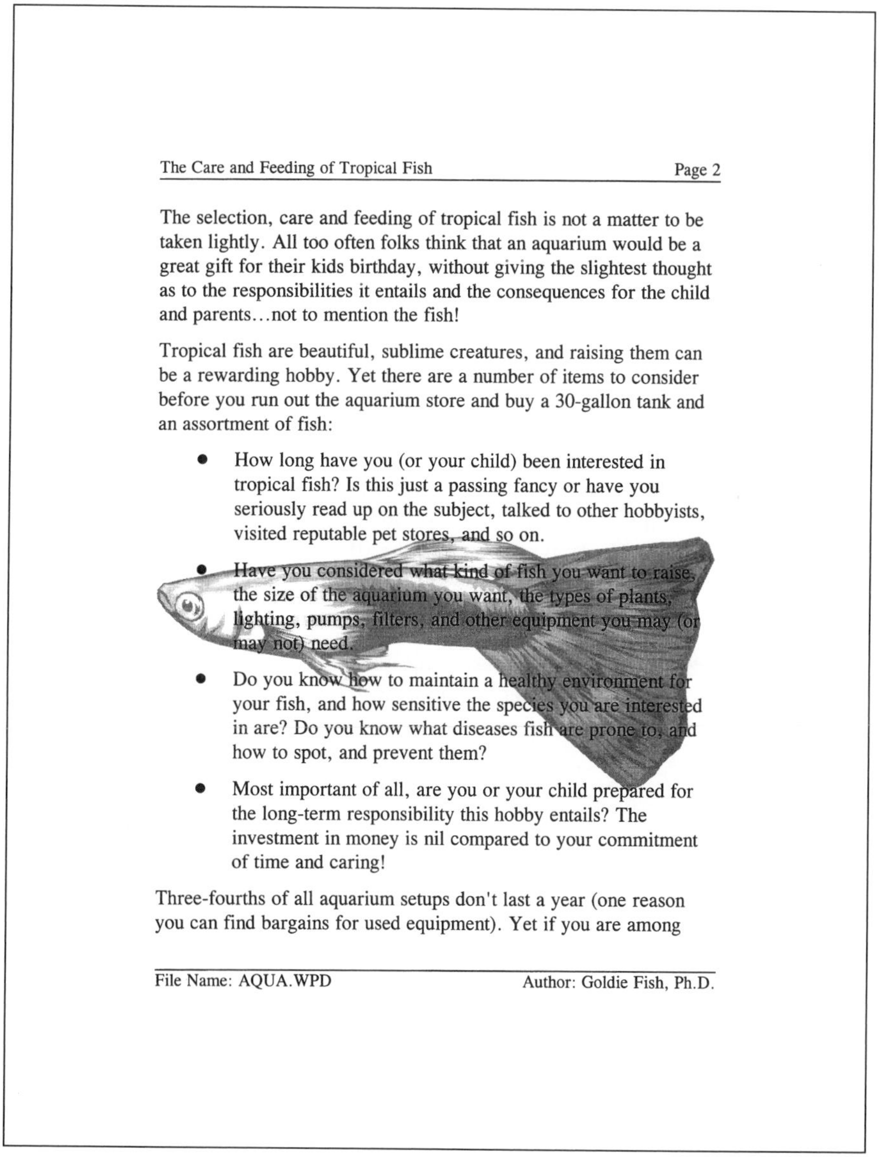

The Care and Feeding of Tropical Fish Page 2

The selection, care and feeding of tropical fish is not a matter to be taken lightly. All too often folks think that an aquarium would be a great gift for their kids birthday, without giving the slightest thought as to the responsibilities it entails and the consequences for the child and parents…not to mention the fish!

Tropical fish are beautiful, sublime creatures, and raising them can be a rewarding hobby. Yet there are a number of items to consider before you run out the aquarium store and buy a 30-gallon tank and an assortment of fish:

- How long have you (or your child) been interested in tropical fish? Is this just a passing fancy or have you seriously read up on the subject, talked to other hobbyists, visited reputable pet stores, and so on.
- Have you considered what kind of fish you want to raise, the size of the aquarium you want, the types of plants, lighting, pumps, filters, and other equipment you may (or may not) need.
- Do you know how to maintain a healthy environment for your fish, and how sensitive the species you are interested in are? Do you know what diseases fish are prone to, and how to spot, and prevent them?
- Most important of all, are you or your child prepared for the long-term responsibility this hobby entails? The investment in money is nil compared to your commitment of time and caring!

Three-fourths of all aquarium setups don't last a year (one reason you can find bargains for used equipment). Yet if you are among

File Name: AQUA.WPD Author: Goldie Fish, Ph.D.

Figure 21-24: Page with a header, footer, and watermark.

At any location in your document, you can have two active definitions for headers, footers, and watermarks: A and B. You can print them both on the same page, but the general idea is that you can create distinct displays for the facing odd and even pages, as in a book. Definitions take effect from the current page on, so you can define different headers, footers, and watermarks in different parts of your document.

When replacing a header, footer, or watermark, specify the same letter for the replacement. For example, only another header A can replace a header A, not a header B. You can turn off any or all headers, footers, and watermarks at any time.

Creating a header or footer

To create a header or footer:

1. Click the first page where you want your header or footer to appear.

2. Click Insert ⇨ Header/Footer.

Tip   In Page or Two Page view, you can also right-click in the top or bottom margin.

3. Click the header or footer you want to create, and then click Create (see Figure 21-25). (If you're working in Page view, you'll be taken directly to the header or footer; if you're working in Draft view, a header or footer window will open, which looks much like a blank document window.)

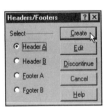

Figure 21-25: Creating a header or footer.

4. Add any text, graphics, and formatting, and make any property bar selections:

  • Click the page numbering button to insert the page, secondary, chapter, volume, or total pages number (see Chapter 20, "Controlling Text and Numbering Pages")

  • Click the horizontal line button to set off your header or footer with a horizontal line (see Chapter 54, "Adding Graphic Lines, Borders, and Fills")

  • Click the header placement button to specify display placement on odd/even pages or on every page

  • Click the header distance button to set the distance between the text and the header or footer

Tip   The default is one blank line, and you can specify spacing in points. For example, type **18p** for a spacing of 1½ lines when using a 12-point font.

- Click the previous button or next button to go to the previous or next header/footer.
- Click the close icon to exit the property bar (in Page view, simply click outside of the header or footer)

To change the header or footer for subsequent pages, create a new header or footer using the same letter as the header or footer you're replacing.

Creating a watermark

To create a watermark:

1. Click the first page on which you want your watermark to appear.
2. Click Insert ➪ Watermark, click watermark A or B, and then click Create (see Figure 21-26).

Figure 21-26: Creating a watermark.

3. Click toolbar insert clipart button or toolbar insert file button to insert a graphic or text.
4. You can type any text you want in the watermark layer, and apply any font or formatting.

Tip   This is a perfect place for TextArt, described in Chapter 8, "Fonts Fantastic."

5. Make any other property bar selections:
   - Click the toolbar watermark placement button to specify display placement on odd, even, or all pages
   - Click the toolbar watermark shading button to adjust the default 25% shading for graphics or text (Figure 21-27)

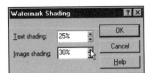

Figure 21-27: Adjusting watermark shading.

- Click the toolbar previous button or toolbar next button to go to the previous or next watermark
- Click the Close icon to exit the feature bar

Editing headers, footers, and watermarks

To edit a header, footer, or watermark, click on any page where it is in effect, click Insert, click Header/Footer or Watermark, click the item, and then click Edit.

In Page view, you can click a header or footer to edit the text directly, or right-click the page and click Watermark to edit a watermark. To change the watermark image, just delete the old one and replace it with the new picture.

Tip   Editing a header, footer, or watermark changes it all the way back to the first page on which it was created. To specify a different header, footer, or watermark from a certain page on, create a replacement or new element of the same letter (A or B).

Ending or suppressing headers, footers, and watermarks

You can discontinue headers, footers, and watermarks at any point. You may also want to suppress them on certain pages, such as title pages or on a page where a graph appears.

To discontinue a header, footer, or watermark, from the current page on, click Header/Footer or Watermark from the Insert menu, and then click Discontinue.

To suppress headers, footers, or watermarks on a particular page, click Format Page⇨Suppress, and then check the items you want to suppress.

To delete a header, footer, or watermark, you can drag its associated code out of the Reveal Codes window, or use Find and Replace, replacing the code with nothing (see Chapter 18, "Editing and Reviewing Techniques").

Using predefined watermarks

When you insert clipart in creating a watermark, you'll find that WordPerfect provides an extensive library of predefined watermark images. Use them to create customized stationery, or stamp your documents with DO NOT COPY, SECRET, or other messages, as shown in Figure 21-28.

Figure 21-28: Two watermark images you can use.

Creating custom watermarks

Any graphics image can be used as a watermark. You may need to change the image to black-and-white and adjust the shading to achieve the effect you want (see Chapter 9, "Working with Graphics"). TextArt is another great tool for creating watermark graphics (see Chapter 8, "Fonts Fantastic").

For More Information . . .

On	See
Formatting with the shadow cursor	Chapter 16
Creating QuickWord entries	Chapter 52
Applying paragraph and page borders	Chapter 54
Using document templates	Chapter 28
Formatting with columns and tables	Chapter 22
Displaying the tab bar	Chapter 16
Numbering paragraphs	Chapter 23
Applying QuickFormats and QuickStyles	Chapter 17
Setting up style libraries	Chapter 28
Numbering pages	Chapter 20
Dragging margin guidelines	Chapter 16
Creating TextArt	Chapter 8
Finding and replacing formatting codes	Chapter 18
Modifying graphics	Chapter 9
Creating labels	Chapter 27

✦   ✦   ✦

Formatting with Columns and Tables

While information is usually displayed from margin to margin (with an occasional tab, indent, or graphic thrown in), columns and tables provide you with other powerful, easy-to-use formatting tools.

Presenting Information in Columns

Columns are a handy way to view many types of information, such as an Address Book, an inventory list, or a restaurant menu. They are useful when writing a script with stage directions or publishing a newsletter with many separate articles.

In WordPerfect, you can specify up to 24 columns across the page and define custom widths and spacing between them. You can set tabs within columns and justify text. Almost anything that can go on a page can go in a column, including graphics and tables.

Columns come in two basic flavors: *newspaper* (up and down) and *parallel* (across). Each type has several variations and options.

Newspaper columns

Columns are a must for newspapers, where the page is far too wide for the reader's eye to grasp. The *standard newspaper columns* seen in Figure 22-1 read from top to bottom, then jump to the top of the next column upon reaching the end of the page or a column break.

The *balanced newspaper columns* shown in Figure 22-2 are especially useful if you have a short text passage that you want to display across the page.

Parallel columns

Parallel columns grouped across the page in rows can be seen in Figure 22-3. The first column in the next row starts below the longest column in the row above. Parallel columns are especially useful in resumes, scripts, lists, and other documents where information is arrayed across the page.

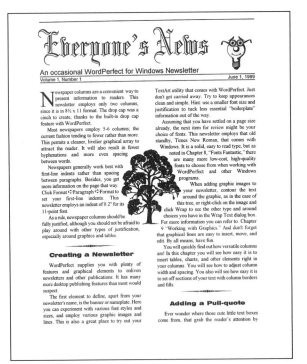

Figure 22-1: Newsletter with standard newspaper columns.

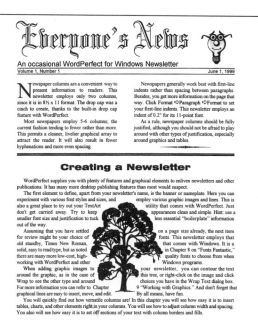

Figure 22-2: Same newsletter with balanced newspaper columns.

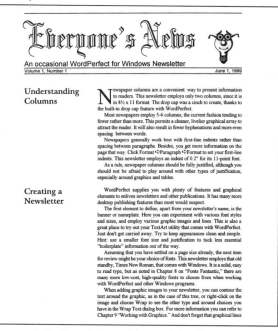

Figure 22-3: Newsletter with parallel columns.

Alternatives to columns

You can also create columns just by setting tabs, as shown with the address list in Figure 22-4. See Chapter 23, "Organizing with Bullets and Outlines," for details on setting tabs.

Sonya Brown	789 Farm Road	Los Gatos	CA	95030
Dr. Helen Wang	2305 Mountain Drive	Boulder	CO	80301
Mathew Chapin	362 Meadow Oak Lane	Manchester	CT	06040
Elizabeth Somner	1795 South Street	Winsted	CT	06098
Nancy Morgan	2532 Chapman Drive, N.W.	Washington	DC	20036
Brian Nelson	15 Federal Street	Middlefield	MA	01243
Judy Davis	375 Hamlet Avenue	Brooklyn	NY	11225
Miranda Sanchez	426 President Street	Westlake	OH	44145
George O'Connor	47 Grove Street	Dallas	TX	75235

Figure 22-4: Tabular column alternative.

Multicolumn tables, found later in this chapter, are an easy-to-use alternative to parallel columns with a number of powerful features. You can remove the lines from the table to make it appear like columnar text.

Defining Columns

To define columns, place the insertion point where you want the columns to begin. Then use either the toolbar or the Columns dialog box to define your columns.

Using the toolbar

The quickest way to define newspaper columns is to click the Columns button on the toolbar, and then click the number of columns you want (see Figure 22-5).

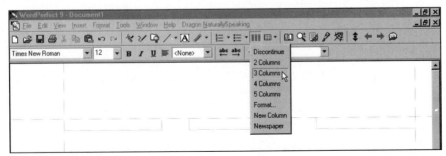

Figure 22-5: Defining columns by using the toolbar.

Using the Columns dialog box

To access the full range of column features and types:

1. Click Format ⇨ Columns, or click the Columns button on the toolbar and click Format.

2. Specify the number of columns you want (see Figure 22-6).

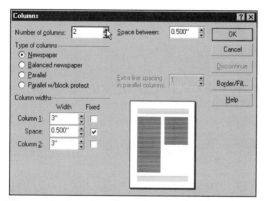

Figure 22-6: Using the Columns dialog box.

3. Specify the column type:
   - *Newspaper*, to wrap text from the bottom of one column to the top of the next
   - *Balanced newspaper*, to adjust the columns to an equal length
   - *Parallel*, to jump text from column to column with each text break, with the next row beginning below the longest block
   - *Parallel w/block protect*, to bump the entire last row to the next page if it doesn't all fit, instead of splitting it

4. Specify any of the following options:
   - *Space between*, to set the default space between columns.
   - *Extra line spacing in parallel columns*, to adjust the number of blank lines between rows of parallel columns.
   - *Width*, to adjust the widths of individual columns (and spaces between columns) to suit the information they contain. Notice that when you change the width of one column, the others adjust in the opposite direction to fit the page margins.
   - *Fixed*, to keep the width of the checked column or space constant when you adjust other columns or spaces. (For a column layout of less than the page width, check Fixed for all the widths and spaces.)

• *Border/Fill*, to apply a graphic border or fill to your columns (see Chapter 54).

Converting regular text into columns

To convert existing text to columns, place the insertion point in the paragraph where you want your columns to begin, or select a block of text. Then define the columns.

Deleting column definitions

To remove columns you have created, go into Reveal Codes and delete the [Col Def:] code. Any column breaks you entered will now act as hard page breaks (with the code [HCol-Spg] in Reveal Codes), so delete them as well.

Working in Columns

As soon as you create your columns, you can start entering text, graphics, and anything else. To end a column before the bottom of the page, press Ctrl+Enter to insert a column break. (You can also click the Columns button on the toolbar and click New Column.)

Tip   To insert a page break while in columns, you must press Ctrl+Shift+Enter, because Ctrl+Enter is used for the column break. You can also click Insert ➪ New Page.

As you enter text in standard newspaper columns, the text fills up the first column and then flows to the next (see Figure 22-7). With balanced newspaper columns, text moves backward across the column break to keep them in balance (see Figure 22-8).

As you type in parallel columns, text flows down the current column until you press Ctrl+Enter to jump to the next column. A column break in the last column ends the row, and the row assumes the width of the tallest section.

Discontinuing columns

To discontinue (turn off) columns:

1. Click where you want the columns to end.
2. Click Format ➪ Columns ➪ Discontinue (or click the Columns button on the toolbar and click Discontinue).

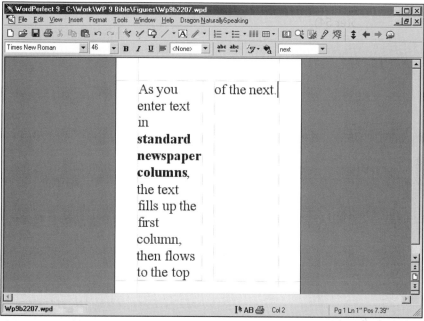

Figure 22-7: Entering text in standard newspaper columns.

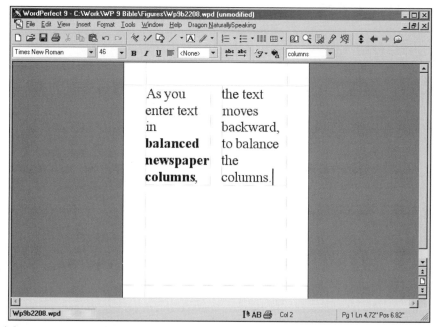

Figure 22-8: Entering text in balanced newspaper columns.

Clicking and typing in columns

When the shadow cursor is on (click the Shadow Cursor button on the application bar, if necessary), working in columns is wonderfully intuitive. Simply click wherever you want and begin typing. You can justify text in columns and snap to tabs or indents, just as you do on the page (see Chapter 18, "Editing and Reviewing Techniques").

To switch columns, point the shadow cursor and click. To turn off columns, point the shadow cursor and click beneath them.

Tip   The only thing the shadow cursor can't do is start a new row of columns across the page.

Maneuvering in columns

If the shadow cursor is off, you can still click to maneuver among columns that aren't empty (or use Alt+← and Alt+→ to move from one column to the next). On the Windows keyboard, Alt+Home takes you to the top of a column; Alt+End takes you to the last line. Go To (Ctrl+G) offers several column position selections.

Formatting and Customizing Columns

You can use the same formatting features within columns that you use in normal document text. You can adjust column widths, set tabs within columns, add line numbers, or apply borders and fills. You may want to apply the following three features to text within columns:

✦ *Full justification* (Format ➪ Justification ➪ Full)

✦ *First-line indent* (Format ➪ Paragraph ➪ Format)

✦ *Hyphenation* (Tools ➪ Language ➪ Hyphenation)

Tip   When using tabs to indent within columns, keep the setting small (such as 0.25 inch) to keep your indents in proportion to the column width.

The surest way to adjust column widths and spacing between columns, as described in the section on creating columns, is to click Format ➪ Columns and specify precise widths for your columns and *gutters* (the spaces between columns). The easiest way, though, discussed in the next section, is to drag the guidelines.

Dragging column guidelines

To adjust the width of a column right on the screen, drag a guideline, as shown in Figure 22-9. (If you don't see the guidelines, click View ➪ Guidelines, and then check Columns to put them on display.)

Column width and spacing

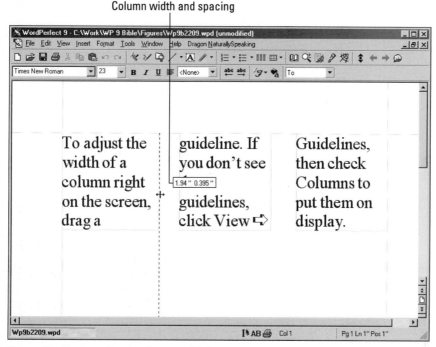

Figure 22-9: Dragging a column guideline.

When you drag a guideline, the space between the columns will increase or decrease. To adjust adjacent columns without changing the space in between, drag the column gutter, as shown in Figure 22-10.

Using the ruler to adjust columns

You can change the tabs within columns, the column margins, and the column widths by clicking and dragging the appropriate ruler bar marker, as described in Chapter 21.

Tip   Sketch out your column widths and margins by using the ruler bar, and then call up the Columns dialog box to make your final adjustments.

Adding line numbers

To add line numbers to newspaper and balanced newspaper columns:

1. Click Format ➪ Line ➪ Numbering.

2. Check "Turn line numbering on."

Column widths

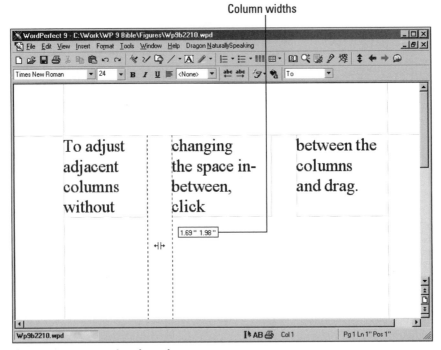

Figure 22-10: Dragging the column gutter.

   3. Uncheck "Restart numbering on each page."

   4. Check "Number all newspaper columns."

The numbers are placed outside the left margins of numbered columns.

Presenting Information in Tables

A picture may be worth a thousand words, but tables are the best way to present many types of information. Report cards, phone bills, baseball standings, and stock listings are only a few of the everyday tables we use. Many charts and graphs (such as the five-day weather forecast on the television screen) are but tabular data in disguise.

What is a table? A *table* is an arrangement of information in horizontal *rows* and vertical *columns*. The intersection of a row and column is a specific *cell* of information. Columns are labeled alphabetically from left to right. Rows are numbered from top to bottom. The *address* of a cell refers to the row and column to which it belongs (see Figure 22-11). Cells can contain numbers, formulas, and graphics, in addition to text.

		Column C	
Row 2		Cell C2	

Figure 22-11: Table row, column, and cell addresses.

While you can arrange information in a tabular form by using tabs or columns, tables offer many formatting advantages, including header rows that repeat from page to page. You can also assign data types to cells and perform calculations, just like in a spreadsheet program (see Chapter 26).

Creating a Table

Chapter 17 showed you an easy way to create and polish up a table: click the Tables button on the toolbar, drag to create the table, QuickFill the headings, and then apply a SpeedFormat style. But the Create Table dialog makes it easy to specify an exact number of rows and columns.

Using the Create Table dialog box

To create a table by using the dialog, click Insert ➪ Table (or double-click the Tables button on the toolbar), and then specify the number of columns and rows (see Figure 22-12).

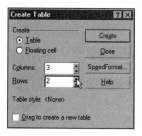

Figure 22-12: Using the Create Table dialog box.

Creating a floating cell

You can also create a *floating cell* — a one-cell table with no lines — from the Create Table dialog box. Use a floating cell to perform calculations right in your document's text, using the same number formats and formulas as tables (see Chapter 26).

Creating a table-in-a-box

You can draw a table-in-a-box (unofficial name), and drag it to any location:

1. Click Insert ⇨ Table, and specify the number of columns and rows you want.

2. Check "Drag to create a new table," click Create, and then drag where you want the table.

Text flows around the table you draw (see Figure 22-13), as with any graphics box, and there's even a space for a caption!

 — Caption

Figure 22-13: Table-in-a-box, with caption below table.

Caution   To go back to creating tables *not* in a box, you must remove the check from "Drag to create a new table."

You can format and edit the table within the box. (Editing the contents of a graphics box is easier in Page view.) The height of the box adjusts as you add or delete rows, or change their heights. The width of the box, however, remains fixed as you add or delete columns.

When you resize the width of the box with a mouse, the width of the columns adjusts. But don't change the height of the box by dragging. Not only will the height of the rows not change, but the box height will also stop adjusting automatically (until you set it back to "maintain proportions").

Creating a table with the shadow cursor

It's even easier to create a table-in-a-box with the shadow cursor. Click and drag out a rectangle, and then click Table. By using this technique, you'll never have to check the "Drag to create a new table" box. (So your next table won't automatically be in a box.)

Converting tabular text or parallel columns to a table

You can convert text in tabbed or parallel columns to a table. Select the text you want to convert, click the Tables button on the toolbar, and click Tabular Column or Parallel Column (depending on the current format). Figure 22-14 shows a table created from the tabular text in Figure 22-4.

Sonya Brown	789 Farm Road	Los Gatos	CA	95030
Dr. Helen Wang	2305 Mountain Drive	Boulder	CO	80301
Mathew Chapin	362 Meadow Oak Lane	Manchester	CT	06040
Elizabeth Somner	1795 South Street	Winsted	CT	06098
Nancy Morgan	2532 Chapman Drive, N.W.	Washington	DC	20036
Brian Nelson	15 Federal Street	Middlefield	MA	01243
Judy Davis	375 Hamlet Avenue	Brooklyn	NY	11225
Miranda Sanchez	426 President Street	Westlake	OH	44145
George O'Connor	47 Grove Street	Dallas	TX	75235

Figure 22-14: Tabular text converted to a table.

Tip

Be sure that the tabular text you're converting has single tabs between items, or you'll get blank columns in your table. (To line up tabular text without inserting extra tabs, display the tab bar or ruler bar, and then drag the settings you don't need off the bar and position the remainder.)

Getting around in tables

The easiest way to get around in a table is to click the cell you want, or use the tab and arrow keys. (Tab at the end of the table to start a new row.)

Because the tab key moves you from cell to cell, you'll need to click Ctrl+Tab to tab within a cell.

Making property bar and menu selections

The Table property bar has buttons for commonly used features, such as selecting the current column or row. Other property bars appear when you select cells or select the entire table.

The complete set of table selections can be found on the Table menu on the property bar (see Figure 22-15).

You can also right-click the table to make selections from the QuickMenu.

Using the selection arrow

When you point to the upper boundary or left boundary of a cell, a selection arrow appears, as shown in Figure 22-16. Click to select the cell, or click and drag to select a group of cells.

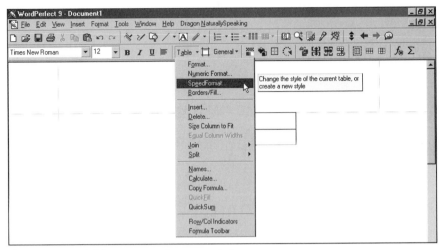

Figure 22-15: Table menu on the property bar.

 Tip Double-click an upward-pointing arrow to select a column, or double-click a left-pointing arrow to select a row.

Figure 22-16: Selection arrow.

Using table row and column indicators

One especially handy selection on the Table menu is the Row/Column Indicators display that provides a clickable road map to columns and rows (see Figure 22-17). You can drag the indicators to select multiple columns or rows, or click in the upper-left corner to select the entire table.

Creating Title and Header Rows

You can use the top table row for the table's title, then designate one or more descriptive rows at the top of a table as header rows that repeat when the table flows to the next page:

1. Click the Select Row button on the property bar to select the top row, then right-click on the selection and click Join Cells. The top row should now be a single cell that you can use for the table's title.

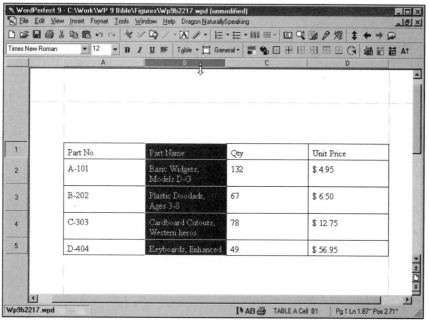

Figure 22-17: Using table row and column indicators.

2. Click anywhere in the second row (or select one or more cells from the rows you want to use for the table headings).

3. Click the Table menu on the property bar and click Format.

4. Click Row, and then check "Header row" (see Figure 22-18).

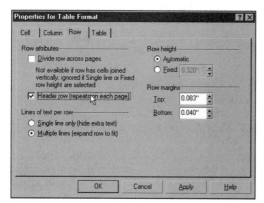

Figure 22-18: Designating header rows that repeat on each page.

Your header rows (but not the title) will now repeat when the table flows to the next page.

Note that when the insertion point is in a header row, an asterisk (*) appears in the application bar after the cell address.

You can join the cells of the top header row to use for a repeating title. See "Joining or splitting cells, columns, and rows," later in this chapter.

Creating a Greeting Card List

To put the table features discussed so far to practical use (and preview some others), create the greeting card list shown in Figure 22-19:

1. Open a new, blank document.
2. Click the Tables button on the toolbar and drag to create a 5×8 table (5 columns by 8 rows).
3. Click Select Row button on the property bar to select the top row, and then right-click on the selection and click Join Cells. The top row should now be a single cell.
4. Drag to select the first two rows. Click the Justification button on the property bar, and then click Center.
5. Type the text in the top two rows, tabbing from cell to cell.
6. Select the first two rows again. Click the Bold button on the property bar. Then right-click, click Format, check "Header row," and click OK. The first two rows of your table are now designated as column header rows that will repeat if your list expands to the next page.
7. Put some people on your greeting card list, and then save it as Greeting Cards.wpd. You'll use the file later in this chapter.

Changing a Table's Structure

Thanks to the context-sensitive property bar and other features, changing a table's structure to fit your information couldn't be easier.

Sizing columns to fit

When you first create a table, all the columns are of the same width. Later you may want to adjust them to conform to the information they contain. For example, the Zip column in your greeting card list doesn't need to be as wide as those for the name and street address.

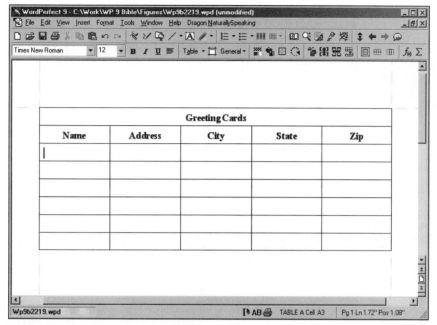

Figure 22-19: Greeting card list table.

Use *Size Column to Fit* to automatically adjust the width of your columns according to the text they contain. Select the column you want to size to fit (or select two or more columns), and then click Size Columns to Fit button on the property bar (or right-click the table and click Size Column to Fit). You're likely to get the best results if you first size to fit the columns that will become smaller, to make room for the columns that you want to expand. The "after" example in Figure 22-20 was achieved by sizing to fit from right to left, starting with the Zip column.

> Size Column to Fit normally sizes a column to accommodate its widest cell. To size it to another cell in the column, first select the cell.

Giving columns equal widths

Instead of sizing columns to fit, you can select an equitable distribution of table widths among two or more columns. To give columns equal widths:

1. Select any part of the columns you want to make the same width.

2. Click Equal Width button on the property bar.

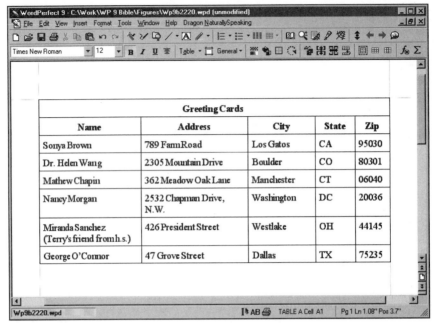

Figure 22-20: Greeting card list after using Size Column to Fit.

Adjusting columns with the mouse or keystrokes

If the Size Column to Fit process does not deliver the results you want, you can drag a table's sides and columns to change their dimensions, as shown in Figure 22-21.

> **Tip** Hold down the Ctrl key to click and drag all the lines from the pointer toward the right at once, while retaining the column widths. Hold down the Shift key to click and drag all the lines from the pointer toward the right at once, while proportionally adjusting the column widths.

To shrink or enlarge the column at the insertion point by using the keyboard, press Ctrl together with the comma or period ("<" or ">" in uppercase).

Sizing columns with the ruler

You can drag the column indicators on the ruler to adjust the width of your columns. You can snap them to grid locations this way (see Chapter 21).

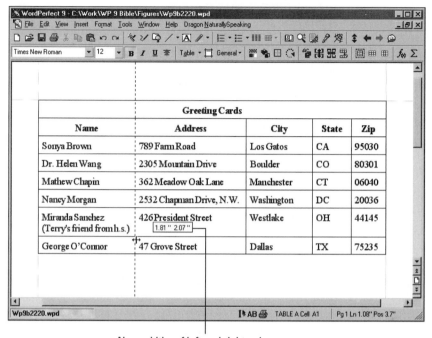

New widths of left and right columns

Figure 22-21: Adjusting a column with the mouse.

Inserting columns and rows

To insert one or more columns or rows at the insertion point, click Table ⇨ Insert, specify the number of columns or rows to add, and then click either Before or After placement (see Figure 22-22).

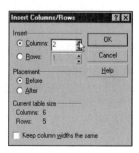

Figure 22-22: Inserting columns or rows.

Inserting a column divides the current column in two. By checking "Keep column widths the same" when inserting columns, the new columns take on the same size as the current one; or, if there isn't room, all the columns are squeezed proportionally.

Added columns or rows retain the formatting attributes of the row or column at the insertion point.

Now practice by adding a column for miscellaneous notes at the right of your greeting card list:

1. Right-click in the last column of the table and click Insert. Specify one column, click After, and then click OK.

2. Type **Notes** in the column header as shown in Figure 22-23.

Greeting Cards					
Name	**Address**	**City**	**State**	**Zip**	**Notes**
Sonya Brown	789 Farm Road	Los Gatos	CA	95030	George's friend
Dr. Helen Wang	2305 Mountain Drive	Boulder	CO	80301	Chem prof.
Mathew Chapin	362 Meadow Oak Lane	Manchester	CT	06040	
Nancy Morgan	2532 Chapman Drive, N.W.	Washington	DC	20036	Kids Nina & Ruth
Miranda Sanchez	426 President Street	Westlake	OH	44145	Terry's friend from h.s.
George O'Connor	47 Grove Street	Dallas	TX	75235	

Figure 22-23: Greeting card list with added Notes column.

3. Select the title row and join the two cells.

4. Adjust the column widths, if necessary, to accommodate the new column.

Joining or splitting cells, columns, and rows

To join a group of cells (such as the top row of the greeting card list), select the cells you want to combine, and then right-click and click Join Cells. The resulting cell has the formatting features of the top-left cell of the original group.

To split a cell, place the insertion point in the cell, click Table ⇨ Split ⇨ Cell, and specify the number of columns or rows. (Text in a cell can affect the way it splits.) You can also split several selected cells at once.

QuickSplitting cells, columns, and rows

You can QuickSplit cells, columns, and rows with your mouse.

To vertically QuickSplit cells or columns:

1. Click Quick Split Vertical button on the property bar.

2. Point and click to split a cell, or drag to split several cells or an entire column (see Figure 22-24).

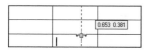

Figure 22-24: QuickSplitting a column.

3. Click Quick Split Horizontal button to horizontally QuickSplit cells or rows.

4. Click the Splitter button again when you're finished.

QuickJoining cells

To QuickJoin cells, click Quick Join button on the property bar, and then drag the cells you want to combine.

Deleting columns, rows, or cell contents

Deleting columns or rows is much the same as inserting, except that you also have the option to delete only the cell contents. To delete columns, rows, or cell contents:

1. Select the cell, or any part of the columns or rows.

2. Click the Table menu on the property bar (or right-click), and then click Delete.

3. Click Columns, Rows, or "Cell contents only" (see Figure 22-25). You can also click "Formulas only" to leave the results of formulas intact.

Figure 22-25: Deleting columns, rows, or cell contents.

If you don't make a prior selection, you can delete any number of columns from the current column to the right, or any number of rows from the current row down.

Using keystrokes to insert, delete, and add rows

You can use the following keystrokes to insert and delete rows, or add rows to the end of a table:

Table Keystroke	What It Does
Alt+Insert	Inserts a row above the insertion point
Alt+Shift+Insert	Inserts a row below the insertion point
Alt+Delete	Deletes the current row
Tab	Adds a row to the bottom of the table (when the insertion point is at the end of the table)

Moving or copying cells, columns, or rows

To move (cut and paste), or to copy (copy and paste) parts of your table or their contents:

1. Select the cells, rows, or columns you want to cut or copy.

2. Right-click and click Cut or Copy.

3. Click one of the following (see Figure 22-26):

- *Selection*, to cut or copy the contents of your selection

- *Row* or *Column*, to cut or copy selected rows or columns and their contents

- *Cell*, to copy the contents of a single, unjoined cell. To copy the cell's contents to several adjacent cells, specify the number of cells down or to the right to copy to, and skip Step 4. To copy the cell elsewhere, click "To clipboard."

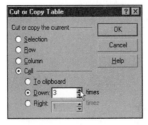

Figure 22-26: Moving or copying cells, columns, or rows.

4. Click OK, place the insertion point where you want to move or copy your selection, right-click, and click Paste. You can paste the selection to another table or into your document's text.

Caution

When copying selected contents to another table location, make sure that there's enough room to the right and below the target cell to hold the whole block, or your pasted information will be truncated.

When you move or copy a selection to another table, table formatting (such as line styles, fills, and text appearance) is moved or copied as well. When you paste into the body of your document, a table structure is created, even for a single cell.

Now it's time for you to practice this delicate operation. Follow these steps to copy three lines from your greeting card list:

1. Drag to select the top three rows of names in your list. (Drag the table row indicators if they're displayed.)

2. Right-click and click Copy ⇨ OK.

3. Place the insertion point somewhere below the table in your document. (You can press Enter a few times to create some space.)

4. Right-click and click Paste. Your page should be similar to the one shown in Figure 22-27.

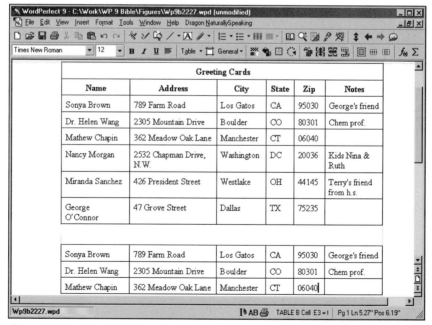

Figure 22-27: Copied table selection.

Using the mouse to move or copy

You can also use the mouse to move or copy table contents and structure. Select the cells, rows, or columns, and then drag the table elements where you want them. (Hold down the Ctrl key or drag with the right mouse button to copy the information instead of move it.)

You can also select and drag the entire table.

QuickFormatting cell and table structures

Click the QuickFormat button on the toolbar to copy cell and table structures to another location. These include the font attributes, fills, lines, borders, and table styles.

Accessing All the Table Formatting Features

WordPerfect's extensive formatting features can be applied to the text in tables and table elements. For example, to change the size or appearance of text in part of a table, select the text and then use the toolbar, property bar, and Font dialog box as you would for text anywhere else.

Certain formatting features, however, apply exclusively to tables (such as center vertical alignment of text in a cell, or a fixed height to a row). Others (such as column margins) may not be exclusive to tables, but they don't apply to general document text. You'll find all these features in the Properties for Table Format dialog box, under the Cell, Column, Row, and Table tabs.

 Tip   You'll find buttons on the property bar for such table formatting features as justification, vertical alignment, and rotating cell contents.

When you apply table formatting, the order of precedence in which the elements apply is as follows:

> ✦ Cell formatting takes precedence over any other settings.

> ✦ Column or row formatting takes precedence over table format settings.

> ✦ Table formatting, the most general, is the same as the underlying document unless you specify otherwise.

Try this exercise: Create a small table, and then click a cell and apply right justification by using the property bar. Next, select the entire table and click Format ➪ Justification ➪ Center. The cell you right-justified will not be centered, because cell formatting takes precedence over the table format.

Because of this, to avoid being surprised when you design your table, follow the format order from general-to-specific by establishing the overall format first, changing specific columns or rows, and finally formatting single cells or small groups of cells.

To format all or part of a table:

1. Place the insertion point in the cell, column, or row you want to format, or select the table elements you want to format.

2. Click the Table menu on the property bar and click Format (or right-click and click Format).

3. Select from the available formatting options for cells, columns, rows, or the entire table, as described in the following sections.

Cells

When using the Table Format dialog cell options (see Figure 22-28), apply any of the features described in Table 22-1. Rotated text and diagonal lines are illustrated in Figure 22-29.

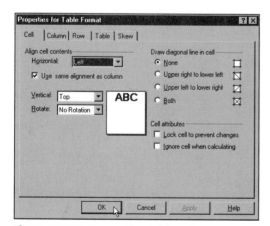

Figure 22-28: Formatting table cells.

Table 22-1
Cell Formatting Features

Feature	*Lets You*
Horizontal alignment	Align cell contents relative to cell margins (left, right, center, full, all, or decimal).
Use same alignment as column	Check to have cell alignment default to that of the column.
Vertical alignment	Align cell contents at the top, bottom, or center of cells. (Displays as mixed when various cells in a selection are aligned differently.)
Rotate	Rotate cell contents in 90-degree increments. (Rotated text is placed in a text box that you can click to edit.)
Diagonal lines	Draw diagonal lines (the cell itself is not split).
Lock cell	Prevent information in the cell from being changed.
Ignore cell	Skip the cell when performing calculations.

Percentage points of the
F Distribution, a = .05

df_1 / df_2	1	2	3
1	161.4	199.5	215.7
2	18.51	19.00	19.16
3	10.13	9.55	9.28
4	7.71	6.94	6.59
5	6.61	5.79	5.41

Milage Chart

	Boston	Cleveland	Chicago	Kansas City	Denver	San Francisco
Boston		657	1004	1435	1998	3128
Cleveland	657		348	819	1362	2483
Chicago	1004	348		542	1021	2173
Kansas City	1435	819	542		606	1861
Denver	1998	1362	1021	606		1255
San Francisco	3128	2483	2173	1861	1255	

Figure 22-29: Cells with rotated text, bottom alignment, and diagonal lines.

Columns

When using the Table Format column options (see Figure 22-30), apply any of the following:

- *Horizontal*, to align contents for columns of cells
- *From right margin* or *Digits after decimal*, to either specify where the decimal is placed or set the number of decimal digits when using decimal alignment

✦ *Width*, to adjust the column width (the combined column widths can't exceed that of the page)

✦ *Always keep width the same*, to keep the column width from changing when you adjust adjacent columns by using the Format dialog box. (You can still drag a fixed-width column to adjust it.)

✦ *Inside margins in column*, to adjust the left and right margins for a column of cells

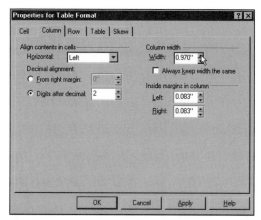

Figure 22-30: Formatting table columns.

Rows

When using the Table Format row options (see Figure 22-31), apply any of the following:

✦ *Divide row across pages*, to continue the row on the next page when there isn't enough room at the bottom. Otherwise, the entire row is bumped to the next page.

> **Tip**
>
> Use block protect, described in Chapter 20, to keep rows together on one page.

✦ *Header row*, to designate rows that repeat at the top of the table when the table spans more than one page.

✦ *Lines of text per row*, to limit the display of information in the row to a single line (additional lines are converted to hidden text). With the multiline default, the row height expands to accommodate additional lines.

✦ *Row height*, to set a specific fixed height. Text that doesn't fit in a fixed row is converted to hidden text. (You can drag the bottom edge of a row to enlarge it.)

✦ *Row margins*, to adjust the top and bottom margins for cells within rows.

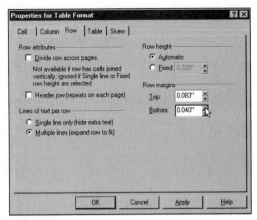

Figure 22-31: Formatting table rows.

The table in Figure 22-32 shows how text can be hidden when you specify "Single line only" or a fixed line height. When the cells' contents are copied into the document below the table, you see the entire text.

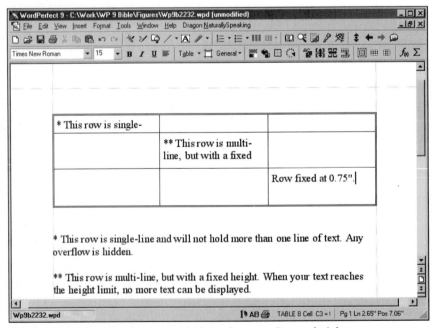

Figure 22-32: Overflow text gets hidden when you fix row heights.

Tables

When using the Table Format table options (see Figure 22-33) apply any of the column options, plus the following:

✦ *Table size*, to adjust the number of columns and rows. Columns are added to or removed from the right; rows from the bottom.

✦ *Table position on page*, to specify the position of the table horizontally within the document: left, right, center, full (the default), or at a specific distance from the left edge of the page.

✦ *Use as Default*, to change the default table position.

✦ *Insert new rows automatically* (on by default), to add a row when you tab in the last cell of the table.

✦ *Disable locks in all cells*, to temporarily unlock all cells for editing or updating. (Remove the check when you're finished, to protect the table's contents.)

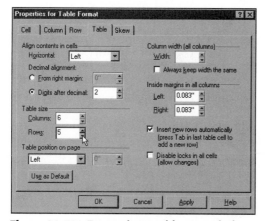

Figure 22-33: Formatting a table as a whole.

Skewing Columns and Rows

New Feature

To really polish up your table's appearance, try skewing its columns and rows:

1. Right-click your table, and then click Format ➪ Skew.

2. Select a skew setting (see Figure 22-34).

3. To customize the selected settings, click More, and then specify various skew options for rows, columns, and text (see Figure 22-35).

Your skew results (see Figure 22-36) become your Current Table settings, which you can easily refine.

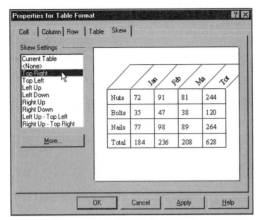

Figure 22-34: Selecting a skew setting.

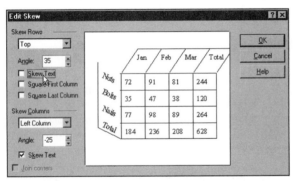

Figure 22-35: Specifying skew options.

Joining and Splitting Tables

You can join and split tables much as you join and split cells, columns, and rows. It's only slightly trickier.

Joining two tables

Joining tables is not as simple as joining cells. To join two tables into one, the last row in the first table and the first row in the second must have the same number of columns.

To join two tables:

1. Remove any text and spacing between the two tables (see Figure 22-37).

2. Click the top table (see Figure 22-38), and then click Table ➪ Join ➪ Table.

Name	Address	City	State	Zip	Notes
Sonya Brown	789 Farm Road	Los Gatos	CA	95030	George's friend
Dr. Helen Wang	2305 Mountain Drive	Boulder	CO	80301	Chem prof.
Mathew Chapin	362 Meadow Oak Lane	Manchester	CT	06040	
Nancy Morgan	2532 Chapman Drive, N.W.	Washington	DC	20036	Kids Nina & Ruth
Miranda Sanchez	426 President Street	Westlake	OH	44145	Terry's friend
George O'Connor	47 Grove Street	Dallas	TX	75235	

Figure 22-36: Skew results become four Current Table settings.

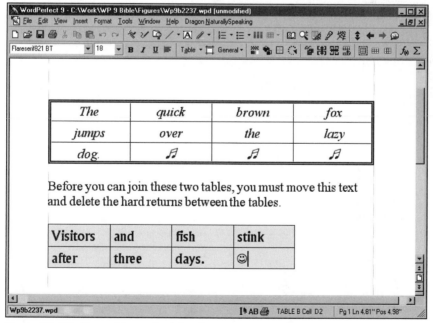

Figure 22-37: Two tables to be joined.

When the tables are joined (see Figure 22-39), the cells in the lower table assume the table-level formatting of the upper table—but formatting applied to particular cells is retained, as with the cell in the lower-right of the figure.

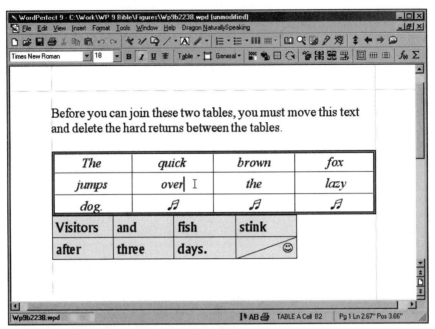

Figure 22-38: Click the top table to join the two.

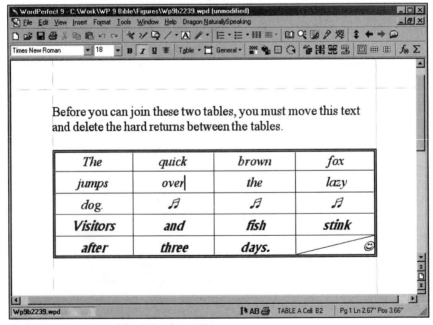

Figure 22-39: Two tables joined together.

Splitting a table

Splitting a table's a little easier than joining:

1. Click anywhere in the row that is to become the top row of the new table (see Figure 22-40).

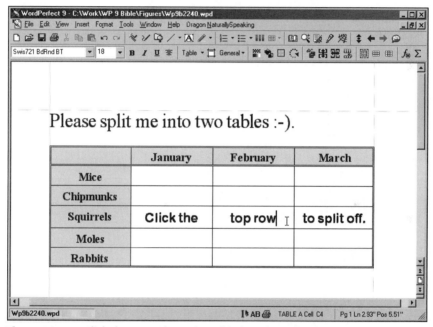

Figure 22-40: Click the row where the table is to be split off.

2. Click Table ➪ Split ➪ Table.

3. Use the left arrow key to place the insertion point between the tables, and then press Enter a couple of times to place some distance between the tables (see Figure 22-41).

Note how the resulting tables retain the formatting features of the original.

Deleting or Converting a Table

Table deletion offers several options for deleting or converting a table, including conversion to tabular text:

1. Select the entire table and press the Delete key, or click Table ➪ Delete.

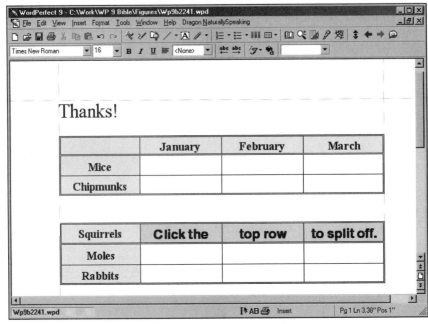

Figure 22-41: Putting some distance between two tables.

2. Select from the following deletion options, as shown in Figure 22-42:

- *Entire table*, to delete the contents and structure

- *Table contents only*, to delete the contents only, leaving the structure intact

- *Formulas only*, to remove only the table formulas, leaving the formula results intact

- *Table structure (leave text)*, to delete the structure only, leaving the contents as tabular text. (Adjust the tabs if you need to straighten out the columns of text.)

- *Convert contents to merge data file*, to turn the table into a merge data file

- *Convert contents to merge data file (use text in first row as field names)*, to turn the table into a merge data file, converting the first (column header) row to field names instead of a merge record

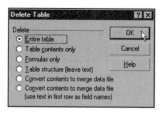

Figure 22-42: Deleting or converting a table.

Editing Table Lines, Borders, and Fills

If none of the table SpeedFormat styles described in Chapter 17 suits your needs, you can edit table lines, borders, and fills as separate graphical elements. You can then save your formatting as a custom SpeedFormat style.

Applying lines, borders, and fills

A table has no border or fill when you create it, and cells are enclosed in single lines. You can click various property bar buttons to change the inside or outside lines for a selected group of cells (you don't have to select a single cell). Select the entire table to apply a border, as shown in Figure 22-43.

Table	with	a
thick	border	⇨
and	alternating	fill

Figure 22-43: Table with a thick border and alternating fill.

You can also click Table ➪ Borders/Fill to apply lines, borders, and fills to selected cells or the entire table.

To create an alternating fill pattern:

1. Click Table ➪ Borders/Fill ➪ Table.

2. Select Rows, Columns, or Both as the alternating fill type.

3. Specify the two fills and the span count (number of rows or columns) for each (see Figure 22-44).

Cross-Reference For more on using graphic lines, borders, and fills, see Chapter 54.

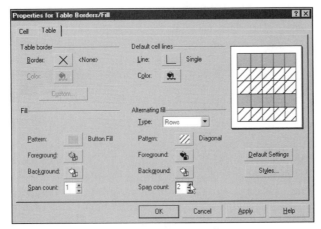

Figure 22-44: Creating an alternating fill pattern.

Saving your custom style

You finally have your table just the way you want it, perhaps with centered, bold headings, a custom alternating fill, plus a drop shadow border to set it off. To apply your styling masterpiece to other tables, save it as a SpeedFormat style:

1. Click the table, and then click Table ⇨ SpeedFormat.

2. Click Create and give your style a name to add it to the SpeedFormat collection (see Figure 22-45).

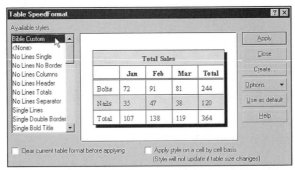

Figure 22-45: Your styling masterpiece added to the SpeedFormat collection.

For More Information . . .

On	See
Setting tabs	Chapter 21
Using the Shadow Cursor	Chapter 16
Applying graphic lines, borders, and fills	Chapter 54
Creating a chart from a table	Chapter 56
Using the ruler bar	Chapter 21
SpeedFormatting a table	Chapter 17
Calculating with WordPerfect tables	Chapter 26
Doing spreadsheet calculations in WordPerfect	Chapter 26

✦   ✦   ✦

Organizing with Bullets and Outlines

W ordPerfect makes it easy to organize and present your ideas with bullets, numbered paragraph lists, outlines, and headings. You can make your points stand out with WordPerfect's Bullets & Numbering feature, or use WordPerfect's outlining tools to organize your ideas and turn them into a polished document.

Creating Bulleted or Numbered Lists

Use bullets or paragraph numbers to set off a list of items or sequence of instructions. There are two ways you can do this:

✦ Use the Format-As-You-Go QuickBullets

✦ Insert single-level bullets and numbering styles

Using QuickBullets

To create a QuickBullet list:

1. On a new line, type preceding tabs if you want to indent the QuickBullets.

2. Type any of the following:
   - **o**, *****, **O**, ^, >, +, or - for a bulleted list (press Ctrl+W to use any other symbol, as shown in Figure 23-1)

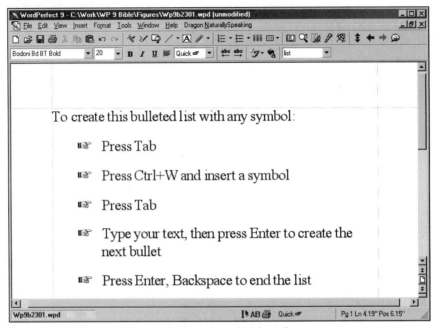

Figure 23-1: QuickBullets employing a WordPerfect character.

- A number followed by . ,) ,or - for a numbered list (type i or I for Roman numerals)
- A letter followed by . ,), or - for an alphabetical list

3. Press Tab, type your text, and then press Enter to create the next QuickBullet.

4. Press Enter ➪ Backspace to end the list.

Tip   Adjust tab settings and paragraph spacing to position the bullets and space the list just right. If QuickBullets isn't working, click Tools ➪ QuickCorrect ➪ Format-As-You-Go to be sure that it's checked.

Using Bullets & Numbering

Use Bullets & Numbering to apply bullets to existing text, or to create a bulleted or numbered list from scratch:

1. Type preceding tabs if you want to indent the list. (You can also select paragraphs of existing text.)

2. Click Insert ➪ Outline/Bullets & Numbering, click the Numbers or Bullets tab (see Figure 23-2), and select the layout you want. (Click "More bullets" to select a different symbol.)

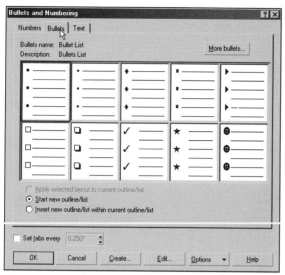

Figure 23-2: Selecting a bullet layout.

3. To adjust the spacing between tabs, check "Set tabs every" and enter the spacing.

4. Type your text, and then press Enter to create the next bullet. (To put a blank line between your bullets, press Enter before typing any text.)

5. Press Enter ➪ Backspace to end the list.

You can save bullet style changes to your style library (see Chapter 28, "Work Quickly with Templates, Projects, and Styles") and use them in future documents.

You can also click the Numbering button or the Bullets button to apply the default number or current bullet layout, or click the arrow to the button's right to select a layout from the palette.

Saving a new layout

If you created a bulleted list with a special symbol, you can save the layout to your default template to make the bullet available in all your documents. Click Insert ➪ Outline/Bullets & Numbering ➪ Bullets and select the bullet; then click Options ➪ Copy ➪ Default Template.

Changing list numbers

When you create a lettered or numbered list, WordPerfect automatically increments the list. When you end a list of items and then start a new list later in your document, WordPerfect normally resumes numbering where you left off. You can change the default list numbering in either of the following ways:

✦ When starting another list later in your document, click Insert ➪ Outline/Bullets & Numbering ➪ "Start new outline/list."

✦ To change the number of the current and subsequent list items, click the Outline Set Paragraph Number button, and then specify the "Start value" and click Set. Use Arabic numbers for letters or Roman numerals (such as 5 for "E").

What's an Outline?

When you're writing a paper, book, or anything in-between, a multilevel outline helps to arrange your ideas. An outline is a powerful aid to the reader as well. This book's table of contents, after all, is really just an outline of parts, chapters, and headings.

For occasional outlines, don't feel obligated to master the outlining tools. However, if you write large documents, WordPerfect's outlining facilities offer powerful assistance.

Understanding Outlining Terms

When you use WordPerfect's tools to create a full-fledged outline, you'll encounter the following terms illustrated in Figure 23-3:

✦ An *outline* is a hierarchical list of "parent" headings and "child" subheadings.

✦ The *outline level* refers to an item's position in the tab-stop hierarchy. Each level can have a distinct numbering type or appearance.

✦ *Outline text* is what you type after a number.

✦ *Body text* is the normal document text that you type on separate lines, between the outline items.

✦ *Outline family* is an outline item at any level, and everything under it until the next item on the same or higher level.

✦ A *level definition* specifies the style applied to a particular outline level, including indents, table of contents markers, and text attributes (such as bold or italic).

Put related level definitions together and you get one of the outline layouts described in Table 23-1.

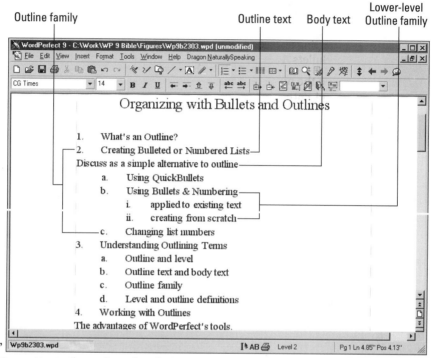

Figure 23-3: Illustration of outlining terms.

Table 23-1
Outline and List Layouts

Layout	Type	Description
Numbers		
Paragraph	Outline	The default layout, with a sequence of indented levels of 1., a., i., (1), (a), (i), 1), a) and i).
Outline	Outline	Another common layout, with a sequence of indented levels of I., A., 1., a., (1), (a), i), a) and 1).
Bullets	Outline	The levels are set off with various bullets (see Figure 23-4).
Numbers	Outline	Similar to the paragraph layout, but with paragraph numbers only (no styles).
Letters	List	Lettered list A, B, C, and so on.

Continued

Table 23-1 *(continued)*		
Layout	**Type**	**Description**
Roman	List	Roman Numeral list I, II, III, and so on.
Numbers 2	List	Numbered list 1, 2, 3, and so on.
Legal	Outline	Levels are sequenced 1, 1.1, 1.1.1, and so on, for legal documents.
Legal 2	Outline	Another legal layout, with levels of 1, 1.01, 1.01.01, and so on.
Legal 3	Outline	Same as Legal, with tabbed text instead of indented.
Legal 4	Outline	Same as Legal 2, with tabbed text instead of indented.
Bullets		
Bulleted lists	List	Bulleted lists employing various bullet characters. Clicking "More bullets" allows you to choose from the full range of WordPerfect special characters.
Text		
Headings	Numbers and styles	Instead of letters or numbers, your text is organized into ready-made headings marked for the table of contents (refer to Figure 23-4).
Definitions	Styles only	Plain Web-publishing layout of progressive indentations from the left margin.
Quotations	Styles only	Plain Web-publishing layout of progressive indentations from both margins.

For information on using the Web-publishing styles, see Chapter 14, "Web Writing and Publishing."

Working with Outlines

WordPerfect's outlining tools give you a sharp-looking outline, with level numbers that are automatically maintained as you rearrange your document.

Creating an outline and changing levels

The best way to learn outlining is to use it. You can try the fancier features after you create your basic outline. Use the headings in this chapter to create an outline for practice, or create your own. To create an outline:

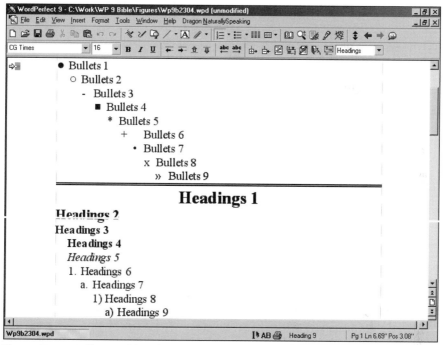

Figure 23-4: Bullets and headings outline levels.

1. Click Insert ⇨ Outline/Bullets & Numbering and select the outline definition you want, and display the outline tools on the property bar (see Figure 23-5).

Figure 23-5: Outline tools.

2. Check "Set tabs every" and specify the level indent amounts.

3. Type the text for the first item, and then press Enter and continue adding several items. (Items you add are always of the same level as the one above.)

4. Click the Outline Left Arrow button or the Outline Right Arrow button to change the level of the current item. (You can also click to the left of the text and press Tab or Shift+Tab.)

5. Click the Outline Up Arrow button or the Outline Down Arrow button to move the current item up or down a line (its level won't change, but numbers automatically re-adjust).

6. To add body text, press Enter twice and then type on the line between the outline numbers or bullets. (To go back and add text under an item, click the end of the item and then press Enter ⇨ Backspace.)

7. To end the outline, press Enter ⇨ Backspace.

Converting text to an outline and back

To create an outline from existing text, select the text, click Insert ⇨ Outline/Bullets & Numbering, and select the outline definition you want. The outline level for each paragraph is based on the number of preceding tabs or indents.

To convert outline text to body text, click at the beginning of the outline text, then press Backspace.

Hiding levels and text

One of the handiest outlining features is the ability to hide outline levels or body text in order to work on your outline in different ways:

✦ Click the Outline Hide Body Text button to show or hide the body text. (Note that the Outline Hide Body Text button remains depressed on the toolbar when body text is hidden.)

✦ Click the Outline Hide Family button to hide the family of an outline item, and the Outline Show Family button to show it again. (Hide a family to move it as a single line.)

✦ Click the Outline Show Levels button to pick how many levels (1–9) you want to display. Select <None> to hide the entire outline, other than the body text.

Information that is collapsed (hidden) doesn't print. This enables you to print your outline to any level, with or without the body text.

Level icon tricks

Click the Outline Display Icons button to display outline level icons in the left margin. The hollow numbers from 1 to 9 indicate the level of an outline item and its associated text (with a hollow "T"). A plus sign (+) indicates that subordinate items are hidden; a minus sign (–) indicates that the entire family is showing.

Tip   Double-clicking an icon alternately hides and shows the subordinate items and text for that family.

When you point to an outline level icon, a double arrow appears. You can then click to select that item's family and drag it to a new location. A horizontal line indicates where the family will be inserted (see Figure 23-6).

Horizontal line indicates new location

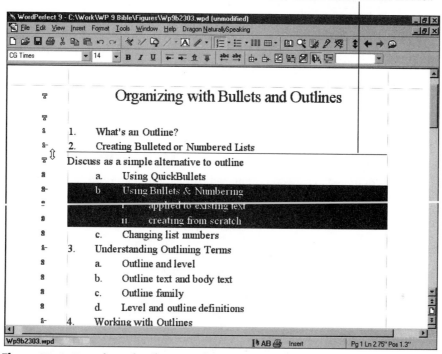

Figure 23-6: Dragging a family to another location.

Tabbing outline items

When you press Tab (or Shift+Tab) at the beginning of an item, you change its level. To tab the item without changing its level, press Ctrl+Tab or Ctrl+Shift+Tab.

Changing an outline item's number

New Feature

To change the number of the current item and subsequent items in an outline family, click the Outline Set Paragraph Number button, specify the "Start value," and click Set (see Figure 23-7). Use Arabic numbers for letters or Roman numerals (such as 5 for "E" or "V").

Figure 23-7: Changing an outline item's number.

Changing an outline's layout

To change your outline's layout, click Insert ⇨ Outline/Bullets & Numbering, select the new layout, and then click either of the following:

✦ *Apply selected layout to current outline/list*, to change the entire outline to the new layout

✦ *Start new outline/list*, to begin the new layout and numbering from that point on

Converting outline level items to headings

After your document has been completed by fleshing out your outline, you can convert the outline level items to formatted document headings, premarked for the table of contents. Go to the beginning of your outline, click Insert ⇨ Outline/Bullets & Numbering ⇨ Text, and select the Headings layout.

Inserting paragraph numbers anywhere in your text

WordPerfect lets you insert a paragraph number anywhere in your document, without upsetting the current numbering format:

1. Click View ⇨ Toolbars to display the Outline toolbar, and then click the Paragraph Number button, or press Ctrl+Shift+F5 on the Windows keyboard. (You can add this keystroke to a DOS keyboard, as explained in Chapter 57, "Customizing Toolbars, Menus, and Keyboards.")

2. Specify the outline level, start value, and number type (refer to Figure 23-7).

3. Check Automatic if you want the level to reflect the number of tabs before the number.

Working with Multiple Outlines or Lists

New Feature   Normally, when you have multiple outlines in a single document, each one is a separate entity, with its own numbering and layout. You can, however, get pretty fancy.

Picking up an outline or list where you left off

To pick up an outline or list where you left off, click the Numbering button and start typing.

Nesting outlines and lists

To insert a new outline within the current one, click Insert ⇨ Outline/Bullets &
Numbering, select the layout, and then click "Insert new outline/list within current
outline/list."

Customizing Outline Layouts and Styles

You can customize an outline's layout or styles (or create new layouts or styles),
and then save them to your default template so that they can be used in other
documents.

Styles associated with outline layouts

Each of the outline layouts (aside from Numbers), employs particular paragraph
styles for each of the nine levels it contains. (Definitions and Quotations outlines
are for Web page formatting, not outlining.)

The eleven layouts used for outlining actually use four sets of outline paragraph
styles, as shown in Table 23-2. Because the Paragraph, Outline, and Bullets outlines
use the same styles (with different numbers or bullets), changing the styles for one
layout changes them for the others as well. Likewise, a change to the Legal
definition styles also affects Legal 2. Only the Headings layout has unique styles.

Table 23-2	
Outline Layouts with Their Associated Styles	
Outline Layout	*Associated Styles*
Paragraph	Level styles 1 through 9
Outline	Level styles 1 through 9
Bullets	Level styles 1 through 9
Numbers	Level style 1
Numbers 2	Level style 1
Roman	Level style 1
Legal	Legal styles 1 through 9
Legal 2	Legal styles 1 through 9
Legal 3	Legal(tab) styles 1 through 9
Legal 4	Legal(tab) styles 1 through 9
Headings	Heading styles 1 through 9

Customizing an outline layout

You can change the delivered outline layouts and styles, but it's usually safer to leave the originals alone and create custom layouts and styles for your particular needs. You might, for example, create a custom headings layout called "MyBook" with its own level styles, to use in writing books or reports.

To create or edit outline layouts and styles:

1. Click Insert ⇨ Outline/Bullets & Numbering.

2. Click Create to create a new layout, or select a layout and click Edit.

3. If you're creating a new layout, give it a name and description (see Figure 23-8).

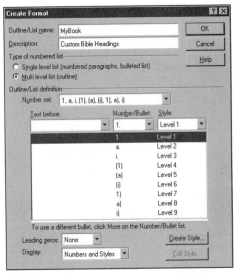

Figure 23-8: Naming and describing a new layout.

4. Use any of the options described in Table 23-3.

	Table 23-3 **Outline Definition Options**
Option	**Lets You**
Type of numbered list	Choose between single-level bullets or paragraph numbers, and multilevel outlines.
Number set	Select a set of numbers on which to base your outline.

Option	Lets You
Number/Bullet	Specify the number or bullet for each level.
Text before	Specify text to precede the number or bullet. (Include a space.)
Style	Select a style for each level.
Leading zeros	Specify leading zeros for particular levels.
Display	Specify whether to use Numbers and Styles, Numbers Only (without styles), or Styles Only (as with headings).
Create Style	Create new styles for various levels of your definition, rather than edit the shipped styles.
Edit Style	Edit the existing styles for various levels of your definition.

Caution

Remember, changes to shipped styles affect other outline definitions using the same styles.

Using custom outline layouts and styles in other documents

Normally, the changes you make to outline layouts or styles (and the new ones you create) affect only the current document. To use a new or modified layout in other documents, click Insert ➪ Outline/Bullets & Numbering, select the layout, click Options ➪ Copy, and then copy it to the default template or additional objects template. See Chapter 28, "Work Quickly with Templates, Projects, and Styles," for more on using templates and styles.

For More Information . . .

On	See
Using Web-publishing outline styles	Chapter 14
Customizing a keyboard	Chapter 57
Numbering lines	Chapter 21
Editing styles and templates	Chapter 28
Generating a table of contents	Chapter 25

✦   ✦   ✦

Adding Document References

If you've never pounded away at a typewriter until five in the morning, adding footnotes to your term paper before the ten o'clock class, you've missed one of life's memorable experiences. You'll never know what it was like to stop in the middle of a page, roll the typewriter carriage back and forth, mark the margin with a pencil to reserve space at the bottom, type more text, add the separator line, and finally the footnote, only to realize that you left out a vital note three pages back.

Footnotes and endnotes are easy to add in WordPerfect. The program is also adept at other document references such as lists of captions, cross-references, and index entries. You can even mark your text to automatically generate a table of contents. Short of the final printing and binding, you can almost publish a book by using WordPerfect alone.

Document references can be classed into two types:

✦ Notes (including footnotes, endnotes, and citations)

✦ Tabulations (such as lists, cross-references, indexes, tables of contents, and tables of authorities)

Inserting Footnotes and Endnotes

Three types of notes are used for document references:

✦ A *footnote* inserts a reference number or other pointer in your text, and then places the explanatory notes, citation sources, or comments at the bottom of the page (see Figure 24-1).

With WordPerfect footnotes are so easy they're almost fun, as are such document references as endnotes, lists of captions, cross-references, and index entries. You can even mark your text to automatically generate a table of contents. Short of the final printing and binding, you can almost publish a book by using WordPerfect alone.

Document references can be classed into two types:

✔ Notes (including footnotes, endnotes, and in-text citations)

✔ Tabulations (such as lists, cross-references, indexes, tables of contents, and tables of authorities)

This chapter shows you how to add notes to your papers, books, and reports, and mark tabulation entries. Chapter 25 shows you how to generate the table of contents, index, and other tabulations.

Using Footnotes and Endnotes

Three types of notes are used for document references:

✔ A *footnote* inserts a reference number or other pointer in your text, then places the explanatory notes, citation sources, or comments at the bottom of the page (see Figure 24-1). A separator line is placed between the text and your footnotes.

✔ An *endnote* is similar to a footnote, except that your notes are assembled together at the end of a paper, chapter, or other part of your work, rather than on the pages where the citations occur.

✔ An *in-text citation* places the author and page of a cited work in parenthesis in the text, such as "(Kant, 156)," instead of a reference number. The reader turns to the bibliography at the end of the work to find the remainder of the reference (such as the title, publisher, and date). WordPerfect doesn't provide an in-text citation feature.[1]

The choice between footnotes and endnotes is primarily one of aesthetics and convenience. Endnotes may present a cleaner appearance, but the reader must flip back and forth to read the notes and to check references. In the typewriter days, endnotes were easier to create, since all the notes could be typed at once, and there was no fussing with separator lines and spacing at the bottom of the page. With a word processor, however, footnotes are just as easy to create, and they save you the work of setting up the endnote page.[2]

[1] Use QwkScreen's In-text Citation feature to create citations that conform to standard styles.

[2] So keep in mind that footnotes are the easiest to create with WordPerfect, with endnotes a close second, and in-text citations a distant third. However, if you are writing for a

Seperation line   Reference numbers

Figure 24-1: A reference number is inserted for each footnote you create.

✦ *Endnotes*, as their name implies, are assembled at the end of a paper, chapter, or other part of your work, rather than on the pages where the citations occur.

✦ An *in-text citation* places the author and page of a cited work in parentheses in the text, such as "(Kant, 156)," instead of a reference number. The reader turns to the bibliography at the end of the work to find the remainder of the reference, such as the title, publisher, and date. (There's no in-text citation feature, as they're easy to type.)

Endnotes may give the main document a cleaner appearance, but the reader must flip back and forth to read the notes or check references. Where you have a choice, footnotes are just as easy to create, and they save you the work of setting up the endnote page.

Creating a footnote or endnote

You can add footnotes and endnotes as you type your text, or you can go back to insert them later:

1. Place the insertion point where you want the reference to appear.

2. Click Insert ➪ Footnote/Endnote ➪ Footnote (or Endnote) ➪ Create.

3. Type the note (see Figure 24-2), and then click the Close icon.

Tip
You can also click outside of your notes when you're in Page view.

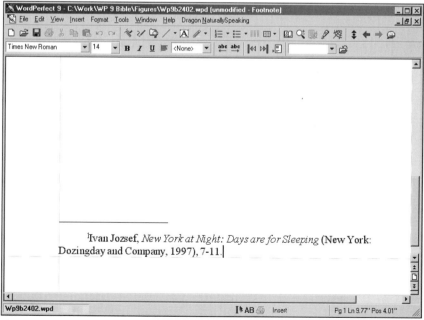

Figure 24-2: Creating a footnote (in Page view).

Tip   WordPerfect automatically provides spacing between the notes, so don't press Enter at the end of a note, or you'll get an extra blank line.

WordPerfect automatically numbers or renumbers the notes you insert. When a footnote can't fit entirely on a page, it carries over to the next.

Caution   A note's number is part of the footnote or endnote style, which includes a Footnote (or Endnote) Number Display code for automatic numbering. If you accidentally delete the number, use Undo (Ctrl+Z) to restore it. Don't retype it.

Viewing footnotes and endnotes

In Draft view, footnotes and endnotes are kept out of sight (as are headers and footers), to help you focus on the body of your text. Switch to Page view (View ➪ Page) if you want to see your notes.

Editing a footnote or endnote

Simply click a footnote or endnote in Page view to edit it, and then click back in your text (or click the Close icon) when you're done. In either Draft or Page view, you can also click Insert ➪ Footnote/ Endnote ➪ Footnote (or Endnote), and then specify the note number and click Edit.

Moving text with footnotes or endnotes

When you move document text, accompanying footnotes and endnotes move with it (be sure to include the reference number). When you change the order of your notes, their numbers automatically adjust.

Deleting a footnote or endnote

Footnotes and endnotes are deleted when you delete the text in which their references are contained. To delete only the note, simply delete the reference number.

Resetting footnote or endnote numbering

At some points in your document, you might want to reset your note numbering — back to 1 at the beginning of each chapter, for example. To reset footnote or endnote numbering:

1. Click where you want to start renumbering your notes.

2. Click Insert ➪ Footnote/Endnote ➪ Footnote (or Endnote) ➪ Options ➪ Set Number.

3. Type a new number, or click Increase or Decrease to change it by one (see Figure 24-3).

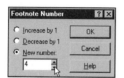

Figure 24-3: Resetting a note's number.

You can also renumber endnote numbers when you specify their placement, as described in the next section.

Specifying endnote placement

Normally, endnotes are placed at the end of your document. That may be fine, but if your document has an index, for example, you'll probably want to place your endnotes before the end. If you're writing a book or journal, you may want to place endnotes at the end of each chapter or article.

To specify endnote placement:

1. Click where you want the endnotes to appear.
2. Click Insert ⇨ Footnote/Endnote ⇨ Endnote ⇨ Endnote Placement.
3. To also restart subsequent endnotes at number 1, click "Insert endnotes at insertion point and restart numbering" (see Figure 24-4).

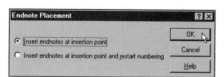

Figure 24-4: Specifying endnote placement.

WordPerfect inserts an Endnote Placement code (which displays as a graphic in Draft view), followed by a hard page break to separate your endnotes from the next page of text.

To also start your endnotes on a new page, press Ctrl+Enter to insert a hard page break, and type a heading for your endnotes just before the placement code.

Endnotes inserted before the placement code appear at the code. Endnotes inserted after the placement code appear at the next placement code, or at the end of your document.

Changing the footnote line separator

To change the length, style, spacing, and position of the line separator between your text and footnotes:

1. Click the page where you want your line separator changes to begin.

2. Click Insert ➪ Footnote/Endnote ➪ Footnote ➪ Options ➪ Separator, and then specify any of the options shown Figure 24-5 and described in Table 24-1.

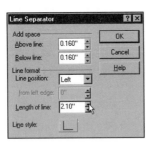

Figure 24-5: Changing the footnote line separator.

Table 24-1
Line Separator Options

Option	*Lets You*
Add space above line	Change the amount of space between the line and the text above it
Add space below line	Change the amount of space between the line and the footnote below it
Line position	Place the line in the left margin, from margin to margin (full), centered between the margins, in the right margin, or at a set position from the left edge of the page
Length of line	Change the length of the line
Line style	Select a different line style from the palette

Setting advanced footnote and endnote options

To set advanced footnote and endnote options:

1. Click where you want the options to take effect.

2. Click Insert ➪ Footnote/Endnote ➪ Footnote (or Endnote) Options ➪ Advanced.

3. Specify any of the options described in Table 24-2 for footnotes (see Figure 24-6) or endnotes (see Figure 24-7).

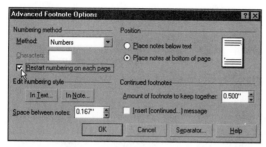

Figure 24-6: Setting advanced footnote options.

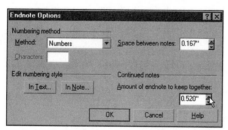

Figure 24-7: Setting advanced endnote options.

Table 24-2
Advanced Footnote and Endnote Options

Option	Lets You
Numbering method	Choose from Arabic numbers, uppercase or lowercase letters or Roman numerals, or characters.
Characters	Specify (when using characters) one to five characters, separated with commas, to use for your notes. (Press Ctrl+W to use symbols.) Each character is used in turn, and then doubled (**), tripled (***), and so on, as needed for additional notes. (One accepted sequence of symbols is *, †, ‡, §, |.)
Restart numbering on each page (footnotes only)	Restart footnote numbers on each page. (This option is especially useful when using characters for your numbering.)

Continued

	Table 24-2 *(continued)*
Option	**Lets You**
Position (footnotes only)	Place footnotes at the bottom of the page (the default) or immediately following your text.
Space between notes	Adjust the amount of space between footnotes or endnotes. (Books often simply indent footnotes, with 0 spacing between them.)
Edit numbering style	Change the style of your in-text note numbers (In Text) or the number and style of the notes themselves (In Note). See "Editing footnote and endnote styles," later in this chapter.
Amount of footnote (or endnote) to keep together	Specify, when there's not enough room to print the entire note, how much of your note must print on the current page before splitting the note to print the remainder on the next page. If there's not enough space left (the default is about three lines), the entire note gets bumped to the next page.
Insert (continued . . .) message	Print a "(continued . . .)" message when footnotes split across pages.

Changing footnote and endnote settings for all new documents

To change footnote settings (other than styles) for all new documents:

1. Click File ➪ Document ➪ Current Document Style and check "Use as default."
2. Select the options you want from the Styles Editor Insert menu (see Figure 24-8).

Editing footnote and endnote styles

You can edit the system styles of your footnotes and endnotes; for example, to print your notes in a different font or smaller font size. Changing the format or font of your notes won't affect your document's text, and vice versa.

You might also want to edit the footnote style so that footnote text lines up after the number. (With reveal codes checked in the Styles Editor, delete the tab code in the footnote style, and place an indent after the note number instead.) The endnote style simply prints the number, so you might want to add a tab or indent after it.

Tip   For notes with tabs or indents, move the tab setting closer to the number so the space between the number and the text is not too large.

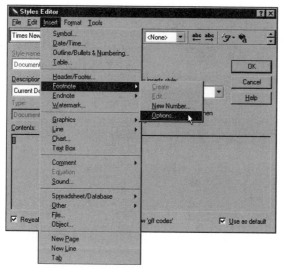

Figure 24-8: Changing footnote and endnote settings for all new documents.

To change the styles of footnotes or endnotes in your document, click Insert ➪ Footnote/Endnote ➪ Footnote (or Endnote) ➪ Options ➪ Advanced, ➪ In Note. For more on editing styles, see Chapter 28, "Work Quickly with Templates, Projects, and Styles."

Changing footnote and endnote styles for all new documents

Changes to your footnote and endnote styles normally affect only your current document. To change the styles for all your new documents, you must edit the system styles in your Default template:

1. Click Format ➪ Styles.

2. Click Options ➪ Settings, and make sure that "WordPerfect system styles" is checked, then click "WordPerfect heading styles and all other system styles" to display the footnote and endnote styles.

3. Select the note style ([Footnote], or [Endnote]) or reference number style ([Ftn#inDoc] or [Endn#inDoc]) that you want to edit, and then click Edit.

4. Edit the tabs, font, margins, and other aspects of the style, and then click OK.

5. Click Options ➪ Copy ➪ Default template ➪ OK, and then click Yes when prompted to override the existing style.

Footnote and endnote tips and techniques

This section provides additional tips and techniques for special footnote and endnote situations you might encounter.

Using both footnotes and endnotes in a document

Some heavily documented works employ a dual system of notes: endnotes for citations and footnotes for substantive notes, definitions of terms, or translations of foreign words and phrases. To distinguish the in-text references, change the footnote numbering to Characters, as described in "Setting advanced footnote and endnote options," earlier in this chapter.

Aligning endnotes

When you type in endnote numbers 1 through 9, they line up nicely, one right under the other. When you get to number 10, however, that extra digit shifts the decimal point over to the right. To line up those decimal points:

1. Click Insert ⇨ Footnote/Endnote ⇨ Endnote ⇨ Options ⇨ Advanced ⇨ In Note.

2. Without moving the insertion point, click Format ⇨ Line ⇨ Tab Set.

3. Select Decimal from the Tab type list and specify 0.25 inches (.63 cm.) in the Tab position box (see Figure 24-9). This flushes the endnote numbers right against the decimal, and allows for the width of a standard 12-point character. (You may need to experiment with the width, or double the amount if your endnotes run to three digits.)

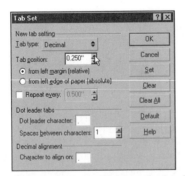

Figure 24-9: Specifying a decimal tab to align your endnotes.

4. Click Set and Close to return to the Styles Editor.

5. Click Insert ⇨ Tab from the Styles Editor menu bar to insert a decimal tab (see Figure 24-10), and then click OK.

Figure 24-10: Adding the decimal tab to your endnote style.

To use this endnote style in all your new documents, see "Changing footnote and endnote styles for all new documents," earlier in this chapter.

Inserting footnotes in tables and columns

You can place footnotes in newspaper columns, but not in parallel columns. You can also place footnotes in tables, but footnotes placed in table header rows are changed to endnotes.

Converting footnotes and endnotes

Suppose you just completed a 28-page paper with 50 footnotes, only to realize that you should have used endnotes instead! Don't panic. Simply click Tools ➪ Macro ➪ Play and run the Footend macro that comes with the program to automatically convert the footnotes to endnotes. There's also an Endfoot macro to convert endnotes to footnotes.

Making Lists

Lists are a form of document reference that we often see, but rarely think about. One example is the list often found in the front of a book that indicates where figures, illustrations, charts, graphs, and other exhibits can be found (see Figure 24-11). The "In This Chapter" sections in this book are lists.

Charts and Tables

World Demand for Nonrenewable Resources 23

Estimated Productivity of the Ocean by Region 41

Millions of US Employed, by Sector, 1950-2000 72

Patterns of International Trade 84

Domestic and Global Income Distribution 107

Federal, State, and local Taxation and Spending 124

Shifting Patterns of Debt 146

Emerging Growth Industries 159

Figure 24-11: A typical list.

Creating a list is a three-step process:

✦ Defining the list and specifying its placement

✦ Marking the text to include in the list

✦ Generating the list

You can mark the text before you specify the list placement, but you must always begin by defining the list. When listing graphics boxes, you don't even have to mark the caption text.

Defining a list and specifying its placement

To define a list and specify its placement in your document:

1. Click where you want the list to appear.

2. If you want the list to start at the top of a new page, press Ctrl+Enter to insert a page break.

3. Type and format the title for the list, and then press Enter at least twice to put some space between the title and the list.

4. Click Tools ⇨ Reference ⇨ List, and then click Define on the List toolbar (see Figure 24-12).

Figure 24-12: The list toolbar.

5. Click the Create button in the Define List dialog box to call up the Create List dialog, and give the list a name (see Figure 24-13).

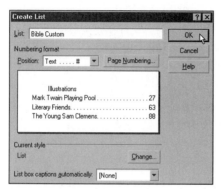

Figure 24-13: Defining a list.

Tip

The name of the list is used for marking list items and generating the list. It doesn't print in your document.

6. Specify any of the following:

- *Position*, to specify how the page number for each list item is displayed and its position relative to the text. You can also choose not to print page numbers.

- *Page Numbering*, to specify a page numbering format different from that of the rest of your document. For more on page numbering, see Chapter 20.

- *Change*, to edit the default hanging indent list style. You might want to leave the default style and then create a custom style to use with your lists. For more on styles, see Chapter 28.

- *List box captions automatically*, to list captions for graphics boxes using the caption type you select, such as Table, Figure, or Text.

7. Click OK, select the definition, and then click Insert. A nonprinting comment, << List will generate here >, displays in your document.

Tip To instantly define a list, type its name in the List box of the List toolbar, and then mark a text item to include in the list. Your list will be assigned the default style, which you can edit later on.

Deleting a list definition

To delete a list definition in a document, click Tools ➪ Reference ➪ List, and then click Define. Select the definition and click Delete.

Retrieving list definitions from another document

To retrieve list definitions from another document and insert them into the current document:

1. Click Tools ➪ Reference ➪ List ➪ Define ➪ Retrieve.

2. Specify the name and path of the document with the list definitions you want, click OK, and then select the definitions you want to retrieve (see Figure 24-14).

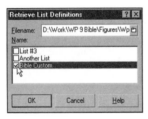

Figure 24-14: Retrieving list definitions from another document.

Marking text to include in a list

To mark the items of text to include in a list:

1. Click Tools ➪ Reference ➪ List, and then select the name of the list in the text box on the toolbar.

2. Select the text for the list item, and then click Mark (or press Alt+Shift+M).

3. Repeat Step 2 to add other items to the list.

Unmarking list items

In Reveal Codes, you can see that each item marked for a list is surrounded by a pair of [Mrk Txt List] codes. If you position the insertion point to the left of a code, you will also see the name of the list for which the item is marked. To unmark an item, simply delete one of its surrounding codes.

Making a list of graphics box captions

You don't need to mark graphics box captions to include them in a list. Select the appropriate caption type in Step 6 of "Defining a list and specifying its placement" above. Note that the Image, Figure, and OLE 2.0 boxes all use Figure Box captions.

Generating lists

Lists are generated along with other document references, including the table of contents, cross-references, and the index. To generate your references at any time, click Tools ➪ Reference ➪ Generate. You can also click Generate on the List toolbar. (Be sure to regenerate your lists when you're done editing your document, so they'll contain the final page numbers for the marked items.)

The list definition must be inserted into your document text in order for the list to generate.

When you generate a list in a master document, text marked in any subdocuments is included. See Chapter 25, "Assembling Multipart Documents," for information on generating master documents.

Creating a Table of Contents

Various types of document references differ more in name than in substance. A table of contents like the one shown in Figure 24-15 is simply a special type of list. Like a list, it automatically updates page numbers each time it's generated.

A table of contents can have up to five levels of headings (for parts, chapters, sections, and so on). As with outlines, each level can have a different style.

As with other lists, creating a table of contents is a three-step process:

✦ Marking the text to include in various levels of the table

✦ Defining the appearance and inserting the definition

✦ Generating the table of contents

Normally you'd mark your text as you go along and define the table of contents when you're about done with your document. You can, however, define the table of contents at any time and continue to mark entries.

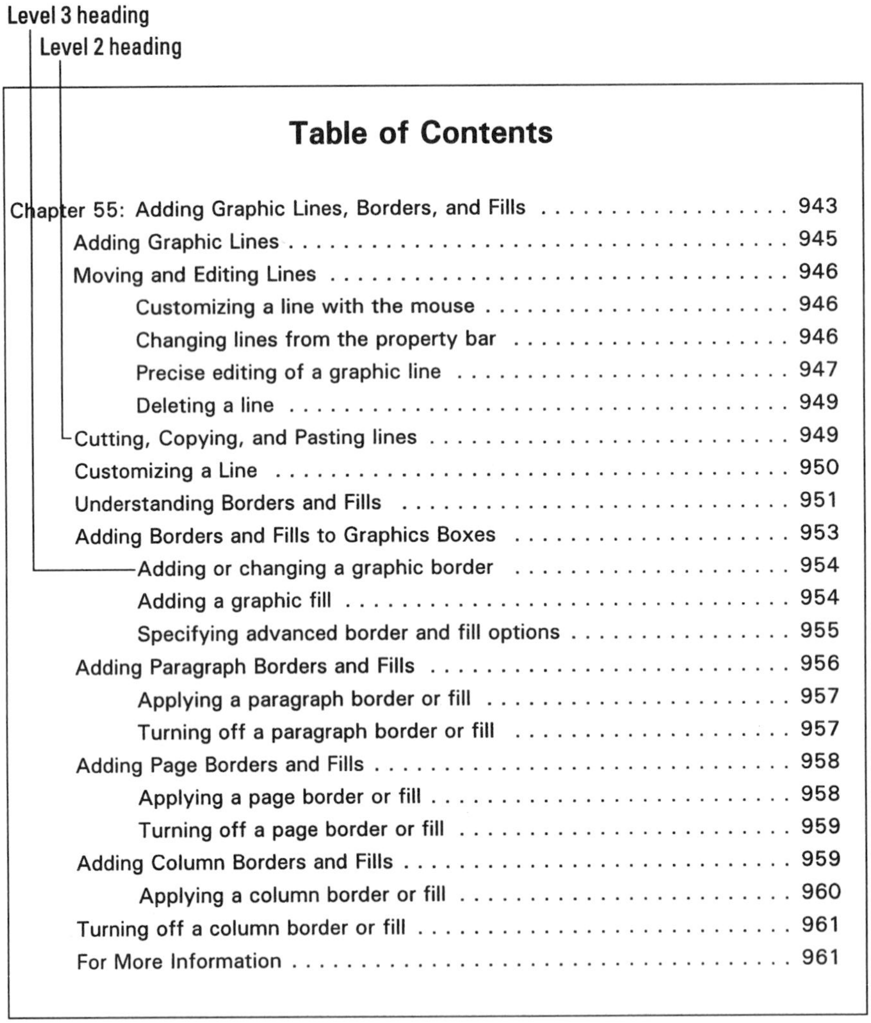

Level 3 heading
Level 2 heading

Table of Contents

Figure 24-15: Table of contents.

Automatically marking text by using heading styles

Items in a table of contents normally include the major divisions of a work, such as chapters, sections, and headings. Items from the front and the back of the work are often found as well, such as the preface, introduction, glossary, bibliography, appendices, and index.

If you apply the built-in heading styles 1–5 to the various levels of titles and headings, your text is automatically marked for levels 1–5 of the table of contents. The rest is easy.

Cross-Reference For more on styles see Chapter 28, "Working Quickly with Templates, Projects, and Styles."

When you create a document from an outline that uses the Headings outline definition, heading levels 1–5 are automatically marked for the corresponding level in the table of contents.

Manually marking table of contents text

You can also mark text manually for inclusion in the table of contents:

1. Click Tools ➪ Reference ➪ Table of Contents to display the Table of Contents toolbar (see Figure 24-16).

Figure 24-16: Table of Contents toolbar.

2. Select the text for your table of contents entry.

Tip The appearance and size of the selected text are retained in the table of contents, as are other formatting codes, such as [HRt]. If you don't want attributes and codes to carry over to the table of contents, turn on Reveal Codes and select the text without its accompanying codes.

3. Click the appropriate Mark button from the toolbar, depending on the level (1–5) on which you want the entry to appear.

4. Repeat Steps 2 and 3 for each of the items you want to include.

Unmarking table of contents items

In Reveal Codes you can see that each item marked for inclusion in the table of contents is surrounded by a pair of [Mrk Txt ToC] codes. (If you position the insertion point to the left of the code, the code's level will be shown.) To unmark an item, simply delete one of the surrounding codes.

Defining the table of contents

To specify the appearance of the table of contents and insert its definition:

1. Click where you want the table of contents to appear.

2. To start at the top of a new page, press Ctrl+Enter to insert a page break.

3. Type and format the title for the table of contents. Press Enter at least twice to put some space between the title and the table.

4. Click Tools ➪ Reference ➪ Table of Contents, and then click Define and specify the number of levels (1–5) you want to include (see Figure 24-17). Text marked for a lower level won't appear in the table of contents.

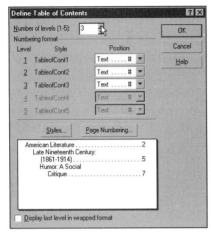

Figure 24-17: Specifying the number of levels for your table of contents.

5. Select any of the following options:

- *Position*, to specify how the page number is displayed for each level, and its position relative to the text. You can also choose not to print page numbers (such as for the top-level part numbers in a larger work.)

- *Styles*, to edit the level styles or define custom styles. See "Customizing table of contents level styles," which follows.

- *Page Numbering*, to specify a page numbering format different from that of the remainder of your document. See Chapter 22 for more on numbering pages.

- *Display last level in wrapped format*, to let text for the last level wrap the left margin instead of using the hanging indent style. This option is especially useful when your table of contents has three levels or more, and you want to use the last level to list minor topics in a compact form. (Don't use the flush right page numbering position on the wrapped level, since that would defeat the purpose of wrapping.)

6. Click OK. A nonprinting comment, << Table of Contents will generate here >, displays in your document.

7. If you want the table of contents to be on a page by itself, press Ctrl+Enter to insert a page break.

8. If you want a new page number to begin after the table of contents (for example, if the table of contents is on page v, and you want the next page to be page 1), set a new number for the page that follows the table of contents (see Chapter 20).

Caution WordPerfect generates a table of contents in each place it finds a definition. If you accidentally end up with two or more definitions in your document, go into Reveal Codes and delete the [Def Mark] codes you don't want.

Customizing table of contents level styles

You can modify the table of contents level styles that come with WordPerfect. A safer approach, however, is to leave the original definitions alone and use them as the basis for creating custom definitions and styles suited to your particular needs. You might, for example, want to create custom level styles TableofCont1a, TableofCont2a, and so on.

Creating and editing table of contents level styles

To create custom table of contents level styles, or to edit level styles:

1. Click Tools ➪ Reference ➪ Table of Contents.

2. Click Define, click Styles, and select the level for the style you want to create or edit (see Figure 24-18).

Figure 24-18: Selecting the level for the style you want to create or edit.

3. Do one or more of the following:

   • Select the style you want to associate with the level.

   • Click Edit, and then edit the style.

   • Click Create, and then create a new style for the level.

Using custom table of contents level styles in other documents

Normally, when you create or edit a table of contents level style, your changes apply only to that document. To use your changes in other documents, you must save them to the Default template or the Additional Objects template. For more on styles and templates, see Chapter 28.

Generating a table of contents

The table of contents is generated along with other document references, including lists, cross-references, and the index. To generate your references at any time, click Tools ⇨ Reference ⇨ Generate. You can also click Generate on the Table of Contents toolbar.

When you generate a table of contents for a master document, text marked in any subdocuments is included. See Chapter 25 for information on assembling multipart documents.

Editing the table of contents

You can edit a table of contents after it has been generated, but keep in mind that any errors you correct in the table of contents — rather than at the source where the text is marked — will reappear the next time you generate document references. So it's usually better to edit the document text, then regenerate the references.

Creating a Table of Authorities

If you don't know what a table of authorities is, you probably don't need one. A *table of authorities* is a list of the cases and statutes cited in a legal brief (see Figure 24-19). The table can be divided into sections (such as for cases, constitutional provisions, statutes, and regulations) that are sorted alphabetically. Citations might occur anywhere in your document, including footnotes and endnotes, not only in the body of your text.

Each section of a table of authorities is actually a single-level table defined and inserted on its own, with its own text citations. There is no definition for the table of authorities as a whole.

Creating a table of authorities involves four steps:

✦ Decide what sections you'll need

✦ Marking the text to include in the various sections of the table

✦ Defining the sections

✦ Generating the table

TABLE OF AUTHORITIES

CASES

Alan MacWeeney, Inc. v. Esquire Associates, Inc., Nos. 43849-43850, Decision of
September 26, 1991 . . . . 41, 42

Blakemore v. Coleman, 701 F.2d 967, (D.C. Cir. 1983) 36

Castorina v. Rosen, 290 N.Y. 445 (1943) 27

Crosby v. 20 Fifth Avenue Hotel Co., 172 Misc. 595, 173 Misc. 604 19

Dearmyer v. Clark, 71 A.D.2d 807, 419 N.Y.S.2d 361 (4th Dep't 1979) 15, 22

E.F. Hutton Group, Inc. v. United States Postal Service, 723 F. Supp. 951 (S.D.N.Y. 1989)
. . . . 34, 35

General Motors Acceptance Corp. v. Grafinger, 61 Misc. 2d 670, 306 N.Y.S.2d 606
(N.Y.C. Civ. Ct., N.Y. Cty 1969) 19

Girard Studio Group. Inc. v. Young & Rubican, Inc. 147 S.D. 2d 357 (1st Dept. 1989)

. . . . 38, 39

Goldstein v. Pullman Co., 220 N.Y. 549 (1917) 29

Guild v. Atlantic-Third Corporation, 18 Misc. 2d 635, 186 N.Y.S.2d 77 (App. Term, 2d
Dep't 1959) 15, 22

Hoffman v. Portogallo. Inc. (Supreme Court, New York County, Index No.
19102/85) June 25, 1987 38

Hunter Trucking Co., Inc. v. Glatzer, 285 App. Div. 314, 136 N.Y.S.2d 857 (1st Dep't
1955) 22, 25, 26

Figure 24-19: Table of authorities.

Deciding what sections you'll need

The first step in creating a table of authorities is to decide what sections you'll need
for grouping your citations. You may want to simply sketch them out on a piece of
paper before you begin.

Automatically marking citations via CiteLink

**New
Feature**

If you have the Legal Edition of WordPerfect Office, you can use the accompanying
CiteLink utility to automatically find and mark the legal citations in your document.
CiteLink can also generate a table of authorities at the top of your document,
sorted into standard categories, with page numbers and links to each citation.

Not only that, CiteLink can hyperlink each citation, so readers can click to see the full text of the citation at the WestDoc Web site (www.westlaw.com). For more on hyperlinks, see Chapter 14, "Web Writing and Publishing."

To automatically mark citations in the current document by using CiteLink:

1. Click the CiteLink Auto Mark icon (Tools ➪ West Group Legal ➪ Auto-Mark Citations Via CiteLink).

2. Click Settings to change any of the displayed settings, and then click OK to run CiteLink (see Figure 24-20).

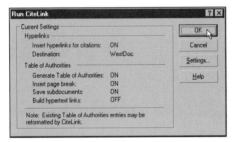

Figure 24-20: Automatically marking citations via CiteLink.

As you update your document, you can re-run CiteLink at any time to remove deleted citations from the table of authorities and add new ones.

You can also manually mark citations for the table of authorities, although they won't have Internet hyperlinks.

Manually marking legal citations

Marking text for a table of authorities is different from marking text for a list or a table of contents. That is because the various cases, statutes, and other items in the table are often cited multiple times, perhaps with different wordings. To be sure that citations for the same source are alike, you define the citation the first time it is encountered, and then insert the same citation in your text at each subsequent occurrence.

The way you mark text for a table of authorities, therefore, depends on whether the citation is a first occurrence or subsequent occurrence:

✦ On the first occurrence, you define both a Full Form for the citation (the way you want the citation to appear in the table) and a Short Form (the name by which you look it up when you mark subsequent occurrences).

✦ On subsequent occurrences, you look up the Short Form from the Table of Authorities toolbar and mark the text.

Creating the first citation of an item

To mark the first citation of a table of authorities item:

1. Click Tools ➪ Reference ➪ Table of Authorities, if necessary, to display the Table of Authorities (ToA) toolbar (see Figure 24-21).

Figure 24-21: Table of Authorities toolbar.

2. Select the text for the citation and click Create Full Form.

3. Type the section of the table in which you want the citation to appear, or select a section from the list.

4. Edit the Short Form text the way you want it to display on the toolbar (see Figure 24-22). (It doesn't appear in the table.)

Figure 24-22: Creating the first citation of an item.

5. Click OK, edit the Full Form text the way you want it to appear in the table, and then click Close.

Revising a citation's Full Form text

To revise a citation's Full Form text, click Edit Full Form on the Table of Authorities toolbar. Next, select the item, click OK, edit the text, and then click Close.

Marking subsequent occurrences of a citation

To mark subsequent citations of a table of authorities item:

1. Click Tools ➪ Reference ➪ Table of Authorities, if necessary, to display the ToA toolbar.

2. Click where you want to mark the item.

3. Select the item's Short Form name from the list (or type it in the text box), and then click Mark.

4. Repeat Step 3 to mark subsequent occurrences.

Unmarking table of authorities items

When you mark an item of text for inclusion in the table of authorities, a [TOA] code is inserted in your document. When displayed in detail in Reveal Codes (if the code is not displayed in detail, place the insertion point to the left of the code), the code for the first citation of an item is in the form of [TOA: section name, short form name, Full Form]. The codes for subsequent markings read [TOA: short form name].

To delete a table of authorities citation, go into Reveal Codes and delete the code. If you delete the Full Form code and leave subsequent markings for the item in your text, you will get a warning during the generation process that WordPerfect can't find the Full Form text. The program will substitute the Short Form text in your table of authorities, preceded by an asterisk.

Defining the table of authorities

Defining a table of authorities is a three-step process:

✦ Typing the headings for the table of authorities and its various sections in your document

✦ Marking where you want the various sections to appear

✦ Defining the format of each section

To define a table of authorities:

1. Click where you want the table of authorities to appear.

2. Type **Table of Authorities** (or whatever title you use) and format the title.

3. Type the heading of the first section (such as "Cases" or "Constitutional Provisions"), and then press Enter at least twice to put some space between the heading and the citations to be generated.

4. Click Tools ⇨ Reference ⇨ Table of Authorities, if necessary, to display the ToA toolbar.

5. Create, Edit, or Retrieve a definition for a section of the table. See either "Creating or editing sections of the table of authorities" or "Retrieving table of authorities section definitions," later in this chapter.

6. Select the section you want and then click Insert. A nonprinting comment, << Table of Authorities will generate here >, displays in your document. (You can only see the section name in Reveal Codes, but it does generate.)

7. Repeat Steps 3 through 6 for each section you want in the table.

Tip Each section can have its own format.

8. If you want the table of authorities to be on a page by itself, press Ctrl+Enter to insert a page break.

9. If you want new page numbers to begin after the table of authorities (for example, if the table of authorities is on page v, and you want the next page to be page 1), set a new number for the page that follows the table of authorities (see Chapter 20).

Creating or editing table of authorities sections

You automatically define a table of authorities section by typing a new section name when you create the first citation of a table of authorities item.

You can then go back to edit its format. You can also define a section before you create any entries for it.

To create or edit a table of authorities section:

1. Click Tools ➪ Reference ➪ Table of Authorities, if necessary, to display the ToA toolbar.

2. Click Define, and then either click Create and type a name for the section or select the section you want to edit and click Edit.

3. Specify any of the options shown in Figure 24-23 and described in Table 24-3.

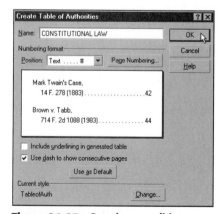

Figure 24-23: Creating or editing a ToA section definition.

Table 24-3
Table of Authorities Editing Options

Option	Lets You
Position	Specify how the page number is displayed (or choose no page numbering)
Page Numbering	Specify a page numbering format different from that of the rest of your document (see Chapter 20)
Include underlining in generated table	Remove citation underlining in the table as well
Use dash to show consecutive pages	Combine groups of sequential page numbers (7–11), rather than list them separately (7, 8, 9, 10, 11)
Use as Default	Click to use your selections with all new ToA sections
Change	Edit the default table of authorities style (for editing styles, see Chapter 28)

Retrieving table of authorities section definitions

To retrieve table of authorities section definitions from another document, such as one that has the standard formats for your office:

1. Click Tools ⇨ Reference ⇨ Table of Authorities ⇨ Define ⇨ Retrieve.

2. Specify the name and path of the document with the definitions you want, and then click OK.

3. Click the window and check the definitions you want to retrieve (see Figure 24-24).

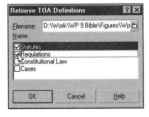

Figure 24-24: Retrieving ToA section definitions from another document.

Deleting a table of authorities section definition

To delete a table of authorities section definition in a document, click Tools ⇨ Reference ⇨ Table of Authorities ⇨ Define. Select the definition you want to delete and then click Delete. (Any markings for the section remain in your text.)

Generating the table of authorities

The table of authorities is generated along with other document references (including lists, cross-references, and the index). To generate your references, click Tools ➪ Reference ➪ Generate. You can also click Generate on the Table of Authorities toolbar.

When you generate a table of authorities for a master document, text marked in any subdocuments is included (see Chapter 25, "Assembling Multipart Documents").

Editing the table of authorities

You can edit a table of authorities after it has been generated, but keep in mind that any errors you correct in the table of authorities — rather than at the source where you defined your entries and marked the text — will reappear the next time you generate your document references. So it's usually better to edit the document text, then regenerate document references.

Creating Indexes

A well-planned, thorough index does much to enhance the accessibility of a book or other large document. The time and care spent in creating an index will be rewarded by the reader's appreciation and loyalty. Creating an index is a personal, as well as a mechanical, process. No computer program can match your judgment in defining entries.

While creating an index takes imagination and patience, WordPerfect's indexing tools can help you get the job done quickly and accurately. In particular, you can create a *concordance file* — a list of index terms and phrases — and then let the program search for and list every occurrence of each item.

An index can include both headings and subheadings, as shown in Figure 24-25. You can also define the format for your index entries.

Creating an index is a three-step process:

✦ Marking the entries in your text (or adding them to a concordance file)

✦ Defining the appearance and placement of the index

✦ Generating the index

Understanding indexes

The purpose of an index is to enable the reader to find every statement pertinent to the topic at hand. An index often includes names of persons as well as subjects. Some scholarly or complex works have additional indexes, such as for authors or titles. A poetry anthology might have an index of first lines. (See "Creating more than one index for a document," later in this chapter.)

Subheading

Index

caption 653, 673-676, 681-683
concordance file 666-669, 671
counter 675-683
Counter feature bar 683
counter levels 677, 678, 681
counters
  changing its numbering method 679
  creating 677
  cross-referencing 683
  deleting 679
  displaying levels 678
  editing 679
  increasing or decreasing 678
  levels 677
  numbering methods 677
  setting the value of 679
  using with macros and styles 680
cross-references
  creating 673
  generating 675
  marking 674
  target 674
  tips and techniques 675
cross-reference 673-676, 683
Cross-reference feature bar 674, 675
document references 642
endnote 642-652, 675, 685
  creating 643
Endnote feature bar 643, 644
endnotes
  deleting 645
  editing 644
  placement 645
  resetting numbers 645
  viewing 644
footnote 642-652, 675, 685
  creating 643
footnote and endnote options 646, 650-652
footnotes
  deleting 645
  editing 644
  moving 645

Figure 24-25: An index with headings and subheadings in the standard format.

An index has three components:

✦ *Heading*. The heading is the principle subdivision of an index, and is normally a noun (“files”) or noun phrase (“file preferences”).

✦ *Subheading*. When a heading has a large number of page references, it usually helps to break it down into topical subheadings, with specific page numbers.

Tip

Leave out the heading page number if the subheadings are widely scattered throughout your work.

Some books have indexes with three or more levels, but WordPerfect can generate only two.

✦ *Cross-reference*. Many indexes have cross-references, which refer to items by different names, or point the reader to additional related information. See "Adding cross-references to indexes," later in this chapter.

Marking individual index entries in your text

You can manually mark each index entry in your text, or use a concordance file to list every occurrence of a word or phrase automatically. You can also combine both methods by putting some items in the concordance file and manually marking others.

To mark individual index entries:

1. Click Tools ➪ Reference ➪ Index to display the Index toolbar (see Figure 24-26).

Figure 24-26: Index toolbar.

2. Select the word or phrase you want to index.

3. Click in the Heading box to display the text you selected. You can edit the text to how you want it to appear in the index, or select a previous heading from your list. (The index heading can be different from the actual words in your document.)

Caution

Be sure to click the Heading box before you mark the entry. Otherwise, the item will be indexed under the previous entry's heading.

4. If this is to be a subheading entry, press the Tab key (or click Subheading box) and edit the subheading text to your liking. For example, if your selected text is "individual index entries," you might want to have a heading of "index" and a subheading of "individual entries." You can also select a subheading from the list.

5. Click Mark. (An [Index] code is placed before your selection.)

Tip You can mark the same text selection more than once, for example to have the Page Layout command appear under both "Printing" and "Formatting" headings. You can also mark an item twice (heading only, and heading plus subheading) if you want its page number to appear under both the heading and subheading.

6. Repeat Steps 2 through 5 to mark additional entries.

Unmarking index entries

To unmark an index entry, go into Reveal Codes and delete the [Index] code preceding the item. To revise an entry, delete the code and mark the text again. Your index will reflect the changes the next time it's generated.

Creating a concordance file

When it comes to efficiently indexing large documents, nothing beats the concordance file. It also spares you the painful process of manually re-indexing a large document that has undergone extensive revision.

The concept of the concordance file is straightforward. You create a list of words and phrases, and then have the program search for the words and create an index entry for every match. When you define your index, you specify where the concordance file is found.

To use concordance files effectively, keep the following points in mind:

✦ Mark the entries in the concordance file just as you mark individual entries in the document text. That way, your generated index contains the precise headings and subheadings you want.

✦ An unmarked concordance entry produces a heading index entry when it finds a match.

✦ Capitalization appears in the index as you type it in the concordance file, not as it's found in the document text. (However, matching is not case-sensitive.)

✦ Matching is performed on whole words and exact spelling ("drag" won't match on "drags" or "dragging").

✦ You don't have to sort (alphabetize) the concordance file, but the index will generate faster if you do. (See Chapter 53, "Sorting Information," for more about sorting.)

To create a concordance file:

1. Open a new blank document and save it with the name you want.

2. Click Tools ➪ Reference ➪ Index to display the Index toolbar.

3. Type an entry for the index.

Tip

Tile your document and the concordance file on your screen, and then drag items from the document while holding down Ctrl to copy them to the concordance file.

4. If desired, enter a custom heading and subheading, and then click Mark as described earlier in "Marking individual index entries in your text."

Tip

Mark the item twice if you want page numbers at both the heading and subheading levels.

5. Press Enter, and then repeat Steps 3 and 4 to create additional items (see Figure 24-27).

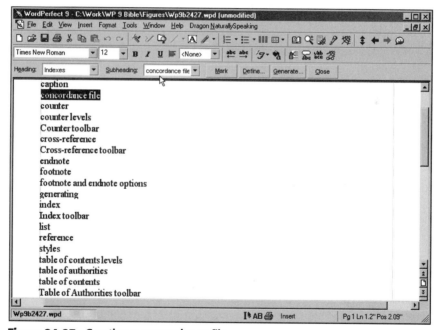

Figure 24-27: Creating a concordance file.

Defining an index

Now that you've marked index entries in your text, created a concordance file, or both, it's time to define the index:

1. Click where you want the index to appear.

2. If you want the index to start at the top of a new page, press Ctrl+Enter to insert a page break.

3. Type and format the title for the index. Press Enter at least twice to put some space between the title and the index.

4. Click Tools ⇨ Reference ⇨ Index ⇨ Define.

5. Specify any of the options shown in Figure 24-28 and described in Table 24-4.

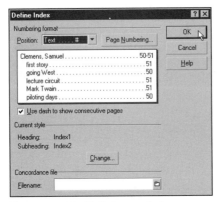

Figure 24-28: Defining an index.

6. Click OK. A nonprinting comment, << Index will generate here >, displays in your document.

Table 24-4	
Index Editing Options	

Option	Lets You
Position	Specify how the page number is displayed in the index and its position relative to the text.
Page Numbering	Specify a page numbering format different from that of the rest of your document (see Chapter 20).
Use dash to show consecutive pages	Combine groups of sequential page numbers (7–11), rather than list each page separately (7, 8, 9, 10, 11).
Change	Edit the styles for the index headings and subheadings. See the next section, "Customizing index heading and subheading styles."
Filename	Specify the name and path of the concordance file you want to use for this index.

Caution WordPerfect generates an index at each place it finds a definition code. If you accidentally end up with two or more definition codes in your document, go into Reveal Codes and delete the [Def Mark] codes you don't want.

Customizing index heading and subheading styles

You can customize index heading and subheading styles (Index1 and Index2), or create new styles or definitions, to suit your particular needs:

1. Click Tools ➪ Reference ➪ Index ➪ Define ➪ Change.

2. Select the level style you want to change (see Figure 24-29).

Figure 24-29: Customizing index heading and subheading styles.

3. Do one or more of the following:

- Select the style you want to associate with the level.
- Click Create to create a style.
- Click Edit to edit the style.

Using custom index level styles in other documents

You can save your custom index styles and definitions to your Default template, so they can be used in other documents. For more on styles and templates, see Chapter 28.

Generating an index

The index is generated along with your other document references, including the table of contents, lists, and cross-references. To generate your references, click Tools ➪ Reference ➪ Generate. You can also click Generate on the Index toolbar.

When you generate an index for a master document, text marked in any subdocuments is included (see Chapter 25).

Editing an index

You can edit an index after it has been generated. Keep in mind, however, that any errors you correct in the index — rather than at the source where you marked the text or in the concordance file — will reappear the next time you generate the document references. So it's generally safer to change the text in the document and then regenerate the index.

Indexing tips and techniques

The indexing topics covered so far should take care of most of your needs. However, if you are indexing a large, complex document, there's a good chance you can make use of one or more of these additional tips and techniques.

Creating more than one index for a document

As noted previously, some scholarly or complex works have more than one index. You can create multiple indexes in either of two ways.

One way is to group all the items for your second index (such as authors and titles) under a single index heading, with each particular item marked as a subheading. After your index is generated, manually create your second index heading, move the collection of subheadings to that location, and edit formatting codes (simply deleting the style codes may do the trick). This method may sound crude, but it can also be simple and effective. Secondary indexes usually require only one heading level, so upgrading all the items from subheading to heading status should give you a second index.

A second (more elegant) way is to create a second concordance file that contains the entries for your secondary index. You can then place a second index definition in your document, specifying the name of your second concordance file. A drawback to this method is that if you have marked individual index entries in your text (in addition to using concordance files), these items will be generated in both indexes and must be manually deleted from one.

Displaying an index in multiple columns

Indexes usually are displayed in multiple columns (for the reader's convenience and in the interests of conserving space). Indexes in multiple columns usually read better if, when you define your index, you change the default page number position (flush right, preceded by a line of dots, or a "dot leader") to one that immediately follows the text (such as, "*Text*, #").

You can define columns for your index either before or after it is generated. Simply place the insertion point before the index definition code (if you go into Reveal Codes you'll see the Index Definition code), and click the Columns button on the toolbar to select the number of newspaper style columns you want. You can also select the entire index, and then apply the column definition. For more on formatting with columns, see Chapter 22.

Creating alpha breaks in an index

Most large indexes are broken into alphabetical sections as a convenience to the reader. At the very least, a blank line is inserted when the next letter is reached. Usually, large capital letters are used to introduce each section, and the breaks sometimes include horizontal bars, reversed text, or other embellishments. These features may be added by editing the generated index manually.

Adding first and last index entries to the tops of pages

There is no way to have the page headers automatically show the first and last index entries for the pages in view at the tops of the pages. If you want to place these locators in your page headers after the index is generated, manually edit the header for each index page. Alternately create and discontinue Header A and Header B with each page. Be careful to type the heading text, even if the locator points to a subheading item. For example, if you're referring to the "creating" item under "footnotes," you should type **footnotes** in the page header. For more on page headers, see Chapter 21, "Formatting Your Document."

Adding cross-references to indexes

Most good indexes contain *cross-references* to aid the reader in finding information on various topics. Index cross-references come in two flavors: *see* (such as, "Leaving, see Exiting"), when the topic is indexed under more than one heading; and *see also* (such as "Fonts 93–105, see also TextArt"), to point the reader to a related topic.

Index cross-references are not to be confused with the document cross-references discussed in the next section. They are simple alphabetic entries with no page numbers of their own, not dynamic links to the document text.

Unfortunately, there is no WordPerfect feature to aid you in adding cross-reference items to your index. You must type them manually after the index is generated. As a word of caution, keep a list of the cross-references for your index in a separate document, because if you regenerate your document references, the cross-references will be wiped out and must be re-created.

Inserting Document Cross-References

Document cross-references are another convenience for the reader of large documents. A *document cross-reference* points to another part of a document that is closely linked to the current discussion. For example, you may be discussing a table or figure and want to add a reference to the page on which the item actually appears.

Cross-references are simple to create in WordPerfect, and their page numbers automatically update each time your document's references are generated.

Understanding cross-reference terms

You need to know the following cross-reference terms:

✦ The *reference* is the item placed in your text (such as "see page 37") to refer the reader to another document location.

✦ The *target* is where the reader can find the item (the page 37 in the reference).

✦ The *target name* is the link between the reference and the target. It enables WordPerfect to place the target page number in the reference automatically during the generation process. In most cases, you need a unique target name for each reference-target pair. (The target name doesn't print.)

In addition to the page number, a cross-reference can display chapter, volume, caption, and other numbers.

Creating cross-references

Creating a cross-reference is a three-step process:

✦ Marking the reference

✦ Marking the target

✦ Generating the cross-references

Marking a reference

To mark a reference:

1. Type the text and punctuation to accompany the reference, such as "(see page),"
   with a space where the number is to appear.

2. With the insertion point in the space, click Tools ⇨ Reference ⇨ Cross-Reference
   to display the Cross-Reference toolbar.

3. If you're not creating a page reference, click Reference and select the reference
   type you want (see Figure 24-30). The Caption Number reference will include
   the caption text, such as "Figure 7."

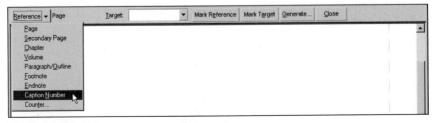

Figure 24-30: Selecting a cross-reference type.

4. Click the Target box and type the target name you want, or select a target name from the list. (Each target name you create is added to the list.) If you type in a name, remember it: you'll need to use the same name when you mark the target. If the name you indicate here and the target name don't match, the reference won't be able to generate.

5. Click Mark Reference to insert the reference code in your document.

A question mark (?) appears where you defined the reference until you mark the target and generate your document references.

Marking a target

To mark a cross-reference target:

1. Click within the text you're referencing. That way, if the text is moved, the target goes with it.

If you're targeting a footnote or endnote, click in the footnote or endnote, not the document text. If your reference is to a caption number, counter, paragraph number, or outline number, place the insertion point to the immediate right of the targeted item.

Tip When targeting a graphics box, use Reveal Codes to place the insertion point immediately to the right of the graphics box code.

2. Click Tools ➪ Reference ➪ Cross-Reference, if necessary, to display the toolbar.

3. Click the Target box and type the target name you want, or select the target name from the list.

4. Click Mark Target to insert the target code.

Unmarking references and targets

To unmark a reference or target, go into Reveal Codes and delete the Ref Pg (reference) or Target code. To revise an entry, delete the code and mark the item again. Your cross-references will reflect the changes the next time they're generated.

Generating cross-references

Your cross-references are generated along with all your other generated document references, including the table of contents, lists, and index. To generate your references, click Tools ➪ Reference ➪ Generate. You can also click Generate on the Cross-Reference toolbar.

If a marked reference still has a question mark (?) after your document is generated, it means that no target by the same name was found in your document. You may have forgotten to mark the target, or marked it by the wrong name (capitalization doesn't matter, but the spelling must be exact). If the name is wrong, delete the target code and mark the target again. Another possible reason for a failure to match is that you accidentally marked the target item as a reference instead of a target.

When you generate cross-references for a master document, text marked in any subdocuments is included (see Chapter 25).

Cross-referencing tips and techniques

Sometimes you may want to depart from the one-reference-one-target theme when creating cross-references. The following tips and techniques may be of help in these situations.

One target with more than one reference

In some cases you might want to cross-reference a target with more than one type of reference. For example, you might want to create a reference in the form of "(see Figure 4, page 37)." In this case, create two references, using the same target name — one for the caption number, the other for the page number. Because both references use the same target name, you only need to mark the target once.

Multiple targets for one reference

One reference can have multiple targets. An example might be "(see pages 2, 14, 50)." In this case, mark the reference once, and then mark each target separately, using the same target name. When you generate the cross-references, commas and spaces are added automatically.

Using Counters

Counters are one of those features that you rarely (if ever) fool with. But once you understand how counters work, you'll find there are some cool tricks you can perform with them.

Understanding counters

WordPerfect already has several built-in features that count and display the number of pages, chapters, paragraphs, lines, footnotes, figures, and other elements in your document. The program also provides two types of counters to keep track of anything else:

✦ User-defined counters for anything not automatically counted (such as sections, exhibits, examples, or problems). You can mark the things you want to count, and manipulate and display counter values at will.

✦ Five *system counters* to automatically count various types of graphics boxes in your document. That is why the default captions for graphics boxes display with the likes of "Figure 1," "Figure 2," and so on. System counters increment automatically, yet they can be edited and set in the same manner as user-defined ones (you just can't edit their names).

Employing user-defined counters is a three-step process in which you

✦ Create the counter

✦ Specify where you want the numbers to increase or decrease

✦ Specify where you want to display the numbers

The important thing to remember is that user-defined counters are not automatic. You must place a code in your document each time you want to change or display its value.

Counter levels and numbering methods

You can create counters with one to five levels, using a variety of numbering methods (such as "I, i, a, 1"). Each level of a counter must be set, increased, or decreased individually. You can display the levels individually as well. You can almost think of each level number as a counter unto itself. The only exception is that when you increase or decrease a counter level, all the levels below it are reset to 1. If you don't want this to happen, set individual levels to particular values (see "Setting a counter value or changing its numbering method," later in this chapter).

Suppose you have a four-level counter set to "II, ii, g, 6." If you increase the second level to "iii," the new value for the counter will be "II, iii, a, 1."

This process only works from higher to lower, not from the bottom up. When you increment the third level in this example beyond "z," it does not reset to "a" and push the second level from "iii" to "iv." Instead, the third level moves to "aa, bb, cc," and beyond.

The initial value of a new counter is 1. It can be decreased or set to 0.

Creating a counter

To create a counter for your document:

1. Click Insert ➪ Other ➪ Counter.

2. Click Create, and then type a name for the counter.

3. To use more than one numbering level, specify the number of levels you want (see Figure 24-31).

4. Click the "Numbering method" lists to specify the numbering method for various levels.

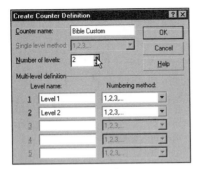

Figure 24-31: Creating a counter.

Increasing or decreasing a counter

Once a counter is defined, you can specify the places in your document where you want its value to increase or decrease (typically with each new section, exhibit, example, or other item that you're counting). While inserting the counter increase or decrease codes is a manual process, the actual count is automatically maintained.

To increase or decrease a counter:

1. Click where you want to increase (or decrease) the counter number.

2. Click Insert ➪ Other ➪ Counter.

3. Select the counter (or level for a multilevel counter) you want to increase or decrease (see Figure 24-32).

4. Click Increase or Decrease.

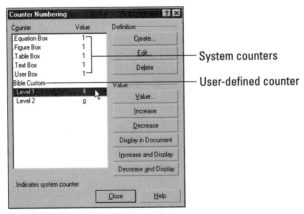

Figure 24-32: Selecting the counter to increase or decrease.

Displaying counter levels

You don't display the counters themselves, but the individual levels of which they are composed. For example, if you have a two-level counter in the form of "22.13" for displaying chapter and figure number, you must display the chapter number, "22," and the figure number, "13," in two separate operations, by using two separate counter display codes.

To display a counter level in your document:

1. Click where you want to display the counter level, and then click Insert ➪ Other ➪ Counter.

2. Select the counter (or level for a multilevel counter) you want to display (refer to Figure 24-32).

3. Click Display in Document.

Increasing or decreasing and displaying counters in one operation

You can both increase or decrease a counter (or a counter level of a multilevel counter) and display its value in one operation:

1. Click where you want to increase or decrease and display the counter level.

2. Click Insert ➪ Other ➪ Counter.

3. Select the counter (or level for a multilevel counter) you want to increase or decrease and display (refer to Figure 24-32).

4. Click Increase and Display, or Decrease and Display.

If you go into Reveal Codes, you'll see that you have inserted two codes in your document, one to increase (or decrease) the counter's value and the other to display it.

Setting a counter value or changing its numbering method

Instead of increasing or decreasing the value of a counter by 1, you can set a counter to a particular value at any point in your document. You can also change a counter's numbering method:

1. Click where you want to set the value of a counter or change its numbering method (the numbers and values before the insertion point are not affected).

2. Click Insert ➪ Other ➪ Counter and select the counter.

3. Click Value, and then specify the new value for the counter, or various levels for a multilevel counter (see Figure 24-33). You can click the lists to change the numbering method at the same time.

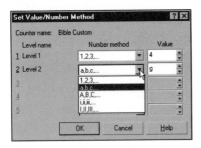

Figure 24-33: Setting a counter value or changing its numbering method.

Deleting a counter

To delete a counter, click Insert ⇨ Other ⇨ Counter, select the counter you want to delete, and then click Delete.

Editing a counter definition

You can edit an existing counter in the same way that you define a new one. Follow the steps described in the earlier section "Creating a counter," but this time select an existing counter and click Edit. You may especially want to edit a system counter in the current document (this doesn't change the system default), as described in the section "Displaying multilevel numbering in captions," later in this chapter. You can't change a system counter's name.

Counter tips and techniques

Counters are not the simplest instruments to use. Following are some tips for using them, with examples of how they can be applied.

Using copy and paste for repetitive counter operations

Counter applications tend to be repetitive by nature. Suppose you are using counters to number problems and solutions in an instructional document. When it comes to numbering the second problem, you might type some text and insert counter increase and display codes (such as "Problem 2").

Instead of repeating this process for the third problem, you can simply select the text and codes for the second problem, copy them to the Clipboard, and paste them in your document to get "Problem 3." You can then repeat the pasting process as many times as you want, and each time the counter display will automatically increase by one.

Using counters with macros and styles

If you frequently repeat a particular counter operation, you might consider incorporating it in a custom macro or style. One example of this might be creating interrogatory statements that take the form of "Question 1:" and "Answer 1:." Each successive pair of questions and answers increases in value by one. To automate this process:

1. Click Insert ⇨ Other ⇨ Counter, and then click Create. Give the counter a name of **Interrogatory** and click OK. Click Decrease to initialize the counter to 0.

2. Click Format ⇨ Styles, and then click Create and give the style a name of **Question**. Click in the Contents box, and type **Question** followed by a space. Click Insert ⇨ Other ⇨ Counter from the Styles dialog box, select the Interrogatory counter, and click Increase and Display. Then type the colon (:), followed by another space.

3. Click OK to return to the Style List dialog box, and then click Create again to create a style named **Answer**. Type **Answer** followed by a space in the Contents box. Click Insert ⇨ Other ⇨ Counter from the Styles dialog box, select the Interrogatory counter, and click Display in Document. Type a colon (:) and a space.

4. If you want to add a blank line between the answer and the next question, check "Show 'off codes.'" Place the insertion point after the [Codes to the left are ON—Codes to the right are OFF] code and press Shift+Enter to insert a Hard Return [HRt] code.

5. To chain the Answer style to the Question style, check the "Enter key will chain to:" box, select Question from the drop-down list, and then click OK. Next, select the Question style, click Edit, and chain the Question style to the Answer style.

Wherever you want to use the Question-and-Answer styles sequence, click Format ⇨ Styles, select the Question style, and then click Apply. Type the text for the first question, press Enter, type the answer, and then press Enter to go to the second question, and so on. To break out of the styles chain and resume normal text, click Format ⇨ Styles and select the <None> style.

Displaying multilevel numbering in captions

Another common counter operation is displaying multilevel numbers in the captions for figures, tables, exhibits, and other document elements (such as "Table 22.3"). You can define a multilevel counter for this purpose, and then increment and display your counter in the captions.

To display multilevel numbers in graphics box captions, modify the program's automatic system counters to assign the number of levels you want. The program increments the lowest level of the system counter when you create a graphics box. However, the default caption styles display only the highest level of the system counter. Therefore, to display multiple counter levels by using the built-in captions, you must modify the caption style as well.

In the following exercise, the system styles are left intact, and new styles are created to display multilevel captions for custom Image or Figure boxes:

1. Click Format ⇨ Graphics Styles, and then select Default Template in the "List styles from" list. (This ensures that the styles you create can be used in future documents.)

2. Select the style you want to customize, click Options ⇨ Copy, give the new style a name (such as "Two-level Caption Box"), and click OK.

3. With the new style selected, click Edit ⇨ Caption, and then click the "Number style" Change button.

4. Click Create in the Style List dialog box, give the new caption style a name (such as "2-level Cptn"), and change the style Type to Document (open).

5. Turn on any formatting codes you need (such as Ctrl+B for bold), and type the text you want (such as "Figure"), followed by a space.

6. Click Insert ⇨ Other ⇨ Counter. Then click Create and assign a name to the new counter definition (such as "Two-level").

7. Specify the number of levels you want for the counter (such as 2 or more), and then click OK.

8. Select Level 1 of your new definitions, and then click Display in Document. This inserts a [Count Disp] code in your style.

9. Type any punctuation separating the level displays (such as a period or a hyphen), and then click Insert ⇨ Other ⇨ Counter, select Level 2 of your counter, and click Display in Document. Repeat this process for any remaining levels.

10. Turn off any formatting codes that you turned on in Step 4 (for example, press Ctrl+B to turn off bold).

11. Click OK to return to the Style List dialog box. With your new style selected, click Insert.

12. Click the Change button for Counter, select the counter definition you created in Step 5 (such as Two-level), click Select, and then click OK ⇨ OK Close.

You can now use the graphics box style you created in any document. Click Graphics ⇨ Custom Box, select the style you created, and click OK. If you right-click the graphics box and click Create Caption, the correct number of levels should appear.

After inserting custom graphics boxes in your document, you may want to set the first levels of the counter you created to number your boxes with the likes of 14.1, 14.2, and so on. To do so, place the insertion point before the first graphics box code, click Insert ⇨ Other ⇨ Counter, select the counter, and click Value to set it.

Note

In addition to creating a new caption style, you have to create a new graphics box style and a new counter style to get multilevel numbering to work. That's because all components of the graphics box are based on styles.

Cross-referencing counters

To include a counter in a cross-reference, click Reference on the Cross-Reference toolbar, and then select Counter (see the section "Marking a reference," earlier in this chapter). If the counter has multiple levels, there will be a period between each level (4.2).

If you are cross-referencing a figure with a multilevel caption number created with counters (see the section "Displaying multilevel numbering in captions," earlier in this chapter), reference the counters instead of the figure box caption.

For More Information . . .

On	See
Creating and editing styles	Chapter 28
Numbering pages	Chapter 20
Generating document references	Chapter 25
Using templates	Chapter 28
Assembling multipart documents	Chapter 25
Creating hyperlinks	Chapter 14
Formatting with columns	Chapter 22
Creating page headers	Chapter 21

✦   ✦   ✦

Assembling Multipart Documents

In writing a book or other large work, it's easier to work on one chapter or part at a time, rather than write the entire document at once. That way, you and your co-workers can focus on manageable tasks and not get overwhelmed by the magnitude of the project. It will also be easier to edit and check your work, and you can send out chunks for criticism and review.

How Master Documents and Subdocuments Work

A *master document* is nothing more than an ordinary document with links to pull in *subdocuments* (other ordinary documents) when it expands (see Figure 25-1). That way, you and others can work on the particular subdocuments and then assemble the whole at publication time.

You'll probably want to put the items that pertain to your document as a whole in the master document (such as a title page, the table of contents, and the index). Other candidates for the master document are a dedication, acknowledgments, credits, a list of charts and tables, and other text too short to merit a document of its own.

You can expand the master (either temporarily or permanently) to display or print the entire document, and automatically generate the table of contents, index, lists, and other document references (see Chapter 24).

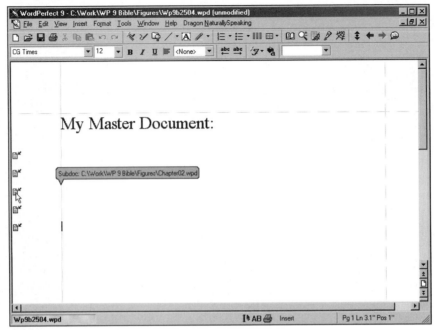

Figure 25-1: Master document with links to subdocuments

.Sometimes there are advantages to editing your expanded master, especially when the document as a whole is nearly complete. For example, you can find and replace a particular word or phrase throughout the entire work. Spell-checking and grammar-checking also can be more efficient, especially when you want to skip particular words or rule classes.

Tip When you make changes at the master document level, be sure to save them to the subdocuments, as explained in "Condensing the master document," later in this chapter. Otherwise, you'll lose your master document changes the next time you expand it.

Assembling a Master Document

With these concepts and cautions in mind, you're ready to assemble a master document. This can involve the following:

✦ Creating subdocuments

✦ Creating the master

✦ Expanding the master

✦ Generating references

✦ Printing the master document

✦ Condensing the master document

Tip

The Reference toolbar (see Figure 25-2) is especially handy when working with master documents. Right-click the toolbar and click Reference to display it. (Right-click the Reference toolbar and uncheck Reference to dismiss the toolbar when you no longer need it.)

Figure 25-2: The Reference toolbar, with handy buttons for master document tasks.

Creating the master document and subdocuments

Wherever possible, styles and codes should reside in the master document (see "Using formatting codes and styles," later in this chapter). You may find, however, that certain features belong in the subdocument, rather than in the master. For example, if the header or footer for each subdocument contains the name of that chapter or section, then the codes for the header or footer must be placed in each subdocument.

The only essential master document items are the subdocument codes. In practice, as noted previously, you're likely to include the contents, index, and other features as well. To create a master document:

1. Open a new or existing document to use as your master.

2. Create pages for your cover, title page, copyright notice, table of contents, and other front matter (such as a list of illustrations). Insert a hard page break (Ctrl+Enter) between each page.

Cross-Reference

For more on creating a table of contents and lists, see Chapter 24, "Adding Document References."

3. Add any formatting codes that you want to use for your entire document (such as for the base font, margins, spacing, page numbering, and headers).

4. Place the insertion point where you want to insert a subdocument link. To begin the subdocument on a separate page, press Ctrl+Enter to insert a hard page break. To begin each subdocument on an odd page (as with chapters in a book), click Format ⇨ Page ⇨ Force Page ⇨ "Current page odd."

5. Click the Subdocument icon on the Reference toolbar (File ⇨ Document ⇨ Subdocument) or right-click in the left margin and click Subdocument.

6. Select the file you want to link, and then click Include (see Figure 25-3).

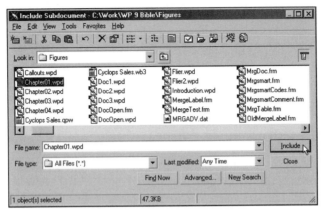

Figure 25-3: Inserting a subdocument link.

Tip

You can specify a filename that doesn't exist (the default path will be the same directory as the master), and create the subdocument later.

7. Repeat Steps 4 through 6 for other subdocuments you want to link.

8. Create a page for your index or other matter for the back of your document.

Cross-Reference

For more on creating an index, see Chapter 24, "Adding Document References."

Tip

When your master and subdocuments reside in your default document folder (click Tools ➪ Settings ➪ Files), the subdocument link contains only the filename, without the path. This makes it easier to transfer them to another location. See "Transferring master documents to another location," later in this chapter.

Viewing subdocument links

The way subdocument links display on the screen depends upon your view mode, as shown in Figure 25-4. In Draft view, a link displays as shaded comment text. In Page or Two Page view, a link appears as an icon that you can click to display the path and filename.

Moving and deleting subdocument links

By going into Reveal Codes, you can cut and paste the link codes in a condensed master to rearrange the subdocuments.

If you no longer want to include a subdocument in the master, simply go into Reveal Codes and delete its [Subdoc] link code.

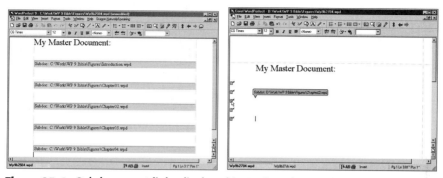

Figure 25-4: Subdocument links displayed in Draft and Page view.

Tip

Do this when the master is in its compressed form. Otherwise, you must delete the [Subdoc Begin] or [Subdoc End] code, and all the expanded text between the codes.

Caution

Deleting a [Subdoc Begin] or [Subdoc End] code in an expanded master breaks the subdocument link, and the remaining text will no longer condense. Restore it immediately with Undo (Ctrl+Z).

Expanding the master document

Once your master document is defined, you can expand all or part of it:

1. Click the Master Document Expand icon on the Reference toolbar (File ➪ Document ➪ Expand Master).

2. Uncheck the subdocuments you don't want to expand; then click OK (see Figure 25-5). (You can also click Mark/Clear, and then click Mark All or Clear All.)

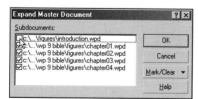

Figure 25-5: Expanding the master document.

The expanded subdocuments appear between a pair of [Subdoc Begin] and [Subdoc End] codes.

When the program can't find a subdocument, a Subdocument Error dialog box appears (see Figure 25-6). You can then specify the correct path and filename, click Cancel to stop the expansion process, or click Skip to bypass that document and expand the remaining subdocuments.

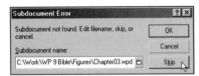

Figure 25-6: Dialog box that appears when a subdocument can't be found.

If a subdocument has a password, you'll be prompted to enter the password when you expand the master.

Caution Close any open subdocuments before you expand the master. Otherwise, you can end up with one version of a subdocument onscreen, and another in your expanded master.

Generating master document references

Many master documents contain definitions for generated references (such as the table of contents, lists, cross-references, and index). You can mark text in the subdocuments, and then generate the references for the document as a whole. Reference definitions in particular subdocuments (such as a list of figures at the beginning of a chapter) generate at the same time.

You can generate references when a master is condensed (for example, to print the table of contents and the index, but not the remainder of the document). When you do, WordPerfect temporarily expands the master, generates the references, and then automatically returns the master to its condensed state.

To generate references for a master document:

1. Click the Generate icon on the Reference toolbar (Tools ⇨ Reference ⇨ Generate).

2. Check any of the following:

    • *Save subdocuments,* to save generated changes to your subdocuments, such as lists (see Figure 25-7)

    • *Build hyperlinks,* to create and generate any hyperlinks to marked text

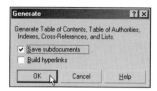

Figure 25-7: Generating master document references.

For more information on hyperlinks, see Chapter 14, "Web Writing and Publishing."

Printing the master document

When the master document is expanded, the subdocuments are formatted for the master document's printer. This ensures that even if several people with different printers work on various parts of the document, the final assemblage will have a consistent look and feel. Thus, fonts and other settings may not appear as they did in the original subdocuments.

Condensing the master document

When you condense an expanded master, you choose which subdocuments to condense (remove from the master), and whether to save editing changes made to the expanded master to the subdocuments:

1. Click the Master Document Condense icon on the Reference toolbar (File ⇨ Document ⇨ Condense Master).

2. Each subdocument is listed twice—once to be condensed (removed) and once to be saved (updated with changes made to the expanded master). Uncheck those you don't want to condense or save. To act on all the subdocuments at once, click Mark/Clear, and then click Condense All, Clear Condense, Save All, or Clear Save (see Figure 25-8).

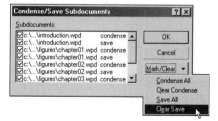

Figure 25-8: Condensing the master document.

If you don't want to save any master document changes to the subdocuments, click Clear Save.

Saving the master document

When you save an expanded master, you'll automatically be prompted as to whether you want to condense it first (see Figure 25-9).

Figure 25-9: Prompt when saving an expanded master.

To save your master document in its expanded form (especially when it is all assembled, polished, and ready to print), click No. (You can still condense it later.) Otherwise, click Yes to condense the master, and then choose whether to save changes to the subdocuments, as explained in "Condensing the master document."

Master Document Tips and Techniques

The following sections provide some tips and techniques to make the most of the master documents.

Placing subdocuments within subdocuments

One interesting technique turns subdocuments into lower-level masters by placing subdocuments within them. This creates a master pyramid, chaining three or more levels, to handle a very large document with a complex structure. You might do this, for example, with a book that has multiple parts and several chapters within each part. When you expand a master that contains lower level masters, the lower-level masters automatically expand as well.

Restarting footnote and endnote numbers

In many large documents, such as scholarly journals or anthologies, you may want to restart your footnote or endnote numbering at the beginning of each subdocument. Unfortunately, with footnote numbering, WordPerfect is too clever for its own good. It figures that there's no need to restart your footnote numbers until after you have created your first footnote, so it won't let you set the footnote number at the beginning of each subdocument. Therefore, you must first expand your master, and then reset the numbering at the beginning of each expanded subdocument. (Click Insert Footnote/Endnote ➪ Options ➪ New Number, and specify a new number of 1.)

You don't have this problem with endnotes, because when you specify endnote placement in a subdocument, you have the option to restart numbering.

Restarting page numbers in subdocuments

If you want to restart page numbering in each subdocument, you will encounter the same problem you have with footnote numbers — you can't set the page number to 1 until after the first page. In this case, you can usually work around the problem without expanding the master. The trick is to insert a hard page break and reset the page numbering (Format ➪ Page ➪ Numbering ➪ Set Value) *before* each subdocument code.

Converting subdocuments from other formats

If subdocuments are in another format, they are converted to the default WordPerfect format when they're pulled into the master. Files from WordPerfect 5.0 and up are automatically converted. Otherwise, WordPerfect tries to determine the format and prompts you for confirmation (see Chapter 10).

Using formatting codes and styles

Whenever possible, formatting codes and styles should be placed in the master, not the individual subdocuments. This is because when you expand a master, subdocument formatting codes and styles are pulled in along with the text, and the codes will remain on until you turn them off.

For example, consider a book of ten chapters (subdocuments) that you want to print entirely in the Book Antiqua font. Suppose the last page of Chapter 3 is inadvertently composed in the Times New Roman font. When you expand your master, everything from the last page of Chapter 3 to the end of the book (or up to the next font code) will be composed in Times New Roman.

To correct this type of problem, locate and delete the offending code.

Tip   Delete offending code in the subdocument as well, so it doesn't reappear.

If special formatting is required within a particular subdocument (such as for margins or tabs), it is generally a good practice to first select the text before you apply the formatting. That way, your special formatting will be turned off before the end of the subdocument, so as not to affect the formatting of subsequent text within the expanded master.

When you expand a master, and then condense it and save the subdocuments, you may see changes to your subdocuments, even when no change is made to the expanded master itself. Possible reasons include the following:

✦ The Document Style (see Chapter 21) of the master replaces that in each subdocument.

Tip   Don't put any codes in subdocument Document Styles for this reason.

✦ Similarly, named styles in the master, or a preceding subdocument, override styles with the same name in successive subdocuments. (The styles currently in effect are saved with the subdocuments.)

✦ WordPerfect's automatic code placement feature deletes codes it considers to be redundant. For example, if a double-space code is already active in your expanded document, it deletes a similar code in a subdocument.

✦ A subdocument has a different character map from that of the master (its map gets replaced by the master's).

Using headers and footers in master and subdocuments

Headers and footers can be defined in either the master document or in subdocuments, depending on how they're used. For example, you may have a header displayed on the even pages (such as the title of a book) that stays the same throughout your expanded document. In that case, define it as Header A in your master. You might also have a Header B that displays the title of each subdocument or chapter on the odd pages. Define the Header B at the beginning of each subdocument. For more on headers and footers, see Chapter 21, "Formatting Your Document."

Transferring master documents to another location

If the subdocument links in your master document contain only the filenames, without the paths, it will be easier to transfer the master and its subdocuments to another location on your computer or to another computer.

The trick here is to have your subdocuments in your default document folder when you create the links and when you expand your master. To specify your default document folder, click Tools ➪ Settings ➪ Files.

For More Information . . .

On	See
Defining and marking document references	Chapter 24
Creating an index or table of contents	Chapter 24
Inserting hyperlinks	Chapter 14
Converting documents	Chapter 10
Changing the Document Style	Chapter 21
Creating headers and footers	Chapter 21

✦   ✦   ✦

Doing Calculations in WordPerfect

While Quattro Pro is the obvious choice for extensive spreadsheet tasks, WordPerfect has impressive spreadsheet capabilities for more general and occasional use. Calculations can be performed on table cells, rows, and columns (see Figure 26-1), or on floating cells that you can place anywhere in your document. The calculated results can be based on mathematical formulas, or a variety of spreadsheet functions.

Understanding Calculations

WordPerfect can calculate the results of any expression for which you can construct a formula. There are about 100 built-in functions you can use in constructing formulas, which are grouped under the following categories and types:

Function Category	Type of Functions
Mathematical	Average, maximum, sine, and sum
Date	Time and date values for minutes, hours, days, months, and years
Financial	Depreciation, payments, rates, and terms
Logical	If, and, or, true, false, and sign
String	Character, currency, length, and trim
Miscellaneous	Cell, block, column, row, index, and match

Cheese 'N Things

Delicatessen

SOLD TO:
Johnson, Harold V.
1256 W. Country Lane
Beaufort Junction, NV

DATE:
May 21, 1999

Invoice

QTY	Item Description	Code	Price	Amount
2	Quarts Milk	N	$0.76	$1.52
1	Lbs. Cheddar	N	$1.84	$1.84
3	Rolls 36mm film	T	$3.98	$11.94
5	Liters soda	D	$1.29	$6.45
1	Box crackers	N	$1.95	$1.95
12	Cans cat food	T	$0.39	$4.68

Subtotal	$28.38
Sales Tax (7.5%)	$1.25
Deposit (@ 5¢ per item)	$0.25
TOTAL DUE	$29.88

N: Non-taxable
T: Taxable
D: Deposit item

Figure 26-1: Invoice employing WordPerfect tables.

WordPerfect also has special shortcuts to calculate subtotals, totals, and grand totals down a column or across a row.

Later in this chapter, under "Creating Formulas," you'll see how to construct formulas by using functions, operators, values, and cell addresses.

WordPerfect or Quattro Pro?

If you're heavily into number-crunching tasks, you might want to use a full-blown spreadsheet program, such as Quattro Pro, that's expressly designed for the job. In that case, you can then either import all or part of the spreadsheet as a WordPerfect table, or create a dynamic link to a spreadsheet, so that the changes made in the spreadsheet program will automatically appear in your document (see Chapter 10, "Working Together and Sharing Data").

If you opt to work in WordPerfect, you'll find that many of WordPerfect's features are similar to Quattro Pro's, particularly the editing and analysis discussed in Chapter 33, "Editing Techniques" and Chapter 35, "Analyzing Data."

Whether you calculate in WordPerfect or link to Quattro Pro, WordPerfect's formatting features can add a professional polish to your results.

Creating Floating Cells

At times you may want to perform calculations right in your document's text, rather than in a separate table. You can do this by creating *floating cells,* which are like one-celled tables with no formatting. You can place these anywhere in your document, like those shown in Figure 26-2. They are used either to calculate a value by referencing data from other tables or floating cells, or to hold a value referenced by another table or cell.

To create a floating cell:

1. Click where you want the floating cell to appear.
2. Click Insert ➪ Table (or double-click the Tables button), and then click Floating Cell (see Figure 26-3).

Your floating cell is assigned a name, and the Formula toolbar appears (see Figure 26-4) so you can customize the name and insert formulas, as described later in this chapter.

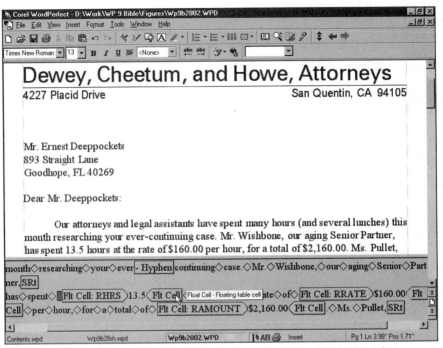

Figure 26-2: Floating-cell letter you'll create (note the paired [FltCell] codes).

Figure 26-3: Creating a floating cell.

Figure 26-4: Formula toolbar.

Using Numbers in Tables

Numbers have many uses in floating cells and tables. They can represent costs, prices, part numbers, temperature readings, barometric pressure, mathematical formulas, addresses, phone numbers, dates, times, percentages, and so on. You can customize how numbers are displayed in your tables: as decimals to the tenth place, with a currency sign, as short or long dates, or in various other ways, both preset and custom. You can also mix and match different number formats in different table columns, or even in different cells. The following sections detail your many options for specifying number formats in tables.

Specifying a numeric format

To change the default General number display to a particular format (such as Accounting, Date/Time, Currency, or Scientific):

1. Select the area of the table you want to change, or click the cell, column, or table.

2. Do one of the following:

   • To apply one of the default numeric formats, click the Numeric list on the property bar and select a format described in Table 26-1.

   • To apply a custom numeric format, click Other at the bottom of the Numeric list on the property bar (or click Table ➪ Numeric Format) and continue with the following steps.

Table 26-1
Numeric Formats

Select	To Display
Accounting	Currency aligned with the currency symbol at the left edge of the column.
Commas	Numbers in fixed format, with commas as thousands separators and negative numbers in parentheses.
Currency	Numbers with up to 15 decimal places, the currency symbol for the language you're using, thousands separators, and a decimal-align character (decimal point, comma, or other special character).
Date/Time	Numbers in the specified date and time format.
Fixed	Numbers rounded to up to 15 decimals, and no thousands separator. If the number contains fewer decimals than specified, empty spaces to the right are filled with zeros.
General (default)	Numbers with no thousands separators or trailing digits, rounded to nearest integer (whole number with no decimals).

Continued

	Table 26-1 *(continued)*
Select	**To Display**
Integer	Numbers without decimals (rounded).
Percent	Numbers as percentages with a percent sign (%) and the specified number of decimals. For example, "0.67222" displays as "67%."
Scientific	Numbers in exponential notation with the specified number of decimals. For example, with three decimals, the number "23,560,000" displays as "2.356e+07."
Text	Numbers display as you enter them (can't be used in calculations).

3. Click the appropriate tab to format cells, columns, or the entire table (see Figure 26-5). (If certain cells were already formatted, they can only be changed again by selecting the cell type.)

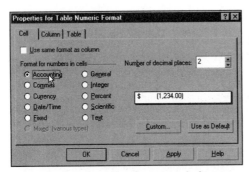

Figure 26-5: Changing the numeric format.

Tip   You don't have the option of Row because calculations are usually done within columns. To specify a numeric format for one or more rows, select all the cells in the row(s).

4. Click the number type you want (or check "Use same format as column" to have cells adopt the number type of their column).

5. Specify the number of digits to display after the decimal place, if applicable. For further customizing options, see the next section, "Customizing a numeric format."

6. To specify the selected format as the default for all new tables, click Use as Default.

Customizing a numeric format

After you've applied basic numeric formats and options (see "Specifying a numeric format," earlier in the chapter), you can further customize various numeric formats. Click Table ⇨ Numeric Format ⇨ Custom, and then select various options as shown in Figure 26-6 and described in Table 26-2. Note that Date and Time formats are customized differently, as shown in the next section.

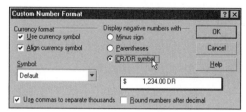

Figure 26-6: Customizing a numeric format.

Table 26-2
Custom Numeric Options

Option	*Lets You*
Use currency symbol	Display currency symbol with numbers
Align currency symbol	Align currency symbol at left edge of cell
Symbol	Select from the available currency symbols
Use commas	Insert commas as thousands separators (does not apply to the Scientific, Date, or Text types)
Minus sign	Display negative numbers with a minus sign
Parentheses	Display negative numbers in parentheses
CR/DR symbol	Display negative numbers to show credits and debits
Round numbers after decimal	Round the display of the numbers to the number of decimal places you specify

Selecting a custom date/time numeric format

To select a custom date/time numeric format, click Table ⇨ Numeric Format, select Date/Time, then click Custom and then select from the list of custom formats (see Figure 26-7).

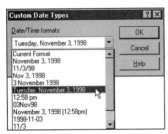

Figure 26-7: Selecting a custom date/time numeric format.

Entering dates and times

You enter most table numbers as you would type any number. But dates and times have a few more rules. After you choose the way you want dates and times to appear, you can enter them in several ways. For example, with the U.S. English defaults, both 12/29/98 and 12-29-1998 become December 29, 1998 when you leave the cell. Plain integer entries are assigned consecutive values starting with January 1, 1900. Thus, 36,525 becomes January 1, 2000.

Enter times using the 24-hour system, with a colon (:) between the hours and minutes. In U.S. English, hours greater than 12 are normally converted to p.m. (14:30 becomes 2:30 P.M.).

Naming Tables, Table Parts, and Floating Cells

WordPerfect assigns names to tables and floating cells in sequence (Table A, Table B, Floating Cell A, Floating Cell B, and so on). You can give them names of your choice, to make them easy to reference in calculations. You can also name cells, selected blocks, rows, and columns.

You can type a cell address in a formula (such as E17) or block coordinates (such as H2:H13) to reference a particular cell or block. However, when you're creating formulas, it's easier to reference cells and blocks by using easy-to-remember names, such as Total Hours, State Tax, or Quarterly Sales. Besides making formulas easy to understand, you're less likely to make a mistake when using names, and the formula will still work if you move the named selection.

Table names can be up to 20 characters long, with any combination of letters, numbers, spaces, or symbols, and must begin with a letter or underscore (_).

Changing the name of a table or floating cell

To get some practice in naming floating cells, tables, and table parts, open a new document and create a floating cell. Then create a 2 × 9 table similar to the one shown in Figure 26-8 and enter text in at least two rows of cells.

City	Fare
London	$259
Paris	$295
Madrid	$545
Budapest	$580
Buenos Aires	$569
Milan	$599
New Delhi	$830
Tokyo	$885

Figure 26-8: Table to which you can assign names.

Now click Table ⇨ Names to see the default names for your floating cell and table (see Figure 26-9).

Tip When you're in a table or floating cell, its name appears at the bottom of the screen.

To change the name of the current table or floating cell:

1. Click Table ⇨ Names.

2. Click the name, click Edit, and type the new name.

Name the table "Air Fares," to use in a later exercise.

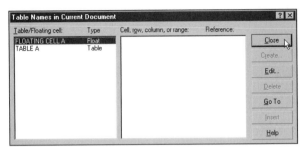

Figure 26-9: Default names for floating cell and table.

Naming table parts

To name a table cell, selected block, row, or column for easy formula reference:

1. Click the cell, row, or column, or select a range of cells.

2. Click Table ➪ Names, and then click Create.

3. Click Cell/Range, Column, or Row, and then type the name (see Figure 26-10).

Tip The Reference line shows the address of the part.

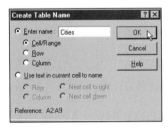

Figure 26-10: Naming a cell, row, column, or range of cells

Using text in cells for names

You can use the text in a cell to name columns, rows, the cells below, or adjacent cells:

1. Click the cell or select the cells with the text you want to use.

2. Click Table ➪ Names ➪ Create.

3. Click "Use text from current cell to name" (see Figure 26-11).

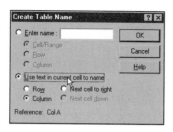

Figure 26-11: Using text in cells for names.

4. Click Row, Column, "Next cell to right," or "Next cell down."

Now let's practice. Using your Air Fares table, select all the cities in the left column to name all the fare cells to their right, as shown in Figure 26-12. (Note that the cell names are automatically sorted in alphabetic order.)

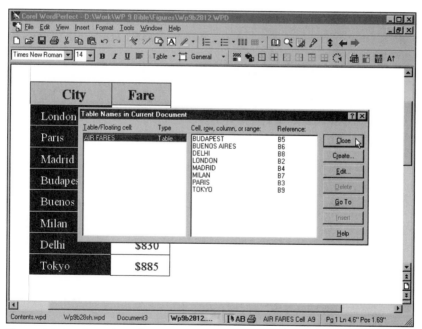

Figure 26-12: Fares in Column B named after the cities in Column A.

Editing and deleting table part names

To edit the name of a table part:

1. Click the table and click Table ⇨ Names.

2. Click the name of the table part, and then click Edit and type a new name.

Tip

To apply the name to a different table part, click the Type list.

3. To delete the name of a table part, click the table, click Table ⇨ Names, click the name, and then click Delete. (You can't delete the name of the entire table or of a floating cell.)

Going to a table by name

If you're looking for a particular table in a large document, you can search for it by name. Click Edit ⇨ Go To (Ctrl+G) to select the table and click OK. You can also go to a floating cell or a named table part, as shown in Figure 26-13.

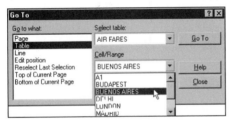

Figure 26-13: Going to a table part by name.

Creating Formulas

Now that you know how to name tables and their parts, you're ready to create formulas to be used in calculations.

Understanding table formulas

Spreadsheet and floating cell formulas can be as simple as summing a column of numbers, or as complex as computing Internal Rate of Return or Net Present Value.

Formulas don't have to be mathematical. They can be *logical functions* that are either 1 (true) or 0 (false), or *text functions* for manipulating text strings or returning a number (such as the number of characters in a cell).

A table formula can contain any of the following:

✦ *Functions* that perform various arithmetic, calendar, financial, logical, and text operations

✦ *Operators*, of either the arithmetic (+, -, *, /) or logical (=, >, |, &) variety

✦ *Values* (constants) that you enter in the formula (such as 8.5%)

✦ *Cell addresses*, such as B2:C4; or *cell names*, such as Budapest

Table 26-3 shows some examples of spreadsheet formulas.

Table 26-3 Spreadsheet Formulas	
Formula	**What It Does**
C12	Inserts the value found in cell C12.
+D13	Adds the values found in all the cells above cell D13.
Rate*Balance	Multiplies the value found in the cell named Rate by the value found in the cell named Balance.
MAX(B2:H2)	Displays the highest value found in the cells of Row 2, from Columns B to H.
AVE(E2:E12)	Calculates the average of the cell values found in Column E, from Row 2 to Row 12.
AND *list of statements*	Returns 1 (true) if all the statements in the list are true; 0 (false) if not.
CELL(*col,row*)	Returns the value found in the specified cell.
IF(Tax="T",0.075*Price,0)	Computes 7.5 percent tax if the entry in the cell named Tax contains "T"; returns 0 if it contains anything else.
LEFT(D4,4)+LEFT(E4,4)	Displays the first four characters of the text in cell D4 together with the first four characters of cell E4.
LENGTH(D11)+2	Displays the number of characters in cell D11, plus 2.

Entering table formulas

Although you can type formulas directly into cells, it's usually easier to use the Formula toolbar, as shown in this chapter's exercises.

1. Click in the table or floating cell in which you want to enter a formula.

Tip   A floating cell is simply a pair of codes. If it's empty, go into Reveal Codes to place the insertion point between the codes.

2. Click the Formula toolbar icon. (You can also click Table ➪ Formula Toolbar, or right-click a table and click Formula Toolbar.)

3. Do any of the following in the Formula toolbar (see Figure 26-14):

- Click the Functions button to select a predefined function (see "Inserting functions and defining arguments," later in this chapter.)

- Click in the Formula Edit box and type a formula (functions, operators, values, and the cells they address).

Tip Click the Row/Column Indicator icon to display the row/column indicators to easily identify a cell address.

- Click a cell or select a range of cells to insert cell addresses.

- Click the Names button, and then double-click a name to insert a table or part name.

4. Click the Table Formula Accept icon to insert the formula into the current cell, or click the Table Formula Cancel icon to cancel the formula changes.

Formula Edit box   Normal editing is suspended

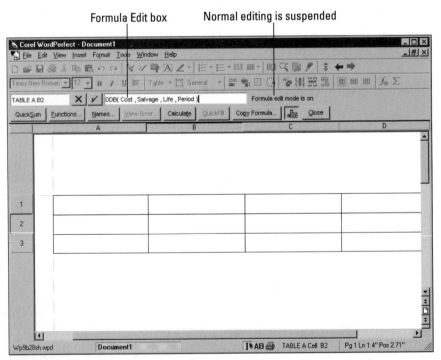

Figure 26-14: Entering a table formula in the Formula Edit box.

When you select a function from the Formula toolbar, or click the Formula Edit box, you go into Formula Edit mode, where normal editing and menu functions are suspended (note the message "Formula edit mode is on" in Figure 26-14). Then, when you click a cell or select a range of cells, the address of the cell or range is inserted into your formula.

Using QuickSum and simple formulas

To practice entering some simple formulas, create a 4 × 5 Product table like the one shown in Figure 26-15.

	1998	1999	Total
Product A	1000	2000	
Product B	2000	3000	
Product C	3000	4000	
Total:			

Figure 26-15: Table on which to practice.

Summing a column

You don't need the Formula toolbar to add a column of numbers. Simply click the bottom cell of column B in your Product table, and then click the Quick Sum icon (you can also click Table ➪ QuickSum, or press Ctrl+=).

Tip   In the case of your Product table, the total will include the year. However, if you assign a number type of Text to the top row of the table, the year will be ignored.

Calculating sums of table cells

When you QuickSum your column, you actually place the total "=" function in the bottom cell of Column B. When the insertion point is in the cell, notice that the cell formula, not the sum, displays at the bottom of the screen.

By using the Formula toolbar, you can sum a column, row, or any selected group of cells. Try these techniques on your Product table:

1. Click the last cell in column C (C5).

2. Click the Formula toolbar icon, and then click the Row/Column Indicator icon, if necessary, to display the row/column indicators.

3. Click the Formula Edit box, type **SUM(C2:C4)**, and then click the Table Formula Accept icon.

4. Drag to select cells B2 through D2, and then click the QuickSum button. (Note how the row is totaled and the formula +SUM(B2:C2) appears in the Formula Edit box.)

5. Click the indicator for Row 3 and click the QuickSum button.

6. Drag the indicators to select Rows 2 through 5 and click the QuickSum button. Your totals should agree with those in Figure 26-16.

	1998	1999	Total
Product A	1000	2000	3000
Product B	2000	3000	5000
Product C	3000	4000	7000
Total:	6000	9000	15000

Figure 26-16: Product table with totals.

Tip

The purpose of this exercise was to give you a feel for entering formulas. In practice, you could simply select the block of cells you want to sum, together with blank cells those below and to the right to hold the sums, and then click Table ➪ QuickSum to get all your totals at once.

Editing and deleting formulas

To edit cell formulas by using the Formula toolbar:

1. Click the cell containing the formula you want to edit or delete.

2. Click the Formula Edit box, and edit or delete the formula.

3. Click the Table Formula Accept icon.

To delete cell formulas:

1. Click the cell (or select the cells) with the formula(s) you want to delete.

2. Click Table ➪ Delete.

3. Click "Formulas only" to delete the formula(s) but leave the formula results (see Figure 26-17).

Figure 26-17: Deleting table formulas.

Inserting functions and defining arguments

To insert a predefined formula function in a cell:

1. Click the Functions button on the Formula toolbar.

2. Select the function you want, and then click Insert (see Figure 26-18). A description of the function appears beneath the list.

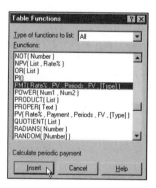

Figure 26-18: Inserting a formula function.

By default, all functions are displayed. You can click the List button to display only Mathematical, Date, Financial, Logical, Miscellaneous, or String functions.

Most functions require one or more *arguments*, as indicated by the keyword in parentheses (see Table 26-4). Replace the keywords with values or references to cells. For instance, replace the "Number" in INT(*Number*) with "56.432," to return the integer "56." A more complicated function, MID(*Text, Position, Count*), looks in a text string (Text) and extracts a number of characters (Count) beginning at a certain place (Position) in the text string.

	Table 26-4 Common Argument Keywords	
Keyword	**Replace With**
Cell	The address or name of a cell.
Block	The address or name of a range of cells.
Date/Time	A date or time number.
List	Any combination of cell or range references, numbers, formulas, functions, or logical statements. Separate items in the list with commas. In some cases, you can leave an item blank. The order of items is critical to some functions.
Number/Count	Numbers you specify in performing a calculation or repetitive operation.

You can also *nest* functions by placing a function within another function. For example, INT(AVE(List)) returns the integer portion of the average of the listed numbers.

Some functions do not require an argument. For example, COL() returns the column number of the cell at the insertion point.

To practice entering functions and arguments, try the following exercise to calculate the amount of money you need now to provide a specified cash flow in the future (Net Present Value):

1. Create the table shown in Figure 26-19. In Column B, assign the percent number type to the first cell, and the currency number type to all the cells below Amount. Enter the annual interest rate of 6.75 percent and the amounts of cash to be paid at the end of each year.

2. Click the last cell in column B, and then click the Formula toolbar icon (Table ⇨ Formula Toolbar).

3. Click Functions, list the Financial functions, and then select NPV(List, Rate%) and click Insert (see Figure 26-20).

4. With the keyword "List" highlighted (see Figure 26-21), select cells B3 through B7 (the amounts for years 1 through 5) to replace it with the cell range.

Annual Rate	6.75%
Year	Amount
1	$5,000.00
2	$5,000.00
3	$6,000.00
4	$6,000.00
5	$7,000.00
Net Present Value	

Figure 26-19: Net present value table.

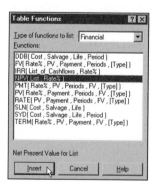

Figure 26-20: Selecting the NPV function.

5. Select the argument "Rate%," and then click cell B1. B1 replaces the keyword "Rate%."

6. Click the Table Formula Accept icon to insert the formula into cell B8, and calculate the Net Present Value (see Figure 26-22).

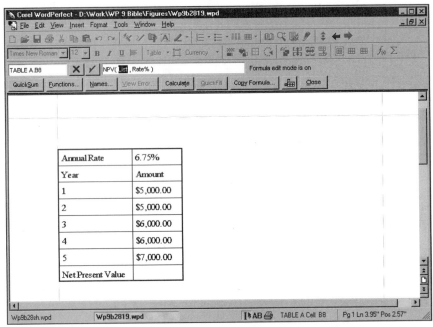

Figure 26-21: Select the cell range to replace the highlighted "List" keyword.

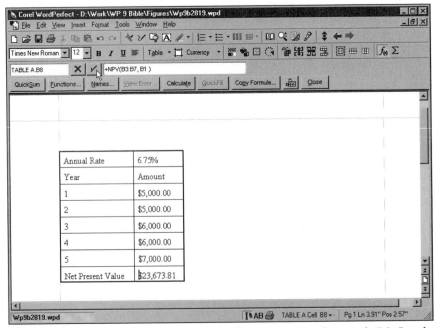

Figure 26-22: Resulting net present value when you replace keywords "List" and "Rate" by cell addresses.

Using arithmetic and logical operators

An *operator* specifies a relationship between two numeric or text values, or two or more logical statements.

The Arithmetic operators shown in Table 26-5 apply only to numbers.

Table 26-5	
Arithmetic Operators	
Arithmetic Operator	**What It Does**
+ (addition)	Adds values.
- (subtraction)	Subtracts value on the right from value on the left.
- (negation)	Changes the sign of the value. For example, -(4) = -4;-(-4) = +4.
* (multiplication)	Multiplies values.
/ (division)	Divides value on the left by value on the right.
% (percent)	Divides value on the left by 100.
% (remainder)	When between two values, returns the remainder of the value on the left divided by the value on the right. For example, 33%6 displays 3 in the cell because 33 divided by 6 equals 5 with 3 remaining.
^ (exponent)	Raises the value on the left to a power specified by the value on the right. For example, $4 \wedge 3 = 4*4*4 = 64$.
! (factorial)	Calculates the factorial product of the integer on the left. For example, $3! = 3*2*1 = 6$.

Caution When using % to represent percent, be sure to follow the % sign with a separator, such as a space or parenthesis, or another operator. If % is enclosed between two values, it is treated as a remainder operator.

Most *logical operators* compare two or more numeric or text values (see Table 26-6). A logical operator returns 1 if the logical statement is true, and 0 if it is false.

A few of the logical operators evaluate and compare a series of logical statements and return a value of 0 or 1, depending on the outcome of the comparison. When comparing text values, they are considered in ASCII order, with A being a lower value than Z.

Table 26-6
Logical Operators

Logical Operator	What It Means or Does
=	Equal to
>	Greater than
<	Less than
<> or !=	Not equal to
>=	Greater than or equal to
<=	Less than or equal to
& or (AND)	Connects two or more logical statements. Returns 1 (true) if all statements are true, and 0 (false) if any are false.
! or (NOT)	Returns the inverse of the function or statement. If, for example, the statement is true, ! returns 0 (false).
| or (OR)	Connects two or more logical statements. Returns 1 (true) if any of the statements are true, and 0 (false) if all are false.
^^ or (XOR)	Connects two or more logical statements. Returns 1 if one of the two statements is true, but not both. Returns 0 if both are true or both are false. When there are more than two statements, returns 1 if an odd number are true and 0 if an even number are true. Known as *exclusive* OR.

You can use logical operators to determine the alphabetic sequence of text strings. For example, the formula "Armstrong" > "Jones" returns 0 (false) because "Jones" appears later in the alphabet and is considered a higher value.

Understanding the operator order of precedence

WordPerfect follows the traditional mathematical order of precedence in calculating the results of formulas.

Table 26-7 shows a list of the order in which operators are calculated, from first to last.

Operators of the same level of precedence are calculated from left to right. The two exceptions are ! (NOT) and - (negation), which are calculated from right to left.

To change the normal order of precedence, enclose the part of the formula to calculate first in parentheses. For example:

```
2 * 3 + 4 = 10
2 * (3 + 4) = 14.
```

Table 26-7 Operator Order of Precedence	
Level of Precedence	*Operator(s)*
1	! (factorial), % (percent)
2	! (NOT), - (negation)
3	^ (exponential)
4	*, / , % (remainder)
5	+, - (subtraction)
6	<, <=, >, >=
7	-, <> or !=
8	& (AND)
9	^^ (XOR)
10	| (OR)

Using logical functions

Logical functions evaluate numeric or text entries in order to choose a course of action. The Cheese 'N Things invoice shown in Figure 26-1, for example, computes sales taxes and deposit amounts after logically evaluating each product's code.

The logical operation is performed by a separate table named TAX+DEP. The table has as many rows as the invoice has line items, so it can compute the applicable taxes and deposits (see Figure 26-23).

The formula in the second row of the Tax column uses a logical function that tests to see if the item is taxable:

```
If(Invoice.C2="T", .075*E2, 0)
```

In this formula, if cell C2 in the table named INVOICE contains a "T," the total cost in cell E2 is multiplied by .075, or 7.5%. If it is not "T," a 0 is put in this cell. The formula is copied down the column to the other line items.

The Deposit column contains similar formulas:

```
If(Invoice.C2="D", .05*A2, 0).
```

Tax	Deposit
0	0
0	0
0.8955	0
0	0.25
0	0
0.351	0
0	0
0	0
0	0
0	0
1.2465	0.25

Figure 26-23: Tax and deposit table used in computing the invoice.

If the item requires a deposit, the number of items is multiplied by .05.

As you enter the line items in the invoice, the tax and deposit amounts for each item are automatically entered in the second table. The cell contents are summed in the bottom cells, and then referenced by the Sales Tax and Deposit lines of the invoice. When all items are entered and the document is recalculated, the totals appear on the invoice.

Using special summation functions

Three special functions, not included in the Table Function lists, are shortcuts to calculating subtotals, totals, and grand totals in a column of numbers:

✦ The *plus sign* (+) calculates a subtotal by adding the cells above it until it reaches the top of the column or another cell with a +.

✦ The *equal sign* (=) calculates a total by adding all the subtotal (+) cells above it, until it reaches the top of the column or another cell with an =.

✦ The *asterisk* (*) calculates the grand total of all the total (=) cells above it.

Try the following exercise to practice using special functions to calculate subtotals, totals, and grand totals:

1. Create the table shown in Figure 26-24. Don't worry about formatting niceties, just the amounts in Column B.

Items by Store	Quantity On Hand
Store 1	512
Store 2	135
Subtotal Item A	
Store 1	575
Store 2	389
Subtotal Item B	
Total A+B	
Store 1	1023
Store 2	543
Subtotal Item C	
Store 1	376
Store 2	279
Subtotal Item D	
Total C+D	
Grand Total	

Figure 26-24: Quantity-on-hand table on which to practice.

2. Click the cell to the right of Subtotal Item A, and then click the Formula toolbar icon to display the Formula toolbar.

3. Click the Formula Edit box, enter + and click the Table Formula Accept icon (see Figure 26-25). You'll see two pluses (++), the first one to indicate that the second is a formula.

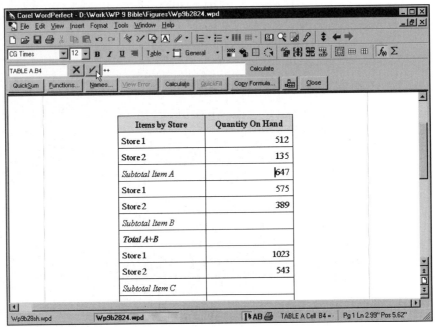

Figure 26-25: Computing the subtotal for Item A.

4. Click the other subtotal cells, repeating Step 3.

5. Click the cell to the right of Total A+B, click the Formula Edit box, enter =, and click the Table Formula Accept icon.

6. Repeat Step 5 for Total C+D.

7. Click the cell to the right of Grand Total, click the Formula Edit box, enter *, and click the Table Formula Accept icon.

8. Click Close to remove the Formula toolbar. Your table should have the totals shown in Figure 26-26.

Items by Store	Quantity On Hand
Store 1	512
Store 2	135
Subtotal Item A	647
Store 1	575
Store 2	389
Subtotal Item B	964
Total A + B	1611
Store 1	1023
Store 2	543
Subtotal Item C	1566
Store 1	376
Store 2	279
Subtotal Item D	655
Total C + D	2221
Grand Total	3832

Figure 26-26: Table with all the totals.

Referencing cells by column and row names

If you've named the columns and rows in your table, you can use their names to reference specific cells. Figure 26-27, for example, shows a table used to tally the weekly occupancy at a local resort. The rows for data are named for weeks 1 to 4; the columns are named for the months in the second row.

Weekly Occupancy - Happy Hollow Hotel				
	March	April	May	June
1				
2				
3		April.Week3		
4				

Figure 26-27: You can reference a cell by its column and row names.

Instead of referencing the cell for the third week of April by using its address of C5, you can specify the column and row names, April.Week3, separated by a period (.).

Using relative, absolute, and mixed cell addresses

Normally, cell formulas reference *relative* addresses. This means that when you copy a formula from one cell to another (see the next section for more information), the addresses in the formula change to maintain the same position relative to the new cell that they had to the old. If, for example, you enter the formula C5+C9 into cell C10, and then copy the formula to cell D10, the new formula will be D5+D9.

If you want to keep the cell references from changing when copying a formula, indicate *absolute* cell addresses with square brackets, as in [C5+C9].

Sometimes you may want either the row or column reference to be absolute, while the other reference remains relative. This is called a *mixed* address. The address [C]4, for example, will increment the row number when the formula is copied down a column, but the Column C reference won't change.

Copying a formula

After you create a formula for a row or column, you can copy that formula to other cells. The invoice shown in Figure 26-1, for example, computes the total amount for each item purchased in Column E. The formula, If(A2>0, A2*D2, 0), was entered in cell E2 and then copied down the nine cells below E2. In cell E3, the formula reads If(A3>0, A3*D3, 0), because the cell references are relative.

To copy a formula:

1. Click the cell containing the formula you want to copy.

2. Click Copy Formula on the Formula toolbar (or click Table ➪ Copy Formula).

3. Click To Cell and enter the address of the cell to which you want to copy the formula, or click Down or Right and enter the number of times to copy the formula (see Figure 26-28).

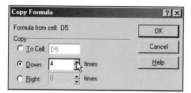

Figure 26-28: Copying a table formula.

All relative cell references are updated to keep their relative positions with the new cells. All absolute references remain unchanged.

QuickFilling cells

Use QuickFill to fill cells with incrementing values across a row or down a column. The values can be numbers, Roman numerals, days of the week, months, or quarters. To use QuickFill with numbers, you must already have two values entered so that the size of the increments can be calculated. With the other types, only one cell entry is needed to set the pattern.

To QuickFill cells:

1. Select the cell or the cells with the starting value(s), plus the cells you want to fill.

2. Click the QuickFill icon (Table ⇨ QuickFill).

To practice using Copy Formula and QuickFill, create a table to compute the monthly payments for a 30-year fixed mortgage, for two different principal amounts, at 12 different interest rates:

1. Create a table with 15 rows and 3 columns. (The precise headings and formatting don't matter.)

2. Right-click the table and click Display Row/Column Indicators, and then select Column A and assign it the Percent numeric format, with three digits after the decimal. Assign the Currency numeric format type to columns B and C.

3. Enter the principal amounts shown in Figure 26-29. Enter the first two interest rates. (Don't type the percent signs or dollar signs.)

Monthly Payments for a 30-year Fixed Mortgage		
	Principal	
Rate	$75,000.00	$100,000.00
6.125%		
6.250%		

Figure 26-29: Mortgage payment table to practice Copy Formula and QuickFill.

4. Click the Formula toolbar icon to display the Formula toolbar.

5. Select the interest rate cells to the bottom of Column A, including the two already filled in. Click QuickFill on the Table Formula bar.

6. Click cell B4. Click Functions, select the payment (PMT) financial function, and then click Insert.

7. Replace the argument keyword "Rate%" with the formula **[A]4/12**. The A column reference is in brackets to keep it absolute when you copy the formula to column C. (Because the payments are monthly, the annual interest rate is divided by 12 to find the monthly rate.)

8. Replace the argument keyword "PV" with the formula **(-[B3])**, the principal amount. (The present value is negative because it is already paid out and the payments will increase the value until it is 0.)

9. Replace the argument keyword "Periods" with **360** (30 years times 12 months per year).

10. Replace the argument keyword "FV" (Future Value) with **0** (because the loan will be paid off entirely at the end of 30 years.)

11. Delete the optional keyword "[Type]," including the comma. Click the Table Formula Accept icon to compute the monthly payment.

12. Click cell B4 and click Copy Formula. Click Down, enter **11**, and then click OK.

13. With the insertion point in cell B4, click Copy Formula. Click To Cell, enter **C4**, and then click OK.

14. Click cell C3 and edit the formula in the Formula Edit box. Change the PV argument from "-[B3]" to **-[C3]**. The formula for C4 should read PMT([A]4/12,-[C3],360,0).

15. Click the Table Formula Accept icon to insert the formula into cell C4. Click Copy Formula, click Down, specify 11, and click OK. The numbers in your table should match those shown in Figure 26-30.

Viewing formula errors

If "??" appears in a cell when you insert a formula, it means that the formula is invalid (WordPerfect can't calculate the result.) If you see "ERR," it means that the formula references a cell with an invalid formula.

Click View Error on the Formula toolbar to see a brief description of the cause of the error.

Calculating Formulas

Table cells automatically calculate when you insert the formula. Floating cells automatically calculate when you move the insertion point out of the cell. However, if you change the contents of a cell to which a formula references, the cell containing the formula is not necessarily recalculated at the same time. You can specify the frequency and extent of automatic recalculation, or turn it off completely.

Tip   If you've changed a referenced cell and formulas haven't been recalculated, the word Calculate appears to the right of the Formula Edit box. The reminder disappears when you click the Calculate button.

Monthly Payments for a 30-year Fixed Mortgage		
	Principal	
Rate	$75,000.00	$100,000.00
6.125%	$455.71	$607.61
6.250%	$461.79	$615.72
6.375%	$467.90	$623.87
6.500%	$474.05	$632.07
6.625%	$480.23	$640.31
6.750%	$486.45	$648.60
6.875%	$492.70	$656.93
7.000%	$498.98	$665.30
7.125%	$505.29	$673.72
7.250%	$511.63	$682.18
7.375%	$518.01	$690.68
7.500%	$524.41	$699.21

Figure 26-30: Computed payment table.

Calculating the current table or the entire document

To calculate the formulas in the current table only, click anywhere in the table, and click Table ⇨ Calculate ⇨ Calc Table (see Figure 26-31). To calculate all the table formulas in the document, click the Calc Document button instead.

If the Formula toolbar is displayed, you can click the Calculate button to recalculate all the formulas in the document.

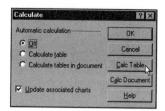

Figure 26-31: Calculating formulas.

Setting automatic calculation

When you change a cell that contains a formula, it is always recalculated—but other cells with formulas containing references to that cell are not necessarily updated. To set the recalculate option:

1. Click Table ⇨ Calculate, and then click one of the following:

   - *Off* to disable automatic calculation

   - *Calculate table* to recalculate the entire table whenever the contents of a cell are changed

   - *Calculate tables in document* to recalculate the entire document when a cell is changed

2. Check "Update associated charts" to update any associated charts when your tables are automatically calculated.

Locking and ignoring cells

To lock cells so their contents can't be changed, select the cells, click Table ⇨ Format ⇨ Cell, and check Lock.

You can also exclude cells from calculations, such as text labels, by checking "Ignore cell when calculating."

To practice excluding cells from calculations:

1. Open or re-create the Product table shown in Figure 26-15. If you had formatted the Year row as "Text," reformat it to "General" for this exercise.

2. Select cells B5 and C5, and then click Table ⇨ Delete ⇨ Cell contents only ⇨ OK to replace any old formulas.

3. Select all the cells in columns B, C, and D, and then click Table ⇨ QuickSum. The calculated totals should include the years in the top row (see Figure 26-32).

4. Select cells B1 and C1 (which contain the years), click Table ⇨ Format ⇨ Cell, click "Ignore cell when calculating," and click OK.

	1998	1999	Total
Product A	1000	2000	3000
Product B	2000	3000	5000
Product C	3000	4000	7000
Total:	7998	10999	18997

Figure 26-32: Column totals before the years were excluded.

5. Click Table ⇨ Calculate. The totals should now exclude the years (see Figure 26-33).

	1998	1999	Total
Product A	1000	2000	3000
Product B	2000	3000	5000
Product C	3000	4000	7000
Total:	6000	9000	15000

Figure 26-33: Column totals after the years were excluded.

Tip   When the insertion point is in a cell that is excluded from calculations, the application bar displays a double quotation mark (") in front of the cell contents.

For More Information . . .

On	*See*
Doing calculations in Quattro Pro	Chapters 32 and 35
Creating dynamic links	Chapter 10
Creating tables	Chapter 22

✦   ✦   ✦

Mass-Producing with Labels and Merge

In This Chapter

♦ ♦ ♦ ♦

Create labels and cards

Create text and table merge data

Design merge form documents

Generate your merged documents

Create mailing envelopes and labels

Select merge records

Merge from the Address Book and other sources

Prompt for keyboard entry during a merge

Create input menus with merge commands

Merge to a table

♦ ♦ ♦ ♦

Suppose you want to mail all your customers a holiday letter or a notice about a great new product. Do you print multiple copies addressed "Dear Valued Customer"?

To send a personal message to each of your clients, try merging your customer list with a form instead. While you're at it, enclose a business card that you created by using the label facilities.

Producing Labels

WordPerfect helps you to bring order to this complex world by offering a sophisticated label-producing application — envelopes, file folders, diskettes, cassettes, name tags, cards, spice jars, merchandise, children, pets, and anything else. You can also use the label facilities to print stuff that doesn't stick, like tent cards, note cards, rotary cards, business cards, and other perforated forms.

You'll start out defining and printing labels on their own. Later in this chapter, you'll learn how to generate labels during a merge.

Creating labels

You can create labels by using any of WordPerfect's predefined formats, including most of the commercially available sheet-fed and tractor-fed styles. To create labels:

1. Open a blank document or place the insertion point in the page where you want to start your labels.

2. Click Format ⇨ Labels, and then click the type of labels you want to display: Laser, Tractor-fed, or Both. (Laser labels are sheet labels used with various types of printers, including inkjets.)

3. Scroll the list to find the definition you want, and then click Select (see Figure 27-1).

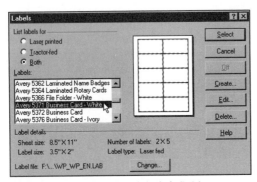

Figure 27-1: Selecting a label definition.

Filling in your labels

You can type label text, add graphics, and use any of WordPerfect's editing or formatting features just as with any other WordPerfect page. (To center label text vertically, click Format ⇨ Page ⇨ Center and select "Current and subsequent pages.")

When you're finished with one label, press Ctrl+Enter (or click Insert ⇨ New Page) to insert a [HPg] code and go on to the next (see Figure 27-2).

Each label on a physical sheet is a logical page, as you can see from their numbers on the application bar. If a label overflows, WordPerfect issues a soft page break to start the next, as with any other page.

When you display labels in Draft view, only the unformatted label texts are displayed, one over the other, separated by page breaks (see Figure 27-3). Note the [Labels Form] and [Paper Sz/Typ] codes used to define and print the labels, and the [HPg] codes between labels.

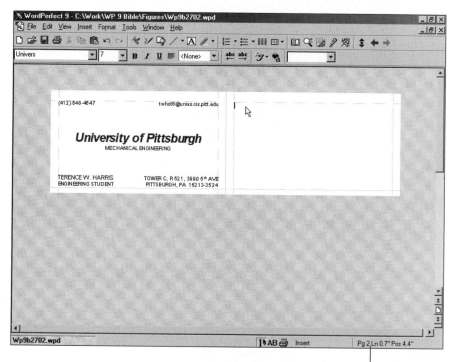

Each label on the physical page is a logical page

Figure 27-2: Press Ctrl+Enter to start the next label.

Point and click to maneuver among labels. Click the Previous Page and Next Page icons at the bottom of the vertical scroll bar to jump between physical pages (sheets) of labels. Using the keyboard, you can Page Up and Page Down, or use Go To (Ctrl+G) to maneuver among logical label pages.

Duplicating labels

To use the merge feature to duplicate labels:

1. Enter the text and graphics for one or more labels. For example, to duplicate labels printed in two columns, complete the first row (logical pages one and two).

2. Click Tools ⇨ Merge ⇨ Perform Merge.

3. Click Output ⇨ New Document.

4. Click Options, specify the number of copies for each label, and then click OK ⇨ Merge.

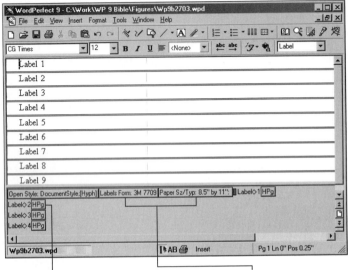

Home page codes between labels   Label Form and Paper Sz/Typ codes

Figure 27-3: Labels in Draft view.

Turning off labels

To stop entering label text, click Format ➪ Labels ➪ Off. (WordPerfect adds blank labels, if necessary, to fill out the sheet.) Note that any page formatting features you may have selected for the labels (for example, centering) will remain in effect, even after the labels have been turned off.

Printing labels

Printing is based on physical pages (sheets) of labels, not logical pages, unless you specify a range of pages:

- ✦ Print the full document to produce all the labels.
- ✦ Print the current page to produce the sheet of labels at the insertion point.
- ✦ Specify a page range to print a range of labels (logical pages).

Click on the toolbar and zoom to Full Page to preview the labels before you print them. Next, print your labels on a blank sheet of paper and hold it up against the labels to make sure that the print lines up correctly. Even then, different paper stock (such as that for business cards) may feed differently, so you may need to adjust the top margin a bit.

If you're printing tractor-fed labels, ensure that the top of the page is properly aligned.

Creating custom labels

The default label file for English versions of WordPerfect WP_WP_US.LAB, contains label definitions for various Avery products (Avery is the leading label manufacturer). You can add custom definitions to this file, or edit and delete existing entries. You can also create and use other label files with a .LAB filename extension. (Install language modules to add country-specific label definitions).

As you can see from Figure 27-3, the label definition code is separate from the label form, and independent of your printer. Label definitions are not special forms, but special formats for standard page sizes. This allows label definitions to be stored in a separate file. It also makes it easy to transfer documents with labels among various systems using different printers.

Creating a label definition

If you have labels not defined in the label file, create a new label definition:

1. Open a blank document or click in the page where you want to start your labels.

2. Click Format ⇨ Labels.

3. Select an existing definition similar to the one you want to create (this is usually helpful, though not essential), and then click Create.

4. Type a Label description (see Figure 27-4), and then click Change if you want to change the label sheet size. This takes you to the Edit Page Size dialog box, with the options explained in the section "Creating a custom page definition," in Chapter 21. (The page Type of "Labels" can't be changed.)

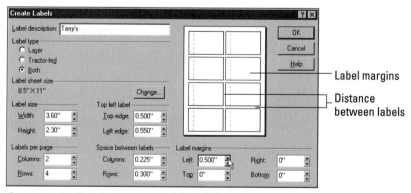

Figure 27-4: Creating a custom label definition.

5. Specify the placement of labels on the page. Preview the resulting label layout as you define the following label arrangement options:

   • *Label type*, to specify whether the definition is for laser printers, tractor-fed printers, or both

- *Label sheet size*, to specify the size of the label stock
- *Label size*, to specify the height and width of a single label
- *Labels per page*, to specify the number of labels across and down the page
- *Top left label*, to specify the position of top-left label, measured from the paper edges to label edges
- *Space between labels*, to specify the horizontal distance between columns and the vertical distance between rows
- *Label margins*, to specify the margins for information within each label

6. Click OK to return to the Labels dialog box. If you get a message that your labels can't fit on the page, go back and adjust your specifications.

7. To use the label definition now, highlight it and click Select. To use it later, click Cancel.

Editing and deleting label definitions

To edit or delete a definition in a label file:

1. Click Format ⇨ Labels, and then select the label definition you want to edit or delete.

2. To delete the label definition, click Delete. To edit the definition, click Edit, and then specify the options described in Steps 4 through 7 in "Creating a label definition" above.

Tip   Rather than edit an original label definition delivered with WordPerfect, create a new definition from a copy.

Creating a new label file

Rather than alter the installed label file, you can store your custom label definitions in a separate file:

1. Click Format ⇨ Labels, and then click Change under "Select label file."

2. Specify the folder for your label file, if necessary, click Create, type a filename and description, and click OK (see Figure 27-5). The .LAB filename extension is automatically added.

Figure 27-5: Creating a new label file.

3. To switch to your new label file, highlight it in the Label File dialog box and click Select.

Tip Because it's easier to customize label descriptions than create new ones, copy an existing file to a new name, rather than start a new file from scratch. Then select the file you copied in the Label File dialog box and click Edit to give it your own description (such as "Custom Label File"). Finally, select the new file and customize it by editing and deleting the label descriptions.

Deleting a label file

To delete a label file, click Format ➪ Labels ➪ Change, select the file you want to delete, and then click Delete.

Tip You can't delete the label file currently in use. If it is currently selected when you open the Label File dialog box, highlight another label file, click Select, and then go back and delete the file you no longer want.

Mass-Producing with Merge

You, too, can create mass mailings that begin "Congratulations, Jane Doe, you're a Grand Prize finalist in our Million Dollar Sweepstakes!" Presumably you have better uses for the Merge feature, such as to send notices or invoices to your clients, or to mail holiday letters to your friends.

The standard merge combines a data source with a form document to produce the merged documents (see Figure 27-6).

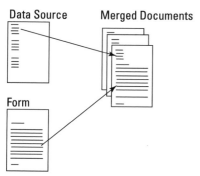

Figure 27-6: Combing a data source with a form document to produce the merged documents.

The *data source* contains the information that changes from letter to letter, such as names and addresses. Your data source can be

✦ A WordPerfect *data file* (document in text or table format)

✦ A file in a format recognized by WordPerfect (such as your Address Book or a Paradox database)

✦ A text file, in a specific format, from another word processor, database, or spreadsheet program

You can also supply keyboard information during a merge.

The *form document* is a standard WordPerfect document that contains your letter, invoice, label, flier, or other text common to each merged document. The form file can also contain commands to control the merge process.

Note Merging files (Tools ➪ Merge) is not the same as combining two documents into one with Insert ➪ File.

Setting up the data file

The first step in performing a merge is setting up the data file with *records* (such as telephone book entries) for every friend, client, CD, or whatever. Each record, in turn, contains all the fields of variable information that get plugged into the merged document.

Tip Set up the data file first, so it will be easy to specify the name and place for each field when you create the form document. (The names in the form document must precisely match those from the data file, or the data won't be found.)

A WordPerfect data file can be either text or a table. (A table can be easier to edit, particularly when you have more than a handful of fields to a record, or when some records have blank fields.)

Note A data file can have up to 65,535 records (if they can fit into your computer's memory). Each record can have up to 255 fields in a text file, and 64 columns in a table.

For the exercises in this book, you'll create a data file of at least three records, with seven fields for each record:

✦ First Name

✦ Last Name

✦ Address

✦ City

✦ State/Province

✦ Zip/Postal Code

✦ Greeting

Tip Breaking the name and address into several fields gives you added flexibility.

To create the data file:

1. Open a new, blank document.

Tip If you're creating a table, a landscape layout (click File ⇨ Page Setup ⇨ Size ⇨ Landscape) with narrow margins and a smaller font lets you fit more columns across the page.

2. Click Tools ⇨ Merge ⇨ Create Data. If the current document isn't blank, you can click "New document window" and click OK (see Figure 27-7).

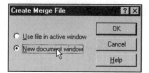

Figure 27-7: Creating a merge data file.

3. To create a data table (instead of a text data file), check "Format records in a table."

4. Type **First Name** in the "Name a field" box, and then press Enter or click Add (see Figure 27-8).

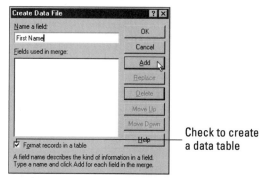

Check to create
a data table

Figure 27-8: Naming fields for the data file.

5. Repeat Step 4 for the Last Name, Address, City, State/Prov, Zip/Postal, and Greeting fields, and then click OK. (You can arrange fields with the Move Up and Move Down buttons.)

6. Click OK and type the first record in the Quick Data Entry dialog box (see Figure 27-9):

First Name	**Fred**
Last Name	**Jones**
Address	**P.O. Box 112**
City	**Middlewood**
State/Province	**MA**
Zip/Postal Code	**12345**
Greeting	**Mr. Jones**

Press Tab or Enter to go to the next field, or click any field. (Press Ctrl+Enter to place multiple lines in a field without jumping to the next field.)

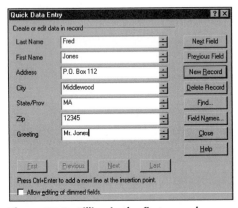

Figure 27-9: Filling in the first record.

7. Click New Record and enter the second record:

First Name	**Alice**
Last Name	**Parker, MD**
Address	**151 Maple Street**
City	**Cottontown**
State/Prov	**KY**

Zip/Postal	**98765**
Greeting	**Dr. Parker**

8. Click New Record and enter the third record:

First Name	**George**
Last Name	**Alton**
Address	**1086 Main Street**
City	**East Tangerine**
State/Province	**NJ**
Zip/Postal Code	**76530**
Greeting	**George**

9. Click Close ➪ Yes, and then provide a name and path for the file (the .DAT extension is automatically added).

Your finished data should look like that in Figure 27-10 if it's in text format, or Figure 27-11 if it's a table. If it doesn't look right, you can correct the screen document or try again from the beginning.

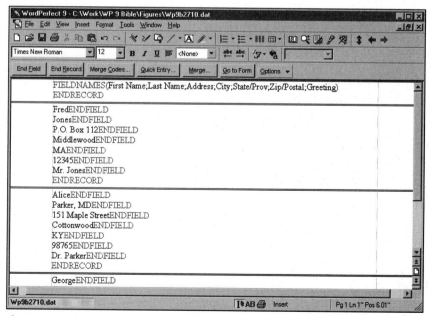

Figure 27-10: Your data file in text format.

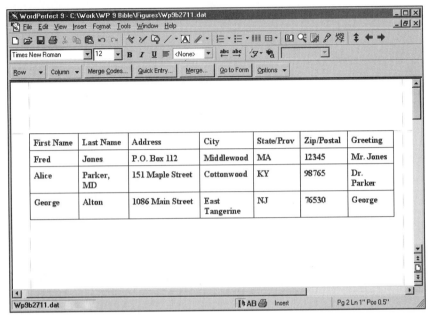

Figure 27-11: Your data file in table format.

Resist the impulse to reformat the text within the cells of a table, as it will unwrap just fine when you merge the data. You may, however, adjust the width of the columns according to the information they contain, just as you would with any other table (see Chapter 22, "Formatting with Columns and Tables").

Examining your data

You can see three types of codes in a text data file:

✦ *FIELDNAMES* specifies the fields in the data file

✦ *ENDFIELD* indicates the end of each field

✦ *ENDRECORD* indicates the end of each record (including the field names record)

Each field begins on a new line and each record begins on a new page, to make them easier to view.

A data table doesn't need special codes, because the header row is used for the field names, and each of the following rows is a separate record.

Creating the form document

Now that your data is defined, you can create the form document with your boilerplate text. Your form document can include codes to control the merge process. However, the initial form for this exercise needs only the DATE code, plus FIELD codes to show where information from the data file gets inserted in the text.

To create the form document:

1. Open a new, blank document. (If you're in the data document, you can click "Go to Form," and follow the prompts.)

2. Click Tools ⇨ Merge ⇨ Create Document. (If you skip Step 1 and your document isn't blank, you can click "New document window" here and click OK.)

3. Enter the name and path of your data file and click OK (See Figure 27-12).

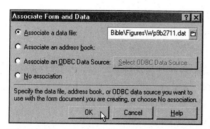

Figure 27-12: Associating a data file with the form document you're creating.

4. Click Date on the Merge bar to insert a date code, and then move down a couple of lines, click Insert Field, and click Insert to place the First Name field in your document (see Figure 27-13).

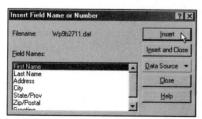

Figure 27-13: Inserting an associated data field in your form document.

5. Insert the other fields (including any punctuation and spaces) and type some boilerplate text, like that in the sample form document shown in Figure 27-14. (The Insert Field dialog box may be left open while typing text.)

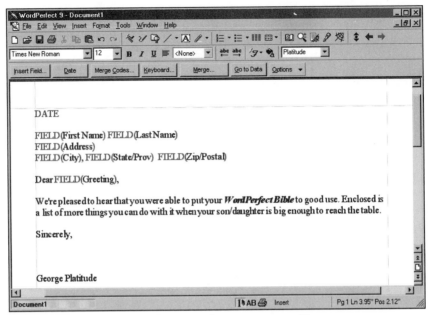

Figure 27-14: Sample form document for your mass mailing.

6. Close the document, saving it as MergeTest.frm.

Tip   Place any formatting for margins, line spacing, and so on, in the Document Style (see Chapter 21, "Formatting Your Document"). This way, the merge won't have to insert individual codes in each merged document. Right-click any graphic, click Contents, and specify Image on Disk so the actual graphic won't be inserted in each merged document (see Chapter 9, "Working with Graphics").

Performing the merge

Now that you've created your form document, perform the merge to produce three form letters, one for each record in the data file:

1. Click Tools ➪ Merge ➪ Perform Merge.

2. Click "Form document" ➪ File on Disk, and select your MergeTest.frm file (see Figure 27-15). Your merge data file should automatically appear as your data source. If not, select it now.

3. Click Output ➪ New Document (if necessary), and then click Merge.

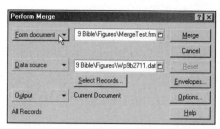

Figure 27-15: When specifying the form document, its associated data source is automatically selected.

During the merge, WordPerfect displays a "Merging" message. With a merge as small as this, the result should be nearly instantaneous (depending on the speed of your computer).

The merged document contains the text for all three letters, separated with hard page breaks. Read through the letters to make sure the proper data was inserted into each field. You can save the document or print it now.

Stopping a merge

To stop a merge in progress, press Esc. If your merge includes keyboard input, you can also click Quit or Stop on the Merge bar.

Including Envelopes in Your Merge

You've seen how to create merged form letters, but what about envelopes to stuff them in? Surprise! You can create envelopes for your form letters at the same time:

1. Click Tools ➪ Merge ➪ Perform Merge.

2. Select the form document and data source (if necessary), and then click Envelopes.

3. Click the Insert Field button on the Merge bar to select fields for the mailing addresses, just as you did for the form letter, as shown in Figure 27-16. Type any additional punctuation.

4. To include the POSTNET bar code with the mailing address, click Merge Codes on the Merge bar and insert the POSTNET code, then insert the field with the postnet number between the parentheses of the POSTNET code.

Tip

Zip+4 codes are required for bulk mailing discounts in the United States.

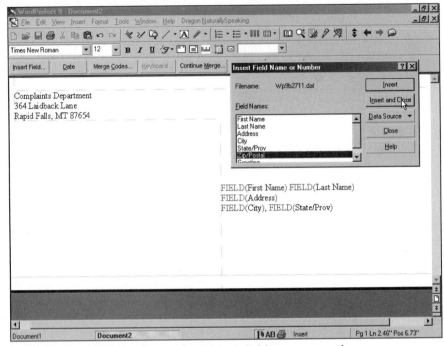

Figure 27-16: Adding mailing address merge fields to your envelope.

5. Type the return address or click the Envelope Return Address button to select from the last 10 return addresses used, or to select one from the Address Book.

6. Select any fonts or formatting from the property bar or menus. You can also insert graphics, such as a logo with your return address.

7. Drag the guidelines or click the Envelope Position button to change the positions of the return and mailing addresses.

8. If necessary, click the Envelope Size button on the property bar to select an envelope size or create a new one.

9. Click Continue Merge ➪ Merge.

The output document now contains all your form letters, followed by all the envelopes.

Your envelope format is retained for the current WordPerfect session. The next time you go to create envelopes with the form document you'll be asked if you want to use edit the envelope or create a new one.

For more information on printing envelopes, see Chapter 19, "Printing Documents, Booklets, and Envelopes."

Using Merge for Envelopes Only

Instead of including envelopes with your merge, you sometimes may only want to produce the envelopes for your mass mailing; when you're sending out wedding invitations or a preprinted brochure, for example:

1. In a blank window, click Tools ➪ Merge ➪ Create Document, and then select the data file, Address Book, or ODBC data source to associate with the envelope.

2. Click Format ➪ Envelope, and then follow Steps 3–8 described in "Including Envelopes in Your Merge," above.

3. Click Merge on the toolbar, click Output, and select Printer to print your envelopes now, or New Document to print them later, and then click Merge.

Tip   Print to a document when testing the merge.

Creating Mailing Labels with Merge

The trick to creating mailing labels instead of envelopes is to set up a separate form document for your labels.

Creating the label form document

To create the label form document:

1. Open a new document window and click Tools ➪ Merge ➪ Create Document, and then click "Use file in active window" and click OK.

2. Specify the associated data source, and then click OK.

3. Click Format ➪ Labels, and select a label definition.

4. Type the return address and any other information that stays the same from label to label.

5. Click Insert Field to insert fields from the associated data file. Because the codes don't print, click Options ➪ Display as Markers, to get a better view of where the data will go (see Figure 27-17).

6. To include the POSTNET bar code for U.S. addresses, click Options ➪ Display Codes (if necessary), click Merge Codes, type **po** to highlight the POSTNET merge code, and then click Insert and Close. Next click Insert Field to insert the Zip/Postal field into the POSTNET code. The codes should appear as "POSTNET(FIELD(Zip/Postal))."

7. Save the file as Mergelabel.frm or any other name to your liking.

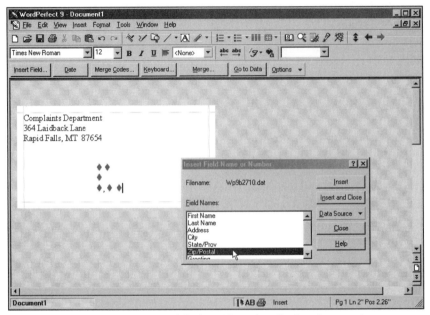

Figure 27-17: Formatting merge labels, with codes displayed as markers.

Printing the labels

To print the labels from the label form document:

1. Open a new document window and click Tools ⇨ Merge ⇨ Perform Merge.

2. Select your label form document and then click Merge.

3. Print the labels.

Tip   Click File ⇨ Print Preview to view your labels before printing

Merge Techniques

Now that you've mastered merge basics, including how to create envelopes and labels, you're ready for some intermediate techniques on using data sources, form documents, and other merge features, to produce precisely the output you want.

Editing data and form documents

Because data files and form documents are WordPerfect documents, you can open and edit them directly. With a table data file, you can edit the structure as well, by using standard table-editing techniques described in Chapter 22, "Formatting with Columns and Labels." For example, you can rename a field by editing the column header, or add a field by inserting a column. You can edit the cells (fields), or insert and delete rows to add or delete records. (Insert and delete rows or columns from the Merge bar.)

Tip Switch between the data file and form document with the "Go to..." button on the Merge bar.

For more controlled editing of a text or table data file, use the Quick Data Entry dialog box:

1. Open the data file, and then click Quick Entry on the Merge bar to edit the current record (see Figure 27-18).

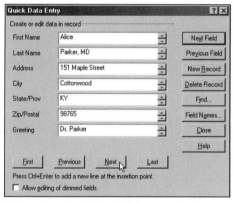

Figure 27-18: Using Quick Data Entry to edit a record.

2. Click any of the following options:
    - *Next Field* (Tab) or *Previous Field* (Shift+Tab), to scroll the fields
    - *New Record,* to add a record
    - *Delete Record,* to remove the current record
    - *Find,* to locate records containing particular text
    - *Field Names,* to edit, add, or delete field names for all your records
    - *First*, *Previous*, *Next*, or *Last,* to move among records

3. To edit fields containing styles, graphics, font changes, and the like, check "Allow editing of dimmed fields." (If you don't want to lose these features, edit the text directly.)

4. To edit the record structure, click Field Names, select or enter a field name (see Figure 27-19), and click any of the following:

   - *Add,* to insert a new field after the highlighted field in every record

   - *Add Before,* to insert a new field before the highlighted field

   - *Replace,* to rename the highlighted field. (Change associated references in the form documents as well.)

   - *Delete,* to remove the field and its contents from every record

Figure 27-19: Editing the record structure.

Directing the merge output

When performing a merge, you can click the Output button to direct the merged text to any of the following locations:

✦ *Current Document,* to append it to the text in the screen document

✦ *New Document* (the default), to send it to a new, blank document

✦ *Printer,* to immediately print the output of the merge

✦ *File on Disk,* to send output directly to a disk file

✦ *E-mail,* to directly send personalized e-mail. You'll be asked to supply the name of the e-mail address field in the data file, and the subject of your message.

Specifying merge output options

When performing a merge, you can click the Options button (see Figure 27-20) to specify any of the following options:

✦ *Separate each merged document with a page break* is the default for producing form letters, mailing labels, and the like. Remove the check to produce a continuous list (such as an inventory of your CDs or a phone directory).

✦ *Number of copies for each record* lets you output multiple copies of business cards and the like from a single copy in your document.

✦ *If field is empty in data source* lets you remove blank lines from your output, such as when you have two address fields but only one is filled.

✦ *Display merge codes* lets you show or hide codes during the keyboard merge, or show them as markers.

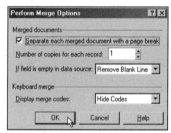

Figure 27-20: Specifying merge output options.

Selecting records

You'll often want to merge with only certain records from an address book, customer file, or other data source. Click Select Records when performing the merge, and then click one of the following:

✦ *Specify conditions,* to designate record-selection criteria (see Figure 27-21)

✦ *Mark records,* to manually check the records you want to use (see Figure 27-22)

Sorting data records

To sort records after you select them (for example, by zip code for mailing), click Options ➪ Sort on the Merge bar, or click Tools ➪ Sort. See Chapter 53, "Sorting Information," for more information on sorting records.

Check to specify a range of records

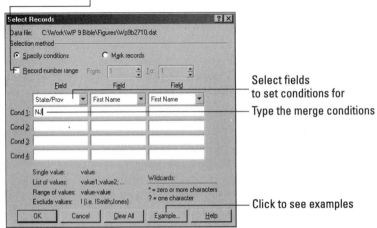

Figure 27-21: Selecting records by specifying conditions.

Specify the records and fields to display in the check list

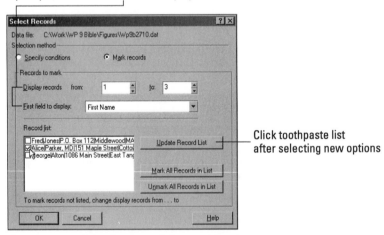

Figure 27-22: Selecting records by marking them.

Merging from the Address Book

To merge from an Address Book:

1. Click Address Book as the data source when performing the merge and select the book you want to use (see Figure 27-23).

2. If you don't want to use all the records in the address book you selected, click Select Records in the Perform Merge dialog to select the addresses you want.

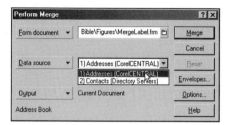

Figure 27-23: Selecting an Address Book as the merge data source.

Merging from other sources

WordPerfect can merge data from many sources, as long as the data format permits the program to identify the fields and records.

Merging from a WordPerfect table

You can merge from any WordPerfect table, as long as you specify the field names in the first row of the table. You can also convert the table (with the field names in the first row) to a merge data file (work from a copy of the table if you want to preserve the original). Select the entire table, press Delete, and then click "Convert contents to merge data file (use text in first row as field names)."

Merging from a spreadsheet or database

To use a file in any of the common spreadsheet or database formats (such as Quattro Pro or Paradox) as your merge data source:

1. Click File ➪ Open and open the spreadsheet or database.

2. Select Merge Data File from the "Import as" list (see Figure 27-24).

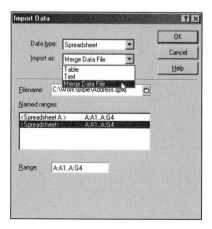

Figure 27-24: Importing a spreadsheet as a merge data file.

3. For a spreadsheet, you can specify the range of data to import. For a database, you can check the fields you want to use (Figure 27-25). (Check "Size table columns to fit data after import" when importing database records.)

Figure 27-25: Selecting fields when importing a database.

4. Click File ➪ Save As, and then save the file to with new name (it will be given the .DAT extension.)

Caution   Be sure to use Save As. A regular save to the same name will wipe out the original spreadsheet or database.

5. If you're importing a spreadsheet, go to the top of the file, click Merge Codes, insert the FIELDNAMES code, and enter the names of the fields.

You can also maintain a link with an imported spreadsheet or database (see Chapter 10, "Working Together and Sharing Data").

Merging from ASCII-delimited text

You can import records from any program that can save records as ASCII-delimited text, in which fields are normally enclosed in quotation marks and separated by commas, and records end with carriage returns:

```
"First Name","Last
Name","Address","City","State","Zip/Postal","Greeting"
"Fred","Jones","P.O. Box 112","Middlewood","MA","12345","Mr.
Jones"
"Alice","Parker","MD","151 Maple
Street","Cottontown","KY","98765","Dr. Parker"
```

```
"George","Alton","1086 Main Street","East
Tangerine","NJ","76530","George"
```

To turn an ASCII file into a merge text file:

1. Click File ➪ Open, open the file, and then select ASCII (DOS) Delimited Text as the convert file format and click OK (see Figure 27-26).

Figure 27-26: Opening an ASCII Delimited Text file.

2. Select Merge Data File from the "Import as" list, specify any delimiters and characters, if necessary, check if the first record has field names, and then click OK (see Figure 27-27).

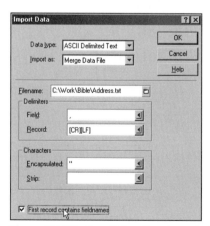

Figure 27-27: Specifying the characteristics of the ASCII text you're converting.

3. Click File ➪ Save As, and then save the file to a new name. (It will be given the .DAT extension.)

4. If field names weren't included in the file, go to the top of the file, click Merge Codes, insert the FIELDNAMES code, and enter the names of the fields.

Gaining Control with Merge Commands

By adding *merge commands* to your form document or data file, you can control the process of your merge and tell it what to do in special situations.

Many merge commands supply additional information with *parameters* (or arguments) that are enclosed within parentheses. The IFBLANK command, for example, requires a field. When two or more parameters are used, separate them with semicolons.

Caution The parentheses for parameters are part of the merge code; don't type them yourself!

Merge commands are similar to those used in macros and in various programming languages. Indeed, you can assign variables, and use hundreds of merge expressions and programming commands, to control the input, processing, and output of your merges. Some commonly used merge commands are described in Table 27-1. Codes used in the examples to follow are indicated by an asterisk (*).

Note A complete list of merge expressions, variables, and commands can be found in the Reference Center that accompanies your suite. The discussion of macro programming concepts in Chapter 58, "Automating with Macros," also applies to merges.

Table 27-1 Commonly Used Merge Commands		
Command	*What It Does*	*Basic Syntax*
ASSIGN	Assigns a value to a *variable* (such as the name or balance due) to be used somewhere in the merge.	`ASSIGN(var; value)`
BEEP*	Gets the user's attention.	`BEEP`
CALL	Tells the merge to transfer execution the labeled subroutine, and then return to the point immediately after the call when RETURN is encountered.	`CALL(label)`

Command	*What It Does*	*Basic Syntax*
CHAINFORM	Tells WordPerfect to continue with an additional form file after the current file is done. (Use this command to create envelopes for your form letters.)	`CHAINFORM(formfile)`
CHAINMACRO	Executes a macro when merging is finished. (Use this to do things merges can't, such as open or save files.)	`CHAINMACRO(macro)`
CHAR	Displays a message box and waits for a single keystroke. A common use of the CHAR command is to display a message asking for a Yes (Y) or No (N) response.	`CHAR(var; prompt; title)`
CODES*	Allows formatting (such as hard returns and tabs) to merge commands without having them replicated in the finished merge.	`CODES(merge codes and formatting)`
COMMENT*	Adds nonprinting comments to your merges. (Use it to hide simple formatting, such as a hard return or tab).	`COMMENT(text)`
DATE*	Inserts the current date.	`DATE`
DISPLAYSTOP	Stops the display of text (normally after the KEYBOARD command).	`DISPLAYSTOP`
DOCUMENT*	Inserts the entire contents of a document into the merged output. (Use it to import boilerplate text as part of the merge.)	`DOCUMENT(documentname)`
ENDFIELD*	Indicates the end of a field in a merge data file.	`ENDFIELD`
ENDRECORD*	Indicates the end of a record in a merge data file.	`ENDRECORD`
FIELD*	References a field defined in a merge, and inserts the field's contents in the merged output.	`FIELD(field)`

Continued

Table 27-1 (*continued*)

Command	What It Does	Basic Syntax
FIELDNAMES*	Specifies the names for fields used in each record in a data file. If the FIELDNAMES command isn't used, the fields must be referenced in the form file by number (FIELD 1, FIELD 2, and so on).	`FIELDNAMES(name1; name2;` `...)`
GETSTRING*	Displays a message with a text box for the user's response. The GETSTRING variable can then be used elsewhere in the merge.	`GETSTRING` `(var;message;title)`
GO*	Tells the merge to skip to the commands located after a specified label, without returning. Compare to CALL.	`GO(label)`
IF / ELSE / ENDIF*	Executes a set of commands if the logical expression you define is true. When ELSE is included, the commands between IF and ELSE are executed when the expression is true; the commands between ELSE and ENDIF are executed when it is false.	`IF(expression)` **Do this if the expression is true** `ELSE` **Do this if the expression is false** `ENDIF`
IFBLANK	Executes a set of commands when the specified field is blank	`IFBLANK(field)`, **followed by** an optional `ELSE`, **and ending** with `ENDIF`, **as with** `IF/ELSE/ENDIF`
IFNOTBLANK	Executes a set of commands when the specified field is not blank.	`IFNOTBLANK(field)`
INSERT*	Writes text within a CODES command. (If you don't use a CODES command, you don't need INSERT, as any text in the form document will appear in the merged output.)	`INSERT(text)`
KEYBOARD*	Pauses the merge so the user can type in data.	`KEYBOARD([prompt])`

Command	What It Does	Basic Syntax
LABEL*	Identifies an area of the merge form file to jump to and execute by using the GO and CALL commands.	`LABEL(label)`
NESTFORM*	Turns control over to another form, and then continues with the next command after the nested form is done.	`NESTFORM(form)`
NESTMACRO	Executes the named macro, and then continues with the next statement.	`NESTMACRO(macro)`
NEXTRECORD*	Tells the merge to stop processing the current merge data record and go to the next.	`NEXTRECORD`
PAGEON / PAGEOFF	Tells WordPerfect whether to insert a page break between each output record (PAGEON) or to print the records continuously (PAGEOFF).	`PAGEON/PAGEOFF`
PROMPT	Displays a message onscreen to the user.	`Prompt(message)`
QUIT	Terminates all merge execution, and outputs any remaining text in the form file. (Compare to STOP.)	`QUIT`
REWRITE*	Rewrites the screen, showing the current state of the merge	`REWRITE`
STOP	Terminates all merge execution and output.	`STOP`
SUBSTDATA	Switches to the beginning of another data file.	`SUBSTDATA(filename)`
SWITCH / ENDSWITCH /	Makes a decision based on specific data in the data file, or data provided by the user.	`SWITCH(expression)` `CASEOF x:` **Do this if expression equals "x"** `CASEOF y:` **Do this if expression equals "y"** `CASEOF z:` **Do this if expression equals "z"** `ENDSWITCH`

Continued

Table 27-1 (*continued*)		
Command	*What It Does*	*Basic Syntax*
VARIABLE*	"Returns" the contents of a variable. For example, if the variable contains the name "Fred Smith," that name is inserted into the merged output.	`VARIABLE(Var)`
WHILE / ENDWHILE	Text and commands within this loop are repeated until the test expression used with the WHILE command is no longer true.	`WHILE(expression)` Repeat this part until the test expression is false `ENDWHILE`

Checking for a blank data field

Suppose you want to be sure that every form letter you're sending out has an entry in the Address field. (It won't get too far without it!) By entering the following IFBLANK command in the form file, the merge will stop and ask you to enter the address from the keyboard whenever it encounters a blank Address field:

```
CODES(
IFBLANK(Address)
     REWRITE KEYBOARD(Address missing: please type it now...)
ELSE
     FIELD(Address)
ENDIF)
```

Tip The CODES command lets you format multiple merge commands for readability, without inserting the extra hard returns and tabs into the output document. The REWRITE command displays the text that has been merged so far, so you can see whose address is missing.

To insert a merge command while editing a form document or data file, click Merge Codes on the Merge bar. Scroll down the list, or type out the first few characters of the merge command you want (see Figure 27-28). Double-click the command or click Insert to place it in your document.

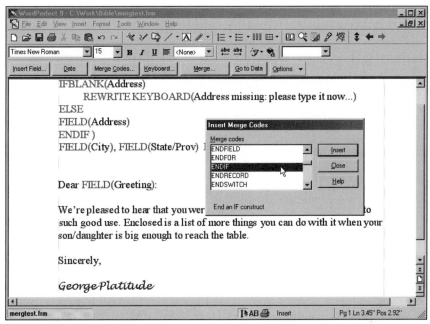

Figure 27-28: Inserting merge codes.

Tip When editing a form document, click the Merge bar buttons to enter the date code or keyboard commands.

WordPerfect automatically prompts for any command parameters. It's best to supply the parameters when you insert the commands, but you can also insert the command as is, and type its arguments later.

Merge commands are inserted into the document like any WordPerfect formatting code. When you open Reveal Codes, you'll see that they aren't like typed text.

The PROMPT command, which displays a message in a box on your screen, is a good example of a one-parameter command. Open your MergeTest.frm document (created in the section "Creating the Form Document," earlier in this chapter), position the insertion point at the top, click Merge Codes, type **prom**, click Insert, and then fill in the prompt parameter with your message, such as "Merging address records to produce form letters and envelopes."

When you click OK ▷ Close, you'll see PROMPT(message) on the screen.

In Reveal Codes you'll see [MRG:PROMPT]message[MRG:PROMPT].

As with formatting codes, deleting one paired merge code deletes the other as well. Merge commands with no parameters display as single codes.

Click Options on the Merge bar to hide your merge codes or display them as markers. To change your default merge code display, click Tools ⇨ Settings, double-click Display, and then click the Merge tab.

Supplying keyboard merge input

There are many uses for the KEYBOARD command described previously in Table 27-1. You can, for example, replace the impersonal "your son/daughter" in the boilerplate merge form with a specific term for each letter:

```
BEEP REWRITE KEYBOARD(Type name of kid or creature . . .  then
press Alt+Enter.)
```

The BEEP is to keep you from falling asleep at the keyboard.

When the merge stops at a prompt, you can either enter the data you're prompted for or

✦ *Skip* the record (don't include it in the output)

✦ *Quit* the merge at the end, but ignore any further commands

✦ *Stop* the merge entirely

Making merges that think

The ordinary merge extracts the data from each record and creates a separate form letter for each. You can make your merges "smart" by testing for some value in one of the fields. For example, if one of the fields is a zip code, you can test whether the zip code is greater or less than some value. That way, you can send out letters just to a select group of people who live in a certain area.

The IF command is most often used to provide decision-making capabilities to merges. The IF expression tests the value in one or more fields, and takes appropriate action depending on whether the outcome is true or false.

For the example in this section, create the merge data table as shown in Figure 27-29, and save it as Mrgadv.dat. (Add more records if you like.)

Fname	Lname	Department	Supervisor	Phone
Laurel	Bunelli	Sales	Mr. Roache	555-9876
Greg	Salazar	Stocking	Mr. Jenkins	555-1212
Arthur	Penner	Marketing	Ms. Ainslee	555-1234

Figure 27-29: Mrgadv.dat data table for this exercise.

Now suppose you want to generate a memo to people in the Sales department. Create the form file as follows:

1. Open a new, blank document.

2. Click Tools ⇨ Merge.

3. Click Create Document and enter Mrgadv.dat as the associated data file.

4. Insert the following codes (in bold) and text into the file as shown in Figure 27-30 (enter a blank IF code, and then insert the Department field within the parentheses):

```
LABEL(loop)
IF("FIELD(Department)"="Sales")
MEMO
DATE
From: Sam Adams, President
To: FIELD(Fname)FIELD(Lname)
Subject: Raises
Starting next week, everyone in the Sales Department will get
a raise.
Good work!
ELSE
NEXTRECORD
GO(loop)
ENDIF
```

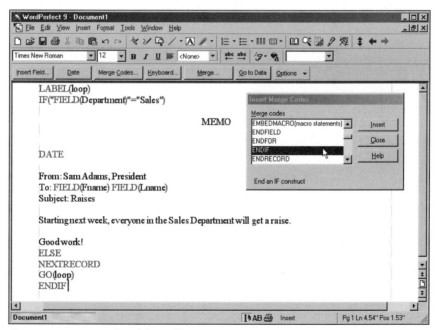

Figure 27-30: Completed form file.

5. Check your work for typographical errors (watch the field names inserted in the FIELD()codes!). Then save the form as Mrgsmart.frm. and close it.

6. Click Tools ⇨ Merge ⇨ Perform Merge, specify Mrgsmart.frm as the form document, with the associated Mrgadv.dat data file, and output to New Document (see Figure 27-31).

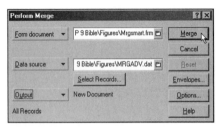

Figure 27-31: Running the merge.

7. Click Merge to output a single memo, to Laura Bunelli in Sales (see Figure 27-32).

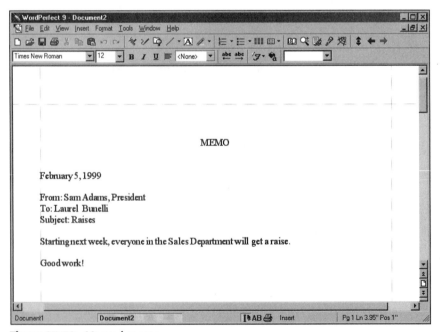

Figure 27-32: Merged memo

The IF expression looks for "Sales" in the Department field, and generates a memo if it is found. If the Department doesn't equal "Sales," that record is skipped by using NEXTRECORD.

Formatting merge codes

If you're familiar with programming WordPerfect macros, you know that commands are a lot easier to read when you format them by using hard returns and tabs. The same is true of merge commands, but with a catch: Most formatting in the commands ends up in the merged output, even though the commands themselves do not. If you noticed in the exercise you just did, the outputted memo didn't start at the top of the page for this reason.

To hide the hard returns in your example from the merge output, you can use the COMMENT command, like so:

```
LABEL(loop) COMMENT(
)IF("FIELD(Department)"="Sales")COMMENT(
)     MEMO
DATE
From: Sam Adams, President
To: FIELD(Fname)FIELD(Lname)
Subject: Raises
Starting next week, everyone in the Sales Department will get a
raise.
Good work!
ELSE COMMENT(
)NEXTRECORD COMMENT(
)GO(loop)COMMENT(
)ENDIF
```

Often, a simpler solution is to enclose whole groups of codes within a CODES command, in which both the codes and their formatting will be ignored:

```
CODES(
LABEL(loop)
IF("FIELD(Department)"="Sales")
) MEMO
DATE
From: Sam Adams, President
To: FIELD(Fname)FIELD(Lname)
Subject: Raises
Starting next week, everyone in the Sales Department will get a
raise.
Good work!
CODES(
ELSE
NEXTRECORD
GO(loop)
ENDIF
)
```

Tip   Select the codes you want to enclose before selecting the CODES command.

You can also enclose the entire form within a single CODES command, and then enclose the text and fields you want to write out within INSERT commands.

Commenting your merge form

You saw how you can use the COMMENT code to hide code formatting, but its main purpose is to document your merge form, to make it easier for you and others to maintain. For example, you might want to include the following comment at the beginning of your raise memo form:

```
COMMENT(Be sure to update the Department before running the
merge.)
```

Generating menus and more

Menus help guide an inexperienced user through the merge process. For example, you might build a merge project that asks the user which of three files, if any, to insert as part of the merge. The user doesn't have to know the names of the files, just enter the number displayed in the menu.

Using the Mrgadv.dat file from the previous example, suppose you have three different form letters, varying according to whether the person get a raise, gets transferred, or gets fired. The menu example shown in Figure 27-33 uses three text documents (Doc1.wpd, Doc2.wpd, and Doc3.wpd), to customize the letter based on the answer to the menu prompt. There's also another form, Opendoc.frm, with standard opening text and codes.

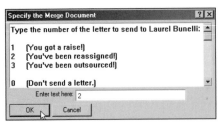

Figure 27-33: Responding to the GETSTRING prompt when running the merge

To create the menu example shown in Figure 27-33:

1. Create the Doc1, Doc2, and Doc3 WordPerfect documents, containing the selectable "raise," "reassigned," and "outsourced" text.

2. Open a new, blank document, click Tools ➪ Merge, click Create Document, and enter Mrgadv.dat as the associated data file.

3. Insert the following codes (in bold) and text into the new file:

```
CODES(
LABEL(Top)
GETSTRING(doc;Type the number of the letter to send to
FIELD(Fname)FIELD(Lname):
     1     (You got a raise!)
     2     (You've been reassigned!)
     3     (You've been outsourced!)
     0     (Don't send a letter.);Specify the Merge Document
IF(VARIABLE(doc)) =1)
     NESTFORM(DocOpen.frm)
     DOCUMENT(Doc1.wpd)
ELSE
     IF(VARIABLE(doc)=2)
          NESTFORM(DocOpen.frm)
          DOCUMENT(Doc2.wpd)
     ELSE
          IF(VARIABLE(doc)) =3)
               NESTFORM(DocOpen.frm)
               DOCUMENT(Doc3.wpd)
          ELSE
               NEXTRECORD
               GO(Top)
          ENDIF
     ENDIF
ENDIF
)
```

Tip Use copy-and-paste to repeat code.

4. Check your work for typographical errors, and then save the form as Mrgdoc.frm. and close it.

5. Create the Opendoc.frm with the following code (you can add more spacing between lines), and associate it with Mrgadv.dat:

```
INSERT(DATE
From: Sam Adams, President
To: FIELD(FName) FIELD(Lname)
Subject: What's Happening to You
Dear FIELD(Fname),
```

Here's the letter you've been waiting for:

6. Click Tools ➪ Merge ➪ Perform Merge, specify Mrgdoc.frm as the form document, with the associated Mrgadv.dat data file, and output to New Document.

7. Click Merge, and then respond to the menu prompt for each record by entering the number of the document to use, or any other character to skip the record (refer to Figure 27-33).

Your resulting letters should resemble the one shown in Figure 27-34.

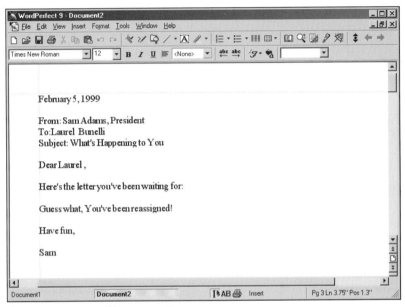

Figure 27-34: Resulting merge letter.

For explanations of the various codes used in the exercise, refer to Table 27-1.

Producing merge lists

Normally, there's a page break between each merge output record, as when you produce form letters and such. To output a continuous list, as with a telephone directory, you can use the PAGEOFF command:

```
PAGEOFF COMMENT(
)FIELD(Lname), FIELD(Fname)  FIELD(Department)     FIELD(Phone)
```

This has the effect of removing the check from the "Separate each merged document with a page break" option when performing a merge.

Merging into tables

In the previous section, you saw how to use merge to create a list. The final list, formatted into columns, lacks visual impact. For that, you can merge data directly into a table, and then format the resulting table (see Chapter 22, "Formatting with Columns and Labels"):

1. In the form file, create a two-row table with as many columns as you need.
2. In the top-left cell of the table, add the following merge commands:

   ```
   WHILE(1) PAGEOFF
   ```
3. Insert the FIELD commands for the data as needed. (Place any fields in the upper-left column after the WHILE and PAGEOFF commands.)
4. In the lower-left cell, enter the following merge commands:

   ```
   NEXTRECORD ENDWHILE
   ```

The merge table form shown in Figure 27-35, uses the Mrgadv.dat file you created earlier to produce the table shown in Figure 27-36.

Including document formatting in your output

Document, paragraph, and character formats in the form merge file are normally transferred to the resulting merge documents. You might, for example, set up tabs in the form document before creating the telephone list described earlier. Or if you want your form letters to have 1½-inch margins, include those formats at the start of the form file.

You can also apply any character format, such as bold or italics, to the boilerplate text of the form merge file. Just write or edit the document in the usual manner and add the appropriate formatting. If you want the variable data from the data file to be formatted in a particular way, apply the formatting to the FIELD code instead.

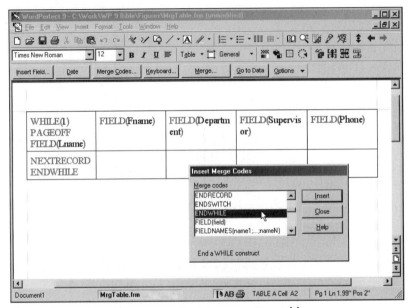

Figure 27-35: Form document set up to merge to a table.

Bunelli	Laurel	Sales	Mr. Roache	555-9876
Salazar	Greg	Stocking	Mr. Jenkins	555-1212
Penner	Arthur	Marketing	Ms. Ainslee	555-1234

Figure 27-36: Result of merging to a table.

For More Information . . .

On	See
Creating a custom page definition	Chapter 21
Editing the Document Style	Chapter 21
Printing envelopes	Chapter 19
Using tables	Chapter 22
Using an image on disk	Chapter 9

On	See
Using the Address Book	Chapter 12
Linking spreadsheets and databases	Chapter 10
Sorting records	Chapter 53
Macro programming concepts	Chapter 58
Merge expressions and commands	WordPerfect Office 2000 Reference Center

✦   ✦   ✦

Working Quickly with Templates, Projects, and Styles

◆ ◆ ◆ ◆

In This Chapter

Use project templates

Add a document
to your projects

List and apply styles

Create your own
styles

Create a custom
set of headings

Set up a style chain

Set style save and
display options

Create a style library

Reset, retrieve,
and turn off or
delete styles

◆ ◆ ◆ ◆

Nothing beats mass production when it comes to turning out CDs, ballpoint pens, or WordPerfect documents. This chapter looks at WordPerfect's features for quickly producing and updating all or part of a document:

✦ *Templates* and *projects,* to automatically apply format, content, and features

✦ *Styles*, to give similar types of text (such as headings and lists) a consistent, easy-to-update appearance

Understanding Templates and Projects

Can you imagine making holiday cookies by painstakingly cutting the dough to form each gingerbread person or tree? Most likely you'd use a cookie cutter for quick, consistent results.

WordPerfect's document cookie cutters are called *templates.* There are dozens of fill-in-the-blanks templates to create calendars, newsletters, business cards, memos, term papers, and other types of documents. They are the files with the filename extension .WPT found in your \PROGRAM FILES\ COREL\WPO2000\TEMPLATE folder.

Templates are less obvious than they used to be, because they are now combined with QuickTasks and Coaches from previous versions of WordPerfect into PerfectExpert projects, described in Chapter 5, "How to Get Help." Nevertheless, every document is ultimately template-based.

While the template feature rarely intrudes on your work, there's nothing mysterious about how templates work. In fact, every time you open a blank document, you're calling upon the default template, with its styles, toolbars, menus, keyboards, and other parts of your working environment. The name of this template is WP9xx.WPT, where xx is the language code, such as US for U.S. English. (You can click Tools ➪ Settings ➪ Files ➪ Template to see where it is.) Without this template, you'd have to specify margins, tabs, justification, spacing, and other formatting every time you opened a document.

You can even try your hand at creating your own templates to automate your personal word-processing tasks. For example, you might create a template that displays your company letterhead and prompts you for the name and address of the recipient.

Using Project Templates

When you click File ➪ Open, you're opening a blank document based on the default template. To use a specialized project template instead:

1. Click File ➪ New From Project, and then select [Corel WordPerfect 9] or the subcategory of projects you want.

2. Select the project you want and click Create (see Figure 28-1).

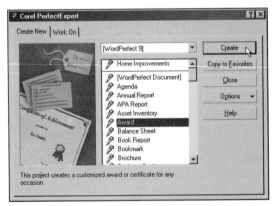

Figure 28-1: Selecting a template-based project to work on.

3. Customize your document with help from the PerfectExpert panel. For example, you can click Change Border to select a different border for an Award certificate (see Figure 28-2).

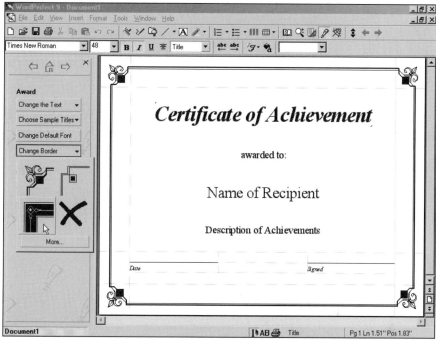

Figure 28-2: Selecting a different Award border from the PerfectExpert panel.

4. Enter your text or data, and make any changes to the document's format, fonts, graphics, and so on.

5. Click Save and give your document a name.

Note

The first time you use a template, you may be asked to supply your personal information that will be automatically inserted in various templates. Fill in the form, or select an entry from the Address Book.

Adding a Document to Your Projects

Chapter 17, "Becoming an Instant WordPerfect Expert," discussed how easy it is to create documents with your custom formats, headings, fonts, and so on, to use as boilerplate for new documents. To add your boilerplate documents, with or without sample text, to your PerfectExpert project list:

1. Set up a new document exactly the way you want, or clean up a copy of an existing document.

2. Click File ⇨ Save As, and save your document under your sample name, such as Boilerplate.wpd, and close the document.

3. Click File ➪ Open, right-click the document name, click Properties, check "Read-only," and click OK (see Figure 28-3). This will prevent anyone from accidentally overwriting your original boilerplate.

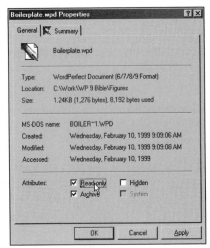

Figure 28-3: Setting your boilerplate document to read-only.

4. Click File ➪ New From Project, and select the category for your project.

5. Click Options ➪ Add Project, and then click "I want to add another document."

6. Click Next and type a project name and description (see Figure 28-4).

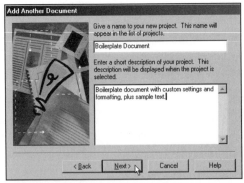

Figure 28-4: Adding your boilerplate document to the PerfectExpert projects.

7. Click Next, specify your document's name and location, and then click Finish.

You can create your own templates, complete with prompts, menus, toolbars, graphics, and so on. Another option is to modify the templates and projects that come with WordPerfect. See online Help for details.

Applying Styles

Whereas templates format your document as a whole, styles format particular sections of text within them. Styles save time in two ways:

✦ Once you package your formatting as a style, you can apply the style to similar text in the same document and other documents.

✦ When changing an underlying style, you can automatically update every place it's applied in your document.

Text and graphics styles

WordPerfect offers two classes of styles:

✦ *Text styles*, composed of formatting codes, and the subject of this chapter

✦ *Graphics styles*, composed of graphic elements that define boxes, borders, lines, and fills (see Chapter 9, "Working with Graphics," and Chapter 54, "Adding Graphics, Lines, Borders, and Fills")

Plain "styles" always refers to text styles, which you can think of as bundles of paired or open formatting codes (see Chapter 16, "Mastering the WordPerfect Interface"). There are three types of text styles:

Type of Style	Paired/Open	What It Does
Character	Paired	Formats text character-by-character
Paragraph	Paired	Formats text paragraph-by-paragraph
Document	Open	Changes the appearance of text from the insertion point on

The Current Document Style is a special document style found at the beginning of every document. This is where you'd modify the default tabs, margins, justification, line spacing, and the like (see Chapter 21, "Formatting Your Document").

Using automatic styles

Character and paragraph styles come in standard and automatic flavors. With an automatic style, changing the format of a paragraph or characters in one location changes the style for all. The QuickStyle and QuickFormat features create automatic styles.

Where styles are stored

To take full advantage of style features, you must know the following four places where styles can be stored:

✦ *In WordPerfect's system.* These built-in system styles support such features as bullets, outlining, footnotes, headers, footers, watermarks, hypertext, and Web publishing. You can change them in a document or template, but not in the system. Apart from the styles for Headings 1–5, which are copied to your current document, they're not usually on display.

✦ *In your document.* Normally, when you create a new style it's stored in your document, and is available for use only in that document.

✦ *In a template.* A style stored in a template is available to all documents using that template.

✦ *In a file.* You can save styles to a separate library file, retrieve them later for use in any document.

Applying styles

Normally, when you open a blank document, only the styles for Headings 1–5 appear in the listings. These styles, used to format titles and various level headings, are premarked to appear automatically in a generated table of contents.

Try the following exercise to see how the heading styles work:

1. Open a new blank document, type **Heading 1 (Title)**, and then press Enter twice. (Don't make your heading text bold.)

2. Go down the line typing **Heading 2**, **Heading 3**, **Heading 4**, and **Heading 5**.

3. Place the insertion point in each heading in turn, and select its style from the property bar list, as shown in Figure 28-5.

Tip You can also select each style, type the text, and press Enter. (Because they're paired paragraph styles, they terminate when you press Enter.)

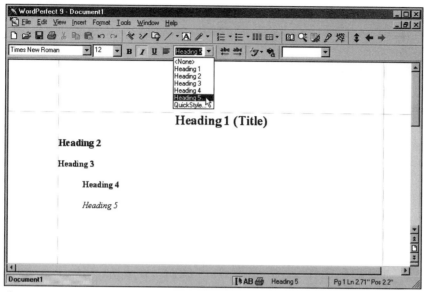

Figure 28-5: Applying the heading styles.

You can also apply styles from the Format menu:

1. Do one of the following:

   • For a character style, select the text you want to be in that style.

   • For a paragraph style, click the paragraph.

   • For a document style, click where you want the style to begin to take effect.

2. Click Format ➪ Styles, select the style, and click Insert (see Figure 28-6). You can also double-click a style in the list.

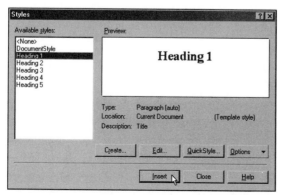

Figure 28-6: Applying a style from the Available Styles list.

Listing styles

Normally, only your document or template styles appear in the Available Styles list, but you can display and select styles from any source. Click Format ➪ Styles ➪ Options ➪ Settings, and check the sources you want to display (see Figure 28-7).

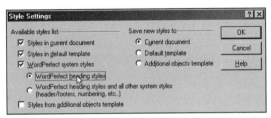

Figure 28-7: Selecting sources for your style listings.

Using keystrokes to turn off or chain styles

The most natural way to turn off a style is by using keystrokes. For a character style, you can simply press the right arrow key to move the insertion point outside of the styled text.

When using a paragraph style, the result of pressing Enter depends on the "inserts style" function assigned to the Enter key, as shown in Table 28-1. When the Enter key inserts a style, you can still turn a paragraph style off by using keystrokes in most cases.

Table 28-1			
Using Enter-key Assignments with Paragraph Styles			
Enter Key Inserts Style	*Result of Pressing Enter*	*Example*	*Keystroke(s) to Turn Off*
<None>	Style turns off	Headings	Enter
<Same Style>	Style turns off, insertion point moves past it, and then style turns back on	Bullets	Enter ➪ Backspace (doesn't work for all styles)
Another style	Style turns off, insertion point moves past it, and the other style turns on	Question-Answer chain (see "Chaining styles," later in this chapter)	Right arrow or Enter ➪ Backspace

When no keystroke is available, you can always turn off a style by selecting <None> from the Style List on the property bar (or click Format ⇨ Styles and insert <None>).

Removing styles

You can usually remove a style by selecting a style of <None> from the styles list on the property bar. One sure way of removing a style (especially a character style) is to go into Reveal Codes and remove its code.

Turning off automatic updating

To turn off automatic updating of an automatic paragraph style:

1. Right-click a paragraph that has the style and click QuickFormat ⇨ Discontinue.

2. Click "Current heading" to turn off the automatic update for just that heading, or click "All associated headings" to discontinue automatic updating of all headings with the associated style (see Figure 28-8).

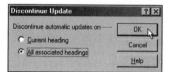

Figure 28-8: Turning off automatic updating.

Tip   You can also switch the style type between "Paragraph (paired-auto)" and "Paragraph (paired)" in the Styles Editor.

Creating your own styles

With that background under your belt, you're ready to create your own styles.

Creating styles by example

The easiest way to create styles in a document is by using the QuickStyle or QuickFormat features described in Chapter 17, "Becoming an Instant WordPerfect Expert":

1. Place the insertion point in your formatted text.

2. Do either of the following:

   • Click Format ⇨ Styles ⇨ QuickStyle, type a name and description, and then click either "Character with automatic update" or "Paragraph with automatic update."

- Click the QuickFormat icon on the toolbar, and then click "Selected characters" or "Headings."

Tip   The QuickFormat Characters option lets you copy character attributes, but it doesn't save them as a style. Use QuickStyle to save attributes as a character style.

You can use either technique to create an automatic paragraph style. QuickFormat initially puts a paint roller in your hands, to help spread the style around. QuickFormat styles are automatically named QuickFormat1, QuickFormat2, and so on, but you can change the names in the Styles Editor.

Using the Styles Editor to create or edit a style

You can also edit a style, or create one from scratch, in the Styles Editor:

1. Click Format ➪ Styles, and then do either of the following:

   - Highlight a style and click Edit.

   - Click Create and type a name and description for the new style.

2. Click the Type pop-up list to select or change a style type. (You can't change the type of a system style.)

3. Add codes and text in the Contents box. You can choose items from the Styles Editor menu, press keystrokes, or type text (see Figure 28-9).

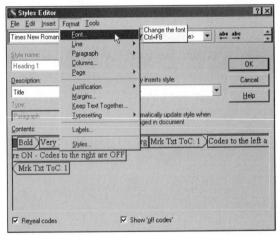

Figure 28-9: Creating or editing a style in the Styles Editor.

Tip   Click Insert ➪ Tab or Ctrl+Tab to insert a tab code. Make sure that "Reveal codes" is checked so that you can see the codes you're inserting.

4. Click OK to save the new or changed style. Existing text based on the edited style is automatically updated.

Creating a new set of headings

Suppose you want to create a set of heading styles similar to the system styles, but using an informal, modern font, such as Futura Medium. One way to do this is to copy the set of system headings and then insert the font code in your custom styles:

1. Open a new blank document and click Format ⇨ Styles.

2. Highlight Heading 1 and click Options ⇨ Copy.

3. Click "Current document," or "Default template," depending on whether you want to use the style for the current document only or have it available for all your new documents (see Figure 28-10).

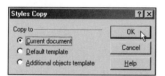

Figure 28-10: Selecting where to copy a style.

4. Click OK, and give the style another name of up to 12 characters and spaces, such as "Inf Head 1" (see Figure 28-11).

Figure 28-11: Naming the style you're copying.

5. Highlight the new style, click Edit ⇨ Format ⇨ Font, select the font you want, and then click OK ⇨ OK to save your changes.

Tip

Give your new styles a description while you're at it.

6. Repeat Steps 2 through 5 for the other four heading styles, and close the Styles dialog.

7. You can now type some text and apply your new styles (see Figure 28-12).

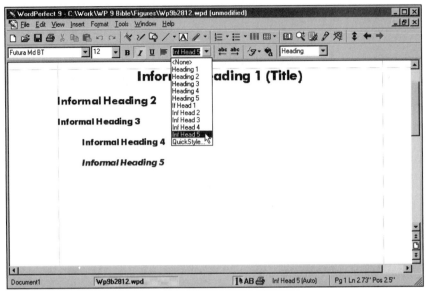

Figure 28-12: Trying out your new heading styles.

 Tip Because the headings are automatic paragraph styles (as you can see on the application bar when the insertion point is in one), you can also update the style by changing the format of document text to which they are applied. To prevent accidental alteration, you can change the style type from "paired-auto" to "paired."

Chaining styles

If you examine your heading styles in the Styles Editor, you'll see that the "Enter key inserts style:" option is set to <None>. This means that when you press Enter, the style is turned off and the insertion point moves to the next line.

If you click the Bullets button on the toolbar to insert a bullet, and then double-click its style code in Reveal Codes, you'll see that "Enter key inserts style" is set to <Same Style>. This means that each time you press Enter, another bullet is created, until you end the list by pressing Enter ➪ Backspace.

Normally, when you create a style, the "Enter key inserts style" is set to <Same Style>, so the style will keep repeating until you turn it off (such as with bullets). If you want your style to behave like a heading, have it chain to <None>.

You can also chain one style to another, even to another and back, in a continuous loop. One practical use of this technique is to create a two-style Question-Answer sheet in the following form:

Question:

Answer:

To create this Question-Answer style chain:

1. Click Format ⇨ Styles ⇨ Create to create the Question style. Type Question: followed by a space in the Contents box of the Styles Editor. Leave the type as Paragraph (paired), but don't change the "Enter key inserts style" option yet.

Tip You can select "Question:" in the Styles Editor and click the Bold button to make it bold, just as you would in a document.

2. Create the Answer style, with a preceding tab (Insert ⇨ Tab). Select Question from the "Enter key inserts style" list.

3. Go back and edit the Question style, setting "Enter key inserts style" to Answer.

To start the chain, select Question from the styles list on the property bar, type some text, and press Enter. You'll automatically switch to the Answer style. Type some text, and then press enter to start the next question.

To turn off the chain, press Enter ⇨ Backspace, or select <None> from the styles list.

Specifying "off codes"

With paired styles, you can insert codes to execute after the style ends.

With the styles created in the previous Question-Answer exercise, the answer follows the question on the next line, with no blank line in between.

To skip a line after each question and answer, you can add hard returns as "off codes" following the end of each style:

1. Click Format ⇨ Styles, highlight the Question style, and click Edit.

2. Check "Show 'off codes'."

3. Click after the ON/OFF separator comment, and then press Enter to insert a [HRt] code (see Figure 28-13).

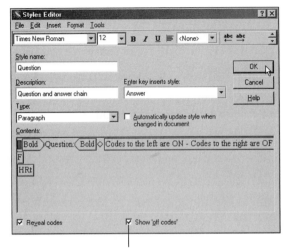

Click here to enter "off codes"

Figure 28-13: Specifying "off codes."

Do the same for the Answer style, and you'll get a blank line after each question and each answer.

Resetting a system style

To reset a system style that you've edited, click Format ➪ Styles, select the style, and click Options ➪ Reset.

Specifying where styles are saved

Normally, the styles you create are saved in the current document. To specify another location, click Format ➪ Styles ➪ Options ➪ Settings and click another location (see Figure 28-14). When you next save a style, it will be saved in the location you chose.

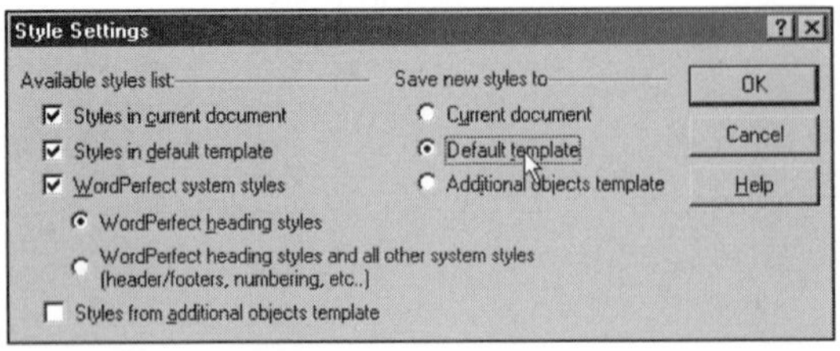

Figure 28-14: Specifying where styles are saved.

Saving styles to a file

To save the listed styles to a library file:

1. Click Format ⇨ Styles ⇨ Options ⇨ Save As.

2. Specify a name and location for the file.

3. Click whether you want to save user styles, system styles, or both (see Figure 28-15).

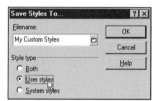

Figure 28-15: Saving styles to a file.

The styles are saved in a blank WordPerfect document.

Retrieving styles from a file

To retrieve styles from a library file and insert them into your current document:

1. Click Format ⇨ Styles ⇨ Options ⇨ Retrieve.

2. Go to the folder and select the file.

 Tip   Look for All Files (*.*) because style files aren't normally saved with a .WPD extension.

3. Click whether you want to retrieve user styles, system styles, or both.

You'll get a warning message if any of the names conflict, so you can choose not to overwrite the existing styles in your document.

 Tip   A styles file is simply another document. You can retrieve styles from any document created in WordPerfect 6.1 and up.

Deleting a style

To delete a (nonsystem) style:

1. Click Format ⇨ Styles, and select the style.

2. Click Options ⇨ Delete, and select either of the following (see Figure 28-16):

    • *Including formatting codes*, to delete all occurrences of the style from the document

    • *Leave formatting codes in document*, to delete the style but leave the style's formatting codes in your document

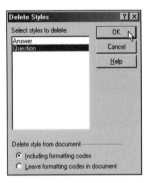

Figure 28-16: Deleting a style.

To remove a style from a section of text, drag the style out of Reveal Codes.

For More Information . . .

On	See
Getting PerfectExpert help	Chapter 5
Creating a boilerplate document	Chapter 17
Using graphics styles	Chapters 9 and 54
Using formatting codes	Chapter 16
Customizing the Document Style	Chapter 21
Using QuickStyle and QuickFormat	Chapter 17
Specifying your default template	Chapter 29
Using styles in master documents	Chapter 25

✦   ✦   ✦

Customizing WordPerfect

Thanks to usability tests and an enhanced graphical inter-face, WordPerfect is easier than ever to use. Still, your needs are unique, and you have a particular way of getting things done.

WordPerfect provides a number of ways to "arrange the furni-ture" in your working environment and screen display. A little time spent in exploring the possibilities can make your work more pleasurable and efficient for years to come. The idea here is to experiment — to find what works best for you. Remember, though, that an incredible amount of work went into designing the WordPerfect environment, so don't feel compelled to change anything.

Understanding WordPerfect's Settings

To properly understand settings, three questions must be addressed:

- ✦ What's a setting?
- ✦ Where do you set them?
- ✦ Where are they stored?

What's a setting?

A setting is any element in your working environment that stays put from session to session. A custom style or macro is not a setting, as it is only applied when called upon. Even a change to your Document Style is not a setting, as it affects only the current document. However, a change to the default Document Style is a setting because it affects all future docu-ments. A custom toolbar or keyboard is also a setting, as it stays put until you change it again.

Where do you set settings?

While most user settings are found among the Settings dialog boxes (the focus of this chapter), there are important exceptions, such as your QuickCorrect options, the guideline display, your Undo history, and your printer default font. Appendix B, "WordPerfect Settings Quick Reference," provides a quick reference to all your user settings, including some Windows 95/98 settings that affect your suite's environment.

Where are your settings stored?

Just as you customize settings at various locations, so are your settings stored at different places.

The Windows Registry

All Windows 95/98 programs (including WordPerfect) store system settings as binary keys in the Windows Registry. This results in a hierarchical tree structure with a dense foliage of obscure entries. Actually, the Registry is composed of two or more files. The standard configuration places a USER.DAT file and a SYSTEM. DAT file in your Windows folder, which are automatically backed up to USER.DA0 and SYSTEM.DA0.

Your Windows Settings Editor (Regedit.exe) lets you edit or export registry settings. The WP registry branches are as follows:

✦ HKEY_CURRENT_USER\Software\Corel\WordPerfect\9

✦ HKEY_USERS\.Default\Software\Corel\WordPerfect\9

✦ HKEY_LOCAL_MACHINE\SOFTWARE\Corel\WordPerfect\9\Location of Files

Caution   The best advice, however, is never to tamper directly with the Registry unless you're an expert systems administrator with an imperative need. Let the suite programs handle your settings, or you'll run the risk of corrupting your Registry and causing the system to fail.

Other places for custom settings

A number of WordPerfect's settings are stored in your default template, rather than the Registry (see Chapter 28, "Working Quickly with Templates, Projects, and Styles"). These include custom toolbars, menus, and keyboards, plus your default Document Style. Click Tools ➪ Settings ➪ Files ➪ Template to see its name and location.

Your QuickWord abbreviations are stored in a separate template (QW9EN.WPT for English) in the same Custom WP Templates folder.

There's also your user word list of QuickCorrect changes, spell-check additions, QuickLinks, and end-of-sentence punctuation exceptions. These files (wt9us.uwl and wt9us.hst for U.S. English) are normally found in your \My Documents\Corel User Files folder.

Your Settings Control Center

Click Tools ➪ Settings to display your Settings control center (see Figure 29-1). From here you can click the particular icon for nearly all of the settings discussed in this chapter.

Figure 29-1: Your Settings control center.

Note

A number of settings in previous releases, such as those for the default view and zoom, symbols display, and the size of the Reveal Codes window are no longer found in the settings dialog boxes. To make your life simpler, these have been made into "sticky" settings, so your latest screen selections carry over from document to document and from session to session.

Setting Up Your Display

The Display Settings dialog box (see Figure 29-2) has tabs for specifying the various settings discussed in the next six sections.

Tip

For a shortcut to your display settings, right-click a scroll bar and click Settings.

Setting your document display

The first display settings you encounter are for your document display, as described in Table 29-1.

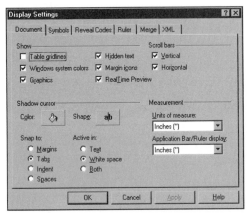

Figure 29-2: Document tab of the Display Settings dialog box.

	Table 29-1 **Document Display Settings**	
Setting	**Lets You**	
Show		
Table gridlines	Speed up your display when checked by turning off shaded fills and showing nongraphic dotted lines in place of the normal table lines. (Leave unchecked and turn on gridlines from the View menu when you need them.)	
Windows system colors	Change black text on white background to Windows system colors. (In Windows' Display Properties, set the Window item under the Appearance tab.)	
Graphics	Hide graphics when unchecked to speed up your display when editing text. (Leave checked and turn off graphics from the View menu when you need to.)	
Hidden text	Display hidden text when checked. (Leave off and use View menu when you want to see it.)	
Margin icons	Display clickable icons for tab settings and comments in Page view.	
RealTime Preview	Preview the results of toolbar selections.	

Setting	Lets You
Scroll bars	
Vertical	Display the vertical scroll bar.
Horizontal	Display the horizontal scroll bar. (If you rarely use the horizontal scroll bar, you can uncheck it to give yourself more screen space.)
Shadow cursor	
Color	Click the palette to change the color of your shadow cursor.
Shape	Click the palette to pick a different shape for when you're pointing to text.
Snap to	Pick whether you want the shadow cursor to snap to (and insert formatting codes for) margins, tabs, indents, or spaces. (Margins, which includes the ability to center text, is normally enough and avoids accidental insertion of tabs, indents, and spaces.)
Active in	Choose to have the shadow cursor appear when your pointer is in text (active in text), in white space, or both.
Measurement	
Units of measure	Select the units of measure for setting margins, line spacing, paper size, and so on.
Application Bar/Ruler display	Select the unit of measure to display on the application bar and ruler.

Setting your symbols display

Suppose you're cleaning up a document written by someone who used spaces, rather than tabs, and used hard returns to end lines in the middle of a paragraph. To save yourself the bother of looking into Reveal Codes, click the Symbols tab in Display Settings and check the particular symbols you want to see. Then click View ➪ Show and the paragraph symbol to toggle your symbols display.

Setting your Reveal Codes display

Tired of squinting at small, black-on-gray text in Reveal Codes? Click the Reveal Codes tab in Display Settings to specify a new font size or color, and several other display options (see Figure 29-3) described in Table 29-2.

Tip   When codes are displayed, you can right-click in the Reveal Codes window and click Settings to change the display options.

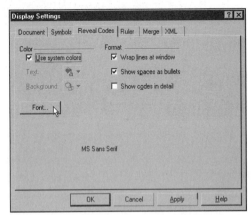

Figure 29-3: Setting your Reveal Codes display.

	Table 29-2
	Reveal Codes Display Settings

Setting	Lets You
Color	Uncheck to select colors from the palettes for your Reveal Codes text (normally black) and background (normally light gray).
Font	Pick a display font and size. Normally stick to the default face for clarity. Use a large size to make your codes stand out (see Figure 29-4). (This feature is especially useful for the visually impaired.)
Wrap lines at window	Wrap the lines in the Reveal Codes window so that you can see all the codes without scrolling (handy when using a larger Reveal Codes font size).
Show spaces as bullets	Display spaces as bullets to make them easier to count.
Show codes in detail	See the formatting details associated with each code. (Otherwise, you must position the insertion point to the left of the code to see them.)

Setting up your ruler

Click the Ruler tab in Display Settings to select either of the ruler (and tab bar) display settings described in Table 29-3. (You can also right-click the ruler, when displayed, and click Settings.)

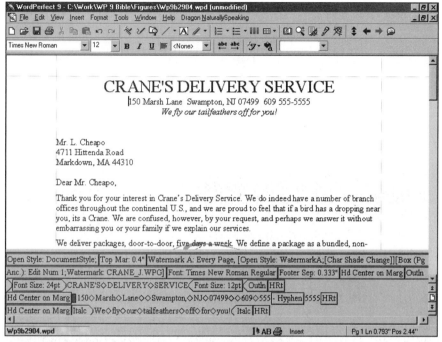

Figure 29-4: Reveal Codes with a 20-point font and line wrap.

Table 29-3 Ruler Settings	
Setting	**Lets You**
Tabs snap to Ruler grid	Have the tabs snap to the nearest invisible grid line, located every ¹/₁₆ of an inch or every millimeter.
Show Ruler guides	Have a vertical, dotted line display on your screen to indicate the new tab location.

Setting your merge codes display

Click the Merge tab in Display Settings to display your merge codes in full (the default), or as markers, to make your document more readable. You can also choose not to display your merge codes at all.

When working with a particular merge file, you can always change the merge code display from the Merge toolbar.

Setting your XML display

Click the XML tab in Display Settings to display your XML codes in full (the default), or as markers (to make your document more readable), or not at all (see Figure 29-5). You can also set the font size, the appearance of tags in Reveal Codes, as well as the text and background colors for various XML components.

Cross-Reference

For a brief explanation of WordPerfect's XML facilities, see Chapter 14, "Web Writing and Publishing."

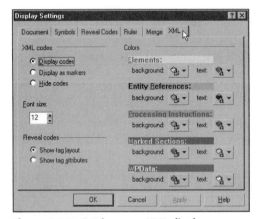

Figure 29-5: Setting your XML display.

Setting Up Your Environment

The Environment Settings dialog box (see Figure 29-6) has tabs for specifying the various settings discussed in the next four sections.

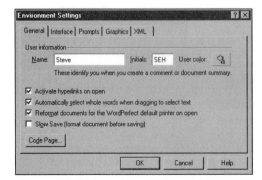

Figure 29-6: General tab of the Environment Settings dialog box.

General environment setup

Your general environment settings are described in Table 29-4.

Table 29-4
General Environment Settings

Setting	Lets You
User name, initials, and color	Automatically insert your name and initials when you create a document summary, review a document, or insert a comment. (Select a distinctive color for your comments or document review.)
Activate hyperlinks on open	Turn on hyperlinks in documents you receive or create. (Documents without hypertext are not affected.)
Automatically select whole words when dragging to select text	Select word-by-word, rather than character-by-character, when you drag the mouse. (To override this feature, hold down the Alt key.)
Reformat documents for the WordPerfect default printer on open	Automatically reformat documents composed on a different printer when you open them. If not checked, WordPerfect looks for the document's printer among your list of available printers. If it finds the printer, the program switches to that printer to edit the document. If the document's printer is not found, however, WordPerfect still reformats the document for the current printer. (Check a reformatted document to see that the pages still look good and the paragraphs, tables, and other elements don't break at awkward places.)
Slow Save (format document before saving)	Ensures that the document is fully formatted before it is saved to disk, so that its components are properly analyzed (parsed) by certain third-party applications. (This is generally equivalent to placing the insertion point at the end of the document, saving the document, and then returning to your original location.)
Code Page...	Change the table that specifies which ASCII and ANSI character sets are used when importing and exporting documents. (Normally, you would not change the code page, especially if you're not switching languages.) For the U.S. language version of WordPerfect, the Windows Code Page should be 1252, which supports the extended TrueType character set.

Setting up your interface

Click the Interface tab of the Environment Settings dialog box to select the interface settings (see Figure 29-7) described in Table 29-5.

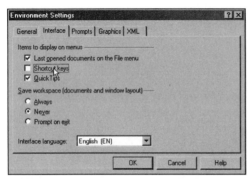

Figure 29-7: Setting up your interface.

Table 29-5 Interface Settings	
Setting	*Lets You*
Items to display on menus	
Last open documents on the File menu	Display or hide the names of the last nine open files at the bottom of the File menu.
Shortcut keys	Show the keyboard shortcuts on the menus. (Leave unchecked for cleaner-looking menus, and use the Quick Tips instead.)
Quick Tips	Pop-up descriptions (including shortcut keys) when you point to toolbar and menu items.
Save workspace (documents and window layout)	
Always	Automatically save your latest changes and place QuickMarks at the insertion points of your open documents when you exit. The next time you start WordPerfect, your documents reopen and you return to where you left off.
Never	Never save your workspace.
Prompt on exit	Choose whether to save your workspace when you exit WordPerfect.
Interface language	Select the language for program dialog boxes, menus, messages, and so on, when you have two or more language versions installed (see Chapter 52, "Writers' Lib").

Setting program prompts and beeps

Click the Prompts tab of the Environment Settings dialog box (see Figure 29-8) to select the prompt and beep settings described in Table 29-6.

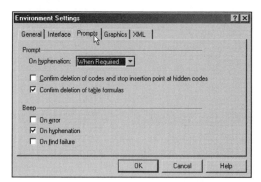

Figure 29-8: Setting program prompts and beeps.

Table 29-6
Program Prompts and Beep Settings

Setting	Lets You
Prompt	
On hyphenation	Select the hyphenation prompt setting discussed in Chapter 20, "Controlling Text and Numbering Pages." (If in doubt, stick to When Required, the default.)
Confirm deletion of codes and stop insertion point at hidden codes	Be prompted when you're about to delete a code while editing character by character.
Confirm deletion of table formulas	Receive a warning when you're about to type over a formula in a table cell or floating cell. (You can't see the formulas, so leave this protection on.)
Beep	
On Error	Hear a warning when an error occurs (off by default).
On hyphenation	Hear a beep when you're prompted to set the hyphenation point (on by default).
On find failure	Hear a beep when what you're looking for in your document can't be found (off by default).

Specifying graphics settings

Click the Graphics tab of the Environment Settings dialog box (see Figure 29-9) to select the settings described in Table 29-7.

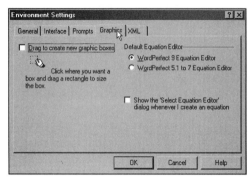

Figure 29-9: Specifying graphics settings.

Table 29-7
Graphics Settings

Setting	Lets You
Drag to create new graphics boxes	Always drag in your document to specify the initial size of your graphics. (You can leave this off and use the shadow cursor instead.)
Default Equation Editor	Choose whether to use the graphical Equation Editor or the text-based Equation Editor from earlier versions of WordPerfect.
Show the 'Select Equation Editor' dialog whenever I create an equation	Always be offered a choice of which Equation Editor to use.

Selecting XML import settings

Click the XML tab of the Environment Settings dialog box to select options for importing HTML, SGML, and XML documents to XML.

Setting Up Your Files

Files Settings (see Figure 29-10) tells WordPerfect where your templates, macros, graphics, and other files are stored. Default folders are specified when you install WordPerfect, but you can change defaults or specify additional folders for various items (such as a separate folder for the macros you write).

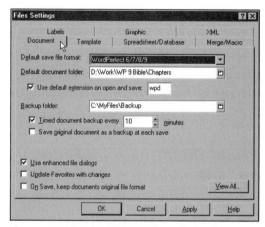

Figure 29-10: The Files Settings dialog box, showing the Document tab.

Updating Favorites

All the Files Settings tabs have an "Update Favorites with changes" selection to automatically update your Favorites folder when you change any of the default folders. You might want to uncheck this item to assume direct control over what appears in your Favorites folder and keep it from becoming cluttered with items you seldom use. (A change to this setting under one tab is reflected under all the others.)

Cross-Reference For tips on setting up your Favorites folder, see Chapter 7, "Managing Your Files."

Selecting document file settings

Click the Document tab in Files Settings to select the document file settings described in Table 29-8.

Table 29-8
Document File Settings

Setting	Lets You
Default save file format	Select the format to which you save your documents. WordPerfect 6/7/8/9 ensures the most powerful feature set and widespread compatibility. WordPerfect 5.1/5.2 ensures even wider compatibility, but sacrifices some advanced formatting. You can also select any of the other formats that WordPerfect can handle, including Microsoft Word, as your default.
Default document folder	Specify the initial open or save folder for a WordPerfect session. After that, you'll always return to the last folder accessed. (Specify the folder you're currently using the most.)
Use default extension on open and save	Specify the extension that's automatically added to the filename when you save a document. Normally leave the check and the extension as "wpd," so programs recognize your files as WordPerfect documents.
Backup folder	Specify where your timed document backups are stored.
Timed document backup every *x* minutes	Have WordPerfect make timed backups of your screen documents at the interval you specify.
Save original document as a backup at each save	Have WordPerfect create a backup copy each time you save a document, with the same filename and a .BAK extension. (This sounds great, because you'll always have two versions of a document. However, it also means that your hard drive will fill up in half the time, and you will have to sort through all those .BAK files. See Chapter 6 for more on backup techniques.)
Use enhanced file dialogs	Use the enhanced Corel Open File dialog box, which lets you perform all the file operations described in Chapter 7, "Managing Your Files," rather than the basic Windows one.
On save, keep document's original file format	Always save the file in its original format. (Normally this option is unchecked, and you're asked to specify the format upon saving if the original differs from the default.)

Tip   To assign another extension when you save a file, put the entire filename in quotes, as with "Test.xyz." By using quotation marks, you can even save a file without an extension, as with "Test."

Setting up your templates

Click the Template tab of the Files Settings dialog box to specify your default and additional template folders and files (see Figure 29-11).

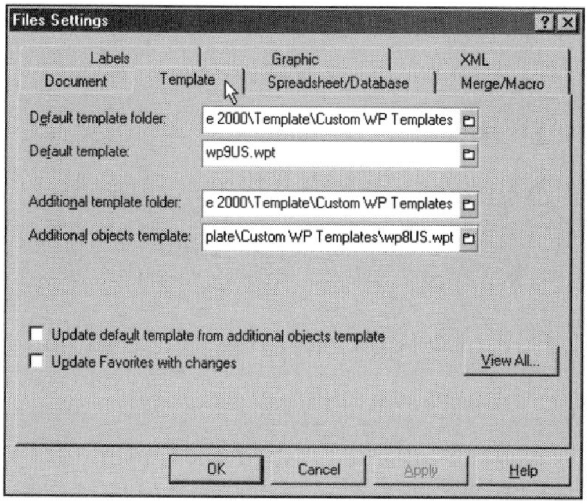

Figure 29-11: Specifying template folders.

The default template is used when you create a new blank document. You can specify an "Additional objects template" to provide other keyboards, menus, toolbars, styles, and template macros. Typically, network users might use a shared folder that contains an additional template customized to corporate standards.

If you specify a default template name that doesn't exist, WordPerfect creates one based on the installation default (such as WP9US.WPT), unless you have also specified an additional objects template, in which case the new template will be based on that.

Updating the default template from the additional objects template

If you want to continually overwrite your default template with the additional objects template, check "Update default template from additional objects template." This option is sometimes used by network system administrators to update every network user's default template with the company standard.

Setting up spreadsheet and database files

Click the Spreadsheet/Database tab of the Files Settings dialog box to specify your default and supplemental folders for spreadsheet and database files (the files you want to share or import, not the programs themselves).

Specifying merge and macro file settings

Click the Merge/Macro tab of the Files Settings dialog box (see Figure 29-12) to specify merge file extensions and macro folders.

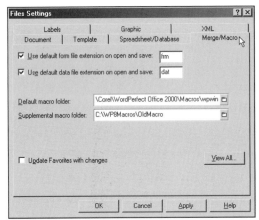

Figure 29-12: Specifying merge and macro file settings.

Normally, when you create merge form and data files, the filename extensions of .FRM and .DAT are automatically applied. You would rarely need to change these defaults.

The default macro folder, upon installation, holds the WordPerfect macros described in Chapter 58, "Automating with Macros." If you have additional macros, it's usually a good idea to keep them in a separate folder. The supplemental folder can also be used to specify the location of shared macros on a network. You can run macros in the default or supplemental folder without specifying their paths.

Setting up your label file

Click the Labels tab of the Files Settings dialog box to specify your default label file (see Figure 29-13).

You can also choose to display only the laser sheet label definitions, only the tractor-fed label definitions, or both. See Chapter 27, "Mass-Producing with Labels and Merge," for more on using labels.

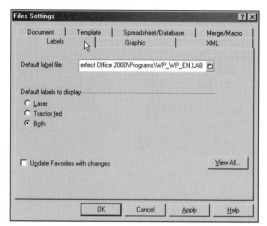

Figure 29-13: Setting up your label file.

Setting up your graphic files

Click the Graphic tab of the Files Settings dialog box to specify the location of your graphic files. The installation sets up a default graphics folder containing a compact clip art scrapbook; you can also designate a supplemental folder. There's also a folder for the fancy page borders WordPerfect installs.

Setting up your XML files

Click the XML tab of the Files Settings dialog box to specify the locations of your XML templates, documents, and graphics, as well as the base template and catalog files to use.

Viewing all your file locations at once

Click the View All button in any of the file settings dialog boxes to get a comprehensive look at all your file settings, as shown in Figure 29-14.

Setting Up Your Document Summaries

Use the Document Summary Settings dialog box (see Figure 29-15) to automate various tasks, as described in Table 29-9. For example, you can have WordPerfect search for "RE:" or "Subject:" in your memos, then extract the text immediately following to fill in the Subject field of the document summaries.

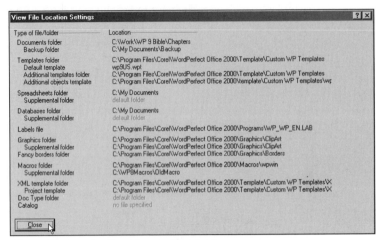

Figure 29-14: Viewing all your file locations at once.

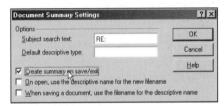

Figure 29-15: Setting up your document summaries.

Table 29-9	
Document Summary Settings	
Setting	*Lets You*
Subject search text	Tell the program what keyword to search for in your documents when automatically selecting text for the Subject field of the document summaries.
Default descriptive type	Specify text for the Descriptive Type field, such as "Report" or "Memo," to be used when you automatically create a document summary. (*Tip:* Leave it blank if you have a diversity of types.)
Create summary on save/exit	Be prompted to automatically create a document summary when you save a document that doesn't yet have one.

Setting	Lets You
On open, use the descriptive name for the new filename	Change a filename in the DOS 8.3 format to one in the long filename (LFN) format taken from the descriptive name field.
When saving a document, use the filename for the descriptive name	Automatically put the filename in the descriptive name field (unless you already filled it in) the first time you save a new document.

Specifying Conversion Settings

Normally, you won't have to change the conversion settings that specify how graphics, ASCII-delimited text records, and documents from other word processors are imported into WordPerfect. An example of when you might want to adjust these settings might be when importing database records during a WordPerfect merge, as not all programs export records with the same delimiters.

You can even have WordPerfect behave like another word processor, or an old version of WP, when formatting certain elements in the current document.

Selecting compatibility settings

Click the Compatibility tab of the Convert Settings dialog box (see Figure 29-16) to select various compatibility settings, described in Table 29-10.

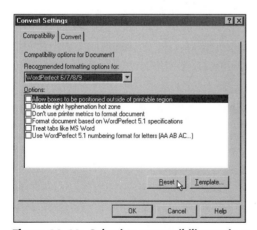

Figure 29-16: Selecting compatibility settings.

Table 29-10 Compatibility Settings	
Setting	*Lets You*
Recommended formatting options for:	Select sets of formatting options particular to MS Word or earlier versions of WP, or create a user-defined set of options.
Allow boxes to be positioned outside of printable region	Allow images to bleed off the edge of the printed page.
Disable right hyphenation hot zone	Use only the left hyphenation zone in determining if a word should be hyphenated.
Don't use printer metrics to format document	Ensure that when you send a document to someone with a different printer, it will print exactly the same way (especially with the addition of font embedding). This is a critical need in the legal industry.
Format document based on WordPerfect 5.1 specifications	Use the WordPerfect 5.1 line height (especially useful for certain standard legal forms).
Treat tabs like MS Word	Have tabs work as they do in MS Word, such as having an automatic tab stop in a hanging indent.
Use WP 5.1 numbering format for letters (AA AB AC ...)	After an outline or list ordered with letters has used A through Z, use AA, AB, AC, and so on, instead of AA, BB, CC, and so on.
Reset	Clear settings and return to WP 6/7/8/9 defaults.
Template	Change compatibility options for all new documents based on the standard template.

Specifying import conversions

Click the Convert tab of the Convert Settings dialog box (see Figure 29-17) to specify how graphics, ASCII-delimited text records, and documents from other word processors are imported into WordPerfect, as described in Table 29-11.

Cross-Reference   See Chapter 10, "Working Together and Sharing Data," for more information about importing files from other programs.

Customizing Your Application Bar

WordPerfect's developers carefully considered which useful features to put on the application bar. From left to right you have the document buttons, the Shadow

Cursor switch, the Caps Lock button, and printer details. Next you have the General Status that displays Insert or Typeover when you're editing text, and special information on such things as tables, columns, macros, merges, and styles at other times. Your combined position display is on the right.

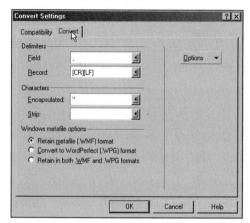

Figure 29-17: Specifying convert settings.

Still, if you want to customize your application bar, you can. For example, if you keep the Windows taskbar tucked behind your application screen (see Chapter 3, "Looking at a Suite Face"), you may want to add the date and time to the application bar. You can then click these buttons to insert the date or time in your document. To customize your application bar:

1. Right-click the application bar and click Settings (Tools ⇨ Settings ⇨ Application Bar).

2. Check or uncheck the features you want from the list of available items (see Figure 29-18).

3. Follow the dialog box instructions to move, delete, or resize an item, or switch it between text and icon display.

Tip   To switch between text and icon display when not in the editor, hold down the Alt key and double-click.

4. Select from the available font sizes.

5. Click OK to keep your new settings, or click Reset to restore the application bar to its default settings.

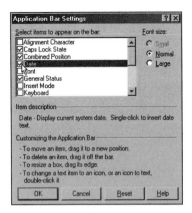

Figure 29-18: Customizing your application bar.

Table 29-11
Convert Settings

Setting	Lets You
Delimiters	
Field	Specify the character or code used to separate fields when importing a spreadsheet or database as ASCII-delimited text.
Record	Specify the character or code used to separate records.
Characters	
Encapsulated	Specify the character (such as a double quotation mark) used to enclose each field, or to mark the place for a field that is not being used.
Strip	Tell WordPerfect the characters you want to remove from the file you're converting.
Windows metafile options	
Retain metafile (.WMF) format	Preserve the original format and attributes when importing a graphic from another Windows program. The graphic works fine in WordPerfect for Windows, but it won't display if you transfer the document to WordPerfect for DOS and other platforms.
Convert to WordPerfect (.WPG) format	Convert the graphic to the .WPG format that displays in all versions of WordPerfect, but you're likely to lose some detail.
Retain in both .WMF and .WPG formats	Create a .WPG file that retains both formats, but you end up with a bigger file.

Customizing Toolbars, Menus, and Keyboards

You can think of toolbars (including property bars and tool palettes), menus, and keyboards as alternative paths to get things done. All three can be customized to activate a feature, run a macro, play keystrokes, or launch a program. You can also customize the toolbar display. See Chapter 57, "Customizing Toolbars, Menus, and Keyboards," for details.

WordPerfect toolbars, menus, and keyboards can also be customized for a particular template. For example, you can create a special toolbar for a specific publishing project, without having it appear among the selections when you create a standard document.

Starting WordPerfect with Custom Options

When launching WordPerfect, you can also make use of one or more of the *startup options*, described in Table 29-12. These environmental variables can be handy at times, especially if your computer is having display or memory problems.

To start WordPerfect with a custom option, click Start on the Windows taskbar, click Run, type **wpwin9** followed by a space, and then type the options you want. For example, type **wpwin9 /fl** to write directly to the screen. To run multiple options, put a space between options.

Table 29-12
WordPerfect's Startup Options

Option	Lets You	Example
:	Open WordPerfect without displaying the startup screen.	
/d-path	Redirect overflow and temporary buffer files to a particular folder.	/d-c:\temp
/DM=90	Reduce screen text display to 90% of true WYSIWYG. (*Tip*: Try this if normal text appears bold or words appear scrunched together.)	
filename	Open a particular file. Include the path if it's not in your default document folder.	Letterhead.wpd
filename /bk-bookmark name	Open a particular file and move to the specified bookmark.	Letterhead.wpd /bk-Address

Continued

Table 29-12 *(continued)*		
Option	**Lets You**	**Example**
/fl	Send text directly to the screen, instead of creating a bitmap that Windows then writes. (This option may increase screen flicker.)	
/l-language code	Specify the language used on opening.	/l-FR
/m-macroname	Start the specified macro on launch.	/m-C:\ Program Files\ Corel\WPO2000\ Macros\WPWin\ Letterhead.wcm
/mt-macroname	Start the specified macro in the default template on launch.	/mt-Letterhead. wcm
/nb	Turn off original document backup.	
/recover	Rebuild document prefix information upon retrieval. (*Tip*: Use the Document Restore utility instead, as described in Chapter 6, "Working Without Worries.")	
/u-name	Identify the initials of the user at startup. (Normally, you should let Windows handle multiple user profiles instead.)	

To use an option all the time, right-click the WordPerfect icon on the taskbar, click Properties, click the WordPerfect icon, click Properties, and then add the option after the target path and program.

For More Information . . .

On	See
Changing the default Document Style	Chapter 21
Locating your settings	Appendix B
Configuring the speech module	Chapter 4
Configuring the shadow cursor	Chapter 16
Changing the default font	Chapter 21
Setting tabs	Chapter 21
Changing the merge code display	Chapter 27
Installing language versions	Chapter 52
Selecting the hyphenation prompt option	Chapter 20
Setting up your Favorites folder	Chapter 7
Selecting backup options	Chapter 6
Customizing toolbars and application bars	Chapter 57
Configuring your Windows desktop	Chapter 3

✦　　✦　　✦

Crunching Numbers with Quattro Pro

A Hands-On Notebook

You can use Corel Quattro Pro to track and compute financial data and other numerical information for home, business, or school.

While you can also use a WordPerfect table to compute totals and formulas, Quattro Pro is a spreadsheet program designed to crunch numbers. It helps you to create a budget, produce an income statement, analyze mortgage terms, or run statistical tests. Quattro Pro answers your "what if" questions, such as "How much money will I make if sales increase by 5 percent each month for the next six months?" You can display the results in a chart or map, or turn them into a slide show production.

This chapter provides hands-on practice, as you create, format, save, and print the spreadsheet shown in Figure 30-1.

Getting Started

To start Quattro Pro, click the Quattro Pro taskbar icon on the Windows taskbar, or Click Start ➪ WordPerfect Office 2000 ➪ Quattro Pro 9. You'll be presented with the blank notebook shown in Figure 30-2 (the notebook window is slightly minimized for clarity).

Choosing how you want to work

New Feature If you're working in an Excel 97 shop, or the rest of the office uses Quattro Pro 8, you can change your compatibility settings to use the same file type, menus, and other features (see Chapter 34, "Formatting Figures and Setting Up Notebooks").

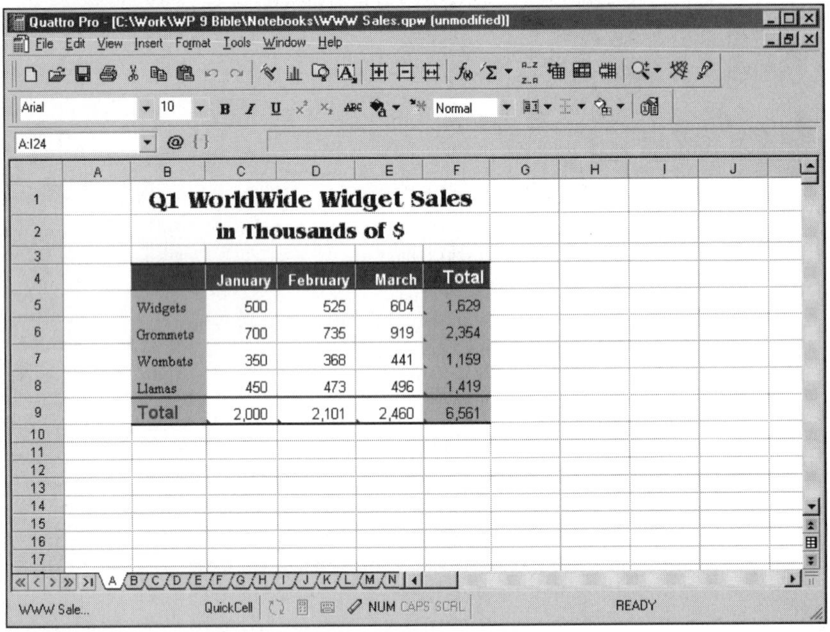

Figure 30-1: Quattro Pro spreadsheet you'll create.

A look at the Quattro Pro screen

Quattro Pro shares the general features of the WordPerfect Office interface described in Chapter 2, "Essential Typing and Editing":

✦ A *menu bar* for general access to features.

✦ A *toolbar* with buttons for frequently performed operations.

✦ A *property bar* with handy lists for changing numeric formats, alignment, and other options, depending on the current task.

✦ An *application bar* displaying the open notebooks, plus various indicators of the program's status. In particular, note the data entry mode indicator showing such states as READY for input, or that the current entry is a VALUE (number) or a LABEL (text).

Unique to Quattro Pro is the *input line* that displays the current cell's address and contents. You can enter data in the input line or directly in the cell.

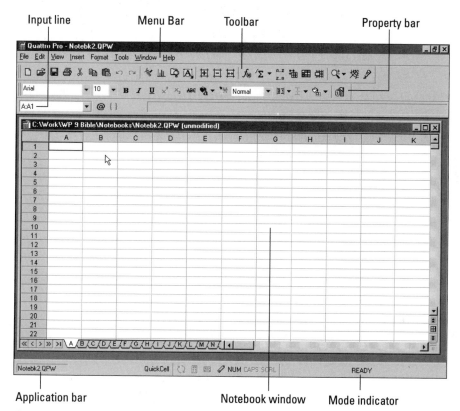

Figure 30-2: Blank notebook shown when you open Quattro Pro.

What's in a name?

New Feature

Each notebook is stored in its own file, initially named Notebk#.QPW, where # is the incremental notebook number. The .QPW filename extension identifies the file as a notebook in the new, compressed format, which permits more than 18,000 columns and a million rows. QP9 can open notebooks created in earlier versions of Quattro Pro, identified by their .WB1, .WB2, or .WB3 extensions.

What are those little tabs for?

Now take a closer look at the notebook window, shown in Figure 30-3. When you click the tabs at the bottom of the window, you'll see that a notebook is a collection of related sheets (spreadsheet pages).

Row border   Select all   Current cell   Selected block   Column border

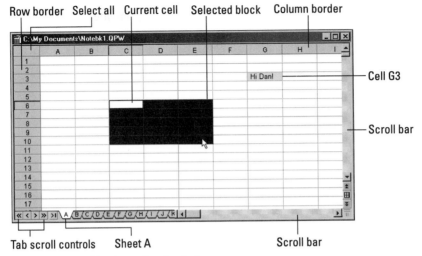

Cell G3

Scroll bar

Tab scroll controls   Sheet A   Scroll bar

Figure 30-3: Tabbed notebook window.

There are, by default, 256 sheets in each notebook, labeled A through Z, then AA through AZ, all the way to IV. (You'll learn later how to give them more descriptive names.) There's also one Objects sheet at the very end to keep the icons for each chart, map, slide show, and dialog box that you've created.

Each sheet is organized into a grid of 256 columns (labeled A through IV) and 65,536 rows (labeled 1 to 65,535).

New Feature   You can specify from 1–18,278 sheets and columns, and as many as 1,000,000 rows! If you ever need this much space to import a large database, it's nice to have, but normally you will probably want to keep the default settings.

Browsing by cell type

New Feature   The *Browse by button* on the vertical scroll bar lets you quickly browse through particular types of cells, such as all cells with formulas or all dependents of the current cell:

1. Right-click the Browse by button to select cells of a particular type (see Figure 30-4).

2. Click the arrow buttons on the scroll bar to move the selector from cell to cell.

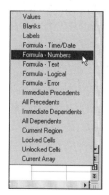

Figure 30-4: Selecting cells of a particular type.

Other workbook screen features

The workbook window also has

- ✦ *Borders* you can click to select columns and rows. Click the upper-left border cell to select the entire sheet.

- ✦ *Tab scroll controls* that work like VCR buttons to fast forward (>) or revert back (<<) to the sheet you want. The Jump to Objects Sheet button jumps you to the Objects sheet and back.

Understanding Addresses

Data is entered into individual cells. The current or *active* cell is the one selected for data entry. A cell's address is the intersection of its column letter and row number, such as cell G3 in Figure 30-3. When referencing a cell, you can qualify its address more fully by specifying the sheet and notebook name. For example, D:C4 is the address of cell C4 on sheet D. [SALES]B:F9 is the address in the SALES notebook of the cell on sheet B, column F, row 9.

What's an object?

An *object* is anything you can change within Quattro Pro, including cells, selections, pages, notebooks, charts, maps, and the Quattro Pro program itself. Each object has properties, such as the border or shading of a cell or block. You'll see the various ways you can edit object properties as you go along.

Entering Data

You can use a number of techniques to enter spreadsheet data, including QuickFill for automatic block completion.

Typing cell entries

When entering data in Quattro Pro, the black-bordered rectangle, or cell selector, indicates the active cell. To enter spreadsheet data:

1. Click a cell.

2. Type its value (number) or label (text).

3. Press one of the following:

   - *Enter* to move the selector one cell down

   - *Tab* to move the selector one cell to the right

   - An *arrow key* to move the selector one cell up, down, left, or right

 Tip If you don't want Enter to move the selector, click Tools ➪ Settings ➪ General, and remove the check from Move Cell Selector/Enter Key.

Later in this chapter you'll learn how to type entries quickly in a selected block, or automatically fill cells with QuickFill.

Moving the selector to a cell

Try the various ways to move the selector around your spreadsheet:

✦ Click a cell

✦ Press the Enter, Tab, and arrow keys

✦ Press Shift+Tab to back tab

✦ Press Home to go to cell A1 (or Ctrl+Home to go to cell A1 on sheet A)

✦ Press End, Home to go to the cell in the last row and the last column in which data is entered (or End, Ctrl+Home for the same location on the last sheet with data)

 Cross-Reference See Chapter 32, "Entering Data and Formulas," for a complete list of navigation shortcuts.

Selecting a block of cells

You can perform many time-saving operations (including data entry) on rectangular *blocks* of selected cells. Selection properties (such as number type and alignment) can be applied to a single cell, as well as to a block.

You identify a selection by its *cell coordinates* — the address of the upper-left cell, followed by one or two periods (..) and the address of the lower-right cell. The selection shown in Figure 30-3 has the coordinates C6..E10.

There are two basic ways to select a block of cells:

✦ Drag from corner to corner with your mouse.

✦ Move the selector to the first cell you want to select, and then hold down the Shift key while pressing the arrow keys.

Hold down the Ctrl key to select multiple blocks. To "unhighlight" or deselect a block, click any cell or press an arrow key.

Understanding labels and values

Before you create a spreadsheet, take a closer look at the two basic types of data they contain: *labels* and *values*.

Labels

A *label* is a text entry such as "January" or "Wombat." Labels can begin with any letter or punctuation mark except + - . ($ = # and @.

Tip   To start a label with a "forbidden" character (as with: $ thousands), precede it with a single quote (') for left alignment, a double quote (") for right-alignment, or a caret (^) for center alignment.

Values

A *value* is a number (47, -47, 47.34, or 4.73E+01), a date (November 9, 1999, 09-Nov-99, or 11/9/99), a formula (+256*8192 or +C5*D5), or a calculated formula result. By default, numbers are right-aligned. Numbers can contain only the following:

✦ A leading minus (-) for negative numbers, a plus (+) for positive numbers, an equal sign (=) for formulas, or currency symbols (such as $, £, or ¥)

✦ Numerals (0 through 9), commas, and periods (.)

✦ A trailing percent (%) or E (for scientific notation)

Any entry that doesn't conform to these conventions (such as 456ABC) is treated as a label. Be sure not to use a lowercase "el" (l) for one (1), or an uppercase "oh" (O) for zero (0).

Tip   You don't need to type the currency symbol, commas, decimal point, or spaces, because the numeric format you apply automatically displays them.

Creating a spreadsheet

Now that you know how to move about and select blocks, as well as the types of data you can enter, it's time to create WorldWide Widget's spreadsheet. To create the spreadsheet:

1. In cell B1, type **Q1 WorldWide Widget Sales**, and then press the down arrow or Enter key.

2. In cell B2, type **in Thousands of $**, and then press the down arrow or Enter key.

3. Fill in the rest of the labels and values shown in Figure 30-5, paying careful attention to the columns and rows. Don't worry if "Grommets" appears cut off when you enter **700** in the cell to its right. The column fills out when you format the spreadsheet.

 Tip   Use the numeric keypad, if you have one, for the numbers.

	A	B	C	D	E	F
1		Q1 WorldWide Widget Sales				
2		in Thousands of $				
3						
4			January			
5		Widgets	500			
6		Grommets	700			
7		Wombats	350			
8		Llamas	450			
9						
10						
11						
12						

C:\Work\WP 9 Bible\Notebooks\Notebk1.QPW

Figure 30-5: Type this much of the sample spreadsheet.

Changing and deleting data

No mistakes so far? Try making some changes or corrections anyway.

Changing the contents of a cell

You can change the contents of a cell by using any of the following techniques:

✦ Click the cell and retype the entire entry.

✦ Double-click the cell (or move the selector to the cell and press F2), and then edit the entry.

✦ Click the cell, and then click the box in the input line above the workbook to edit the entry.

Press Enter, Tab, or an arrow key to apply the change.

Undoing changes

To cancel any of your last 200 changes, click the Undo button (Ctrl+Z, or click Edit ⇨ Undo). Click the Redo icon to restore your changes (Ctrl+Shift+Z, or click Edit ⇨ Redo).

If Undo doesn't work, click Tools ⇨ Settings ⇨ General, and check Enable Undo.

Deleting the contents of a cell or selection

To delete the contents of a selected cell or block, press Delete. (Press Ctrl+Z to restore the deletion.)

Changing the appearance of your data

You have many ways to spiff up a cell or selection, or your entire spreadsheet. To change your spreadsheet's headings:

1. Drag to select the spreadsheet titles in block B1..B2.
2. Click the Font Face list and select another font, such as Benguiat Bk BT (see Figure 30-6).

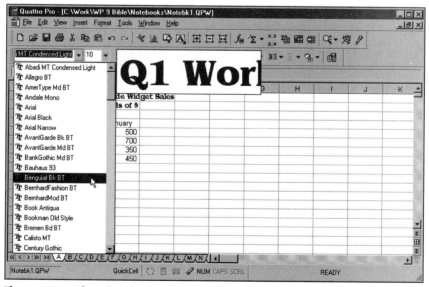

Figure 30-6: Changing the font of the selected headings.

3. Click cell B1, click the Font Size list on the property bar, and select a font size (16-pt. was used in Figure 30-7).

	A	B	C	D	E	F
1		Q1 WorldWide Widget Sales				
2		in Thousands of $				
3						
4			January			
5		Widgets	500			
6		Grommets	700			
7		Wombats	350			
8		Llamas	450			
9						
10						

Figure 30-7: Spreadsheet after changing the font face and sizes for the headings.

4. Click cell B2 and apply a font size to the subheading (14-pt. in the figure).

Using QuickFill

Instead of typing February and March headings into cells D4 and E4, use QuickFill to automatically enter the months:

1. Select cells C4..E4.

2. Click the QuickFill button (or right-click the selection and click QuickFill).

QuickFill takes the starting month, day, number, formula, or other pattern from the first cell or cells.

Fast data entry in a selected block

To speed up your data entry, first select the block you want to fill. You can then press Enter after every entry, without worrying about where one column ends and the next one begins.

To enter your February and March sales numbers:

1. Select block D5..E8.

2. Type the numbers shown in Figure 30-8 (press Enter after each entry).

3. Click the mouse or press an arrow key to exit block entry mode.

At the end of the block, the next Enter takes you back to the beginning. Shift+Enter takes you in the reverse direction.

	A	B	C	D	E	F
1		**Q1 WorldWide Widget Sales**				
2		**in Thousands of $**				
3						
4			January	February	March	
5		Widgets	500	525	604	
6		Grommets	700	735	919	
7		Wombats	350	368	441	
8		Llamas	450	473	496	
9						
10						

C:\Work\WP 9 Bible\Notebooks\Notebk1.QPW

Figure 30-8: Fill in the February and March sales numbers as a block.

Calculating Values with Formulas

The real power of a spreadsheet lies in its ability to calculate values by using formulas. You'll learn all about creating formulas in Chapter 32, "Entering Data and Formulas." In the meantime, don't worry if your algebra skills are rusty — Quattro Pro offers many formula-entry shortcuts, such as the Sum QuickFunction you get to try in this chapter.

Entering formulas

To enter a formula:

1. Click the cell in which you want the formula's results to appear.

2. Type the formula using the following guidelines:

   • The formula must start with . + - (@ # $ or =

   • The formula can include numbers; cell addresses; block cell coordinates or block names; arithmetic operators for add, subtract, multiply, divide, or exponentiation (+ - / * or ^); built-in functions; and parentheses for grouping

3. Press Tab, Enter, or an arrow key.

New Feature

If the formula is valid, its result instantly appears in the cell, along with a blue *formula marker* in the lower-left corner of the cell. If it can't be calculated, you get an "ERR" or other message.

Table 30-1 shows examples of the types of formulas you can create.

Table 30-1 Examples of Formulas	
Formula	*What It Does*
+C5*C6	Multiplies the value in cell C5 by the value in cell C6.
=C5*C6	Multiplies the value in cell C5 by the value in cell C6. (Using = to start a formula is the same as using +.)
+C5-C6	Subtracts the value in cell C6 from the value in cell C5.
+(C5+C6)*1.05	Adds the value in cell C5 to the value in cell C6, and then multiplies the result by 1.05.
+1.05*(C5/C6)	Divides the value in cell C5 by the value in cell C6, and then multiplies the result by 1.05.
@SUM(C5..C8)	Totals (sums) the values in cells C5, C6, C7, and C8.
@UPPER(B5)	Converts the text value in cell B5 to uppercase letters.

Using the Sum QuickFunction to automatically enter formulas

Now that all your sales data has been entered, use the Sum QuickFunction to add up the totals in a flash:

1. Select the cells you want to total, plus the blank cells in which you want the totals to appear (see Figure 30-9).

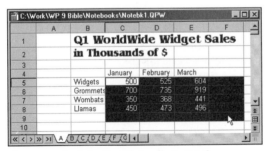

Figure 30-9: Selecting the cells to total.

Tip   As soon as you select the cells, the sum previews on the application bar, together with the average, count, maximum, and minimum values.

2. Click the QuickSum button to total the values in the selected block (see Figure 30-10).

Figure 30-10: Totaling a block using QuickSum.

Tip

If the sum sign isn't displayed on the QuickFunctions button, click the arrow on the right to select the QuickSum function. Any headings in a selected block will not affect the totals, as only values are summed.

New Feature

Point to the blue formula marker in one of the total cells to display its formula, such as @SUM(C5..E5). Now click the cell to display its formula on the input line.

Automatically totaling columns and rows

Now, press Ctrl+Z to undo your totals, and you'll learn an even easier way to total columns and rows.

New Feature

Type **Total** under "Llamas" in cell B9, and then press Enter, Tab, or an arrow. Presto, your totals automatically appear! Do the same after "March" in cell F4.

Quattro Pro recognized "Total" as a special word in your heading, and automatically inserted the formulas for you.

Formatting Your Spreadsheet

Your number-crunching is done. You can now add the final formatting touches to WorldWide Widget's spreadsheet.

Using SpeedFormat

To use SpeedFormat to apply an attractive format to your spreadsheet:

1. Select the block you want to format (B4..F9 for this example).

2. Click the Speed Format button (Format ➪ SpeedFormat).

3. Click the format you want to apply (see Figure 30-11). For the example here, click Conservative 2.

4. Click OK.

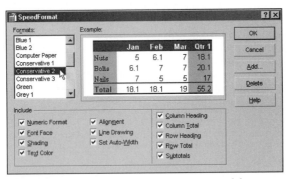

Figure 30-11: SpeedFormatting your spreadsheet.

Applying a numeric format

The values you type in a blank cell normally display as entered, without any commas, decimals, currency symbol, or other formatting. Because your spreadsheet subheading already indicates that WorldWide Widget's sales are in thousands of dollars, the numbers need only commas, without decimals or a currency symbol.

To apply a numeric format:

1. Click the cell or select the block you want to format (C5..F9 for this exercise).

2. Right-click the block and click Cell Properties ➪ Numeric Format.

3. Select the format and specify any options, as shown in Figure 30-12. (Specify the Number format with zero decimals and check "Use 1000 Separator" in this exercise.)

Tip   You can also apply the basic formats (but not their options) from the property bar.

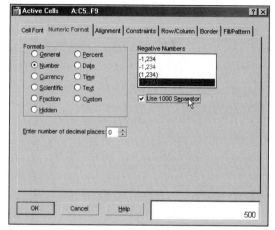

Figure 30-12: Applying a numeric format.

Your spreadsheet should now resemble the one shown in Figure 30-13.

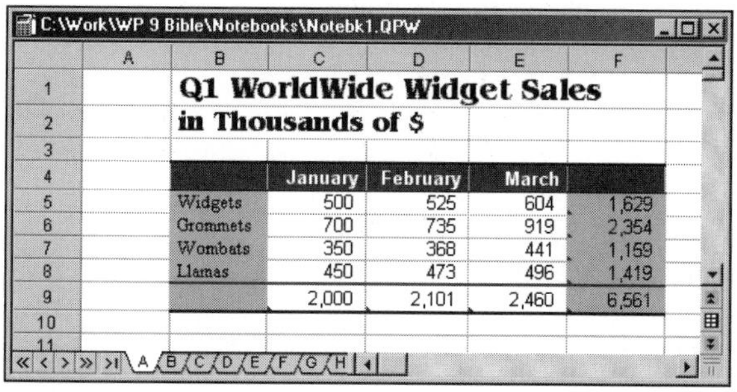

Figure 30-13: Your spreadsheet after applying the SpeedFormat style and numeric format.

Centering text across cells

Lookin' good! Your last task is to center the headings over the spreadsheet:

1. Select the cell with the text you want to center, plus the cells to the right in the columns you're centering it over (Block B1..F2 in this case).

2. Click the Horizontal Alignment button (see Figure 30-14), and then click the alignment you want (Center Across Block here).

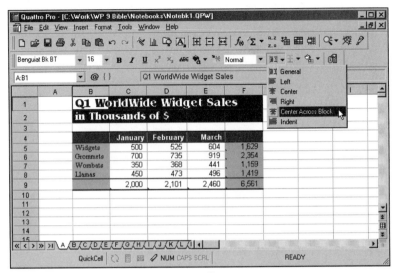

Figure 30-14: Centering text across cells.

That's it! Press an arrow key to deselect the block. Your finished spreadsheet should now resemble the one shown in Figure 30-1.

Inserting Comments

To insert nonprinting comments to document your spreadsheet:

1. Click the cell you want to comment, and click Insert ➪ Comment.

2. Type your comment, using any fonts and attributes you desire, and then click outside of the comment.

An indicator displays in the upper-right corner of a commented cell. Point anywhere in the cell to view its comment (see Figure 30-15).

Displaying and dragging comments

New Feature

Click View ➪ Comments to put comments on permanent display. While on display, you can click and drag the edge of the box to move it out of the way of adjacent cells (a connecting line to the comment appears).

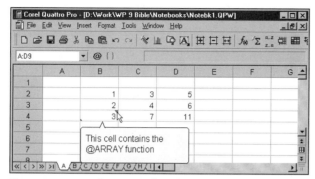

Figure 30-15: Point to a cell with a comment indicator to view its comment.

Deleting a comment

To delete a comment, click the cell and click Edit ⇨ Clear ⇨ Comments. To edit a comment, click the cell and click Insert ⇨ Comment.

Tip   To change a comment's font, select the text, right-click the bubble, and click Cell Comment Properties.

Saving, Printing, Closing, and Opening a Notebook

Your mastery of the basic techniques will be complete as soon as you save, print, and close your notebook, and then learn how to open it again.

Saving a notebook

As mentioned in Chapter 6 "Working Without Worries," you should regularly save your work in any program. To save your Quattro Pro notebook:

1. Click the Save button (you can also click File ⇨ Save or press Ctrl+S).

2. Because this is the first time you're saving the notebook, type a "real" filename (**WWW Sales** for this practice notebook) to replace the generic "Notebk1.QPW." (If you want, select a different drive or folder in which to store the notebook.)

3. Click Save.

The new filename appears with its .QPW extension. The next time you save this notebook, you won't be prompted for a filename. You can always use File ➪ Save As to save a copy of your notebook to a different filename.

Tip   Click Tools ➪ Settings ➪ File Options to specify your default notebook folder, automatic timed backup interval, and other file options. See Chapter 7, "Managing Your Files," for general file-management techniques.

Printing a spreadsheet

Now that you've saved your work, try printing your spreadsheet:

1. If you want to print less than the entire sheet (from cell A1 to the last row and the last column in which data is entered), select the area you want to print.

2. Click the Print button. (You can also press Ctrl+P or click File ➪ Print.)

3. Select the print area, copies, and other options described in Chapter 37, "Printing Notebooks, Charts, and Maps."

4. If you want to center what you're printing between the left and right margins, click Page Setup ➪ Options, check Center Cells (see Figure 30-16), and click OK.

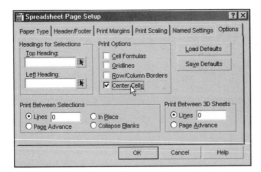

Figure 30-16: Centering what you're printing between the left and right margins.

5. Before you sacrifice any trees, click Print Preview. To zoom in quickly so that the text is more readable, click the Zoom in button on the toolbar (see Figure 30-17).

6. Click the Print button to print what you see, or click the Don't Print button (Esc) to return to the Spreadsheet Print dialog box.

7. To print from the Spreadsheet Print dialog box, click Print.

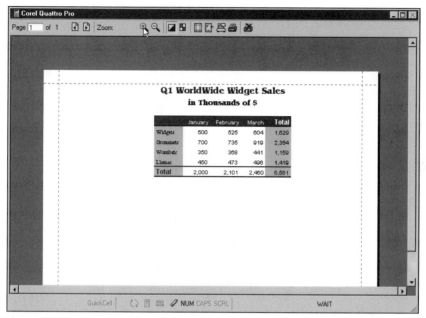

Figure 30-17: Zooming the print preview.

 Cross-Reference   See Chapter 37, "Printing Notebooks, Charts, and Maps," for information on print scaling and other print options.

Congratulations! You've created, saved, and printed a great-looking spreadsheet in record time. Now, try just a few more file-management techniques to round out your repertoire.

Closing a notebook

To close a notebook, click File ➪ Close (Ctrl+F4).

Opening a new or existing notebook

After the notebook window is cleared, you can

✦ Start working on a new notebook

✦ Click File ➪ New from Project to work from a predesigned template or project (see Chapter 31, "Becoming an Instant Quattro Pro Expert")

✦ Click the Open button (File ➪ Open) to open an existing notebook, or select one of the last notebooks you worked on from the File menu

Exiting Quattro Pro

To exit Quattro Pro, click File ⇨ Exit (Alt+F4). You'll be prompted to save any outstanding changes.

You've now mastered the spreadsheet basics. You'll learn how to save time and create instant spreadsheets in Chapter 31, "Becoming an Instant Quattro Pro Expert."

For More Information . . .

On	See
Specifying compatibility settings	Chapter 34
Using navigation shortcuts	Chapter 32
Using the WordPerfect Office interface	Chapter 3
Creating formulas	Chapter 32
Saving and protecting your work	Chapter 6
Managing your files	Chapter 7
Specifying print options	Chapters 13 and 37
Using templates and projects	Chapter 31
Naming cells	Chapter 32
Creating charts and maps	Chapter 36
Editing techniques	Chapter 33
Entering labels, values, and formulas	Chapter 32
Formatting your spreadsheet	Chapter 34
Getting help	Chapter 5
Selecting cells, blocks, and pages	Chapter 32

✦   ✦   ✦

Becoming an Instant Quattro Pro Expert

Now that you know how to set up a notebook, what else can you do? A lot. In fact, Quattro Pro puts an incredible amount of spreadsheet power in the hands of the novice. This chapter is your key to accessing that power, plus some handy tricks for setting up your display, and more. You may not be an expert by the end of this chapter, but that will be hard to tell from your results.

Jump-Starting Your Projects

Quattro Pro comes with the flexible, PerfectExpert Help facilities, including many projects to get you off to a flying start.

A Quattro Pro project is a preformatted notebook template, for business or home use, that's ready to receive your particular data. You'll find more than 100 projects in such categories as auto, business and home budgets, finance, investment, marketing, mortgage, and retirement planning.

If you don't have all the projects installed, you can click Start ⇨ WordPerfect Office 2000 ⇨ Setup and Notes ⇨ Corel Setup Program, and then click Add New Components to select projects from the Quattro Pro components.

To create a notebook based on a PerfectExpert project:

1. Click File ⇨ New from Project, and then select [Quattro Pro 9] or the subcategory of projects you want.

2. Select the project you want and click Create (see Figure 31-1).

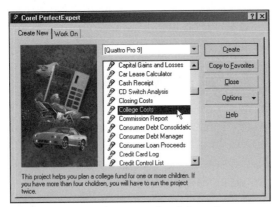

Figure 31-1: Creating a notebook based on a PerfectExpert project.

3. Fill in your data with help from the PerfectExpert panel. For example, you can click Insert Sample Data to see how College Costs are computed, and then substitute your own data (Figure 31-2).

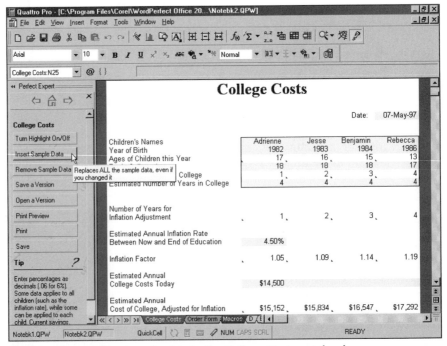

Figure 31-2: Inserting sample data in the College Costs notebook.

Tip   If the data is hard to read, click the Turn Highlight On/Off button.

4. Enter your data and change any parameters or formulas, and then click Save and give your notebook a name.

5. Click Save a Version to save a version of your calculations (see Figure 31-3) that you can later open to compare results. (Not all templates offer this option.)

Figure 31-3: Saving a version of your calculations.

 Cross-Reference   For more on using PerfectExpert, see Chapter 5, "How to Get Help."

Importing and Exporting Data

New Feature   You can import all or part of a file into the current notebook, or extract all or part of the current notebook to a file, including one formatted for Microsoft Excel 97. Quattro Pro automatically translates to or from any of the spreadsheet and database formats shown in Table 31-1.

Cross-Reference   See Chapter 10, "Working Together and Sharing Data," for more on sharing text and other information between programs.

Table 31-1	
Spreadsheet and Database Formats Quattro Pro Translates	
Program Format	*Extension*
Quattro Pro for Windows, version 7/8	.WB3
Quattro Pro for Windows, version 6.0	.WB2
Quattro Pro for Windows, versions 1.0 and 5.0	.WB1
Quattro Pro for DOS, versions 5.0 and 5.5 (import only)	.WQ2
Quattro Pro for DOS, through version 4.0	.WQ1
Paradox	.DB
Excel 97	.XLS

Continued

Table 31-1 *(continued)*	
Program Format	**Extension**
Excel versions 5 and 7	.XLS
1-2-3, versions 4 and 5	.WK4
1-2-3, version 3.x	.WK3
1-2-3, version 2.x	.WK1
1-2-3, version 1.0	.WKS
1-2-3, educational version	.WKE
DBASE IV	.DB4
DBASE III	.DBF
DBASE II	.DB2
ASCII text, tab or comma delimited	.TXT
Comma-separated values	.CSV
VisiCalc	.DIF
Multiplan (SYLK)	.SLK
HTML version 3 (tables only)	.HTM, .HTML
Quicken Interchange Format (import)	.QIF
WordPerfect (import as text)	.WPD

Inserting and Combining Data

You can insert all the data from another file into the one you're working on. You can also copy data into your current sheet, or *combine* data, performing arithmetic and other operations.

You can insert, copy, and combine spreadsheet data with any of the following features:

✦ *Insert File*, to insert another entire file in the current spreadsheet

✦ *Copy and Paste*, to copy spreadsheet selections

✦ *Paste Special*, to copy a selection, with the option to combine the copied data with existing data at the new location

✦ *Copy Cells*, to specify a part of a file to copy to a new location

This chapter describes working with whole files and file parts. Chapter 33, "Editing Techniques," describes working with selections.

Inserting all the data from another file

To insert all the data from another file on new sheets:

1. Close the file whose data you want to insert (if it's open).
2. Click the sheet that will follow the inserted data.
3. Click Insert ⇨ File, and specify the file (see Figure 31-4).

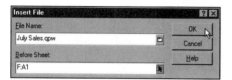

Figure 31-4: Inserting a file.

When inserting a notebook, every sheet with data is inserted, pushing back existing sheets.

Combining data

New Feature

You can paste spreadsheet selections with Edit ⇨ Paste, overwriting existing data with the contents of the Windows Clipboard. Or use Paste Special when you need a flexible, intuitive tool that lets you select what to paste, perform arithmetic operations, and more. See Chapter 33, "Editing Techniques," for details.

Model Copy, described in Chapter 33, "Editing Techniques," lets you adjust the absolute references in the block you're copying to the new location. The Consolidator (see Chapter 35, "Analyzing Data") lets you combine blocks of data to a destination block using various statistical operations.

Extracting Data to a File

You might want to save a part of the current notebook to another file, to share information with colleagues or to start a new notebook. Although you can copy and paste the data to another notebook, you have more options when you extract data to a file:

1. Select the data you want to extract, and then click Tools ⇨ Data Tools ⇨ Extract to File.
2. Type a filename (see Figure 31-5). Include the extension for the type of file you're extracting to, such as QPW for Quattro Pro 9, TXT for ASCII text, or XLS for an Excel file.

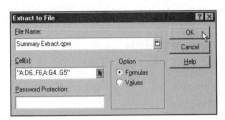

Figure 31-5: Extracting data to a file.

3. Enter a password if you want to protect a Quattro Pro notebook.

4. Click whether you want to extract the formulas in selected cells, or only their resulting values.

Getting Expert Help with Complex Tasks

Sometimes you get expert help at a critical moment, without even asking. When you click Insert ⇨ Chart, for example, the Chart Expert appears, providing step-by-step guidance, with an accompanying preview of your results (see Figure 31-6). Other experts appear when you create a data map, consolidate data, build what-if tables, and so on. For more on using the Chart Expert in particular, see Chapter 36, "Creating Charts, Maps, and Shows."

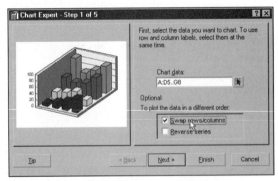

Figure 31-6: One of the "experts" that appears at critical moments.

Fine-Tuning Your Quattro Pro Display

Quattro Pro provides a number of tricks for managing your screen display, including a Page Break view to help you arrange your data for printing.

Choosing how your spreadsheet appears

Click the View menu to choose from three sheet views:

✦ *Draft* gives you a clear working view of your data, without the headers, footers, and margins that appear in print.

✦ *Page* displays the spreadsheet pages exactly as they will print, complete with headers, footers, margins, and so on (see Figure 31-7).

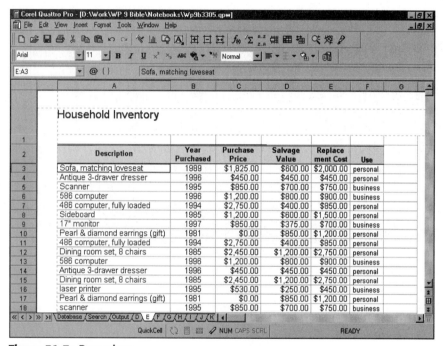

Figure 31-7: Page view.

New Feature *Page Break*s adds horizontal and vertical lines to show how the data divides across pages when printing.

Your last display selection becomes your default view.

Viewing comments and formulas

You can also check selections on the View menu to display hidden comments, and to display formulas, instead of their results. Normally, leave these selections unchecked and point to the comment and formula markers instead.

Selecting your display settings

You can hide, show, or customize various items in your screen display. Depending on the item, you set it either for all your notebooks, for the current notebook, or for the current sheet.

To change the default display for all your notebooks, click Tools ⇨ Settings ⇨ Display, and then specify any of the following (see Figure 31-8):

✦ *Show Input Line*, to display the Input Line

✦ *Show Formula Markers*, to display pop-up markers for viewing cell formulas

✦ *Show File History*, to display the last opened notebooks on the File menu

✦ *Show Scroll Indicators*, to display the row or column as you drag scroll boxes

✦ *Show Shortcut Keys*, to display keystroke shortcuts on the menus

✦ *Show Comment Marker*, to display markers and pop-up bubbles for normally hidden comments (when comment markers are off, you must click view ⇨ Comments to toggle comment display on and off)

✦ *Show Quick Tips*, to show pop-up descriptions when you point to toolbar and menu items

✦ *Real-Time Preview*, to display the results of toolbar selections before you make them

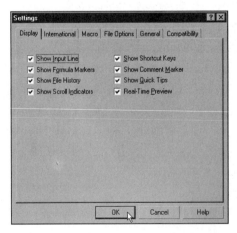

Figure 31-8: Selecting application display settings.

You'll find other display settings under the Compatibility tab:

✦ *3D Syntax*, to specify how 3-D selections appear in formulas

✦ *Sheet Tab Display*, to show default sheet tabs as numbers instead of letters

✦ *Minimum number to display*, to limit the default number of sheets per notebook (you can still insert additional sheets)

To show or hide zeros, row and column borders, or grid lines for the current sheet, click Format ⇨ Sheet ⇨ Display.

Splitting windows into panes

You can split a window into two panes in order to view two sheets at once (or two separate parts of the same sheet):

1. Point to the pane splitter icon in the lower-right, where the horizontal and vertical scroll bars meet. Depending on where you point, a vertical or horizontal double-arrow appears.

2. Drag the pane splitter up or across to where you want to divide the window (see Figure 31-9).

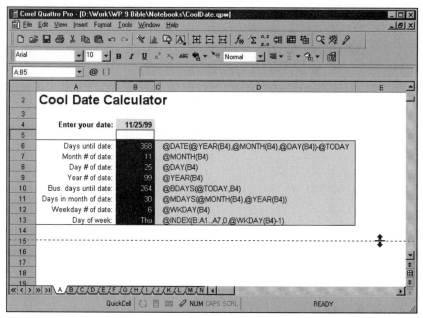

Figure 31-9: Dragging the pane splitter.

3. Tab and scroll to the information you want to see in the other pane.

4. To resize the panes or close the second pane, drag the splitter in either direction.

To split panes without using the mouse, or to *synchronize* panes so they scroll as one:

1. Click where you want to split the window.

2. Click View ➪ Split Window.

3. Click Horizontal or Vertical (see Figure 31-10). You can also click Clear to remove the split.

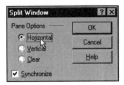

Figure 31-10: Splitting windows and synchronizing panes.

4. Click Synchronize to turn synchronization on or off.

Tip

Your synchronize selection stays in effect until you change it again, and applies when you drag to split panes.

Opening new views

To open a new view of the current notebook, click Window ➪ New View. Click the Window menu again to tile or cascade the windows. The title bar of the new window shows the notebook filename, followed by a colon and a number to indicate at which view you're looking (see Figure 31-11).

Views are similar to split panes, except they appear as separate windows and always scroll independently.

Hiding and showing windows

When you have multiple windows open, you can temporarily hide those you're not working on. Click Window ➪ Hide to hide the active window. To redisplay a hidden window, click Window ➪ Show and select the window you want to see.

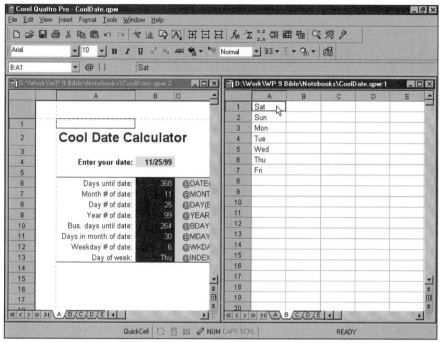

Figure 31-11: Two views of the same notebook.

Locking the title display

You can lock upper-left rows and/or columns to keep titles in view as you scroll your data:

1. If necessary, use the scroll bars to position the rows and/or columns you want to lock at the upper-left corner of the window.

2. Click the cell below and to the right of the titles you want to lock. For example, click cell B2 to keep row 1 and column A in view.

3. Click View ⇨ Locked Titles and scroll your data (see Figure 31-12).

To unlock titles, click View ⇨ Locked Titles again.

	A	B	C	D	E	F	G	H
1	Year	Quarter	Winery	Appellation	Region	Cost Per Case	Cases Sold	Sales
23	1992	Q4	Beaulieu	Cabernet Sauvignon	South	$165	388	$64
24	1992	Q1	Beaulieu	Cabernet Sauvignon	North	$165	620	$102
25	1992	Q1	Beaulieu	Cabernet Sauvignon	East	$165	400	$66
26	1992	Q2	Beaulieu	Cabernet Sauvignon	East	$165	411	$67
27	1992	Q3	Beaulieu	Cabernet Sauvignon	East	$165	419	$69
28	1992	Q4	Beaulieu	Cabernet Sauvignon	East	$165	423	$69
29	1992	Q1	Beaulieu	Cabernet Sauvignon	West	$165	200	$33
30	1992	Q2	Beaulieu	Cabernet Sauvignon	West	$165	213	$35
31	1992	Q3	Beaulieu	Cabernet Sauvignon	West	$165	223	$36
32	1992	Q3	Beaulieu	Cabernet Sauvignon	North	$165	650	$107
33	1992	Q4	Beaulieu	Cabernet Sauvignon	West	$165	233	$38
34	1991	Q2	Beaulieu	Chardonnay	North	$163	425	$69
35	1991	Q3	Beaulieu	Chardonnay	North	$163	460	$74
36	1991	Q4	Beaulieu	Chardonnay	North	$163	450	$73
37	1991	Q1	Beaulieu	Chardonnay	South	$163	230	$37

Figure 31-12: Scrolling data with locked titles.

Keeping a Cell's Value in View

The QuickCell on the application bar lets you see a cell's value update as you change referenced cells at other locations:

1. Click the cell (normally one with a formula that references other cells).

2. Click QuickCell on the application bar.

Repeat the process to display another cell's value.

Tip   Display a blank cell to clear the QuickCell.

Customizing the Quattro Pro Interface

Normally, the property bar and one toolbar provide all the screen options you need. On occasion, you may want to right-click a toolbar or click View ➪ Toolbars to put an additional toolbar on display (see Figure 31-13).

New
Feature   You can adjust the size of toolbar buttons and borders, create new toolbars, or customize existing ones. You can also customize menus and keyboards. See Chapter 57, "Customizing Toolbars, Menus, and Keyboards," for details.

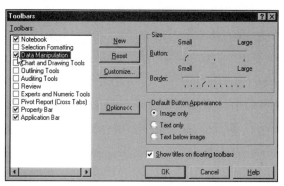

Figure 31-13: Putting an additional toolbar on display.

Creating a Boilerplate Notebook

Do you find yourself repeating the same settings, formats, headings, fonts, and so on, in many of the notebooks you create? To set up a boilerplate notebook, with or without sample data, much like the project notebooks that come with Quattro Pro:

1. Set up a new notebook exactly the way you want, or clean up a copy of an existing notebook.

2. Click File ➪ Save As, and save your notebook under your sample name, such as Boilerplate.qpw, and close the notebook.

3. Click File ➪ Open, right-click the notebook name, click Properties, and check Read-only (see Figure 31-14).

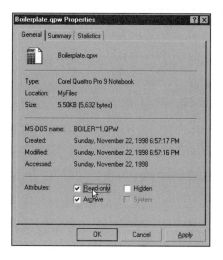

Figure 31-14: Setting your boilerplate notebook to read-only.

By setting your notebook to read-only, you won't accidentally mess up your boilerplate. Normally you would click "Open as copy" to keep the original notebook intact. But even if you don't, you'll only be able to open the notebook as read-only (see Figure 31-15). Either way, you'll have to save any new work under another name.

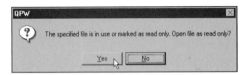

Figure 31-15: Opening a read-only notebook.

Cross-Reference   For more on managing files, see Chapter 7, "Managing Your Files."

To add your boilerplate notebook to the Quattro Pro list in the PerfectExpert:

1. Click File ⇨ New from Template, and select the category for your project.

2. Click Options ⇨ Add Project, and then click "I want to add another document."

3. Click Next and type a project name and description (see Figure 31-16).

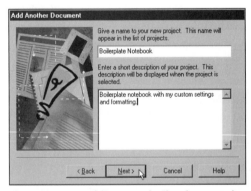

Figure 31-16: Adding your boilerplate notebook to the PerfectExpert projects.

4. Click Next, specify your notebook's name and location, and then click Finish.

Saving Your Workspace

One handy Quattro Pro trick is to save your current workspace (all your notebooks on display and your positions in them), so that you can pick up later exactly where you left off:

1. Click File ➪ Workspace ➪ Save.

2. Specify the name and location for your workspace (the program gives it a .WBS filename extension).

Note that saving a workspace does not save the contents of your notebooks. You can save as many workspaces as you want.

 Tip   To update a workspace, save it again to the same name.

To restore your workspace, select from the last nine items on your File menu, or click File ➪ Workspace ➪ Restore and select the workspace.

For More Information . . .

On	*See*
Using PerfectExpert Help	Chapter 5
Sharing information between programs	Chapter 10
Combining data with paste special	Chapter 33
Consolidating data	Chapter 35
Using the data analysis tools	Chapter 35
Using the Chart Expert	Chapter 36
Working in Page view	Chapter 34
Customizing toolbars	Chapter 57
Hiding columns and rows	Chapter 34
Zooming the screen	Chapter 34
Managing files	Chapter 7

✦   ✦   ✦

Entering Data and Formulas

The hands-on practice in Chapter 30, "A Hands-On Notebook," gave you a taste of selecting blocks and entering data. Now you're ready for some in-depth experience.

This chapter lets you in on some more tricks for selecting blocks and getting about, and then shows you how to do advanced data and formula entry, and how to import and export spreadsheet data. Skim the chapter if you like, or complete all the topics and become a pro.

More Ways to Select Cells

You're always working with selected cells in Quattro Pro, when you consider that even clicking a single cell selects that cell. Chapter 30, "A Hands-On Notebook," discussed the two basic techniques for selecting a multicelled block:

✦ Click and drag from corner to corner with the mouse.

✦ Hold down the Shift key while pressing the arrow keys.

When you select a multicell block, the current cell is outlined and the remainder of the block is highlighted. To deselect a multicelled block, simply click the mouse or press an arrow key.

Other keyboard selection tricks

One keyboard selection trick is to hold down the Shift key while pressing any of the navigational keystrokes described in Table 32-1. For example, Shift+Home highlights cells from the selector position to cell A1.

You can even use this method with Go To. Click one corner of the block, click Edit ⇨ Go To (Ctrl+G), specify the opposite corner (on the same or another sheet), and then hold down the Shift key as you click OK (see Figure 32-1).

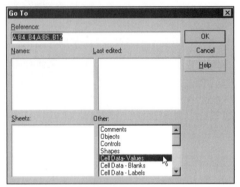

Figure 32-1: Select a block with Go To, holding down the Shift key as you click OK.

Using borders to select rows or columns

The easiest way to select rows or columns is to click row or column borders (see Figure 32-2). To select a range of rows or columns, either drag the border or hold down the Shift key while you click to extend the selection. To select the entire sheet, click the unlabeled border cell in the upper-left corner.

	A	B	C	D	E	F	G	H
1		**Q1 WorldWide Widget Sales**						
2		**in Thousands of $**						
3								
4				January	February	March	Total	
5		Widgets	500	525	604	1,629		
6		Grommets	700	735	919	2,354		
7		Wombats	350	368	441	1,159		
8		Llamas	450	473	496	1,419		
9		**Total**	2,000	2,101	2,460	6,561		
10								
11								

C:\MyFiles\WWW Sales.qpw (unmodified)

Figure 32-2: Click and drag borders to select rows or columns.

Selecting multiple blocks

To select two or more blocks of cells, hold down the Ctrl key as you select the next block. The Ctrl key works with any block-selection method, so you can mix and match, as shown in Figure 32-3.

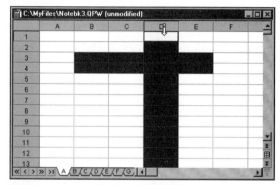

Figure 32-3: Hold down the Ctrl key to select multiple blocks.

You can then perform a block operation, such as applying a numeric format, on several blocks at once.

Selecting a 3-D block or multiple sheets

To select a 3-D block, with the two-dimensional coordinates extending through multiple sheets:

1. Select a 2-D block on the first sheet of the 3-D block.

2. Hold down the Shift key and click the tab for the last sheet of the 3-D block. (Hold Shift and press Ctrl+Page Down to select one sheet at a time.)

A black line appears under the tabs for the sheets containing your selection. To select multiple sheets instead of a 3-D block, click the tab for the first sheet, and then hold down the Shift key and click the last sheet tab.

Using Keyboard Navigation Shortcuts

Quattro Pro has several keyboard shortcuts for moving the selector, as shown in Table 32-1.

Table 32-1
Keyboard Navigation Shortcuts

To Move	Press
One cell up/down	up arrow/down arrow
One cell right/left	right arrow/left arrow or Tab/Shift+Tab
In the direction of the arrow to the next filled cell or to the edge of the sheet	End, followed by an arrow key
Cell A1 of the current sheet	Home
Cell A1 of the first sheet	Ctrl+Home
Lower-right nonblank cell of the current sheet	End, Home
Last nonblank cell in the entire notebook	End, Ctrl+Home
To cell you specify	F5 or Ctrl+G
One screen up/down	PgUp/PgDn
Right/Left one screen	Ctrl+Right arrow/Ctrl+Left arrow
Next sheet	Ctrl+PgUp
Previous sheet	Ctrl+PgDn

Naming Cells and Blocks

You can type a cell address (such as E17) or block coordinates (such as H2..H13) to reference a particular cell or block. However, when you're creating formulas, it's easier to reference cells and blocks by using easy-to-remember names, such as Total Hours, State Tax, or Quarterly Sales. Besides making formulas easy to understand, you're less likely to make a mistake when using names, and the formula will still work if you move the named selection.

Naming a cell or block

To name a cell or block of cells:

1. Select the cell or block you want to name.

2. Click Insert ⇨ Name ⇨ Cells, or right-click your selection and click Name Cells.

3. Type a name; then click Add (see Figure 32-4).

Figure 32-4: Naming a cell or block.

Cell names are not case-sensitive. You can use any keyboard characters except operators (+, -, *, /, ^, =, <, >, #, or &), $, or open and close parentheses. You can't name cells with numbers alone (such as 37), or use valid cell addresses (such as C7).

Naming cells after their adjacent labels

To name cells after their adjacent labels (such as column headings):

1. Select the labels.
2. Click Insert ⇨ Name ⇨ Cells ⇨ Labels, and then click Right, Left, Up, or Down, depending on the relative position of the cells you want to name (see Figure 32-5).

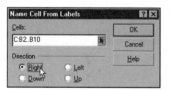

Figure 32-5: Naming cells after their adjacent labels.

Creating a table of names

To create a reference table of named cells:

1. Click Insert ⇨ Name ⇨ Cells ⇨ Output.
2. Specify the top left cell where you want the table to appear (see Figure 32-6).

Figure 32-6: Creating a table of named cells.

The table is not automatically maintained, so you must regenerate it manually if you update the names.

Tip You can easily view the cell names without creating a table. See "Viewing and selecting named cells and blocks," later in this chapter.

Naming multicelled blocks automatically

To name multicelled blocks automatically, select the block and click Insert ⇨ Name ⇨ Cells ⇨ Generate. Click Help in the Generate Cell Names dialog box for more information.

Changing the coordinates of a name

To change the coordinates assigned to a cell name:

1. Click Insert ⇨ Name ⇨ Cells, and click the name you want to reassign.

2. Do either of the following:

   • Enter the new block coordinates in the Cell(s) box.

   • Click the Block Select button to select a block from the notebook (the dialog box will be minimized), and then press Enter or click the Maximize button.

3. Click Add.

Deleting or changing a name

To delete a cell name, click Insert ⇨ Name ⇨ Cells, click the name you want to delete, and click Delete (or, click Delete All to delete all the block names). To change a cell name, select the name, type the new name, click Add, and then delete the old name.

Viewing and selecting named cells and blocks

To view the cell names in your notebook, click the list at the left of the input line. Click a name in the list to go to, and to select, the cells (see Figure 32-7).

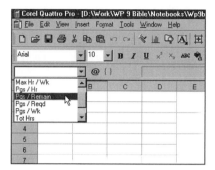

Figure 32-7: Click the Block Names hand icon next to input line to go to and select named cells.

You can also press Ctrl+G (Go To) and select a name to go to and to select the cells.

Renaming Sheets

You can give your sheets descriptive names for easy identification. (You just can't rename the Objects sheet at the end of the notebook.) Formula references to the renamed sheets automatically use the new names.

To name a sheet, double-click its tab and type the new name. (You can also right-click the tab and click Edit Sheet Name.) To restore a sheet's default tab display, click Format ➪ Sheet ➪ Name ➪ Reset.

You can also use QuickFill to name a number of sheet tabs at once (see "QuickFilling Cells," later in this chapter).

Entering Labels (Text)

The data you enter in Quattro Pro is either a label (such as "Total") or a value (a number, date, formula, or formula result), according to the rules explained in Chapter 30, "A Hands-On Notebook." As you enter data in a cell, the READY indicator in the application bar changes to LABEL or VALUE, depending on your entry.

Tip   Set cells for telephone numbers to Labels Only, so the dashes won't be interpreted as minus signs.

Viewing and editing labels

Text you enter in a cell displays horizontally across the spreadsheet. If the adjacent cell contains data, only as much text as can fit in the cell displays after it's entered, although if you click the cell, you can see more text on the input line (see Figure 32-8). If you double-click the cell, you can see (and edit) the entire entry.

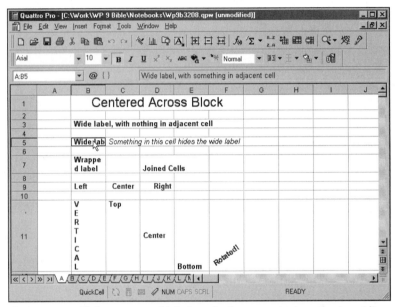

Figure 32-8: Click a truncated label to display more text on the input line.

Aligning text

The default general alignment is left for text and right for data. Figure 32-8 also displays various other text-alignment possibilities:

✦ *Center Across Block* centers text in the left cell across adjacent selected cells.

✦ *Wrap Text* displays the entire label by widening the row.

✦ *Join Cells* combines selected cells, keeping only the data in the upper-left cell.

✦ *Left/Center/Right* aligns text within the cell.

✦ *Vertical* displays text from top to bottom within the cell.

✦ *Top/Center/Bottom* aligns text vertically within the cell.

✦ *Rotated* turns the text from 0–359 counterclockwise degrees.

To align text:

1. Select the cells for which you want to align the text (include adjacent cells for Center Across Block).

2. Click Format ⇨ Selection ⇨ Alignment (or right-click the selection and click Cell Properties ⇨ Alignment).

3. Select the alignment you want (see Figure 32-9).

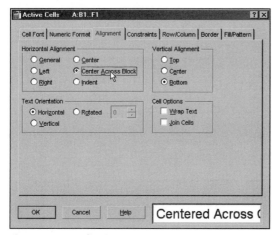

Figure 32-9: Aligning text.

You'll learn a lot more about formatting cells and other spreadsheet elements in Chapter 34, "Formatting Figures and Setting Up Notebooks."

Repeating characters

To repeat a pattern of characters in a cell, precede the entry with a backslash, as in \= (to fill the cell with equal signs); or \XO (to fill the cell with the pattern "XOXOXO..."). The pattern will repeat as many times as will fit in the cell. (To begin a label with a backslash without repeating characters, precede the backslash with ', ", or ^.)

Entering Numbers and Dates

Entries conforming to the standard numeric and date formats are automatically recognized by Quattro Pro. Otherwise, they're treated as labels.

Tip

To enter a number or date as a label, precede it with a single quote for left alignment, a double-quote for right alignment, or a caret (^) for center alignment. To enter the formula result without the formula, type the formula (such as **447*1.25** or **+A4/100**), and then press F9.

Viewing and aligning numbers

Numbers that exceed the cell width don't display across the adjacent cells as labels do. Instead, Quattro Pro rounds decimals and translates numbers into scientific notation. Your entry of **5000.55555** may display as "5000.556" and **500055555** may display as "5E+08". If you click the cell, however, you'll see the entire entry on the input line.

Numbers are normally right-aligned as you enter them, although any of the label-formatting possibilities also apply to numbers.

If you've changed the number format from General to Currency or another format, numbers too wide for the cell may appear as a series of asterisks. Again, the complete entry displays if you click the cell or widen the column.

Changing the numeric format

The default, General numeric format displays numbers exactly as you enter them. You can apply several other display formats (such as Fixed, Scientific, Currency, or Date), or even create a custom display format.

Changing the display format has no effect on the entry's value. For example, if you type **12345** in a cell, and then change the display to Fixed with two decimals, the number appears as 12345.00.

To change the numeric format of selected cells:

1. Click Format ⇨ Selection ⇨ Numeric Format (or right-click the selection and click Cell Properties ⇨ Numeric Format).

2. Select a format, plus any options, such as the number of decimals, currency symbol, or date format (see Figure 32-10).

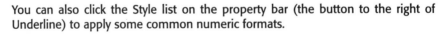

Tip　You can also click the Style list on the property bar (the button to the right of Underline) to apply some common numeric formats.

Table 32-2 describes the available numeric formats.

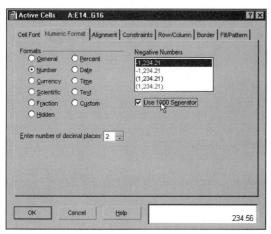

Figure 32-10: Changing the numeric format.

Table 32-2
Numeric Formats

Format	Number Display	Example [Typed Entry]
General	The default display of numbers as you enter them.	-12345.6789 [-12345.6789]
Number	Up to 15 decimal places with an optional thousands separator and a choice as to how negative numbers display.	12,345.68 [12345.6789]
Currency	Displays with currency symbol for the language you specify, thousands separators, decimal-align character, choice of negative number display, and accounting alignment option (left-aligned currency symbol).	£12,345.68 [12345.6789]
Scientific	Exponential notation with the specified number of decimal places.	1.23+08 [123456789]
Fraction	Displays numbers with set or maximum denominators, plus reduced fraction option.	Reduced: 234 2/3 [234 4/6]; Denominators <=100: 235 11/23 [235.478]
Percent	Percentages with a percent sign (%) and the specified number of decimals.	167.22% [1.67222]

Continued

	Table 32-3 *(continued)*	
Format	*Number Display*	*Example [Typed Entry]*
Date/Time	Displays numbers in the specified date or time format.	See "Calculating dates and times," later in the chapter.
Text	Displays formulas instead of their results, or numbers as you enter them.	@SUM(D4..D7)
Custom	Displays numbers as bars, "K Meg Gig," months, years. Click Edit to customize a format to your needs (see online Help on editing).	

Entering dates and times

You can enter dates and times by using any of the formats shown in Table 32-3. Leading zeros can be omitted. (For example, 03/04/99 and 3/4/99 are equivalent.)

Table 32-3 Valid Date and Time Formats		
Format	*Example*	*Comment*
DD-MMM-YY	09-Nov-99	
DD-MMM	09-Nov	Assumes the current year
MMM-YY	Nov-97	Assumes the first day of the month
Long International	11/09/99	Uses the current setting (Tools ⇨ Settings ⇨ International ⇨ Date Format)
Short International	11/09	Shortened version of the current setting
HH:MM:SS AM/PM	12:01:47 A.M.	
HH:MM AM/PM	12:01 P.M.	
Long International	23:45:32	Uses the current 24-hour time setting (Tools ⇨ Settings ⇨ International ⇨ Time Format)
Short International	23:45	Shortened version of the current 24-hour setting

Tip To restrict selected cells to valid date entries, click Format ⇨ Selection ⇨ Constraints ⇨ Dates Only.

Changing the default numeric formats

To change the default appearance and punctuation for your numeric formats, click Tools ➪ Settings ➪ International, and then click the item you want to change (see Figure 32-11).

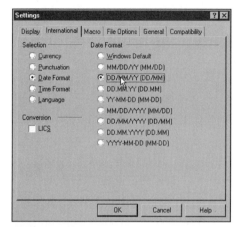

Figure 32-11: Changing the default numeric formats.

Displaying two-digit years in four-digit format

The Windows default date format uses the regional settings specified in the Windows Control Panel (click Start ➪ Settings ➪ Control Panel, and then double-click Regional Settings).

If you want your two-digit year entries in cells with the Date number type to display in four-digit format:

1. Change the "Short date style" from "M/d/yy" to "M/d/yyyy" (see Figure 32-12).

2. In Quattro Pro, click Tools ➪ Settings ➪ International, and then select Windows Default as your international date format.

Now when you type 12/29/99, Quattro Pro displays "12/29/1999." The value of your entry is not affected.

Entries typed in a cell with the Normal number type will expand to the Windows long date style. If you want two-digit year entries in cells with the Normal number type to display in four-digit format, select a Quattro Pro date format with "YYYY."

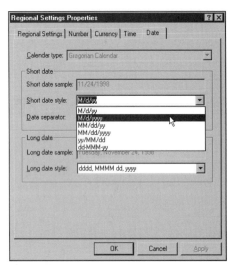

Figure 32-12: Changing the Windows default date format.

Calculating dates and times

Entries recognized as dates appear as a single integer on the input line. Type **12/29/99**, for example, press Enter, and then click back on the cell and you'll see that it's automatically translated to "36523."

This allows Quattro Pro to perform calculations on your dates and times. For example, you can subtract 7/1/99 from 12/29/99 to arrive at the number of days between the two dates. You can work with any date between January 1, 1600 (-109,571) and December 31, 3199 (474,816). The integer 0 is December 30, 1899.

The time is expressed as a decimal fraction of the day, where the beginning of the day is 0.0 (00:00:00 or 12:00:00 A.M.), noon is 0.5, and one minute to midnight is 0.9993 (23:59:00 or 11:59:00 P.M.).

Mixed numbers indicate the date and time. Thus, 36523.5 represents 12/29/99 at noon.

Two-digit years and the year 2000

Now that the twenty-first century is upon us, how does Quattro Pro interpret a two-digit year date, such as 12/29/03?

The rule is, any year below the year "30" is taken to be in the twenty-first century; years 30 and above are assumed to be in the twentieth century:

Typed Entry	Quattro Pro Sees It As	Numeric Value Assigned
12/29/29	December 29, 2029	47481
12/29/30	December 29, 1930	11321

When typing pre-1930 dates, use a four-digit format, such as 10/24/1929.

Entering Functions and Creating Formulas

Every calculated result in Quattro Pro is based on a formula, even one as simple as 2*2. The operators (symbols for expressing mathematical operations) in many formulas reference values (variables) found in other cells. For example, the formula (B3+C3)/D3 divides the sum of the values in cells B3 and C3 by the value in D3, and displays the result.

Try creating the following formula yourself to see how it works:

1. Open a notebook or click a fresh sheet.
2. Enter **4** in cell B3, **5** in cell C3, and **6** in cell D3.
3. Type **(B3+C3)/D3** in cell E3, and then click the OK button on the input line or press Enter.

The result, 1.5, should display in cell E3. Click the cell to see the formula in the input line, or double-click the cell to edit the formula on the spot. (Try changing the / to * to get the result of 54.)

The algebraic expression you created references cell coordinates. You'll also learn how to reference blocks or block names, and how your parentheses alter the operator order of precedence.

Beginning a formula

A formula must begin with one of the following characters:

+ - $ (@ . # =

Formulas can include numbers, cell coordinates, block references, or block names as well as operators. Uppercase and lowercase letters are equivalent, unless they appear inside double-quotation marks within a text string. Any spaces between operators and values are deleted by the program.

To identify a formula that begins with a letter (such as for a cell address or block name), precede it with a plus sign (+C4-C5). Otherwise, the program will think it's a label.

Operators and their order of precedence

Formulas use operators to act on two or more values. The arithmetic operators (+, -, /, *, and ^) perform addition, subtraction, division, multiplication, and exponentiation. The concatenation operator (&) joins text strings. The logical operators (<, >, <=, >=, <>, =, #NOT#, #AND#, and #OR#) determine whether an expression is true (1) or false (0).

Operations are performed according to their *order of precedence*, from highest to lowest. Operations on the same level are performed from left to right. For the common arithmetic operations, just remember "**My Dear Aunt Sally**" (multiplication, division, addition, subtraction).

Table 32-4 shows the operators, in their order of precedence, and provides some examples. In the examples, A3 contains 100, A4 contains 50, A5 contains "Hi," and A6 contains "there!"

Table 32-4
Operators (in Descending Order of Precedence) and Sample Formulas

Operator	Meaning	Precedence	Example	Result
^	To the power of (exponentiation)	7 (highest)	+A3^A4	1E+100
+, -	Positive, negative	6	-A3	-100
*, /	Multiply, divide	5	+A3/A4	2
+, -	Add, subtract	4	+A3-A4	50
=, <>	Equal, not equal	3	+A3<>A4	1 (because A3 is not equal to A4)
<, >	Less than, greater than	3	+A3<A4	0 (because A3 is not less than A4)
<=	Less than or equal	3	+A3<=A4	0 (because A3 is not less than or equal to A4)
>=	Greater than or equal	3	+A3>=A4	1 (because A3 is greater than or equal to A4)

Operator	Meaning	Precedence	Example	Result
#NOT#	Logical NOT	2	#NOT# (A3<A4)	1 (negates the result of A3<A4)
#AND#	Logical AND	1	+A3<A4 # AND# A3>=A4	0 (because both conditions aren't true)
#OR#	Logical OR	1	+A3<A4 #OR# A3>=A4	1 (because at least one condition is true)
&	Concatenate	1 (lowest)	+A5&" "&A6	Hi there! (combine text)

Changing the operator order of precedence

You can use parentheses to change the operator order of precedence:

$$3 + 2 * 5 = 13$$

$$(3 + 2) * 5 = 25$$

When parentheses are nested, the innermost parentheses are executed first:

$$(3 + 2) + (4 * 5) * 3 = 65$$

$$((3 + 2) + (4 * 5)) * 3 = 75$$

Note

As you enter an opening (, [, or { in a formula, notebook link, or macro command in the formula, the opening character appears red until you type the closing),], or }. Then, both characters turn green. If the characters are unbalanced when you press Enter or move to another cell, Quattro Pro attempts to supply the closing characters. If it can't, you'll get an error message (click OK and fix the mistake).

Using @functions

Rather than define every operation in a mathematical formula from scratch, you can make use of nearly 500 ready-made functions to perform database, date, engineering, financial, logical, mathematical, statistical, string, and miscellaneous operations. These are often referred to as *@functions*, because they begin with an "at" sign.

Two commonly used statistical functions are @SUM to add cells in a block and @AVG to compute their arithmetic mean.

You can enter @functions in several ways:

✦ Type the function manually.

✦ Click the Function (@) button on the input line (Insert ⇨ Function), select a function from one of the categories, and then click Next to go to the Formula Composer.

✦ Click @formula to go directly to the Formula Composer.

See "Using the Formula Composer," later in this chapter.

Figure 32-13 shows a Cool Date Calculator employing several handy date functions.

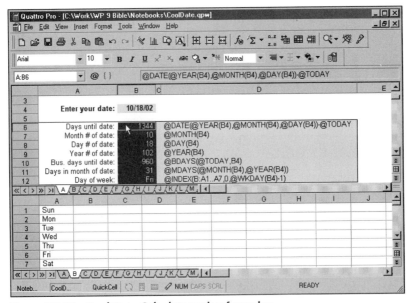

Figure 32-13: Cool Date Calculator using formulas.

To set up a similar notebook:

1. Enter the text labels shown in block A2..A13 of sheet A and block A1..A7 of sheet B.

2. In cells B6..B13 of sheet A, carefully type the formulas shown in block D6..D13.

3. Test your date calculator by typing various dates into cell B4.

When typing formulas with @functions, it is important to follow the exact *syntax,* or format.

Specifying cells and blocks in formulas

You can specify the cells and blocks referenced by formulas either by typing their coordinates or by pointing to them.

Typing cell or block coordinates

You can type the coordinates for cells and various types of blocks in formulas, as shown in Table 32-5.

Table 32-5
Typing Cell and Block Coordinates in Formulas

To Specify a	Enter	Example
Single cell	The cell address	@UPPER(A5) displays the contents of cell A5 in uppercase
2-D block on the current sheet	The address of the top-left cell, followed by one or two periods, followed by the address of the bottom-right cell	@SUM(A3..B10)
2-D block on another sheet	The sheet name followed by a colon, followed by the block reference	@SUM(B:A3..B10)
2-D block in a different notebook	The notebook filename in brackets, followed by the sheet and block	@SUM([C:\MyFiles\ Money.wb3]B:A3..A10)
Multiple blocks	Each block, separated with a comma	@SUM(A3,C4..E7,B:A3..B10)
3-D block	The sheet range followed by the 2-D block coordinates	SUM(A..C:A3..B10)
Named cells or blocks	The cell or block name	@SUM(MyBlock)

Pointing to cells and blocks

Rather than type the coordinates for cells and blocks, you can point to them with your mouse:

1. In an empty notebook sheet, type **2** in cell A2, type **3** in cell A3, and **4** in cell A4.

2. Click cell A6 and type **@SUM**.

3. Drag to select Cells A2 through A5.

4. The total "9" displays. Double-click cell A6 to reveal the formula it's based upon: @SUM(A2..A5), with the cells themselves enclosed in a blue rectangle (see Figure 32-14).

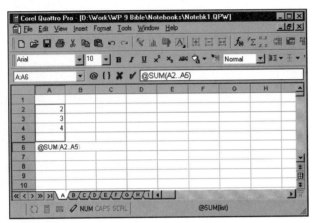

Figure 32-14: Cell coordinates filled in by pointing.

Try another example in the same spreadsheet:

1. Click cell B6 and type +.

2. Click cell A3.

3. Type * and click cell A4.

4. Type / and click cell A2.

5. Press Enter to complete the formula and display the result (6).

You can also use the pointing technique in any dialog box that offers a place to fill in cell or block references. In the same spreadsheet:

1. Click Insert ➪ Name ➪ Cells.

2. In the Name box, type **Add Me Up**.

3. Click the Block Select button next to the Cell(s) box. (The Cell Names box shrinks to its title bar.)

4. Drag to select cells A2 through A5. The selected block coordinates appear below the Cell Names title bar (see Figure 32-15). (If you select the wrong cells, simply drag again.)

5. Press Enter or click the Maximize button to redisplay the Cell Names box with the coordinates you selected.

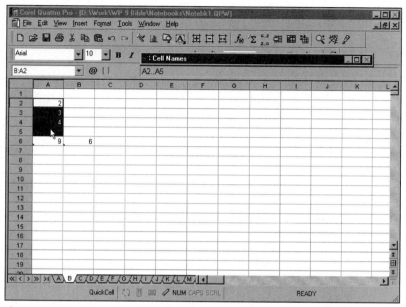

Figure 32-15: When you click the Block Select button, the Cell Names dialog box shrinks so you can drag to select cells.

6. Click Add ⇨ Close to finish the job. (Click cell A6 and you'll see that the formula now uses the block name instead of A2..A5.)

Tip

When the Cell(s) entry is highlighted, you don't have to click the Block Select button. Simply move the dialog box out of the way (if necessary) and click or drag in your spreadsheet to replace the cell coordinates. Also (when the entry is highlighted), you can automatically name the selection — just press F3, and then double-click a name in the pop-up dialog box.

Using the Formula Composer

Use the Formula Composer to create, edit, and debug formulas visually:

1. Click the cell in which you want to create or edit a formula.

2. Click the Formula Composer button on toolbar, and then use any of the following methods to enter or change the formula (see Figure 32-16):

   • To put all or part of the current expression into the Expression box, click the expression or snippet in the outline pane on the left.

- In the Expression box, revise the expression as needed. You can position the insertion point in the usual way, click the Function (@) button on the input line to insert a function, the Block Name button on Formula Composer toolbar to insert a cell name, the Block Select button in Formula Composer to point to a cell or block reference, or the Convert to Values button on Formula Composer toolbar to convert the formula to a value. To clear the Expression box, press Ctrl+Backspace.

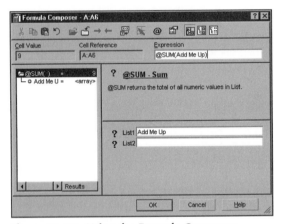

Figure 32-16: Using the Formula Composer.

Tip

For an in-depth explanation of a function or argument displayed in the Formula Composer, click the appropriate Help button in the Formula Composer. For help on other features, click the Help button. For a detailed description of all the @functions, click Help ⇨ Help Topics ⇨ Contents, double-click the "Reference information" book, and then double-click the "Quattro Pro spreadsheet functions" book.

3. Click OK to save the new or modified formula, or click Cancel to exit without saving your changes.

Try using the Formula Composer to enter a simple formula in your practice notebook:

1. Click cell C6, and then the Formula Composer button on toolbar.

2. Click the Function (@) button on the input line, and then click the Statistical - Descriptive function category (see Figure 32-17).

3. Scroll the Function list, click the SUM function, and click Next.

4. Click in the List1 argument box, click the Block Select button in Formula Composer, drag to select block A2..A5, and then press Enter. (You can also click the Block Name button on Formula Composer toolbar, select Add Me Up, and click OK.)

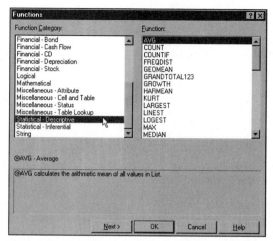

Figure 32-17: Displaying the descriptive statistical functions.

5. Your formula should be the same as the one shown in Figure 32-16. Click Finish to enter the formula in cell C6, and click Enter.

QuickFilling Cells

Chapter 30, "A Hands-On Notebook," showed you how you can quickly type data in selected cells by pressing Enter after each entry. Still, there's nothing more tedious than typing a sequence of dates or numbers, such as January, February, March . . . , Monday, Tuesday, Wednesday . . . , 1, 2, 3, 4, 5, 6, 7 . . . , you get the idea. With QuickFill, you can type one or two entries and let the program fill in the rest. For a defined series, like the days of the week, you don't even have to type a single entry! Sounds good, eh?

QuickFilling cells from "seed" entries

You can QuickFill a series of numbers, times, dates, quarters, or formulas, based on one or two seed or starter entries:

1. Type one or two seed labels (such as "Sunday"), or values (such as a number, date, time, or formula). Multiple entries must be in adjacent cells.

2. Select the seed entry or entries, together with the blank cells you want to fill.

3. Click the QuickFill button on toolbar, or right-click the selection and click QuickFill.

Couldn't be easier. In the QuickFill Sampler shown in Figure 32-18, the white cells are the seeds and the black cells are QuickFilled. Cell J3 is the calculated result of the formula +H3/2. Note how QuickFill automatically adjusted the formulas in the cells below it to +H4/2, +H5/2, and so on. Similarly, cell H14 contains the formula +H3+J3, and cell J14 contains the formula +H14+10.

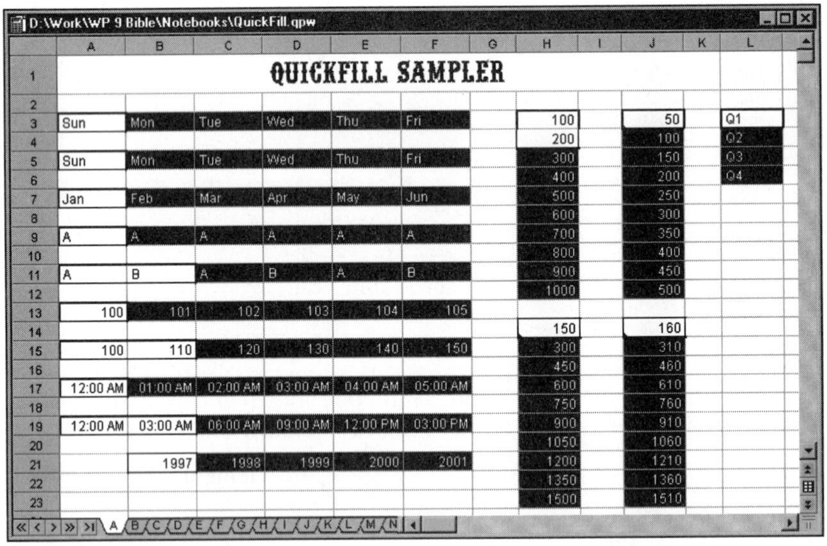

Figure 32-18: QuickFill sampler.

Applying a predefined QuickFill series

When you apply a predefined QuickFill series to cells or sheet tabs, you don't have to type a single entry. To apply a predefined QuickFill series:

1. Select the cells you want to fill (or click any cell to fill the sheet tabs).

2. Click the QuickFill button on toolbar, and select a series name from the list (see Figure 32-19). The series elements appear below the selected series.

3. If you selected a rectangular block or a single cell (for tabs), click Columns, Rows, or Tabs.

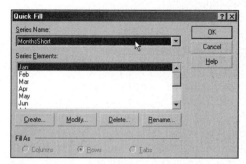

Figure 32-19: Selecting a predefined QuickFill series.

Creating a custom QuickFill series

You can create a custom QuickFill series based on a list (series of labels) or a formula applied to a seed value. (The series can start anywhere; for example, a fiscal year series can start with October.) To create a custom list series:

1. Click a cell, and then click the QuickFill button on toolbar ⇨ Create.

2. Give the series a name, click List, type the series elements, and then add them to the list (see Figure 32-20).

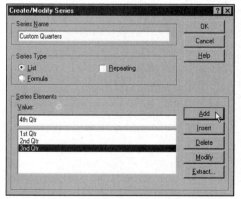

Figure 32-20: Creating a custom QuickFill list series.

3. Check Repeating if you want the series to start over when more cells are selected than there are items in the series.

To create a formula series, check Formula in Step 2, and then click the Help button for further information. You can also modify or delete an existing series.

Working with Arrays

Quattro Pro has a special @ARRAY function and other features to operate on *data arrays*, or blocks of data you work with as a group. A single formula performs an operation on an entire array.

Using block arrays

Quattro Pro recognizes when you're performing an array operation, and converts your formula to one specifying the @ARRAY function. Simply type the first block (preceded by a +), the operator, and the second block. To see how arrays work:

1. On a blank sheet, type numbers in the B2..D3 block, as shown in Figure 32-21.

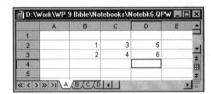

Figure 32-21: Create a block of entries to try out arrays.

2. Click cell B4 and type the formula **+B2..D2+B3..D3**.

3. Press Enter to add the two rows.

4. Click cell B4 to see that your entry was automatically converted to the array formula: @ARRAY(B2..D2+B3..D3). This saves you the trouble of typing the @ARRAY formula directly.

5. Note that there are no formula markers in cells C4 and D4 — the @ARRAY function in cell B4 took care of their totals, without the need for additional formulas.

To try another array experiment in the same sheet:

1. Click cell F2, and type the formula **+B2..D4*2**.

2. Press Enter to create a corresponding array, @ARRAY(B2..D4*2), in which all the values are doubled (see Figure 32-22).

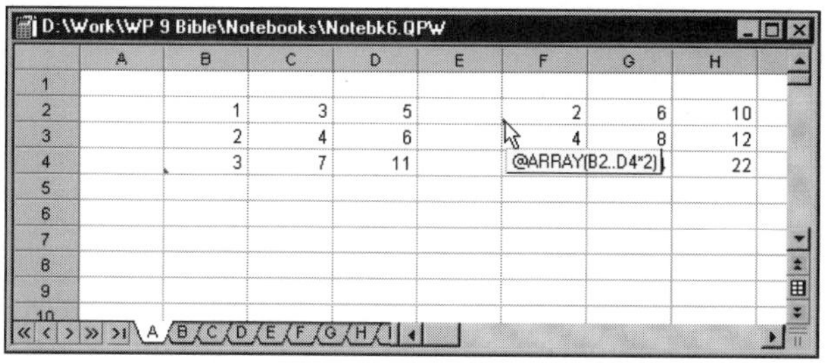

Figure 32-22: Second array created by the formula in cell F2.

Using other @functions with arrays

Many @functions in addition to @ARRAY accept array arguments and operate on arrays. Try the following example:

1. Click a blank cell in the same sheet, click the input line, and type the formula **@Sum(B2..B4*C2..C4)**.

2. Press Enter to display the total from multiplying entries in column B by the corresponding entries in column C, and summing the products. You should get 32 (1*3+2*4+3*7).

How arrays are handled depends on the @function you're using.

Specifying array constants

In the previous examples you created *block arrays*, or block references to cells with variables, rather than exact values. You can also specify *array constants* in a formula, a string of exact values enclosed in braces ({}), and separated by row and column *delimiters*, to indicate the shape of the array. Try the following experiment to get the idea:

1. Open a blank sheet and click cell B2.

2. Click the input line and type the formula +{1;2;3;4 | 5;6;7;8 | 9;10;11;12}*4, using semicolons to separate numbers across the row and the pipe symbol (|), Shift+\, to separate rows.

> **Note** Your separator for numbers in rows may be a period, comma, or other character, depending on your international punctuation (Tools ⇨ Settings ⇨ International ⇨ Punctuation).

3. Click the OK button on input line to create the array shown in Figure 32-23.

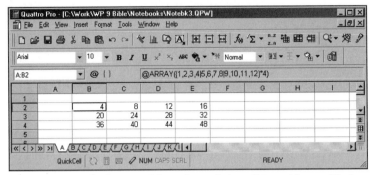

Figure 32-23: Block created from formula in cell B2 with specified array constants.

For More Information . . .

On	See
Basic block selection and data entry	Chapter 30
Formatting spreadsheet elements	Chapter 33
Sharing data between programs	Chapter 10
Using Model Copy	Chapter 33
Consolidating blocks of data	Chapter 35

✦   ✦   ✦

Editing Techniques

◆ ◆ ◆ ◆

In This Chapter

Edit entries in the cell or input line

Find and replace data

Clear cell contents and formatting

Insert and delete cells, rows, columns, and sheets

Move and copy data

Manage address references in formulas

Edit a group of sheets in 3-D

◆ ◆ ◆ ◆

Quattro Pro offers many convenient ways to edit entries within a cell and to delete, move, copy, insert, find, and replace data within your notebook. In this chapter, the point isn't to master every technique, but to pick up the editing tricks that work best for you.

Editing Cells

You can replace, edit, or delete the contents of cells. You can also clear their formatting.

Replacing a cell's contents

To replace a cell's contents, click the cell and type the new entry.

Editing a cell's contents

You have two ways to edit a cell's contents:

◆ Click the cell, and then click anywhere in the input line to edit its contents.

◆ Double-click the cell to edit its contents directly.

When editing a cell, you can use any of the basic editing techniques described in Chapter 2, "Essential Typing and Editing" (including cut, copy, and paste). You can also use QuickCorrect's automatic word replacement in Quattro Pro.

Tip Click Tools ⇨ Spell Check from Ready mode, when you're done editing.

To exit Edit mode and save the revised entry, do any of the following:

✦ Press Enter or an arrow key.

✦ Click the OK button on the input line.

✦ Click elsewhere in the spreadsheet.

To cancel your changes as you're replacing or editing an entry, press Esc or click the Cancel button on the input line.

Correcting errors

When entering or editing data, various error messages can display. For example, a CIRC message on the application bar means the notebook contains a *circular reference* — a formula with a direct or indirect reference to its own cell. An ERR message appears when you attempt to reference a non-existent block, column, row, or sheet. NA in a cell means a value is not available. If you enter an invalid function, a dialog box displays an "unknown function" message.

Click OK to clear the error message and return to Edit mode. Often the insertion point will be positioned at the problem character in the input line. If you need some help tracking down errors, click Format ⇨ Notebook ⇨ Recalc Settings to see the source of circular references, or to turn the Audit Errors feature on or off. (Click Help in the Active Notebook dialog box for more details.)

Finding and Replacing Data

Suppose you want to quickly locate a certain value in your notebook, or change all "Salary" labels to "Big Bucks," or change all "+C4+C5+C6" formulas to "@SUM(C4..C6)." For jobs like these, use Find and Replace:

1. Select the cells or blocks you want to search. You can select a 2-D block, a 3-D block, or a block in Group mode. (Click tabs to select sheets. Hold down the Ctrl key to select multiple sheets, or hold down the Shift key to select a range of sheets.)

2. Click Edit ⇨ Find and Replace (Ctrl+F).

3. Enter your Find and Replace entries, and specify the cells you want to search (if you didn't select them already), as shown in Figure 33-1.

Tip   Drag the Find and Replace dialog box away from the area you're searching.

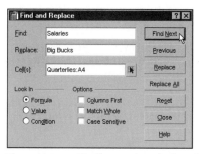

Figure 33-1: Finding and replacing data.

4. Select what to look in:

   - *Formula,* to look in formulas, as they appear in the input line.

   - *Value,* to look at the results of the formulas, as they appear in cells.

   - *Condition,* to compare cells in the spreadsheet with the condition in the Find box (using the logical operators <, >, <>, =, >=, and <=). For example, enter **? >= 400** to look for the first value that's greater than or equal to 400. You can also begin the search from a specific cell, as with **C6 >=400**. (You can only find values, not replace them, when doing a conditional search.)

5. Check the options you want:

   - *Columns First,* to search down columns first, instead of across rows.

   - *Match Whole,* to match only on the entire Find entry. If you enter cat, for example, you'll match only on the three-letter word, not "cats" or "scatter."

   - *Case Sensitive,* to match only on the exact capitalization. An entry of Cat won't match on "cat" or "CAT."

6. Select one of the following:

   - *Find Next,* to find the next occurrence

   - *Previous,* to find the previous occurrence

   - *Replace,* to replace the found item and search for the next

   - *Replace All,* to replace all found items without stopping

   - *Reset,* to clear the search boxes and return to the default options

Clearing Cell Contents and Formatting

Rather than delete a cell or selected block (as described in the next section), you can clear cell contents (data and formulas), cell formatting (alignment, numeric format, borders, fill, and so on), or both. To clear a cell's contents:

1. Select the cell or block.

2. Do any of the following:

   - *To clear both the contents and formatting*, click Edit ⇨ Clear ⇨ Cells (or right-click the selection and click Clear).

   - *To clear just the contents*, press Delete (or click Edit ⇨ Clear ⇨ Values).

   - *To clear just the formatting*, click Edit ⇨ Clear ⇨ Formats.

Figure 33-2 provides a before-and-after display of the three types of clearing operations. Note that in no case were the cells themselves deleted.

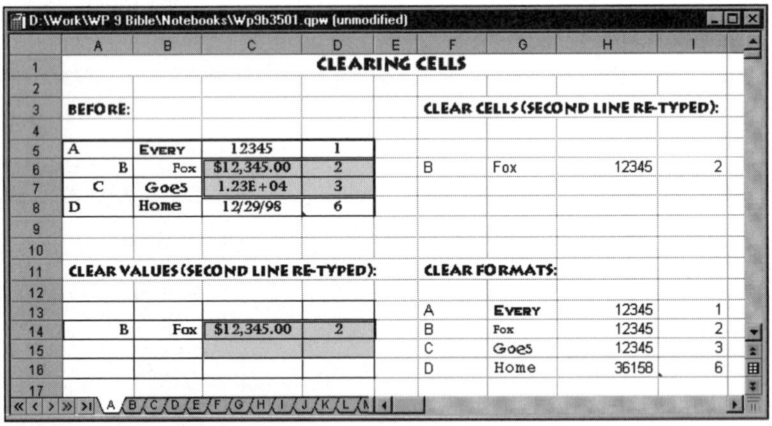

Figure 33-2: Clearing cell contents and formatting.

Deleting cells, rows, columns, or sheets

Deleting a cell or block is not the same as clearing its contents. You're deleting the actual space in the spreadsheet — causing the elements below or to the right to fill the gap.

The difference between clearing and deleting is illustrated in Figure 33-3. Note how the cells below the deleted block moved up to fill the vacant space. The same closing occurs when you delete rows, columns, or sheets. (When you delete a sheet, the sheets behind it move up.)

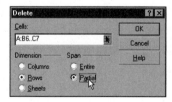

Figure 33-3: Deleting, rather than erasing cells, causes the cells below to fill the gap.

To delete cells, blocks, rows, columns, or sheets:

1. Select the elements you want to delete.

2. Click the Delete Cells button (Edit ➪ Delete, or right-click the selection and click Delete Cells).

3. If you're deleting cells, select from the following options (see Figure 33-4):

   • *Columns, Rows,* or *Sheets,* to specify what to delete

   • *Entire,* to delete all the rows, columns, or sheets in your selection

   • *Partial,* to delete only the selected cells

Figure 33-4: When deleting cells, you can delete all the rows, columns, or sheets in your selection, or only the selected cells.

Caution Quattro Pro automatically adjusts references in cell names and formulas affected by your deletion. However, if one of the deleted cells is a corner cell that defines a block, the block becomes invalid and any formulas or names that reference the block produce an error (ERR). ERR also appears for formulas that reference a cell within a deleted column, row, or sheet.

Inserting Cells, Rows, Columns, or Sheets

When you insert blank cells, rows, columns, or sheets, existing data moves down, to the right, or toward the back of the notebook to make room.

Quattro Pro automatically expands references in block names or formulas to account for the inserted space. You will get an ERR message only if you push a referenced cell beyond the limits of the current sheet, or beyond the last sheet in the notebook.

Inserting blank cells

To insert blank cells:

1. Select the size of the block you want to insert, beginning in the upper-left corner of where you want to insert it (see "Selection Before" in Figure 33-5).

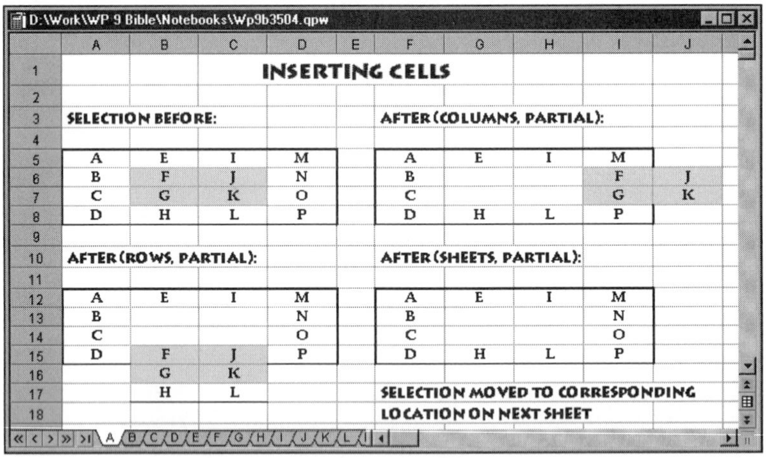

Figure 33-5: How existing data shifts when you insert a block, after selecting the Columns, Rows, or Sheets dimension.

2. Click the Insert Cells button (Insert ➪ Cells, or right-click the selection and click Insert Cells).

3. Click Columns to shift to the right, Rows to shift down, or Sheets to shift to the next sheet (see Figure 33-6).

Figure 33-6: Specifying where to shift the selected block.

4. Click Partial. (If you select Entire, the block's entire columns, rows, or sheet will shift.)

Inserting blank rows, columns, or sheets

To insert blank rows, columns, or sheets:

1. Select the number of rows (see Figure 33-7), columns (see Figure 33-8), or sheets you want to insert.

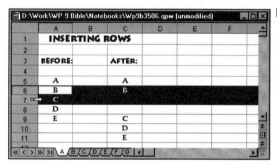

Figure 33-7: Inserting rows.

Figure 33-8: Inserting columns.

Tip

Click anywhere on a sheet to insert one sheet. To insert multiple sheets, click the last tab while holding down the Shift key.

2. Click Insert Cells button (or click Insert, and then click Row, Column, or Sheet).

Tip

Select a single row or column, and then click Insert Cells button multiple times.

Moving and Copying

Chapter 32, "Entering Data and Formulas," detailed the various techniques for selecting cells, rows, columns, and sheets. Here you can try your hand at the four techniques for moving and copying your selections:

✦ Drag-and-drop

✦ Cut or copy-and-paste

✦ Cut or copy and Paste Special

✦ Copy Cells

You can also move entire sheets.

Table 33-1 compares the four methods.

Table 33-1 Comparison of Moving and Copying Techniques				
Feature	**Drag & Drop**	**Paste**	**Paste Special**	**Copy Cells**
Visual and intuitive	✔	Somewhat	No	No
Warn of data overwrite	✔	No	No	No
Handle multiple blocks	No	✔	✔	✔
Multiple copies	No	✔	✔	No
Copy between applications	✔	✔	✔	No
Copy cells by name	No	No	No	✔
Override absolute references	✔	No	✔	✔
Select paste items	No	No	✔	✔
Perform arithmetic operations	No	No	✔	No
Link copy to original data	No	No	✔	No
Formulas as values	No	No	✔	No
Skip blanks and hidden data	No	No	✔	No
Transpose columns and rows	No	No	✔	No

Caution   Whatever technique you choose, leave enough space for your move or copy, so you don't overwrite data you want to keep.

Using drag-and-drop

To move or copy selected cells with drag-and-drop:

1. Select the cell(s).

2. Point to the edge of your selection, so the pointer changes to a four-way arrow.

3. Drag the selection to the new location, and do one of the following:

   • Release the mouse button to move the selection (see Figure 33-9).

   • Hold down the Ctrl key as you release the mouse button to copy the selection.

   • Press Esc to cancel the operation.

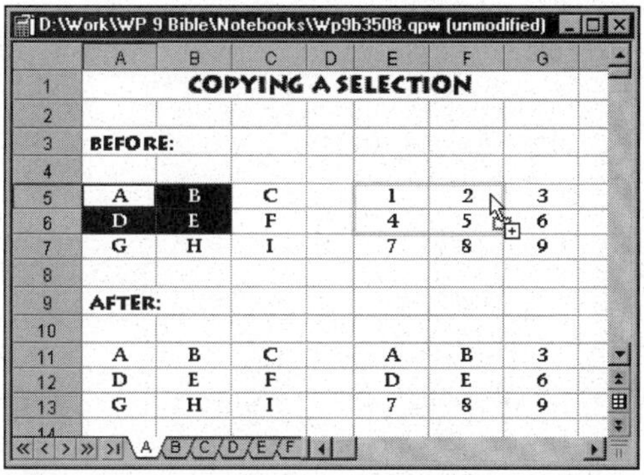

Figure 33-9: Hold down the Ctrl key to copy with drag-and-drop.

If your move or copy is about to overwrite existing data, a warning gives you the chance to change your mind (see Figure 33-10).

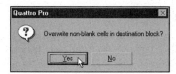

Figure 33-10: Warning you get when you're about to drop a selection over existing data.

Tip   You can also click on a selection and hold to drag it, as in previous versions of Quattro Pro. The drag-and-drop delay is set to 5 seconds (5,000 ms) to avoid accidental dragging, but you can adjust it (Tools ⇨ Settings ⇨ General).

To drag-and-drop a sheet:

1. Click the sheet you want to move or copy (you can also select multiple sheets).

2. Drag its tab to the new location (see Figure 33-11). Hold down the Ctrl key as you release the tab to insert a copy of the sheet.

Figure 33-11: Move a sheet by dragging its tab.

Moving and copying via the Clipboard

To move or copy a selection via the Clipboard:

1. Do one of the following:

   • To move the selection, click the Cut button (you can also click Edit ⇨ Cut or press Ctrl+X).

   • To copy the selection, click the Copy button (you can also click Edit ⇨ Copy or press Ctrl+C).

2. Click the upper-left cell of the new location.

3. Click the Paste button (you can also click Edit ⇨ Paste or press Ctrl+V).

Caution   Be careful where you paste because, unlike moving and copying with drag-and-drop, you get no warning before overwriting existing data.

You can paste as many copies of the Clipboard contents as you want. You can also cut, copy, and paste information within a cell or in the input line.

Using the Clipboard is also a handy method for transferring information between programs (see Chapter 10, "Working Together and Sharing Data").

Making enhanced copies with Paste Special

New Feature

Quattro Pro's old Copy Cells facility has been replaced with intuitive, automatic enhancements to Paste Special that let you select what to paste and other options:

1. Select the cells you want to copy, and then click the Copy button (Edit ⇨ Copy).

2. Click the upper-left cell of the new location, click Edit ⇨ Paste Special, and select the spreadsheet elements you want to paste (see Figure 33-12).

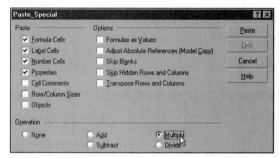

Figure 33-12: Making super copies with Paste Special.

3. Check the options you want:

   • *Formulas as Values,* to copy formula results, not the formulas themselves

   • *Adjust Absolute References,* to perform a Model Copy, as described later in this chapter

   • *Skip Blanks,* to avoid pasting blank cells over existing data

   • *Skip Hidden Rows and Columns,* to not paste information in any hidden columns or rows

   • *Transpose Rows and Columns,* to have the pasted rows and columns change places

4. Click any mathematical operation you want performed by the pasted values on the existing values.

5. Click either of the following:

   • *Paste,* to paste your selection with whatever operations you selected

   • *Link,* to paste values and labels as formulas linked to the original data

Using Copy Cells

The Copy Cells facility is not as intuitive as drag-and-drop or cut-and-paste, but you get the options to reference cell names, and override absolute references (Model Copy) when copying formulas:

1. Select the cells, and then click Edit ⇨ Copy Cells. (Press F3 to select a named block.)

2. Select the reference in the To box, and then click the upper-left cell of the destination block (see Figure 33-13).

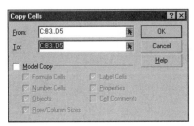

Figure 33-13: Using Copy Cells.

3. Check Model Copy, if applicable, and select the items to include in the copy.

For an example of the Model Copy using Paste Special, see "Adjusting absolute references with Model Copy," later in this chapter.

Transposing Data

Paste Special gives you the option to transpose the data you're copying. To transpose data already in your notebook:

1. Select the rows and columns you want to transpose.

2. Click Tools ⇨ Numeric Tools ⇨ Transpose.

3. Select the reference in the To box, click the upper-left cell for the transposed data, and then click OK. (Just make sure that the To range doesn't overlap the From range.)

Managing Address References in Formulas

When you move or copy formulas and the data they reference, Quattro Pro attempts to maintain the integrity of your formulas, based on what it thinks you want to do. Sometimes you may need to override the defaults, to specify how you actually want to handle address references.

Working with relative addresses

Normally, cell formulas refer to *relative* addresses. This means that when you move (or copy) cells with formulas, data referenced by the formulas, or both, Quattro Pro adjusts the formula (if necessary) to maintain its integrity. To see how relative addresses work:

1. Open a sheet and type **2**, **4**, **6** in cells A2-A4; and **3**, **5**, **7** in cells C2-C4.

2. Click cell A5, and then click the QuickSum button to insert the formula @SUM(A2..A4) in the cell (see Figure 33-14).

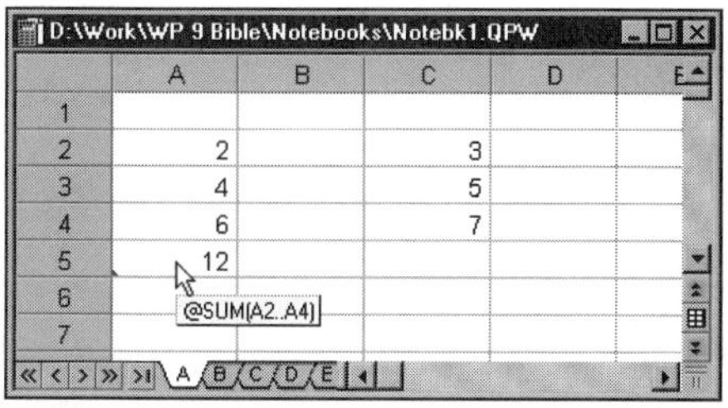

Figure 33-14: Setting up a relative address experiment.

3. Drag cell A5 to cell C5, hold down the Ctrl key, and drop a copy into place. Note how the copy of your formula automatically adjusts its references to read @SUM (C2..C4) for a new total of 15 (see Figure 33-15).

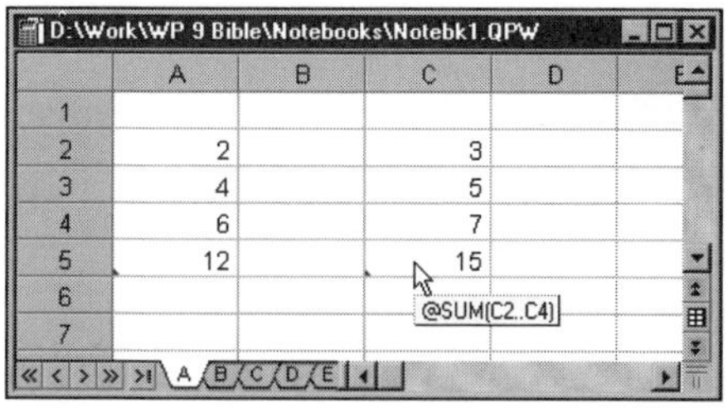

Figure 33-15: Cell references automatically adjust when you copy a formula.

4. Click the label above column C to select the column, and then point to either side of the column and drag it to column D. Note how the formula adjusts to @SUM (D2..D4) when you move the data it references.

5. Now move (don't copy) cell A5 to cell B5. This time the formula doesn't change, because the data it references stays in place.

6. Next, drag cell A3 over to cell B3. Note how it drops out of the total because it no longer falls within the A2..A4 block coordinates (see Figure 33-16). (Had the formula been +A2+A3+A4, it would have adjusted to +A2+B3+A4, because each cell would be treated as a separate block.)

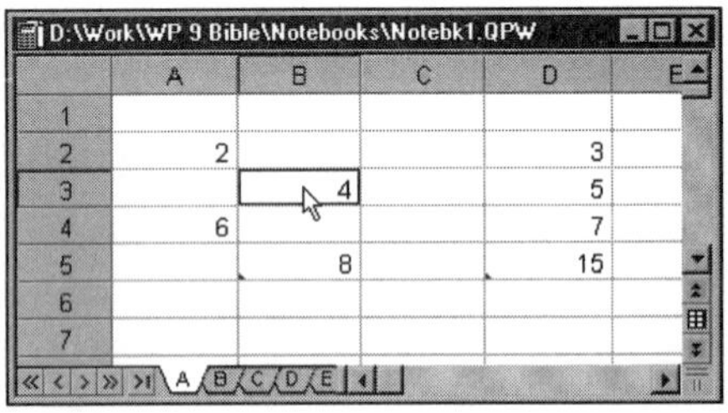

Figure 33-16: Cell A3 drops out of the total when it's moved outside the block coordinates in the formula.

7. Finally, drag cell A2 over to cell B2. Because A2 is one of the block coordinates, the formula in A5 now changes to @SUM(B2..A4), and cell B3 again falls within the coordinates (see Figure 33-17).

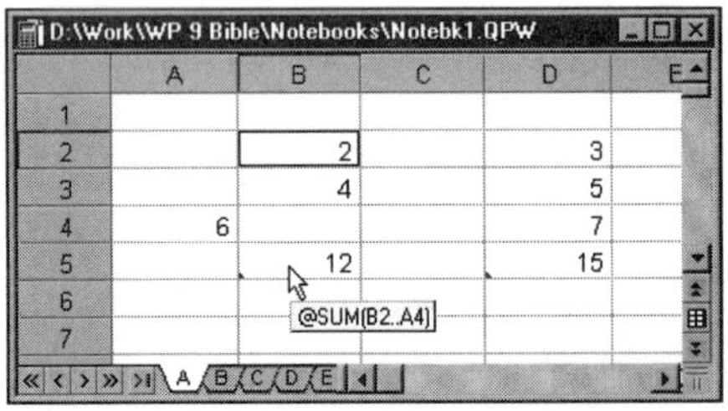

Figure 33-17: After dragging cell A2 to column B, cell B3 once again falls within the formula's block coordinates.

Specifying absolute addresses

Normally you'll want to use relative addresses, which is why the program changes them automatically. But situations may arise in which you don't want address references to change. For example, all the monthly payment formulas for the Auto Loan Calculator in Figure 33-18 reference the same absolute addresses for the Annual Rate and Periods cells in column F.

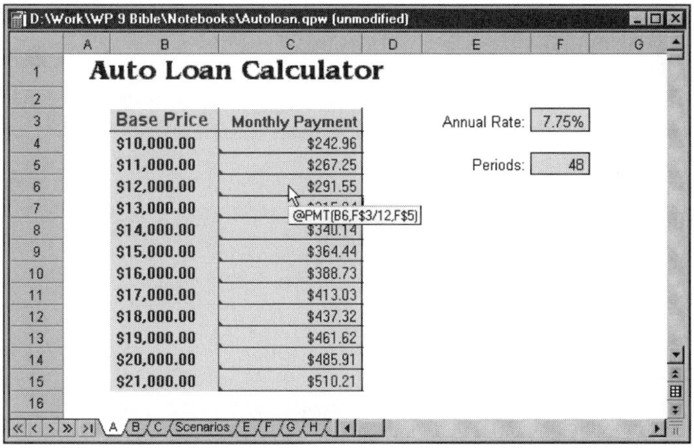

Figure 33-18: Auto Loan Calculator with absolute references to the rate and period cells.

In creating the first monthly payment formula in cell C4, dollar signs ($) were placed before the row references for the rate (F$3) and periods (F$5), so they wouldn't increment as the formula was copied (by using QuickFill) down column C.

In specifying absolute references, place a dollar sign before each reference you want to keep fixed:

✦ *F4* locks both the column and row references to cell F4.

✦ *$F4* locks only the column reference (the row can adjust).

✦ *F$4* locks only the row reference (the column can adjust).

✦ *$A:F$4* locks the sheet and row references (the column can adjust).

✦ *$Profit* locks all the column and row references of the named Profit block.

Instead of typing the dollar signs, you can insert them with the Abs key (F4). Position the insertion point in or just after the cell address you want to make absolute, and then press F4 until the dollar signs appear where you want them (you'll cycle through eight possibilities).

Using the Cell Reference Checker

The Cell Reference Checker automatically suggests corrections for cell references that should have referred to a specific cell (an absolute reference), but referred instead to a cell relative to a new location (relative reference) when moved, filled, or pasted.

For example, suppose that you don't specify absolute addresses in the payment formula in cell C4 of the Auto Loan Calculator. Now, when you QuickFill the formula down cells C5–C15, the Cell Reference Checker (in effect) says, "Hey! Are you sure you want to reference those blank cells in column F, or should I make the references absolute?" Click the << Details button for a full explanation (see Figure 33-19).

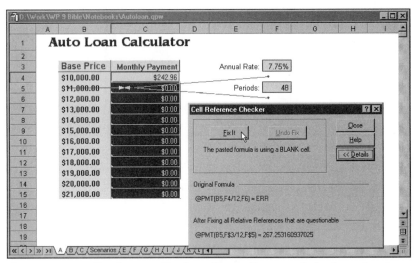

Figure 33-19: Cell Reference Checker offers to fix your relative formula references.

Click Fix It, and the Cell Reference Checker automatically changes the Annual Rate and Periods references to absolute addresses. Any wonder that computers can play chess!?

Adjusting absolute references with Model Copy

Sometimes you may want the absolute references in the block you're copying to adjust to the new location. This "Model Copy" procedure is especially useful when your selection has absolute references to cells within it.

The Auto Loan Calculator shown in Figure 33-20 has the absolute references B3 (the loan amount) and E3 (the number of months). If you copy the calculator (other than with drag-and-drop, or to the corresponding location on another sheet), the formulas will not reference the loan amount or number of months in the new location. (A copy in the same sheet will reference the correct cells.)

Tip

The spreadsheets shown in Figures 33-18 and 33-20 show what you can do with the @PMT function. They also display Quattro Pro's "What-If" capabilities, by instantly updating the monthly payment when you change the annual rate, periods, or loan amount.

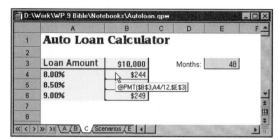

Figure 33-20: Calculator with absolute references you want to adjust when copying.

Paste Special lets you automatically adjust absolute references to the new location:

1. Select the cells you want to copy, and then click the Copy button (Edit ➪ Copy).

2. Click the upper-left cell of the new location, and then click Edit ➪ Paste Special and check "Adjust Absolute References (Model Copy)," as shown in Figure 33-21.

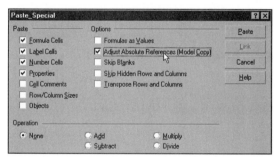

Figure 33-21: Adjusting absolute references when copying.

Working on a Group of Sheets

Suppose you want to set up a budget for Q1 through Q4, using separate notebook sheets for each quarter. The budget items, headings, and formulas on each sheet are the same, although the budget numbers may be different (see Figure 33-22). By grouping the sheets, you can apply labels, formulas, and formatting to all the sheets at once.

To work on a group of sheets, you must first name the group, and then turn on Group mode editing.

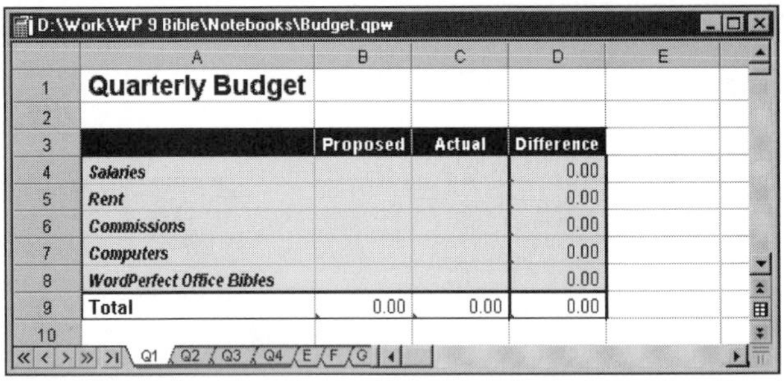

Figure 33-22: Working on a group of sheets (note bottom bar connecting tabs).

Naming a group of sheets

To name a group of sheets:

1. Click Insert ➪ Name ➪ Group of Sheets.

2. Give the group a name (other than the name of a sheet), and specify the first and last sheets in the group (see Figure 33-23). (If you preselect the sheets, the sheet entries automatically appear.)

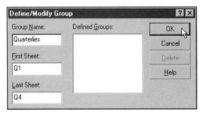

Figure 33-23: Naming a group of sheets.

You can name as many groups as you want, although a particular sheet can belong to only one group. To revise or delete a group, click Insert ➪ Name ➪ Group of Sheets, and then click the group name.

Working in Group mode

Click View ➪ Group Mode (Alt+F5) to work in 3-D on a named group (the tabs in your named groups will be underlined in blue). Any change you make to the properties of one sheet in the group, such as the column width, is applied to all the sheets in the group. You can press Ctrl+Enter to have an entry to one sheet "drill" up or down to the other sheets in the group. Likewise, you can press Ctrl+Delete to delete in 3-D.

To return to 2-D mode, click View ➪ Group Mode again.

Table 33-2 describes some group operations you can perform.

Table 33-2 **Some Group Mode Operations**	
In Order to	*Do This*
Apply a cell entry to all the sheets.	Press Ctrl+Enter.
Delete cell contents in all the sheets.	Select the cell or block on any sheet, and then press Ctrl+Delete.
Delete cells, blocks, rows, or columns on all sheets.	Select the elements you want to delete, and then click the Delete Cells button.
Sum the same cells on all the sheets.	Select the cells on any sheet, and then click the QuickSum button.
Add 2-D or 3-D references in formulas.	Turn Group mode off to point to 2-D references; turn it on to point to 3-D references.

Tip   When using Group mode, be sure Undo is enabled (Tools ➪ Settings ➪ General ➪ Enable Undo).

Note that normal cell editing and block clearing affect only the current sheet, even when Group mode is on (unless you hold down the Ctrl key as you press Enter or Delete).

Group mode also works with other operations, such as inserting and resizing rows or columns, copying and moving blocks, and changing sheet properties.

Sometimes, you'll need to turn Group mode off and on to do a particular task. For example, to copy data from one sheet in a group to the remaining sheets in the group:

1. Turn off Group mode.

2. Select the source data and then press Ctrl+C.

3. Turn on Group mode.

4. Click the upper-left destination cell in any sheet and then press Ctrl+V.

Caution   Turn off Group mode when you don't need it, and be careful when using Cut, Clear, or Clear Values in Group mode. If you accidentally make an unwanted change to all the sheets, press Ctrl+Z (Undo) immediately.

For More Information . . .

On	See
Using basic editing techniques	Chapter 2
Using selection techniques	Chapter 32
Auditing errors	Quattro Pro's online help
Transferring information between programs	Chapter 10
QuickFilling sheet tabs	Chapter 32

✦   ✦   ✦

Formatting Figures and Setting Up Notebooks

This chapter shows you many ways to enhance the appearance of blocks, rows, columns, spreadsheets, and notebooks. You'll also discover some handy tricks for creating an efficient, attractive, secure environment.

The main idea of a spreadsheet is to line up numbers in little boxes and then run them through your mathematical operations. That's fine for the number-crunching mechanics, but sometimes you'll want to dress up your results. This chapter shows how Quattro Pro makes it easier than ever to present your data in an attractive format (see Figure 34-1).

Figure 34-1: Before-and-after formatting.

Beyond Quattro Pro's formatting capabilities, you can employ a number of other settings to customize your working environment.

Working in Page View

When it comes to formatting, nothing beats working in the Page view display, viewing margins, headers, page breaks, and other formatting exactly as they will print.

Click View ➪ Page to perform all your normal spreadsheet tasks, plus any of the following:

✦ Adjust margins by dragging the dotted guidelines (see Figure 34-2).

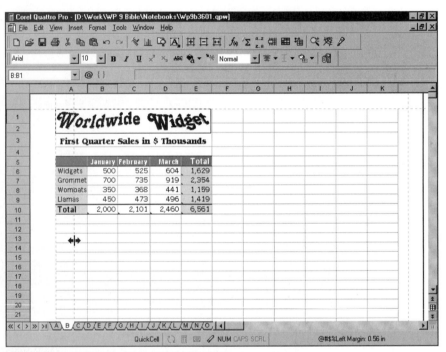

Figure 34-2: Adjusting a margin in Page view.

✦ Move hard page breaks by dragging the solid lines.

✦ Right-click (or double-click) in the margins to set up the page.

✦ Right-click in the margins to create (or remove) a header or footer. (Double-click a header or footer to edit it.)

Click the Zoom button (or View ➪ Zoom) and select a smaller zoom percentage, to view more of your sheet onscreen.

Once your formatting is finished, you can click View ➪ Draft to return to the normal spreadsheet view.

Cross-Reference For more information on setting up your print page, see Chapter 37, "Printing Notebooks, Charts, and Maps."

Formatting Cells

You have four ways to access all the formatting and other properties that apply to a selected cell or block:

✦ Click the Cell Properties button.

✦ Click Format ➪ Selection.

✦ Right-click your selection and click Cell Properties.

✦ Press F12.

You can then change the text color, numeric format, alignment, row height, column width, and so on (see Figure 34-3).

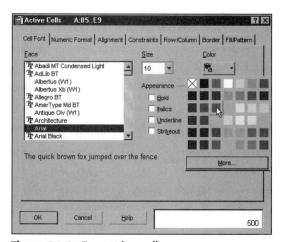

Figure 34-3: Formatting cells.

This chapter will mostly refer to Format ➪ Selection, but use whatever method you prefer.

Tip To save your custom formatting as a style, see "Doing Data in Style," later in this chapter.

Changing text appearance

The property bar is the quickest route to changing the font face, size, color, or appearance of selected cells. You can also press Ctrl+B (bold), Ctrl+I (italic), or Ctrl+U (underline).

Tip   The row height automatically adjusts to its largest font size.

Click Format ➪ Selection ➪ Cell Font to display cell entries in strikeout, or to apply single or double accounting-style underlines.

Cross-Reference   For more information on fonts, including custom TextArt, see Chapter 8, "Fonts Fantastic."

Changing the numeric format

Click Format ➪ Selection ➪ Numeric Format to apply or customize any of the numeric formats described in Chapter 32, "Entering Data and Formulas." (Use accounting alignment with the Currency format to left-justify the currency sign and right-justify the amount.)

Aligning data

Click the Horizontal Align button on the property bar, or click Format ➪ Selection ➪ Alignment, to change the alignment of selected cells, as described in Chapter 32, "Entering Data and Formulas." The General (default) horizontal alignment places text at the left and numbers at the right.

You can also align data by using the prefix characters ' (left), " (right), and ^ (center).

Locking and constraining cell data entry

You can lock cells in a sheet to prevent them from being changed at all, or you can constrain them to a particular type of entry (labels only or dates only).

This may sound confusing (because it is), but locking is performed at the sheet level, while unlocking and constraining are performed at the cell level. Here's how it works: To prevent the contents of any cell in the current sheet from being altered, click Format ➪ Sheet ➪ Protection, and then check Enable Cell Locking. (You can also lock other objects on the sheet.)

Now, to *allow* editing of selected cells in a locked sheet, click Format ➪ Selection ➪ Constraints ➪ Unprotect (see Figure 34-4).

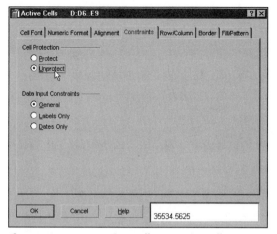

Figure 34-4: Removing cell protection allows entries when the sheet is locked.

You can't delete a row or column that has a locked cell.

To constrain the type of entries allowed in a selection, click Format ⇨ Selection ⇨ Constraints, and then click Labels Only or Dates Only. Select General to remove any constraints.

Set cells for phone numbers to Labels Only, so the dashes won't be interpreted as minus signs.

Applying lines in and around cells

You can click the Line-drawing palette on the property bar to quickly apply lines in and around selected cells. To access all the border options for selected cells:

1. Click Format ⇨ Selection ⇨ Border.

2. Select the line segments you want to change (hold down the Shift key to select multiple segments):

   • *All,* to select all the segments

   • *Outline,* to put a border around your selection

   • *Inside,* to select the segments within your selection

3. Check "Hide grid lines in filled regions on all sheets" (see Figure 34-5) to blank out the screen grid display within your selection. (Screen grids don't print, but this option can improve your screen display.)

4. Click the Border Type palette to select the line style or to remove border lines.

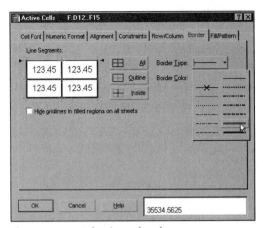

Figure 34-5: Selecting a border type.

5. Click the Border Color palette to change the color.

Applying cell fills

To change fill (background) for selected cells, click the Cell Fill button to apply the current fill color, or click the arrow to the right of the button to select a color from the palette. From the palette you can select from the following:

✦ A previous selection under Custom Colors

✦ *More,* to select from 256 colors and shades of gray (see Figure 34-6)

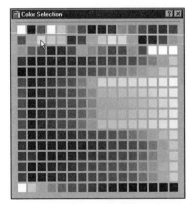

Figure 34-6: Selecting from 256 colors and shades of gray.

✦ *No Fill,* to turn off shading

Formatting Columns and Rows

Formatting your columns and rows has nothing to do with your calculations, but everything to do with your presentation. In particular, you have several ways to size columns.

Resizing columns and rows with a mouse

The quickest way to resize a column or row is to drag the right side of a border cell for a column or the bottom of a border cell for a row. You can also select several rows or columns, and then drag the border of one to change them all at once (see Figure 34-7).

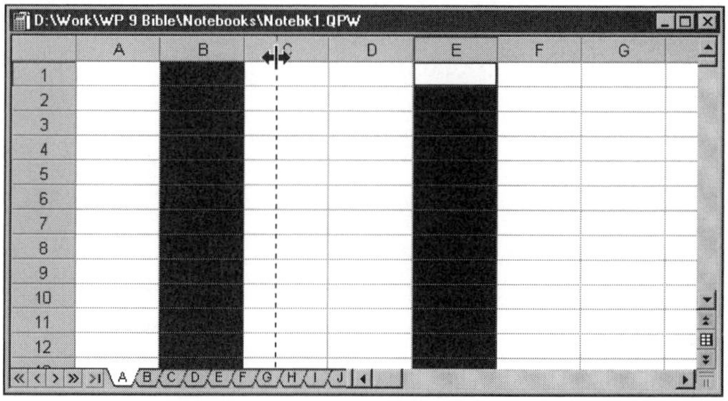

Figure 34-7: Drag one column's border to adjust all the selected columns at once.

QuickFilling columns

To resize a column to its widest entry plus one character, click the column (or select adjacent columns), and then click the QuickFit button. You can also double-click the column border or click Format ➪ QuickFit.

Tip   Select part of the column to QuickFit to a size other than its widest entry.

Using Fit-As-You-Go

When a column is too narrow to display a number, the Fit-As-You-Go feature (Tools ➪ Settings ➪ General) automatically widens the column. (General numbers display in scientific notation, rather than expand the column.)

When Fit-As-You-Go is off, a number displays as asterisks (*) if it's too wide to fit in the column. (A general number that's too big switches to scientific notation, if there's room.)

If you narrow a column that was expanded by Fit-As-You-Go, asterisks display for numbers that no longer fit.

Specifying precise column and row sizes

To set columns or rows to a precise size:

1. Select the column(s) or row(s), or any cells within them.

2. Click Format ➪ Selection ➪ Row/Column, and select from the following options:

   • *Set width* or *Set height*, to specify the units (characters, points, inches, or centimeters) and the number of units (see Figure 34-8)

   • *Reset width* or *Reset height,* to restore the default column width or row height

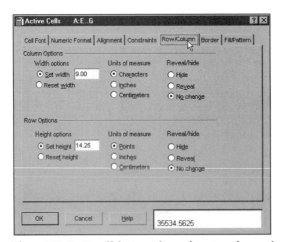

Figure 34-8: Specifying precise column and row sizes.

Hiding columns and rows

Sometimes it's convenient to hide columns and rows, to focus on a particular area of a spreadsheet (see Figure 34-9).

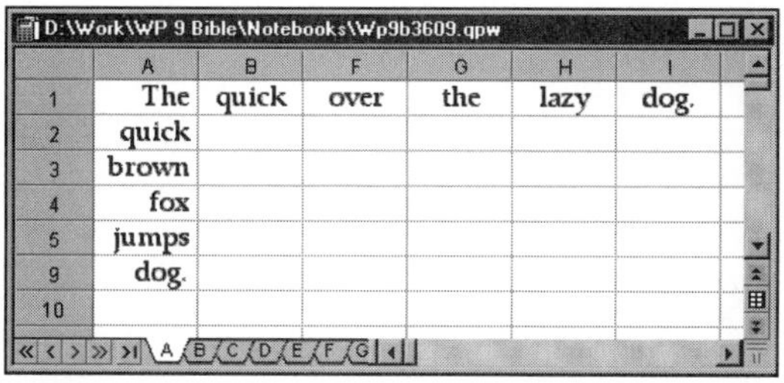

Figure 34-9: A spreadsheet with hidden rows and columns. Note the missing column and row labels.

To hide rows or columns:

1. Select the columns or rows, or any cells within them.

2. Right-click your selection and click Hide.

Hidden information doesn't print, but it's still used in calculations. Copy and paste operations work as if the data were not hidden.

To redisplay the hidden data, select the surrounding columns or rows, and then right-click your selection and click Reveal.

Doing Data in Style

Quattro Pro comes with a few simple styles to change the numeric format or point size (for headings).

Applying styles

To apply a style to selected cells, click the Styles list on the property bar to switch from Normal to a particular style, or click Format ⇨ Styles, and select the style you want. The Normal style returns you to the system defaults.

Customizing styles

To customize a notebook's built-in styles, or add a custom style of your own:

1. Click Format ⇨ Styles.

2. Select the style you want to revise, or type a name for the style you want to create (see Figure 34-10). Note that the Normal style cannot be revised.

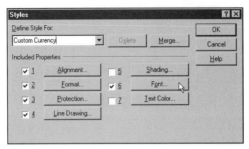

Figure 34-10: Type a name to create a custom style.

3. Click the button (Alignment, Format, Protection, and so on) for any property you want to modify, change its settings, and click OK.

Tip   Uncheck properties you don't want to change, so the style won't override other editing you've done to a cell or block. Note how several built-in styles have only one property checked.

4. To copy property settings from another style or preformatted cell, click Merge, click Style or Cell, specify the style name or cell address, and then click OK (see Figure 34-11).

Figure 34-11: Merging (copying) from another style or preformatted cell.

A new style is added to the Style list. Any cells to which a style has been applied are automatically updated when you revise the style.

To delete a style, click Format ➪ Styles, select the style, and click Delete. You can't delete the Normal style.

To copy a style to another notebook, copy a cell to which the style has been applied. The new style automatically appears in the Styles list for that notebook.

QuickFormatting Cells

Instead of fussing with styles, use QuickFormat to quickly apply the current numeric format, font, fills, lines, and so on, to other parts of your notebook. To use QuickFormat:

1. Click the cell whose formatting you want to copy, or select multiple cells to copy a block of formatting.

2. Click the QuickFormat button.

3. Drag the roller over the cells you want to format, or click the upper-left cell if you're copying a block of formatting.

4. Click the QuickFormat button to turn off QuickFormat.

Zooming the Screen

If you're visually impaired and need to enlarge the figures on the screen, or you want a bird's-eye view of your entire masterpiece, click the Zoom button and select another magnification for the current sheet.

Tip   Click Selection to zoom in on selected cells, or the current cell and contiguous cells with data.

You can also click Other (or View ⇨ Zoom), to pick another percentage, or specify a custom setting from 10 percent to 400 percent (see Figure 34-12).

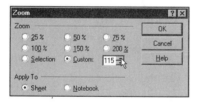

Figure 34-12: Zooming the screen.

Click Notebook to change the zoom for all the sheets. Zooming your display doesn't affect printed output.

SpeedFormatting Techniques

In Chapter 30, "A Hands-On Notebook," you used SpeedFormat to polish up your spreadsheet in a flash. Now you'll get an in-depth look at SpeedFormat options and learn how to create custom formats you can apply repeatedly.

SpeedFormat styles are especially powerful because they automatically recognize a block's column headings (cells in the top row), column totals (cells in the bottom row), row headings (cells in the left column), row totals (cells in the right column), subtotals (column and row totals within the block), and the body (remaining cells).

Applying a SpeedFormat style

To SpeedFormat selected cells:

1. Click the SpeedFormat button. (You can also click Format ⇨ SpeedFormat, or right-click the selected block and click SpeedFormat.)

2. Click the format you want to apply (see Figure 34-13).

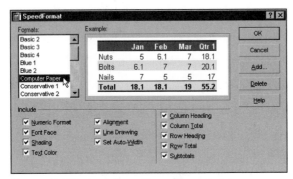

Figure 34-13: Applying a SpeedFormat style.

3. Uncheck any properties you don't want to include, or any block parts you don't want to change. (Checked items override any existing property settings.) Your choices are reflected in the Example display.

 Tip   Click Undo (Ctrl+Z) immediately if you don't like the result.

Creating a custom SpeedFormat style

To create a custom SpeedFormat style to apply to other tables you create:

1. Format a block of cells (at least three rows by three columns in size) with the properties you want for headings, totals, subtotals, and body cells.

2. Click Format ⇨ SpeedFormat ⇨ Add, and give your format a name (see Figure 34-14).

3. Specify the block coordinates, if necessary.

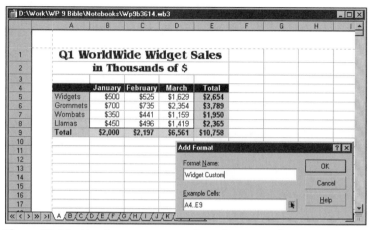

Figure 34-14: Naming your custom SpeedFormat style.

Specifying Sheet Properties

You can set a number of properties by the sheet, including cell lock, grid display, and tab colors. To set sheet properties:

1. Select the sheet or sheets (hold down the Shift key and click a tab to select a range of sheets).

2. Click Format ➪ Sheet (or right-click a tab and click Sheet Properties), and then click the tab for the settings you want to change (see Figure 34-15).

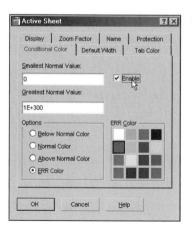

Figure 34-15: Setting sheet conditional colors.

Table 34-1 provides a quick reference to the settings you'll find under the various tabs.

Table 34-1		
Sheet Settings Quick Reference		
Tab	**Settings**	**Defaults**
Display	Display or hide zeros, borders, and grid lines	Everything displayed
Default Width	Column width in characters, inches, or centimeters	Nine characters
Name	Sheet name	Alphabetic letter
Protection	Cell and object locking	Not checked (see "Locking and constraining cell data entry," earlier in this chapter)
Conditional Color	Flag data outside the "normal" range, such as a stock with a high price-earnings ratio, or a sales entry that might be in error, and set their values and colors	Not enabled
Tab Color	Tab color	System Color (white)
Zoom Factor	Zoom (magnification)	Your last zoom selection

Specifying Notebook Properties

You can set several properties for the notebook as a whole, such as the scroll bar display, the zoom factor, and the recalculation mode. To set notebook properties, click Format ➪ Notebook, and then click the tab for the setting you want to change (see Figure 34-16).

Table 34-2 provides a quick reference to the settings you'll find under the various tabs.

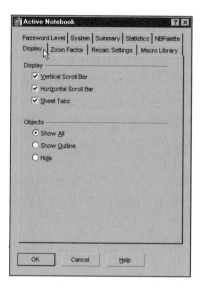

Figure 34-16: Notebook display settings.

Table 34-2
Notebook Settings Quick Reference

Tab	Settings	Defaults
Display	Display or hide scroll bars, sheet tabs, and objects	Everything displayed
Zoom Factor	Zoom (magnification)	Your last zoom selection
Recalc Settings	Recalculation and audit error settings	Background mode, natural order, one iteration, no audit errors
Palette	Edit color palette, or reset to default	42 colors
Macro Library	Macro library notebook	No (see Chapter 38, "Automating with Macros and Buttons")
Password Level	Level of protection	None
System	System notebook (remains open until you exit Quattro Pro)	No
Summary	Title, subject, author, keywords, and comments	All blank except user name for Author
Statistics	View statistics	Displays filename, folder, creation and saved dates, last saved by, and revision number

Setting the recalculation and audit modes

Click Format ➪ Notebook ➪ Recalc Settings to select the recalculation mode (see Figure 34-17):

✦ *Automatic*, to pause the program and recalculate formulas as soon as a change is made

✦ *Manual*, to recalculate formulas manually when data changes. (The calculator on the application bar is highlighted when formulas require manual recalculation. Click the calculator or F9.)

✦ *Background* (the recommended default), to recalculate formulas automatically between keystrokes. (Recalculations always finish before a notebook is saved, extracted, or printed.)

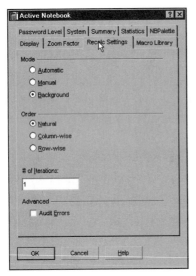

Figure 34-17: Setting recalculation and audit modes.

Recalculation is normally performed in the *natural order* in which cells depend on each other. You can change this order to "Column-wise" or "Row-wise" in special situations, such as for a complicated series of engineering formulas with circular references. When you have *circular references* back to the original formula, you'll probably need to set a higher number of iterations to achieve accurate results (255 is the maximum). (If you don't have circular formulas and the recalculation order is set to Natural, the number of iterations is ignored.)

The Audit Errors option displays the sheet and cell at which the problem started for each cell containing NA or ERR.

Password-protecting a notebook

To password-protect your notebook, click File ⇨ Save (File ⇨ Save As for a notebook you've already named), check Password Protect, and then enter the password twice for verification (see Figure 34-18).

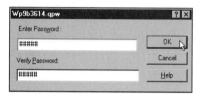

Figure 34-18: Password-protecting a notebook.

To set a particular level of security for your notebook:

1. Click Format ⇨ Notebook ⇨ Password Level, and then select the security level (see Figure 34-19):

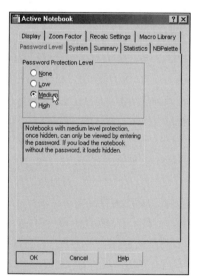

Figure 34-19: Assigning a notebook security level.

Security Level	Requires a Password to
None	View and edit all elements (removes all password protection)
Low	See cell formulas
Medium	View the notebook
High	Open the notebook

2. Enter and verify your password when prompted.

Passwords are case-sensitive ("Top Secret" and "top secret" are not the same). And if you lose the password, you're out of luck, because the Password Level tab doesn't appear on a protected notebook.

Designating system notebooks

One use for passwords (medium level) is to hide the system notebooks for a Quattro Pro application. System notebooks are hidden notebooks containing macros and other objects for general use that you want to keep available, but you don't want the user to alter. To designate a system notebook, click Format ⇨ Notebook ⇨ System, and then click Yes.

Changing Application Settings

Last, but not least, click Tools ⇨ Settings to change settings that affect the appearance or behavior of Quattro Pro itself. Click the tabs to change the settings as needed (see Figure 34-20). For more information on a particular option, click the What button, and then click the desired item.

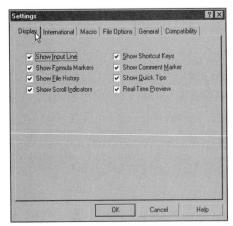

Figure 34-20: Changing application settings.

Table 34-3 provides a quick reference to the settings you'll find under the various tabs.

Table 34-3
Application Settings Quick Reference

Tab	Settings	Defaults
Display	Markers for formulas and comments, real-time preview, and other display items (see Chapter 31, "Becoming an Instant Quattro Pro Expert")	Everything displayed
International	Set formats for currency, punctuation, date, time, and language, plus Lotus character set option	Installation defaults; Lotus characters off
Macro	Redraw suppression while macro is running, plus startup macro	Both for redraw, \0 for startup macro
File Options	Default folder, timed backup, and other options	Timed backup and URL refresh off; full path and enhanced file dialog boxes
General	Various automatic features	All checked except compatibility keys and math formula entry; drag-and-drop delay of 5,000 ms (5 seconds) to effectively turn it off
Compatibility	Operational settings for QP9, QP8, Excel 97, or custom; plus other interface and size options (see Chapter 30)	QP9; WPW files, 256 sheets and columns; 65,536 rows

For More Information . . .

On	See
Setting up your print page	Chapter 37
Using fonts and TextArt	Chapter 8
Selecting numeric formats	Chapter 32
Aligning data in cells	Chapter 32
Renaming sheets	Chapter 32
Choosing how you want to work	Chapter 30
Creating macros and macro libraries	Chapter 38

✦   ✦   ✦

Analyzing Data

Once your data is entered, edited, and formatted, you'll find that there's much more Quattro Pro can do with it. Sure, you can create lovely charts, maps, and slide shows, but its real power turns on when you need to analyze data and deliver results.

Chapter 31, "Becoming an Instant Quattro Pro Expert," showed how you can jump-start your analysis with projects and templates that help you to do everything from a 401K Planner to a Year-End Tax Plan (didn't quite make it to Z). Here you'll try out some of the great data-handling tools that make these projects possible, to directly manipulate and analyze your data in many ways. While some tools involve sophisticated mathematical concepts (such as solving simultaneous equations), you don't have to be a math genius to answer what-if questions, find an optimum solution, or come up with next year's sales projections. Pick up the right tools to solve your problem, and then let Quattro Pro do the work.

Opening the Toolbox

A spreadsheet program is only as good as its tools, and Quattro Pro's are as good as they get. Click the Tools menu to browse the data-related tool categories, described in Table 35-1. This chapter gives you a hands-on look at tools in each of these categories.

Analyzing with the Experts

Before you embark on your own, check out the available experts to help you perform advanced analysis of financial or statistical data:

1. Set up the input block you want to analyze. The data must be numeric. In many cases you can use column and row labels.

2. Click Tools ⇨ Numeric Tools ⇨ Analysis.

3. Select the expert you need (see Figure 35-1), and then follow the step-by-step procedures.

Table 35-1 Data Tool Categories	
Tool Category	**Lets You**
QuickFilter	Quickly sift and sort through the data on your screen
Sort	Sort a selection by using as many as five sort keys
Hyperlink	Link to another file or Web site
Outline	Summarize groups of data in rows or columns, while hiding the details
Auditing	Visually connect your screen data and formulas to help in analyzing data and tracing errors
Numeric Tools	Perform many types of statistical, optimizing, matrix, multivariable, and budget analyses
Data Tools	Query, combine, extract, and arrange data
Consolidate	Combine data from two or more blocks using a specific operator (such as sum, average, or sample variance)
Scenario	See what happens to "snapshots" of your models as you change data or variables

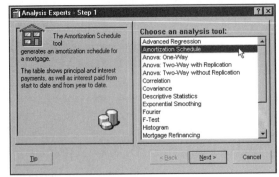

Figure 35-1: Using the analysis experts.

Setting Up a Database

Before you try out the data analysis tools, take a look at how data is set up and organized. Most collections of information are one form of database or another. An imposing term perhaps, but as Chapter 43, "The Secrets to Database Success," explains, a *database* is nothing more than a collection of related records of information (such as a phone list or checkbook ledger). The CorelCENTRAL Address Book is an excellent example of a database, but a household inventory table also qualifies. The important point is that each record is composed of similar items of information, or *fields* (first name, last name, street, zip code, phone number, and so on), so they can be easily searched, sorted, or analyzed.

A heavy-duty *database manager*, such as Paradox, is designed to organize, maintain, and report on large, diverse collections of data. Quattro Pro can import or link data from such a system for manipulation and analysis. (See Chapter 10, "Working Together and Sharing Data," for more information on importing and sharing data.)

A database in Quattro Pro consists of a single table, on one sheet, with as many as 18,278 fields and one million records. Each row is a record, with the first, column-header row defining the field names. To set up a database:

1. Enter unique field names for the database in the top, header *row*. (Names aren't case-sensitive, and you can put spaces between words.)

2. Enter the data for each record (row) in the appropriate fields (columns). All entries in a particular column, other than the field name, should normally be of the same data type.

Tip   Don't leave a blank row between the column header row and the first record, because it will be interpreted as a blank record. Instead, drag the bottom border at the left of the first data row, or use lines, shading, and other formatting to set off the header row.

Records   Field names

	A	B	C	D	E	F
1	Description	Year Purchased	Purchase Price	Salvage Value	Replacement Cost	Use
2	486 computer, fully loaded	1994	$2,750.00	$300.00	$700.00	personal
3	Pentium computer	1997	$1,200.00	$800.00	$900.00	business
4	Laser printer	1995	$530.00	$250.00	$350.00	business
5	Scanner	1995	$850.00	$400.00	$600.00	business
6	19" monitor	1998	$850.00	$375.00	$650.00	business
7	Pearl & diamond earrings (gift)	1981	$0.00	$850.00	$1,200.00	personal
8	VCR	1992	$375.00	$175.00	$325.00	personal
9	Sofa, matching loveseat	1989	$1,825.00	$600.00	$2,000.00	personal
10	Antique 3-drawer dresser	1996	$450.00	$450.00	$500.00	personal
11	Dining room set, 8 chairs	1985	$2,450.00	$1,200.00	$2,750.00	personal
12	Sideboard	1985	$1,200.00	$600.00	$1,500.00	personal
13						

D:\Work\WP 9 Bible\Notebooks\Inventory.qpw

Database / Search / Output / D / E / F / G / H / I /

Figure 35-2: Household inventory database you can create.

The household inventory shown in Figure 35-2 is an example of a simple database you can create.

Searching a Database

The new QuickFilter tool is probably all you need for searching and sorting your data (see "Quick Data Sorting and Filtering," later in this chapter). But if you have, for example, a corporate inventory with hundreds or thousands of records, you may want to look at the more formal search and sorting tools described in this and the next section.

Searching a database is a three-step process:

1. Initialize the field names.

2. Specify your search criteria.

3. Define an output block.

Select records, excluding the header, then click Insert ➪ Name ➪ Cells to give them a name to which you can refer when searching or sorting.

Tip   Database searches are easier in a true database manager like Paradox. However, if you have database tables, you can click Insert ➪ External Data ➪ Expert to query the data before you insert it.

If you have a Paradox query, you can click Insert ➪ External Data ➪ Table Query to query the tables from Quattro Pro.

Initializing field names

By initializing your field names, you can include them in your search criteria:

1. Select the database block (*including* the header row).

2. Click Tools ➪ Data Tools ➪ Notebook Query ➪ Field Names ➪ Close.

Click the drop-down list on the left of the input line, and you'll see that you've created a group of names from the header row. (You get the same result when you select the header row and then click Insert ➪ Name ➪ Cells ➪ Labels ➪ Down.)

Specifying search criteria

Your next step is to specify the conditions, or criteria, by which you want to search the database.

Quattro Pro uses the *Query-By-Example* (QBE) search technique, which matches records against the examples you provide. You can specify either *exact matches* (for example, the word "scanner"), or *logical conditions* (for example, any year after 1995). You can use any of the true/false type formulas for logical matches described in Chapter 32, "Entering Data and Formulas."

Specify your search conditions in a *criteria table*, like that shown in Figure 35-3. The table can be on a different notebook sheet, but it must have at least two rows: the first to specify the exact field name(s) on which to search, and subsequent rows for the search criteria. The fields can be in any order, and you need only specify those on which you're searching.

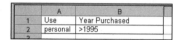

Figure 35-3: Search criteria table.

 Tip   To display formulas rather than their results (0 for false and 1 for true), use cell properties (Format ⇨ Selection ⇨ Numeric Format) to set the format of your criteria table to text.

The table in the example matches on personal items acquired after 1995 (all conditions in the row must be satisfied). If you search just on column A (A1..A2), you'll match on all personal items, regardless of date. A search on column B (B1..B2) returns all items purchased after 1995, for either business or personal use.

Use multiple rows to specify multiple sets of search criteria. The criteria table in Figure 35-4, for example, matches on all items with either "computer" or "printer" in the description. Note the use of the asterisk (*) wildcard to replace zero or more characters. You can also use "?" for a single character, or "~" to exclude matching entries. For example, by using "~*computer*" to search the descriptions, you'll return all items that don't contain "computer" anywhere in the description.

Figure 35-4: Using multiple rows for multiple sets of search criteria.

Setting up the output block

If you plan on extracting a copy of the matched records, reserve a big enough output block in any part of your notebook. Enter the field names you want to extract, in any order, in the first row of the output block.

Tip   The field names must be precise, so copy them from the first row of the database just to be sure.

Searching the database

Now that you've initialized the database, specified your search criteria, and set aside an output block, you're ready to search the database:

1. Click Tools ⇨ Data Tools ⇨ Notebook Query, and specify the database block, including the field names (see Figure 35-5).

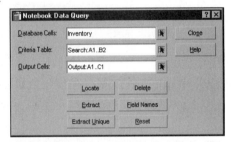

Figure 35-5: Searching the database. Note how the name for the block of records (if you assigned one) can be used in place of the coordinates.

2. Specify the criteria table, including field names and search conditions.

3. If you're extracting data, specify the cells of the first row containing the column headings of the output block. (Select down multiple rows to limit the number of output records.)

4. Click a search option:

   • *Locate*, to highlight matching records. (Browse and edit the resulting matches by using the arrow keys, and then press Esc or Enter when you're finished.)

   • *Extract*, to copy data from matching records to the output block.

   • *Extract Unique*, to eliminate duplicate records when copying.

   • *Delete*, to erase matching records. (Use Locate to examine or delete records one at a time.)

   • *Field Names*, to assign cell names to fields so you can use them in your searches.

   • *Reset*, to clear the entries in the Notebook Data Query dialog box.

Quick Data Sorting and Filtering

For basic sorting, the QuickFilter tool provides an intuitive, visual way to sift and sort through a large number of records onscreen. To follow the examples used here, open the Wines notebook found in the Samples folder.

Sorting and filtering records

To sort and select records with QuickFilter:

1. Select the block of data you want to QuickFilter, including a blank row (or a row with header labels) above the data for the QuickFilter buttons.

Note   In some cases you can let the program select the block of data, such as the entire Wines database.

2. Click Tools ⇨ QuickFilter, and then click the QuickFilter button for the field you want to sort or *filter* (select) on (see Figure 35-6).

Other filtering options   Ascending or descending order

	A	B	C	D		Regio	Cost Per Cas	Cases Sol	Sales
1	Yea	Quarte	Winery	Appellation					
2	1991	Q1	Beaulieu	Cabernet Sau	(Show All)		$165	450	$74,250
3	1991	Q2	Beaulieu	Cabernet Sau	(Top 10...)		$165	550	$90,750
4	1991	Q3	Beaulieu	Cabernet Sau	(Custom...)		$165	575	$94,875
5	1991	Q4	Beaulieu	Cabernet Sau	(Blanks)		$165	650	$107,250
6	1991	Q1	Beaulieu	Cabernet Sau	(Non Blanks)		$165	320	$52,800
7	1991	Q2	Beaulieu	Cabernet Sau	(Sort A-Z)		$165	325	$53,625
8	1991	Q3	Beaulieu	Cabernet Sau	(Sort Z-A)		$165	330	$54,450
9	1991	Q4	Beaulieu	Cabernet Sau	East		$165	350	$57,750
10	1991	Q1	Beaulieu	Cabernet Sau	North		$165	350	$57,750
11	1991	Q2	Beaulieu	Cabernet Sau	South		$165	360	$59,400
12	1991	Q3	Beaulieu	Cabernet Sau	West		$165	370	$61,050
13	1991	Q4	Beaulieu	Cabernet Sauvignon	East		$165	375	$61,875
14	1991	Q1	Beaulieu	Cabernet Sauvignon	West		$165	230	$37,950
15	1991	Q2	Beaulieu	Cabernet Sauvignon	West		$165	235	$38,775
16	1991	Q3	Beaulieu	Cabernet Sauvignon	West		$165	240	$39,600
17	1991	Q4	Beaulieu	Cabernet Sauvignon	West		$165	260	$42,900
18	1992	Q2	Beaulieu	Cabernet Sauvignon	North		$165	625	$103,125

F:\Program files\Corel\WPO2000\Suite9\Samples\wines.qpw

Filter on a particular label or value

Figure 35-6: QuickFiltering records onscreen.

3. To sort on the field, select a sort of A–Z for an ascending sort, or Z–A for a descending sort. (To sort on more than one field, such as Sales by Region, click Tools ⇨ Sort.)

4. To filter on a particular label or value, select:

- A value from the bottom of the list
- *Show All,* to undo previous filtering on the field
- *Top 10,* to display only the leading numeric values based on rank or percentage
- *Blanks,* to display records for which the field isn't filled in
- *Non Blanks,* to display only those records with an entry in the field
- *Custom,* to define more multiple filtering conditions (see Figure 35-7)

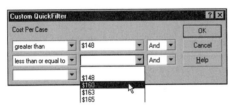

Figure 35-7: Defining multiple filtering conditions.

The arrow on a filtered column is highlighted in blue.

Copying filtered data

 When you copy and paste QuickFiltered data, only the records on view are copied.

Sophisticated Sorting

Once you've set up a database, you may want to sort your records to view them in a particular order. You may want to look at your inventory, for example, by date, with the most recent purchases on top. You can also separate business from personal items, or arrange items according to their replacement costs.

 In Chapter 53, "Sorting Information," you'll find a general explanation of sorting, together with examples in WordPerfect. You already know the concepts of records and fields, however, from setting up your database. Sorting is pretty simple in Quattro Pro.

Sorting principles

Before you get down to sorting, you should understand the following principles:

✦ Even though you're sorting rows, sorting works by the block in Quattro Pro, not by the record. So if you don't select all the columns, the sort can jumble up the rows (records). The data in the selected columns will switch rows, while data in the rest of the columns stays put. (Click Undo immediately if this happens.)

✦ Sorting is done according to the sort keys (columns), in either ascending or descending order. You can have as many as five sort keys, which execute in the order specified. If your first key, for example, is last name, make your second key first name, to put records with identical last names in order.

✦ Sorting moves blank rows to the beginning or end (a good reason to avoid them). If necessary, delete blank rows before sorting and add them after the sort is completed.

✦ Do not sort the header row containing the field names.

✦ If the sort block contains formulas that reference cells outside the block, use absolute addresses such as +E9 before sorting. If you use relative addresses such as +E9, the formulas won't adjust properly. (To quickly change a relative address to an absolute address, double-click the cell containing the formula you want to change, click the cell address in the formula, and press F4.)

Sorting your data

With these principles in mind, it's time to sort your data:

1. Select the block you want to sort (include all the columns and omit the field names), as shown in Figure 35-8. (If you assigned a name to your block of records, you can enter the name instead.)

2. Click Tools ⇨ Sort.

3. Type your sort keys, or click the list to select them (see Figure 35-9).

   Click the Previous Sorts list to use or modify a previous sort.

4. If your selection *includes* a header row, check "Selection contains a heading" to exclude it from the sort.

5. Check the Ascending box next to each sort key to sort in ascending order (blanks, special characters, 0–9, A–Z), or remove the check to sort in reverse, descending order (Z–A, 9–0, special characters, blanks).

	A	B	C	D	E	F	G	H	I
1	Year	Quarter	Winery	Appellation	Region	Cost Per Case	Cases Sold	Sales	
2	1991	Q1	Beaulieu	Cabernet Sauvignon	North	$165	450	$74,250	
3	1991	Q2	Beaulieu	Cabernet Sauvignon	North	$165	550	$90,750	
4	1991	Q3	Beaulieu	Cabernet Sauvignon	North	$165	575	$94,875	
5	1991	Q4	Beaulieu	Cabernet Sauvignon	North	$165	650	$107,250	
6	1991	Q1	Beaulieu	Cabernet Sauvignon	South	$165	320	$52,800	
7	1991	Q2	Beaulieu	Cabernet Sauvignon	South	$165	325	$53,625	
8	1991	Q3	Beaulieu	Cabernet Sauvignon	South	$165	330	$54,450	
9	1991	Q4	Beaulieu	Cabernet Sauvignon	South	$165	350	$57,750	
10	1991	Q1	Beaulieu	Cabernet Sauvignon	East	$165	350	$57,750	
11	1991	Q2	Beaulieu	Cabernet Sauvignon	East	$165	360	$59,400	
12	1991	Q3	Beaulieu	Cabernet Sauvignon	East	$165	370	$61,050	
13	1991	Q4	Beaulieu	Cabernet Sauvignon	East	$165	375	$61,875	
14	1991	Q1	Beaulieu	Cabernet Sauvignon	West	$165	230	$37,950	
15	1991	Q2	Beaulieu	Cabernet Sauvignon	West	$165	235	$38,775	
16	1991	Q3	Beaulieu	Cabernet Sauvignon	West	$165	240	$39,600	
17	1991	Q4	Beaulieu	Cabernet Sauvignon	West	$165	260	$42,900	
18	1992	Q2	Beaulieu	Cabernet Sauvignon	North	$165	625	$103,125	
19	1992	Q4	Beaulieu	Cabernet Sauvignon	North	$165	670	$110,550	
20	1992	Q1	Beaulieu	Cabernet Sauvignon	South	$165	310	$51,150	
21	1992	Q2	Beaulieu	Cabernet Sauvignon	South	$165	314	$51,810	

C:\Program Files\Corel\WordPerfect Office 2000...\wines.qpw (unmodified)

Figure 35-8: When selecting the block to sort, include all the columns and omit the header row.

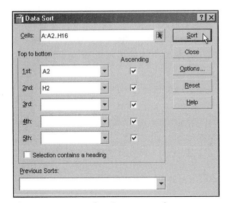

Figure 35-9: Selecting a sort key.

6. In special situations, click Options and select from the following (see Figure 35-10):

- *Left to right,* to sort data across rows, instead of down columns (top to bottom)

- *Sort blank cells first,* to always output records with blank keys on top

- *Sort numbers last,* to always place labels (for example, 19" monitor) before values (for example, $850) in the sort order

- *Heading size,* to specify the number of rows in your heading (if "Selection contains a heading" is checked)

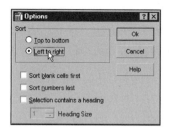

Figure 35-10: Selecting search options.

If you don't like your sort results, click Undo (Ctrl+Z) immediately.

Keeping track of your pre-sort order

To keep track of your pre-sort order, you can add a record key field, and then increment the key as new records are added. You can even leave gaps in your numbering to allow you to insert records later on (see Figure 35-11). You can then sort on the record key to restore your pre-sort order.

Sort on your key to restore the pre-sort order.

Sort on your key to restore the pre-sort order

	A	B	C	D	E	F
	Description	Record Key	Year Purchased	Purchase Price	Salvage Value	Replacem Cost
2	486 computer, fully loaded	1000	1994	$2,750.00	$300.00	$700
3	Pentium computer	1010	1997	$1,200.00	$800.00	$900
4	Laser printer	1020	1995	$530.00	$250.00	$350
5	Scanner	1030	1995	$850.00	$400.00	$600
6	19" monitor	1040	1998	$850.00	$375.00	$650
7	Pearl & diamond earrings (gift)	1050	1981	$0.00	$850.00	$1,200
8	VCR	1060	1992	$375.00	$175.00	$325
9	Sofa, matching loveseat	1070	1989	$1,825.00	$600.00	$2,000
10	Antique 3-drawer dresser	1080	1996	$450.00	$450.00	$500
11	Dining room set, 8 chairs	1090	1985	$2,450.00	$1,200.00	$2,750
12	Sideboard	1100	1985	$1,200.00	$600.00	$1,500
13						

D:\Work\WP 9 Bible\Notebooks\Inventory.qpw

Database / Search / Output / D \ E / F / G /

Figure 35-11: A record key lets you restore your pre-sort order.

Creating Outline Summaries

The outline tools let you summarize groups of data in rows or columns, while hiding the details. Outlining is a two-step process in which you

✦ Add formulas and headings to summarize your records

✦ Automatically or manually create your outline

Unfortunately, there is no facility to generate the headings and formulas themselves, so outlining can be a time-consuming process.

A notebook can contain several outlines, but you can have only one outline per sheet.

Adding formulas and headings

Before creating your outline, arrange your data in the order you want it to appear. (For the example here, sort a copy of the Wines spreadsheet by year, by quarter, and by winery.) Then add the formulas and headings to summarize your data:

1. Insert a blank row beneath each group of records you want to summarize. (Insert blank columns if your records are arranged horizontally.) For this example, you can insert blank rows for each winery's quarterly sales, total sales for all wineries by quarter, and total annual sales for all wineries.

2. Add text to describe your summaries and formulas to create your totals. (Click the QuickSum button to perform common arithmetic functions, such as sum or average, on an adjacent group of values.)

Creating an outline

To create an outline from your summary headings, click any cell on the sheet, and then click Tools ➪ Outline ➪ Auto Outline.

Creating a multilevel outline

To create a multilevel outline, summarize your data to multiple levels of detail. With your sorted copy of the wines spreadsheet, your first outline level is likely to be the quarterly totals for each winery. You can insert additional rows and formulas to show total quarterly sales for all wineries and annual sales for all wineries. This results in a four-level outline:

1. Yearly total

2. Quarterly total

3. Quarter by winery

4. Quarterly sales for each winery for each appellation and region

Viewing outlined data

To control the appearance of your outlined data:

1. Click Tools ➪ Outline ➪ Show Outline Toolbar, and then click the Outline Show button to display the outline panels at the side and top of your sheet. (You can also click Tools ➪ Outline ➪ Show Outline to display or hide the panels.)

2. Click the Outline Plus button or the Outline Minus button on the toolbar or in the panel to expand or collapse the details of the current outline group (see Figure 35-12).

		A	B	C	D	E	F	G	H
	1	Year	Quarter	Winery	Appellation	Region	Cost Per Case	Cases Sold	Sales
	14	1991	Q1	Beaulieu			$163	3800	$618
	15	1991	Q1	Duckhorn	Merlot	South	$148	325	$48
	16	1991	Q1	Duckhorn	Merlot	West	$148	275	$40
	17	1991	Q1	Duckhorn	Merlot	North	$148	200	$29
	18	1991	Q1	Duckhorn	Merlot	East	$148	480	$71
	19	1991	Q1	Du			$148	660	$97
	20	1991	Q1	Du			$148	289	$42
	21	1991	Q1	Du			$148	2229	$329
	22	1991	Q1	Total				6029	$948
	35	1991	Q2	Beaulieu			$163	3965	$645
	42	1991	Q2	Duckhorn			$148	2243	$331
	43	1991	Q2	Total				6208	$977
	56	1991	Q3	Beaulieu			$163	4115	$669
	63	1991	Q3	Duckhorn			$148	2268	$335
	64	1991	Q3	Total				6383	$1,005
	77	1991	Q4	Beaulieu			$163	4360	$709
	84	1991	Q4	Duckhorn			$148	2320	$343
	85	1991	Q4	Total				6680	$1,052

(Outlining Tools window shown over the sheet; title bar: D:\Work\WP 9 Bible\Notebooks\Outline.qpw [unmodified])

Figure 35-12: Click the + and – buttons to expand or collapse details. Your outlined data prints as it appears onscreen.

3. Click the level numbers at the top of the control panel to display or collapse the entire outline to various levels.

Copying outlined data

New Feature

When you copy and paste outlined data with collapsed levels or details, only the records on view are copied.

Editing an outline

To add or remove outline groups:

1. Click Tools ➪ Outline ➪ Show Outline Toolbar, and then click the Outline Show button to display the outline panels.

2. Do any of the following:

- To add an outline group, select the data, including summary text and formulas, and then click the Outline Add Group button (see Figure 35-13).

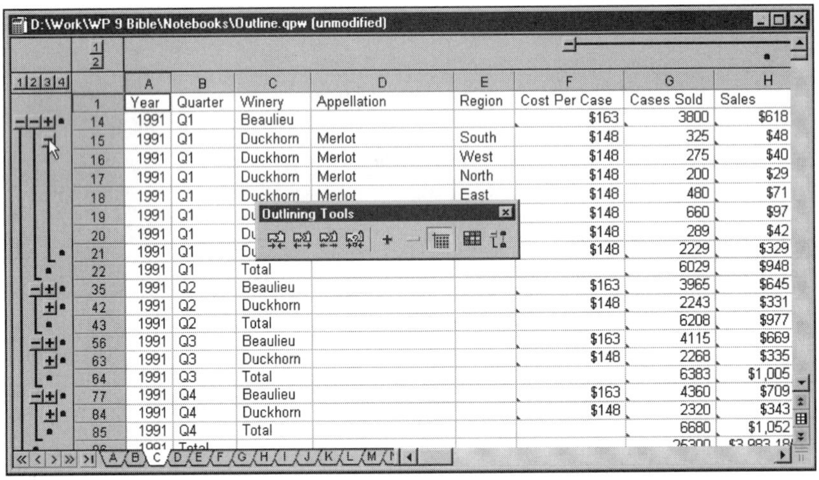

Figure 35-13: Adding an outline group.

- To ungroup selected cells, click the Outline Ungroup button.
- To remove all the outline groups, click the Outline Remove Groups button.
- To automatically create an outline from selected cells, click the Outline Create Outline button.
- To apply a predefined format to selected outline cells, click the Speed Format button.
- To position an outline's summary cells, click the Outline Position Summary button.

Arranging Data with Cross-Tabs Reports

You can quickly create a *cross-tabs report* of your data, with fields displayed in a variety of ways.

To follow the examples used here, use a copy of the Wines notebook found in the Samples folder. This notebook shows two vineyards' quarterly sales of various wines to different regions. You can use any other 2-D or 3-D table, as long as it conforms to the database block standards described in "Setting up a database," earlier in this chapter. You can place report items in any order, and then experiment with different arrangements.

To create a cross tabs report of the data in your current sheet:

1. Select the block of data for your report.

2. Click Tools ⇨ Data Tools ⇨ Cross Tabs ⇨ Report.

3. Quattro Pro selects the source data (see Figure 35-14), which you can change, if necessary.

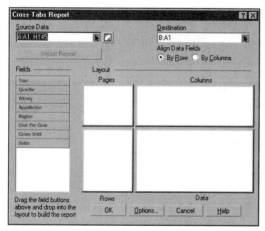

Figure 35-14: Creating a cross-tabs report.

4. The report destination defaults to the upper-left cell of the first blank sheet. (If you specify a sheet that isn't blank, leave enough room for the report.)

5. Drag the fields that you want to summarize to the layout. To report the total number of cases sold for each winery by year, drag the Year field to Columns, the Winery field to Rows, and the Cases Sold field to Data (see Figure 35-15).

6. Double-click a field to change its summary type, or to add another summary (see Figure 35-16). For example, you can display the average number of cases sold as well as the total number of cases. You can also opt to hide field items (such as data for a specific year) or compare data with other fields. (Don't add another summary for this exercise.)

7. To add a dimension to your report, such as cases sold by Appellation, drag a field to the Pages section (see Figure 35-17).

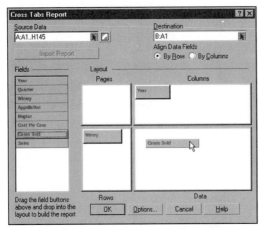

Figure 35-15: Assigning fields to the label and data areas.

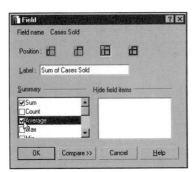

Figure 35-16: Changing the type of value for an area.

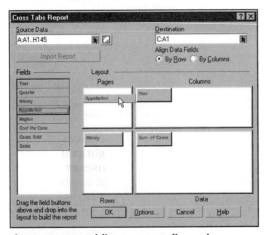

Figure 35-17: Adding a report dimension.

8. Click Options to customize your report (see Figure 35-18). Name your report, add row and column summaries, choose to update data or not, choose an entry for empty cells, and choose to apply formatting or keep the original formatting.

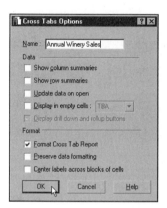

Figure 35-18: Customizing your report.

9. Click OK to generate your report (see Figure 35-19). To change the report properties, click the report, and then click Tools ➪ Data Tools ➪ Cross Tabs and pick the appropriate option.

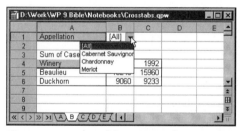

Figure 35-19: Resulting cross-tab summary. (Note the Appellation dimension.)

Predicting Results with Scenarios

You can create *scenarios* (models of real situations and choices) to show how the results change as your data or formulas change. You might examine a worst-case scenario (what happens to the town budget if a plant closes or there's a cold winter with a lot of snow) or a best-case scenario (a mild winter or interest rates fall). Often, scenarios are used to find the optimum possible outcome.

Creating scenarios is a two-step process in which you

✦ Set up the baseline data and formulas.

✦ Record the results of changing values.

Tip
Try Model Copy if you just need to run a quick test of substitute values (see Chapter 33).

Setting up baseline data and formulas

To set up your scenario, create a baseline model with data and formulas that includes *changing cells* that you vary with each scenario.

For example, when buying a car, you may find several fine specimens from which to choose. Some are new, some are used, and the loan terms vary.

Instead of deciding on gut feelings or the color of the paint, you're going to use an *auto loan calculator* like that shown in Figure 35-20 to determine how big your monthly payments will be.

	D:\Work\WP 9 Bible\Notebooks\Autoloan.qpw (unmodified)				
	A B	C	D	E	F
1					
2	**Auto Loan Calculator**				
3					
4	Annual Rate	Monthly Payment		Loan Amount	$10,000
5	6.75%	$238.30			
6	7.00%	$239.46		Months	48
7	7.25%	$240.62			
8	7.50%	$241.79			
9	7.75%	$242.96			
10	8.00%	$244.13			
11					
12					

Figure 35-20: Auto Loan Calculator for your scenarios.

So, fasten your seat belt, open a notebook, and set up your Auto Loan Calculator:

1. Type **Annual Rate** in cell B4, **Monthly Payment** in cell C4, **Loan Amount** in cell E4, and **Months** in cell E6.

2. In cells B5..B10 type the interest rates shown in Figure 35-20 (or whatever interest rates your lender is offering). Type either the percent (**6.75%**) or decimal equivalent (**.0625**). (Type the first two rates, and then select the block and click the QuickFill button.)

3. In cell F4, type the baseline loan amount, such as **$10,000**. In cell F6, type the baseline number of periods, such as **48** for a four-year loan.

4. In cell C5, type the formula **@PMT(F$4,B5/12,F$6)**. This formula calculates monthly payments based on the loan amount, monthly interest rate (B5/12), and the number of months. (The "$" before the Loan Amount in F4 and Months in F6 keeps their row references fixed when the formula is copied down the rows.)

5. To copy the payment formula down, select cells C5..C10, and click the QuickFill button. Click Format ⇨ Selection ⇨ Numeric Format and set the format to currency.

Headings and formatting are optional. Save your notebook when you're finished (Ctrl+S).

Recording the results of your changes

Now that you have your baseline data and formulas, you can use the Scenario Expert to find out what happens as you change their values:

1. Click Tools ⇨ Scenario ⇨ New, specify the changing cells (**F4,F6** in our example), and then click Next (see Figure 35-21). (Hold down the Ctrl key to select multiple cells.)

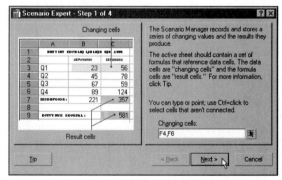

Figure 35-21: Specifying the changing cells for your scenario.

2. Give your first, *base scenario* a descriptive name such as "$10K, 48 months," type a new value in one or more of the changing cells, and then click Add Scenario (see Figure 35-22).

3. Repeat Step 2 until you've defined all the scenarios you want, and then click Next. Table 35-2 provides names and values for this example.

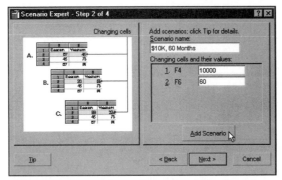

Figure 35-22: Specifying the name and values for each scenario.

Table 35-2 Scenario Names and Values for This Example		
Scenario Name	**F4 Value**	**F6 Value**
$10K, 60 months	10000	60
$15K, 48 months	15000	48
$15K, 60 months	15000	60
$20K, 48 months	20000	48
$20K, 60 months	20000	60

4. Drag the Scenario Expert out of the way of your model, click the various scenarios in the list, and click Show Scenario to display the changing values (in yellow) and new results (in green). The Show Scenario button changes to Undo Show (see Figure 35-23).

5. You can delete any scenarios you don't find useful, or retrace your steps to create new scenarios. Click Undo Show to restore the spreadsheet to its baseline data.

6. Click Next, and then click Exit to leave the Scenario Expert immediately, or click Create Report to generate a summary report for all the scenarios (see Figure 35-24).

Note   Each time you run the Scenario Expert, a new group of scenarios is defined (Group2, Group3, Group4, and so on). The expert's Scenario Summary Report shows the changing cells and the result cells for the current group of scenarios only. To create a report for all the groups of scenarios in the notebook, use the Scenario Manager, described next.

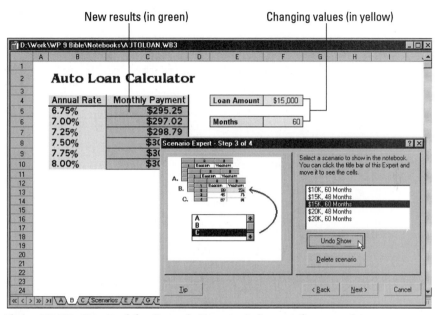

New results (in green)   Changing values (in yellow)

Figure 35-23: Step 3 of the Scenario Expert — trying out the scenarios.

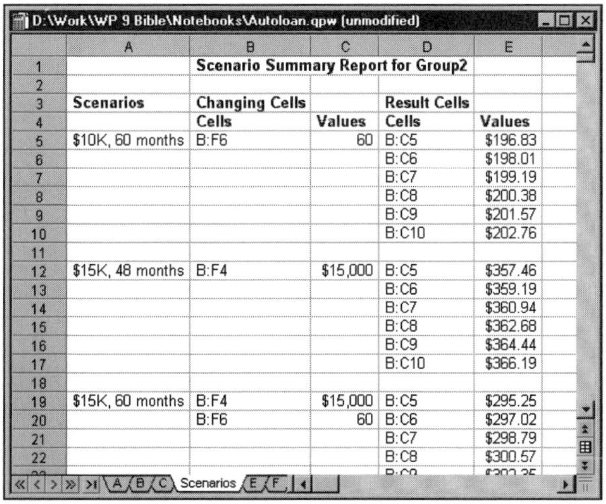

Figure 35-24: Summary report showing the results of all your scenarios.

Viewing and editing scenarios

To view or edit your scenarios:

1. Go to the sheet that contains your scenarios, click Tools ➪ Scenario ➪ Edit, and drag the Scenario Manager to a convenient location (see Figure 35-25).

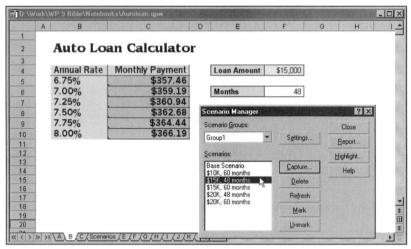

Figure 35-25: Viewing and editing scenarios with the Scenario Manager.

2. Select the group of scenarios you want from the Scenario Groups list.

3. Click a scenario to view its results, or to set any of the options described in Table 35-3.

Table 35-3	
Scenario Manager Options	
Click	**In Order to**
Capture	Create a baseline scenario for a new group, or take a new snapshot of an existing group.
Delete	Remove the selected scenario.
Refresh	Automatically identify change and result cells in the capture area from alterations to entries and formula results since the baseline capture.
Mark/Unmark	Highlight selected cells manually.
Report	Create a new Scenario Summary Report.
Highlight	Turn off highlighting or change the color of change and result cells.

4. Click Settings to change the group name or capture area, to delete the current group with all its scenarios, or to create a new group with its own baseline.

Tracking scenario versions

To use the Scenario Manager for version control of your capture area, click Settings in Step 4, and then uncheck "Adjust for cell movement." Your scenarios will now register all moves, insertions, and deletions. To register changes to shading, click the Highlight button and uncheck "Highlight changes to Base Scenario." Be sure to capture a final version before closing the notebook.

Solving for Goals

Your loan scenarios started with some existing numbers (loan amount, interest rates, and number of periods) in order to calculate a result (monthly payment). But suppose you have a desired monthly payment in mind and want to calculate the size of the loan you can take on, given a particular interest rate and number of periods. In that case, use the Solve For tool to start from a desired goal (resulting monthly payment) and work backward to the value of the input (loan amount) to achieve it.

Consider the loan calculator in Figure 35-26. It solves for the target monthly payment by using the formula **@PMT(Loan,Rate/12,Months)** in cell A6. The referenced variables are found in cells D5..D7. Solve For figures out the missing variable to achieve the target, as long as you give it the other two.

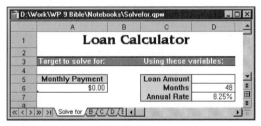

Figure 35-26: Loan Calculator you can use with Solve For.

To use Solve For, create your model spreadsheet with a formula whose target value you want to solve for, and specify any values the formula needs.

Tip   Name variable cells to make the process more intuitive.

You can leave the variable you're solving for blank. Next, follow these steps:

1. Click Tools ➪ Numeric Tools ➪ Solve For.

2. Specify the Solve For cells, target value, and options (see Figure 35-27) described in Table 35-4.

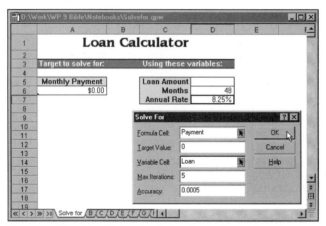

Figure 35-27: Specifying the Solve For cells, target value, and options.

Table 35-4
Solve For Cells, Target Value, and Options

Item	Lets You Specify
Formula Cell	The cell with the formula you're solving for
Target Value	The formula result you want to attain (or a cell containing the amount)
Variable Cell	The cell that's changed to arrive at the target
Max Iterations	The number of successive approximations (1 to 1,000) Solve For can make to arrive at the target (the default is 5)
Accuracy	How close Solve For must come to the desired target before it stops (the default is 0.0005)

The example shown solves for the loan amount (D5) that results in a target monthly payment of $400 when number of months and annual rate are given. The results are inserted in your model (see Figure 35-28), or an error message appears if the equation can't be solved.

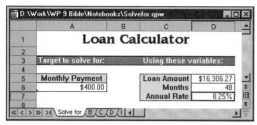

Figure 35-28: Solve For's calculation of the amount of an 8.25% loan that requires 48 $400 monthly payments.

Finding the Optimum Solution

Solve For substitutes values in a single formula to meet a goal. You can use the Optimizer instead if you need to (1) evaluate more than one formula, (2) find a minimum or maximum solution instead of an exact target, (3) find values that satisfy specified limits (or constraints), or (4) solve sets of linear and nonlinear equations and inequalities.

To find an optimum solution:

1. Click Tools ➪ Numeric Tools ➪ Optimizer.

2. Specify the Solution Cell and the target value you're aiming for (see Figure 35-29).

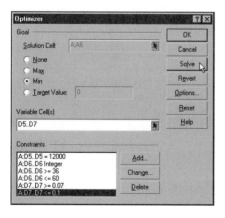

Figure 35-29: Using Optimizer.

3. Specify the cell or cells that can be varied to achieve the target.

4. Add any constraints to particular variables.

5. Click Options to specify various modeling, reporting, limit, estimate, search, and other options. See online Help for more details.

Exploring Possibilities

Instead of following scenarios one-by-one, you can lay out a whole range of possibilities at once by creating *what-if tables* of variables (also called *sensitivity tables*). You can create two types of what-if tables:

✦ A table of one variable that's used in one or more formulas

✦ A table of two variables, which can be used in only one formula

Suppose you're getting a short-term loan for your business, and the bank wants to know the present value of your projected cash flow (@NPV). You might have a range of possibilities, for both the cash flow estimate and the interest rate at which it is discounted. By creating a two-variable what-if table, you can explore their effect on the present value:

1. Set up your table of substitute values (see Figure 35-30), with one set of values in a column (projected cash flow in A4..A9), and the other set of values in a row (possible interest rates in B3..E3).

C:\Work\WP 9 Bible\Notebooks\What-If.qpw (unmodified)				
	A	B	C	D	E
1	Present Value of Projected Cash Flow				
2					
3	0	6.00%	6.50%	7.00%	7.50%
4	$100,000				
5	$110,000				
6	$120,000				
7	$130,000				
8	$140,000				
9	$150,000				
10					

Figure 35-30: Two-variable what-if table for projected cash flow and interest rates.

2. Set up the formula (in cell A3) of **@NPV(B2,C2)**, referring to two blank input cells (B2 for the discount rate; C2 for the cash flow).

3. Click Tools ➪ Numeric Tools ➪ What-If.

4. Check Two Free Variables to indicate the type of table to build (see Figure 35-31).

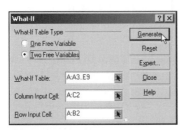

Figure 35-31: Defining the what-if table.

5. Specify the table cells (A3..E9) containing the formula and substitution values.

6. Specify the blank Input Cells referenced by the formula (C2 for the cash flow column, and B2 for the rate row).

7. Click Generate to apply the formula to the various row-column combinations in the table (see Figure 35-32).

	A	B	C	D	E
	C:\Work\WP 9 Bible\Notebooks\What-If.qpw				
1	Present Value of Projected Cash Flow				
2					
3	0	6.00%	6.50%	7.00%	7.50%
4	$100,000	$94,340	$93,897	$93,458	$93,023
5	$110,000	$103,774	$103,286	$102,804	$102,326
6	$120,000	$113,208	$112,676	$112,150	$111,628
7	$130,000	$122,642	$122,066	$121,495	$120,930
8	$140,000	$132,075	$131,455	$130,841	$130,233
9	$150,000	$141,509	$140,845	$140,187	$139,535
10					

Figure 35-32: Resulting what-if table with the formula applied to various row-column combinations.

Another example of a two-variable what-if situation might be calculating the cost of driving various distances when gas costs varying amounts per gallon, and the car's miles per gallon is fixed.

A one-variable what-if example might be calculating total price, given various unit prices and variable number of units sold. Refer to the online Help for how to handle one-variable situations.

Consolidating Data

The Consolidator makes it a cinch to combine two or more blocks of data into a single destination block, using a choice of statistical operations. Normally, you'd combine blocks with the same dimensions, although the example here uses the unequal-sized blocks shown in Figure 35-33.

Tip   Use the Consolidator within the Scenario Manager to take before and after snapshots of your source and destination blocks.

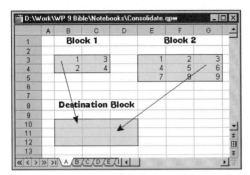

Figure 35-33: Consolidating two blocks of data.

To consolidate blocks:

1. Click Tools ➪ Consolidate ➪ New, and then select the source cells and click Add for each block you want to consolidate (see Figure 35-34). Hold down the Ctrl key to select both blocks at once.

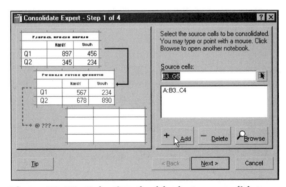

Figure 35-34: Selecting the blocks to consolidate.

2. Click Next and select the operator to use in combining source cells (see Figure 35-35).

3. Click Next and specify the Destination Block (only the top-left cell need be specified for a rectangular destination block). Check the "Top row" or "Left column" label options if your blocks contain labels that you want to use in matching cells during the consolidation process.

4. Click Next and give your consolidation a name, and then click Consolidate to generate your results (see Figure 35-36).

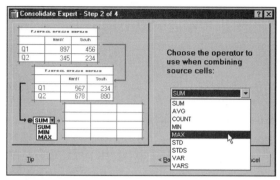

Figure 35-35: Selecting a consolidation operator.

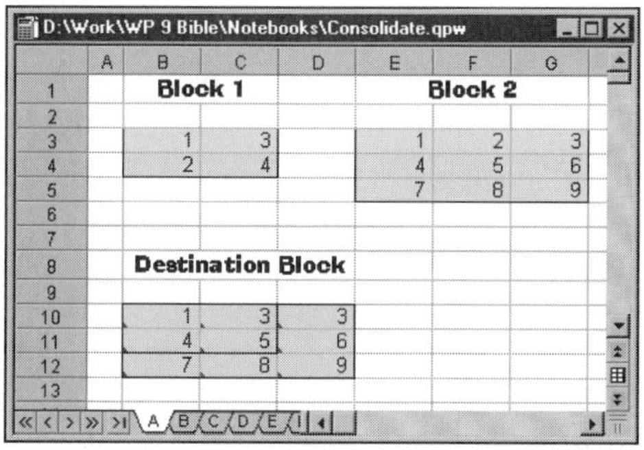

Figure 35-36: Resulting consolidation using the MAX operator. Note how matching begins at the upper left, and the largest of each matched pair of cells is output.

To modify your consolidation, click Tools ➪ Consolidate ➪ Edit.

Creating a Frequency Distribution

Create a *frequency distribution table* to count how many values in a block fall within given value intervals (bins). The example in Figure 35-37 counts the number of times certain job categories fall into specified earnings ranges.

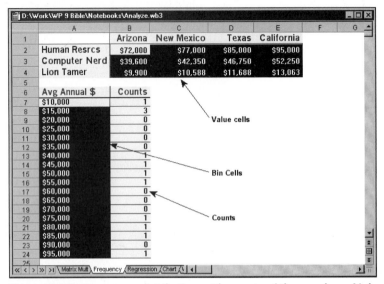

Figure 35-37: Frequency distribution with counts of the number of job categories that fall into specified earnings ranges.

To create a frequency distribution table:

1. Set up a column bin of ascending values to set the range boundaries, with a blank column to the right to store the counts.

2. Click Tools ⇨ Numeric Tools ⇨ Frequency.

3. Specify the Value Cells (the cells you're counting) and the Bin Cells (see Figure 35-38). Separate multiple blocks with commas (,).

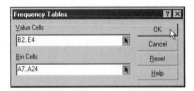

Figure 35-38: Creating a frequency distribution.

4. Click OK to count how many values fall within each range.

If you change any of the value cells, you'll need to recompute the frequency distribution.

Performing a Linear Regression

Another common statistical operation is the *linear regression,* to show how one set of *dependent variables* is affected by one or more sets of *independent variables.* For example, you may have data on the number of ads placed versus weekly sales, as shown in Figure 35-39.

D:\Work\WP 9 Bible\Notebooks\Analyze.qpw (unmodified)

	A	B	C	D	E
1	Number of Ads vs. Weekly Sales				
2					
3	Week	Ads	Sales		
4	1	42	3745		
5	2	77	4278		
6	3	34	3892		
7	4	23	3346		
8	5	67	4182		
9	6	11	3811		
10	7	45	4723		
11	8	32	3689		
12	9	71	3397		
13	10	33	3422		
14	11	27	3155		

Regression / Chart

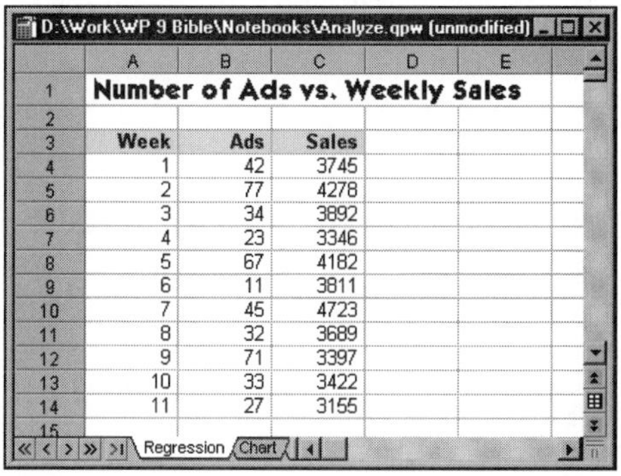

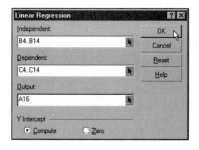

Figure 35-39: Data for a linear regression.

Your job is to perform a regression to see the effect of ads (the independent variable) on sales (the dependent variable):

1. Click Tools ➪ Numeric Tools ➪ Regression.
2. Specify the columns of independent and dependent variables, and the upper-left cell for your output (see Figure 35-40).

Figure 35-40: Performing a linear regression.

3. Select whether to compute the Y-intercept, or force it to zero.

Using the Matrix Tools

Use the matrix tools to perform operations on rectangular arrays of numbers:

✦ *Multiply* the elements of one matrix by the elements of another. For example, you may want to compute the costs of various fixed-time jobs using workers in different hourly rate categories (see Figure 35-41).

✦ *Invert* the numbers (the first step in solving sets of linear equations).

✦ *Transpose* columns and rows in copying the matrix.

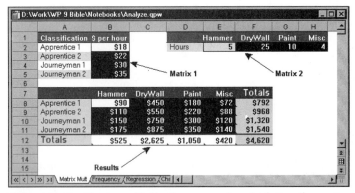

Figure 35-41: Matrix multiplication example calculating the costs of assigning workers in various hourly pay categories to specific fixed-time jobs.

To multiply matrices:

1. Click Tools ➪ Numeric Tools ➪ Multiply.

2. Specify the two matrices, and the upper-left destination cell (see Figure 35-42). Note that the row and column headers are not included in the coordinates of the matrices.

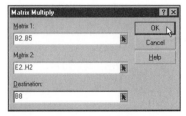

Figure 35-42: Multiplying matrices.

Tracking Down Analytical Errors

Auditing tools help you to track down analytical errors by visually connecting data and formulas. You can trace both *precedents* (all cells that provide data to a formula cell), and *dependents* (all formulas that use data from a particular cell):

1. Click Tools ➪ Auditing ➪ Show Auditing Toolbar.

2. To show cells that provide data to a formula, click the formula cell, and then click the Audit Precedents button (see Figure 35-43). Click the link buttons to be carried back and forth between formulas and data.

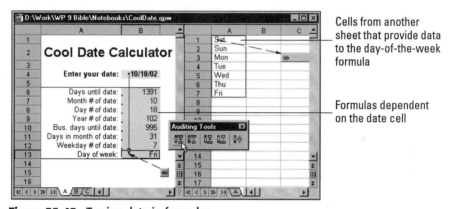

Figure 35-43: Tracing data in formulas.

3. To show all formulas that use data from a particular cell, click the data cell, and then click the Audit Dependents button.

4. If you have multilevel precedents or dependencies (such as when a formula cell is used by other formulas), click the buttons multiple times to trace back through the levels.

5. Click the buttons with upside-down pencils to erase the precedent or dependent arrows, or click the Audit Erase button to erase all the arrows.

For More Information . . .

On	See
Using built-in projects and templates	Chapter 29
Sorting information	Chapter 53
Importing and sharing information	Chapter 10
Specifying logical conditions	Chapter 32
Using Model Copy	Chapter 33
Creating a Paradox database	Chapters 43–46

✦   ✦   ✦

Creating Charts, Maps, and Shows

No matter how great your data is, it's not of much use if
you don't get your point across. Chapter 34,
"Formatting Figures and Setting Up Notebooks," showed you
how to improve the format of your data; general charting
terms, types, and techniques are covered in Chapter 56,
"Charting Data." Here you'll learn how to use charts and maps
to interpret your data and convey your message. You'll even
learn how to create a slide show in Quattro Pro.

To Float or Not to Float

You can create a Quattro Pro chart or map either as a floating
object on the same sheet as your data or on a sheet by itself,
to print separately or to use as a slide. Either way, an icon for
each chart and map appears automatically on the Objects
sheet (the last sheet in the notebook).

Creating Charts

You can create a chart in Quattro Pro in three ways:

◆ Click Insert ➪ Chart, and then let the Chart Expert
prompt you through the steps.

◆ Select the data you want to chart, click the Chart button,
and then click or drag in the sheet to create the size of
chart you want. (Quattro Pro will pick a default type,
based on your data.)

◆ Right-click the cell in which you want the chart, click
New Custom Chart, and fill in the dialog box from
scratch.

You can easily change a chart's type and appearance, no matter which method you use. Changes to your data automatically update the chart.

Setting up your chart data

It's easier to create good-looking charts if you heed the following tips in setting up your data (see Figure 36-1):

✦ Don't leave any blank columns or rows.

✦ Type your chart labels in the top row and first column.

✦ To create multiple pie or column charts, place the legend labels in the first row, and the pie slice labels in the first column.

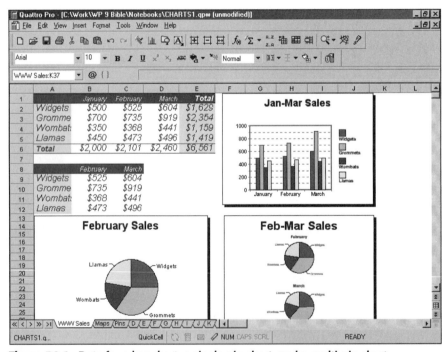

Figure 36-1: Data for a bar chart, a single pie chart, and a multi-pie chart.

Creating a chart

To create the charts from the data shown in Figure 36-1, use the Chart Expert:

1. Click Insert ➪ Chart, click the Block Select button, and select your chart data (see Figure 36-2). (Select A1..D5 for the bar chart, A9..B12 for the February Sales pie, or A8..C12 for the Feb–Mar Sales pies.)

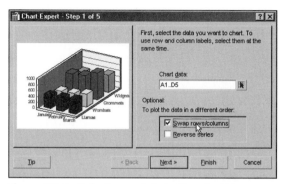

Figure 36-2: Select your data in Step 1 of the Chart Expert.

2. Check any data ordering options:

   • *Swap rows/columns,* to swap the x-axis and y-axis displays. (Check this option for the bar chart in the example, to put the months, with only three labels, on the x-axis.)

   • *Reverse series,* to reverse the order of the series. For example, you may want to move taller items to the back in a 3-D chart.

3. Click Next to select the general chart type, and then click Next to pick a specific chart type (see Figure 36-3).

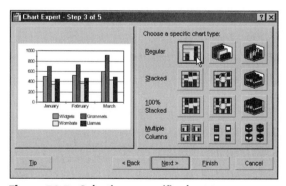

Figure 36-3: Selecting a specific chart type.

4. Click Next to specify the title, subtitle, and axis titles (see Figure 36-4). Click a destination of Current Sheet (the default) or Chart Window to create it as an object in the notebook's Objects sheet.

5. Click Next to pick a color scheme.

6. Click Finish. If you chose a destination of Current Sheet, click the cell for the chart's upper-left corner, or drag to define the chart's position and size.

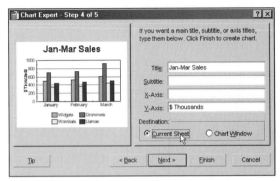

Figure 36-4: Adding chart titles and selecting the destination.

Cross-Reference   For more information on creating and editing data charts, see Chapter 56, "Charting Data."

Creating Analytical Series

Once you've created a data chart in Quattro Pro, you can perform various types of statistical analysis on a chart series, and graph the results without changing underlying data. You can also save a table of the analysis results.

For example, you can set up a column of the weekly sales figures for WorldWide Widget, chart the data, and then perform any of the types of analysis described in Table 36-1.

Table 36-1
Types of Analysis

Type	What It Does
Aggregation	Combines multiple data points into aggregate points (such as days to weeks or months) based on their sum, average, standard deviation, variance, minimum, or maximum
Moving average	Highlights trends by displaying a moving average of your fluctuating data
Linear Fit	Generates a straight line that best fits the trend of your data
Exponential Fit	Generates a best-fit curve for data that increases or decreases geometrically

To include your regular data, along with as many types of analysis as you want, use the same data for more than one series (see Figure 36-5).

Figure 36-5: Chart showing weekly sales plus a moving average analytical series for the same data.

Analytical series usually work best as line displays.

To create an analytical series:

1. Click Insert ⇨ Chart and follow the steps to create a line chart.

2. Right-click the series you want to analyze (such as weekly sales for the quarter), click Line or Bar Series Properties, click Analyze, and then select the method you want to use and specify the particular options (see Figure 36-6).

Figure 36-6: Creating an analytical series.

3. To chart the same data in another way, click Chart ⇨ Series, and specify the same data for another series.

4. To change the appearance of the raw data from a line to a bar display, right-click the series, click Line Series Properties, click Series Options, and then select Bar as the Override Type (see Figure 36-7).

Figure 36-7: Overriding the appearance of a line series.

Creating Bullet Charts

Bullet charts in Quattro Pro are nothing like their animated cousins in Presentations (see Chapter 41, "Mastering Presentations Techniques"), but they're useful for slide shows or just to get your point across. Your bullet chart has a title, an optional subtitle, and one or two levels of bulleted items. To create a bullet chart:

1. Type your title and the optional subtitle directly beneath it (see Figure 36-8).

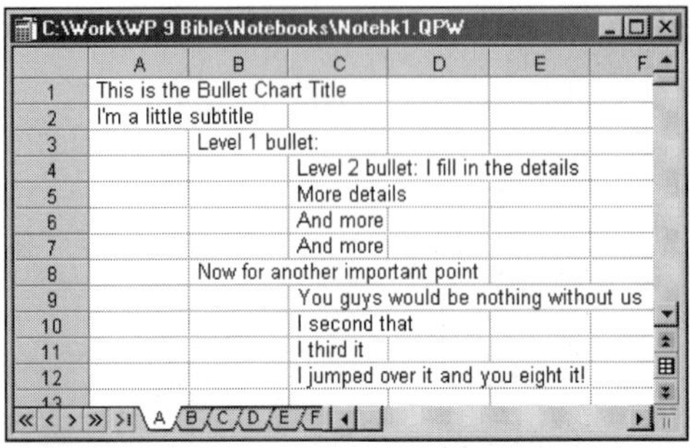

Figure 36-8: Creating a bullet chart.

2. Type your level-1 bulleted entries one column to the right, and level-2 items two columns to the right. Do not include blank rows between any of the rows of text.

3. Select all cells (A1..C12 in this example), right-click your selection, and click New Custom Chart ➪ OK to create your chart (see Figure 36-9). (Or click the Chart button and then click your sheet to insert the bullet chart in the current sheet.)

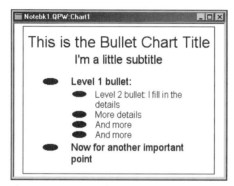

Figure 36-9: Resulting bullet chart.

Because your selection is all text, it's automatically recognized as a bullet chart, rather than a data chart.

To edit a bullet chart's text, edit the cells from which it was created.

To change the overall appearance of a bullet chart, click the chart, click Chart ➪ Gallery, and select the style you want (see Figure 36-10).

Figure 36-10: Selecting a bullet chart style from the Chart Gallery.

To customize your bullets, right-click a bullet for the level style you want to change, click Bullet Series Properties, and then change the bullet line spacing, text font, indentation, bullet style, and other properties (see Figure 36-11).

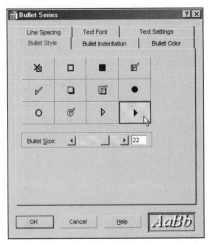

Figure 36-11: Customizing your bullets.

Creating a Slide Show

You can create bullet chart slide shows in Quattro Pro, and then enhance them with any other charts and maps in your notebook. To create a slide show:

1. Enter your text just as you would for a single bullet chart, leaving blank rows between your slides (see Figure 36-12).

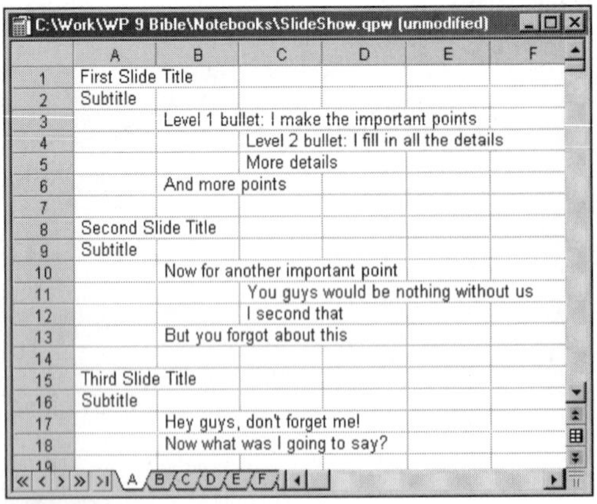

Figure 36-12: Text for a slide show.

2. Click Tools ➪ Slide Show ➪ New, and then select the cells with your slide show text (see Figure 36-13).

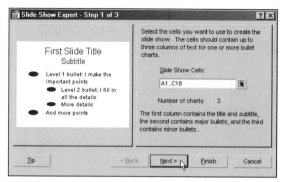

Figure 36-13: Selecting the cells with your slide text.

3. Click Next and select a layout from the Gallery.

4. Click Next and give your show a title, and then select a transition effect and click Finish (see Figure 36-14).

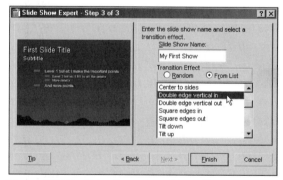

Figure 36-14: Selecting a transition effect.

Your slide shows are stored in the Objects sheet of the current notebook. To edit or play your slide show, click View ⇨ Objects (if you're not already in the Objects sheet), double-click the show's icon, and then select various options from the Slides menu (see Figure 36-15).

You can drag the slide thumbnails to rearrange them on the light table, and create slides from new or existing charts and maps. Click the Cell Properties button to change transition effects and other slide properties.

If you get seriously into slide shows, you'll probably want to use Corel Presentations instead of Quattro Pro.

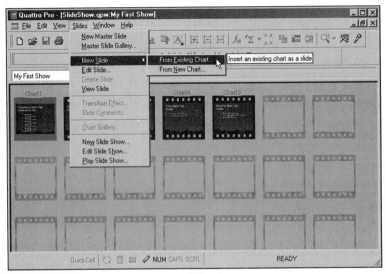

Figure 36-15: Editing or playing a slide show.

Creating Maps

When your data is geographic in content (such as the profits by state shown in Figure 36-16), presenting it in a map can provide a powerful visual impact.

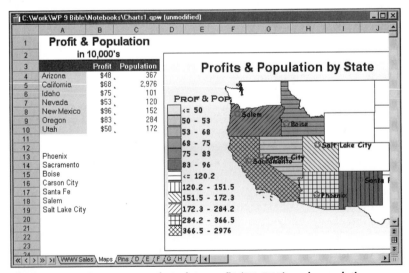

Figure 36-16: Custom map that plots profit (B4..B10) and population (C4..C10) in seven states (A4..A10).

The default map created depends on the data you select. Quattro Pro offers a host of maps and overlays for you to choose from.

Installing the map module

The mapping features take up about 8MB of disk space, so they aren't normally added to your system. To install the data maps, you'll need to perform a custom installation as described in Appendix A, "Setting Up WordPerfect Office 2000":

1. On the Windows taskbar, click Start ⇨ Programs ⇨ WordPerfect Office 2000 ⇨ Setup and Notes ⇨ Corel Setup Program .

2. Select Add New Components (Figure A-11), then follow the prompts and select the Data Maps.

Setting up your map data

To map your data, it must be associated with recognizable geographic divisions or cities. Creating maps is more automatic if you arrange your data in columns:

✦ Put region names (such as the country, state, or prefecture) in the first column.

Note   The names must be of the same type. For example, you can't have Mexico, California, and Canada, as you'd be mixing whole nations with parts.

✦ Put data you want to map as colors in the second column.

✦ Put data you want to map as patterns in the third column.

To create a map with patterns and no colors, leave the second column blank.

Using the mapping notebooks

You can map data from any source, as long as Quattro Pro can recognize the geographic entities. You'll also find some special notebooks in your maps folder (\PROGRAM FILES\COREL\WPO2000\ PROGRAMS\DATAMAPS) with population and statistical data (see Figure 36-17). You can select the data you need from one of these notebooks and then copy it to your working notebook for editing and mapping. (The sheets in these notebooks are write-protected, so you won't accidentally delete or alter the data.)

To use the special notebooks to set up some data for the exercises to follow:

1. Save a blank notebook to MAPDATA.QPW, or some such name.

2. Open the WORLD.QPW notebook and click the World 1 tab.

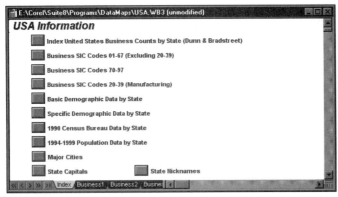

Figure 36-17: One of Quattro Pro's special notebooks, with handy data for your maps.

3. Select columns A, C, and D (holding down the Ctrl key as you do so) and then copy and paste them to sheet A of your test notebook. (You can use either the country name in column A or the abbreviation in column B.) You may now close the WORLD.QPW notebook if you wish.

4. Select some geographically related countries, such as the South American countries listed in Figure 36-18 (Peru deliberately misspelled), and copy their data (including the column labels) to sheet B of your test notebook. Delete any blank rows and columns, and double-click the border labels to size the columns to fit.

C:\Work\WP 9 Bible\Notebooks\MapData.qpw

SHORT_NAME	POPULATION	BIRTHRATE
Argentina	33,100	20.70
Bolivia	7,802	36.10
Brazil	150,794	26.20
Chile	13,600	23.40
Colombia	34,252	26.00
Ecuador	9,996	30.90
French Guiana	105	27.90
Guyana	805	25.40
Paraguay	4,519	33.90
Puru	22,454	31.00
Surinam	437	26.30
Uruguay	3,131	18.30
Venezuela	18,883	29.90

Figure 36-18: Data copied from the WORLD. WB3 notebook.

Creating a map

To call on the Map Expert for step-by-step assistance once the data is set up:

1. Select the data you want to map, without the headings. (You don't have to preselect the data, but it makes the process more automatic.)

2. Click Insert ⇨ Graphics ⇨ Map.

3. Select the map that matches your data, if necessary (see Figure 36-19).

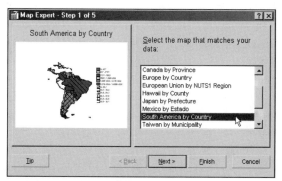

Figure 36-19: Selecting the map.

4. Click Next, and select the Region Names, Color Data, and Pattern Data, if necessary (see Figure 36-20).

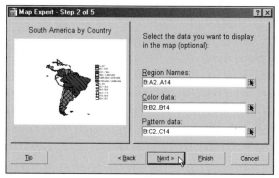

Figure 36-20: Selecting your map data.

5. Click Next and select a color scheme for your map.

6. Click Next and specify any overlays or cities, as explained later in this chapter.

7. Click Next. You'll be prompted about any region names that can't be identified (see Figure 36-21).

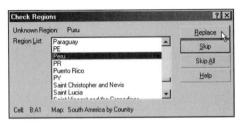

Figure 36-21: Specifyany region names that can't be identified.

8. Specify the title, subtitle, and axis titles (see Figure 36-22). Click a destination of Current Sheet (the default) or Map Window to create it as an object in the notebook's Objects sheet.

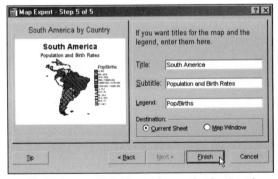

Figure 36-22: Adding map titles and selecting the destination.

9. Click Finish to create the map. If you chose a destination of Current Sheet, click the cell for the map's upper-left corner, or drag to define the map's position and size.

Unfortunately, you may find that the numbers in the map's legend are in scientific notation, making them difficult to decipher.

Editing a map

You can edit the map's data or appearance, just as you can for charts, as described in Chapter 56, "Charting Data." Click in the map to select it, and then do any of the following:

✦ To add or change the title, subtitle, or legend, right-click the map and click Titles.

✦ To change the font or appearance of a title, subtitle, or legend, double-click the item.

✦ To reposition the map or legend, click and drag the item (see Figure 36-23).

Figure 36-23: Repositioning a map.

✦ To change the background or fill (or convert it to a slide show button), click Chart ⇨ Background.

✦ To change the data blocks or overlays, right-click the chart and click Data.

Setting the redraw mode

Unless you have fast graphics, you may not want to redraw your chart after every change to your data. To set the Redraw mode:

1. Click the map, right-click the region, click Map Properties, and then click the Redraw Options tab.

2. Click Automatic to redraw the map with every change to your data, or click Manual to update the chart only when you click the Redraw button (see Figure 36-24).

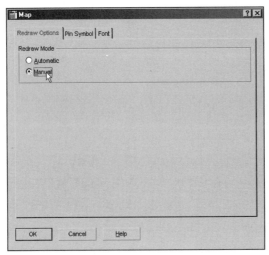

Figure 36-24: Setting the Redraw mode.

Zooming a map

To zoom a map, click in the map to select it, and then right-click the map and select from the following:

✦ *Zoom In,* to double the magnification

✦ *Zoom Out,* to halve the magnification

✦ *Zoom to Normal,* to return the map to its original magnification

✦ *Center,* to make the point where you right-click the center of the map

Customizing a map

To customize a map's border, box type, and other features, right-click the map and click Map Properties (see Figure 36-25).

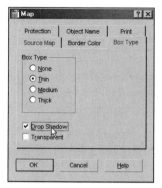

Figure 36-25: Customizing a map.

Overlaying a world grid or U.S. highway grid

To overlay the appropriate map with a world grid or with a U.S. highway grid:

1. Right-click the map, click Data ➪ Add Overlay ➪ Static.
2. Select the overlay you want (see Figure 36-26).

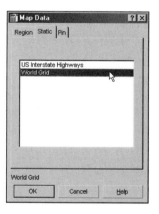

Figure 36-26: Overlaying the U.S. highway grid.

Adding other regions to a map

To extend a map to other regions, such as to append Canadian provinces to a map of the U.S.:

1. Right-click the map, click Data ➪ Add Overlay, and then select the overlay and click OK.
2. Specify the data blocks for the region names, colors, and patterns, and then click OK (see Figure 36-27).

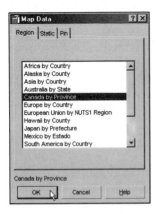

Figure 36-27: Adding another region to a map.

Adding cities to a map

Various mapping notebooks contain the names of capitals and other major cities, together with their latitude and longitude (see Figure 36-28).

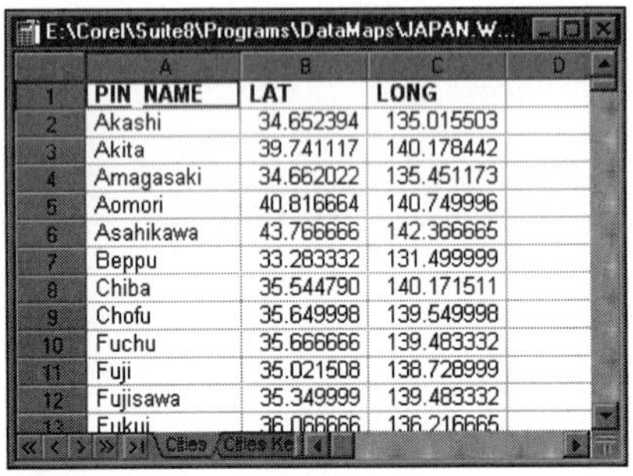

Figure 36-28: Major Japanese cities you can add to a map.

If your notebook contains the names of any of these cities, you can add them as pins (with optional text) to your map:

1. Right-click the map, and click Data ⇨ Add Overlay ⇨ Pin.

2. Select the category of cities and click OK.

3. Specify the data blocks and optional labels for your cities. Click "Use pin names as labels" to use the same names for your labels (see Figure 36-29).

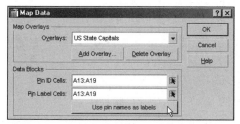

Figure 36-29: Adding cities to a map.

Customizing your pins

To change the color, symbol, or other properties for the pins in your map, click the map, then right-click the map and click Map Properties ⇨ Pin Symbol (see Figure 36-30).

Adding any location to a map

You can add any location to a map, such as a town, factory, or camp, as long as you identify its latitude and longitude. See online Help for more details.

Removing an overlay

To remove a geographic, world grid, U.S. highway, or pin overlay, right-click your map, click Data, select the overlay, and click Delete Overlay.

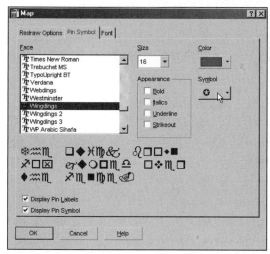

Figure 36-30: Customizing your pins.

For More Information . . .

On	See
Formatting data	Chapter 29
Charting terms and techniques	Chapter 56
Creating bullet charts in Presentations	Chapter 41
Copy, cut, and paste with the Clipboard	Chapter 2
Setting up your WordPerfect Office 2000	Appendix A
Printing charts and maps	Chapter 37

✦   ✦   ✦

CHAPTER 37

Printing Notebooks, Charts, and Maps

✦ ✦ ✦ ✦

In This Chapter

View and zoom pages

Customize your print page

Create headers and footers

Save and reuse your page settings

Preview before you print

Print your data

Print charts, maps, and slide shows

✦ ✦ ✦ ✦

While general printing for WordPerfect Office is covered in Chapter 13, "Printing and Faxing Information," Quattro Pro has particular features to select what to print and how you want the output to appear. This chapter also shows you how to set up your print page and preview before you print.

Setting Up the Print Page

Spreadsheets are designed to work with numbers, not to print them. Nevertheless, you can specify a number of options in setting up the printed page in Quattro Pro.

Viewing and zooming pages

Page setup is intuitive and visual in Page view (View ➪ Page), as shown in Figure 37-1. As noted in Chapter 34, "Formatting Figures and Setting Up Notebooks," you can

- ✦ Adjust margins by dragging the dotted guidelines
- ✦ Move hard page breaks by dragging the solid lines
- ✦ Right-click (or double-click) in the margins to set up the page
- ✦ Right-click in the margins to create headers and footers, and then double-click a header or footer to edit it (see Figure 37-1)

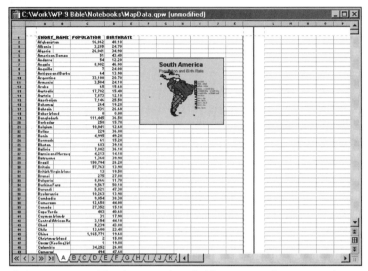

Figure 37-1: Working in Page view (with a zoom of 50 percent).

It also helps to zoom (View ➪ Zoom) to a smaller percentage when looking at your page setup.

Customizing your print page

To specify the page size, orientation, and other options for the printed page:

1. Click File ➪ Page Setup (or double-click in a margin in Page view).

2. Click the tabs to specify various options:

- *Paper Type* (see Figure 37-2), to select the size of the page you're printing on and its orientation: Portrait (vertical) or Landscape (horizontal).

- *Header/Footer,* to type the text that you want to appear at the top or bottom of each printed page. Also see "Editing headers and footers," later in this chapter.

- *Print Margins,* to change the measurements of the top, bottom, left, and right margins (see Figure 37-3). Type **in** for inches (as in 1.0 in) or **cm** for centimeters (as in 2.54 cm). Leave Break Pages checked unless you're printing multiple pages on a continuous form.

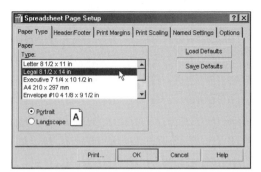

Figure 37-2: Selecting a page size and orientation.

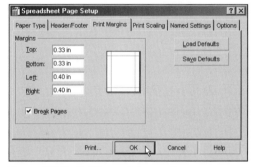

Figure 37-3: Setting print margins.

Note The breaks referred to are soft page breaks that automatically occur when you're printing more data than can fit on a single page. Removing the check will not affect any hard page breaks (Insert ⇨ Page Break ⇨ Create) that you've inserted to control your formatting.

- *Print Scaling,* to expand or shrink your text to a specified percentage of its normal size on the print page. You can also reduce the size of the printed spreadsheet to a desired number of pages in width and height (see Figure 37-4).

- *Named Settings,* to save the current sheet options and print settings as a named group to reuse later (see Figure 37-5). These are saved with the current notebook, and don't affect the Quattro Pro defaults (see "Saving and loading default settings," later in this chapter).

Tip Named settings are handy for printing notebooks with more than one report.

- *Options* (see Figure 37-6), to specify any of the print options described in Table 37-1.

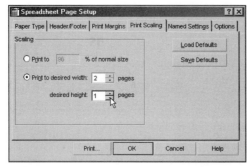

Figure 37-4: Scaling the size of your printed text.

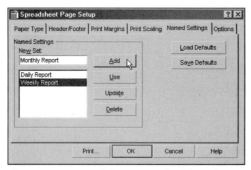

Figure 37-5: Specifying named settings for a particular notebook.

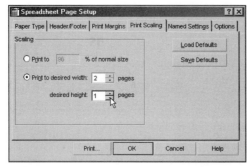

Figure 37-6: Specifying page setup print options.

Table 37-1
Page Setup Print Options

Option	Lets You
Headings for Selections	When printing selected cells, specify any cell in the row or column you want to use for a top or left heading on every page. (Don't include the heading row or column in your selection, or it will print twice on the first page.)
Print Between Selections/3D Sheets	Separate printed multiple blocks or notebook sheets with any number of blank lines, or with a page break (advance). You can also have multiple selections print in their actual relative positions (In Place), or with no blanks between them (Collapse Blanks).
Cell Formulas	Print each cell's address and contents (including formulas) instead of its calculated results.
Gridlines	Print the lines that appear on your screen.
Row/Column Borders	Print the borders that appear on your screen.
Center Cells	Print your selections midway between the left and right margins. (Don't select blank columns or they'll throw off the center.)

Saving and loading default settings

When setting up your printed page, you can click Save Defaults under any of the tabs to save your current settings as the default for all your notebooks. Be sure you want to do this. To save your current settings for the current notebook only, use the named settings instead.

Click Load Defaults to load the latest defaults you saved (not the factory settings).

Editing headers and footers

Page view provides an intuitive way to edit your headers and footers. Right-click in the appropriate margins to create headers or footers, and double-click a header or footer to edit it.

Header and footer text is enlarged as you enter it, so you can see what you're typing. You can change your font or insert symbols from the property bar. Click the Header Codes button to insert various codes for the notebook name, date, time, and page numbers (see Figure 37-7). Text after the first vertical bar (|) is centered; text after the second vertical bar is right-justified. Text after an "n" (#n) prints on the second line.

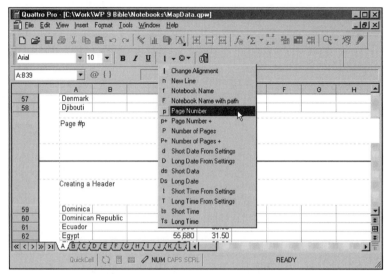

Figure 37-7: Editing headers and footers in Page view.

Previewing Before You Print

Click File ➪ Print Preview to see how your print job is going to come out (see Figure 37-8). You might end up saving a tree or two.

Tip   To print part of the current sheet, or a chart, select it before you preview.

Click the various preview buttons to scroll your pages, zoom your display, or toggle between color and black and white. You can't edit in print preview, but you can change your page setup.

When you print from the preview, the information displayed is immediately printed, using the latest print settings for the number of copies, and so on. Click the End Preview button or press Esc to exit the preview without printing.

Printing Data

Compared to all the page setup options you have, printing is a pretty straightforward affair. To print data:

1. Click the sheet you want to print, or select whatever data, charts, and so on you want to print.

2. Click the print icon. (You can also press Ctrl+P, or click File ➪ Print.)

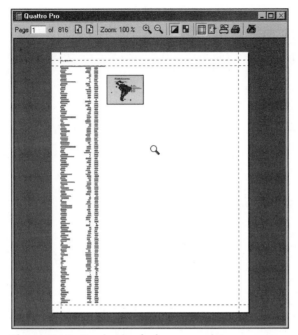

Figure 37-8: Previewing before you print.

3. Specify what you want to print, the number of copies, and other options (see Figure 37-9). (You can also go to Page Setup or Print Preview.)

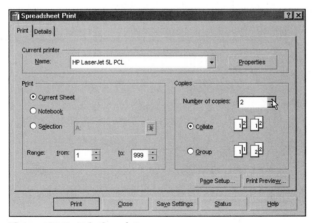

Figure 37-9: Printing data.

4. Click Print.

When you print a sheet, Quattro Pro knows to print only the active area with data, not a million blank columns and rows (although it does print blank rows or columns within the active area). If the active area is bigger than the printed page, Quattro Pro fits as many columns as possible across the page and prints all the rows in those columns. It then prints the next group of columns, and so on, until all your data is printed. With some transparent tape and a bit of work, you can assemble the printed pages into one large display.

Caution   When printing a selection, don't select blank columns to the left or right, because they'll print too. And don't select by the row or column, or you'll print several blank pages.

When cell labels spill over into empty cells to the right, do extend the selection around those cells, so the labels aren't truncated.

Printing a Chart, Map, or Slide Show

To print a chart, map, or slide show, click the Jump to Objects Sheet button to go to the Objects sheet, and then click the item's icon. To select multiple objects, hold down the Shift key as you click the icons. You can also print a selected chart or map from any sheet.

For More Information . . .

On	See
Basic printing	Chapter 13
Creating custom print settings	Chapter 13
Formatting data	Chapter 34
Printing to a file	Chapter 13
Controlling your print jobs	Chapter 13

✦   ✦   ✦

Automating with Macros and QuickButtons

Suppose you have a series of keystrokes or commands that you perform over and over again. Maybe you need to type your name, address, e-mail address, Web page address, and favorite animal. Or, perhaps you must regularly review a daily or weekly report. Thanks to macros and buttons (such as those shown in Figure 38-1), you can make quick work of such repetitive tasks.

Quattro Pro's Two Types of Macros

Quattro Pro macros, like those in WordPerfect, make your life easier by playing back a series of commands or keystrokes. However, in Quattro Pro, macros come in two flavors:

✦ *Quattro Pro* macros, compatible with older (pre-7) versions of the program, that are stored and edited as notebook labels

✦ *PerfectScript* macros, like those in WordPerfect and Presentations, that are stored and edited as WordPerfect documents

Quattro Pro macros are stored in any notebook, or in a shared macro library (dedicated notebook) for all to use. PerfectScript macros are stored in a designated folder.

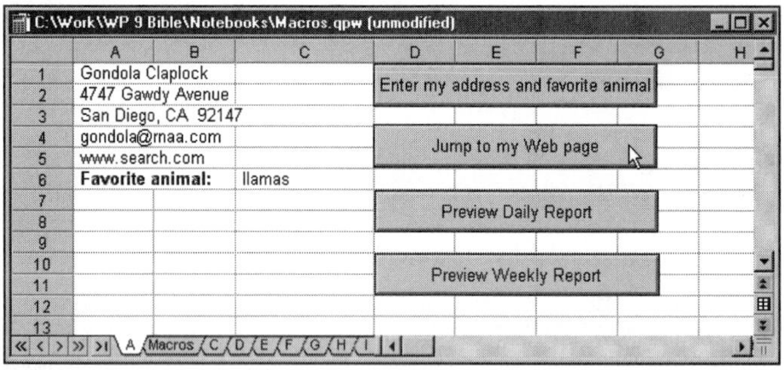

Figure 38-1: Automate your notebooks with macros and buttons.

Compare the Quattro Pro recorded macro shown in Figure 38-2 with the PerfectScript recorded macro shown in Figure 38-3. Notice that the macros are similar, though each one uses slightly different syntax (rules) for its commands.

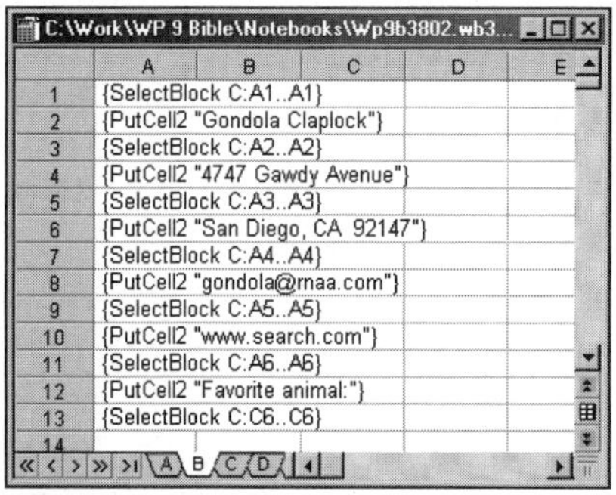

Figure 38-2: Quattro Pro macro.

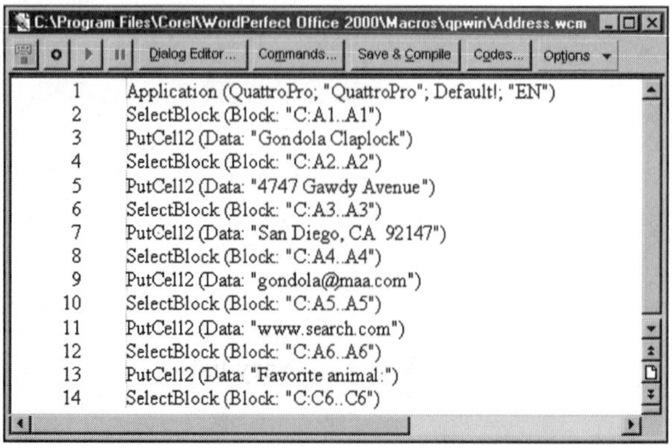

Figure 38-3: The same macro in PerfectScript.

When played back, both macros type the same text in the same location, as shown in Figure 38-4.

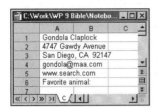

Figure 38-4: Playing either macro produces this result.

Which should you use? Each has its advantages. Quattro Pro macros can go in a notebook or button, and you can edit them right in Quattro Pro. PerfectScript macros can perform cross-application tasks. They also share a common syntax and use the WordPerfect Office superb macro-editing facilities.

This chapter provides a brief introduction to the Quattro Pro macro language. Chapter 58, "Automating with Macros," introduces the PerfectScript commands.

New Feature

You can also use Visual Basic for Applications (VBA) to build cross-product business solutions.

Creating Quattro Pro Macros

You can start by recording a simple macro. Later, you'll add some flexibility with typed commands, and assign the macro to a QuickButton like the one shown in Figure 38-1. Open a new notebook for this exercise.

Recording a Quattro Pro macro

To record a Quattro Pro macro:

1. Click Tools ➪ Macro ➪ Record, and click Quattro Pro Macro (see Figure 38-5).

2. Specify the location (cell address) where your macro commands should start (B:A1 for this example). (You can specify either a starting cell or a block. It's easiest to specify the starting cell in a blank sheet.)

3. To store the new macro in an open macro library instead of the current notebook, select the notebook from the Macro Library list. (See "Creating a Quattro Pro macro library," later in this chapter.)

4. To record over an existing macro, click the macro name in the Macros/Named Cells box. (See "Naming a Quattro Pro macro," later in this chapter.)

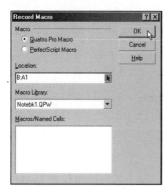

Figure 38-5: Recording a Quattro Pro macro.

5. Click OK. The recording icon appears on the application bar.

6. Perform the task as you normally would. For this exercise, do the following:

- Click cell A1 on sheet C.

- Type your name and press Enter.

- Type your street address and press Enter.

- Type your city, state, and zip code and press Enter.

- Type your e-mail address and press Enter.

- Type your favorite Web page address and press Enter.

- Type **Favorite animal:** and press the right-arrow twice.

7. Click Tools ⇨ Macro ⇨ Record to stop recording.

Click sheet B and note how Quattro Pro records the results of your keystrokes as macro commands, not the keystrokes themselves (such as the Enter or arrow keys).

Macro recording tips

Following are some tips to help you in recording a macro:

✦ To suspend recording at any time, click Tools ⇨ Macro ⇨ Pause (and do whatever you want). Click Tools ⇨ Macro ⇨ Pause again to resume recording.

✦ It doesn't matter how you access commands. You can click a menu or QuickMenu, click toolbar and property bar buttons, or press shortcut keys.

✦ If you notice a small typo after leaving a cell while recording your macro, continue recording and fix it later. If you make a big typo or record the wrong commands, stop recording, and then re-record the macro in the same location. (Your new macro commands will replace the old ones.)

✦ You can't record a command that pauses for user input. However, you can enter {GET}, {GETLABEL}, and {GETNUMBER} user-input commands manually.

Naming a Quattro Pro macro

It's handy to give the macro a name so that you can run it more easily:

1. Click the first cell of the macro.

2. Click Insert ➪ Name ➪ Cells.

3. Type a name for the macro in any of the following ways (see Figure 38-6):

   • To create a Ctrl+Shift keystroke macro, type a backslash (\) followed by a letter from A to Z. (For the macro in your exercise, type **\A** so that you can run the macro by pressing Ctrl+Shift+A.)

   • To assign an easy-to-remember name, type the name, such as **Address**.

   • To create a startup macro that runs automatically anytime you open the notebook, type **\0** (backslash zero) or **_nbstartmacro**. (When you open a notebook, Quattro Pro looks for a _nbstartmacro macro to play. If it doesn't find that, it looks for a \0 macro.)

   • To create an exit macro that runs just before you close the notebook, type **_nbexitmacro**.

Figure 38-6: Naming a Ctrl+Shift macro.

4. Click Add ➪ Close.

Give your new macro a whirl. Return to sheet C of your notebook, select cells A1..A6 and press Delete to clear the cells, and then press Ctrl+Shift+A to run the macro you named \A. Instantly, the macro types the name, address, and other information you recorded. Cool stuff!

Creating Quattro Pro macro libraries

Macro libraries are notebooks reserved for macros; you can access them from any notebook. Any time a macro library is open, you can play macros from it or add macros to it. To create a macro library:

1. Open or create and name a notebook to use as a library.

2. Create the macros you want to store in the notebook, or copy them from another notebook.

3. Click Format ➪ Notebook ➪ Macro Library ➪ Yes (see Figure 38-7).

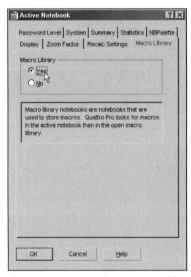

Figure 38-7: Creating a macro library.

Recording a PerfectScript Macro

Recording a PerfectScript macro is similar to recording a Quattro Pro macro. To record a PerfectScript macro:

1. Click Tools ➪ Macro ➪ Record ➪ PerfectScript Macro.

2. Give the macro a name (the .WCM macro extension is automatically added). You can also click the locate button at the right of the Filename text box to pick another location for your macro (see Figure 38-8).

3. Perform the tasks you would when recording a Quattro Pro macro.

4. To stop recording, click Tools ➪ Macro ➪ Record.

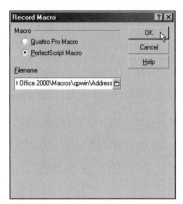

Figure 38-8: Naming a PerfectScript macro.

Quattro Pro Versus PerfectScript Macros

When you compare Quattro Pro and PerfectScript macros, you notice the following:

✦ Like Quattro Pro macros, PerfectScript macros record only the logical results of your keystrokes and commands.

✦ The command syntax, as noted earlier, is not the same.

✦ PerfectScript macros are stored in .WCM macro files that you can edit in WordPerfect, instead of in a Quattro Pro notebook.

✦ Unlike Quattro Pro macros, PerfectScript macros have no shortcut names in Quattro Pro for running keystroke, startup, or exit macros.

✦ You can play PerfectScript macros by name, in the folder in which they reside, much as you play a Quattro Pro macro from a library notebook.

Playing a Quattro Pro Macro

To play a Quattro Pro macro:

1. Click Tools ➪ Macro ➪ Play (Alt+F2) and click Quattro Pro Macro.

2. To play a macro in the current notebook, specify its location or select it by name (see Figure 38-9).

Figure 38-9: Playing a named macro in the current notebook.

3. To play a macro in an open macro library notebook, select the library from the list (see Figure 38-10), and then select the macro to play.

Figure 38-10: Selecting an open macro library notebook.

You can also play a Ctrl+Shift keystroke macro by pressing Ctrl+Shift+letter. Quattro Pro first looks for a macro in the current notebook, and then it searches any open macro library notebooks.

Tip To avoid confusion, it's best to have only one macro library notebook open at a time.

While the macro runs, the Macro icon appears on the property bar. Playback starts with the first cell in the macro block and continues down through the column until it finds an empty cell, a cell containing a numeric value, the {QUIT} or {RETURN} macro command, or an invalid macro entry.

Playing a PerfectScript Macro

To play a PerfectScript macro:

1. Click Tools ⇨ Macro ⇨ Play (Alt+F2) and click PerfectScript.

2. Type the macro name (the .WCM extension is assumed), or browse the folder to select the macro you want (see Figure 38-11).

Figure 38-11: Playing a PerfectScript macro.

Stopping Macro Playback

If you're quick, you can stop a Quattro Pro or PerfectScript macro while it's running. Just press Ctrl+Break (or click Tools ⇨ Macro ⇨ Play). Then, click OK or press Enter to return to Ready mode.

Editing Macros

It's easy to edit a macro, but be careful. If you type an invalid macro command, you'll get an error message similar to the one shown in Figure 38-12 when you play the macro.

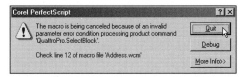

Figure 38-12: Error message explaining invalid macro command.

A full treatment of macro programming would require a book of its own, but it's helpful to know how to add nonrecordable commands that will make your macros more flexible.

Tip   Record commands wherever you can, to ensure proper syntax. You can cut and paste recorded commands with both Quattro Pro and PerfectScript macros (but not between them).

Editing a Quattro Pro macro

To edit a Quattro Pro macro, retype or edit the macro commands as spreadsheet text. Insert rows, if necessary, when adding commands. Delete rows to eliminate unwanted commands. Don't leave a blank cell (or a blank row) within the macro, as it will stop the playback.

Editing a PerfectScript macro

To edit a PerfectScript macro, start WordPerfect, click Tools ⇨ Macro ⇨ Edit, and select the macro. Edit the macro as you would any WordPerfect macro, as described in Chapter 58, "Automating with Macros."

You can also use the PerfectScript Macro Facility to edit PerfectScript macros (see Figure 38-13). Click Start on the taskbar, and then click WordPerfect Office 2000 ⇨ Utilities ⇨ Corel PerfectScript. From there, you can click the toolbar buttons to play, stop, pause, record, compile, edit, or debug a macro. You can edit macro dialogs, get help in using PerfectScript, and fill in macro commands with a command browser.

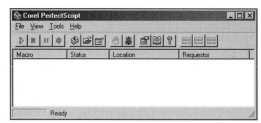

Figure 38-13: PerfectScript macro editor.

Typing macro commands

Return to the Quattro Pro macro you recorded earlier (refer to Figure 38-2). The {SelectBlock} commands select specific cells, and the {PutCell2} commands type data into the selected cells. This macro isn't very flexible because it always places text into specific cells on sheet C. To change the macro so that it inserts text at the current location:

1. Click sheet B (the sheet with your macro) and delete row 1 by selecting the row and clicking Edit ➪ Delete.

2. Click cell A1, click Insert ➪ Name ➪ Cells, select **\A**, and then click Add ➪ Close. This reestablishes the macro name as \A.

3. Click cell A2, type **{Down}**, and press Enter to replace the current contents. Do the same for cells A4, A6, A8, and A10. (Copy and paste to save time.) Your macro should now resemble the one shown in Figure 38-14.

	A	B	C	D
1	{PutCell2 "Gondola Claplock"}			
2	{Down}			
3	{PutCell2 "4747 Gawdy Avenue"}			
4	{Down}			
5	{PutCell2 "San Diego, CA 92147"}			
6	{Down}			
7	{PutCell2 "gondola@rnaa.com"}			
8	{Down}			
9	{PutCell2 "www.search.com"}			
10	{Down}			
11	{PutCell2 "Favorite animal:"}			
12	{SelectBlock C:C6..C6}			

Figure 38-14: Macro with lines 1–10 edited to type text at the current location.

Recording commands within a macro

Now suppose you want to put "Favorite animal:" in bold type. You can type the bold command if you know it, or you can let Quattro Pro fill in the command from your keystrokes:

1. Click cell A12 (your recording will overwrite its contents).

2. Click Tools ➪ Macro ➪ Record ➪ Quattro Pro Macro. Leave the location set to B:A12 and click OK.

3. Click the Bold button to insert {Setproperty "Font.Bold";Yes} into cell A12. As a side-effect, cell A12 is set to bold.

4. Click the Bold button again to insert {Setproperty "Font.Bold";No} in cell A13 and turn off the unwanted boldface in cell A12. (You'll replace this "Bold off" command in a moment.)

5. Click Tools ➪ Macro ➪ Record to stop recording.

6. To move the selector two cells to the right of "Favorite animal:" during playback, click cell A13 (with the unwanted "Bold off" command), and then type {Right 2} and press Enter.

Recording relative addresses

Normally, the commands you record refer to absolute addresses, such as A:A1. No matter where you play your macro from, it will always go to that address when it plays.

To record relative addresses instead of absolute addresses (in order to have the macro play at an offset from the current address):

1. Click Tools ➪ Macro ➪ Options.

2. Click Relative (see Figure 38-15).

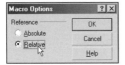

Figure 38-15: Specifying relative addresses for your macro recordings.

Now the addresses in your macro will look something like {SelectBlock C(-4)R(-10).. C(-4)R(-10)}, telling the macro to execute the command starting four columns to the left and ten rows up from the current location.

Typing a nonrecordable command

You now need to add a command that prompts for user input (the animal name). This is a nonrecordable command, so click cell A14 and type the following:

```
{GETLABEL "Enter the name of your favorite animal:",
@CELLPOINTER("address")}
```

Your completed macro should resemble the one shown in Figure 38-16. Save your work (File ➪ Save).

	A	B	C	D	E	F	G	H
1	{PutCell2 "Gondola Claplock"}							
2	{Down}							
3	{PutCell2 "4747 Gawdy Avenue"}							
4	{Down}							
5	{PutCell2 "San Diego, CA 92147"}							
6	{Down}							
7	{PutCell2 "gondola@rnaa.com"}							
8	{Down}							
9	{PutCell2 "www.search.com"}							
10	{Down}							
11	{PutCell2 "Favorite animal:"}							
12	{Setproperty "Font.Bold";Yes}							
13	{Right 2}							
14	{GETLABEL "Enter the name of your favorite animal.", @CELLPOINTER("address")}							
15								

C:\Work\WP 9 Bible\Notebooks\Wp9b3816.qpw (unmodified)

Figure 38-16: Your completed macro, with the prompt for user input.

Getting help with macro commands

To get help with any of Quattro Pro's macro commands, click Help ➪ Help Topics ➪ Index, and then type "macro" to highlight "Macro Command List." Then click Display to display the list of commands (see Figure 38-17).

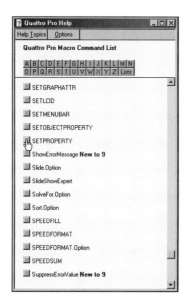

Figure 38-17: Displaying the macro command list.

Click a letter, and then click a particular command (SETPROPERTY in this case) for a detailed explanation and examples (see Figure 38-18).

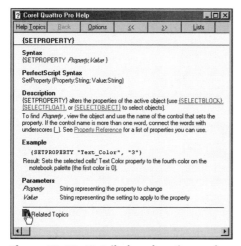

Figure 38-18: Detailed explanation and examples for a particular command.

Another handy trick is to press Shift+F3 when you're back in Quattro Pro to display the various categories of commands (see Figure 38-19). You can then look up the commands in each category, and insert the command you need or display its help.

Figure 38-19: Press Shift+F3 to look up and insert commands by category.

For general macro help, click Help ➪ Help Topics ➪ Contents, and then double-click the "Using macros" book.

Testing your revised macro

Now the moment of truth — testing the macro. Click any cell in any sheet (such as D:B3), and then press Ctrl+Shift+A. Your macro types the sample text (at the current location), puts "Favorite animal:" in bold, and displays the prompt shown in Figure 38-20.

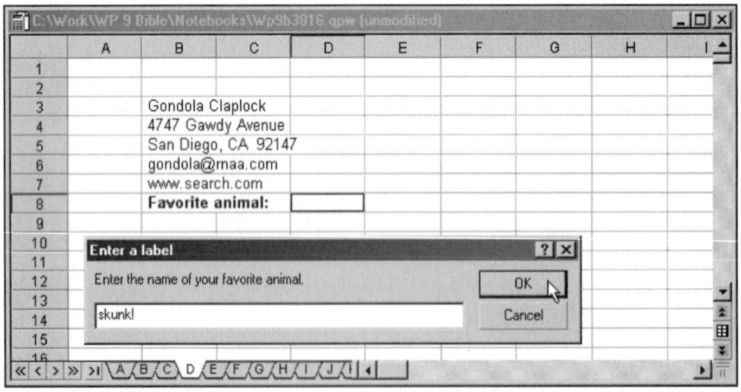

Figure 38-20: Now your macro works anywhere!

Type the name of your favorite animal and click OK. Now your macro not only types text, but also prompts for user input and types that as well.

If something didn't work right or you got an error message, it's probably just a typo. Fix whatever it is, and play the macro again.

Debugging Macros

Creating recorded macros is a snap. But typing macros from scratch and setting up fancy macros from recorded snippets requires some programming expertise, meticulous attention to detail, accurate typing, and a lot of patience. A single typo, a misplaced cell reference or command, or a logic error can make your macro behave strangely or fail completely.

That's where the debugger comes in. To help locate and identify programming bugs (errors), the debugger can

✦ Play back macro commands one at a time

✦ Display both the macro code and the spreadsheet as it updates

Starting and stopping the debugger

To start or stop the debugger, click Tools ➪ Macro ➪ Debugger, or press Shift+F2.

Debugging a macro

To debug your sample macro:

1. Click Tools ➪ Macro ➪ Debugger.

2. Click an empty cell on any sheet and press Ctrl+Shift+A to start your macro.

3. Press any key or click within the debugger window to go from step to step (see Figure 38-21).

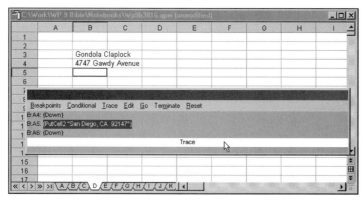

Figure 38-21: Debugging your test macro.

4. At any step, pick any of the debugger menu selections described in Table 38-1.

Table 38-1 Macro Debugger Menu Selections	
Menu Selection	*Lets You*
Breakpoints	Set up to four breakpoints that pause the macro at specified macro instruction cells. Click Go to play back the macro to the next breakpoint.
Conditional	Set up to four conditional breakpoints that pause the macro at specified macro instruction cells only if certain conditions are true. Click Go to play back the macro to the next conditional breakpoint.
Edit	Stop the macro to edit a specified cell.
Trace	Display (below "Trace" in the debugger window) the contents of up to four specified cells while the macro runs. (If necessary, resize the debugger window to show all the trace cells.)
Go	Run the macro to completion at full speed. (Same as pressing Enter.)
Terminate	Stop the macro in its tracks. (Same as pressing Ctrl+Break.)
Reset	Clear all breakpoints and trace settings.

Note   The PerfectScript debugger works differently from Quattro Pro's. Click Start on the taskbar, and then click WordPerfect Office 2000 ➪ Utilities ➪ Corel PerfectScript. Click File ➪ Debug ➪ Play, and then select the macro you want to debug.

Creating Buttons

Buttons and other form controls are handy inventions for playing macros and special dialogs, or jumping to a notebook or Internet location. To create a form button:

1. Click Insert ➪ Form Control ➪ Button, and then click or drag to insert the QuickButton.

2. To resize the button, right-click and press Esc to select it, and then drag a side or corner handle.

3. To move the button, click and drag.

4. To customize the button, right-click the button, click Button Properties, and then click the various tabs:

   • *Label text,* to customize your button's text (see Figure 38-22)

Figure 38-22: Customizing a QuickButton's text.

- *Macro,* to type up to 200 characters of macro commands. Use the SelectBlock command to jump to another location, as with {SelectBlock A:A1}. To play a macro, use the Branch command. For this example, type **{Branch \A}** to play your notebook macro (see Figure 38-23).

Figure 38-23: Using the Branch command in a QuickButton to play a macro.

- *Link to URL* (under the Macro tab) to create a hyperlink to an Internet address (see Figure 38-24)

Figure 38-24: Linking your QuickButton to an Internet address.

- *Box Type,* to specify the thickness of the border or a drop shadow
- *Border Color,* to specify a custom border color
- *Protection,* to prevent your QuickButton from being moved or altered when sheet-level object protection is on
- *Object Name,* to change the name by which the button can be referred to in macros
- *Print,* to select whether to print the button with the spreadsheet

For more information on using form controls, see Chapter 14, "Web Writing and Publishing."

More automation tools

Quattro Pro has additional tools for automating spreadsheets, which you can explore at your leisure:

✦ Menu-building macro commands such as {AddMenu}, {DeleteMenuItem}, {AddMenuItem}, and {SetMenuBar]

✦ Dialog boxes created with the Dialog Designer (Tools ➪ Macro ➪ Dialog Designer)

✦ Text buttons within a chart in a slide show

Now you know some quick and easy ways to automate your spreadsheets. This chapter concludes your introduction to Quattro Pro. Happy number-crunching!

For More Information . . .

On	See
Using PerfectScript commands	Chapter 58
Naming cells and blocks	Chapter 32
Editing techniques	Chapter 33
Managing files and folders	Chapter 7

✦   ✦   ✦

Showing Your Stuff with Presentations

◆ ◆ ◆ ◆

A Hands-On Slide Show

When it's not enough to put your ideas in writing, you can use Presentations to put them into a multimedia show. This chapter serves up a platter of possibilities as you create your own slide show. While most of your creations are destined for individual perusal in print or onscreen, you may have occasion to make a high-level presentation of your ideas or proposals. At such times, your text, while still critical, is likely to be kept to the minimum that can be grasped at a glance. Instead, you'll use graphics, audio, animation, and visual effects to impress folks with short attention spans and media-saturated brains.

What You Can Present

With a little help from Corel Presentations, you can deliver a professional show as

- ✦ A monitor presentation
- ✦ An Internet (or intranet) show
- ✦ Overhead transparencies
- ✦ Printed color or black-and-white copies

These publishing options are covered in Chapter 42, "Publishing Alternatives," where you'll also see how to print speaker notes, or export your show to a service bureau, to be turned into actual 35mm slides.

A *slide show* presents text, charts, drawings, and graphics in self-contained frames, enlivened with sound and animation. Text and graphics don't wrap from page to page as they do in a WordPerfect document — instead you have transitions from one bullet, paragraph, animated image, or slide to the next.

Presentations also let you create drawings; or graphic containers with charts, drawings, paintings, or text for use in other documents.

Raising the Curtain

To start Presentations, click the Taskbar Presentations icon on the Windows taskbar, or click Start ➪ WordPerfect Office 2000 ➪ Corel Presentations 9. You'll be given the choice of starting (or resuming) a slide show, master, or drawing, as shown in Figure 39-1.

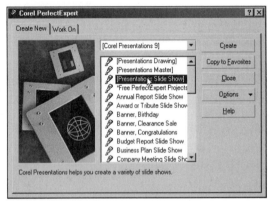

Figure 39-1: Upon starting Presentations, you choose to work on a slide show or drawing.

Looking at the Drawing Window

You'll be creating a slide show in this chapter, but for the moment, select [Presentations Drawing] and click Create, to take a peek at the drawing window. Click a shape button on the tool palette on the left of your screen, and then drag to draw the object, noting how your property selections change (see Figure 39-2).

The drawing and charting facilities, while a part of the Presentations module, are covered separately in Chapter 55, "Creating Your Own Art," and Chapter 56, "Charting Data."

Creating a Slide Show

Now it's time to go on-stage to set up your own slide show.

Property bar   Toolbar

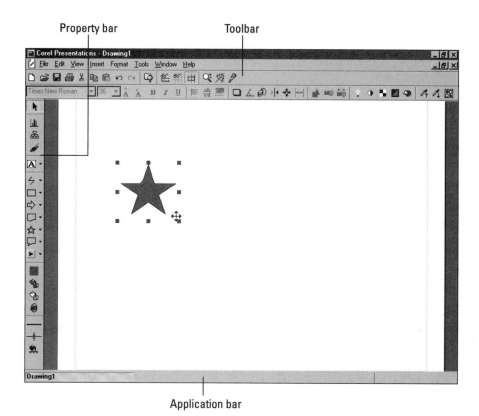

Application bar

Figure 39-2: Presentations drawing window, showing property bar selections when you draw an object.

Setting up your scenery

Click File ➪ New from Project, select [Presentations Slide Show] and click Create. The first thing you're asked to do is pick a master for your show's scenery from one of the design categories (see Figure 39-3):

> ✦ *35mm*, for creating color slides or transparencies
>
> ✦ *Business*, *Color*, *Design*, *Nature*, and *Theme*, for presentations on a monitor
>
> ✦ *Printout*, for crisp print handouts or black-and-white transparencies

Tip

> To install additional masters, click Start ➪ WordPerfect Office 2000 ➪ Setup and Notes ➪ Corel Setup Program, and then select the masters under the Presentations components.

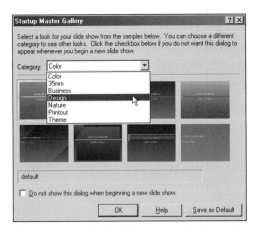

Figure 39-3: Picking the scenery for your show.

Each selection you see is a professionally designed master (a template of layout and background layers) for opening titles, bullet charts, organization charts, and so on.

To specify your selection as the default design, click Save as Default. You can check "Do not show this dialog when beginning a new slide show" to pick the default automatically from now on.

To change the scenery later on, click the Master Gallery button on the property bar, or click Format ➪ MasterGallery. In Chapter 41, "Mastering Presentations Techniques," you'll learn how to customize the templates and create your own masters.

Looking around the stage

As soon as you pick out your scenery and click OK, you'll enter the slide show stage (see Figure 39-4).

Now there's an interesting window! The Presentations slide screen has these clever, intuitive features:

- ✦ Each slide has its own tab, just like a Quattro Pro notebook sheet.
- ✦ Other tabs on the right let you quickly switch the view of your slides, or QuickPlay your show on the spot.
- ✦ The New Slide button lets you instantly create any type of slide.

You'll get to use these features as you go along.

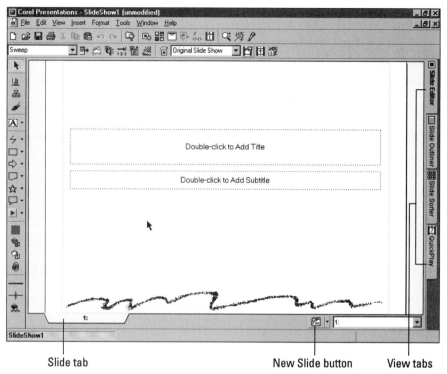

Figure 39-4: Slide show stage.

Adding titles and graphics

Your title slide should be in the Slide Editor, awaiting some content. To add titles and graphics:

1. Double-click the title box and type a title (see Figure 39-5), and then click outside of the box when you're finished. Do the same for the subtitle.

Figure 39-5: Adding a title.

Tip   A slide's title appears on its tab.

2. To add a clip art graphic to the first page, click the Clipart button (or click Insert ⇨ Graphics ⇨ Clipart), and then drag the clip art you want from the Scrapbook and position it in your slide (see Figure 39-6).

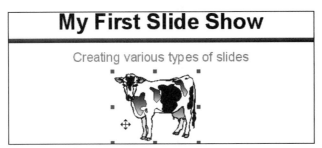

Figure 39-6: Adding a clip art graphic.

You can drag, resize, and customize the text and graphics boxes in your slides. See Chapter 9, "Working with Graphics," for detailed techniques.

Creating different types of slides

To add some more slides to your show:

1. Click Insert ⇨ New Slide, click the type of slide you want (see Figure 39-7), and click OK to add the specified number of slides. Add one of each of these types in turn:

   • A *Bulleted List* slide of your show's contents

   • A *Text* slide with a brief introduction to the show, using any fonts or formatting you want

   • A *Data Chart* slide, using the sample data, with a chart style picked from the gallery (charting in its full glory is covered in Chapter 56, "Charting Data")

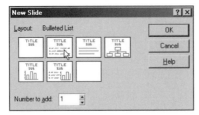

Figure 39-7: Adding a new slide.

Tip Click the New Slide button to insert a slide of the selected type, or click the arrow on its right to select another type from the pop-up list.

2. Double-click, as before, to type a title and subtitle on each slide.

3. Double-click the designated area to add the specific feature for each type of slide.

Deleting a slide or changing its type

If you accidentally create a slide you don't want, click Edit ➪ Delete Slides. To change a slide's layout, click the Slide Layout icon on the property bar.

Viewing, Arranging, and Previewing Your Show

So far, you've been working in the Slide Editor on each slide, one at a time. Now click the tabs on the right to take in three other views:

✦ *Slide Outliner* lets you create your slide show from an outline of titles, subtitles, slide types, and even speaker notes (see Figure 39-8). Press Ctrl+Enter to insert a new slide, and type the title, optional subtitle, and any text for text boxes or bullet points. You can then switch to the Slide Editor to complete individual slides. See Chapter 40, "Becoming an Instant Presentations Expert," for more on outlining shows.

✦ *Slide Sorter* gives you a bird's-eye view of your slide show. You can double-click a thumbnail to edit a particular slide, double-click an icon beneath a slide to change its properties, or drag the thumbnails around to rearrange the slides (see Figure 39-9). Click the zoom buttons to enlarge or shrink the thumbnails.

Tip Hold the Ctrl key down to select multiple slides to drag, or hold the Alt key down to select a range of consecutive slides.

✦ *QuickPlay* instantly plays your show, starting with the current slide. Click the screen or press Enter to go to the next transition. You can press Esc to end the show at any time.

Saving the Show

Not bad! You've already picked a master, and created, edited, and played a slide show, complete with graphics, bullets, text, and a chart. Now click Ctrl+S (File ➪ Save) to save your show and give it a name. Presentations automatically adds the .SHW extension, to identify it as a show.

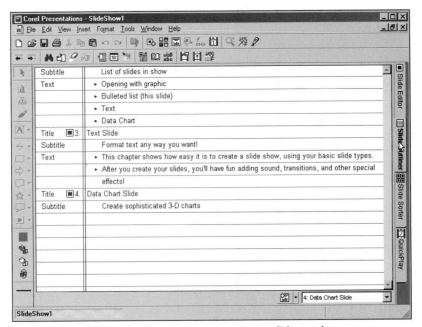

Figure 39-8: Slide Outliner, where you can create slides and text contents from outlines.

Changing Slide Transitions

Click the Slide Sorter tab, click the first slide, and then click the QuickPlay tab to play your slide show again. Notice how each slide sweeps in from left to right as you click the screen or press Enter. Sweep, the default, is a nice transition, but you can choose from many others:

1. Click the Transition list in the property bar. (You can also click Format ➪ Slide Properties ➪ Transition.)

2. Point to the transitions for previews and click the one you want (see Figure 39-10).

3. Click the Transition Direction button to change the transition's direction (if applicable).

4. Click the Transition Speed button to change the transition's speed.

Adding Sound

That does it for the video. Now how about a little audio for your show? (Of course, you need a sound card and speakers to hear it.)

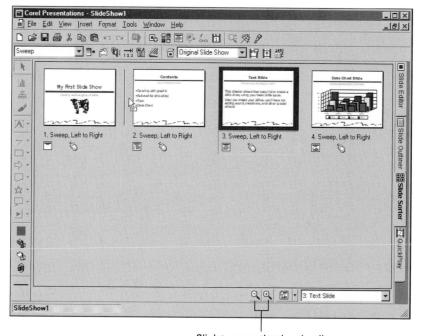

Click to zoom the thumbnails

Figure 39-9: Click and drag the Slide Sorter icons to rearrange your slides.

Understanding MIDI and .WAV files

Windows has two types of sound files: MIDI (.MID) and Digital Audio Waveform (.WAV).

✦ *MIDI (Musical Instrument Digital Interface)* files enable computers to record, edit, and play back music with MIDI-compatible instruments (such as keyboard synthesizers and drum machines). MIDI files are small, because they record code rather than the actual sounds, which is why you can't record speech in MIDI.

✦ *Waveform* files can be recorded from any sound source, including speech or music. Sound quality can be excellent, but the files can be many times larger than MIDI files for the same playback time. Just how large depends on the sample rate at which analog sounds are converted to digital codes. A sample rate of 11 KHz (11,000 per second) delivers telephone-quality sound. A sampling rate of 44.1 KHz is comparable to CD sound quality, but a one-minute .WAV file recorded at that rate can be as large as 11MB. The little ding in Windows takes 11,586 bytes.

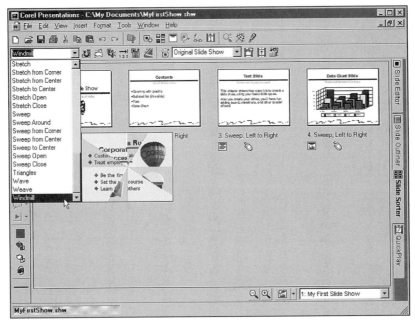

Figure 39-10: Previewing and selecting a transition.

Tip To install additional sound files, click Start íWordPerfect Office 2000 í Setup and Notes ⇨ Corel Setup Program, and then select the sound files under the Presentations components.

Adding a sound clip or CD track

To add a sound clip or CD track to your show:

1. Select a slide in any of the views, and then click the Sound button (or click Format ⇨ Slide Properties ⇨ Sound).

2. Specify the Wave clip, MIDI clip, or CD track you want to play, as shown in Figure 39-11. Click Play Sound to preview a clip and adjust the slide between Soft and Loud to control the volume.

3. If you selected a Wave or MIDI clip, you can check the box to save a copy of the clip with your show. (The show file will be bigger, but the sound will be portable.) You can also check to loop (continuously repeat) the sound (most Wave files are short).

4. To play a CD selection, click the icon to the right to enter a description, select a track, and specify a start and end location on the CD. You can also click Play, and then mark the start and end locations (see Figure 39-12).

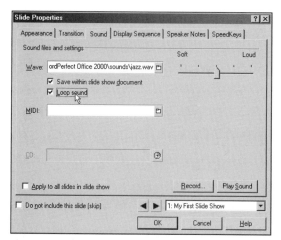

Figure 39-11: Adding sound to your slides.

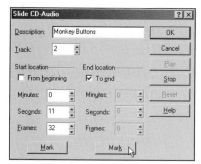

Figure 39-12: Marking the start and end locations when playing a CD track.

Recording your own voice

Now for the fun part. Got your microphone hooked up? To record your own voice:

1. Click Format ➪ Slide Properties ➪ Sound, and then click Record to launch the Windows Sound Recorder.

2. Click the Record button (see Figure 39-13), and sing away (or let your baby do the talking).

3. Click the Stop button to stop recording. You can click Record again to resume where you left off, or adjust the slide to where you want to start over.

4. Click the Play button to review your audio masterpiece.

5. When you're happy with your recording, click File ➪ Save to save it to disk. Save it as a .WAV file, so you can add it to your slides.

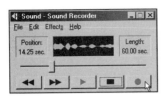

Figure 39-13: Recording a sound clip.

Note   The longer the recording, the bigger the file.

Playing Your Show

And now, the moment you've been waiting for! To play your show:

1. Click the Play Show button or click View ⇨ Play Slide Show.

2. Select any of the play options (see Figure 39-14):

   • *Beginning slide*, to specify where your show should start

   • *Audience*, to select a custom version of the show

   • *Create QuickShow*, to create a bitmap version of your show. It will play instantly (when you check "Use QuickShow file"), but it will take up a lot more memory; you'll also have to re-create the QuickShow every time you make a change to a slide

   • *Repeat slide show until you press 'Esc'*, to play your show in a continuous loop

   • *Highlighter color*, to pick another color from the palette

   • *Width*, to select another width for the highlighter from the palette

Figure 39-14: Playing your slide show.

3. Click Play, and then click the mouse to advance the show or drag to draw with the highlighter (see Figure 39-15).

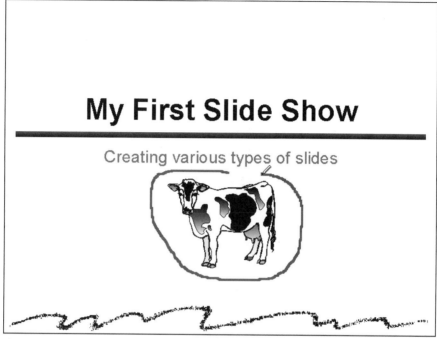

Figure 39-15: Drag the mouse to highlight a slide.

4. Control your show with any of the keystrokes described in Table 39-1. (You can also specify custom QuickKeys, as described in Chapter 40, "Becoming an Instant Presentations Expert.")

Table 39-1
Keystrokes for Playing Slide Shows

Action	*Keystroke(s)*
Next Transition	Space, Enter, right arrow, or down arrow
Previous Transition	Left arrow or up arrow
Next Slide	PgDn
Previous Slide	PgUp
Go to Slide	Ctrl+G
Backtrack	Backspace

Continued

Table 39-1 *(continued)*

Action	Keystroke(s)
Increase Volume	+
Decrease Volume	-
Stop Sound	End
Replay Sound	Home
Erase Highlighter	Ctrl+E
Quit Show	Esc, or Ctrl+F4

That should give you a taste of what can be done. Save your show again and take a break! Chapter 40, "Becoming an Instant Presentations Expert," will show you the automated tools for creating a show. In Chapter 41, "Mastering Presentations Techniques," you'll learn about bouncing bullets, flying graphics, and other Presentations tricks.

For More Information . . .

On	See
Publishing slide shows	Chapter 42
Creating your own art	Chapter 55
Creating charts and graphs	Chapter 56
Customizing templates and creating masters	Chapter 41
Working with clip art and text boxes	Chapter 9
Outlining shows	Chapter 40
Using predesigned shows	Chapter 40
Using SpeedLinks and SpeedKeys	Chapter 40
Customizing slide layers	Chapter 41
Mastering Presentations tricks and techniques	Chapter 41

✦   ✦   ✦

Becoming an Instant Presentations Expert

Now that you've mastered the basics for creating a show, it's time to move on to some expert techniques for achieving professional-quality results in no time flat.

Planning and Testing a Show

A slide show demands a little planning and testing, just as a written proposal or report does. You should ask

- ✦ Who is my audience?
- ✦ What is my message to them?

These simple questions can be tough to answer in a sentence or two. Just make sure your purpose is clear by the time you're finished!

Don't let the multimedia razzle-dazzle muddle your message. It's better to have a few simple slides, each conveying a specific portion of your message. Organize your slides with the following:

- ✦ An *opening,* to present the subject and objective of your show. You might use an attention-grabbing question or statement, followed by a slide with a quotation or anecdote to draw in your audience.

- ✦ The *body* of your show with several slides, each making a specific point, bolstered by facts and figures. Use the Slide Sorter to organize your argument.

✦ The *conclusion,* employing bulleted charts to summarize your key points. The closing can artfully repeat the title theme, thank the audience, and then have a dissolve transition (see Chapter 39, "A Hands-On Slide Show") to a blank slide with a black background (see Chapter 41, "Mastering Presentations Techniques").

Test out your show on volunteer victims, to see if you're grabbing their attention, addressing their questions, and getting your message across.

Opening an Existing Show

To open an existing show when entering Presentations, click the Create New or Work On tab and select the show you want (see Figure 40-1). Once you're in Presentations, you can click the File menu, and then click New or Open, or select a recent project from the bottom of the menu.

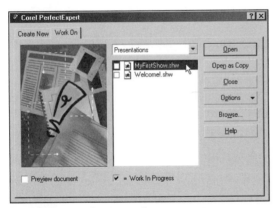

Figure 40-1: Selecting a show as you enter Presentations.

Following the Expert Examples

Click the Create New tab as you enter Presentations, or click File ➪ New from Project when you're there, to check out a number of predesigned projects that you can tailor to your needs, starting with the Annual Report slide show shown in Figure 40-2. You can also click Free PerfectExpert Projects to download new projects from Corel's Web site.

To install additional projects, click Start l WordPerfect Office 2000 l Setup and Notes l Corel Setup Program, and then select the projects under the Presentations components.

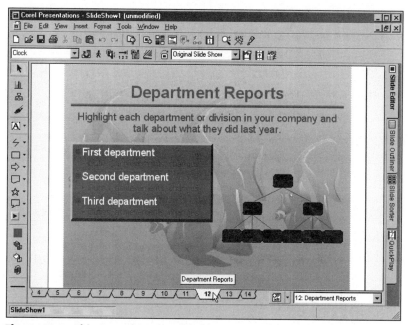

Figure 40-2: This Annual Report slide show is one of many projects you can tailor to your needs.

Creating a Show from an Outline

One handy Presentations trick is to work from an outline when creating a new slide show:

1. Click File ➪ New and select a master, if necessary; and then click the Outliner tab and type the title for the first slide (see Figure 40-3).

2. Press Enter, and then type the (optional) subtitle.

3. Type additional lines of text for a bulleted list, text, or combination slide. Click the Outline Left Arrow button or the Outline Right Arrow button to change the level of the current item. (You can also press Tab or Shift+Tab.)

4. Press Ctrl+Enter to create additional slides. (You can also press Enter and then click the Outline Left Arrow button as many times as necessary.)

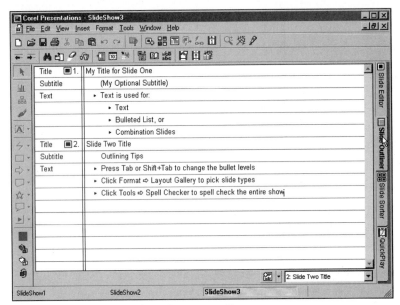

Figure 40-3: Creating a show from an outline.

5. Click Format ➪ Layout Gallery to specify the appearance of your slides.

6. Switch to the Slide Editor to add clip art, charts, and other objects to your slides.

 Tip   To spell-check your entire show, switch to the Outliner and click Tools ➪ Speller.

Importing a WordPerfect outline

You can create a slide show directly from a WordPerfect outline. To import a WordPerfect outline:

1. Click the Outliner tab.

2. If you're inserting the WordPerfect outline in an existing show, press Ctrl+Enter where you want to insert the slides.

3. Do either of the following:

   • Select the outline in WordPerfect, copy it to the Clipboard, and then paste it in the Outliner.

   • Click the Insert File button (Insert ➪ File) to insert an outline that's been saved to a file.

4. To add subtitles, click the end of the title lines, press Enter, and type your subtitles.

Tip You can also click the first text line of a slide, and then press Shift+Tab to turn it into a subtitle.

Sending an outline to WordPerfect

To send your slide show outline to WordPerfect and work on it there, click File ➪ Send to ➪ Corel WordPerfect, and then check Outline (see Figure 40-4).

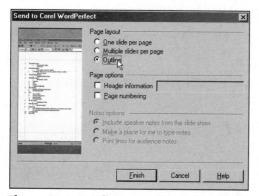

Figure 40-4: Sending an outline to WordPerfect.

Creating Custom Versions of a Show

You can tailor a show to different audiences, without having to save it under different names. To create a show with every slide and then specify which slides to skip for particular audiences:

1. Click the Slide Sorter tab, and then select Custom Audiences from the Audience drop-down list in the middle of the property bar.

2. Click New and type a name for your custom audience, and then click OK (see Figure 40-5).

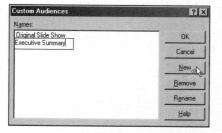

Figure 40-5: Creating a custom version of a show.

3. Select each slide you want to skip for this audience, and then click the Slide Skip button (the skipped slides will appear dim in the sorter).

Any changes you make to a particular slide will apply to all versions of your show. For more on playing shows, see Chapter 39, "A Hands-On Slide Show."

Adding SpeedLinks and SpeedKeys

When you play a slide show, *SpeedLinks* and *SpeedKeys* enable you to

✦ Jump to another place in the show

✦ Open the Web browser and jump to an Internet address

✦ Launch an application

✦ Play a sound clip

When you point to an object with an attached SpeedLink, the pointer turns into a hand and you can click the object to activate the link. A SpeedKey is activated by pressing the assigned keystroke when the slide is in view.

Creating a SpeedLink

To attach a SpeedLink to a clip art image, text box, or other object in the slide layer:

1. From the Slide Editor, right-click any object you've added to the slide and click SpeedLink.

2. Give your SpeedLink a name (see Figure 40-6), and then specify a link assignment:

- *Go to*, to go to the slide you select from the list

- *Action*, to play a sound clip (see Chapter 39), stop the sound, go to an Internet location (see Chapter 14), launch a program, or quit the show

Creating an invisible SpeedLink

You can turn any part of your slide (such as the title) into an apparent SpeedLink, by drawing an invisible SpeedLink on top of it:

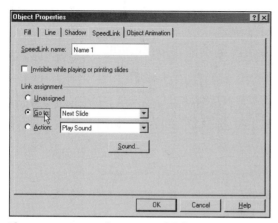

Figure 40-6: Creating a SpeedLink.

1. Click the Draw Closed Object button on the tool palette, and then drag where you want to create a rectangle or other closed object.

2. Right-click the object you created, click SpeedLink, and then check "Invisible while playing or printing slides." (To make the object less intrusive as you work on your slides, leave a thin border and remove the fill.)

3. Specify the "Go to" location or action assignment for the link, as described previously.

When playing the show, a hand pointer appears when you point to the spot, even though the object is invisible. When playing a show on the Internet, a colored border also appears around the slide when a SpeedLink is present.

Clearing a SpeedLink

To clear a SpeedLink from an object, right-click the object, click SpeedLink, and then click Unassigned.

Specifying SpeedKeys

To assign SpeedKeys to a particular slide:

1. Right-click a blank spot on the slide and click SpeedKeys.

2. Select a key, and then specify any "Go to" location or action assignment, as described earlier in the section "Creating a SpeedLink" (see Figure 40-7).

3. Check "Apply to all slides in slide show" if you want the keystroke to work with all your slides.

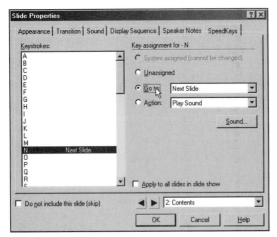

Figure 40-7: Specifying SpeedKeys.

For the standard keystrokes to use when playing a show, see Chapter 39, "A Hands-On Slide Show."

Clearing a SpeedKey

To clear a SpeedKey from a slide, right-click the slide, click SpeedKey, and then select the keystroke and click Unassigned.

For More Information . . .

On	See
Specifying slide transitions	Chapter 39
Specifying slide backgrounds	Chapter 41
Playing slide shows	Chapter 39
Adding sound clips	Chapter 39
Specifying Internet locations	Chapter 14
Using keystrokes when playing a show	Chapter 39
Mastering Presentations tricks and techniques	Chapter 41
Printing and publishing shows	Chapter 42

✦   ✦   ✦

Mastering Presentations Techniques

With Presentations, you can dazzle your audience by using the latest multimedia features and tools. This chapter shows you how to customize and automate your show for maximum impact.

Chapter 39, "A Hands-On Slide Show," gave you the basics for putting together a show, and Chapter 40, "Becoming an Instant Presentations Expert," showed you how to plan your presentation, tailor your show to different audiences, and use SpeedLinks and SpeedKeys when playing your show. This chapter is devoted to techniques and refinements to dazzle and persuade your audience. Plus, you learn how to create organization charts.

Peeling Back the Slide Layers

Before you start getting creative with slides, take a closer look at what they're made of. Select the opening title slide from the show you created, and then click Edit ➪ Layout Layer. Note that the tabs at the bottom are for your template layouts, not your individual slides (see Figure 41-1). The tabs on the right of the screen indicate that your slides are made up of three layers:

✦ The topmost *Slide* layer, where you double-click the placeholders to add specific titles, bullets, and so on. You can also add slide-specific text, clip art, and other objects (see Figure 41-2).

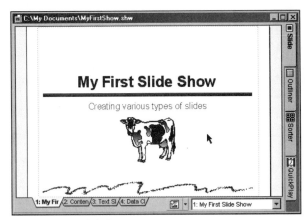

Figure 41-1: Slide layer.

✦ A middle *Layout* layer, with placeholders for titles, subtitles, bulleted lists, and so on.

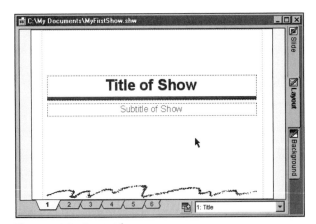

Figure 41-2: Layout layer.

✦ A bottom *Background* layer, for the slide's overall color, pattern, and size. You can add clip art, bitmaps, text, and other objects in the background layer (see Figure 41-3).

Together, the layout and background layers constitute a template, and determine the general appearance and contents of a slide. A *master* is a collection of related templates for various types of slides.

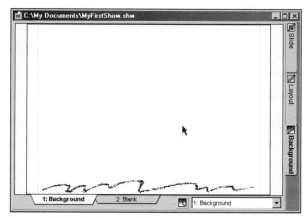

Figure 41-3: Background layer.

Changing a slide's background

To change a slide's background:

1. Click Edit (or right-click the slide) and then click Background Layer.

2. Click the Slide Background Gallery button (Format ⇨ Background Gallery), and then select a Category from the list.

3. Select a background from the gallery (see Figure 41-4), or click Browse to select a bitmap background from another file.

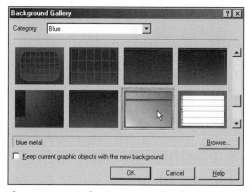

Figure 41-4: Selecting a new background from the gallery.

Check "Keep current graphic objects with the new background" if you want to keep any bitmap, clip art, or text that you've added to your current background.

 Tip   To install additional masters and backgrounds, click Start ⇨ WordPerfect Office 2000 ⇨ Setup and Notes ⇨ Corel Setup Program, and then add the Presentations components you want.

Changing a slide's color or fill

You can customize the color or fill of a slide's foreground or background:

1. From the Slide Editor (slide layer) or the background layer, click File ⇨ Page Setup (or right-click in the drawing window and click Page Setup).

2. Click the Page Color tab, and then click one of the fill style buttons from left to right:

   • *Use Master's Page Color*, to default to the master background.

   • *Pattern*, to specify a background and pattern color.

   • *Gradient*, to pick a gradient fill and colors. You can then click Gradient Settings to pick the gradient type, offset, and other options, as described in Chapter 54, "Adding Graphic Lines, Borders, and Fills."

   • *Texture*, to select a background from such categories as fabrics, paper, wood, or stone (see Figure 41-5), or click Browse to locate another texture.

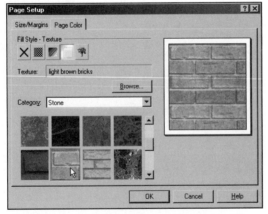

Figure 41-5: Selecting a textured background.

- *Picture*, to select a picture from one of the categories (see Figure 41-6), or click Browse to locate another bitmap image. You can then click Picture Settings to pick the layout for the image, such as Tile, or "Scale to fit area."

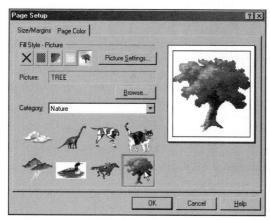

Figure 41-6: Selecting a picture fill.

Creating custom layouts

Once you have selected or defined a background, you can define custom layouts for a particular show, or to save as a new master:

1. Click Edit ➪ Layout Layer.

2. Click the tab for the type of slide (title, bulleted list, text, and so on) that you want to modify, or click the Slide New Layout button (Insert ➪ New Layout), and give the new layout a name (see Figure 41-7).

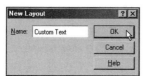

Figure 41-7: Adding a custom layout to the master.

3. You can move, resize, or delete the placeholders for the title, subtitle, and other elements. You can click Format ➪ Font to specify the font face, style, size, color, outline, and fill.

4. You can add various items from the menus and toolbars. For example, click Insert ⇨ Bulleted List, drag to create a placeholder, and select the type of text placeholder you want (see Figure 41-8).

Figure 41-8: Adding a text placeholder to your layout.

5. To assign a background to layouts, click the Slide Assign Background button (Format ⇨ Assign Background), and then highlight and select a background for each of the layouts you want to change (see Figure 41-9).

Figure 41-9: Changing the backgrounds for selected layouts.

6. To rename a layout, click the Slide Rename Layout button (Edit ⇨ Rename Layout).

7. To delete a selected layout, click the Slide Rename Layout button (Edit ⇨ Delete Layout).

Saving your custom template as a new master

After you've customized your backgrounds and layouts, you can save them as a new master that can be applied to other shows:

1. Click File ⇨ Save As, and select a "File type" of Presentations Master 7/8/9.

2. Go to the Masters category folder in which you want to save your master.

3. Type a new name in the "File name" box (otherwise you'll overwrite an existing master).

Your new master should now appear in the Master Gallery, in the category under which you saved it.

Putting Objects on a Slide

You can put any object you want on a slide. Add it to the background if you want it to appear on several slides, as with a company logo. Use the Slide Editor to add an object to a single slide. Select from the Insert menu and drag to add the following:

Object	Described in Chapter
Clip art	9
Bitmaps	55
Charts	56
Text boxes	9
Bullet charts	36
TextArt	8
Spreadsheets	30
Various shapes and arrows	55

Click Insert ➪ Spreadsheet to create and edit a Quattro Pro spreadsheet right on your slide (see Figure 41-10).

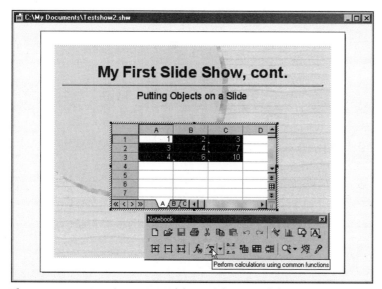

Figure 41-10: Creating a spreadsheet right on a slide.

Customizing Bullets

To customize bullets:

1. Right-click in a bulleted list and click Bulleted List Properties.

2. Specify any of the options under the various tabs:

   - *Fonts*, to change any of the font characteristics for the various levels

   - *Bullets*, to change the bullets' justification, character, size, color, or fill properties (select a bullet shape of Other, as shown in Figure 41-11, to specify special characters for your bullets)

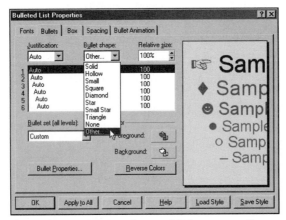

Figure 41-11: Select a shape of Other to specify special characters for your bullets.

   - *Box*, to create a custom box for the entire list

   - *Spacing*, to adjust the line spacing for main and subordinate levels

   - *Bullet Animation*, for some real fun (see the following section, "Animating Your Show")

Cross-Reference For more on working with bulleted lists, see Chapter 23, "Organizing with Bullets and Outlines."

Animating Your Show

Few show topics are so lively that they won't benefit from the animation effects you can apply (in moderation) to bullets, clip art, and other objects.

Animating bullets

To make your points stand out, try having your bullets fly in and land, one at a time, with each click of the mouse. To animate your bullets:

1. Right-click your bullets and click Object Animation (or click Bulleted List Properties ⇨ Bullet Animation).

2. Preview the sample (see Figure 41-12) as you select various combinations of effects:

   • *Animation type*, to apply various transition and animation effects in place (within the list), or across the screen (to emerge from outside the list)

   • *Direction* and *Speed*, to control the way and how fast bullets emerge

   • *Display one at a time*, to have each bullet appear as you click your mouse, or at a specified time delay

   • *Highlight current bullet*, to have the previous points fade into the background as a new one emerges

   • *Display in reverse order*, to have the bottom bullet emerge first

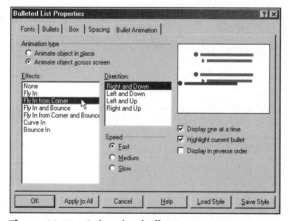

Figure 41-12: Animating bullets.

Animating any object

You can apply animation and transition effects to any slide object (such as a graphic or chart), just as you do to individual bullets:

1. Right-click the object and click Object Animation.

2. Apply any of the type, effect, direction, and speed options that you can use for bullets (see Figure 41-13).

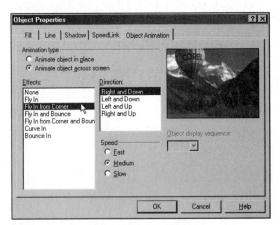

Figure 41-13: Animating any object.

3. If you're animating two or more objects (not counting bullets) in a single slide, you can click the "Object display sequence" list to specify the order in which your objects appear.

Animating titles

To animate a title or subtitle, delete the existing text and its placeholder, create a text box in the Slide Editor, and then enter and format your text. You can then select the text box and animate it.

If your slide has both an animated title and animated bullets, the title will normally appear last. To have the title appear first, click Format ➪ Slide Properties ➪ Display Sequence, and then click either "Immediately after the slide transition" or "Before the bulleted list."

Automating and Controlling the Display Sequence

Normally the sequence of transitions for slides, animated bullets, and animated objects is controlled by mouse clicks or keystrokes. However, to apply "no hands" automation and other sequence controls to all or part of your show:

1. Click the Slide Display Sequence button (Format ➪ Slide Properties ➪ Display Sequence).

2. Select from the various groups of options:

- *Display next slide*, either manually, or after a specified delay in seconds (see Figure 41-14)

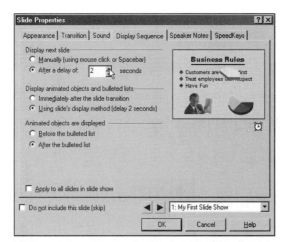

Figure 41-14: Automating and controlling the display sequence.

- *Display animated objects and bulleted lists*, immediately after the slide transition, or using the delay you specified for the slide

- *Animated objects are displayed*, either before or after the bulleted list

- *Apply to all slides in slide show*, to use the same display sequence with all your slides

Transitions control how slides and animated objects are introduced. You can also specify sound clips to play when a slide is introduced, or when you click a SpeedLink.

Going to the Movies

A judiciously placed movie clip can enhance the mood of your show:

1. Click Insert ➪ Movie, and select a video file (.AVI, .MOV, .MPEG, .QT), insert it in your slide, and then size and position it with your mouse (see Figure 41-15).

2. Click the Slide Movie Properties button, or right-click the movie clip and click Movie Properties to specify any of the following (see Figure 41-16):

   - *Movie name*, for the particular movie you want to play.

   - *Movie border*, of none, thin, or 3-D.

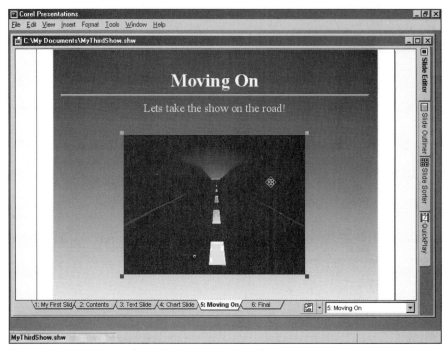

Figure 41-15: Sizing and positioning a movie with your mouse.

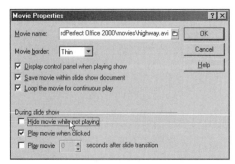

Figure 41-16: Specifying movie properties.

- *Display control panel when playing show*, to show the Slide bar, Stop, and Pause buttons. (Leave this off for a clean display, and click the movie to play it.)

- *Rewind movie when playing is stopped*, to return to the first frame.

- *Save movie within slide show document*, to let you send the show elsewhere or play it on another computer.

- *Loop the movie for continuous play*, to keep it going. (Click the movie any time you want to stop it.)

- *Hide movie while not playing*, to surprise your audience when you click the spot. The movie disappears again when it's finished.

- *Play movie when clicked*, to keep it still until you want it to play.

- *Play movie* x *seconds after slide transition*, to automatically play it without clicking.

Creating Speaker Notes

You can attach speaker notes to your slides, to print as cue cards or as audience handouts, or to include in an Internet show:

1. Click the Slide Speaker Notes button or right-click on a blank spot in the slide and click Speaker Notes.

2. Click Insert Text from Slide (if you want to include it), and then type your notes.

3. Click the arrows to add notes to other slides (see Figure 41-17).

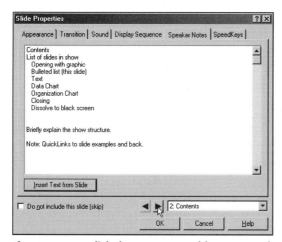

Figure 41-17: Click the arrows to add notes to other slides.

Creating an Organization Chart

Organization charts show an organization's structure, the relationships among people and positions, or any other hierarchy (such as a family tree). You can add other information (such as phone numbers, locations, or dates of birth).

Tip   Keep details to a minimum to present a clear visual display.

How you initially create an organization chart depends on where you are:

✦ *In a WordPerfect document,* (1) click where you want to place the chart; (2) click Insert ➪ Graphics ➪ Draw Picture; (3) click the Organization Chart button (Insert ➪ Organization Chart); or (4) click inside the drawing frame that appears.

✦ *In a Presentations drawing window or slide,* click the Organization Chart button (Insert ➪ Organization Chart), and then drag the size frame you want, or click to fill the entire window or slide. (Specify a slide layout of None if you're filling the entire slide.)

✦ *In an Org Chart slide,* double-click the designated area.

Unless you're creating an Org Chart slide, you'll be asked to pick a layout structure and orientation (see Figure 41-18).

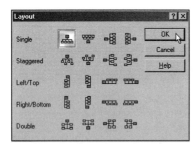

Figure 41-18: Picking a layout for your organization chart.

Editing your organization chart

To edit an organization chart:

1. Double-click the chart in the drawing window so that a border of slashes appears around it.

2. Double-click a box to fill in the placeholder name and title.

3. Select the chart elements you want to edit:

   • Click to select a box (see Figure 41-19).

   • Hold down the Ctrl key to select multiple boxes.

   • Right-click a box to select all the boxes in its branch or level.

   • Right-click in the chart and click Select All to edit all the boxes at once.

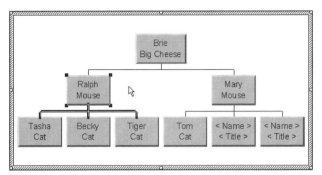

Figure 41-19: Selected box with its attached subordinates.

4. Perform any of the following operations on selected elements:

   • Click the Organization Chart Subordinates button to add subordinates, or click the Insert menu to add subordinates, co-workers, staff, or a manager to selected boxes.

   • Right-click a box and click Replace Manager to promote it.

   • Click the Organization Chart Branch Structure button (Format ➪ Branch Structure) to change the layout structure and orientation of selected boxes and subordinates.

   • Click the Organization Chart Box Fields button (Format ➪ Box Fields) to add, delete, move, or rename fields for selected boxes (see Figure 41-20).

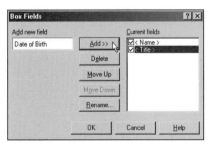

Figure 41-20: Adding a new field to selected boxes.

   • Click the Organization Chart Connectors button (Format ➪ Connectors) to change the connectors between chart levels.

   • Click Format ➪ Box Properties to change the box type, border, fill, and size of selected boxes (see Figure 41-21).

   • Click the Organization Chart Box Spacing button (Format ➪ Box Spacing) to adjust the spacing between boxes.

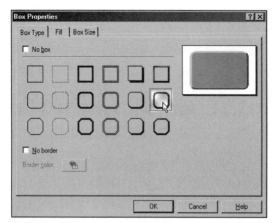

Figure 41-21: Changing the properties of selected boxes.

- Click various buttons to change the font and line attributes. (Normally, select all the boxes before you do.)

- Click the Organization Chart Collapse/Expand View button to collapse or expand your view of selected branches.

- Click the Organization Chart Zoom Branch button to zoom your view in or out for a selected branch.

Dragging boxes to rearrange your chart

You can also drag boxes to rearrange your chart:

✦ Drag the selected box over to the side or middle of another box to place it as a co-worker or subordinate (see Figure 41-22). Its subordinates move with it.

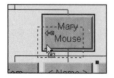

Figure 41-22: Dragging a box to another location.

✦ To move or copy the contents of a selected box, drag the box to another using the *right* mouse button.

You can also move branches around by cutting or copying them to the Clipboard and then pasting the branch to the selected box. (See Chapter 2, "Essential Typing and Editing," for more information on cutting, copying, and pasting.)

Saving your organization chart style

To save the style of your current organization chart (box properties, font, color, structure, spacing, and so on):

1. Click Chart ➪ Save Style.
2. Type a name and click Save (the .CHS extension is automatically added).

You can then click Chart ➪ Retrieve Style to apply it to other charts you create.

Displaying your organization chart

When displaying your organization chart, you may want to change the orientation of your chart or page, depending on where your chart is and how it is structured. You can decrease page margins to fit more boxes in your display.

You can also print your organization as a poster (see Chapter 42, "Publishing Alternatives").

Saving your organization chart

If you intend to keep your organization chart, save it in your WordPerfect document, Presentations drawing, or your slide show. Click File ➪ Save As to save a selected chart as a separate .WPG graphic.

For More Information . . .

On	See
Slide show basics	Chapter 39
Planning your show	Chapter 40
Tailoring shows to different audiences	Chapter 40
Using SpeedLinks and SpeedKeys	Chapter 40
Applying gradient fills	Chapter 54
Adding clip art and text boxes	Chapter 9
Creating shapes, arrows, and bitmaps	Chapter 55
Creating charts and graphs	Chapter 56
Creating TextArt	Chapter 8
Creating spreadsheets	Chapter 30
Working with bulleted lists	Chapter 23
Outlining your shows	Chapter 39
Using cut, copy, and paste	Chapter 2
Printing posters and notes	Chapter 42

✦   ✦   ✦

Publishing Alternatives

Now that you've learned how to put together a dazzling presentation, this chapter shows you various ways to produce and publish your show.

Producing a Show on the Go

Show on the Go enables you to turn your show into a portable file that can be played on another computer. The other machine doesn't need to have Presentations installed, just Windows 95/98/NT, a sound card that can play any clips in your show, and the standard Windows drivers for video and sound.

You can create a run-time version that plays on Windows 3.*x* as well, but all transitions will revert to the default type, object animations will be removed, and any Object Linking and Embedding (OLE) objects appearing on slides won't function.

Creating a Show on the Go

To create a Show on the Go:

1. Click File ⇨ Show on the Go, save your show if prompted, and specify if you want to Repeat slide show until you press 'Esc' (see Figure 42-1).

2. Click Change to specify a different name, destination, system, or display type. In particular, you can send the file to a floppy, or as an e-mail attachment. You can also create a portable show that runs on Windows 3.*x*, as well as Windows 95/NT.

3. Click Create to produce your run-time show (such as MyFirstshow.exe) at the destination specified, and then send it on its way.

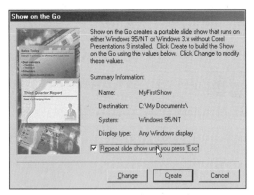

Figure 42-1: Creating a Show on the Go.

Playing a Show on the Go

To play a Show on the Go in Windows 95:

1. Click Start ➪ Run on the Windows 95 taskbar.

2. Specify the run-time show and click OK.

The run-time show employs any play options and automated controls you specified in Presentations. Use the mouse or keystrokes to control the show, as described in Chapter 40, "Becoming an Instant Presentations Expert." Press Esc to quit the show at any time.

Publishing to PDF

Click File ➪ Publish to PDF, to publish a slide show to PDF (Portable Document Format).

Your show won't have the animation and multimedia effects you get with Show on the Go, but anyone with the freely distributable Adobe Acrobat Reader will be able to view the results (see Figure 42-2).

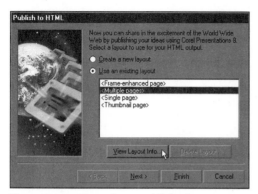

Figure 42-2: Your show published to PDF, as viewed in the Adobe Acrobat Reader.

Cross-Reference For more information on publishing to PDF, see Chapter 14, "Web Writing and Publishing."

Putting on a Web Show

You have two ways to publish your show and put it on the Internet, where it can be viewed with most browsers:

✦ As a Hypertext Markup Language (HTML) or Web document, with slides converted to graphics

✦ As a Show It! presentation, embedded in an HTML page, complete with graphics, animation, transitions, sound, and video

Publishing your show to HTML

To publish the current show to HTML:

1. Click File ➪ Internet Publisher, and save the file, if prompted.

2. Click Layout in the panel on the left (or click the Next button), and then choose whether to create a reusable custom layout or apply an existing one (see Figure 42-3). You'll have to create a new layout the first time around.

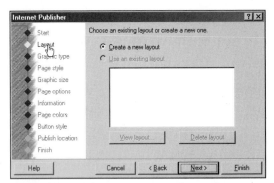

Figure 42-3: Selecting a custom layout for your show or creating a new one.

3. Click Graphic type to select the GIF, JPEG, or PNG graphic format for your show, as shown in Figure 42-4. (The Show It! selection is discussed in the next section.) Click a graphic type for a detailed description. You can try compressing JPEG images to reduce the size of your files.

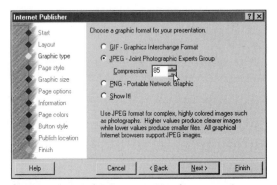

Figure 42-4: Selecting an HTML layout option.

4. Click Page style to select from alternative HTML page layouts (see Figure 42-5).

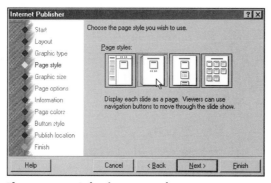

Figure 42-5: Selecting a page layout.

5. Click Graphic size and select the display size (not all users have the higher resolution displays), along with the size and type for the slide graphics. You can also put a border around your slides (see Figure 44-6).

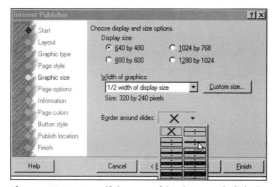

Figure 42-6: Specifying graphic sizes and slide borders.

6. Click Page options to select the navigation aids for your show (see Figure 44-7). The self-running presentation provides an additional automatic advance option, at the interval you specify. A Table of Contents slide is added to the beginning of your show. (Omit slide titles and numbers to leave more room for the images.)

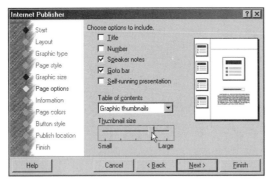

Figure 42-7: Selecting page option navigation aids.

7. Click Information to specify items to display at the bottom of the Index page at the beginning of your show (see Figure 42-8). You can also attach a copy of the original show for visitors to download and play in Presentations.

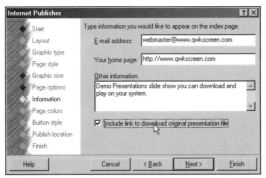

Figure 42-8: Specifying information to appear on the Index page at the beginning of your show.

8. Click Page colors to customize the colors of your links and background, or to select a wallpaper bitmap (see Figure 42-9).

9. Click Button style to choose the look of the navigation buttons on your slides.

10. Click Publish location to specify the title and folder for your show. Click Advanced for various additional options (see Figure 42-10). Don't change the name for the initial file, but you may need to change the extension from HTML to HTM to play on certain systems. Normally you'll want to keep your graphics in a subfolder.

11. Click the Finish button to publish your presentation. You'll be prompted to save and name your current layout so you can use it again. Click Show Me at the final prompt to display the results in your browser (see Figure 42-11).

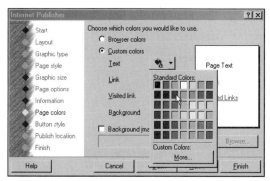

Figure 42-9: Customizing your link colors or background.

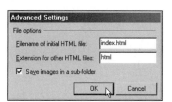

Figure 42-10: Specifying advanced settings for your show.

Figure 42-11: Your published presentation, ready for posting on the Web!

You can now upload your pages (along with graphics and sound clips) to your Web site. (See Chapter 14, "Web Writing and Publishing," for more information.) You won't get the transition or audio effects, but the format, fonts, and symbols display faithfully in the slide graphics. SpeedLinks work, too, except for those that launch programs.

Creating a Show It! presentation

To create a Show It! presentation from the current show:

1. Click File ⇨ Internet Publisher, and save your show if prompted.

2. Click Layout in the panel on the left (or click the Next button), and then choose whether to create a reusable custom layout or apply an existing one (see Figure 42-12). You'll have to create a new layout the first time around.

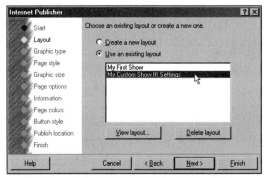

Figure 42-12: Selecting a custom layout for your show or creating a new one.

3. Click Graphic type and select Show It!

4. Click Page style to select whether to display your slides in a single page or to use browser frames with a collapsible outline (see Figure 42-13).

5. Select additional items to customize, as described in Steps 5–10 of the preceding "Publishing your show to HTML" section. Note that under Page options you can check whether you want the show to play once or to repeat until "Esc" is pressed.

6. Click the Finish button to publish your presentation. You'll be prompted to save and name your current layout so you can use it again. Click Show Me at the final prompt to display the results in your browser (see Figure 42-14).

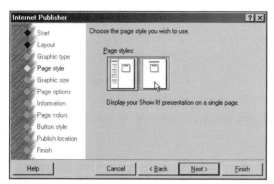

Figure 42-13: Selecting the page style for your Show It! presentation.

Figure 42-14: Your published Show It! presentation in your Web browser.

The resulting show includes all the formatting, graphics, fonts, transitions, and sounds of your original presentation. Advance the show with mouse-clicks.

Your show will include a Show It! link to the Presentations site, where visitors can download the required Show It! plug-in for Netscape Navigator. Users of Internet Explorer 3 and above can automatically download the plug-in when they visit your site. You must be running Windows 95/98/NT to install the plug-in.

The Web server with your Show It! files must also be configured to recognize and handle the MIME types for Show It!, so that others can view your presentation on the Web. Ask your system administrator to apply the following MIME binary file extension/application mappings:

```
.pqf @--> application/x-cprplayer
.pqi @--> application/cprplayer
.shw @--> application/presentations
```

Printing a Slide Show

You print a slide show much like any other document (see Chapter 13, "Printing and Faxing Information"), with certain options particular to the medium:

1. Click Print (File ➪ Print) and select what you want to print (see Figure 42-15):

    • *Full document*, to print your entire show

    • *Current view*, to print the current slide

    • *Selected objects*, to print the selected items in the slide layer

    • *Slides*, to print the specified number of slides

    • *Speaker notes*, to print the slide text and accompanying notes

    • *Audience notes*, to print pictures of the slides with ruled lines for taking notes

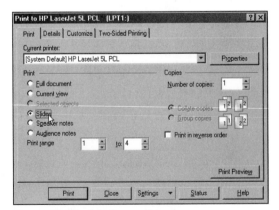

Figure 42-15: Printing a slide show.

2. Specify, where applicable, the page range and number of slides per page.

3. Click the Details tab to print slide backgrounds, numbers, and titles.

4. Click Print Preview to see how your selections will print.

Turning Your Show into Slides

You can turn your show into high-resolution slides, either by printing them to an accompanying film recorder or by sending a file to a service bureau for processing. When creating slides, you may want to select a master from the 35mm category, designed specifically for this purpose. You can also click File ⇨ Page Setup, and select the 35mm page definition with 0" margins.

Printing to a film recorder

To print to an installed film recorder:

1. Click File ⇨ Print and select the film recorder from your list of printers.

2. Click Print and follow the film recorder's options (such as film type and exposure time) and procedures.

Sending your show to a service bureau

To send your show by way of a modem to the Graphicsland service bureau:

1. Click File ⇨ Send To ⇨ Graphicsland.

2. Follow the step-by-step procedures that appear.

To send your show to another service bureau, click File ⇨ Save As, select the "File type" the bureau requires, and then save the file and deliver it for processing.

Printing posters and thumbnails

You can enlarge or reduce the printed image of your slide or drawing to produce multipage posters, thumbnail prints, or anything in between:

1. Click File ⇨ Print and select Current view if you intend to print only the current slide.

2. Click the Enlarge/Reduce tab, and then click any of the following:

   • *Poster,* to select a multiple page size from (four pages) to (36 pages!), as shown in Figure 42-16

   • *Enlarge/Reduce,* to adjust the size of the image from 10 to 600% (pages)

   • *Scale to fit output page,* to fit the slide or drawing to the output page size you specify

   • *Print thumbnails,* to put up to 64 miniature images on a single sheet, with options for page order, numbers, and borders

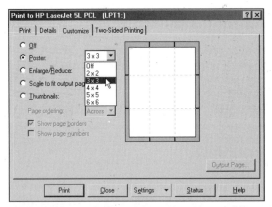

Figure 42-16: Printing a poster from your slide or drawing.

3. If you enlarged your output to print on multiple pages, tape the pages together to create your enlargement or poster. Most printers have a nonprinting "dead zone" at the page margins, so you'll probably need to trim some edges.

For More Information . . .

On	See
Slide show basics	Chapter 39
Mastering Presentations tricks and techniques	Chapter 41
Using keystrokes when playing a show	Chapter 39
Publishing to PDF	Chapter 14
Web publishing	Chapter 14
Printing techniques	Chapter 13

✦   ✦   ✦

Managing Information with Paradox

The Secrets to Database Success

Never used a database? Sure you have! Your telephone directory and address book are just two examples of databases that you use all the time. This chapter explains database concepts and outlines the steps of a successful database project.

What's a Database?

A database is a collection of related information, grouped as a set of records. A database can be a metal filing cabinet with customer records, a card file with names and phone numbers, or a notebook with a handwritten listing of a store's inventory. However, just putting miscellaneous information in a filing cabinet, card file, notebook, or even a computer doesn't make it a database. The information has to be organized.

A computerized database is generally organized into one or more tables, with a row for each *record* and columns for the *fields*, or data items. A computerized address book, for instance, has a record for each person, with fields for the name, address, telephone number, and so on.

The power of databases

A computerized database permits efficient storage and flexible information retrieval. With a computerized phone directory, for example, you can search by address when you don't know the name of a business or individual. When your customer database is in a computer instead of a filing cabinet, you can easily retrieve records by geographic area, order date, total sales, and so on.

What's a relational database?

You can store records in a Quattro Pro spreadsheet or even in a WordPerfect table. The resulting *flat-file* database can be quite efficient as long as the amount of information to be handled is relatively small.

A full-featured database lets you organize, update, and examine large amounts of data. A relational *database manager*, such as Paradox, also lets you access multiple tables simultaneously by linking records via a common field. Paradox is the database manager that is a part of the WordPerfect Office suite.

For example, a *relational database* might store customer information for a mail-order supplier of car stereos in one table and order information in another table. The two tables might be linked by a common customer number. Figure 43-1 shows an example of this with two tables linked by Customer ID.

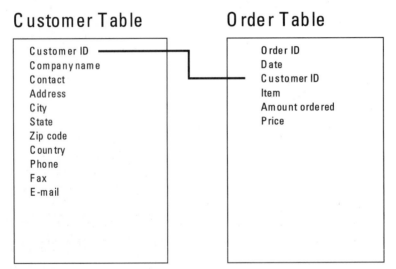

Figure 43-1: How a relational database works.

By searching on the customer number field in the mailing list and matching it to the customer number field in the orders table, the database manager can determine what the customer ordered and the total cost of the purchase.

Linking tables via a common field makes it easy to organize and maintain your data. Information entered once in one table can be accessed many times by others. For example, if your customer orders were in a flat-file database, you'd have to enter customer information for every order.

Handling different types of data relationships

Database tables can be related in several ways:

✦ In a *one-to-one* relationship, a unique value in a field of one table is directly linked to a unique value in a field of another. Figure 43-2 illustrates a one-to-one relationship between an Employee table and a Benefits table, linked via a common social security number.

✦In a *one-to-many* relationship, a unique value in a field of the master (parent) table is linked to a non-unique value in the detail (child) table. Figure 43-3 illustrates a one-to-many relationship in which each record in the Customer table has a unique Customer ID field, related to any number of records in the Sales table. Most table relationships are one-to-many.

✦ In a *many-to-one* relationship, several non-unique records in the master table are linked to a unique value in the detail table. For example, the records in an Orders table can be linked to a table with zip codes. There can be many orders for each zip code. Just reverse the tables in Figure 43-3 to see what a many-to-one relationship looks like.

✦ In a *many-to-many* relationship, many records in the master table can be linked to many records in the detail table. Figure 43-4 illustrates a many-to-many relationship between inventory items and possible suppliers.

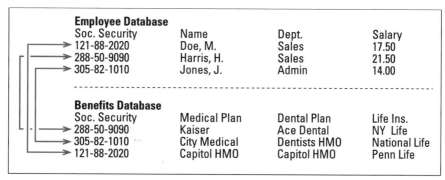

Figure 43-2: One-to-one relationship.

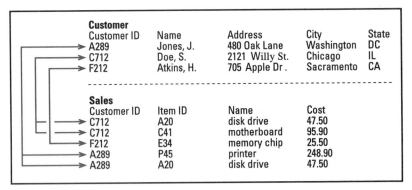

Figure 43-3: One-to-many relationship.

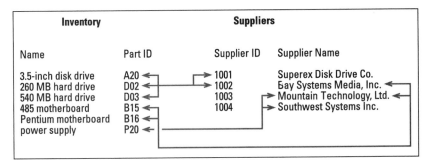

Figure 43-4: Many-to-many relationship.

Because there is no unique value on either side of a many-to-many relationship, record matching is ineffective.

Note With Paradox and most other PC-based relational database managers, many-to-many relationships are created by linking two separate one-to-many relationships. Paradox does not support this relationship for display and reporting purposes.

Using relationships

As you create a relational database, you'll find yourself asking the following questions:

✦ When do I break data into separate tables?

✦ How should I structure their relationships?

While there are no hard-and-fast rules, a prime consideration in your answers is how your data is to appear in forms and reports.

Typically, you'll want to create additional tables when the amount of information becomes hard to handle, or when you find yourself duplicating data repeatedly. For example, if you find that you're entering the same customer number or part name over and over in a single table, you'll probably be better off with two tables, linked by a common field. Your job is to figure out which fields belong in each table, the common field you should link by, and the type of relationship to establish between the tables.

Planning Properly

Proper planning is key to the success of any database project, whether it's for personal use or for a corporate system involving hundreds of users.

Before doing any work on a database, you should have a clear statement of purpose and precise goals for your project.

During the planning phase, you'll determine what fields you need, the type of data for each (characters, numbers, currency, and so on), and how to organize your tables. You can use flowcharts to illustrate how data is processed and the relationships between tables.

Above all, your users, or clients, must be actively involved in the planning process, if your project is to be a success.

Designing the Database

Just as you wouldn't build a house without a plan, you must design your database before you build it. This may sound obvious, but many database projects start with little or no design. Key components of your design include the following:

✦ Data access

✦ The user interface

✦ Processing needs

✦ Program interaction

✦ Output requirements

Data access

Determine what tables your application requires for data entry and reporting. You'll also want to consider what kinds of operations are to be performed, such as mass updates to the values in various fields.

The user interface

Decide what your database application will look like to the users. For example, data entry clerks may need customized forms that are easy to fill in.

Processing needs

Determine how your application will work once data is entered. For example, decide what queries are necessary to retrieve data used in reports.

Program interaction

Determine what (if anything) your application must do to support other programs. For example, you may need to design queries to send specific data to a WordPerfect mail-merge operation, or your tables may need to be accessible as HTML data on a corporate intranet.

Output requirements

Work closely with users to determine precisely what kinds of reports are needed, and how they should appear. Output can include data files, crosstab summaries, or new Paradox tables.

Creating a Project Checklist

As you develop your specifications, keep a checklist of the planning steps, such as the example shown in Table 43-1.

Table 43-1 Sample Checklist of a Project Plan	
Item	*Description*
Database purpose	To track Help Desk calls
End-users	Four telephone support technicians and one department manager
Target completion date	March 1
User-interface needs	Data entry forms with search buttons to allow a support technician to quickly find records entered by other support technicians
Processing needs	Queries to report on calls by a range of days, and by the name of the technician

Item	Description
Program interaction needs	Query to produce a Quattro Pro table for numeric analysis
Output requirements	Reports of daily calls, calls by technicians over a range of days, and total of calls by type for the month

Finalizing your plan

Once you have your design on paper, present it to all your users, from the data entry clerks to the managers who use the reports. You may have to go back to your users several times before all the details are correct. Obtain their final feedback and sign-off before you develop the application.

Keep in mind that the development of a complex database application is by nature an evolving process. Users can't anticipate every need, and business requirements change over time, necessitating further refinements to your system. But with a solid foundation of planning by you and the users, future changes will be a lot less painful.

Identifying data needs

Once you have the project plan in place, identify data needs by

- ✦ Defining the data
- ✦ Refining the data
- ✦ Normalizing the data
- ✦ Specifying primary keys
- ✦ Specifying foreign and relational keys

Defining data

The first step in identifying data needs is known as *data definition*, in which you lay out your planned requirements into hierarchies of related fields. List every conceivable data category. At this point, don't worry about what fields go into what tables, or whether some of the items are redundant or unnecessary.

Refining Data

During *data refinement*, you'll show users your proposed list of fields and sample reports. This step is instrumental in eliminating unnecessary fields. For example, your users may tell you that a proposed male/female field is never needed in any reports.

Normalizing data

In the next step you *normalize* your database, to improve its structure and eliminate potential problems. At the end of the normalization process, your data will be organized into a group of tables, and nonkey information generally won't have to be entered in more than one table. A normalized database requires less updating and is less prone to errors and inconsistencies.

The process of normalization can be divided into successive steps, known as *normal forms*. Normal form is a programming term. You could just as easily refer to these steps as three successive processes in the database design that are intended to make database management more efficient. Don't confuse the term "normal form" with data entry forms that you'll learn about in a later chapter—the two terms have absolutely no relationship to each other.

1. In the first normal form, you remove *repeating groups* of data by placing them in separate tables.

   For example, in creating an Orders table, you realize that each order can include several parts, so you place the repeating part information in a separate Items Ordered table, linked via the order number:

   - **Orders table**—Order Number, Part Number, Customer Number, Customer Name, Customer Location, Customer Contact Number

   - **Items Ordered table**—Order Number, Part Number, Part Description, Unit Price, Quantity Ordered, Supplier, Supplier Location, Supplier Contact Number

2. In the second normal form, you remove partial key dependencies to other tables.

   Look to see that the Orders table contains customer information that is repeated with every order, and the Items Ordered table has a particular part description and unit price that is repeated for every order including that part. If the customer location or unit price changes, you'll have an *update anomaly*— an inconsistency between the database tables—unless you change the location or unit price for every order that includes that customer or part. Or suppose an order is canceled and deleted; the customer or part information will be deleted as well, resulting in a *delete anomaly*—important information might be lost—unless another order contains the same customer or part.

   To achieve the second normal form in our example, separate the attributes dependent on the order or parts key alone from those dependent on both the order and parts key. This can be achieved by creating separate Customer and Parts tables:

   - **Orders table**—Order Number, Customer Number

   - **Customer table**—Customer Number, Customer Name, Customer Location, Customer Contact Number

- **Items Ordered table** — Order Number, Part Number, Quantity Ordered
- **Parts table** — Part Number, Part Description, Unit Price, Supplier, Supplier Location, Supplier Contact Number

Now the customer information is not repeated and each part has only one description and unit price. Customer and part updates instantly apply throughout the database.

3. In the third normal form, you remove *non-key dependencies* to other tables.

In our example, we see that the part supplier, location, and contact number describe only the supplier, not the part. To achieve the third normal form, put these items in a separate Supplier table, with the supplier number as the key.

- **Parts table** — Part Number, Part Description, Unit Price, Supplier Number
- **Supplier table** — Supplier Number, Supplier Name, Supplier Location, Supplier Contact Number

Note

You can have additional, higher levels of normalization (entire college texts are devoted to the topic), but the third level is enough for most real-world PC applications. The total elimination of duplicate data entry can result in a confusing structure with many tables and links.

Identifying primary indexes or keys

For most tables in a multi-table database, you must designate a primary key to index the records. The primary key is made up of one or more fields that uniquely identify a record. For example, a table of employees at a company might be indexed by each employee's social security number. A table of customers might use a unique customer ID.

Any table on the one side of a one-to-many relationship must have a primary key. Even if your database uses only a single table, a primary key can speed up sorts and searches, and prevent duplicate entries.

If a unique field doesn't exist, look for a unique combination of fields instead. For example, in a table that tracks data from weekly employee timesheets, a combination of the Employee ID field and a Week Ending field may serve as the primary index.

Identifying foreign and relational keys

When your database uses relationships among multiple tables, you must decide which fields will serve as the relational keys. In at least one of the tables, the field or fields used to establish the relationship must be a primary key.

With one-to-many relationships, you'll need to include a foreign key in the child or detail tables that relates to the primary key in the parent or master table. For example, you might have a table of sales reps and a table of multiple phone calls made by each sales rep. The call records could include the sales rep ID, in addition to a unique call ID, to relate the records to the Sales Rep table.

With one-to-one relationships, your relational keys are the primary keys in both tables. For example, you might have a personnel database, with one table containing employee names and addresses, and another table containing medical insurance information on each employee. You can designate the employee ID code as a primary key in each table, and link the tables by means of that field.

Considering the Alternatives

Although WordPerfect Office 2000 includes the powerful database manager Paradox, there are simpler data-management alternatives within WordPerfect Office 2000. Take a look at WordPerfect tables (Chapter 22), Quattro Pro notebooks (Chapter 30), and especially the CorelCENTRAL card files (Chapter 12).

For More Information . . .

On	See
Mastering the Paradox interface	Chapter 44
Using Experts	Chapter 45
Creating tables	Chapter 46
Creating forms	Chapter 48
Building queries	Chapter 49
Creating reports	Chapter 50
Using Paradox output in other applications	Chapter 51

✦   ✦   ✦

Mastering the Paradox Interface

Welcome to Paradox, the database manager of WordPerfect Office 2000 Professional. This chapter explains what Paradox does and how you can master the Paradox interface.

Working with Objects

Almost every component of the Paradox environment can be referred to as an *object*, much like cats and dogs and pigs and horses are all "animals." Objects include any database component that stores, displays, retrieves, or presents data — such as tables, forms, queries, and reports.

Tables

Tables are the heart of your database. Paradox stores your data in one or more tables that display in separate windows, as shown in Figure 44-1.

Creating a table to store your data is a simple task. You can design a table manually, or choose from several predefined formats by using the Table Expert (see Chapters 45 and 46).

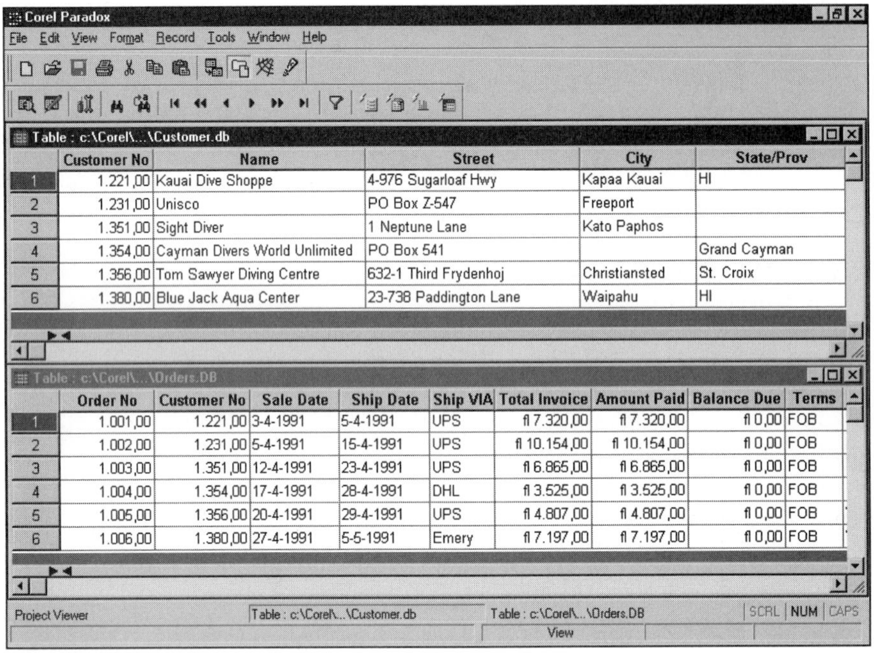

Figure 44-1: Two Paradox tables.

Forms

You can type data directly into your table while in Edit mode. Better yet, create a user-friendly form to enter and view data, one record at a time (see Figure 44-2).

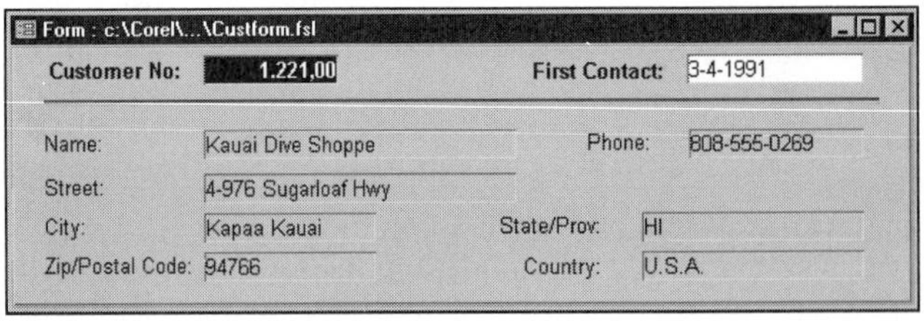

Figure 44-2: User-friendly form for entering and viewing data.

You can use the Form Expert to quickly create a data entry form. You can also design custom forms with fields at any location, along with descriptive text and graphics (see Chapter 48).

Queries

Queries retrieve specific data from one or more tables. You typically ask questions about the data such as, "How many salespersons beat their June quota?" You create a query by filling in a graphical Query-by-Example (QBE) form or by using the new Query Expert (see Chapter 49). The response to your query is displayed in an *answer table* (see Figure 44-3).

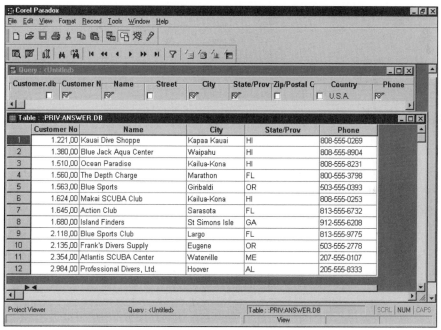

Figure 44-3: Answer table in response to a query.

Reports

Reports display data from one or more tables in various formats, from tabular to free-form to mailing labels (see Figure 44-4).

You can use the Report Expert to quickly build several types of reports. If you need additional flexibility, you can use the powerful report designer to create custom reports in either a tabular or free-form format (see Chapter 50).

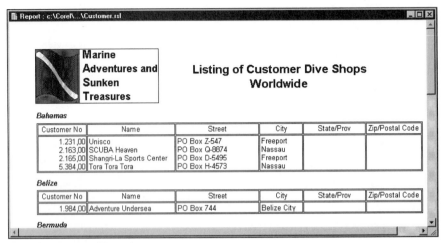

Figure 44-4: Paradox report.

Other objects

Other Paradox objects include scripts, libraries, data models, and SQL statements. These are mostly used by advanced Paradox users, and with the exception of data models, they aren't discussed extensively in this book. For further information on any of these objects, including ObjectPAL (the Paradox programming language), refer to online Help or the Paradox guide in your WordPerfect Office 2000 Reference Center.

Paradox also makes use of various *design objects*, to improve the layout of forms and reports. These include text, boxes, lines, charts, and graphics.

Object *properties* are the attributes of an object. For example, text properties include an object's font, style, size, and color.

Customizing Your Desktop

When you start Paradox, the first thing you see is the desktop (see Figure 44-5). This is the working space for all your Paradox objects.

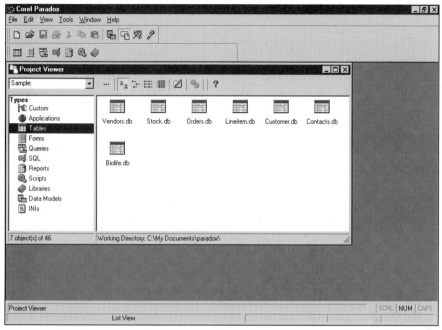

Figure 44-5: Paradox desktop.

To customize your desktop, click Tools ⇨ Settings ⇨ Preferences, click the General tab, and then change any of the following (see Figure 44-6):

✦ *Title*, to change the wording of the title bar at the top of your display

✦ *Background bitmap*, to pick a wallpaper background for your desktop

✦ *Desktop state*, to determine the state of the desktop when Paradox is started. When both options are checked, the desktop will look just like it did when you last exited. If you only check "Restore on startup," and then click "Save Now," Paradox will always start with the current set of files.

✦ *Default system font*, to change the default font used by Paradox for tables, forms, and reports

✦ *Project Viewer settings,* to display the Project Viewer on startup (recommended)

Figure 44-6: Customizing your desktop.

Click other tabs in the Preferences dialog box to change settings for Tables, Forms/Reports, Queries, and other objects. To customize your toolbars, right-click the toolbar and click Customize (see Chapter 57).

Using the Project Viewer

Unless you've closed it, you see the Project Viewer inside the desktop when you start Paradox (see Figure 44-7). If you don't see the Project Viewer, click the Project Viewer button, or click Tools ⇨ Project Viewer.

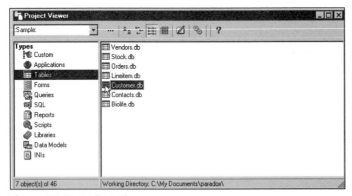

Figure 44-7: Project Viewer.

Icons for the objects in your *working directory* (your default folder for opening and saving files) are displayed on the left.

Tip Click the Types heading at the top of the list to display all the objects.

To view a particular group, click the corresponding icon. (The Scripts and Libraries groups contain ObjectPAL code.) Right-click an icon to create a new object.

From the Project Viewer, you can double-click a table or other object to perform the default action for that object (to open it, in most cases). You can right-click an object to change its properties.

Using Directories

In addition to your working directory or folder, you can have private folders and aliases.

When you install Paradox on a local drive, your working directory is placed under your system folder, usually in Program Files\Corel\WordPerfect Office 2000\Paradox\Working.

As you work with Paradox, you'll probably want to create one or more additional folders for various projects. For example, you might have an attendance database in C:\Data\Attendance, or a purchasing database in C:\Data\Purchasing.

Changing the working directory

To change the working directory, click File ➪ Working Directory and specify the path, or select an alias from the Aliases list (see "Assigning aliases" later in this chapter).

Changing private directories

In a multi-user environment, you need a place to put the objects you're working on. By design, this is a nonshared folder known as your *private directory*. The default private directory is named Private, and it is created below the Paradox folder on your hard drive (or in your Home folder on the network).

To change your private directory, click Tools ➪ Settings ➪ Preferences, click the Database tab, and enter the path. When you change your private directory, Paradox deletes any temporary tables, such as an answer table with query results.

Assigning aliases

In Paradox, an *alias* is a name that you can assign to a folder as a shortcut. By default, the working directory is assigned the alias :WORK: and the private directory is assigned the alias :PRIV:.

To assign new aliases at any time:

1. Click Tools ➪ Alias Manager ➪ New, and type an alias name (see Figure 44-8). (Leave the "Driver type" box as Standard when using Paradox tables.)

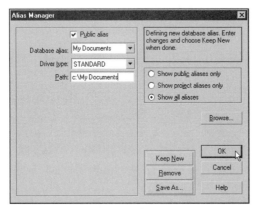

Figure 44-8: Assigning Aliases.

2. Enter the path of your alias folder. Check "Public alias" if you want to use the alias from any working folder. (Project aliases are only available from the working directory in which they were created.)

If you want to use the alias again after the current Paradox session, click Save As.

Exiting Paradox

To exit Paradox, click File ➪ Exit. Paradox prompts you to save changes to open objects before you exit. Data changes in tables are automatically saved.

For More Information . . .

On	See
Using Experts	Chapter 45
Creating tables	Chapter 46
Creating forms	Chapter 48
Building queries	Chapter 49
Creating reports	Chapter 50
Customizing toolbars	Chapter 57
Using advanced objects	Paradox guide in the Reference Center
Programming with ObjectPAL	Paradox guide in the Reference Center and ObjectPAL Reference
Using Paradox in a network environment	Paradox guide in the Reference Center

✦   ✦   ✦

Becoming an Instant Paradox Expert

◆ ◆ ◆ ◆

In This Chapter

Get started with the
Welcome Expert

Create a custom
project by using the
Database Expert

Start directly from a
predefined project

Get Expert help with
other tasks

◆ ◆ ◆ ◆

Paradox 9 comes with a number of ready-to-use projects
that make it easy to get started. You'll also find a number
of Experts to help you perform complex tasks.

Now that you know how to plan a database project and you're
familiar with the Paradox interface, it's time to get started on
your own database! Paradox offers a number of powerful
projects and Experts that make it easy to get started, even if
you're a database novice.

Getting Expert Help When You Start Paradox

When you launch Paradox, the Welcome Expert (see Figure
45-1) lets you open an existing database or create a new one
from scratch. (If you don't see the Welcome Expert, click
Tools ⇨ Settings ⇨ Preferences ⇨ Experts and check Run
Welcome Expert each time Paradox loads.) The Welcome
Expert also offers easy access to other Experts and the
Paradox 9 tutorial.

When the Welcome Expert appears, click one of the following:

- ◆ *New Database*, to create a database from scratch by using
  the Visual Database Designer, discussed in Chapter 46

- ◆ *Open Database*, to select an alias and then open an
  existing database

- ◆ *Database Templates*, to open the Database Expert and
  create a database from a template (see "Using the
  Database Expert").

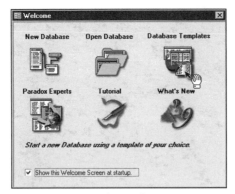

Figure 45-1: Paradox Welcome Expert.

✦ *Paradox Experts*, to choose another Expert to help you with various tasks (see "Getting Expert Help with Other Tasks," later in this chapter)

✦ *Tutorial*, for step-by-step instructions for creating a table, running a report, or performing other tasks

✦ *What's New*, to discover the latest features in Paradox 9

Using the Database Expert

The Database Expert lets you select a ready-to-use, multi-table database, and customize it to your needs:

1. Click Tools ➪ Experts, click the Database Expert, and click Run Expert (or start the Database Expert from the Welcome Expert).

2. Choose the type of personal, business, or corporate database you want to create (see Figure 45-2).

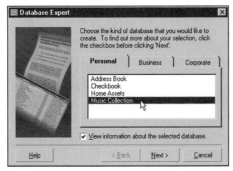

Figure 45-2: Choosing the type of database you want to create.

3. Check the View information about the selected database box and click Next to get information on the database structure, including the tables, forms, and reports that will be created (see Figure 45-3).

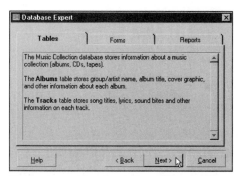

Figure 45-3: Viewing information on the database structure.

4. Click Next to customize the tables you're about to create. Select the table you want to customize, and then add, remove, and rename fields (see Figure 45-4).

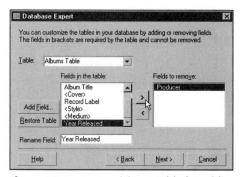

Figure 45-4: Customizing a table by adding, removing, and renaming fields.

5. Click Next, specify the name and location, then click Finish to create your database.

Your new database comes complete with forms and reports, plus a handy tabbed form to provide quick access to its tables, forms, and reports (see Figure 45-5).

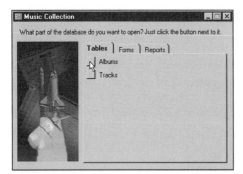

Figure 45-5: Tabbed access form created by the Database Expert.

Using a Predefined Project

If you don't need to customize your database at the start, you can create it directly from a predefined project, rather than using the Database Expert:

1. Click the New button (File ⇨ New) and select a PerfectExpert project from the Paradox section (see Figure 45-6).

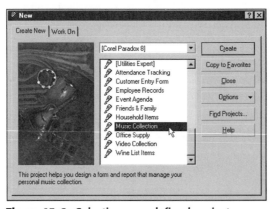

Figure 45-6: Selecting a predefined project.

2. Click Create, and start adding data (see Figure 45-7).

3. Use the PerfectExpert for help in changing the layout of forms and reports, and with other project tasks (see Figure 45-8).

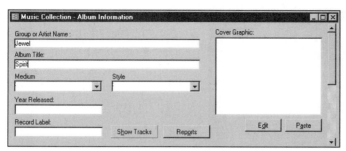

Figure 45-7: Adding data to your project.

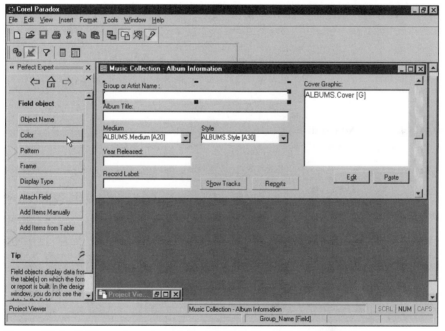

Figure 45-8: Editing a form template with help from the PerfectExpert.

Getting Expert Help with Other Tasks

You'll find more Paradox Experts, described in later chapters, to help you create tables, forms, reports, mailing labels, and so on. Click Tools ➪ Experts to display them all or click the PerfectExpert button to access them from the PerfectExpert panel. Then click the Expert you want to use (see Figure 45-9), click Run Expert, and follow the steps on the screen.

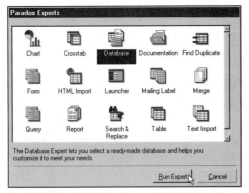

Figure 45-9: Getting Expert help with other tasks.

For More Information . . .

On	See
Creating tables with the Table Expert	Chapter 46
Using the Visual Database Designer	Chapter 46
Entering and editing data	Chapter 47
Creating forms with the Form Expert	Chapter 48
Creating reports with the Report Expert	Chapter 50
Using the other Paradox Experts	Chapter 51

✦　　　✦　　　✦

Creating and Linking Tables

The previous chapters showed you how to plan a database project, get started with Paradox, and use Experts to create databases from templates.

Now comes the fun part, creating your own tables and linking them together in a relational database. Although templates can be quite powerful, building your own tables is often the best way to create a tailor-made database based on your plans and designs.

Creating a Table

To create a Paradox table:

1. Click the New icon (or click File ➪ New From Project...), select New Table, and click Create (see Figure 46-1).

Tip   Even quicker, right-click Tables in the Project Viewer, and click New.

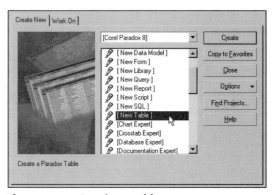

Figure 46-1: Creating a table.

2. Click Blank to create a table from scratch. You can also get help from the Table Expert (see "Using the Table Expert" later in this chapter).

3. Select the table type, normally Paradox 7,8,9 (see Figure 46-2). If you select another type, some field types or features may not be available.

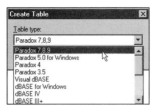

Figure 46-2: Selecting the table type.

4. Click OK, and type a field name (see Figure 46-3), up to 25 characters. Any key fields you are indexing on (as discussed in Chapter 43) must appear at the top of the field roster.

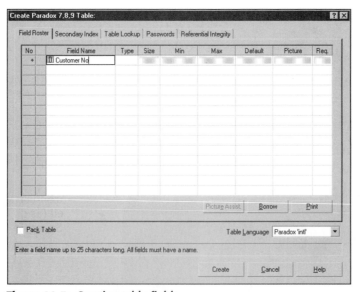

Figure 46-3: Creating table fields.

Tip

Keep names short so your report columns won't be too wide.

Field names can include spaces, numbers, and any characters other than double quotation marks, square brackets, left or right parentheses, curly braces, or the -> character combination.

Caution Spaces in field names are allowed, but not recommended. Don't use spaces if you want to share your databases with users of other database products.

5. Click the cell in the Type column to select one of the 17 field types (see Figure 46-4) described in Table 46-1 (located at the end of this procedure).

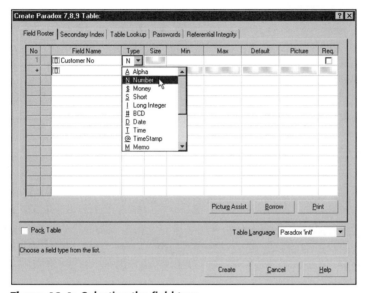

Figure 46-4: Selecting the field type.

6. Specify the field size, where required, based on the actual data you want the field to hold.

7. Validity checks can be specified to restrict entries to a particular range of values. Default values and pictures can be specified as well (as discussed in the next section, "Specifying Validity Checks and Picture Strings").

8. Use the Min, Max, Default, Picture, and Req'd columns to restrict entries to a particular range of values or assign default values, as discussed in the next section, "Specifying Validity Checks and Picture Strings."

9. If the field is to be part of a primary index (as discussed in Chapter 43), click the Key column on the left to display a key (see Figure 46-5).

10. Tab or press the down arrow key to add more fields to the table.

11. Click Create when you're done, enter the table's name and location, and then click Save.

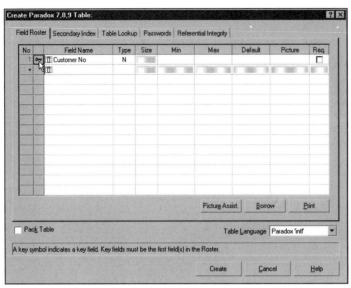

Figure 46-5: Designating a key field.

Table 46-1
Field Types in Paradox

Field Type	Lets You
Alpha	Store up to 255 characters, including letters, numbers, punctuation marks, blank spaces, and special symbols.
Number	Store numeric values other than currency. (Use the alpha type for numbers you don't calculate on, such as postal codes or phone numbers.)
Money	Store currency values, rounded to a default of 2 decimal places. (The $ symbol appears, but the currency symbol selected in your Windows Control Panel is actually used.)
Short	Store integer values from –32,767 to +32,767. Caution: Avoid this field type unless you're sure that the entries will fall within this range.
Long Integer	Store integer values from –2147483647 to +21147483647.
BCD	Store binary-coded decimal numbers, with up to 32 decimal places. Use this type when you need to store decimal values with more accuracy than the 15 decimal places provided with number fields.
Date	Store date values from 1/1/9999 B.C. through 12/31/9999 A.D. (Paradox checks the validity of dates as you enter them.)

Field Type	Lets You
Time	Store times in a default format of HH:MM:SS A.M./P.M. (Entries are checked for validity.)
Timestamp	Insert the current date and time when you add a record to the table.
Memo	Store unlimited text for employee evaluations, product descriptions, and the like. You can specify how many characters get stored with the table. The complete memo is stored in a separate file on disk, and retrieved as you view the record.
Formatted Memo	Store unlimited, formatted text. You can specify how many characters get stored with the table. The complete memo is stored in a separate file on disk, and retrieved as you view the record.
Graphic	Store graphic images.
OLE	Paste Object Linking and Embedding (OLE) data, such as sound clips, video clips, or parts of a spreadsheet or document.
Logical	Store logical (yes or no) values.
Autoincrement	Automatically increment a numeric value in the field for each record that you add. (Use for customer ID numbers and the like, to uniquely identify each record. Autoincrement values can't be changed.)
Binary	Store binary data such as sound. (The contents of binary fields can only be accessed with ObjectPAL.)
Bytes	Store from one to 255 characters. (The contents of bytes fields can only be accessed with ObjectPAL.)

Note   Two-digit years in Paradox, like those in Quattro Pro, are Year 2000–compliant. For more information, you may want to visit the Corel Year 2000 Web site at `http://www.corel.com/year2000/index.htm`.

Specifying Validity Checks and Picture Strings

When defining a table, you can restrict entries to a particular range of values by specifying *validity checks* for a field, or specify a *default value* for Paradox to enter when the field is left blank. You can also format entries with picture strings.

To specify a validity check, default value, or picture string while defining a table, click the field in the roster (previously shown in Figure 46-3), and then do any of the following:

✦ Specify minimum and/or maximum values in the Min and/or Max boxes.

✦ In the Default box, specify a value to assign to the field if no other value is entered.

Tip

Use the TODAY and NOW keywords with Date, Time, or Timestamp fields to make them default to the current date or time when a record is added. NOW enters both the date and time in a Timestamp field.

✦ Check the Req box to ensure that the field is filled before the record is accepted.

✦ Select a *picture string* from the drop-down list in the Picture box to restrict data entry to a precise format. Click the Picture Assist (Assistant) button to create your own pictures using any of the symbols in Table 46-2. For example, type **(###) ###-####** to specify the telephone number with the hyphen and parentheses, and constrain user entry to ten numbers (as shown in Figure 46-6).

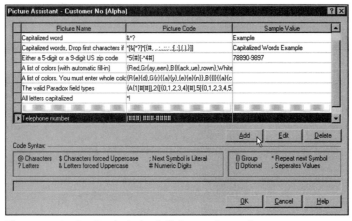

Figure 46-6: Getting help in defining a picture format.

Table 46-2
Picture Symbols

Symbol	What It Does
#	Allows any numeric digit
?	Allows any letter
@	Allows any character
!	Allows any character (converts letters to uppercase)
&	Allows any letter (converts to uppercase)

Symbol	What It Does
;	Indicates that the following character is a literal character
*	Allows repetition of the following character any number of times
[ ]	Indicates that the characters inside the brackets are optional
{ }	Indicates a grouping of characters inside the brackets
,	Separates alternate values

Note   Not all field types support all types of validity checks. For example, you cannot specify a maximum or minimum value for a logical field.

Defining Table Lookups

Table lookups provide a sophisticated way to restrict data entry to a particular range of values in a related table, and assist the user by displaying a list of acceptable entries. Normally, an existing table is used for the lookup, but you can create a separate table for the purpose. Validity checks and picture strings are used to ensure that a value entered in a table meets certain criteria; a lookup table ensures that a value entered in a table matches an existing value in another table. For instance, use a lookup table to add customer numbers from an existing customer table to a new order table to make sure that all the customer numbers entered in the order table match a customer number in the customer table.

To define a table lookup while creating a table:

1. Click any field in the field roster, and then click the Table Lookup tab.

2. Double-click the field for which you want to restrict data entry (see Figure 46-7), and double-click the table with the range of acceptable values defined.

Tip   You can also select the field and table and click the arrow buttons.

Note   The type of the field for which you define the lookup must be the same type as the first field in the lookup table.

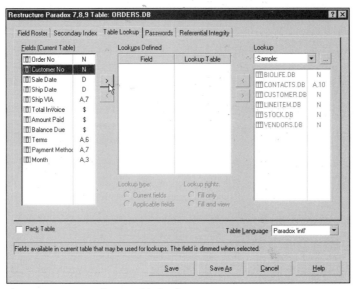

Figure 46-7: Creating a table lookup.

3. Select the type of lookup access:

- **Fill only** checks whether a value entered exists in the lookup table
- **Fill and view** lets the user display the lookup table when entering data (see Figure 46-8)

Figure 46-8: Displaying the lookup table when entering data.

Specifying a Secondary Index

Most tables have a primary index (as discussed in Chapter 43). You can also specify a *secondary index* to maintain an internal ordering of the records by another field and to speed up searching and reporting.

For example, you may have a table of employees with a primary index on the social security number, but you regularly generate reports in last name order. If the table is a sizable one, you can create a secondary index on the Last Name field to speed up reporting.

To specify a secondary index when creating a table:

1. Click the Secondary Index tab.

2. Click Add, and then specify a name for the secondary index.

3. Click the field or fields to index on, and then click the right arrow to add them to the Selected Index Fields (see Figure 46-9).

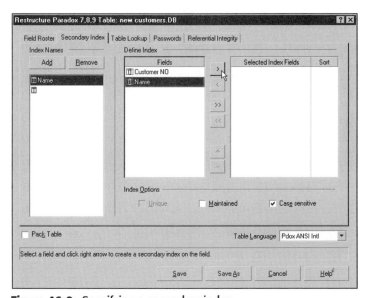

Figure 46-9: Specifying a secondary index.

Changing a Table's Structure

You're often likely to change the structure of your tables. You may need to add new fields, delete fields that aren't used, or change the names or other properties of existing fields. You may also need to change the order of your fields, either to put them in a more logical order, or to change their default order of appearance when you generate forms and reports by using the Experts.

To change a table's structure:

1. Right-click the table in the Project Viewer and click Restructure.

2. Do any of the following:

- **To change a field's name, type, or size**, click within the field and make the change.

- **To insert a new field**, click the roster number for field below the new field and press Insert.

- **To move a field to a new location,** drag the field's roster number.

- **To delete a field,** click the field's roster number and press Delete.

Note

When you delete a field used in a form or report, you'll get a warning when you open the form or report that the underlying field can't be found. You must open the form or report in Design mode and remove the field reference (see Chapters 48 and 50).

Borrowing Another Table's Structure

Why re-invent the wheel? Instead of creating a new table from scratch, you can borrow the design of an existing one:

1. Click the New icon (or click File ➪ New From Project...), select [New Table], and click Create. Now create a blank Paradox 7,8,9 table (as discussed in the first section of this chapter) and wait for the field roster to appear.

2. Click Borrow to display the Select Borrow Table dialog box (as shown in Figure 46-10) and select the table whose structure you want to borrow.

Figure 46-10: Borrowing another table's structure.

3. Check any optional properties you want to borrow (such as validity checks and indexes), and then click Open.

4. Edit the new table to meet your needs. Insert and delete fields and change the properties of fields (as discussed previously in "Changing a Table's Structure").

Using the Table Expert

When creating a table from scratch, you can save a lot of manual drudgery by using the Table Expert. The Table Expert lets you select the fields to be included in your database (field names can be edited) and helps you create a key field.

To use the Table Expert:

1. Click the PerfectExpert icon (or click Tools ➪ Experts), and then click the Table Expert (and click Run Expert if necessary).

2. Click the Business or Personal button in the bottom left corner of the Table Expert, and then follow the onscreen instructions to complete the table (see Figure 46-11).

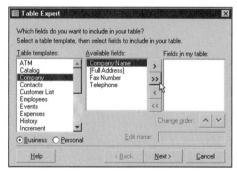

Figure 46-11: Creating a table with the Table Expert.

Linking Tables by Using the Visual Database Designer

Once you've defined individual tables, how can you make them work together? The Visual Database Designer makes this a simple task.

WordPerfect's new Visual Database Designer feature enables you to easily *link* individual tables into a multiple-table database. The tables you want to link must have a common field, and at least one of their fields must have an index. The fields you link should match in type and size, and the parent table's field should be the key field.

In the following exercise you'll use the Paradox samples to create a multi-table data model for your company, with information on customers, orders, items, stock, and vendors.

You'll need two separate tables for this example. You'll have a customer table that's linked to an orders table by a common customer number. For a complete database you would need additional tables that won't be shown in this example.

Rather than creating the tables for this exercise from scratch, you can copy them from the Sample folder to your Private folder. To copy the tables:

1. Make certain the :Sample: alias is selected in the drop-down list box in the Project Viewer.

2. Hold down Ctrl as you click customer.db and orders.db.

3. Right-click the selected tables and choose Copy from the pop-up menu.

4. Select the :PRIV: alias in the drop-down list box in the Project Viewer.

5. Right-click in the right-hand pane of the Project viewer and select Paste.

6. Click the Set Current Directory as Working Directory button on the Project Viewer toolbar.

To link the sample tables:

1. Click Tools ➪ Visual Database Designer.

2. Select Edit ➪ Add Table to display the Add Table dialog box (see Figure 46-12).

3. Select the tables that will be linked and click Add (see Figure 46-13). In this case you'll want to add the two tables that you copied earlier.

4. Click Close to close the Add Table dialog box.

5. Right-click a table to expand or collapse its view. To expand or collapse all the tables, click the Expand All or Collapse All icon (View ➪ Expand All or View ➪ Collapse All). Click the New Paradox Table icon to add a new table.

6. Right-click each of the tables in turn and select Restructure. Click in the key column and make the first field in each of the tables a key field; as described earlier, the field you want to link must be a key field. Click Save to save the table.

7. Select the field of the table you want to link, drag the field to the field of the table you want to create a link with, and then give the link a name (see Figure 46-14). For this example, drag the Customer No field of the Orders table to the Customer No field of the Customer table.

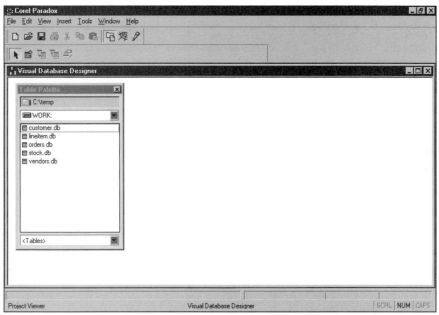

Figure 46-12: Specifying the tables to be linked.

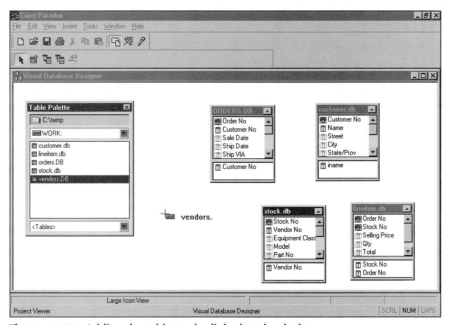

Figure 46-13: Adding the tables to be linked to the desktop.

Figure 46-14: Naming a link.

8. The link you create is indicated with an arrow (see Figure 46-15). Select the arrow and click the Link Property icon to show the link's properties.

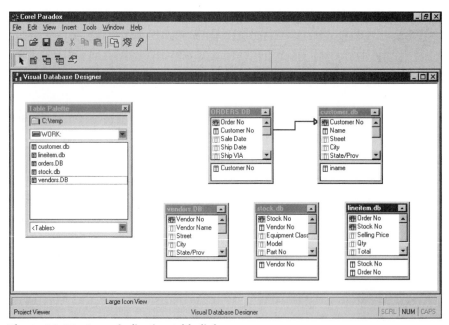

Figure 46-15: Arrow indicating table link.

Your multi-table database is now complete.

Protecting Referential Integrity

By using the Visual Database Designer to link your tables, the *referential integrity* of your database is automatically ensured. This means that record changes or deletions in one table will not break the links to records in related tables. For example, when you change the primary key in a record of the parent table, the linked fields in all corresponding child table records are automatically updated.

Referential integrity also prevents "orphan" records. You can't delete a record in the parent table unless all matching records in the child table have been deleted. Likewise, you can't add a record to the child table unless it matches a record in the parent table.

You can also define referential integrity in the field roster, as follows:

1. If the parent table is open on the desktop, close it.

2. Click Tables in the Project Viewer, right-click the child table, and click Restructure (see Figure 46-16).

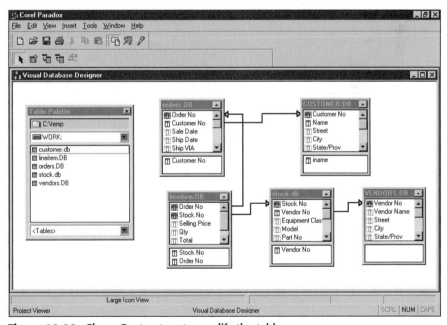

Figure 46-16: Chose Restructure to modify the table.

3. Click the Referential Integrity tab.

4. Click Add to name the link.

5. Click the parent table in the Parent Table list. The table's key now appears in the Parent's Key listing.

6. In the Fields list, double-click the field of the child table that corresponds to the key field of the parent table. The field name then appears in the Child Fields listing (see Figure 46-17).

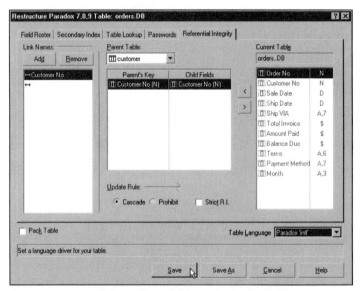

Figure 46-17: Defining referential integrity in the field roster.

7. Select any of the following options:

- **Cascade** automatically updates corresponding fields in the child table when the key field in the parent table is changed.

- **Prohibit** prevents changes to the parent key when the child table has records with the same key value.

- **Strict referential integrity** prevents older DOS versions of Paradox from opening tables created in Paradox for Windows that make use of referential integrity.

For More Information . . .

On	See
Planning your database	Chapter 43
Year 2000 compliance	Chapter 32
Building a database with the Database Expert	Chapter 45
Working with tables	Chapter 47
Creating forms	Chapter 48
Creating reports	Chapter 50

✦   ✦   ✦

Entering, Editing, and Viewing Data

Your tables aren't really a database until you put some data in them! This chapter shows you how to directly enter data in your tables. Chapter 48, "Creating Input Forms," shows you how to create user-friendly data input forms.

Working with Data in Table View

Table view presents the direct and obvious way to work with your data (see Figure 47-1). You have two ways to enter Table view:

♦ Click Tables in the Project Viewer and double-click the table you want to see (or right-click it and click Open).

♦ Click the Open Table icon (File ➪ Open ➪ Table), select the table, and click Open.

Freezing your column display

One unique feature of the Table view is the scroll lock marker above the horizontal scroll bar (previously shown in Figure 47-1). By dragging the marker to the right, you can "freeze" one or more columns at the left side of the window while the rest of the columns are scrolled.

Navigating records

Instead of scrolling records, you can click various toolbar buttons to go to the first, last, next, or previous record, or to the next or previous set (see Figure 47-2). You can also click Record ➪ Go to, and select a destination.

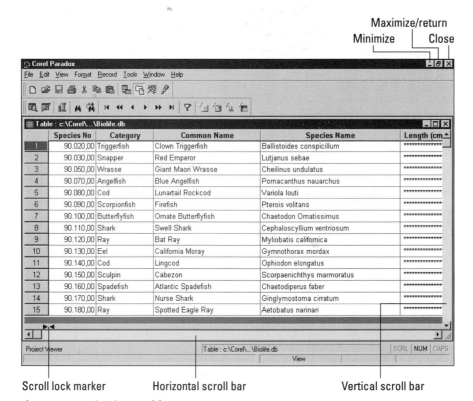

Figure 47-1: Viewing a table.

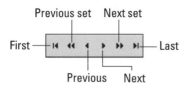

Figure 47-2: Toolbar navigation buttons.

You can also navigate and edit records with any of the keyboard shortcuts described in Table 47-1.

Table 47-1 Shortcut Keys in Table View	
Key	**Lets You**
Home	Move to the first field of the current record
Ctrl+Home	Move to the first field of the first record
End	Move to the last field of the current record
Ctrl+End	Move to the last field of the last record
Ctrl+Backspace	Delete the word to the left of the insertion point when editing a field's contents (see "Changing part of a field" later in this chapter)
Insert	Insert a record
Ctrl+Delete	Delete the current record
Ctrl+D	Duplicate (copy) the data in the field directly above the current record into the current field
Esc	Undo an edit
Spacebar	Enter the current date, time, or both into a Date, Time, or Timestamp field

Editing records

You can toggle in and out of the record Edit mode by doing any of the following:

✦ Click the Edit icon to enter Edit mode; click the View button to return to View mode.

✦ Click View ➪ Edit Data to enter Edit mode; click View ➪ View Data to return to View mode.

✦ Press F9 to enter Edit mode when you're in View mode and vice versa.

When you're not in Edit mode, the message "Not in Edit mode" appears on the property bar when you attempt to edit a record.

Caution

Paradox automatically saves your edits as you move off a record, so be sure of your changes before you move to a different record.

Inserting and deleting records

To add a new record in Edit mode, click Record ➪ Insert, or press the Insert key. If you're at the last record of the table, you can also click the Next Record icon.

To delete the current record, click Record ➪ Delete or press Ctrl+Delete.

Changing part of a field

When you edit a field, the entire contents of the field are normally replaced. To change just part of a field in Edit mode (for example, to correct a mistyped word) do the following:

1. Double-click the field, press F2, or click View ➪ Field View.

2. Edit the field.

Once you move off the current field, Paradox automatically switches back to the normal Edit mode.

Tip   Press Ctrl+F2 to perform partial edits on several fields in the persistent field view, and then press F2 to return to normal Edit mode.

Displaying and editing memo fields

To display the entire Memo field you're editing, double-click the field, press Shift+F2, or click View ➪ Memo View (see Figure 47-3). Press Shift+F2 to close the memo editing window.

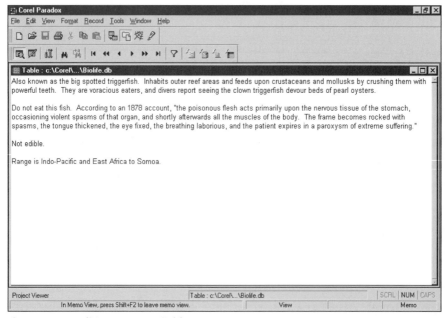

Figure 47-3: Editing a Memo field.

You can also format text in a Formatted Memo field, as follows:

1. Right-click the field and click Properties.

2. Click the Font tab to change the font, size, spacing, and/or color.

3. Click OK.

When you're not in Edit mode, you can double-click a Memo field to view it.

Editing fields with cut, copy, and paste

When editing fields, you can cut, copy, and paste data via the Clipboard, following the procedures described in Chapter 2, "Essential Typing and Editing."

Inserting graphics

When editing graphic fields, you can insert graphics via the Clipboard by using cut, copy, and paste. To insert a graphic from another location, click Edit ⇨ Paste From to display the Paste From Graphic File dialog box. (see Figure 47-4). Then locate and select the graphic file you want to insert, and click Open.

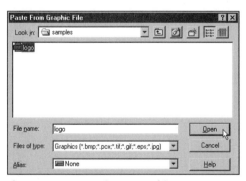

Figure 47-4: Inserting a graphic.

Paradox supports the BMP, PCX, TIFF, GIF, JPG, and EPS graphic formats. Graphics you store are converted to the Windows Bitmap (.BMP) format.

Cross-Reference   See Chapter 9, "Working with Graphics," for a description of graphic formats.

Viewing a Graphic

You can see all or part of a graphic in Table view, depending on the size of the columns and rows (see Figure 47-5).

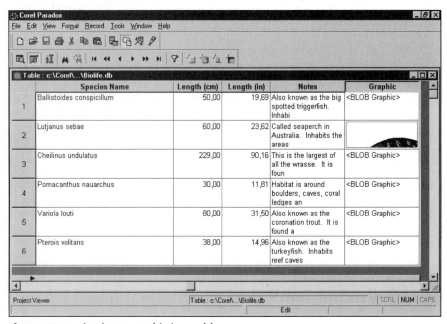

Figure 47-5: Viewing a graphic in a table.

Double-click the field to view the graphic in a separate window (see Figure 47-6).

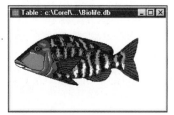

Figure 47-6: Viewing a graphic in a separate window.

Copying graphic and binary data to external files

One little-known feature of Paradox is its capability to copy data from a graphic or binary field into an external file. To use this feature:

1. Click the field and click Edit ➪ Copy To.

2. Enter the filename and location, and then click Save.

Using Speech to Enter Data

Paradox supports Dragon NaturallySpeaking for data entry and navigating your tables. To start Dragon NaturallySpeaking from Paradox, click Tools ➪ Dragon NaturallySpeaking. For more information on using Dragon NaturallySpeaking, see Chapter 4, "Hello Hal!" For a listing of Paradox speech commands, see Appendix C, "NaturallySpeaking Quick Reference."

Spell-Checking Your Data

Spelling errors make it look like you don't care enough to do things correctly. No matter how carefully you type, anyone can make a spelling error. Spelling errors can also prevent you from correctly matching records if the same item is spelled differently in other records.

Click Tools ➪ Spell Check to spell-check a field while editing a table or form. Select multiple fields or records to spell-check them all at once.

You must be in Edit mode to run Spell Checker.

Changing a Table's Appearance

As you work with tables in Table view, you can rearrange the appearance of the data in several ways.

To change your table's appearance with your mouse:

✦ Drag any horizontal grid line to change the height of all the rows.

✦ Drag a vertical grid line on either side of a column to change its width.

✦ Drag a column heading button to move a column to another location (the underlying order of the data does not change).

To change the appearance of fields or column headings:

1. Right-click the field or column heading, and then click Properties.

2. Click the General, Alignment, and/or Font tab and make your changes (see Figure 47-7).

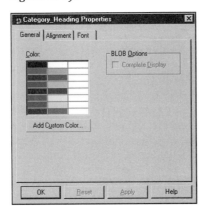

Figure 47-7: Changing the appearance of a field or column heading.

To change the appearance of all your fields or column headings, hold down the Shift key as you right-click in any field or column heading.

To change the appearance of the table grid lines, right-click the grid, and then choose the settings.

Note   Changes made to data in tables are automatically saved, while changes made to the appearance of tables have to be saved manually. You'll be prompted to save changes to table properties when you close the table or exit Paradox.

Locating Records

There are several ways to locate particular records in a large table. You can search for a specific field value, search for a record number or field, find and replace field values, and/or find and replace Memo field text.

Locating field values

You can locate records in the current table by specifying a field value that you want to find, as follows:

1. Click the Locate icon (Record Í Locate Í Value), and select the field you want to search on (see Figure 47-8).

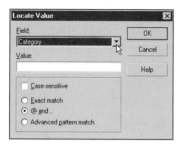

Figure 47-8: Selecting a field to search on.

2. Enter the value you want to find.

3. Click the Case-sensitive check box if you want to match on the exact capitalization.

4. Click one of the following:

   - *Exact match,* to only locate records that precisely match the search term. For example, if you enter **California** as the Value and then select this option, you won't get a match if a field contains "California Burgundy."

   - @ and .. lets you use either or both these wildcard operators in your search, @ stands for any character; .. stands for any number of characters, including none. For instance, enter ..house.. to find, boathouse, houses and houseboat.

   - *Advanced pattern match,* to specify any of the extended wildcard characters described in Table 47-2.

5. Click OK to locate the first matching record. To find successive values, click the Locate Next icon or click Record ➪ Locate ➪ Next.

Locating record numbers or fields

To locate a record by its record number, click Record ➪ Locate ➪ Record Number. You can also drag the vertical scroll bar while observing the record numbers on the application bar.

To locate a particular field in a wide table, click Record ➪ Locate ➪ Field.

| | Table 47-2 |
| **Extended Wildcard Search Characters** | |
Wildcard	*Represents*
@	Any single character
..	Any number of characters, including none
^	Beginning of field
$	End of field
*	Any number of characters, including none
+	Match one or more of the characters before the +
?	Match one or none of the characters before the ?
|	Match either of the characters before or after the vertical bar
[abc]	Match any of the characters enclosed within the brackets
[^abc]	Match any characters not enclosed within the brackets

Locating and replacing values

You can locate and replace every occurrence of a value. For example, you can change every "keyboard" entry in a description field of an inventory to "computer keyboard."

To locate and replace values:

1. Click View ⇨ Edit Data to enter Edit mode (if you're not already in it).

2. Click Record ⇨ Locate ⇨ Replace, and select the field to perform the replacement on.

3. Enter the value to locate and the value to replace it with.

4. Specify the search options as previously described in Steps 3 and 4 of "Locating field values" (see Figure 47-9).

Note   You can search for a portion of the field, but the entire value of the field will be replaced. For example, you can search for "..computer..", and this will match "computer keyboard", but replacing it with "PC" will result in a value of "PC", not "PC keyboard".

Figure 47-9: Locating and replacing values.

Using Find and Replace with Memo fields

To find and/or replace text in any Memo field:

1. Click the Memo field.

2. Click View ➪ Edit Data to enter Edit mode (if you're not already in it).

3. Click Edit ➪ Find and Replace.

4. Specify the text you want to find.

5. Specify the replacement text.

6. Click Find to locate the next occurrence, Replace to replace a single occurrence and move on, or Replace All to replace all occurrences.

Sorting and Filtering Records

The records in a table appear in key field order. If there is no key field, records appear in the order in which they were entered. However, you may want to sort your table to view records in a different order, or *filter* your table to display a particular subset of records. For example, you may want to view your customer table by last name instead of by customer ID key, or you may want to see only the records for customers in the Netherlands.

When you sort a table, you are creating a copy of the table in the order you specify. Even if you specify "same table," it simply replaces your original table with the new, sorted one. When you use a filter to order the table, the underlying data is still in the original order; it is just displayed the way you specify. This is usually the preferred way of "sorting," as it does not require that a copy of the table be made.

Sorting a table

To sort a table:

1. Click Format Í Sort, and select whether you want to sort to the current table or to a new table by clicking the Same table or New table option (see Figure 47-10).

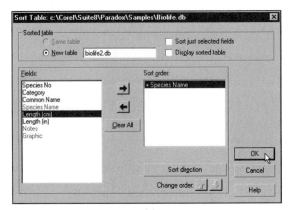

Figure 47-10: Sorting a table.

Note   The "Same table" option is not available on an indexed table.

2. If you want to include just the selected fields in the results, click the Sort Just Selected Fields box.

3. If you want to display the table after it has been sorted, click the Display Sorted Table box.

4. Select the fields you want to sort on by clicking the right-arrow button to add them to the sort order list. List the fields in the sort order you want (for example, Last Name, followed by First Name).

Tip   Use the up and down arrow buttons to rearrange the listing.

5. Select any field in the sort order list and click the Sort Direction button to toggle its sort order between ascending (+) and descending (–).

Cross-Reference   For general information on sorting, see Chapter 53, "Sorting Information."

Filtering records

You can use the Filter feature to view the records you want, or to sort them on a secondary index, as follows:

1. Click the Filter icon (Format ➪ Filter) to display the primary index (with an asterisk) in the "Order by" list, along with any secondary indexes, on the Filter Tables screen (see Figure 47-11).

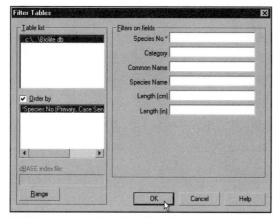

Figure 47-11: Using the Filter feature to sort on a secondary index.

2. Select the index you want to sort on.

Sort on the primary index to restore the default sort order.

3. Enter selection criteria in the appropriate field or fields (such as "9000" in the Species No field).

4. To filter records with a range of values, click Range, and then click the Set Range box and specify a range of values (see Figure 47-12).

For more complex record filtering (such as all species in the Shark category with a length under 100cm), use the query facilities described in Chapter 49, "Building Queries."

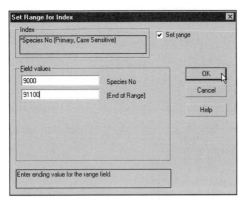

Figure 47-12: Filtering records on a range of values.

Printing a Table

To print the contents of the current table:

1. Click the Print icon (File ➪ Print).

2. Select any of the following options (shown in Figure 47-13):

- *Current printer,* to select another printer.

- *Properties,* to set the printer properties such as resolution or paper source.

- *Full file,* to print the entire table.

- *Page range,* to specify a starting and ending page.

- *Number of copies,* to change the number of copies.

- *Collate copies,* to print multiple copies as complete sets.

- *Group copies,* to print multiple copies by printing a complete run of each page before printing the next page.

- *Number on first page,* to change the value of the starting page number.

- *Print in reverse order,* to print the highest-numbered pages first, such as when your printer outputs pages face up, rather than face down.

- *Overflow handling,* to specify how to print data that is too wide to fit on a sheet of paper. You can clip the printout to the width of the current page, create horizontal overflow pages, or panel the overflow vertically.

3. Click Print.

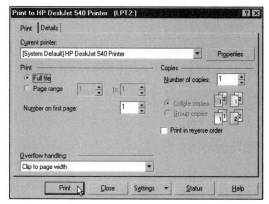

Figure 47-13: Printing a table.

A printout of a table in Table view resembles the table's onscreen appearance. If you want a fancier format, you must design a report, as described in Chapter 50, "Creating Reports and Labels."

Cross-Reference For general information on printing, see Chapter 13, "Printing and Faxing Information."

For More Information . . .

On	See
Creating Tables with the Table Expert	Chapter 46
Using the Visual Database Designer	Chapter 46
Creating forms with the form expert	Chapter 48
Creating Reports with the report expert	Chapter 50
Using the Paradox experts	Chapter 51

✦　　✦　　✦

Creating Input Forms

While Chapter 47 showed you how to directly enter data in a table, it's usually much easier to create and use input forms, as you'll see in this chapter.

Why Forms?

Input forms present a controlled, formatted, screen environment for entering data, often one record at a time. You can design different forms to provide different views of the same data, from one or more tables. Forms also let you place text and graphic fields in a convenient arrangement for the viewer (see Figure 48-1).

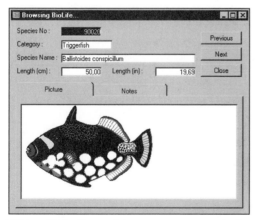

Figure 48-1: Forms let you arrange your text and graphics.

Forms are the primary user interface in many database systems, so careful consideration should be given to their design. You should always have users test forms out before you implement them. You'll often find existing paper-based forms to start from, and these can be a good design tool because users will already be familiar with using them.

Creating an Input Form

You have two ways to create input forms in Paradox:

✦ With the Quick Design tool

✦ With the Form Expert

You can use each method individually or combine them. For example, you might use the Form Expert to design the basic form, and then refine the layout by hand.

Creating forms with Quick Design

The fastest way to create an input form is to open the table in Table view, and then click the Quick Form icon (Tools ➪ Quick Design ➪ Quick Form). Paradox creates a default form with a simple, single-column layout of all the fields (see Figure 48-2).

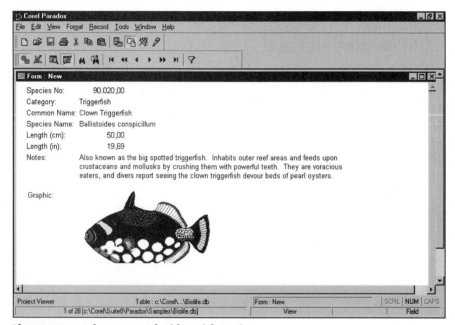

Figure 48-2: A form created with Quick Design.

Creating forms with the Form Expert

For help in creating more sophisticated input forms with selected fields from one or more tables, use the Form Expert.

Creating a one-table input form

To create a form that updates a single table:

1. Click the PerfectExpert icon (Tools ⇨ Experts), and then click Form and click Run Expert.

2. Click the Data from one table button, and then click Next (see Figure 48-3).

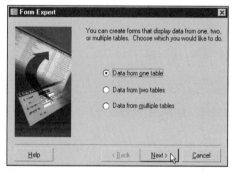

Figure 48-3: Creating a form from one table.

3. Click the Browse button, select a table, click OK, select the fields to display in your form, click the right arrow button, and then click Next (see Figure 48-4).

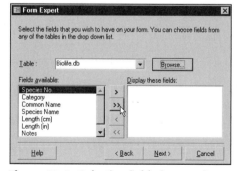

Figure 48-4: Selecting fields for your form.

Tip

Click the double-arrow buttons to select or remove all the fields.

4. Select a one- or multiple-record form type. Multiple records can be displayed in columns or tables (see Figure 48-5). Click Next.

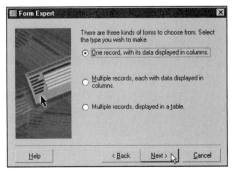

Figure 48-5: Selecting the form type.

5. Select a style for your form (the right side of the dialog box shows a sample of how the form will appear), and then click Next (see Figure 48-6).

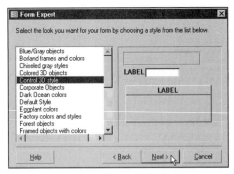

Figure 48-6: Selecting a style for your form.

6. Enter a filename, and specify the location for the form, normally your working directory (see Figure 48-7). Also choose whether you want to view the form in Run mode (containing data from the table) or Design mode (where you can make additional changes to the design of the form). Click Finish to create your form.

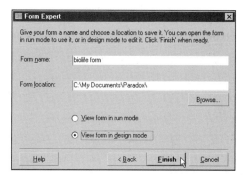

Figure 48-7: Specifying your form's name and location.

Creating a two-table input form

To create a form to update two tables:

1. Click the PerfectExpert icon (Tools ⇨ Experts), click Form, and then click Run Expert.

2. On the Form Expert dialog box (previously shown in Figure 48-3), click the Data from Two Tables button and then click Next.

3. Select the *master table* (see Figure 48-8), click Next, select the *detail table* (see Figure 48-9), and then click Next.

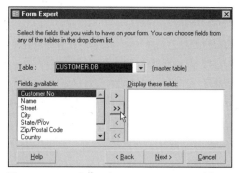

Figure 48-8: Selecting your master table.

The detail table provides detailed information on the records in the master table. For instance, an invoice detail table might contain a list of items ordered on each invoice in an orders table; or a customer table might provide detailed client information for each order.

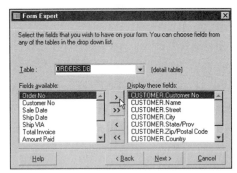

Figure 48-9: Selecting your detail table.

4. Select fields from the master table to display on your form (see Figure 48-10) and click the right arrow button to add them to the Display These Fields list box.

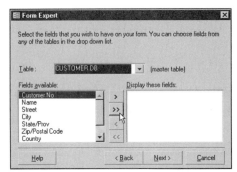

Figure 48-10: Selecting fields from the master table.

5. Select the detail table from the Table drop-down list, select detail fields for your form, click the right arrow button to add them to the Display These Fields list box, and then click Next (see Figure 48-11).

6. Select a form type. You can build a form that displays one master table record in columns and multiple detail table records in a table, or one that displays all the information in columns or tables (see Figure 48-12).

7. Click Next to select the style and name your form, as described previously in Steps 5 and 6 under "Creating a one-table input form."

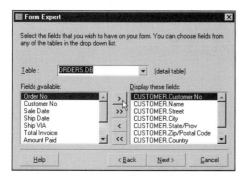

Figure 48-11: Adding fields from the detail table.

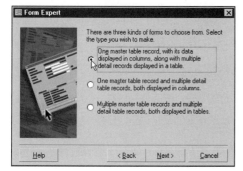

Figure 48-12: Selecting the form type.

Design tips for multi-table forms

Creating a multi-table form is a bit trickier than creating a form for one table. Here are some tips for designing user-friendly relational forms:

✦ *Limit the number of fields from the detail table.* You'll need to fit detail table fields within the overall form, so select only the necessary fields.

✦ *Don't place master record data in the detail portion of the form.* Because every detail record contains the same key information, common (linking) fields should be placed in the master portion of the form.

✦ *Protect the referential integrity of your database.* If you didn't protect the referential integrity when you created your tables, you should definitely do so now, before using the input forms.

Cross-Reference

See Chapter 46 for more information on protecting a database's referential integrity.

Creating a data model for multi-table forms

You can also use the Form Expert to create multi-table input forms based on a *data model*. First, create the model by using the Data Model Designer:

1. Click File ➪ New ➪ Data Model, and then use the Add Object Palette to switch to the folder with the tables you want to use in the data model.

2. Select each table and click Add to place it on the Data Model Designer. Once all your tables have been added, click Close to close the palette (see Figure 48-13).

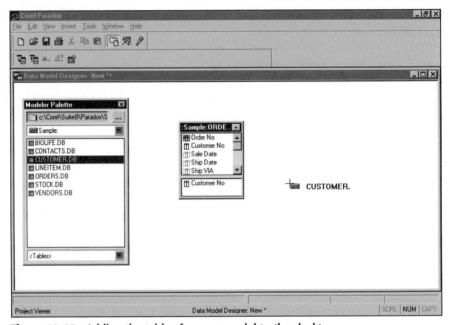

Figure 48-13: Adding the tables for your model to the desktop.

3. Right-click a table to expand or collapse its view. To expand or collapse all the tables, click the Expand All or Collapse All icon (View ➪ Expand All or View ➪ Collapse All).

4. Link the tables together: Select the field of the table you want to link, and then drag the field to the field of the table you want to create a link with.

5. If you did not use the Visual Database Designer to establish referential integrity among the tables that you're linking, specify the common fields in the tables you want to link (see Figure 48-14).

When you link two tables, the detail table must be indexed on the linked field.

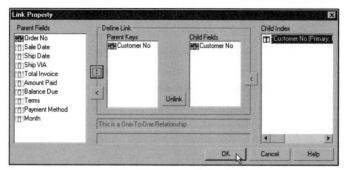

Figure 48-14: Specifying link properties.

6. After linking all the tables, click File ⇨ Save to save the data model.

Tip

Another way to create a multi-table form is to create and save a relational query (as described in Chapter 49), and then use that query as the data source for the form.

Creating multi-table forms

Now that you've created a data model, you can use it to create multi-table forms. The easiest way is to use the Form Expert, but you have more options when you create them manually.

Using the Form Expert to create a multi-table form

To create a multi-table form by using the Form Expert:

1. Click the PerfectExpert icon (Tools ⇨ Experts), click Form, and click Run Expert.

2. On the Form Expert dialog box (previously shown in Figure 48-3), click the Data from Multiple Tables button and then click Next.

3. Select the data model you want to use.

4. Select fields from tables in the data model to add to your form and click the right arrow button to add the selected fields to the Display These Fields list box (see Figure 48-15).

5. Click Next, select a form type and style, and then name your form as you would when creating a two-table form.

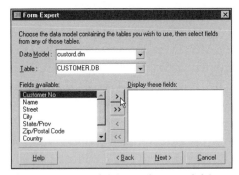

Figure 48-15: Selecting a data model for a multi-table form.

Manually creating a multi-table form

To manually design a form based on a data model:

1. Do either of the following:

- In the Project Viewer, right-click the Forms icon at the left and click New. Choose Data Model (see Figure 48-16).

- Click File ➪ New ➪ Form, and then click Data Model.

Figure 48-16: Creating a form based on a new data model.

2. Click the drop-down list in the lower-left corner of the Data Model New dialog box to switch from Tables to Data Models, and then double-click the data model you want to use to add it to the desktop.

3. Click OK, and then select the way you want the fields laid out by clicking the By Columns button (see Figure 48-17). (Figure 48-18 shows the by rows method.)

Note   You must use columns if you're creating a single-record style form (which you'll specify in the next step).

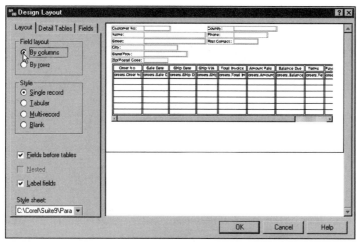

Figure 48-17: Laying out fields by columns.

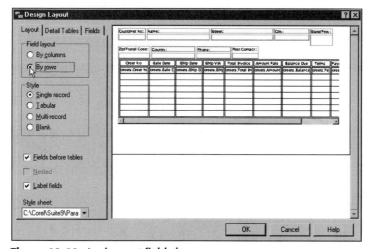

Figure 48-18: Laying out fields by rows.

4. Select a style of Single record (one record per screen), multiple records in Tabular rows (see Figure 48-19), Multi-record, or Blank (with no initial fields). With the multi-record layout, you can select to repeat records horizontally, vertically, or both (see Figure 48-20).

5. Pick a style sheet (optional) and click the Label Fields box to disable (no check mark) or enable (check mark) field labels.

6. Select Nested to display the master records in the multi-record object, and Fields Before Tables to display the current record's fields first.

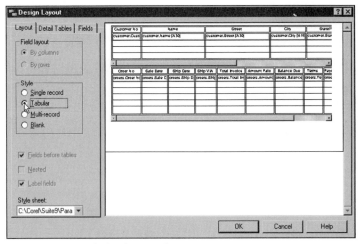

Figure 48-19: Tabular form style.

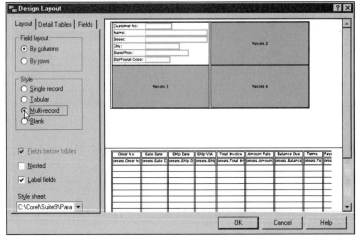

Figure 48-20: Multi-record style with records repeated horizontally and vertically.

7. Click the Fields tab to select, rearrange, and remove fields (see Figure 48-21). Click Reset Fields if you want to restore all the fields to the layout.

8. Click the Detail Tables tab, and then click the Table or Record button to display the subordinate records of the detail tables in tabular or record style (see Figure 48-22).

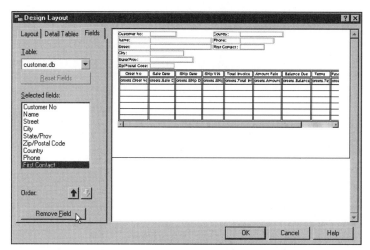

Figure 48-21: Selecting, rearranging, and removing fields.

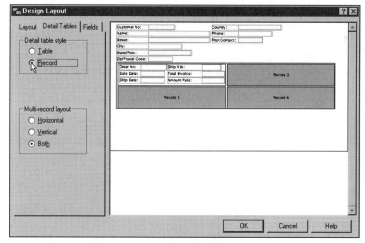

Figure 48-22: Selecting a detail table style.

9. Click OK to display the form in Design mode (see Figure 48-23). From there you can perform any of the following:

- Drag fields and labels around on the form.

- Click toolbar buttons to select various objects, and then click the form where you want to place them (or click and drag to size them as well).

- Right-click fields, labels, and objects to change their properties.

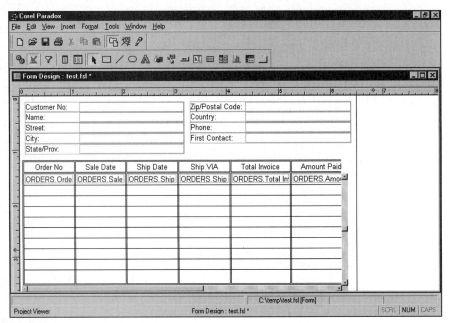

Figure 48-23: A form in Design mode.

10. Click the Save button (File ➪ Save) to save your completed form. (Paradox adds an .FSL extension.)

11. Click the Run Form icon to exit Design mode and run the form. Click the Design Form icon (View ➪ Design Form) to return to Design mode.

Form Design Techniques

Now that you've gone through the entire design process by using the data model, you can look at some more design techniques that you can employ while in Design mode.

Press F8 (or click the Run Form and Design Form icons) whenever you want to toggle between Design (editing) mode and View mode, where you can see what your form looks like with actual data.

Selecting objects

Many form design operations, including those defined in Table 48-1, are performed on selected objects.

Table 48-1
Working with Objects in Forms

In Order To	Do This
Select a group of objects	Hold down the Shift or Ctrl key as you click the objects.
Select all the objects	Click a blank area in the form, and then click Edit ⇨ Select All.
Move objects	Click and drag the object or group.
Resize an object	Click the object and drag a sizing handle.
Delete an object	Click the object and press Delete.
Change an object's label	Click the object, click anywhere above the label portion of the object, and then click within the label. Make the desired corrections, and then click anywhere outside of the label.

To select a field or other object, select it as shown in Figure 48-24.

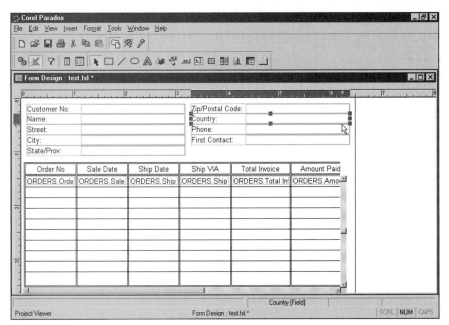

Figure 48-24: Selecting a field in Design mode.

Aligning objects

To align a group of selected objects, click Format ➪ Alignment and select from the various options. You can choose to align objects horizontally using Align Left, Align Center, or Align Right. You can align them vertically using Align Top, Align Middle, or Align Bottom.

Adjusting object sizes

To equalize the size of selected objects in a group, click Format ➪ Size, and then select from the following options:

✦ *Minimum Width,* to change the width of all the objects to that of the narrowest object

✦ *Maximum Width,* to change the width of all the objects to that of the widest object

✦ *Minimum Height,* to change the height of all the objects to that of the shortest object

✦ *Maximum Height,* to change the height of all the objects to that of the tallest object

Equalizing object spacing

To equalize the spacing within a group of selected objects, click Format ➪ Spacing, and then select from the following:

✦ *Horizontal,* to equalize the horizontal spacing

✦ *Vertical,* to equalize the vertical spacing

Editing a field's description or format

Every field in a form is composed of two parts: the edit region (containing the data) and the attached descriptive label.

Click a field once to select the entire field object. You can click a second time to edit the descriptive label.

To change the formatting of the label or of the text in the field, right-click the label or edit region and click Properties.

Adding fields

To add a field to your form in Design mode:

1. Click the Field icon, and then click the form to place a field at its default size, or click and drag to size the field.

2. Select the type of field you want from the Field Expert (see Figure 48-25).

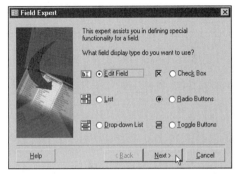

Figure 48-25: Selecting the type of field to add.

3. Click Next and follow the onscreen instructions for the type of field selected. For the common Edit field, you'll next be asked what field, if any, you want to attach to it (see Figure 48-26).

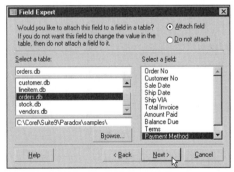

Figure 48-26: Selecting the database field to attach to the form field.

4. The remaining steps of the Field Expert may ask you to enter the field label and tooltip, attach a default value to a field not attached to a table, select from various ObjectPAL functions, or pick a style for the field (see Figure 48-27).

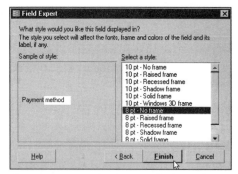

Figure 48-27: Selecting a style from the Field Expert.

5. After you have made all the desired selections for your new field, click Finish to exit the Field Expert.

Adding text boxes

You'll often want to add text boxes to your forms for titles, explanatory labels, and notes to the user. To add a text box to a form:

1. Click the Text icon, click the form where the text box should begin, and then drag to the size you want.

2. Follow the online instructions in the Text Expert dialog box to type your text and apply various styles, formatting, and special effects (see Figure 48-28).

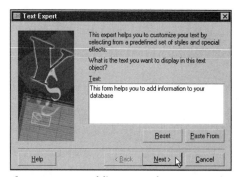

Figure 48-28: Adding a text box to your form.

Cross-Reference

For more on text boxes, see Chapter 9.

Changing a form's background color

To change the background color of a form, right-click a blank area in Design mode, click Properties, and then click the General tab.

 Tip The user entering data typically needs clarity more than beauty.

Adding graphics

To add a graphic to a form in Design mode:

1. Click the Graphic icon, and then drag where you want the graphic to appear.

2. Right-click the undefined graphic and click Paste to paste a graphic from the Clipboard, or click Paste From to select a graphic on disk.

Adding lines, rectangles, and ellipses

Other selections on the property bar let you draw lines, rectangles, and ellipses on your forms. See Chapter 55 for more on drawing objects.

Adding calculated fields

Sometimes you may want to add a calculated expression to a form that is based on one or more fields in the underlying table or query. For example, you might calculate and display a sales tax, based on 6 percent of the Total Invoice field.

To add a calculated field to a form in Design mode:

1. Click the Field icon and then click the form to place a field at its default size, or click and drag to size the field.

2. When the Field Expert appears, click Cancel.

3. Click the Edit Region of the Field, right-click the Edit Region, and click Define Field.

4. Check Calculated and enter the expression to perform the calculation, with fields specified as [tablename.fieldname]. For example, "[Orders.Total Invoice] * .06" would display the value in the Total Invoice field of the Orders table, multiplied by 6 percent (see Figure 48-29).

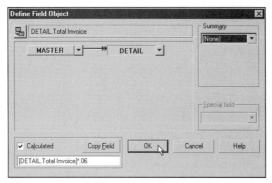

Figure 48-29: Adding a calculated field.

Adding command buttons

You can add user-friendly command buttons to your forms in Design mode, to perform common data-management operations (such as moving around in the underlying table or printing the current record). To add a command button to a form:

1. Click the Button icon, and then click the location for the button.

2. Follow the onscreen instructions in the Button Expert, selecting from the various categories and actions (see Figure 48-30).

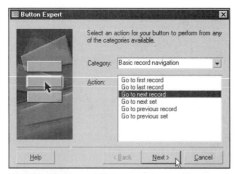

Figure 48-30: Adding a command button.

3. When you are done making your selections, click Finish to exit the Button Expert.

Protecting your form design

To let others use your completed form but not change it in any way, create a delivered version of the form that can't be opened in Design mode, as follows:

1. Click the Save button (File ➪ Save).

2. Click Format ➪ Deliver.

    Paradox saves a copy of the form to the same name, but with an .FDL extension.

Caution

Delivered forms cannot be "undelivered," so keep a copy of the original form (with the .FSL extension) in case you want to make changes later on.

Using Forms

To open a form you created, click Forms in the Project Viewer, and then double-click the form (or right-click the form and click Open). You can also click the Open icon (File ➪ Open ➪ Form), and select the form.

When using a form to add records, many of the techniques (such as sorting and filtering records) are the same as those you can use when updating a table directly.

Cross-Reference

See Chapter 47 for information on direct table updates.

To add records to a form:

1. Click the Edit icon or press F9 to enter Edit mode.

2. Click the Last Record icon and then click the Next Record icon to move to a blank record.

To move among the fields and records of a form, press the various keystrokes described in Table 48-2.

Table 48-2	
Navigation Keys in Forms	
Press	*To Move*
Home	To the first field in current record
End	To the last field in current record

Continued

	Table 48-2 *(continued)*
Press	**To Move**
Ctrl+Home	To the first field in first record
Ctrl+End	To the last field in last record
Tab or Enter	To the next field
Shift+Tab	To the previous field
Up arrow	To the next field
Down arrow	To the previous field
PgUp	Up one record
PgDn	Down one record
F3 and F4	Between tableframes and multi-record objects

Click the Print icon (File ➪ Print) to print the contents of a form. This prints a copy of the form for each record in the table that the form is based on.

For More Information . . .

On	See
Building queries	Chapter 49
Referential integrity	Chapter 46
Drawing objects	Chapter 55
Adding data to a table	Chapter 47
Creating reports	Chapter 50

✦   ✦   ✦

Building Queries

The beauty of having your data in Paradox tables is that you can get instant responses to every imaginable question, without manually sorting and tabulating piles of data. This chapter shows you how easy this is by using the query facilities. Queries offer a powerful, easy-to-use way to retrieve information from your tables, and even to update records.

What Queries Can Do

In addition to answering your questions, a query can

+ Perform calculations and summarize data
+ Create new fields
+ Change or delete records
+ Create a new table from selected data in other tables

Building Queries

You can ask all sorts of questions of your data by using the visual, intuitive query facilities in Paradox.

Paradox provides two basic tools for building queries:

+ The new Query Expert
+ Query-By-Example (QBE)

The Query Expert is quickest, but QBE gives you more options for creating complex queries.

Note Paradox also provides a Visual Query Builder and an SQL editor for advanced users. These tools are not discussed here.

Building queries with the Query Expert

The new Query Expert makes it easier than ever to build simple queries.

New Feature The Query Expert guides you, step-by-step, through identifying the tables you want to search, your search criteria, and the type of search you want to perform—detailed or summary.

To use Query Expert to build a query:

1. Click Tools ⇨ Experts, click Query, and the click Run Expert.

2. Specify the directory containing the tables you want to search on, using the Browse button to locate the directory if necessary (see Figure 49-1).

Figure 49-1: Locating your tables' directory in the Query Expert.

3. Click Next, select the fields to include, and click the right arrow button (see Figure 49-2).

Tip You can select fields from more than one table.

4. Click Next and select the type of query you want to perform: detail or summary (see Figure 49-2). (If you are performing a summary query, see "Calculating Summary Values," later in this chapter.)

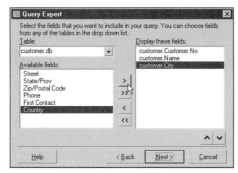

Figure 49-2: Selecting fields to include in the query.

5. Click Next and set selection criteria for one or more fields (see Figure 49-3). Click Preview to check out the results.

   • Select an operator to specify how to compare the values, such as "is equal to."

   • Select a field or a value to compare, such as "U.S.A." Some operators require two fields or values.

   • Select Preview to verify that your selection criteria work properly. The preview doesn't produce an actual output table or sort the results.

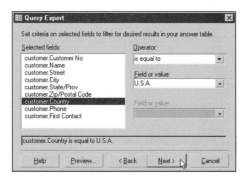

Figure 49-3: Setting query selection criteria.

6. Click Next to select fields to sort by (see Figure 49-4). The results will be sorted in the order in which the fields appear in the Sort Order box. Click Ascending or Descending to change the sort direction. Click Preview again to make certain the results are what you want.

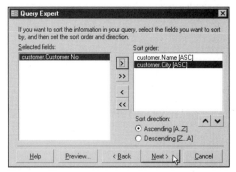

Figure 49-4: Selecting sort fields and order.

7. Click Next and specify a name and location for your query. Specify whether you want to run the query, edit the query in Design mode, or save and exit by clicking the corresponding button (see Figure 49-5).

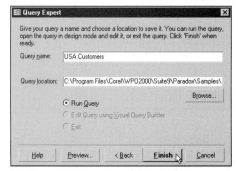

Figure 49-5: Naming and choosing a mode for your query.

8. Click Finish to run the query and display the results (see Figure 49-6).

Building queries using Query-by-Example

The remaining queries in this chapter are created by using Query-by-Example. This is a three-step process in which you perform the following:

1. Select a *datasource* of one or more tables.

2. Select fields to display in the Answer table.

3. Specify selection conditions (criteria).

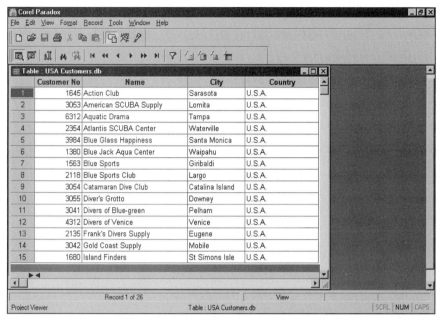

Figure 49-6: Query results.

Here you'll start by creating a simple one-table query, and then try out more advanced multi-table queries, options, and selection criteria.

Creating a query

Try creating a query based on the sample database that comes with Paradox:

1. Click File ➪ Working Directory to set the working directory to that for the sample files if it is not already the working directory (normally C:\Program Files\Corel\WordPerfect Office 2000\Paradox\Samples). You can also select the :Sample: alias in the Project Viewer and click the Set Current Directory as Working Directory button on the Project Viewer toolbar to make it the working directory.

2. Click File ➪ New from Project, and then select [New Query] and click Create (or right-click the Query icon in the Project Viewer and click New).

3. Select the CUSTOMER.DB table and click Open (see Figure 49-7).

4. Check the Name, City, Country, and Phone field check boxes to display these fields in the answer table (see Figure 49-8).

Tip   Use the scroll bar to see all the fields.

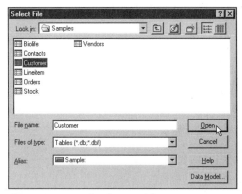

Figure 49-7: Selecting a table to query.

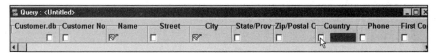

Figure 49-8: Selecting query fields.

5. Click the blank area under the Country heading, type U.S.A., and press Enter or Tab (see Figure 49-9). This specifies a selection condition for that particular field.

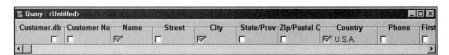

Figure 49-9: Selection condition for the Country field.

6. Click the Run Query icon, press F8, or click Query ⇨ Run Query and view the resulting answer table (see Figure 49-10).

You can query any other database in the same manner. Note how in Steps 3 and 4 you

✦ Checked the fields to include in your answer table

✦ Specified a selection condition for a particular field

Other than those queries that modify your database (discussed in "Using Queries to Change Data" later in this chapter), most queries produce a temporary *answer table* named ANSWER.DB. Any changes you make to data in an answer table have no effect on the tables you queried.

	Name	City	Country
1	Action Club	Sarasota	U.S.A.
2	American SCUBA Supply	Lomita	U.S.A.
3	Aquatic Drama	Tampa	U.S.A.
4	Atlantis SCUBA Center	Waterville	U.S.A.
5	Blue Glass Happiness	Santa Monica	U.S.A.
6	Blue Jack Aqua Center	Waipahu	U.S.A.
7	Blue Sports	Giribaldi	U.S.A.
8	Blue Sports Club	Largo	U.S.A.
9	Catamaran Dive Club	Catalina Island	U.S.A.
10	Diver's Grotto	Downey	U.S.A.
11	Divers of Blue-green	Pelham	U.S.A.
12	Divers of Venice	Venice	U.S.A.
13	Frank's Divers Supply	Eugene	U.S.A.
14	Gold Coast Supply	Mobile	U.S.A.

Figure 49-10: Resulting answer table.

Records in the answer table are normally sorted in ascending order on the first field in the answer. (Adjacent fields are called upon when sorting two or more records with the same first field.) You can re-sort the answers on any field, as with any other table.

Cross-Reference

For more information on sorting tables, see Chapter 47.

You can even query the answer table, just like any other table. When you do, the original answer table will be overwritten by the new results. To save your answers permanently, click Format ➪ Rename Table while the answer table is open, or click Tools ➪ Utilities ➪ Rename and change the name of ANSWER.DB in the :priv: alias.

Saving a query

To save the current query, click the Save icon or click File ➪ Save, and give the query a name — Paradox automatically assigns the .QBE extension. You can also click File ➪ Save As to copy a query to another name.

Retrieving a query

Once you've saved a query, you can retrieve it from the Project Viewer. Click the Queries icon on the left and then double-click the query (or click the Open Query icon and select the query).

Creating Multi-Table (Relational) Queries

You can create *relational queries* that access two or more tables in your database. In Step 3 of the previous "Creating a query" section, hold down the Ctrl key and click to select more than one table.

You can also add tables to the current query, as follows:

1. Click the Add Table icon (Edit ⇨ Insert Table).

2. Select the tables you want to add, and then click Open.

When you base queries on more than one table, you must also use example elements to designate the common field that links the related tables (as described next).

A relational query example

To see how relational queries work, try listing all orders for all customers in the Bahamas:

1. Click File ⇨ Working Directory to select the Samples folder as your working directory if it is not already the working directory.

2. Click File ⇨ New ⇨ Query or right-click the query icon in the Project Viewer and click New.

3. Click Customer.db, hold down the Ctrl key and click Orders.db, and then click Open (see Figure 49-11).

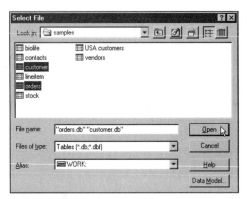

Figure 49-11: Selecting tables for your relational query.

4. Click the Join icon and then click underneath the Customer No field. The Customer table displays "join1" in red, indicating the common field (see Figure 49-12).

5. Click underneath the Customer No for the Orders table, to place a matching "join1" in that field (see Figure 49-13).

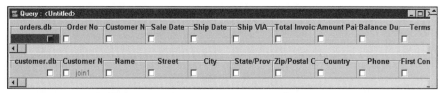

Figure 49-12: Selecting the common (join1) field in the Customer table.

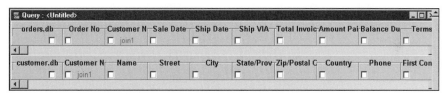

Figure 49-13: Selecting the common field in the Orders table.

6. Click the Customer check boxes for the Name, City, and Country fields for display in the answer table, and then click the Orders check boxes for the Sale Date, Ship Date, and Total Invoice fields (see Figure 49-14).

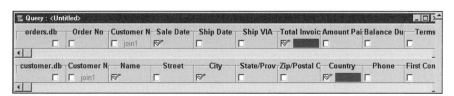

Figure 49-14: Selecting fields to be displayed in the answer table.

7. Click the Country field for the Customer table, type Bahamas for your selection condition, and press Enter (see Figure 49-15).

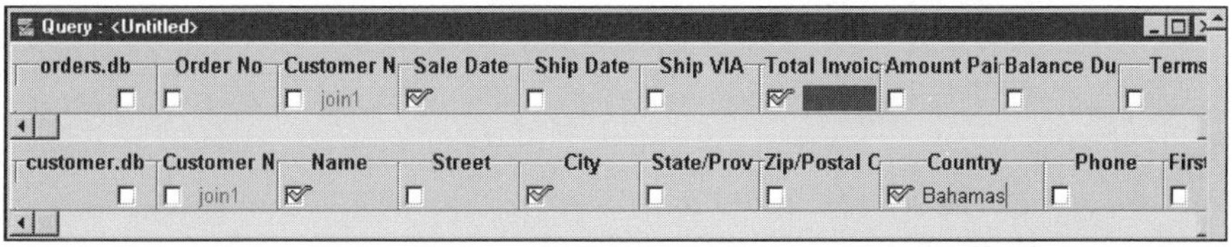

Figure 49-15: Specifying a selection condition.

8. Click the Run Query icon (Query ➪ Run Query) to create the answer table with all orders for all customers in the Bahamas (see Figure 49-16).

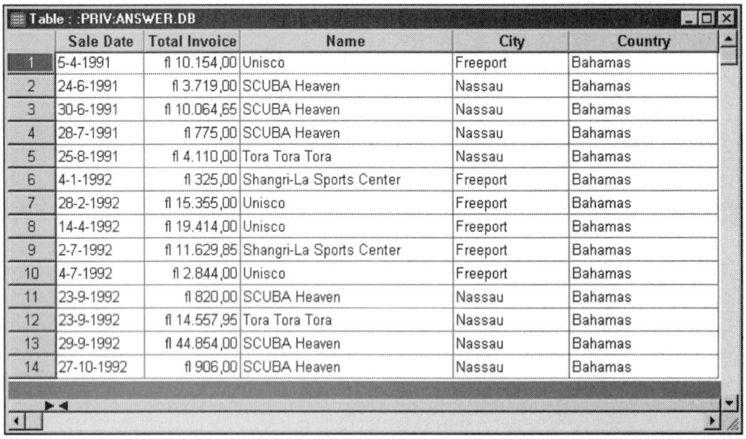

Table : :PRIV:ANSWER.DB

	Sale Date	Total Invoice	Name	City	Country
1	5-4-1991	fl 10.154,00	Unisco	Freeport	Bahamas
2	24-6-1991	fl 3.719,00	SCUBA Heaven	Nassau	Bahamas
3	30-6-1991	fl 10.064,65	SCUBA Heaven	Nassau	Bahamas
4	28-7-1991	fl 775,00	SCUBA Heaven	Nassau	Bahamas
5	25-8-1991	fl 4.110,00	Tora Tora Tora	Nassau	Bahamas
6	4-1-1992	fl 325,00	Shangri-La Sports Center	Freeport	Bahamas
7	28-2-1992	fl 15.355,00	Unisco	Freeport	Bahamas
8	14-4-1992	fl 19.414,00	Unisco	Freeport	Bahamas
9	2-7-1992	fl 11.629,85	Shangri-La Sports Center	Freeport	Bahamas
10	4-7-1992	fl 2.844,00	Unisco	Freeport	Bahamas
11	23-9-1992	fl 820,00	SCUBA Heaven	Nassau	Bahamas
12	23-9-1992	fl 14.557,95	Tora Tora Tora	Nassau	Bahamas
13	29-9-1992	fl 44.854,00	SCUBA Heaven	Nassau	Bahamas
14	27-10-1992	fl 906,00	SCUBA Heaven	Nassau	Bahamas

Figure 49-16: Results of your relational query.

You can extend the relational query with as many tables as you need. Figure 49-17 shows a four-table relational query with three sets of common fields to link the Customer table with the Orders table (join1), the Line Item table with the Stock table (join2), and the Line Item table with the Orders table (join3).

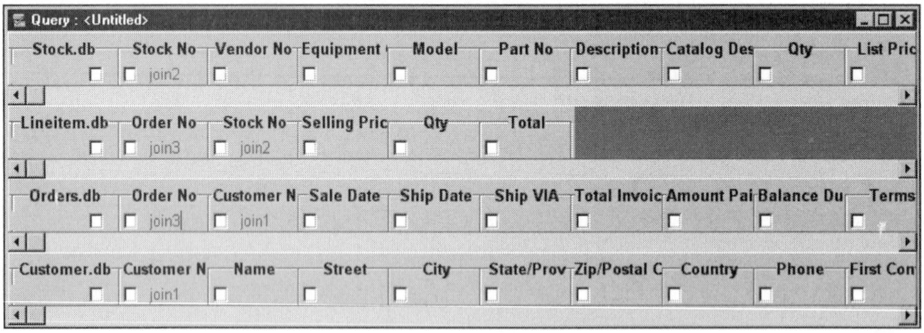

Figure 49-17: Four-table relational query employing three sets of common fields (join1, join2, and join3).

To select all of a table's fields at once, check the box under the table name at the left (see Figure 49-18). Remove the check to deselect all the fields.

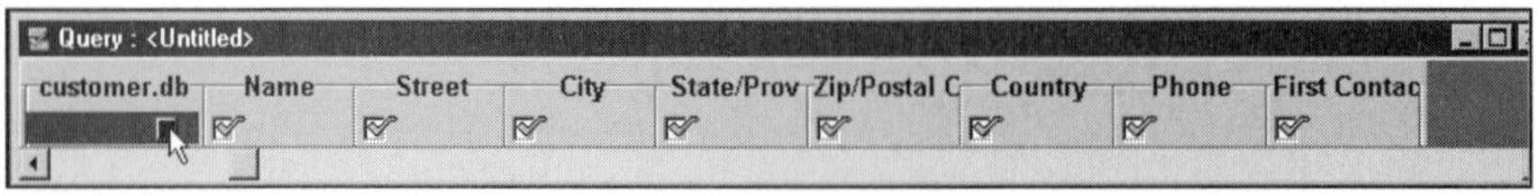

Figure 49-18: Selecting all of a table's fields at once.

Removing tables from a query

To remove tables from a query, click the Remove Table icon, select the table (or tables), and then click OK. There are many possible reasons for wanting to remove a table from a query. For instance, you can base a query on the tables that contain data for the most recent two years, you can continue to use this query by adding the most recent year once a year and removing one year. Or, you have a customers database and regional additions that are integrated in the complete database a couple of times a year. After the database has been updated you can remove the regional additions from the query.

Selecting a check option

Normally when you check a field, the results appear in ascending order, only the first of duplicate entries appears, and all checked fields appear in the answer table. However, you can change this by right-clicking a check box and selecting from the following four check options (shown in Figure 49-19):

✦ A *plain check* to display the normal results

✦ A *check with a plus* (+) to display all values, including duplicates; when you use a check-mark-plus with any field, it overrides any sorts and excludes duplicates of any check-with-an-arrow fields

✦ A *check with an arrow* (↓) to display the results (without duplicates) in descending order

✦ A *check with a G* to group the records by this field, without showing the field in the answer table

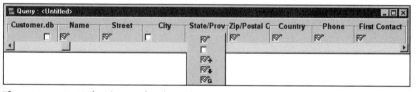

Figure 49-19: Selecting a check option.

Caution

When you define a query that calculates summary values, don't use the default check mark unless you intend to exclude duplicates from your totals. Instead, use check-mark-plus to include all values.

Changing the sort order

You can change the sort order of your query to sort your answers on any field or combination of fields, as follows:

1. Click the Sort icon (Query ➪ Properties ➪ Sort).

2. Select the answer fields you want to sort on, and then click the right-arrow button to add them to the Sort Order list (see Figure 49-20). List the sort fields in the order you want (for example, Country, followed by zip code).

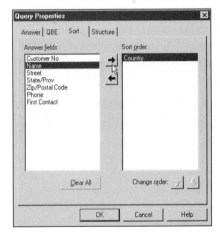

Figure 49-20: Changing the sort order of your answer table.

Tip   Use the up and down arrow buttons to rearrange the listing.

Adding Selection Criteria

You can refine your selections with many types of selection expressions, as you did in the first query example by typing U.S.A. in the Country field to select only the records meeting that condition. You can add a selection expression to a field whether or not it is checked (included in the answer table).

To enter a selection condition:

1. Click to the right of the check box for the desired field.

2. Type an expression.

Specifying AND-based criteria

If you type U.S.A. in the Country field and CA in the State/Prov field (see Figure 49-21), your query retrieves all records with "U.S.A." in the Country field and "CA" in the State/Prov field. This is an example of an AND condition, because *all* conditions must be true to select a record.

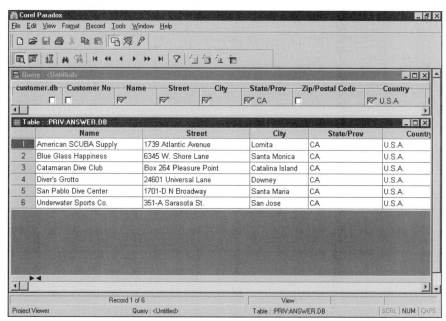

Figure 49-21: Specifying AND-based selection criteria.

You can enter as many AND conditions as you need to select specific records.

Specifying OR-based criteria

By contrast, if you type CA OR HI in the State/Prov field (see Figure 49-22), you'll retrieve all records from either California or Hawaii. This is an example of an OR condition, because a record is retrieved when *any* one of the conditions is true.

You can also indicate multiple OR conditions by pressing the down arrow to add rows to the query, checking desired fields, and entering criteria.

For example, you can type Bahamas in the Country field, and then press the down arrow key to add another row. Then check the desired fields in the second row, and enter U.S.A. in the Country field. Add another row for Bermuda. This query, shown in Figure 49-23, selects the records for all three countries.

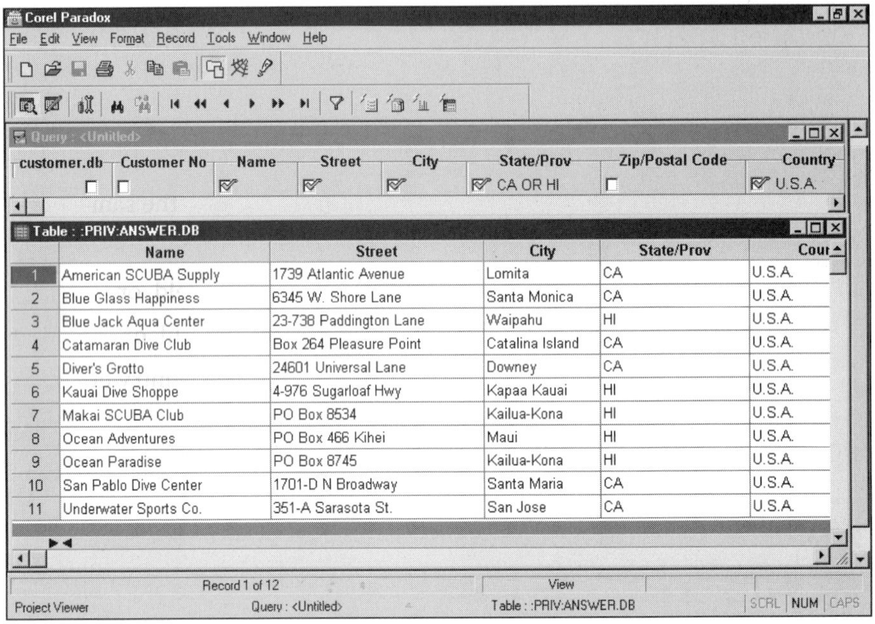

Figure 49-22: Specifying OR-based selection criteria.

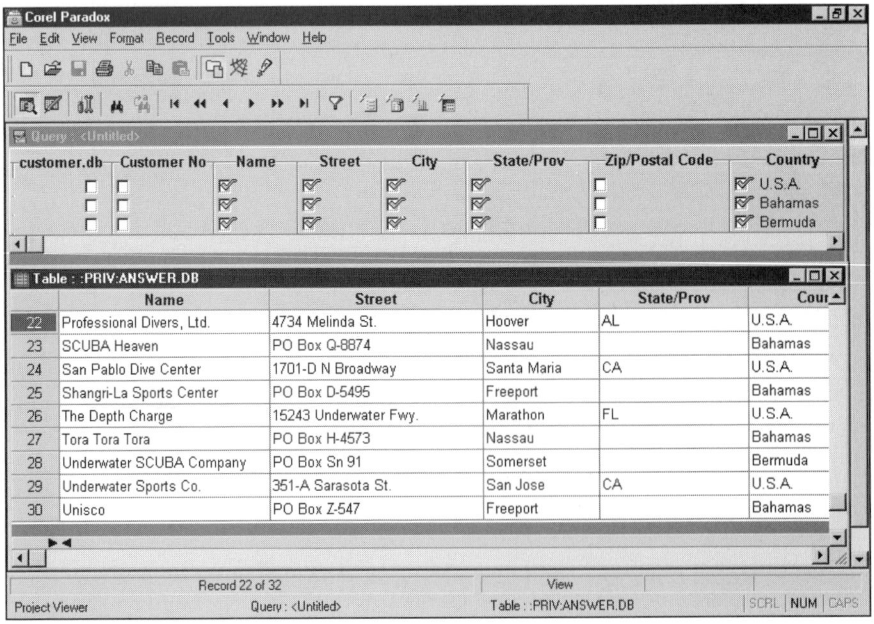

Figure 49-23: OR-based query using multiple rows.

Tip   When you build OR queries with multiple rows (instead of using the word OR), check the same fields in each line of the query. Otherwise, you'll get an error message when you run the query.

Combining AND- and OR-based criteria

You can use any combination of AND- and OR-based criteria in the same query. The query shown in Figure 49-24 selects records that have

✦ "CA" in the State/Prov field and "U.S.A." in the Country field, or

✦ "FL" in the State/Prov field and "U.S.A." in the Country field, or

✦ "Manitoba" in the State/Prov field and "Canada" in the Country field, or

✦ "Venezuela" in the Country field

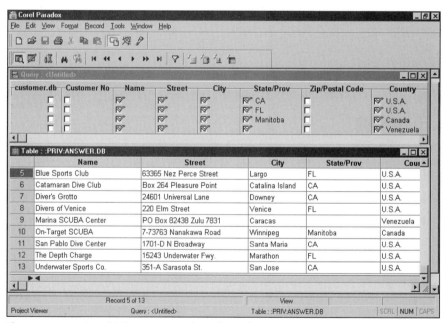

Figure 49-24: Combining AND- and OR-based criteria.

Using query operators

You can use any of the query operators shown in Table 49-1 to construct expressions that select records based on a wide variety of numeric conditions, ranges, and pattern matches.

Table 49-1
Query Operators

Operator	Indicates
+	Addition
–	Subtraction
*	Multiplication
/	Division
( )	Grouping
=	Equal to
<	Less than
>	Greater than
<=	Less than or equal to
>=	Greater than or equal to
..	Pattern matching any characters
@	Pattern matching a single character
like	Similar to (spelling does not have to be an exact match)
not	Not a match
blank	Contains no value
today	Date value matches today's date
average	Average of values
max	Maximum of the values
min	Minimum of the values
sum	Sum of the values
count	Number of values
unique	Include only the first occurrence of each unique value in a group of records
all	Include all occurrences of identical values in a group of records
calc	Create a new value based on the calculation
and	Boolean AND
or	Boolean OR
as	Rename a field in the answer table

If you are looking for an exact match, you can simply type the value you're seeking. To match on a range of values, use the range operators (such as >9999,<20001 to retrieve records containing values between 10,000 and 20,000). You'll find more examples of criteria usage in the following sections.

Creating query expressions

You can create a variety of query expressions, employing multiple selection criteria and operators. Table 49-2 provides some examples.

Table 49-2 Examples of Query Expressions		
Field	**Expression**	**Selects**
Last Name	O'Malley	Records with O'Malley in the Last Name field
Country	Bermuda or Bahamas	Records with Bermuda or Bahamas in the Country field
Country	not Venezuela	Records containing any country name other than Venezuela in the Country field
Total Invoice	>=10000	Records with a value of $10,000.00 or more in the Total Invoice field
Total Invoice	>9999,<20001	Records with a value between $10,000.00 and $20,000.00 in the Total Invoice field
Sale Date	> 12/31/98, <1/1/00	Records with any 1999 Sale Date

Specifying text expressions

You can specify text expressions in a variety of ways. Thus, all of the following expressions are interpreted as London:

London

"London"

=London

="London"

Text expressions are case-sensitive, so london is not the same as London.

Using range operators

In fields with number or currency values, you can use the range operators such as =20.00 and > 5, <12 to obtain the desired data.

You can also use range operators with text. For example, entering >M as a criterion would return values beginning with any letter in the second half of the alphabet. You cannot, however, use range operators and wildcards together.

Queries are case-sensitive, and you can't use wildcards and range operators together.

Specifying date ranges

In fields with dates, you can use the reserved word today to specify the current date. For example, the expression >=6/15/96, <=today selects all records with dates from June 15, 1996 to the current date. The expression >=today, <=today+30 retrieves all records from the present date to 30 days in the future.

Matching on wildcards

Normally, records must exactly match a search condition to be selected. For example, an entry of FL in a State field selects records containing "FL," but not "fl," "Fl," or "Florida." You can use wildcards to create a query that's not case-sensitive, or one that allows additional characters beyond those specified.

In queries, you can use the same wildcards that you use to locate records in table view: @ for any single nonblank character, and .. for any series of zero or more characters. Hence, if you enter FL@ in a State field, your query will return records containing "FLA" but not "FL." Entering FL.. returns "FL," "FLA," "Fla," and "Florida." You could enter 100@@ in a Zip Code field to return records with five-digit zip codes beginning with "100."

The .. wildcard is especially handy when searching dates. For example, an entry of 7..98 returns all dates in July of 1998, and ..30.. returns all dates on the thirtieth of any month of any year.

Using reserved words and symbols

Query operators (such as and, or, blank, not, today, *, and @) are reserved words or symbols that are interpreted in special ways. To employ any of these terms as normal search text, you must put them in double quotes. For example, you can type "today" in a query expression to search for the word "today," instead of the current date.

By the same token, when selecting U.S. addresses by their state abbreviations, an entry of WA OR OR to select all records from "Washington OR Oregon" would be rejected as a double-OR statement. You would have to type WA OR "OR" to obtain the desired results.

Calculating Summary Values

You can use various operators (such as MAX, MIN, COUNT, AVERAGE, and SUM) to summarize the values in a group of records. To calculate with one of these operators, enter your selection criteria as you normally would, and then enter the calculation operator preceded by the word CALC.

For example, to total the invoice amounts for a particular customer, you could enter the customer's number in the Customer No field, and then enter the expression CALC SUM in the Total Invoice field.

Try the following exercise to summarize sample data provided with Paradox:

1. Click File ➪ Working Directory to select the Samples folder as your working directory if it is not already the working directory.

2. Click File ➪ New from Project, select [New Query], and click Create.

3. Select the ORDERS.DB table, click Open, and click the Customer No field to check it.

4. Click under the Total Invoice heading, and then type CALC SUM.

5. Leave all the other fields unchecked, and click the Run Query icon. The result should show the sum of the invoices for each customer (see Figure 49-25).

6. Close the answer table, and then change the calculation expression from CALC SUM to CALC AVERAGE and run the query again. This time you'll get the average invoice amount for each customer.

Linking Fields by Using Example Elements

One of the more powerful features of Query-by-Example (QBE) is the capability to link fields in a query. By linking fields, you can use the values stored in one field as a selection condition for another field.

For example, you can ask questions such as, "How many employees at our consulting firm are billed at hourly rates that are the equivalent of at least three times their salary?" Assuming the Hourly Rate and Salary fields are in the same table, this type of query would require you to refer to the value stored in the Hourly Rate field as part of the condition for the Salary field.

You link fields in a query by using *example elements* — symbols or variables that you assign to one field and then use in another to refer to the assigned field's values. These links let you combine two or more tables in a single query.

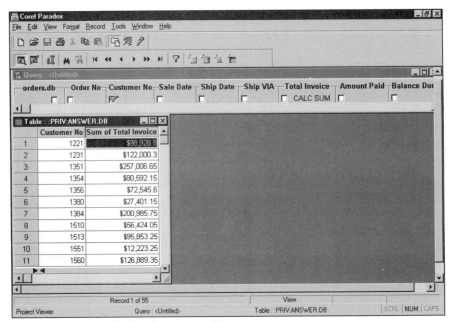

Figure 49-25: Calculating the sum total.

Using example elements in a query is a two-step process:

1. Assign an example element to a field by using the Example (F5) key.

2. Use the same example element as a condition or calculation in another field.

Try the following exercise to find which orders have a ship date that's no later than two days after the sale date:

1. Click File ➪ Working Directory to select the Samples folder as your working directory if it is not already the working directory.

2. Click File ➪ New from Project, select [New Query], and click Create.

3. Select the ORDERS.DB table, and then click Open.

4. Check the boxes to include the Customer No, Sale Date, Ship Date, and Total Invoice in your query results.

5. Click under the Sale Date, press F5, and type ABC (or any other name).

   The characters should appear in red, indicating that you're creating an example element.

Note   If the characters aren't red, delete the entry, press F5 again, and re-type the entry.

6. Click under the Ship Date and type the less-than symbol (<).

7. Press F5 again and type ABC, and then type a plus sign (for addition) followed by the number 3.

    At this point, your query should look like the one shown in Figure 49-26. The letters ABC in the Ship Date field should also be red, to identify this part of the entry as an example element.

Figure 49-26: Query design using example elements.

Note The plus sign is not highlighted because it is not part of the example element.

8. Click the Run Query icon.

    The results should list all records for which the Ship Date is no more than two days later than the Sale Date (see Figure 49-27). In this case, you've used the example elements to retrieve data based on a comparison between two fields.

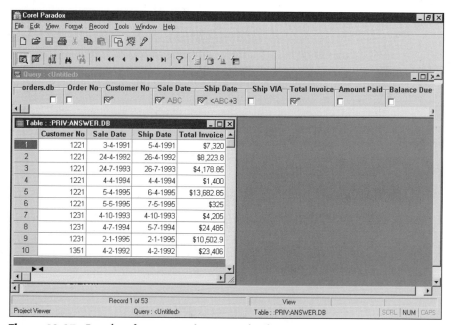

Figure 49-27: Results of a query using example elements.

Using Queries to Change Data

A query can be used for more than just answering questions. By using any of the following operators, you can use a query to change data:

✦ *Insert,* to add new records having certain values

✦ *Delete,* to remove all records meeting a given condition

✦ *ChangeTo,* to alter values in specified fields within records that meet specified criteria

Whenever a query involves more than one table, example elements are used. You can press F5, and then type common example expressions in the query columns, or you can click the Join icon.

Note   You can't use check marks in Insert, Delete, or ChangeTo queries.

Inserting data

An Insert query lets you copy data from one or more source tables to a target table. You can include specific criteria to select records to insert. To create an Insert query:

1. Create a new query and add the source table or tables to the query design.

2. Add the target table.

3. Place example elements in the fields from which you want to move the data, with a matching element between each field that you want to transfer from the source table (or tables) and the matching field in the target table. You must also place the reserved word Insert in the leftmost column of the query.

Tip   Click the leftmost column in the query and type the letter I to display the reserved word Insert.

4. Add selection criteria if you only want to insert certain records from the source table.

5. Run the query to insert the records into the target table.

For example, suppose a regional office has a table of vendors that you want to add to your vendor table. You could create an Insert query like the one shown in Figure 49-28 to insert each record from the regional office vendor table into your own.

Figure 49-28: An Insert query that inserts records from a source table into a target table.

First, the source table (CAVENDORS.DB) was added to the query design, and then the target table (VENDORS.DB) was added. Next, example elements (named join1 to join8) were added for each field from the source table that was to have data added to the target table (in this case, elements were added for all the fields). Finally, the reserved word Insert was added to the leftmost column of the query. (See "Linking Fields by Using Example Elements" earlier in this chapter for a detailed description of these steps.)

When the query runs, a temporary table named INSERTED.DB appears, which shows the records that are inserted into the target table.

Deleting data

You can remove records from a table by using a Delete query. This is particularly useful when you're removing a large number of records (such as all students who graduated in a particular year.)

To construct a Delete query, design the query to select the desired records, and then place the reserved word Delete in the leftmost column (click the leftmost column and type **D**).

Caution   If you provide no selection criteria, Paradox deletes all records from the table!

The example shown in Figure 49-29 deletes all customers from the Bahamas.

When the query runs, a temporary table named DELETED.DB appears, which shows the records that were deleted.

Tip   To recover records accidentally deleted, save the DELETED.DB table to a different name and create an Insert query to add the records back to the table.

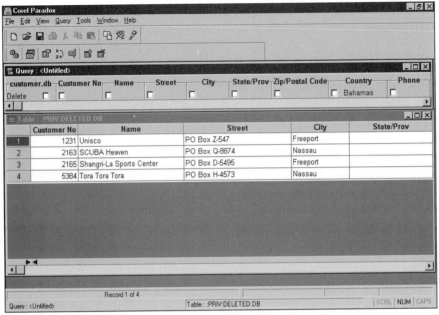

Figure 49-29: A Delete query and the resulting deleted records.

Changing data

You can update (change) records with a ChangeTo query. This is handy for global updates, such as when you want to change the salary of every employee in a certain department by a given amount, or when you want to change all telephone area codes for records of a particular city.

The operator ChangeTo is different from the Delete and Insert operators in that you can put ChangeTo in any column except the leftmost column of the query. (The Delete and Insert reserved words always go in the leftmost column.)

Type ChangeTo in the field whose contents you want to change, followed by an expression to change the data. For example, to change (212) to (617), enter the following:

> 212, ChangeTo 617

Most ChangeTos employ selection criteria in one or more fields to determine when the change takes effect. The example in Figure 49-30 changes all 212 entries in the Area Code field of the table to 617 whenever the Zip Code field contains the value 10020.

Figure 49-30: A ChangeTo query.

When the query runs, a temporary table named CHANGED.DB appears, with copies of the original records (before the changes).

Viewing Your Query Source Code

Although you design the query in a visual environment, Paradox translates your design into QBE statements when it processes your query. You can convert your QBE queries into SQL statements.

For example, when you create the relational query shown in Figure 49-31, you can click the Show SQL icon (View ➪ Show SQL) to view the underlying SQL code shown in Figure 49-32.

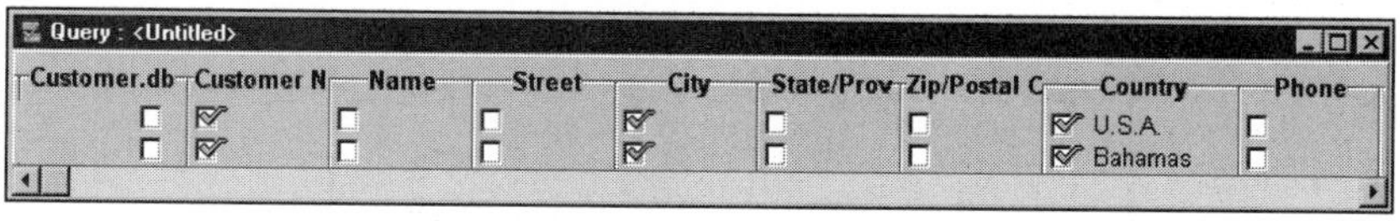

Figure 49-31: Visual design of a relational query.

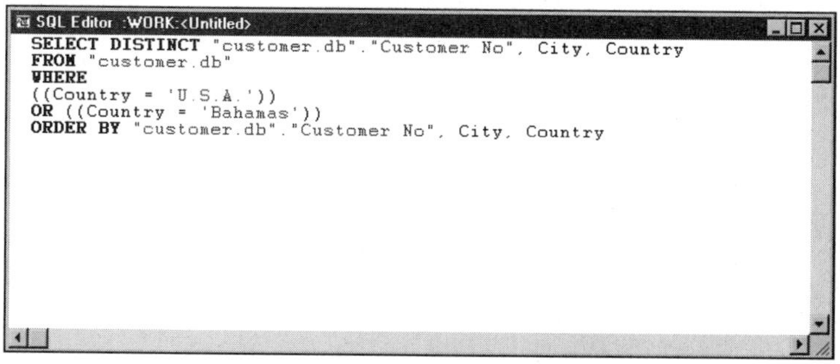

Figure 49-32: SQL statements underlying the query.

Advanced users can use these SQL statements directly when programming with ObjectPAL, the programming language of Paradox.

Updating Tables in Live Query View

Normally, the answer tables created by your queries contain static copies of the data. That is, changes to the answer table have no effect on the underlying tables. However, you can create a *live query view* that lets you update the underlying table(s) by making changes to the answer table.

To create a live query view:

1. Open the query by right-clicking it in the Project Viewer and click Design.

2. Click the Query Properties icon (Query ⇨ Properties).

3. Click the Answer tab and click the Live Query View button (see Figure 49-33).

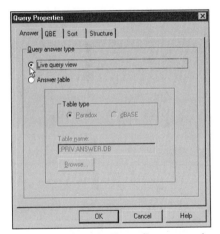

Figure 49-33: Creating a live query view.

When you run the query, the answer table shows the data as a live query view, where any changes you make are stored in the underlying table.

Live query views can be useful when you want to allow editing of a specific subset of records (such as all the employees in a single department). However, the live query view has two major limitations:

✦ It can only be based on a single table.

✦ You must use the check-mark-plus option.

With more than one table, or with check options other than check-mark-plus, the live query view answer table will be read-only, so you won't be able to edit it.

Finding Duplicate Information

Can a query find duplicate information in a table? Yes, in fact this is easy when you use the new Find Duplicate Expert.

New Feature

Find Duplicate Expert leads you, step-by-step, through identifying fields in a table that contain duplicate information. By running the Find Duplicate Expert query, you can ensure that each field contains unique data.

To use the Find Duplicate Expert:

1. Click Tools ⇨ Experts, click Find Duplicate, and click Run Expert. Click Next.

2. Select a table, select the fields within the table that you want to search for duplicate information, and then click the right arrow button to add the selected fields to the Duplicate Value Fields list (see Figure 49-34). Or use the double right arrow button to add all the fields. Use the Order button to change the order in which the fields appear in the answer table. Click Next.

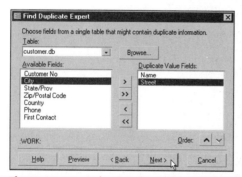

Figure 49-34: Selecting the table and fields that might contain duplicate information.

3. Select and click the right arrow button to add additional fields you want to see in the answer table to the Displayed Fields list (see Figure 49-35). Use the Order button to change the order in which the fields appear in the answer table. Click Next.

4. Name the table that will contain the records with duplicate information (see Figure 49-36) and click Finish to create the table.

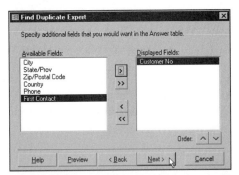

Figure 49-35: Selecting fields for the duplicate record answer table.

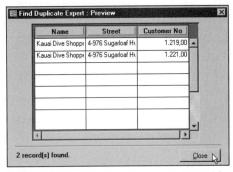

Figure 49-36: Naming the duplicates table.

For More Information . . .

On	See
Sorting tables	Chapter 47
Joining tables	Chapter 43
Creating relational forms	Chapter 48

✦   ✦   ✦

Creating Reports and Labels

Although you can structure queries to obtain specific data, only reports can satisfy many general and recurring data-presentation needs. You can quickly create reports in Paradox to display data in virtually any format, with various levels of detail.

So far you learned how to set up a database, get data in and create queries. Now you'll see how to get data out with reports and labels. This chapter shows you how to create reports from one, two, or multiple tables.

Understanding Report Types

Nearly all reports that you'll create fall into one of the following categories:

✦ *Groups/totals reports,* also known as *tabular reports,* display data in rows, with each field's data occupying a separate column (see Figure 50-1).

✦ *Columnar reports,* also known as *form-oriented reports,* display all fields in a single column (see Figure 50-2). The field names shown in the figure are optional.

✦ *Mailing label reports* print mailing labels (see Figure 53-3).

Designing Reports

To produce effective, relevant reports, follow these steps in planning and design:

1. *Lay out the report's design.* Lay out the report's design on paper, and then show it around to ensure that it effectively serves the users' needs.

2. *Assemble the needed data.* Determine the tables, records, and fields needed for your reports.

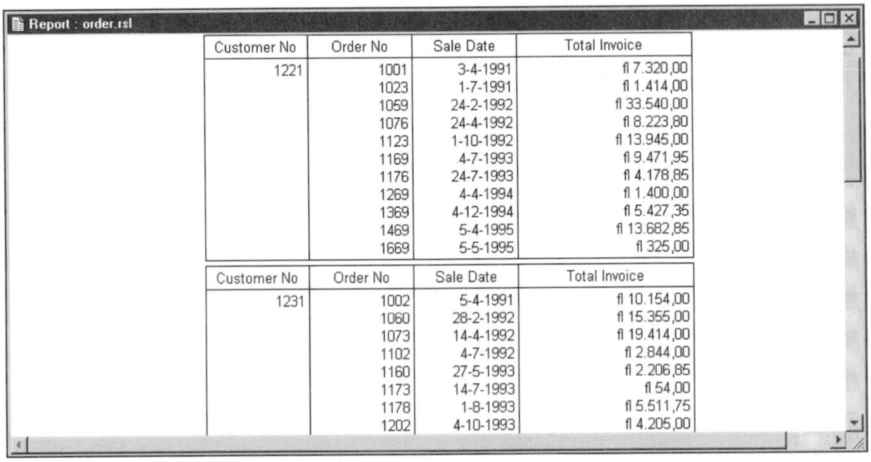

Report : order.rsl

Customer No	Order No	Sale Date	Total Invoice
1221	1001	3-4-1991	fl 7.320,00
	1023	1-7-1991	fl 1.414,00
	1059	24-2-1992	fl 33.540,00
	1076	24-4-1992	fl 8.223,80
	1123	1-10-1992	fl 13.945,00
	1169	4-7-1993	fl 9.471,95
	1176	24-7-1993	fl 4.178,85
	1269	4-4-1994	fl 1.400,00
	1369	4-12-1994	fl 5.427,35
	1469	5-4-1995	fl 13.682,85
	1669	5-5-1995	fl 325,00

Customer No	Order No	Sale Date	Total Invoice
1231	1002	5-4-1991	fl 10.154,00
	1060	28-2-1992	fl 15.355,00
	1073	14-4-1992	fl 19.414,00
	1102	4-7-1992	fl 2.844,00
	1160	27-5-1993	fl 2.206,85
	1173	14-7-1993	fl 54,00
	1178	1-8-1993	fl 5.511,75
	1202	4-10-1993	fl 4.205,00

Figure 50-1: Groups/totals report.

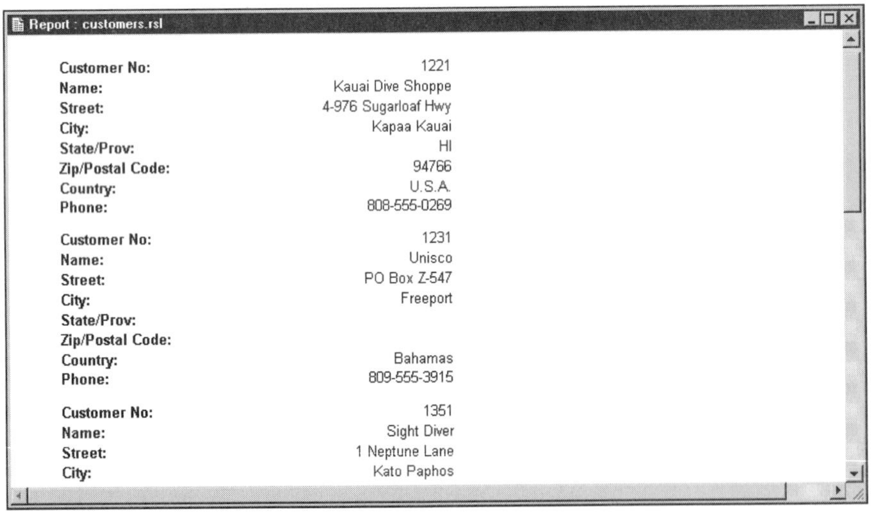

Report : customers.rsl

Customer No:	1221
Name:	Kauai Dive Shoppe
Street:	4-976 Sugarloaf Hwy
City:	Kapaa Kauai
State/Prov:	HI
Zip/Postal Code:	94766
Country:	U.S.A.
Phone:	808-555-0269
Customer No:	1231
Name:	Unisco
Street:	PO Box Z-547
City:	Freeport
State/Prov:	
Zip/Postal Code:	
Country:	Bahamas
Phone:	809-555-3915
Customer No:	1351
Name:	Sight Diver
Street:	1 Neptune Lane
City:	Kato Paphos

Figure 50-2: Columnar report.

3. *Design the report.* Design your report with the help of the Report Expert, or manually in the Report Design window.
4. *Preview and print the report.* Create and view the report. You can then go back to refine your design, or print the final results.

When designing a report, you can employ the same techniques that are available when designing a form. You can:

✦ Select objects

✦ Align objects

Figure 50-3: Mailing label report.

✦ Adjust object sizes

✦ Adjust object spacing

✦ Edit field objects

✦ Add fields

✦ Add lines, rectangles, and ellipses

✦ Add text boxes

✦ Add graphics

✦ Add calculated fields

✦ Add command buttons

Forms Versus Reports

Because you can print both forms and reports in Paradox, and they have many features in common, it's sometimes hard to decide which to use.

Forms can be used to input data, and they are fine for printing individual records and screens. Reports can also print individual records, but only reports can display or print details or summaries for groups of records. You might print a form if you are viewing a record and need a copy of only the data shown in that single record — such as one customer's address information. You would use a report to print an entire address list showing all of the customers.

See Chapter 48 for details on using any of these techniques.

You can also add page breaks to reports (click the Page Break icon), or insert charts and crosstabs.

See Chapter 51 for more information on inserting charts and crosstabs.

Creating Reports

Paradox provides three ways to create reports:

✦ With the Quick Report tool

✦ With the Report Expert

✦ Manually, in the Report Design window

You can also combine the methods. For example, you might use the Report Expert to design the basic report, and then refine its layout by hand.

You can also combine queries and reports in many situations. Use the query to extract specific records and fields, sorted in a particular order, and then generate the report from the query answer table. (See Chapter 49 for more information about queries.)

Creating reports with Quick Report

The fastest way to create a report is to open a table in Table view (or run a query to produce an answer table that appears in Table view), and then click the Quick Report icon (Tools ➪ Quick Design ➪ Quick Report, or press Shift+F7). You get an instant report, in a basic, single-column layout, with the current date and the name of the underlying table or query on the first page (see Figure 50-4).

Creating reports with the Report Expert

For help in creating more sophisticated one- and two-table reports, use the Report Expert as follows:

1. Click the PerfectExpert icon (Tools ➪ Experts), click Report, and click Run Expert.

2. Specify whether the report will display data from one or two tables by clicking the corresponding button (see Figure 50-5).

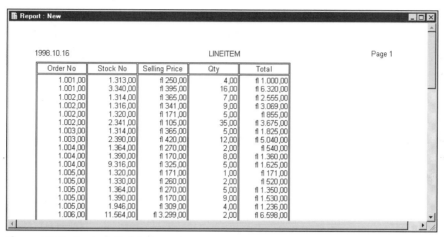

Figure 50-4: Instant Quick Report.

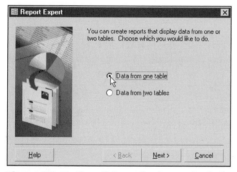

Figure 50-5: Specifying whether to include data from one or two tables.

   3. Click Next, choose the table(s) to use in the report, select the fields to include in your report, and click the right arrow button to add the fields (see Figure 50-6). If you are using two tables, pick the fields you are linking on.

Tip   Click the double-arrow buttons to select or remove all the fields.

   4. Click Next and select fields to group your reports by, in order of group priority (see Figure 50-7). For example, group the orders by customer number to get an overview of all the orders for a customer. Use the group priority arrows to specify which groupings are most important.

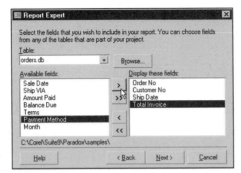

Figure 50-6: Selecting fields for your report.

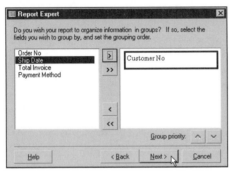

Figure 50-7: Selecting fields to group your report by.

5. Click Next and select the summaries, if any, to calculate for each group (see Figure 50-8). Select the field to summarize, click the right arrow button, and choose the type of summary from the drop-down Summary list box. For instance, summarize the Total Invoice field to show the amount each customer has ordered.

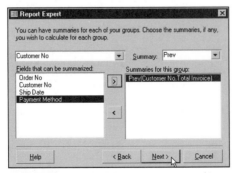

Figure 50-8: Specifying group summaries.

6. Click Next, select a style for your report, and specify whether individual or multiple records will be printed per page by clicking the corresponding button (see Figure 50-9). As you select styles, they will be previewed in the right pane of the dialog box.

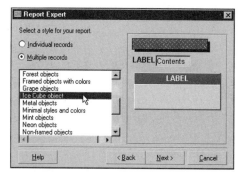

Figure 50-9: Selecting a report style and records per page.

7. Click Next and specify a title, page numbering, and date and time displays as desired (see Figure 50-10). Choose the location for the elements that you add.

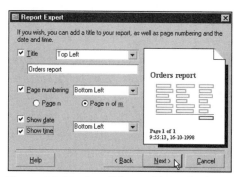

Figure 50-10: Specifying a title and other report options.

8. Click Next and enter the filename and location for the report (normally your working directory). You can also print the report now, if desired, by clicking the Print Report button (see Figure 50-11).

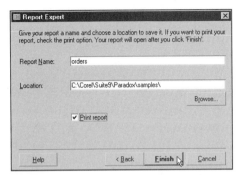

Figure 50-11: Specifying your report's name, location, and whether to print it.

9. Click Finish to create your report and display it on the screen (see Figure 50-12). Click the Print icon (File ⇨ Print) to print the report. Click View ⇨ Zoom to get an overview or a detailed view of your report.

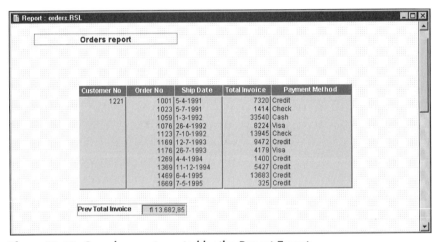

Figure 50-12: Sample report created by the Report Expert.

Note that if you're creating a report with data from two tables, you'll be asked to select a master table and a detail table in Step 3. Once you do, you have to choose a link to relate the two tables (see Figure 50-13). All the other steps are similar to the steps used to create a single-table report.

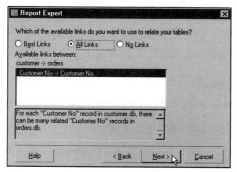

Figure 50-13: Linking tables for a two-table report.

Manually creating reports with the data model

You can create reports manually in either of two ways:

✦ Open a blank report, and then add the desired text, text boxes, graphics, lines, rectangles, and other objects.

✦ Create a report based on a data model (the method described here).

Reports that use a data model are based on the tables and relationships within the model. This method is generally the best way to create multi-table reports.

To begin designing a report based on a data model:

1. Do either of the following:

   • In the Project Viewer, right-click the Reports icon and click New ➪ Data Model.

   • Click File ➪ New From Project, click [New Report], and then click Create ➪ Data Model.

2. Choose the data model.

3. Choose the layout options and the fields to include.

4. Click OK to create the basic report.

5. Edit the layout as necessary.

6. Save your report.

Because the steps and options for creating a report based on a data model are similar to those for creating a form based on a data model, refer to Chapter 48 for complete step-by-step details.

Fine-Tuning Your Report's Layout

Once you've specified your report layout options in the data model, your report appears in the Report Design window (see Figure 50-14).

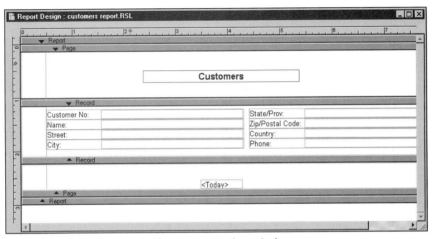

Figure 50-14: Your report in the Report Design window.

Note how Paradox uses horizontal *bands* to control how sections of a report break—a technique commonly used by database managers. Bands can include the following:

✦ A *report header* at the beginning of the report, with such information as the report title, date, and company name

✦ A *report footer* at the end, that can include overall summaries and end-of-report indicators

✦ A *page header* and a *page footer*, for such items as the column headers, date, title, page number, and page summary

✦ A *group header* and a *group footer* when reporting on groups. The report shown in Figure 50-15 includes a group band for the City field.

✦ A *record* or *detail band* for the data in the body of the report. You can include identifying labels in this band.

By default, your new report has bands for the Page Header, Page Footer, and Records. The others are optional.

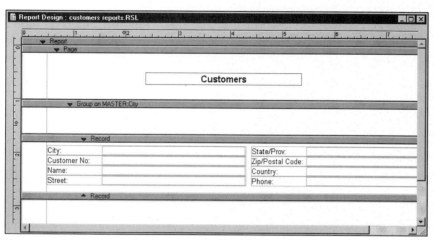

Figure 50-15: A report with a group band for the City field.

To resize a band, click within the band, and then click on the border where the pointer changes to a double-headed arrow and drag the border.

Cross-Reference See online Help for more information on creating, viewing, selecting, editing, and deleting bands.

Adding a report grouping

You can add *group bands* to your reports to subdivide data into specific categories, such as by country or department. A group band is inserted between the page band and the record band.

To add a group band to a report in Design mode, click the Add Band icon or click Insert ➪ Group Band, and then do either of the following:

✦ Click the Group by Field Value button and select the field to group by (see Figure 50-16). If you also want to group on the first characters in the field, check the Range Group button and enter the number of characters in the text box below it. Click the OK button to add the group band to your report design.

✦ Click the Group by Record button and enter the number of records per group (see Figure 50-17). Click the OK button to add the group band to your report design.

Figure 50-16: Adding a report grouping by field values.

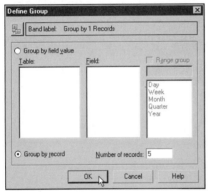

Figure 50-17: Adding a report grouping by number of records.

Previewing Your Report

View mode enables you to see what your report looks like with actual data (see Figure 50-18). Click the Run Report icon, press F8, or click View ⇨ Run Report whenever you want to toggle between Design (editing) mode and View mode.

Use the toolbar navigation buttons, shown in Figure 50-19, to move from page to page in your report.

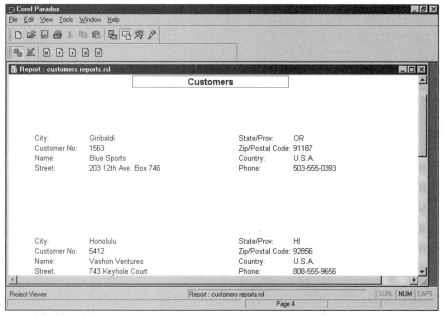

Figure 50-18: Previewing your report.

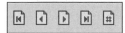

Figure 50-19: Toolbar buttons for report navigation.

Saving Your Report

To save your completed report, click the Save icon (File ➪ Save). If you're saving the report for the first time, specify its name (Paradox adds the .RSL extension) and location (normally the working directory).

Protecting Your Report Design

If you've completed the design of a report and want to protect it from being altered, you can create a delivered version of the report that can't be opened in Design mode. Follow these steps:

1. Click the Save icon (File ➪ Save) to save the latest changes.

2. Click Format ➪ Deliver.

Paradox creates a copy of the report and saves it with the same name as the report, but with an .RDL extension.

Caution   Delivered reports can't be "undelivered," so keep a copy of the original report (with the .RSL extension) in case you want to make changes later on.

Printing Reports

Click the Print icon (File ➪ Print) to print the current report on the screen. You can also right-click a report in the Project Viewer and click Print.

Cross-Reference   See Chapter 13, "Printing and Faxing Information," for general information on printing.

Creating Mailing Labels

Creating mailing labels is one of the routine chores required of a database system. Paradox provides a Label Expert to make this an easy task. In addition, before creating the labels, you can run a query to provide an answer table, with specific records to generate the labels from.

To create mailing labels:

1. Click the PerfectExpert icon (Tools ➪ Experts), click Mailing Label, and then click Run Expert.

2. Select the label category and type, and then click Next (see Figure 50-20). You can define a custom size label using the New Label button.

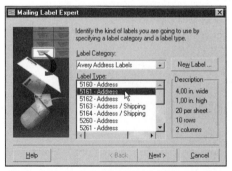

Figure 50-20: Selecting the label category and type.

3. Select the table or query that contains the data for your labels, and then click Next (see Figure 50-21). If the table or query you want is not shown, use the Browse button to locate it.

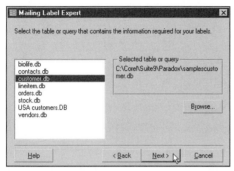

Figure 50-21: Selecting the table or query that contains label data.

4. Select the font size, style, and type for your labels, and then click Next (see Figure 50-22). As you choose the options, the Sample box shows how your selections appear.

 Tip

You should normally keep the font small and simple so that your labels will fit into the available space.

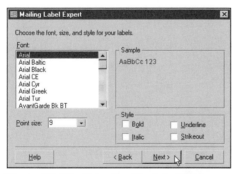

Figure 50-22: Selecting the label font.

5. Specify whether the labels should be printed from left to right or by columns; then click Next (see Figure 50-23).

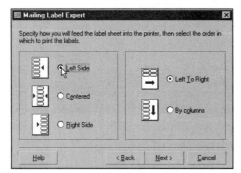

Figure 50-23: Selecting print options.

6. Select the fields to include in your labels and click the Place Field button to add them to the layout (see Figure 50-24). Add any punctuation or spacing necessary to produce the correct layout.

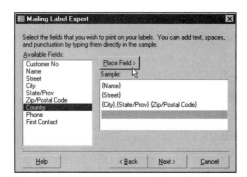

Figure 50-24: Selecting fields for your labels.

7. Click Next, and specify the name and location for your label report (see Figure 50-25). You can also choose to view the labels onscreen, print the labels, or modify the labels in a design window by clicking the corresponding button. Click Finish to create the labels.

Using Report Information to Create Merge Files

Instead of producing the mailing labels in Paradox, you can use the Merge Expert to create a WordPerfect merge file.

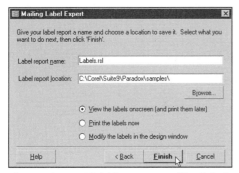

Figure 50-25: Finishing your mailing labels.

To create a WordPerfect merge file:

1. Click the PerfectExpert icon (Tools ➪ Experts), click Merge, and then click Run Expert.

2. Click the appropriate button to specify whether you want to create new merge settings or, if you have created a merge before, to use existing settings (see Figure 50-26). If you want to use existing settings, choose the settings from the drop-down list box.

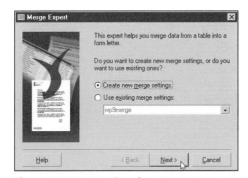

Figure 50-26: Starting the Merge Expert.

3. Click Next and select the merge application and form file you want to use (see Figure 50-27). If you don't want to use any of the existing form files, you can click No and Paradox will help you create a new one later in this procedure.

4. Click Next and select the table that has the merge data (see Figure 50-28).

Tip   Run a query first to merge selected data only.

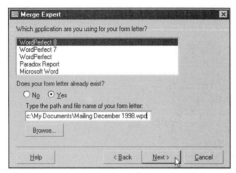

Figure 50-27: Selecting the application and form file.

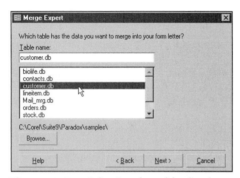

Figure 50-28: Selecting the table that has your merge data.

5. Click Next, select the fields to sort by, and click the right arrow button (see Figure 50-29). Use the Change Order and Sort Direction options to further refine the sort.

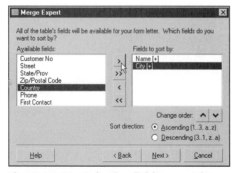

Figure 50-29: Selecting fields to sort by.

6. Click Next and, if necessary, adjust the formats of various fields for use in the merge file (see Figure 50-30). To adjust a format, click the field you wish to adjust and choose the field type from the drop-down Format list box.

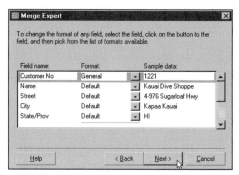

Figure 50-30: Adjusting the field formats.

7. Click Next, save the merge settings for later use, and run the merge (see Figure 50-31). If you did not select an existing form letter in Step 3, Paradox displays Help information for creating one in the merge application you chose.

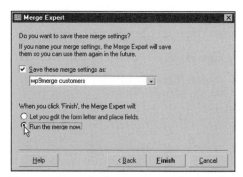

Figure 50-31: Saving merge settings and running the merge.

For more information on WordPerfect's mail merge facilities, see Chapter 27.

Reporting to WordPerfect

In addition to using report information to create mailing labels, you can also save it so it can be displayed as a standard WordPerfect document.

New Feature

WordPerfect now lets you save reports in the Rich-Text Format (RTF) so you can open it in WordPerfect and apply all the standard formatting (see Figure 50-32). To save a report in RTF, click File ➪ Publish As ➪ RTF.

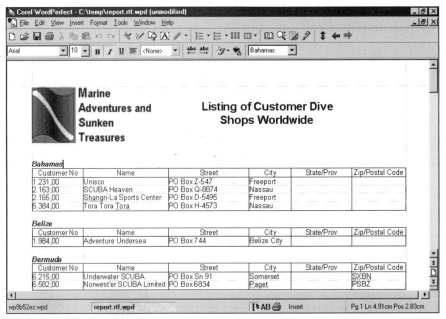

Figure 50-32: Using your report in WordPerfect.

For More Information . . .

On	See
Creating forms	Chapter 48
Using Paradox queries	Chapter 49
Printing reports	Chapter 11
Using WordPerfect merge	Chapter 27
Creating charts	Chapter 51
Creating crosstabs	Chapter 51

✦   ✦   ✦

Paradox Tricks and Techniques

♦ ♦ ♦ ♦

In This Chapter

Create and
edit charts

Create cross-tab
summaries of
your data

Publish Web pages
with your data

Import and export
data in a variety of
formats

Create a launcher
for your project

♦ ♦ ♦ ♦

Knowing a few tricks and techniques about Paradox will help you to take advantage of its unique power. This chapter lets you in on some powerful Paradox secrets to charting and analyzing data, posting data on the Web, and more.

Working with Charts

In Paradox, you can create area, bar, column, line, and pie charts, and then display them within a form or report (see Figure 51-1).

Note   Paradox's charting facilities are rudimentary compared to those in Presentations (see Chapter 56), so you might want to export the Paradox data you want to chart as an ASCII text file or spreadsheet file, and then import the data into Presentations. (See "Exporting data as text," later in this chapter.)

Creating a chart

To create the chart shown in Figure 51-1 in Paradox:

1. Create and run a query, if necessary, to create an answer table with the data you want to chart (see Chapter 47).

2. Click the PerfectExpert icon (Tools ⇨ Experts), click Chart, and then click Run Expert.

3. Select whether you want to place the chart on a new form or a new report, and then click Next (see Figure 51-2).

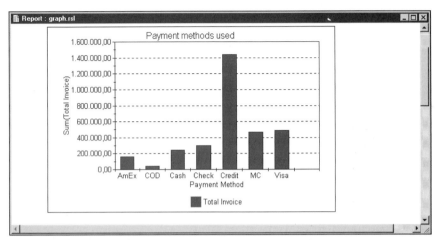

Figure 51-1: Paradox chart.

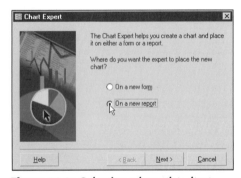

Figure 51-2: Selecting where the chart should go.

4. Select the table or query with the data you want to chart, and then click Next (see Figure 51-3).

5. Select whether you want a single chart, or a chart for each group or page in the report, and then click Next (see Figure 51-4).

6. Select the field to group information by, and then click Next (see Figure 51-5).

7. Select whether you want to create a tabular chart that takes data directly from the table, or a chart that summarizes the values in a field, and then click Next (see Figure 51-6).

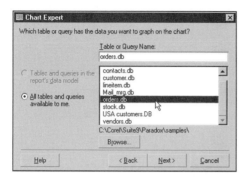

Figure 51-3: Selecting the data you want to chart.

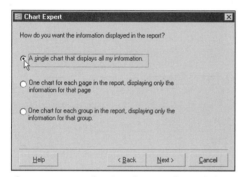

Figure 51-4: Selecting the number of charts to create.

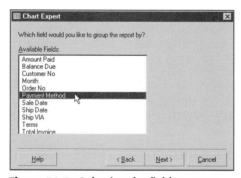

Figure 51-5: Selecting the field to group information by.

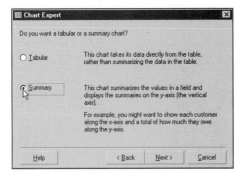

Figure 51-6: Selecting a tabular or summary chart.

8. If you're creating a summary chart, select whether to summarize data by one or two categories (other fields), and then click Next (see Figure 51-7).

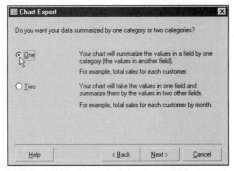

Figure 51-7: Selecting the number of categories to summarize data by.

9. Select the type of chart you want, and whether it should be two-dimensional or three-dimensional, and then click Next (see Figure 51-8).

10. Select the field for the horizontal (X) axis, and then click Next (see Figure 51-9).

11. Select the field or fields for the vertical (Y) axis. If you're creating a summary chart, select one field and select the summary operation you want to see (see Figure 51-10). Click Next.

12. Specify the chart's title, subtitle, and axis titles, and then click Next (see Figure 51-11).

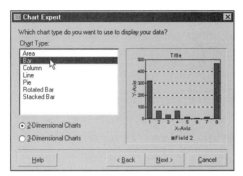

Figure 51-8: Selecting the chart type.

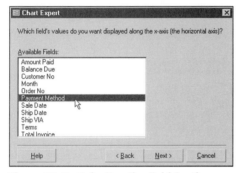

Figure 51-9: Selecting the field for the horizontal axis.

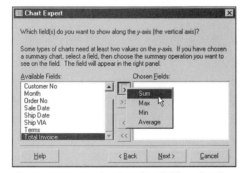

Figure 51-10: Selecting the field(s) for the vertical axis (and the summary operation for a summary chart).

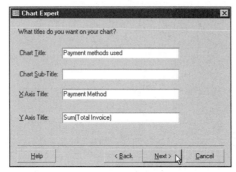

Figure 51-11: Adding titles to your chart.

13. Finally, specify a filename for the chart, and whether you want to view the chart when you finish, or bring it up into the design window to make further changes (see Figure 51-12). Click Finish to create the chart.

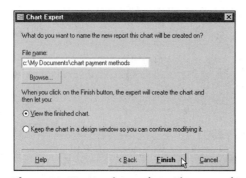

Figure 51-12: Naming and creating your chart.

Note   If you selected "On a new form" in Step 3, the chart is saved with your forms and given an .FSL extension. If you selected "On a new report," the chart is saved as a report with an .RSL extension.

Editing a chart

Once a chart is created, you can edit it in Design view:

1. Double-click the form or report with the chart in the Project Viewer, and then click the Design mode button or press F8 to switch to Design mode.

2. To change the chart type, right-click any blank area of the chart and click Chart Type.

3. Right-click various items in the chart (such as markers, axes, or titles), and then click Properties to change them.

Creating a Quick Chart

 New Feature In Paradox 9 you can create a Quick Chart directly from a table, without placing it in a report or form. Simply open a table and click the Quick Chart button (Tools ⇨ Design ⇨ Quick Chart).

Creating Cross-Tab Summaries

You can create cross-tab queries to summarize numeric or currency data, and display it in a spreadsheet-like format. A cross-tab has

✦ *Column labels* across the top row

✦ *Category labels* on the left side of the cross-tab

✦ *Summaries* of the data within individual cells

The chart shown in Figure 51-1 breaks down total invoices by the payment method used. To break down the totals by customer, create the cross-tab shown in Figure 51-13.

	AmEx	COD	Cash	Check	Credit	MC	Visa
1221			$33,540	$15,359	$37,627		$12,403
1231				$33,262	$69,271	$19,468	
1351					$227,012	$25,500	$4,495
1354				$55,198			$25,394
1356			$3,596		$17,592		$51,358
1380					$16,672		$10,729
1384			$1,238	$33,071	$60,651		$106,026
1510	$7,514						$48,910
1513			$26,502	$14,050		$14,217	$38,392	$2,693

Payment methods used by customers

Figure 51-13: Cross-tab summary of table data.

Creating a cross-tab

To create a cross-tab summary:

1. Click the PerfectExpert icon(Tools ⇨ Experts), click Crosstab, and click Run Expert.

2. Select whether you want to place the cross-tab on a new form or a new report (see Figure 51-14) and then click Next.

Figure 51-14: Selecting where the cross-tab summary should go.

3. Select the table for your cross-tab, and then click Next (see Figure 51-15). (Use the answer table from a relational query to cross-tab data from multiple tables).

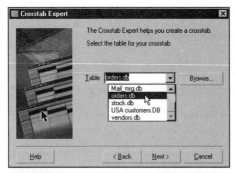

Figure 51-15: Selecting the table for your cross-tab.

4. Select the fields for the top (column) and left (category) labels, click the top two buttons in the center to position the fields, and then click Next (see Figure 51-16).

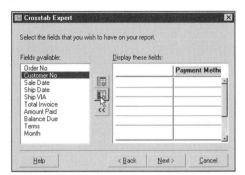

Figure 51-16: Selecting fields for the column and category labels.

5. Select the fields on which you want to perform a calculation, along with the type of calculation you want to perform, and then click Next (see Figure 51-17).

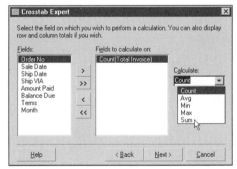

Figure 51-17: Selecting the calculation fields and the type of calculation.

6. Preview the structure of your cross-tab report (see Figure 51-18). If it's not what you want, click Back to change your selections; otherwise, click Next.

7. Finally, specify a filename and location for your cross-tab, and whether you want to view it in Run mode when you finish, or bring it up in Design view to make further changes (see Figure 51-19). Click Finish to create the cross-tab.

Note   If you selected "On a new form" in the first dialog box of the Crosstab Expert, the cross-tab is saved with your forms and given an .FSL extension. If you selected "On a new report," the cross-tab is saved as a report and given an .RSL extension.

Figure 51-18: Previewing your cross-tab report structure.

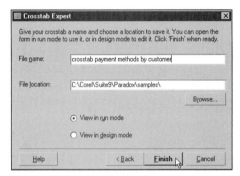

Figure 51-19: Naming and creating your cross-tab.

Editing a cross-tab

A cross-tab can also be edited in Design view. All the tools that are available to customize a form or report are available for cross-tabs as well (see Chapters 48 and 50).

Creating a Quick Cross-tab

New Feature

In Paradox 9 you can create a Quick Cross-tab directly from a table, without placing it in a report or form. Simply open a table and click the Quick Crosstab button (Tools ➪ Design ➪ Quick Crosstab).

Publishing to HTML

You can easily publish your data to HTML, for display on the Internet or to post within a corporate intranet (see Figure 51-20).

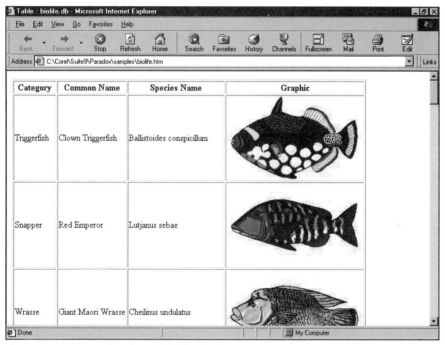

Figure 51-20: Paradox data published to HTML.

To publish data to HTML:

1. Open the table with data you want to publish (or run the desired query to produce an answer table).

2. Click File ⇨ Publish to HTML, select the fields for your HTML table, and then click Next (see Figure 51-21). (Click the up and down arrow buttons to change the order of the selected fields.)

3. Give the Web page a meaningful title, select other display options, and then click Next (see Figure 51-22).

4. Select whether to publish the table as a static Web document or a dynamic document generated by the Corel Web Server each time it's requested. Type a filename for your document, click Save As Template if you want to save its format for use in other HTML documents, and then click Finish to create your document (see Figure 51-23).

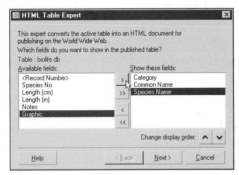

Figure 51-21: Selecting fields for your HTML table.

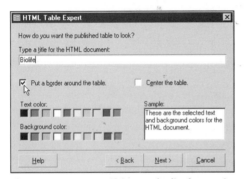

Figure 51-22: Specifying Web display options.

Figure 51-23: Specifying how you want to publish the table.

See Chapter 14 for details on creating HTML documents and displaying them on the Web. To see online Help about using the Corel Web Server, start the Corel Web Server, right-click its icon on the Windows taskbar, click View Connections, and view the online Help.

Importing and Exporting Data

As with the other applications in the WordPerfect suite, Paradox has robust import and export capabilities. You can transfer data between a Paradox table and the following popular file formats:

✦ Microsoft Access tables

✦ dBase tables

✦ HTML tables

✦ ASCII delimited text

✦ ASCII fixed-length text

✦ Quattro Pro

✦ Lotus 1-2-3

✦ Excel

✦ WordPerfect documents and merge files (export only)

Note You can only import and export table data between other products and Paradox. You can't import or export forms, reports, or queries.

Note Using Microsoft Access tables in Paradox 9 requires some configuration. You need to have the Jetengine .DLLs installed on your system to be able to use Microsoft Access tables in Paradox. If Microsoft Access 95 or Microsoft Access 97 is installed on your system, you already have these DLLs. Otherwise, download the MS Data Access Components (MDAC) from the Microsoft Web site (http://www. microsoft.com/data). More information on this topic can be found in the Paradox help system.

Cross-Reference For general information on transferring and sharing data, see Chapter 10, "Working Together and Sharing Data."

Importing databases

To import tables created by other database software into Paradox:

1. Click File ➪ Import, and then click Import.

2. In the From box, enter the path and the filename of the database (Paradox will select the appropriate file type).

3. In the To box, enter the name of the Paradox table that is to receive the data.

4. If you're importing data into an existing table, click "Overwrite existing table" to overwrite existing records, or click "Append to existing table" to add the imported records to the end of the table (see Figure 51-24).

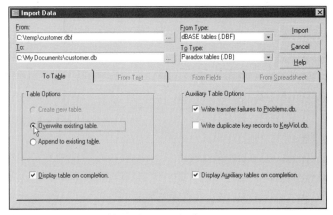

Figure 51-24: Specifying import options.

5. Check "Write transfer failures to Problems.db" if you want to log any import errors. Check "Write duplicate key records to KeyViol.db" if you want to save duplicate key records.

6. Click Import to import and display the data.

Importing spreadsheets

Before importing spreadsheet data into Paradox:

✦ Remove any unnecessary characters (such as hyphens, underscores, asterisks, or exclamation points).

✦ Ensure that each column contains just one kind of data.

✦ Note the coordinates of the range of data you want to import (if you're not importing the entire spreadsheet).

To import spreadsheet data into Paradox:

1. Follow Steps 1 and 5 of "Importing databases."

2. Click the From Spreadsheet tab and check "Use first row of data as field names" if you want Paradox to use the first row of the spreadsheet as column labels (see Figure 51-25).

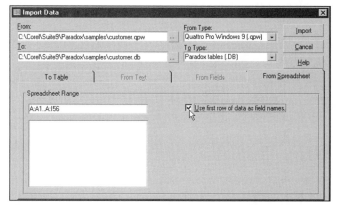

Figure 51-25: Specifying more spreadsheet import options.

3. Specify the range of spreadsheet data you want to import, and then click Import to import and display the data.

Importing text files

While you can use File ➪ Import to import a text file, you can use the Text Import Expert to walk you through the process:

1. Click Experts (Tools ➪ Experts), click Text Import, and click Run Expert. (You can also click File ➪ Import ➪ Text Expert.)

2. Choose whether to create new import settings, use settings you previously saved, or modify existing settings, and then click Next (see Figure 51-26). If you haven't imported text files yet, the options to use existing settings will be unavailable.

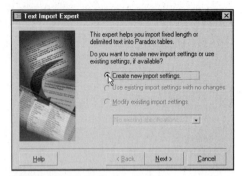

Figure 51-26: Selecting text import settings.

3. Select the file you want to import, click whether it was created by DOS or Windows, and then click Next (see Figure 51-27).

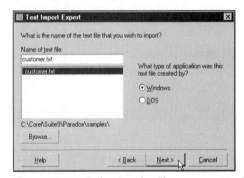

Figure 51-27: Selecting the file you want to import.

4. Enter the name of the table that is to receive the data. If you're importing data into an existing table, choose whether to overwrite the existing table or append the data to the end of the table, and then click Next (see Figure 51-28).

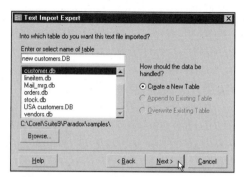

Figure 51-28: Specifying the table to receive the imported data, and where the data should go.

5. Select the row of text where the import process should begin, and then click Next (see Figure 51-29).

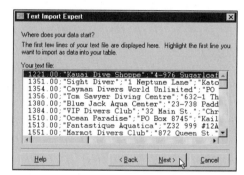

Figure 51-29: Selecting the first line you want to import.

6. Check whether you're importing fixed-length or delimited text, and then click Next (see Figure 51-30).

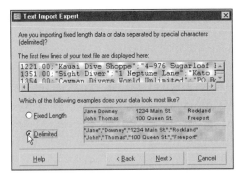

Figure 51-30: Specifying the type of text you're importing.

7. Specify the delimiters and separators used to identify fields and records, and then click Next (see Figure 51-31). (For more on text delimiters, see Chapter 29.)

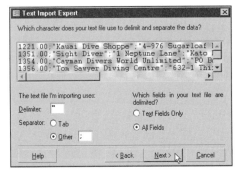

Figure 51-31: Specifying text delimiters and separators.

8. Make any changes to the proposed field names, types, and sizes, and then click Next (see Figure 51-32). (Click Borrow to copy the structure of another Paradox table that will match your imported data.)

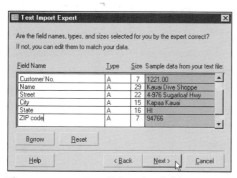

Figure 51-32: Specifying the field names, types, and sizes.

9. Check if you wish to save for future use the import settings you just specified. You can also check to create an ObjectPAL script that, when run, will perform the import. Choose whether or not to open the finished table when the import process is complete, and then click Finish to import the text file (see Figure 51-33).

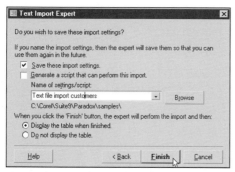

Figure 51-33: Specifying whether to save the current import settings and other options.

Importing HTML data

Paradox provides an HTML Import Expert that lets you import tables or lists from Web pages directly into Paradox tables:

1. Click Experts (Tools ➪ Experts), click HTML Import, and click Run Expert. (You can also click File ➪ Import ➪ HTML Expert.)

2. Select the HTML file that contains the data you want to import, and then click Next (see Figure 51-34).

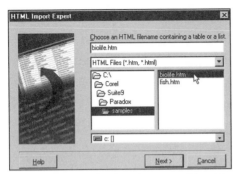

Figure 51-34: Selecting the HTML file with the data you want to import.

3. Select the HTML table you want to import, check if you want to use the first row in the preview for column headings, and then click Next (see Figure 51-35).

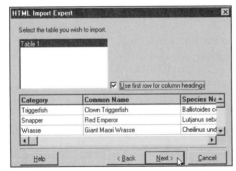

Figure 51-35: Selecting the HTML table you want to import.

4. Select whether you're creating a new table or adding the HTML data to an existing table. Click Next (see Figure 51-36).

5. Link the data in the HTML table to fields in the new or existing table, and then click Next (see Figure 51-37).

6. Specify your table and path, select if you want to view the finished table, and then click Finish to import the HTML data (see Figure 51-38).

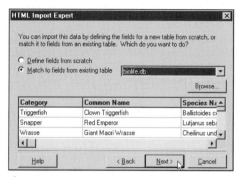

Figure 51-36: Importing data to a new table or an existing one.

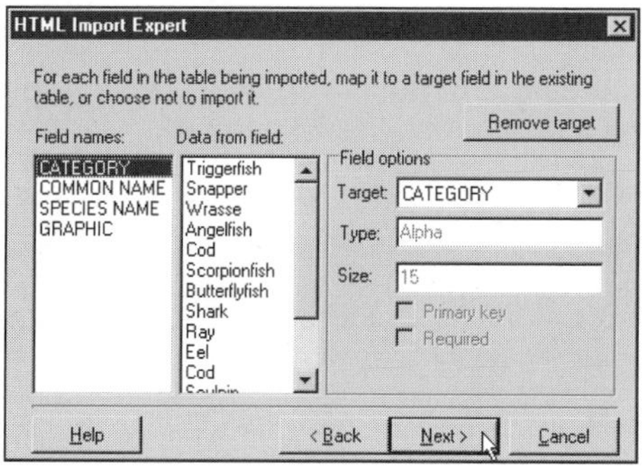

Figure 51-37: Linking the HTML data to fields in the Paradox table.

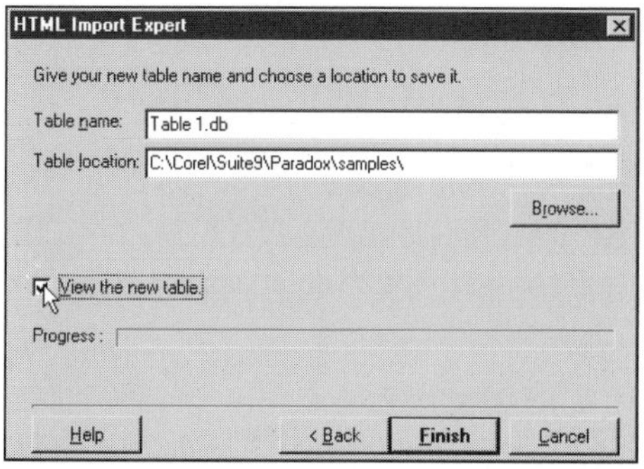

Figure 51-38: Completing the import process.

Exporting data to spreadsheets and databases

When you export table data to a spreadsheet file, Paradox exports each record as a row and each field as a column. When you export to a database, records and fields from the Paradox table become records and fields in the other database's file format.

Note Memo, graphic, binary, and OLE fields are not exported, unless you're exporting to dBASE 5 for Windows or to another version of Paradox that supports those field types.

To export table data to a spreadsheet or database file:

1. Click File ➪ Export and select the table with the data you want to export.

2. Click the To Type list and select the spreadsheet or database format you want. In the To box, enter the path and filename for the exported file.

3. If you want to place table field names in the first row of the spreadsheet or database file, check "Use first row of data as field names."

4. Click Export to export your Paradox table (see Figure 51-39).

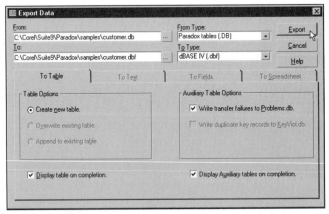

Figure 51-39: Exporting data to a spreadsheet or database.

Tip Instead of exporting Paradox data to Quattro Pro, use Quattro Pro's External Data Expert to open Paradox tables and queries directly (see Chapter 35) or copy and paste Paradox data into a Quattro Pro notebook (see Chapter 10).

Exporting data as text

You can export the data in Paradox tables as delimited text with fields separated by characters, or as a fixed-text file with fields separated by a fixed amount of space. (Memo, graphic, binary, and OLE fields are not exported.)

To export Paradox table data to a delimited text file:

1. Click File ➪ Export and select the table with the data you want to export.

2. Select ASCII Delimited from the To Type list (see Figure 51-40), and then specify the following:

Selection	Lets You
Fields Separated By	Select the character to separate fields
Fields Delimited By	Specify the characters, if any, to surround particular values
Delimited Fields	Choose whether to enclose the data from all the fields with delimiters, or only the text fields
Character Set	Click whether to export using your computer's OEM character set (code page), or the ANSI character set that can only be read by other Windows programs
Field Names	Check if you want to use the first row of data as field names

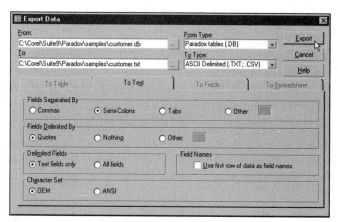

Figure 51-40: Exporting data as text.

3. Click Export to create the text file.

To export Paradox table data to a fixed-width text file:

1. Click File ➪ Export and select the table with the data you want to export (refer to Figure 51-42).

2. Select ASCII Fixed from the To Type list.

3. In the Character Set section, click whether to use the OEM or ANSI set for the exported data.

4. Click the To Fields tab. To use an export specification you've saved previously, click Load Spec and select the specification. To save the current export specifications for future use, click Save Spec and name the specification (see Figure 51-41).

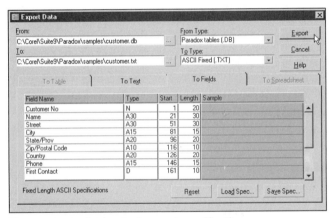

Figure 51-41: Setting text export specifications.

5. Click Export to create the text file.

Exporting to WordPerfect

To export a Paradox table to a WordPerfect table:

1. Click File ➪ Export and select the table with the data you want to export (refer to Figure 51-40).

2. Select WordPerfect 9 from the To Type list, and then click Export.

For general information on working with WordPerfect tables, see Chapter 22. To merge Paradox data with a WordPerfect form letter, see Chapter 50.

Creating an Application Launcher

To set a professionally packaged application apart from a mundane collection of objects, create an application launcher as the starting point for common database tasks.

For example, you might typically work with a customer form and need to regularly print a customer report. Rather than hunting for these objects in the Project Viewer every day, you can create a launcher with buttons for updates and reporting. You can then select the launcher from the Paradox Project Viewer or even the Windows Start menu.

Paradox comes with a Launcher Expert to quickly create an application launcher (see Figure 51-42) with buttons for tables, queries, forms, and reports.

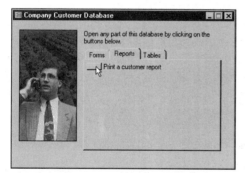

Figure 51-42: Launcher to update forms and reports.

To create an application launcher:

1. Click the PerfectExpert icon (Tools ⇨ Experts), click Launcher, and then click Run Expert.

2. Click "Create new launcher settings" or click "Use existing launcher settings," select the settings you want to use, and then click Next (see Figure 51-43). If you haven't created a launcher yet, the option to use existing settings will be unavailable.

3. Select the forms, reports, scripts, tables, queries, and other items that the launcher should run, and then click Next (see Figure 51-44). (Click the up and down arrows for each category to rearrange its items.)

4. Change the filename prompts for each launcher button to something meaningful to the user, and then click Next (see Figure 51-45).

5. Type a caption for the launcher, select various location, style, and positioning settings, and then click Next (see Figure 51-46).

Figure 51-43: Creating or selecting launcher settings.

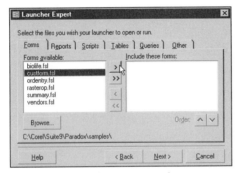

Figure 51-44: Selecting items for your launcher to run.

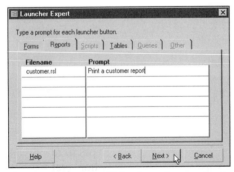

Figure 51-45: Specifying launcher prompts.

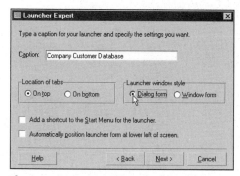

Figure 51-46: Specifying the launcher caption and other options.

6. Select an image to personalize your launcher, and then click Next (see Figure 51-47).

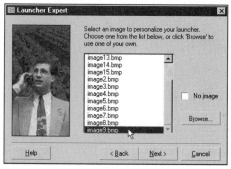

Figure 51-47: Selecting an image to personalize your launcher.

7. Specify the launcher name and location, save your launcher settings, and then choose whether to run the launcher or open it in Design view to make further changes (see Figure 51-48). Click Finish to create the launcher.

Once you've created the launcher, you can open it from the Project Viewer and use it to access your tables, queries, forms, reports, and scripts in the project. If you checked "Add a shortcut to the Start Menu for the launcher" (refer to Figure 51-46), you'll be able to click Start ➪ Programs, and then select the launcher from the "Paradox Launchers" group to start Paradox with your launcher.

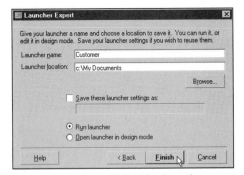

Figure 51-48: Specifying the launcher name, location, and other options.

A Few Words About ObjectPAL

A launcher form can be seen as a simple database application. If you want more control over your databases and want to create a customized environment for end-users, check out ObjectPAL. ObjectPAL is an object-oriented programming language that lets you create full-featured database applications. Explaining the use of ObjectPAL would require a separate book, but the Paradox Guide in the Reference Center will get you started.

For More Information . . .

On	*See*
Creating charts in Presentations	Chapter 56
Creating charts in Quattro Pro	Chapter 36
Creating cross-tabs in Quattro Pro	Chapter 35
Web writing and publishing	Chapter 14
Using databases in Quattro Pro	Chapter 35
Working with WordPerfect Tables	Chapter 22
Using WordPerfect Merge	Chapter 27
Transferring and sharing data	Chapter 10
Specifying text delimiters	Chapter 31
Programming with ObjectPAL	Paradox guide in the Reference Center

✦   ✦   ✦

Suite Techniques

Writers' Lib

Writing is work. No program can think for you, and there's no substitute for your own eye and ear for language. However, the WordPerfect suite's superlative writing tools can speed up your work and deliver a lively document that's free from spelling and grammar mistakes. You'll be amazed at how freely your thoughts flow once the program is looking after the mechanics. As you saw in Chapter 2, "Essential Typing and Editing," your basic error-correction is now fully automatic with:

+ Spell-As-You-Go

+ Grammar-As-You-Go

+ Prompt-As-You-Go

+ QuickCorrect

+ Automatic typo correction

You also have Formatting-As-You-Go (Chapter 17, "Becoming an Instant WordPerfect Expert") for automatic sentence corrections, instant bullets, and other conveniences.

This chapter covers QuickCorrect tricks in more detail, and shows you how to create formatted abbreviations with QuickWords. (Although QuickWords is WordPerfect-only, it's covered in this suitewide chapter because it's closely related to QuickCorrect.)

Using Spell Checker

If you had to name the most indispensable writing tool, it would have to be spell-checking. It's hard not to love Spell-As-You-Go, which even catches duplicate words as you type. Spell Checker enables you to correct your whole document at once, and customize your replacement word lists.

◆ ◆ ◆ ◆

In This Chapter

Spell-check your document

Use QuickCorrect to make your typing fly

Insert QuickWords with formatting and graphics

Find a better word with the Thesaurus

Proofread your documents

Use abbreviations to insert text and graphics

Write in other languages

◆ ◆ ◆ ◆

Understanding word lists

Spell Checker and the Grammatik proofreader (including their Spell-As-You-Go and Grammar-As-You-Go tools) match the words in your document against three types of word lists:

✦ *Main word lists* (dictionaries) that come with the program. You can chain as many as ten compatible lists.

✦ *User word lists* containing your personal skip and replacement words. A default user word list (which also displays your list of QuickCorrect entries in its editor) comes with the program. You can add to that list or create and chain additional lists.

✦ *Document word lists* (built-in word lists) where you can place skip and replacement words just for that document.

When checking a word, lists are searched in reverse order (from document to personal to main).

Spell-As-You-Go can add skip words to the default user list.

Checking your spelling

To spell-check text:

1. Click the Spell button on the toolbar. (You can also click Tools ➪ Spell Checker, or right-click a WordPerfect document and click Spell Checker.)

2. Spell Checker normally checks your entire document or selected text (including headers, footers, footnotes, and endnotes). When it stops at a word, you can click the Check list to select other elements to check, such as the current page.

3. When Spell Checker finds a word it doesn't recognize (see Figure 52-1), click one of the replacement buttons described in Table 52-1.

Checking part of your document

Click the Check list in Spell Check, and click the portion of the document to check, such as the current paragraph or page. Better yet, try the following before you start the spell-check:

✦ Select a portion of your document to check.

✦ Place the insertion point on a misspelled word to check from the insertion point on.

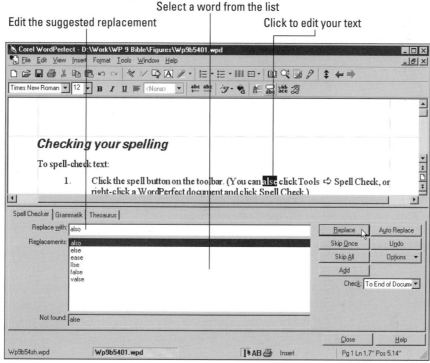

Figure 52-1: Checking your spelling.

Table 52-1
Spell Checker Replacement Options

This Option	Lets You
Replace	Swap the word in your document with the suggested "Replace with" word. You can edit the suggestion or click another word in the Replacements list.
Skip Once	Remove the marking and keep your spelling of the word.
Skip All	Add the word to the document list so it's no longer flagged in this document.
Add	Put the flagged word in the user word list, so it will be skipped in all your documents.
Auto Replace	Add the flagged word and your replacement to the QuickCorrect list.
Undo	Retrace your spell-checking steps, but not undo your corrections.
Options	Customize the spell-checker, edit word lists, and change languages, as discussed in the following sections.
Resume	Go back to checking your spelling. The button appears if you've clicked outside of the Spell Checker to edit your text.

Customizing the Spell Checker

To customize the spell checker, click the Spell Checker button (Tools ➪ Spell Checker), and then click Options (see Figure 52-2) and check or uncheck the checking and notification options described in Table 52-2.

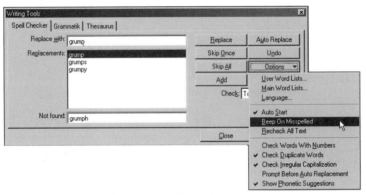

Figure 52-2: Customizing the spell checker.

Table 52-2 Spell Checker Options	
This Option	**Lets You**
Auto Start (on by default)	Start spell-checking immediately when you select spell-check. (You can still change options as soon as you stop at a misspelled word.)
Beep on Misspelled	Sound a warning at each word not found.
Recheck All Text	Remove words from "skip all" status, so they're flagged once more in the next spell-check.
Check Words With Numbers	Flag certain words with numbers as possible errors ("4c" but not "32nd").
Check Duplicate Words (on by default)	Delete second occurrence of duplicate words (such as "of of").
Check Irregular Capitalization (on by default)	Flag words with irregular capitalization, such as "JULy" and "helP," as possible errors. "GOOD" is OK.
Prompt Before Auto Replacement	Swap a word with its replacement entry from the user word list.
Show Phonetic Suggestions (on by default)	Include words that sound similar to the flagged word in the replacement suggestions, such as "spiller," "spoiler," and "spooler" for "speler."

Adding, removing, and selecting word lists

As noted earlier, you can check your spelling and grammar against as many as ten main word lists. You might want to have Spell Checker chain two or more main word lists if, for example, your document contains both English and Spanish words, or it includes specialized medical or legal terms.

The lists are searched in the order you specify, and the chain must begin with the .MOR or .LEX file for the language you're using. (The .MOR extension indicates a morphological list, meaning it uses rules to check word variations.)

The main English word list for WordPerfect 9 is WT9EN.MOR. Other languages with morphological lists are French, Spanish, German, Italian, and Dutch. The word list for Spanish, for example, is WT9ES.MOR.

Word lists for other languages sport a .LEX extension, indicating that they don't use morphological rules. That for Greek is WT9GR.LEX; Russian is WT9RU.LEX, and so on. Third-party WordPerfect-compatible dictionaries are also available for medical, legal, and other specialized fields.

You can also chain as many as ten user word lists for various specialized uses or projects. These are used by QuickCorrect, as well as by Spell Checker and Grammatik. The chain begins with the default user list WT9XX.UWL where, again, XX indicates the language. (If you're on a network, your default user word list is in a form such as WIUUUUXX.UWL, where UUUU represents your network initials, and XX indicates the language.)

To add, remove, or select a list in the main or user word list search order, as well as to change the spell-check language:

1. Click Tools ⇨ Spell Checker ⇨ Options.

2. Click Main Word Lists to add or remove supplemental word lists in other languages. You can then check the word lists you want to use now (see Figure 52-3).

Figure 52-3: Selecting word lists in other languages you want to use.

Tip Removing a word list from the search order doesn't delete the list.

3. Click User Word Lists to create, select, and edit custom user word lists (see Figure 52-4). (Click the first blank line or the line below where you want the list to appear in the search order.)

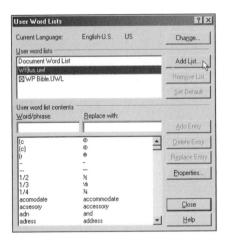

Figure 52-4: Creating, editing, and selecting user word lists.

4. Click Set Default to specify which user word list receives the words when you click "Add" during a spell-check. (When the current "receiving word list" is selected, Set Default is grayed out.)

5. To also change the current spell-checking language, click the Change button in the User- or Main Word Lists dialog box and select the language (see Figure 52-5). (See "Writing in Other Languages" at the end of this chapter.)

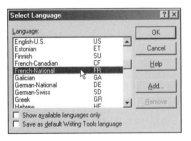

Figure 52-5: Changing the spell-checking language.

Tip To change a word list's place in a search-order chain, you must delete its name, and then add it back in the position you want.

Editing a user word list

You can automatically add words to the default user word list during a spell-check. (The words you add with Spell-As-You-Go and QuickCorrect are sent to the original user word list for the language you're using.) You can also manually edit any user word list, to add or delete words or phrases.

To edit a user word list:

1. Click Tools ➪ Spell Check ➪ Options ➪ User Word Lists.

2. Click the list you want to edit, and then do any of the following:

   • To add a skip word or abbreviation, type it in the Word/phrase box, and then click Add Entry (see Figure 52-6).

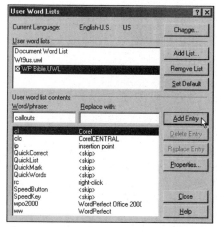

Figure 52-6: Editing a user word list.

   • To add a replacement word or phrase, type the word or abbreviation to be replaced in the Word/phrase box, type the replacement word or phrase in the "Replace with" box, and then click Add Entry.

Tip If you're adding a capitalized word, such as the name of a person or place, type all the letters in lowercase in the Word/phrase box. The word will be capitalized automatically.

   • To edit an existing entry, click the entry, edit the replacement word or phrase, and click Replace Entry. To delete an entry, click the entry, and then click Delete Entry.

Defining alternative replacements

Sometimes you may want to define alternative replacements for a word, particularly if it's one you want to avoid. If you abhor "finalize" for example, you may want to recommend "finish," "complete," and "put the finishing touches on" as replacements. Manually edit a user word list to create three separate "finalize" replacement entries — one for each of the replacement alternatives.

The next time "finalize" is used, Spell Checker and Grammatik will flag it and offer the alternative replacements (see Figure 52-7). It won't be flagged by Spell-As-You-Go.

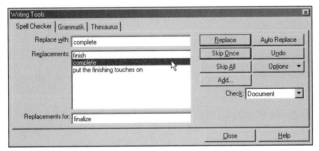

Figure 52-7: You can select from your alternative replacements when performing a spell-check.

Speed Typing with QuickCorrect

How do you describe QuickCorrect? It's fast. It's accurate. It's automatic. It's habit-forming.

Fixing typos on the fly

Click Tools ➪ QuickCorrect in WordPerfect, and you'll see a new "Correct other mistyped words when possible" option (see Figure 52-8). Check this feature to fix most typographical errors (typos) automatically when the word is five characters or more, it's not capitalized, and there's only one replacement word close to what you typed.

This new feature is off by default because (1) it's so quick and automatic that most users won't know what's happening, and (2) it can, on occasion, make a fix that you hadn't intended. But unless you're heavily into scientific, technical, or foreign words that aren't in the dictionary, you'll love the way it fixes mistakes as fast as you make them.

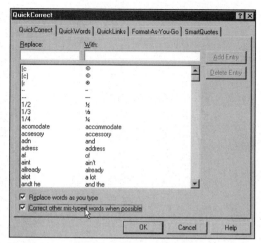

Figure 52-8: Fixing typos on the fly.

Replacing words as you type

QuickCorrect keeps an extensive list of mistypes (such as "antarctic" and "aparent") that it fixes on the fly. To speed up your typing, you can also create abbreviations for words you often use (such as "cl" for "Corel"). Just check the "Replace words as you type" option to automatically correct or expand your entries.

QuickCorrect changes "adn" to "and" the moment you press the spacebar, Enter, Tab, or Indent. Your entry is replaced even if it has quotation marks, an apostrophe, or other punctuation attached. For example, if you have a "cl" entry for "Corel," "cl's" followed by a space expands to "Corel's."

Tip
If QuickCorrect fixes something that you want to let stand (such as switching a lowercase "i" in quotation marks to "I"), you don't have to turn off QuickCorrect to put it back. Type another word or two, go back and change the text, and then slip away by using the arrow key.

Creating QuickCorrect entries

QuickCorrect entries are a snap to create. If you find yourself repeating a particular typing mistake (such as "comming" instead of "coming"), Spell-As-You-Go can usually create the entry for you. If you find yourself typing a long word or phrase over and over, create a QuickCorrect abbreviation (such as "ilu" for "I love you"). Once you add a few personal entries to the QuickCorrect list, you'll be amazed at how pleasurable typing becomes.

To add a QuickCorrect entry:

1. Click Tools ➪ QuickCorrect.

2. Type your mistake or abbreviation in the Replace box, and then type the replacement word or phrase in the With box (see Figure 52-9).

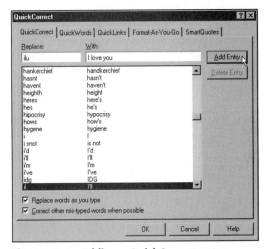

Figure 52-9: Adding a QuickCorrect entry.

3. Click Add Entry.

To delete a QuickCorrect entry, type or click the entry, and then click Delete Entry. To revise an entry, type or click the entry, type your revision in the With box, and then click Replace Entry.

Caution   Don't type an actual word in the Replace box. If you set up an abbreviation to replace "win" with "Windows," for example, you might end up typing "I hope you Windows the prize." You could use "wi" or "wn" for the abbreviation instead. Use your judgment when it comes to rarely used words (such as replacing "cant" with "can't").

You can't create multiple QuickCorrect entries for different cases (such as "dt," "Dt," and "DT" for different forms of "document"). However, a single "dt" (for "document") expands in various ways, depending on how you type it:

Typing	Expands To
dt or dT	document
Dt	Document
DT	DOCUMENT

Note that the case sensitivity for the replacement entries extends from lowercase to uppercase, not the reverse. If you create a "DT" entry for "DOCUMENT," for example, you'll still get "DOCUMENT" when you type **dt**.

If you use a term in both its abbreviated (WP) and expanded (WordPerfect) forms, use a variation of the abbreviation for your expanded entry ("ww" for WordPerfect).

You can create variations of QuickCorrect entries to cover plural, possessive, or other forms. For example, you can use "dts" for "documents," "dtg" for "documenting," and "wws" for "WordPerfect's." Frequently used contractions are excellent candidates. Use "dont" for "don't," "im" for "I'm," and so on. And why bother with the Shift key? Set up capitalized entries for names you type, such as "lorraine" for "Lorraine," and "becky" for "Becky."

Press Ctrl+W to use any special character or symbol in the With box. For example, you can automatically replace "ra" with ⇨ or put the accents on names and words such as "René" and "cliché."

And try this: replace two periods (..) with one (.) for automatic correction in case you accidentally type two periods at the end of a sentence.

Inserting Formatted QuickWords

QuickCorrect replacements are text-only, and always appear in the current font type and style. To insert formatted text or graphics in WordPerfect, including TextArt, use QuickWords abbreviations instead (see Figure 52-10).

For example, you can create a "lhd" abbreviation that expands into a personal or business letterhead, with a top margin of three-quarters of an inch, the name and address in particular fonts, plus a logo graphic. You can section it off with a graphic line, followed by two hard returns and the date code. All this and more can be included in one simple abbreviation.

QuickWords replace formatted abbreviations from previous versions of WordPerfect. Unlike abbreviations, QuickWords are instantaneous, and easier to create and manage.

Figure 52-10: TextArt QuickWord.

Creating a QuickWord

To create a QuickWord:

1. Create the formatted text and graphics.

2. Select your creation, and then click Tools ➪ QuickWords.

3. Type the letters you want in the "Abbreviated form" box, and then click Add Entry.

Make your QuickWord names short, simple, unique, and easy to remember. QuickWords expand automatically as you type, like QuickCorrect entries. They are not case-sensitive. For example, "lhd" or "LHD" expands to the same QuickWord.

Deleting, renaming, or replacing QuickWords

To delete or rename a QuickWord:

1. Click Tools ➪ QuickWords, and click the abbreviation.

2. Click Delete Entry to delete the QuickWord, or Options ➪ "Rename entry" to rename it.

To replace a QuickWord, type the same abbreviation for the new QuickWord, and then click Options ➪ "Replace entry."

Inserting QuickWords as plain text

To insert QuickWords as plain text and without graphics, click Tools ➪ QuickWords ➪ Options ➪ Expand as Plain text.

Inserting QuickWords manually

To turn off automatic QuickWords, click Tools ➪ QuickWords and remove the check from "Expand QuickWords when you type them." To insert a QuickWord manually, click Tools ➪ QuickWords, click the abbreviation, and then click "Insert in text."

You can also type the abbreviation and then, without typing a space, expand it by pressing Ctrl+Shift+A (Ctrl+A on a DOS keyboard).

To expand an abbreviation later, place the insertion point on it and perform the same operation. To expand all the abbreviations in your document at once, run the Expndall.wcm macro that comes with WordPerfect. (See Chapter 58, "Automating with Macros," for help on running macros.)

Finding a Better Word

If you're looking for a better word, look no further than WordPerfect's Thesaurus.

Finding a word in the Thesaurus

To select a replacement (synonym) for a word, click the word, and then click the Prompt-As-You-Go list on the property bar to select the word you want. (Click Tools ➪ Proofread and check Prompt-As-You-Go, if necessary, to turn the feature on.)

For an in-depth search of synonyms, click the word, and then click Tools ➪ Thesaurus. From the list of replacement words (see Figure 52-11), you can

- ✦ Click any word in the list to display its synonyms.
- ✦ Type any word in the "Replace with" box, and then click Look Up to find its synonyms.
- ✦ Click a replacement for your original word, and then click Replace.

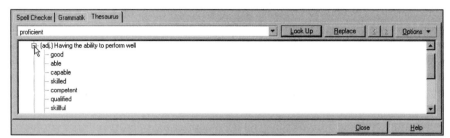

Figure 52-11: Looking for a better word in the Thesaurus.

For example, if you don't like any of the replacements offered for "proficient," you can click "skilled" or any other word to display a secondary list. You may scroll this list and find the word "practiced" more to your liking. Click "practiced" (see Figure 52-12), and then click Replace to swap it for "proficient."

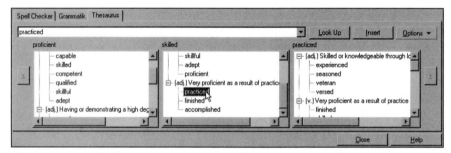

Figure 52-12: Selecting a replacement word from a secondary list.

You can cascade as many lists as you want. The scroll arrows activate when you have selected more than three lists.

To display just the meaning of various replacement words, click Options, click Synonyms to remove its check, and then click any of the replacement words (see Figure 52-13).

Checking Your Grammar

While Grammatik's Grammar-As-You-Go does a great job of catching many common errors of usage and punctuation, proofreading your work with a separate run of Grammatik can perform a more thorough check of grammar, usage, and style. It can also find word roots, examine sentence parts, and check sentence and paragraph construction.

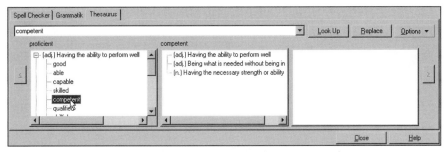

Figure 52-13: Displaying just the meaning of replacement words.

Proofreading a document

To proofread a document:

1. Click Tools ➪ Grammatik.

2. For each problem encountered (see Figure 52-14), do one of the following:

- Click a replacement suggestion and click Replace. (The "New sentence" box previews the replacement.)

- Click your text to edit it directly, and then click Resume to continue.

- Click Skip Once to tell Grammatik you don't want to change the highlighted text, or Skip All to ignore this phrase for the rest of the session.

- Click Turn Off to ignore all errors associated with the rule for the rest of this session.

- Click Add to put the flagged word in the user list, so it will be skipped in all your documents.

- Click Auto Replace to add the flagged word and your replacement to the QuickCorrect list.

- Click Undo to cancel the last replacement.

To get a detailed explanation of a flagged problem (including helpful examples), click the name of the error rule class displayed. You can also click any underlined hypertext term in Grammatik's explanation.

Grammatik normally checks your entire document or selected text. If you turn off Auto Start, you can also select To End of Document to check from the insertion point on. You can also click and scroll your document during a session to change the current checking location.

Grammatik's pretty amazing, but it's not perfect. So don't be afraid to decline its advice.

Click a suggested replacement   Problem text

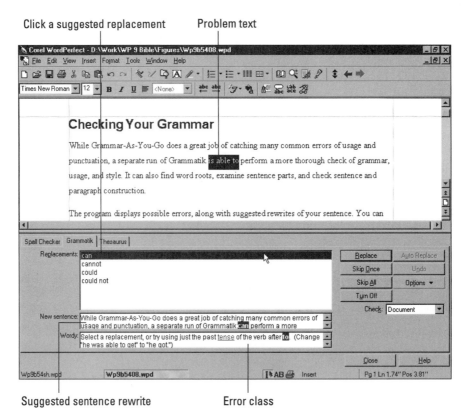

Suggested sentence rewrite   Error class

Figure 52-14: Proofreading a document with Grammatik.

Selecting Grammatik options

While Grammatik works fine from the start, it pays to take a look at its options. Click Tools ➪ Grammatik ➪ Options, and then check the options you want (see Figure 52-15), as described in Table 52-3.

Selecting a checking style

Grammatik flags various types of possible errors, depending on the checking style you select. Different styles set different thresholds (such as for the length of a long sentence) and turn on different style, grammar, and mechanical rule classes. Each writing style also has a formality level—informal, standard, or formal—determining how strictly it follows the rule classes of usage and diction.

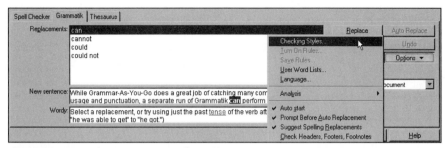

Figure 52-15: Selecting Grammatik options.

Table 52-3 **Grammatik Options**	
Option	**Lets You**
Checking Styles	Select and customize checking styles
Turn On Rules	Reactivate rules you've suspended during this session
Save Rules	Save your modified session settings to a new checking style
User Word Lists	Specify your user word list chain, or edit particular lists
Language	Change the language for your writing tools
Analysis	Analyze the sentence or document
Auto start	Start proofreading immediately, from the top of your document, if you haven't selected text
Prompt before auto replacement	Decide whether to swap a word with its replacement in the user word list
Suggest spelling replacements	Select a suggested replacement for a flagged word
Check headers, footers, footnotes	Check parts of a WordPerfect document normally skipped by Grammatik

Click Tools ➪ Grammatik ➪ Options ➪ Checking Styles, and then select one of the predefined styles described in Table 52-4 (see Figure 52-16).

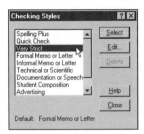

Figure 52-16: Selecting a checking style.

<table>
<tr><td colspan="2" align="center">Table 52-4
Checking Styles</td></tr>
</table>

Checking Style	*What It Does*
Spelling Plus	Checks spelling, punctuation, date format, hyphenation, and other basic mechanics.
Quick Check	Supplements the Spelling Plus style with basic grammar (such as incomplete sentence, incorrect verb form, questionable usage, subject-verb agreement, and tense shift). This default style is designed for standard documents aimed at a general audience.
Very Strict	Follows every rule in the book for formal writing (such as a legal document).
Formal Memo or Letter	Adheres to almost every rule, with some relaxation on sentence length and split infinitives.
Informal Memo or Letter	Uses a relaxed style with loose thresholds and doesn't check for such things as colloquial or overstated usage, passive voice, or weak sentences.
Technical or Scientific	Uses a formal style for scientific publications that permits the passive voice, and long, complex sentences with technical wording.
Documentation or Speech	Follows a nontechnical style of average formality, using the active voice. Doesn't check for colloquial usage and jargon, formalisms, end-of-sentence prepositions, and the like.
Student Composition	Upholds the correct, formal usage expected of a college paper or business report.
Advertising	Allows for the informal style of advertising copy and marketing literature, with emphasis on mechanics and grammar.
Fiction	Grants artistic license for informal, creative writing with relaxed thresholds.
Grammar-As-You-Go	Defines the basic rules used by Grammar-As-You-Go.

Analyzing a sentence

As Grammatik proofreads a sentence, it identifies each clause and part of speech. Viewing this analysis may help you to see why Grammatik has flagged a particular error:

1. Click Options ➪ Analysis.

2. Click Parse Tree or Parts of Speech.

The parse tree shows the types of clauses to which various groups of words belong (see Figure 52-17). Parts of Speech identifies each word as a noun, verb, adjective, and so on (see Figure 52-18). (Don't you wish you had had this little tool available when you were in junior high school!)

Figure 52-17: Parse tree.

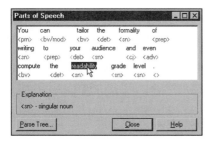

Figure 52-18: Parts of speech.

Writing in Other Languages

WordPerfect is an international program, with versions in more than 20 languages. Whatever your *package language* (the language and country listed on the outside of your WordPerfect package), you can still type documents in other languages by using the accents and punctuation marks particular to each. You can also use another language's conventions for date, time, thousands separator, footnote continuation, and so on. You can even use a non-Roman alphabet (Greek, Cyrillic, Japanese, Hebrew, or Arabic) included in your character sets.

Using the writing tools and versions for other languages

New Feature

WordPerfect Office 2000 lets you do spell checking, proofreading, word lookup, and automatic hyphenation in more than 15 languages. You can install writing tools for additional languages at any time (see Appendix A, "Setting Up WordPerfect Office 2000").

To change the language for the screen and keyboard, as well as for the writing tools, you must purchase the version of the WordPerfect suite for that language. You'll then be able to switch among the language versions (by selecting Tools ⇨ Settings ⇨ Environment ⇨ Interface ⇨ Interface language).

Tip

You can create your own foreign language keyboard definition, without purchasing another version, by assigning characters you frequently use in that language to particular keys (see Chapter 57, "Customizing Toolbars, Menus, and Keyboards").

Using another language in the current document

To specify another language to use for all or part of your current document:

1. Click where you want to start using the conventions for another language, or select the text to which you want to apply the conventions.

2. Click Tools ⇨ Language ⇨ Settings.

3. Select the language you want to use (see Figure 52-19). If the writing tools for that language aren't on your system, you'll be prompted to install them.

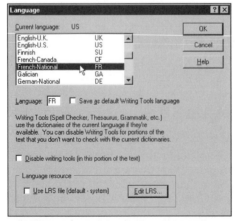

Figure 52-19: Using another language in the current document.

4. To use that language's tools for all your new documents, check "Save as default Writing Tools language."

5. To turn off the writing tools temporarily (for example, if you're writing a passage in a language for which you have no tools), check "Disable writing tools."

When you specify a language other than your package language, WordPerfect inserts a language code [Lang:*xx*] (or a pair of language codes around selected text) in your document, where *xx* represents the code for the language (such as GR for Greek).

For More Information . . .

On	See
Spell-As-You-Go	Chapter 2
Grammar-As-You-Go	Chapter 2
Prompt-As-You-Go	Chapter 2
Format-As-You-Go	Chapter 17
Inserting SmartQuotes	Chapter 17
Running macros	Chapter 58
Customizing keyboards	Chapter 57
Comparing documents	Chapter 18

✦　　✦　　✦

Sorting Information

◆ ◆ ◆ ◆

In This Chapter

Sort text lines and table rows

Identify sort records and their subdivisions

Define sort keys

Sort from an input file or to an output file

Sort by the last word

Connect words so they sort as one

Sort dates

Extract records with sort

◆ ◆ ◆ ◆

A great deal of information is more accessible when sorted — arranged in a particular order. This chapter introduces the sorting concepts that apply to all programs, demonstrating the WordPerfect particulars.

When searching through a mountain of information, how can you find what you're looking for? Fortunately, a great deal of information is sorted. Imagine trying to locate a number in a telephone book if it weren't!

The information in your document, spreadsheet, or database is no different. It's more useful in an arranged, rather than random, order. The arrangement can differ according to need. You'll generally want your list of friends or customers to be in alphabetical order, but sometimes you may want to sort your friends by birth date, a mailing by zip code, or your customers by total sales in descending order.

Basic sorts are easy in WordPerfect, and this chapter also shows you how to do some sophisticated sorting and extracting. If you're publishing a newsletter, you can extract the names and addresses for subscriptions that are about to expire. If you're a teacher, you may want a list of students in danger of failing. These sort and extraction techniques are often used when performing a merge (see Chapter 27, "Mass-Producing with Labels and Merge"). Chapter 35, "Analyzing Data," shows you how to sort Quattro Pro spreadsheets. Sorting Paradox tables is covered in Chapter 47, "Entering, and Editing Data."

Doing Simple Sorts

Before you get to the fancy sorts, you will be glad to see just how easy regular sorts can be.

Sorting lines of text

Open a new document and type a list of names, such as those shown in Figure 53-1. Any names will do, as long as they're not in alphabetical order.

Bill Shakespeare
James Joyce
Franz Kafka
Alice Walker
Kurt Vonnegut
Milan Kundera
Toni Morrison
Colin Dexter

Figure 53-1: List of names to sort.

To sort the names:

1. Select the names.

2. Click Tools ⇨ Sort, then click "First word in a line" and click Sort (see Figure 53-2).

Presto! The names are sorted, as shown in Figure 53-3.

But wait! You want the list sorted by last name, not by first name. That's a little more complicated, but still easy enough. To sort the list by last name:

1. Select the names and click Tools ⇨ Sort again, only this time click New to create a custom sort definition.

2. Change the number of the Word parameter in the key to 2, as shown in Figure 53-4, and then click OK ⇨ Sort. This time the names come out sorted by the second word in the first field (the last name), as shown in Figure 53-5.

Tip   If some of the names happen to contain middle name or middle initial, you can connect them with a hard space (Ctrl+Space) to treat them as a single word during sorting. See "Connecting words to sort them as one," later in this chapter.

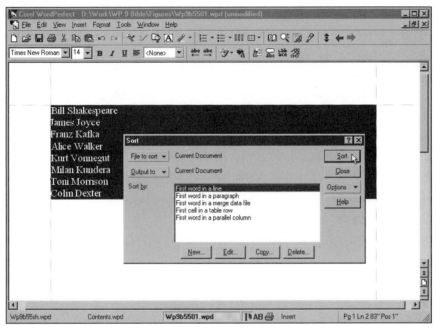

Figure 53-2: Sorting the list of names.

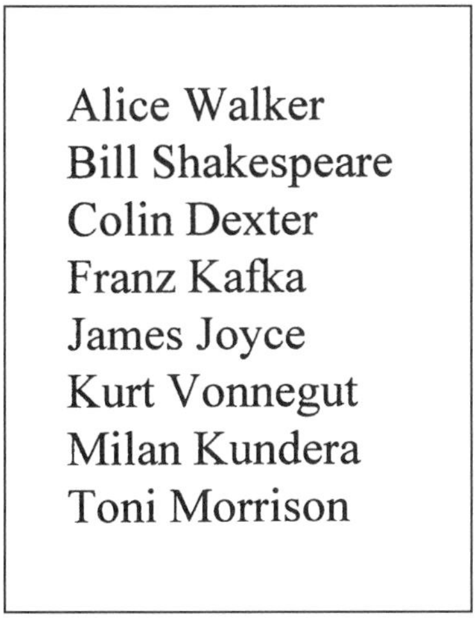

Alice Walker
Bill Shakespeare
Colin Dexter
Franz Kafka
James Joyce
Kurt Vonnegut
Milan Kundera
Toni Morrison

Figure 53-3: Sorted names.

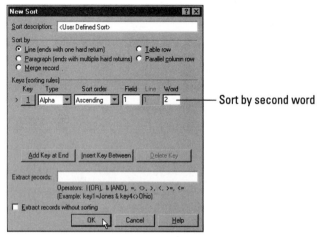

Figure 53-4: Specifying the sort by last name.

Colin Dexter
James Joyce
Franz Kafka
Milan Kundera
Toni Morrison
Bill Shakespeare
Kurt Vonnegut
Alice Walker

Figure 53-5: List sorted by last name.

Sorting table rows

Sorting table rows can be even easier than sorting lines of text. Just click the column on which you want to sort, click the Select Column button to select the column, and then click the Table Sort button and select the way you want to sort (see Figure 53-6).

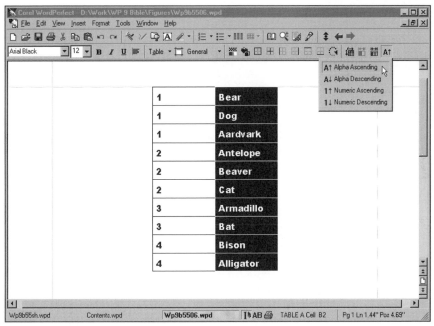

Figure 53-6: Sorting table rows by the cells in the selected column.

You can also select only the cells for the rows you want to sort.

 Tip Designated header rows are automatically excluded from the sort.

Sophisticated Sorting with Records and Keys

It's nice to know that basic sorts are easy and intuitive in WordPerfect. Once you get the hang of a few more concepts and features, you'll be able to sort any records that are thrown your way into whatever order you need.

Sort records: the types of things you can sort

Obviously, it doesn't help to sort every kind of information, like the words in a sentence. What you want to sort are *records*, or related bundles of information (such as telephone book entries) that are easier to find if they're in a particular order. If you're familiar with a database manager such as Paradox, you already know that a collection of records (your telephone book, for example) is called a *data file* or *database*. When you talk database language, each distinct item within a record (last name, first name, street address, zip code, and so on) is called a *field*.

Don't be put off by the terminology—you can use many collections of sorted records in everyday life. In addition to the telephone book, there are dictionaries, encyclopedias, recipe files, and checkbook ledgers. A book's index is nothing but a sorted collection of records, with fields for the heading text and page numbers.

Identifying sort records and their subdivisions

Because WordPerfect is text-based (not record-based, like a full-fledged database system), it uses its standard formatting codes to identify records and their subdivisions, down to individual words in a line. WordPerfect can recognize five types of sort records. Each type of record can, in turn, be subdivided in particular ways:

Record Type	*How the Record Is Recognized*	*Record Subdivisions*
Line	Each line ends with a hard return.	field, word
Paragraph	Paragraphs are separated by two or more hard returns.	line, field, word
Merge text data	Each record ends with an ENDRECORD code.	field, line, word
Table row	Each row of cells is a record.	column, line, word
Parallel column	Each row of columns is a record.	column, line, word

Line, paragraph, and parallel column records are illustrated in Figure 53-7.

Even though the names of the record subdivisions depend on how they're formatted, the sorts work the same way. When you create or edit a sort for a particular record type, its proper sequence of subdivisions automatically displays.

All you need to know is how WordPerfect identifies the record subdivisions within your document:

John B. Moseley   420 Seaview Dr.   La Jolla   CA   92037
Nancy Peterson   987 Haight St.   San Francisco CA   94109
Florence Byrnes   5240 Main St.   Woodbury   CT   06798
Alicia E. Eberhardt 1500 Golden Ave.   Atlanta   GA   30327
William B. Wattson 468 Hereford Rd.   Palestine   TX   75801

Forty-niner   Hybrid Tea   Red
More of a bi-color, with the outside of the petals a creamy yellow and the inside a bright red that turns blue as it ages. Nicely formed buds and a compact, upright bush.

French Lace   Flonbunda   White
Very full-petaled flowers in clusters of six or more open to resemble charming old-fashioned roses. Large, buff-white blooms on spreading plants with dark green foliage. Vigorous and disease resistant.

America   Climber   Pink
Plentiful coral buds open into huge pink blossoms with a silver sheen. Fragrant and disease resistant. Used well when grown as a pillar rose.

Peru   South   496,222 square miles. Crops include barley, beans,
            America   cacao, casava, coca, corn, cotton, grapes, oca and
                           olluco, potatoes, quinua, rice, sugar, sweet potatoes,
                           and wheat.

France   Europe   212,821 square miles. Crops include apples,
                           artichokes, barley, buckwheat, corn, grapes, oats,
                           potatoes, rye, sugar beets, and wheat.

Jamaica   Central   4,692 square miles. Crops include bananas, cacao,
            America   casava, citrus fruit, coffee, copra, corn, ginger,
                           pimentos, rice, sugar cane, and sweet potatos.

Figure 53-7: Line records with tabs between fields; paragraph records separated by two hard returns; and parallel column records.

Record Subdivision	How It Is Identified
Field	Tab, indent, center, or flush-right codes separate fields in lines of text. ENDFIELD codes separate fields in merge data files.
Line	Lines are separated by a hard or soft return.
Word	Words for sort purposes are separated by spaces, or the date and time separators (/, hard hyphens, and : for U.S. English). For example, "12/29/02" is three sort words.
Column	Columns in a table row are numbered from left to right, starting with cell 1. Columns in a row of parallel columns are separated by hard page codes, and are numbered from left to right.

What are sort keys?

The fields you sort on are known as *sort keys*. When you sorted your list of names by last name, you used the second word in each line as your sort key.

You can specify as many as nine keys in a single sort. The records are first sorted by key 1; then the matching records within key 1 are further sorted by key 2; and so on. For example, the address list entries in Figure 53-8 were sorted by state (key 1) and then by last name (key 2), so that the names within each state are in order.

Last name is key 2   State is key 1

Sonya Brown	789 Farm Road	Los Gatos	CA	95030
Dr. Helen Wang	2305 Mountain Drive	Bolder	CO	80301
Mathew Chapin	362 Meadow Oak Lane	Manchester	CT	06040
Joseph Guss	1207 Spring Road	Sommerville	CT	06072
Elizabeth Somner	1795 South Street	Winsted	CT	06098
Nancy Morgan	2532 Chapman Drive	Washington	DC	20036
Brian Nelson	15 Federal Street	Middlefield	MA	01243
Judy Davis	375 Hamlet Avenue	Brooklyn	NY	11225
Miranda Sanchez	426 President Street	Westlake	OH	44145
George O'Connor	47 Grove Street	Dallas	TX	75235

Figure 53-8: Records sorted by two keys (last name, within state).

Sort keys can be alphanumeric (blanks, followed by symbols, numbers, and letters) or numeric (numbers only). The sort order can be ascending, numbers from negative to positive; or descending, letters from A to Z (the reverse).

Defining Keys and Performing Sorts

With these sort concepts in hand, you're ready to do some sophisticated sorting. For the exercises that follow, open a new document and create an expanded list of writers, such as the list shown in Figure 53-9. The particular names, dates, countries, and types don't matter, as long as you have a variety of records, including two to three records for some particular countries and types.

Amos Oz	1939-	Israeli	novelist
Naguib Mahfouz	1911-	Egyptian	novelist
Ngũgĩ Wa Thiong'o	1938-	Kenyan	novelist
Emily Dickinson	1830-1886	American	poet
Kornel Ujejski	1823-1897	Polish	poet
Heinrich Heine	1797-1856	German	poet
Miguel de Cervantes Saavedra	1547-1616	Spanish	novelist
Anton Chekhov	1860-1904	Russian	playwright
Li Bo	701-762	Chinese	poet
Henrik Ibsen	1828-1906	Norwegian	playwright
Gloria Naylor	1950-	American	novelist
Mario Vargas Llosa	1936-	Peruvian	novelist
Murasaki Shikibu	978?-1026	Japanese	novelist
Honoré de Balzac	1799-1850	French	novelist
William Shakespeare	1564-1616	British	playwright
Sylvia Plath	1932-1963	American	poet

Figure 53-9: List of writers on which to practice.

You are creating line records, although paragraph, table row, and parallel column records work equally well. Separate the fields in each record with a single tab code, and end each record with a hard return, including the last. It also helps to set the tabs (see Chapter 21, "Formatting Your Document") so that the fields line up. Save your list when you're finished and make a backup copy, and then try out variations on the general sort instructions that follow.

Caution If you begin your lines with a tab or indent, keep in mind that the name following the first tab will actually be field 2.

To sort records in a document:

1. Select the records you want to sort, unless you're sorting the entire document. (When sorting table row or parallel column records, select the records you want to sort, or click anywhere in the table or parallel columns to sort all the records.)

Note To use a document on disk for your sort input or sort output, see the section "Sorting from an Input File or to an Output File," later in this chapter.

2. Click Tools ➪ Sort.

3. Click Options to ensure that "Allow Undo after sorting" is checked (see Figure 53-10). That way, you can easily reverse the sort if you don't like the results. (If "Allow Undo after sorting" is already checked, click outside the list so you don't remove the check.)

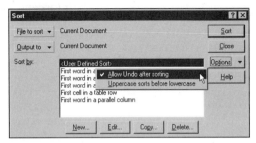

Figure 53-10: Make sure that "Allow Undo after sorting" is checked.

4. To use an existing sort definition as is, select it from the list of defined sorts and click Sort. To change a sort definition or to create a new one, continue with the following steps.

5. To define your sort criteria, do either of the following:

   • Click New, and then specify the name of your sort in the "Sort description" box.

   • Select an existing sort definition and then click Edit, or click Copy and specify a new name in the "Sort description" box (see Figure 53-11).

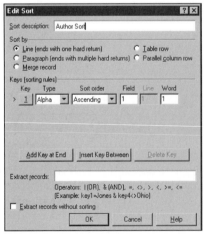

Figure 53-11: Describing your sort definition.

6. Click the record type (line, paragraph, merge record, table row, or parallel column) by which you want to sort.

7. For key 1, specify the Type (alpha or numeric), Sort order (ascending or descending), and record subdivision (such as field 3, word 1) on which you want to sort.

8. To specify additional keys, click Add Key at End to add lower-level key definitions at the end of the list (see Figure 53-12), or Insert Key Between to insert keys before the highlighted key (the key numbers automatically adjust). When your definition has more than one key, you can also click Delete Key to remove the selected key.

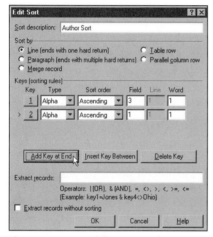

Figure 53-12: Adding a sort key.

9. Click OK to save your new or modified sort definition. If you created a new sort definition, it now appears among the defined sorts in the Sort dialog box.

10. Click Sort to run the sort now, or click Close to use your definition later.

If the sort doesn't work the way you expected, press Ctrl+Z (Undo), edit your sort criteria, and try again.

Use your list of authors to practice sorting in different orders on various record subdivisions. Try sorting by last name (field 1, word 2), date of birth, nationality, and type of writing. Be sure to try out multiple keys, such as by nationality (key 1: field 3, word 1), and then by name within nation (key 2: field 1, word 1), as shown in Figure 53-12.

Tip

If some of your writers' names are more than two words (as with Honoré de Balzac), see the section "Sorting by the Last Word," later in this chapter.

Sorting from an Input File or to an Output File

In most cases, you'll be sorting the document on your screen. Sometimes, however, you may want to sort from the document to another file on disk. That way, for example, you can keep your address list sorted by name intact, and make a working copy sorted by state. You can also sort from a file on disk without bringing it up to the screen. To specify a sort input or output file on disk:

1. Click Tools ⇨ Sort.
2. Click the List button for "File to sort" or "Output to," and then click "File on Disk" and specify the file.
3. Specify the sort order as described earlier in this chapter, then click Sort.

Caution You must sort tables or parallel columns on the screen. Do not specify an input file or output file for a table or column sort.

Using Word Sorting Tricks

Here are some tricks you can use when sorting on particular words, including the last word in a row, two words you want to sort as one, and dates.

Sorting by the last word

Use negative numbers in your sort keys to designate record subdivisions in reverse order. A common application of this technique is sorting by last name, as with the list of names to be sorted shown in Figure 53-13.

Bill Shakespeare
James Joyce
Mario Vargas Llosa
Alice Walker
Honoré de Balzac
Milan Kundera
Toni Morrison
Colin Dexter

Figure 53-13: Use -1 to sort these last names.

The last name in the list can be either the second or third word from the left, but it's always the last word on the right (except for Vargas Llosa). By sorting on -1 you'll get the desired results.

Connecting words to sort them as one

Use a hard space (Ctrl+Space) between words you want to sort as one. For example, if some names in your list contain middle name or middle initial, you can connect them with a hard space (Ctrl+Space) to treat them as a single word during sorting. Another example would be the name Mario Vargas Llosa, where you can put a hard space between Vargas and Llosa, so that the last name will sort as "Vargas Llosa" instead of "Llosa."

Sorting dates

The date and time separators work the same way as spaces do in separating words. For example, the dates 2/14/99 or 2-14-99 sort as three words if you are using U.S. English. (The hyphens are hyphen characters, or "hard" hyphens, not the hyphen codes that are entered when you press the hyphen key.)

When sorting dates in these formats, specify a key for word 3 (the year), and then specify keys for words 1 and 2 (the month and day).

Extracting Records with Sort

Sometimes you may not want to use all the records in your list. Say, for example, that you want to notify your clients in a particular state of an upcoming seminar, or you must send out notices to those in your organization whose memberships are about to expire. In such cases, you can use sort to extract (select) the particular records you need.

Defining extraction statements

Record extraction is a two-part process. You define the keys (the same type of keys you use for sorting), and then construct an extraction statement to pick out the records you want. For example, the following statement tells WordPerfect to extract only the records for American poets:

```
key 1=American & key 2=poet
```

This extraction statement makes use of three operators: the greater than or equal to (>=) symbol, the ampersand (&) symbol, and the equals sign (=). Table 53-1 describes the sort-extraction operators you can use.

Table 53-1
Sort-Extraction Operators

Operator	What It Does
| (OR)	Selects records that meet either key condition. (You must type the | symbol, not the word OR.) Example: key 1=Johnson | key 3=CA extracts all records with Johnson in key 1, as well as all records with CA in key 3.
& (AND)	Selects records that meet both key conditions. (You must type the & symbol, not the word AND.) Example: key 1=Johnson & key 3=CA extracts records for those Johnsons living in California.
=	Selects records with keys equal to the designated value. Example: key 4=92037 selects records with a 92037 zip code.
<>	Selects records with keys not equal to the designated value. Example: key 4<>poet selects records for all nonpoets.
>	Selects records with keys greater than the designated value. Example: key 3>Jones selects records for people whose names fall later in the alphabet than Jones, such as Kelly or Randolf, but not Johnson.
<	Selects records with keys less than the designated value. Example: key 2<5000 selects records with values less than 5,000 in key 2.
>=	Selects records with keys greater than or equal to the designated value. Example: key 5>=Kansas selects records for Kansas and states that follow it alphabetically.
<=	Selects records with keys less than or equal to the designated value. Example: key 5<=Kansas selects records for Kansas and states that precede it alphabetically.

The space after "key" is optional ("key 1" and "key1" are the same), and values are not case-sensitive ("American" and "american" are the same).

Extracting records

When you extract particular records, you normally keep your original list intact, and send your output to a separate file. To extract records:

1. Select the records from which you want to extract, unless you are extracting from the entire document. (When extracting from table row or parallel column records, click anywhere in the table or parallel columns to use all the records.)

2. Click Tools ➪ Sort.

3. Click the List button to the right of the "Output to" box, and then click "File on Disk" and specify the file for your extracted records. (The file is created or updated by the sort.)

Caution Unless you specify a different output file, the records not meeting your extraction criteria will be deleted from the file you're sorting.

4. Click New, Edit, or Copy, and then specify the key definitions, following Steps 5–8 in the earlier section "Defining Keys and Performing Sorts."

5. Using your key definitions and the extraction operators shown in the dialog box, type the record-extraction statement (see Figure 53-14).

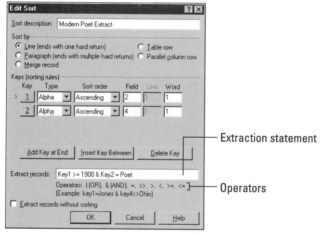

Figure 53-14: Constructing a record-extraction statement.

6. To extract the selected records in their original order, check "Extract records without sorting."

7. Click OK to save your new or modified sort definition.

8. Click Sort to extract the records now, or click fClose to use your definition later.

Creating extraction statements with multiple operators

You can create extraction statements with multiple operators, and any combination of AND and OR conditions. For example, the following example extracts all French novelists, plus all German writers, novelists or not:

```
key 4=novelist & key 3=French | key 3=German
```

Notice in this example that the operators in the extraction statement read sequentially from left to right. You can modify this order with the help of parentheses. For example, the following statement extracts all novelists from France and Germany.

```
key 4=novelist & (key 3=French | key 3=German)
```

The addition of parentheses causes WordPerfect to read the OR statement in its entirety before activating the AND condition.

Using the global extraction key

You can also use a *global* extraction key (key g) to extract on a word or value, regardless of its location in the record. For example, the following statement extracts all records with the word "Japanese":

```
key g=Japanese
```

Use the global key only with the "=" operator. For example, if you specify "key g>Peruvian" instead, you will still get Mario Vargas Llosa's record, because the global key finds that his family name (Vargas Llosa) meets the extraction condition. If you specify "g>1800", you will extract every record, because numbers come before letters in the alphabetical sort sequence.

For More Information . . .

On	See
Performing merges	Chapter 27
Sorting spreadsheets	Chapter 33
Sorting Paradox tables	Chapter 47
Setting tabs	Chapter 21

✦   ✦   ✦

Adding Graphic Lines, Borders, and Fills

There's no better way to polish up your desktop publications than with graphic lines, borders, and fills. WordPerfect's graphic lines, borders, and fills give your documents a polished, professional look. Plus, they're fun. The newsletter in Figure 54-1 illustrates how lines and borders can organize text and graphic elements in an aesthetically pleasing way. Fills direct the reader's eye to key information in text boxes, columns, tables, and paragraphs.

This chapter focuses on WordPerfect because of its unique features, and it's where these elements are used the most. Presentations enables you to change the lines and fills used in clip art objects, and Quattro Pro enables you to apply borders and fills to inserted graphics. Chapter 55, "Creating Your Own Art," covers the general facilities for drawing graphic lines and other objects. Graphic fills and borders, when used, are the same throughout the suite.

Adding Graphic Lines

Graphic lines (or rules) have been a part of printing since before the invention of type. WordPerfect's graphic lines come in two directions: horizontal and vertical. (To draw curved or diagonal lines, see Chapter 55, "Creating Your Own Art.") The default single, black line is 0.013 inches wide and extends from margin to margin, but you can place lines of any length, thickness, color, spacing, or style at any location.

Figure 54-1: Illustration of graphic lines, borders, and fills.

By default, a horizontal line is placed at the text baseline; a vertical line is placed at the insertion point (see Figure 54-2). To insert a line:

1. Position the insertion point where you want the line to appear. (The text line can be blank.)

2. Click Insert ⇨ Line, and then click Horizontal Line or Vertical Line.

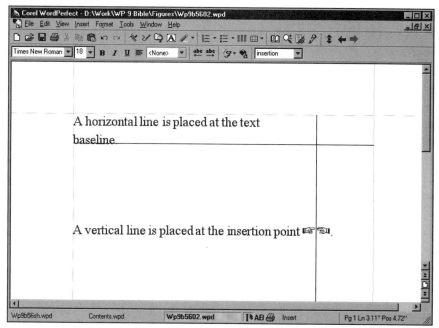

Figure 54-2: Default horizontal and vertical lines.

When you place a vertical line at the left or right margin, the line shifts slightly into the margin away from the text.

Tip   You can type four or more hyphens (-) or equal signs (=) at the beginning of a line, and then press Enter to insert a single or double horizontal line. (For more on Format-As-You-Go options, see Chapter 17, "Becoming an Instant WordPerfect Expert.")

Moving and Editing Lines

Moving and editing graphic lines with a mouse is simple and intuitive. You can also use a dialog box for additional options and more precise control.

Customizing a line with the mouse

Click a line to select it. Six resizing handles appear (as shown in Figure 54-3), which you can drag to change the line's length or width.

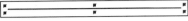

Figure 54-3: Resizing handles on
a selected line.

Drag the end handles to change the length. To change the width, it's best to grab one of the middle handles, as shown in Figure 54-4. When you grab an end handle, it's hard not to change the length as well.

Tip   Thicker lines have a middle handle at the ends that you can drag to adjust the length.

Figure 54-4: Dragging a middle
handle to change the thickness
of a line.

Point to a line and click to drag it to another location.

Changing lines from the property bar

Click a graphic line, and then click buttons on the property bar to change its style, thickness, or color (see Figure 54-5). You can also change a horizontal line to vertical, and vice versa.

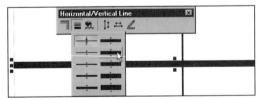

Figure 54-5: Changing the thickness of a line
from the property bar.

Precise editing of a graphic line

For more precise (if less intuitive) line adjustments, select the line and click the Edit Line button to open the Edit Graphics Line dialog box (see Figure 54-6). You can also double-click or right-click a line to edit it.

Tip   Make your rough adjustments to a graphic line with the mouse, and then, with the line still selected, click the Edit Line button (or double-click the line) to do any fine-tuning.

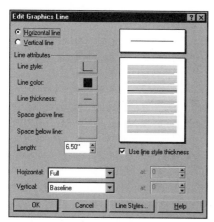

Figure 54-6: Precise editing of a graphic line.

Options for adjusting the line's length and position are discussed in this section. To edit other line attributes, see "Customizing a line," later in this chapter.

Editing horizontal lines

The default horizontal position for a horizontal line is Full, from margin to margin. Click the Horizontal list to change it to Left, Right, Centered, or Set. Set permits you to specify a precise offset from the left edge of the page (not the left margin). When you switch from Full to Set, WordPerfect automatically adjusts the length of the line as you change the offset.

The default vertical positioning of a horizontal line is the text baseline at the insertion point. You can also select Set from the Vertical list, to designate a precise distance from the top of the page.

A horizontal line set to Full automatically switches to Left when you specify a length.

To create a centered horizontal line, three inches long, placed one-third of the way down the page:

1. Click Insert ⇨ Line ⇨ Horizontal Line to place a horizontal line at the insertion point.

2. Double-click the line, click the Horizontal list, click Centered, and specify a length of 3 inches.

3. Click the Vertical list, click Set, and then specify an offset of 3.67 inches. The preview window should match the one shown in Figure 54-7.

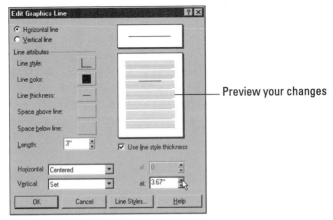

Preview your changes

Figure 54-7: Editing the horizontal line.

4. Click OK.

To edit the same line with the mouse:

1. Click the line and drag it to where you want.

2. Drag one of the handles at either end of the line to adjust the length and thickness of the line (see Figure 54-8).

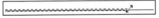

Figure 54-8: Adjusting the line
with a mouse.

3. Double-click the line and note how its parameters have changed.

Editing vertical lines

The default vertical position for a vertical line is Full, from the top to bottom margins. You can also select Top, Bottom, Centered, or Set.

Set permits you to specify a precise offset from the top of the page (not the top margin). When you switch from Full to Set, WordPerfect automatically adjusts the length of the line as you change the offset.

You have several horizontal placement options for a vertical line, including Column Aligned, to place vertical lines between columns. When you do, you also specify the column after which the line should appear.

A vertical line set to Full automatically switches to Top when you specify a length.

To insert a vertical line midway between the margins, extending from the line at the insertion point down to the bottom margin:

1. Click anywhere in a text line, about one-third of the way down the page, and then click Insert ➪ Line ➪ Vertical Line.

2. Point to the line and double-click, and then click the Horizontal list and click Centered.

3. Click the Vertical list, click Set, and then enter the line position (such as "Ln 3.96") you see displayed on the right of the property bar. The preview window should resemble the one shown in Figure 54-9.

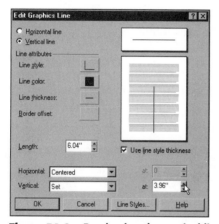

Figure 54-9: Previewing the vertical line.

4. Click OK, and then click and drag the line to move it around the page. Double-click the line and note how its parameters have changed.

Deleting a line

To delete a line, click the line to select it, and then press Delete. You can also delete its [Graph Line] code in reveal codes.

Cutting, copying, and pasting lines

You can right-click a line to cut or copy it, and then paste it just as you would ordinary text (see Chapter 2, "Essential Typing and Editing").

Creating a custom line

You can create a custom line, or customize an existing line, to specify the style, position, length, spacing, color, and thickness you want.

You can even create a custom line style to apply to your lines. The styles you create are listed along with the system styles (see Chapter 28, "Working Quickly with Templates, Projects, and Styles"). Anytime you want to apply the customized width, color, pattern, and so on, to another line, simply select your style by name from among the line styles.

To create a custom line or customize an existing line:

1. Click where you want to insert the line, and then click Insert Line ➪ Custom Line (or double-click the line you are editing).

2. Click "Horizontal line" or "Vertical line."

3. Specify the horizontal position, vertical position, and length, as described in the section, "Precise editing of a graphic line," earlier in this chapter.

4. Specify any of the line options described in Table 54-1.

Table 54-1 Custom Line Options	
Option	**Lets You**
Line color	Change the line's color, or check "Use line style color" to return the line to its default color
Line Style	Select a line style from the palette or the list at the bottom of the palette (see Figure 54-10). (The list has all the styles, including your custom styles.)
Line thickness	Change the line's thickness. You can also click "Use line style thickness" beneath the preview window to return the line to its default thickness.
Space above/below line	For a horizontal line at the default vertical baseline, specify the spacing above and below the line. For a left- or right-aligned vertical line, specify the border offset of the line from the margin (see Figure 54-11).
Line Styles	Select a line style or create a custom style using all the line and pattern options

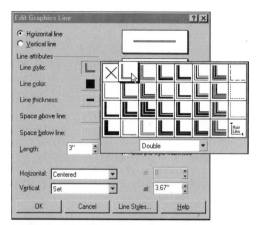

Figure 54-10: Selecting a line style.

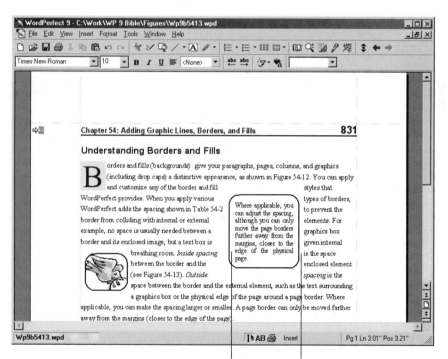

Inside spacing   Outside spacing

Figure 54-11: Horizontal and vertical lines.

Understanding Borders and Fills

Borders and fills (backgrounds) give your paragraphs, pages, columns, and graphics (including drop caps) a distinctive appearance, as shown in Figure 54-12. WordPerfect provides an array of border and fill styles that you can automatically apply to your documents; you can also customize any of the preset styles to fit your needs.

Drop cap fill   Page border   Paragraph border

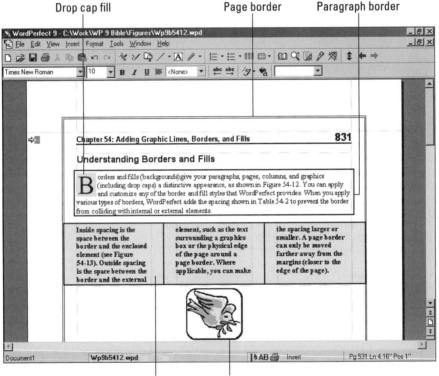

Column border and fill   Graphics box border

Figure 54-12: Examples of borders and fills.

To apply borders, you need to understand the two types of border spacing: *inside spacing* and *outside spacing* (see Figure 54-13). Inside spacing is the space between the border and the enclosed element. Outside spacing is the space between the border and the external element, such as the text surrounding a graphics box or the physical edge of the page around a page border. Where applicable, you can make the spacing larger or smaller. A page border can only be moved farther away from the margins (closer to the edge of the page).

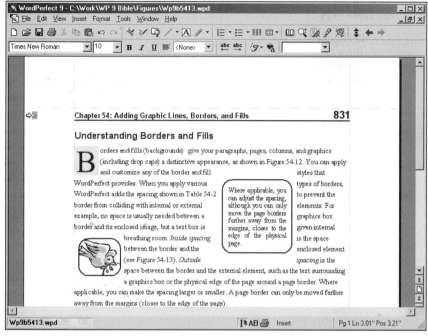

Figure 54-13: Inside and outside border spacing.

When you apply various types of borders, WordPerfect adds the spacing described in Table 54-2 to prevent the border from colliding with internal or external elements. For example, text in a box needs some internal space, while a graphic can go against the box border.

Table 54-2
Default Inside and Outside Border Spacing

Border Type	Inside Spacing	Outside Spacing
Paragraph	Bottom 0"; top/left/right .028"	Top 0"; bottom .028"; left/right N/A
Page	N/A	3/4 of margin, minus line thickness
Column	Top/bottom 0"; left/right (smallest adjacent column space - line thickness) /2	Top/bottom 0"; left/right N/A
Graphics box with image	0"	.167"
Graphics box with text	.083"	.167"

Adding Borders and Fills to Graphic Boxes

This section discusses the general options you have when adding borders and fills, illustrated by their application to graphics boxes. The particulars on adding graphic borders and fills to paragraphs, pages, and columns are covered in later sections.

Adding or changing a graphic border

You can click the Graphic Border button to change the border style, thickness, or color of a selected graphics box (see Figure 54-14), or click the Graphic Fill button to add or change its fill. To access all the options, click More on either palette. (You can also right-click a graphic and click Border/Fill.)

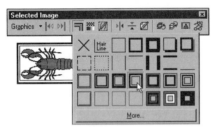

Figure 54-14: Making a selection from the Graphics border palette.

Adding a drop shadow

To add a drop shadow to a graphic:

1. Right-click the graphic, click Border/Fill, and then click the Shadow tab.

2. Click an image on the left, and then make finer shadow adjustments by using the scroll bars or spin boxes (see Figure 54-15).

3. Click the color palette to pick a shadow color.

Applying a graphic fill

When applying a graphic fill, you have a variety of solid, patterned, and gradient fills from which to choose (see Figure 54-16).

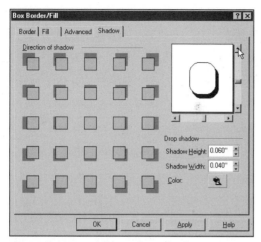

Figure 54-15: Adding a drop shadow to a graphic border.

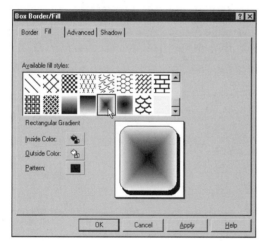

Figure 54-16: Selecting a fill type.

You can then click the Inside Color palette to select a foreground color for the fill. With pattern or gradient fills, you can click the Outside Color palette to pick a background color as well. Click Pattern to select any of the patterns from the palette (see Figure 54-17).

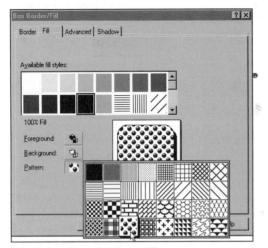

Figure 54-17: Selecting a fill pattern.

Specifying advanced border and fill options

When applying borders and fills to graphics boxes, paragraphs, pages, and columns, you can click the Advanced tab (see Figure 54-18) to specify various options described in Table 54-3.

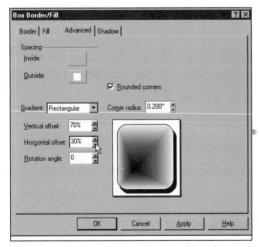

Figure 54-18: Specifying advanced border and fill options.

Table 54-3
Advanced Border, Fill, and Shadow Options

Option	Lets You
Spacing	Specify the inside and outside spacing.
Gradient	Specify a gradient fill pattern, plus offsets from center and a rotation angle.
Corner radius	Check "Rounded corners" and specify a radius. Not applicable to paragraphs and columns. (Rounded page borders print, but they don't display onscreen.)

Using Paragraph Borders and Fills

Paragraph borders and fills are an excellent way to highlight critical information in your document. They produce a powerful visual impact, so use them judiciously.

Applying a paragraph border or fill

You can put a border around a single paragraph or a series of selected paragraphs. You can apply a paragraph border or fill to existing text, or specify a border or fill and continue typing. If you apply a border to a paragraph that extends beyond the bottom of the page, the border is closed at the end of the page and begins anew at the top of the next page.

To apply (or change) a paragraph border or fill:

1. Click where you want the paragraph border or fill to begin, or select a group of paragraphs.

2. Click Format ➪ Paragraph ➪ Border/Fill, and select a border style (see Figure 54-19). (Scroll to the bottom of the list and select the Column Between or Column All border style to put a separator line between paragraphs.)

3. Check "Apply border to current paragraph only," or leave the check box empty to let the border (and fill) surround subsequent paragraphs as well.

4. Specify any other border and fill options described in the section "Adding Borders and Fills to Graphic Boxes," earlier in this chapter.

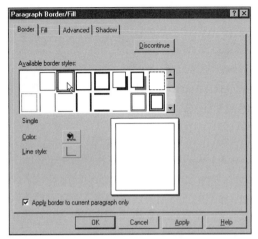

Figure 54-19: Applying a paragraph border or fill.

Turning off a paragraph border or fill

Click Format ➪ Paragraph ➪ Border/Fill ➪ Discontinue to turn off a paragraph border or fill. To remove the border or fill from all the paragraphs, you can also go to the beginning of the border or fill, open reveal codes, and delete the [Para Border] code.

Using Page Borders and Fills

Use page borders and fills to visually encompass the entire page, including headers and footers. Page borders come in two flavors:

✦ The standard borders and fills that are also used with paragraphs, columns, and graphics

✦ Fancy borders that employ border graphics, such as those in Figure 54-20. These are great for party invitations, award certificates, love letters, and other special occasions.

Tip   You won't see a page border in Draft view. The best observation point is Page view, at a zoom of Page Width or Full Page.

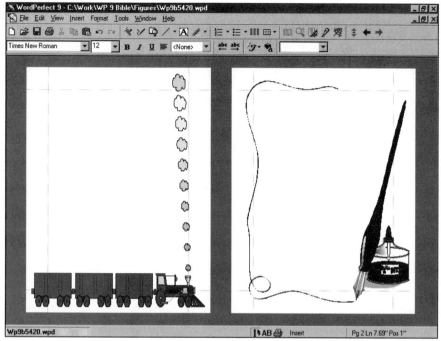

Figure 54-20: Fancy page borders.

Applying a page border or fill

To apply (or change) a page border or fill:

1. Click anywhere in the page where you want the border or fill to begin. You can also select any part of several pages to which you want the border to apply.

2. Click Format ⇨ Page ⇨ Border/Fill, and then select a border style.

3. To apply a fancy border, select Fancy from the Border Type list, and then select a border (see Figure 54-21). You can click the Change button to look for borders in other folders.

4. Check "Apply border to current page only," or leave the check box empty to let the border (and fill) surround subsequent pages as well.

5. Specify any other border and fill options described in the section "Adding Borders and Fills to Graphic Boxes," earlier in this chapter.

Tip

You can't adjust the spacing for a fancy page border, so it's best to apply the border *before* you type and format your text.

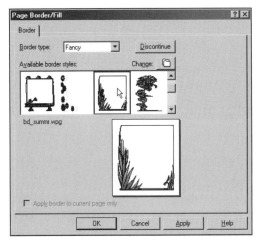

Figure 54-21: Applying a fancy page border.

Turning off a page border or fill

Click Format ➪ Page ➪ Border/Fill ➪ Discontinue to turn off a page border or fill. To remove the border or fill from all your pages, you can also go to the beginning of the border, open reveal codes, and delete the [Pg Border] or [Fancy Border] code.

Using Column Borders and Fills

You can use borders and fills with columns much as you do with paragraphs and pages. Two of the border styles — Column Between and Column All — are designed especially for columns. Column Between draws vertical lines between the columns. If you have three columns, for example, it will draw two lines. Column All draws a box around the columns, as well as lines between them.

Applying a column border or fill

When you apply a column border or fill, it surrounds a group of columns, not just the column at the insertion point. You can, as with the Column All border style, include separator lines between the columns.

Tip   To apply a border or fill to particular text within a column, select the text and apply a paragraph border instead.

To apply (or change) a column border or fill:

1. Click anywhere in a column where you want the column border or fill to begin.

2. Click Format ➪ Columns ➪ Border/Fill and select a border style (see Figure 54-22).

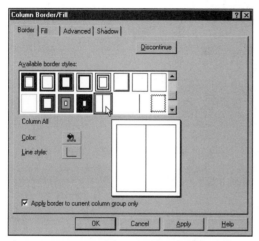

Figure 54-22: Applying a Column All border.

3. Do either of the following:

   • Check "Apply border to current column group only" to apply the border or fill only to the columns you clicked on.

   • Leave the check box empty to have the border or fill surround all subsequent columns in your document as well.

4. Specify any other border and fill options described in the section "Adding Borders and Fills to Graphic Boxes," earlier in this chapter.

Note   Don't worry if a column border doesn't look the way you expect it to in the document window. Sometimes the lines do not show all the way, but they print fine.

A fill pattern (such as shading) applies to the entire width of the columns on the page. Parallel columns have spacing between their rows, causing breaks in the borders or fills.

Tip   To place lines between parallel columns, create vertical graphic lines and position them between the parallel columns (see "Moving and Editing Lines," earlier in this chapter).

When you use the Column Between or Column All border style, keep the fill shading light, so the lines separating the columns show clearly.

Turning off a column border or fill

Click Format ⇨ Column ⇨ Border/Fill ⇨ Discontinue to turn off a column border or fill. To remove the border or fill from all the columns, you can also go to the beginning of the border, open reveal codes, and delete the [Col Border] code.

For More Information . . .

On	See
Drawing graphic lines and objects	Chapter 55
Format-As-You-Go	Chapter 17
Cutting, copying, and pasting	Chapter 2
Creating and saving styles	Chapter 28
Working with graphics	Chapter 9
Creating drop caps	Chapter 17

✦   ✦   ✦

Creating Your Own Art

While WordPerfect Office comes with an extensive collection of clip art and backgrounds, a hand-drawn object may be just the touch you need for your slide, drawing, menu, or brochure. This chapter shows you how to draw and edit a variety of shapes in WordPerfect and Presentations, and then goes on to show you how Presentations can be used to create and edit text objects and bitmaps. You'll get hands-on tips for editing shapes, and applying fills, shadows, 3-D, and other special effects.

Types of Graphic Objects

The WordPerfect suite comes with a variety of graphic objects that you don't have to draw by hand:

- ✦ WordPerfect's horizontal and vertical graphic lines
- ✦ Clip art
- ✦ Charts
- ✦ TextArt
- ✦ Borders and fills

These, plus scanned images, are covered elsewhere in this book, as noted in "For More Information..." at the end of this chapter. In this chapter you'll learn how to create shapes, text objects, and bitmaps.

Drawing Shapes

New Feature WordPerfect Office 2000 offers more than 100 new shapes that can be used in WordPerfect, Quattro Pro, and Presentations (see Figure 55-1). The various types are described in Table 55-1.

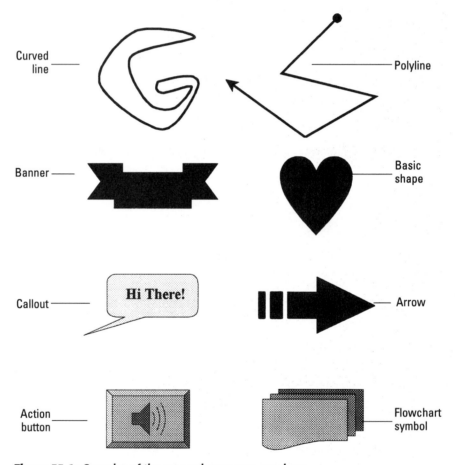

Figure 55-1: Samples of the many shapes you can draw.

Available Shapes

You'll find the largest collection of shapes on the Presentations tool palette and Insert menu. WordPerfect provides most of these shapes in its Draw Object Shapes dialog box, while Quattro Pro offers a more limited selection of shapes.

Any object you create in Presentations can be cut and pasted to WordPerfect, Quattro Pro, and other applications. In both WordPerfect and Quattro Pro, you can also click Insert ➪ Graphics ➪ Draw Picture to use the Presentations tools directly in a document or spreadsheet.

Table 55-1
Shapes You Can Draw in WordPerfect and Presentations

Shape Category	Some of the Shapes You Can Draw
Lines	Straight line, polyline (line with joints), curve, freehand line, arc, line arrow
Stars	Star, burst, ribbon, banner
Basic	Circle, triangle, rectangle, diamond, heart, cube, cylinder, lightning bolt
Callout (text enclosure)	Rectangular, rounded, cloud, rectangle with connecting line
Arrows	Various shaped solid arrows
Action	Buttons for forward, reverse, stop, sound
Flowchart	Standard flowchart template symbols

This chapter also shows you how to draw more complex shapes and bitmaps, in addition to these basic shapes. When you create more complex drawings in WordPerfect or Quattro Pro, the Presentations menus and tools appear.

Creating Shapes in WordPerfect

To create a shape in WordPerfect:

1. Click Insert ➪ Shapes.

2. Select the shape category, and then select the particular shape you want (see Figure 55-2).

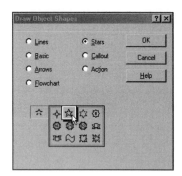

Figure 55-2: Creating a shape in WordPerfect.

3. Click OK, and then do one of the following, depending on the shape you're drawing:

- To create a regular shape, such as a square, cube, circle, or horizontal line, click where you want the shape to appear.

- Drag to insert and size or angle a shape at the same time (or to draw freehand lines).

- If you're drawing a complex curve or polyline with twists and turns, click at each inflection point, and then double-click to complete the shape.

Sizing and stretching a shape

Your shape is inserted in a graphics box. You can drag a corner handle of a selected box to size the shape proportionally, or drag a side handle to stretch the shape (see Figure 55-3).

Figure 55-3: To size or stretch a selected shape, drag a handle of its graphics box.

Altering a shape's form

If your shape has a red, diamond-shaped *glyph*, you can drag the glyph to alter the form of the shape (see Figure 55-4).

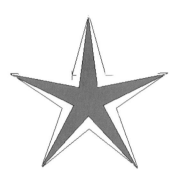

Figure 55-4: To alter a shape's form, drag its diamond-shaped glyph.

Changing a shape's attributes

From the property bar, you can change the attributes of a selected shape, such as adding ends to a line to turn it into an arrow, or changing a shape's foreground or background fill (see Figure 55-5).

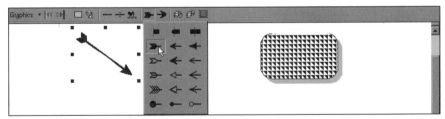

Figure 55-5: Use the property bar to change the attributes of a selected shape.

Skewing a shape

To skew (slant) a shape, right-click the shape, click Skew Shape, point to one of the green diamonds that appear, then drag to skew the shape (see Figure 55-6).

Figure 55-6: Skewing a shape.

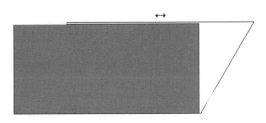

Rotating a shape

To rotate a shape, right-click the shape, click Rotate Shape, point to one of the green circles that appear, then drag to rotate the shape (see Figure 55-7).

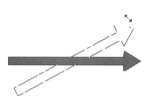

Figure 55-7: Rotating a shape.

Adding text to a shape

To add text to a shape, right-click the shape, click Add Text, and then type text in the box that appears (see Figure 55-8). The text stays attached if you move the object.

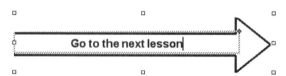

Figure 55-8: Adding text to an object.

Applying other graphics box techniques to shapes

You can apply other graphics box techniques to shapes in WordPerfect, including layering, grouping, or changing the anchor. For more on handling graphics boxes, see Chapter 9, "Working with Graphics."

Creating shapes in Quattro Pro

You can draw several types of shapes directly on a Quattro Pro spreadsheet, as well as in WordPerfect or Presentations. Click Insert ⇨ Shapes and select from the menu to draw any of the objects shown in Figure 55-9.

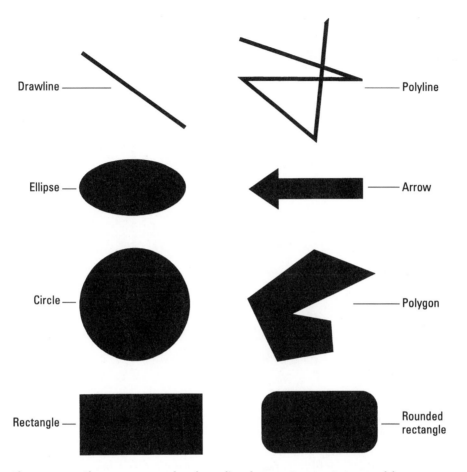

Figure 55-9: Shapes you can also draw directly on a Quattro Pro spreadsheet.

Drawing Shapes in Presentations

To create more complex shapes, use the Presentations drawing tools. Objects you create in Presentations can be copied to other applications. You can also click Insert ⇨ Graphics ⇨ Draw Picture to use the tools directly in a WordPerfect document or Quattro Pro spreadsheet (see Figure 55-10).

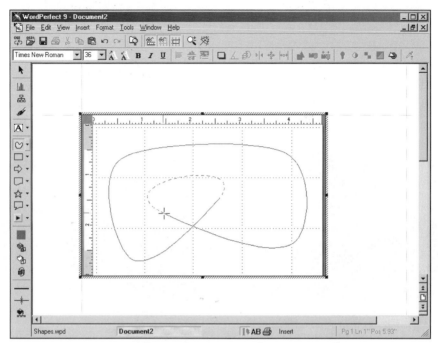

Figure 55-10: Drawing a complex shape in WordPerfect by using the Presentations tools.

Using the rulers, grid, and Snap To

The rulers and grid help you to draw and position objects exactly (see Figure 55-11). You can have the objects you create "snap to" grid intervals, much the way you can line up text with invisible tabs. You can also drag multiple red alignment guides off the ruler (or back) to aid you in lining up objects. (The ruler, grid, and alignment guides do not print.)

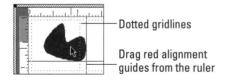

Dotted gridlines

Drag red alignment guides from the ruler

Figure 55-11: Use the ruler, grid, and alignment guides to position objects exactly.

Click the Ruler icon to toggle the display of the ruler; the Grid button to toggle the grid display; and the Snap button to toggle Snap To Grid. You can also turn these features on and off from the View menu.

To customize grid and Snap To features, click View ➪ Grid/Guides/Snap ➪ Grid/ Guides/Snap Options, and then specify any of the following:

✦ The horizontal and vertical Snap To spacing between dots (see Figure 55-12)

Figure 55-12: Specifying grid and Snap To options.

✦ The interval between dotted grid lines (normally every sixteenth dot)

✦ The *snap zone*, or how close an object can get to an alignment guide before it snaps to the guide

Drawing more complex shapes

With Presentations, you can draw the basic shapes, plus the more advanced shapes described in Table 55-2. As in WordPerfect, you can click instead of drag to insert a regular shape, such as a square or circle when inserting a rectangle or ellipse. You can also hold down Shift while you draw certain shapes to *constrain* them to a regular shape or angle. For example, you can constrain a rectangle to a square, an ellipse to a circle, and a line or polyline to exact vertical, horizontal, or 45-degree diagonal angles.

Table 55-2
Shapes You Can Draw in Presentations

Shape	How to Draw It	Constraint When Holding Shift
	Drag to create the line	90-degree and 45-degree angles
	(1) Click wherever you want to change the direction of the curve (2) Double-click to stop	Creates a circular arc
	Same as curve	Places points at horizontal, vertical, and 45-degree angles
	See "Drawing a Bézier curve	Places points at horizontal, vertical, and 45-degree angles

Drawing a Bézier curve

A Bézier curve is a smooth, curved line formed from a series of segments. To draw a Bézier curve:

1. Click the Bézier button from the Line Object tools, and click the starting point.

2. Click where you want the line to curve in another direction, drag to shape the curve, and then release (see Figure 55-13).

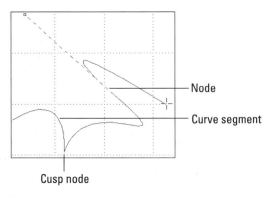

Figure 55-13: Drawing a Bézier curve.

Node

Curve segment

Cusp node

3. Repeat Step 2 for as many segments as you need.

4. Double-click to finish the curve.

To add a cusp (sharp change in direction), drag and release to create a segment, move the mouse to size and curve the segment, hold down the Alt key and click where you want to change direction, and then drag to create the next segment.

Selecting objects

You must select objects (including clip art, TextArt, charts, and images) before you can edit them. To select objects in the drawing window, click the Select button if necessary, and then click the object. Hold down Ctrl or Shift to select multiple objects.

To select all the objects at once, you can also press Ctrl+A or right-click a blank area and click Select All.

Tip   Press Ctrl and click to deselect objects one at a time.

Moving, copying, and sizing objects

Objects in the drawing window are in graphics boxes that you can move, copy, or size like any other, using any of the techniques described in Chapter 9, "Working with Graphics."

Precisely positioning or sizing an object

To precisely position or size an object in the drawing window:

1. Select the object.
2. Position the arrow in the object to move it, or on a handle to size it.
3. Hold the spacebar while clicking the arrow keys.
4. Release the spacebar when the object has reached the desired size or position.

Editing objects

You can edit the attributes of selected objects (such as the border, fill, shadow, color, or line style) by selecting options from the property bar. See "For More Information..." at the end of this chapter for details on editing particular attributes.

Editing points

To edit the points of a selected object:

1. Right-click the object and click Edit Points.
2. Drag any of the points to reshape the object.
3. If the object is a curve, closed curve, freehand line, curved arrow, or Bézier curve, you can also click a point and drag a control handle on the direction line (see Figure 55-14).

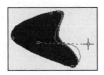

Figure 55-14: Click a point and drag a control handle to reshape a curved object.

Right-click points for additional options, depending on the type of object. You can add points, change a straight line into a curve, connect the first and last point, and so on.

Using Undo and Redo

When moving or editing objects, you can click the Undo or Redo buttons to undo or restore your latest ten editing actions.

Arranging the order of overlapping objects

When you have two or more overlapping objects, you can arrange their order in the stack (see Figure 55-15). Select an object, click the order button on the property bar, and then click

+ *To Front,* to move the object to the foreground
+ *To Back,* to move the object to the background
+ *Forward One,* to move the object up in the stack
+ *Back One,* to move the object down in the stack

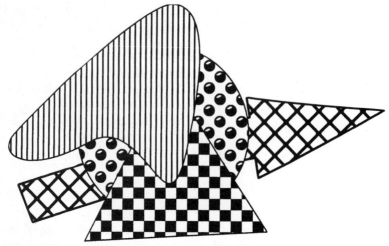

Figure 55-15: You can arrange the order of overlapping objects.

Grouping objects

Once you've arranged your objects the way you want, you can group them into a single object:

1. Click the graphic while holding Shift, or press Ctrl+A to select all the objects.

2. Click the Group button, or right-click any one of the selected graphics boxes and click Group.

The grouped objects can now be moved, sized, and edited as one. To separate the group back into individual objects, click the Separate button, or right-click an object and click Separate Objects.

Combining objects

To combine two or more drawn objects into a single figure:

1. Select the objects you want to combine.

2. Click the Combine button, or Graphics ⇨ Combine on the property bar.

Overlapping areas become transparent, and the combined figure assumes the fill pattern and colors of the bottom object (see Figure 55-16).

Figure 55-16: Combining objects.

You can only combine drawn objects, not bitmaps, text objects, or charts.

Blending objects

To blend two selected objects into any number of intermediate objects:

1. Select the objects and click Tools ➪ Blend.

2. Specify the number of intermediate objects you want.

The intermediate objects gradually go from the shape, size, color, and fill of one object to the other (see Figure 55-17). The objects can be saved individually, or as a grouped object.

Figure 55-17: Blending objects.

Rotating, skewing, and flipping objects

You can right-click an object to rotate or flip it, or click the Graphics menu on the property bar when objects are selected. (To create a mirror image, drag a copy while holding down Ctrl+Shift, and then flip the copy.)

To skew (slant) or rotate an object, right-click the object, click Rotate, and then drag a side handle to skew the object or a rounded corner handle to rotate the object (see Figure 55-18).

Tip You can drag the rotation point to any location within or outside of the object.

Figure 55-18: Rotating an object.

Adding depth to an object

To add depth to a selected object in the drawing window:

1. Click Tools ➪ Quick 3-D.

2. Select a rotation from the palette (see Figure 55-19).

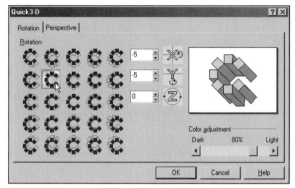

Figure 55-19: Selecting a 3-D rotation.

3. Adjust the lightness or darkness of the 3-D effect, relative to the object.

4. Click the Perspective tab, and then click Linear, Parallel, or Inverse and specify the depth of the 3-D effect.

The 3-D effect becomes a permanent part of the object (see Figure 55-20). Applying 3-D to text turns it into a drawing object.

Figure 55-20: Object with 3-D effect.

Warping an object

To warp a selected object in the drawing window, click Tools ⇨ QuickWarp, and select a shape from the palette (see Figure 55-21).

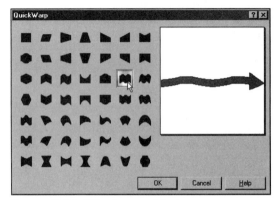

Figure 55-21: Warping an object.

The warp becomes a permanent part of the object. Applying warp to text turns it into a drawing object.

Aligning objects

You can align drawing objects individually (see Figure 55-22) or, when multiple objects are selected, in relation to one another:

1. Select the object(s) you want to align.

2. Click the Align button on the property bar, and then click the alignment option you want.

Spacing objects evenly

To proportionally space three or more objects in relation to one another:

1. Select three or more objects to space.

2. Click the Space icon on the property bar, and then click Space Left/Right or Space Top/Bottom.

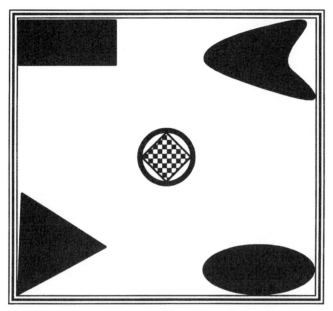

Figure 55-22: Aligning objects.

Making an object transparent

To make an object transparent, allowing an object underneath to show through:

1. Right-click the object and click Object Properties.

2. Click the fill tab and click Pattern Settings.

3. Make either the foreground or background color transparent (see Figure 55-23).

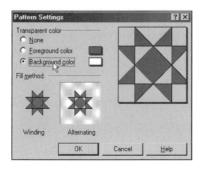

Figure 55-23: Making an object transparent.

Only pattern fills can be made transparent (see Figure 55-24), although picture fills have transparent spaces when they're tiled or stacked.

Creating Text Objects in Presentations

You can create a text box or line of text in the drawing window, much as you create a text box (see Chapter 9, "Working with Graphics") or line of text in WordPerfect. Text created this way becomes a graphic object to which various effects can be applied.

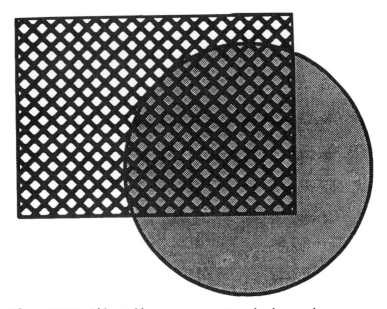

Figure 55-24: Object with transparent pattern background.

Creating a text box or line

To create a text box or line in the drawing window:

1. Click the Text Box button from the Text Object Tools and drag the width of the box you want, or click the Text Line button and click where you want the line to begin

2. Right-click and click Font, to select the font face, style, size, and color you want.

Tip   Select various effects and tools from the property bar, including shadow and spell-check.

3. Type your text.

4. Click outside the box or line when you're finished.

A text box expands downward as you type (drag a side handle to widen or narrow it). Text on a line cuts off beyond the right end.

Applying effects to text objects

You can apply effects to text objects, such as size, skew, and rotate (see Figure 55-25), just like any other object.

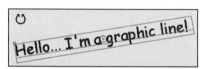

Figure 55-25: Rotating a text object.

To turn your text into graphics with fills and outlines, right-click the text, click Font, and then click the Fill Attributes and Outline tabs. To create 3-D text or to warp text, see "Adding depth to an object," or "Warping an object," earlier in this chapter.

<table>
<tr><td>**Cross-Reference**</td><td>For more extensive font effects, use the TextArt utility (see Chapter 8, "Fonts Fantastic").</td></tr>
</table>

Contouring text

To contour a line of text in the drawing window to another line or object:

1. Create the line (or box) of text.

2. Draw an object with the contour you want.

3. Select both objects (see Figure 55-26).

Figure 55-26: Select both the text and the contour object.

4. Click Tools ➪ Contour Text, and select a text position (see Figure 55-27).

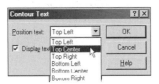

Figure 55-27: Positioning the contoured text.

5. Check "Display text only" to make the object disappear, leaving only the text (see Figure 55-28).

Figure 55-28: Resulting contoured text.

Tip

If you don't like the resulting contour, click Graphics on the property bar, click Separate Objects, and then redraw or edit the line. You can also use Undo to back up or start from scratch.

Adding text to clip art

It's easy to superimpose text on clip art, especially with the drawing layer in WordPerfect, but the text can just as easily separate from the graphic during editing. For permanent results, add the text directly to the clip art:

1. Click the drawing window to use the whole window for the image area.

2. Drag the image you want from the Scrapbook to the drawing window.

3. Create your text box or line, and any contouring object, if necessary.

4. Position and size the text over the graphic.

5. Press Ctrl+A to select both text and graphic, and then click @drgroup on the property bar.

6. Click File ⇨ Save to save the grouped object.

In Figure 55-29, a text line was superimposed on the image.

Figure 55-29: Text line combined with an image.

In Figure 55-30, the text was contoured around an ellipse drawn around the figure.

Figure 55-30: Text contoured around an ellipse drawn on the clip art.

Working with Bitmaps in Presentations

As explained in Chapter 9, "Working with Graphics," there are two broad categories of graphics:

✦ *Vector,* or drawn objects made up of lines defined by mathematical equations

✦ *Bitmap,* or painted images composed of thousands of individual pixels

So far, all the lines and shapes you've worked on in this chapter are vector objects. Presentations also has facilities for creating and editing bitmaps, although if you're heavily into creating original art or retouching photos, you'll probably use more specialized software such as CorelDRAW or Corel Photo-Paint.

Creating a bitmap

To create a bitmap image:

1. If you're starting from WordPerfect or Quattro Pro, click Insert ➪ Graphics ➪ Draw Picture.

2. Click the Bitmap button (Insert ➪ Graphics ➪ Bitmap), and then drag to define a bitmap area, or click to use the entire drawing window.

Tip   You can expand or shrink the bitmap area after you drag it.

3. Use the tools, such as the paint brush, air brush, and flood fill, to create your bitmap (see Figure 55-31).

4. Click the End button when you're finished to return to the drawing window.

Editing a bitmap file

To edit a bitmap file in the drawing window, double-click the image. Use the bitmap editing tools, and click the End button when you have finished.

Scanning an image

If you have a scanner hooked up and ready to go, you can scan a photograph or drawing as a bitmap image into the drawing window:

1. Click the Acquire Image button when no objects are selected, or click Insert ➪ Graphics ➪ Acquire Image.

2. Click "Page bounded," "Area bounded," or "Fixed size," depending on how you want to scale the image (see Figure 55-32).

3. Follow your software's procedures to scan the image.

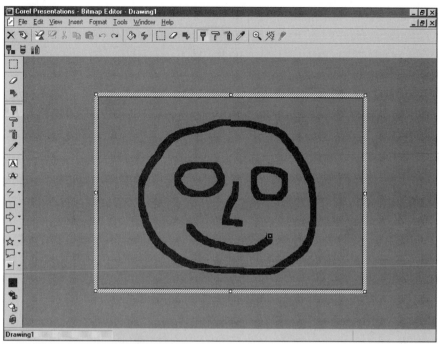

Figure 55-31: Drawing a bitmap.

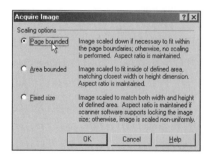

Figure 55-32: Scaling the scanned image.

Zooming in

To get a pixel-by-pixel view of your bitmap, click the Zoom icon (or click View ➪ Zoom) and drag the rectangle to the area you want to edit (see Figure 55-33).

Click the Zoom icon to zoom back out.

Figure 55-33: Zooming in on your pixels.

Using the bitmap tools

When editing a bitmap, you can use any of the additional bitmap tools described in Table 55-3.

	Table 55-3 Bitmap Tools	
Tool	**How to Use It**	**Tips**
	Click the Paint Brush button, select a fill and color, and then drag to paint.	Select a brush shape and size from the property bar. Hold Ctrl to use the background color from a pattern or gradient fill.
	Click the Flood Fill button, select a fill and color, and then click to fill a contiguous area.	All the pixels you're replacing must be the same color. Zoom to flood part of an area.
	Click the Air Brush button, select a color, and then drag to spray paint.	The slower you drag, the denser the spray. Select an air brush density from the property bar.
	Click the Selective Replace button, select the foreground color you want to replace, select the background color to replace it with, and then drag over the pixels you want to replace.	Only pixels of the exact foreground color are replaced.
	Click the Pickup Color button and click the pixel in your image. Hold Ctrl down to pick up the color for your background.	Lets you apply a precise color from one part of your image to another.

Tool	How to Use It	Tips
	Click the Eraser button, and then drag to erase areas of your image.	Erased pixels are transparent, allowing the page color to show through.
	Click the Select Area button, and then drag to select an area.	Lets you edit, move, duplicate, or erase a particular area of your image. Click outside an area to deselect it. Hold Ctrl down while dragging to duplicate the area.
	Click the Erase Selection button.	Erases a selected area.
	Click the Clear button.	Erases the entire bitmap.

Applying special effects

You can enhance all or part of a bitmap image with a variety of special effects, including brightness, contrast, mosaic, wind, stereogram, and many others:

1. Select, if necessary, the area of the image you want to enhance or exclude.

2. Click the Special button, and select the effect you want to apply (see Figure 55-34).

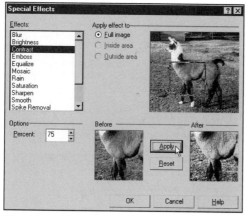

Figure 55-34: Enhancing a bitmap with special effects.

3. Specify the area and options, where applicable.

4. Click Apply to apply the effect, or Reset to undo the enhancement.

Resampling a bitmap

To resample a resized bitmap to improve its display:

1. Size the bitmap.
2. With the bitmap selected, click the Resample button, or right-click the bitmap and click Resample Bitmap.

Resampling the bitmap increases or decreases its file size.

Saving a bitmap

To save your bitmap objects:

1. Select the objects you want to save.
2. Click File ➪ Save As ➪ Selected items.
3. Specify the filename and type.

For More Information . . .

On	See
Adding clip art and text boxes	Chapter 9
Applying borders and fills	Chapter 54
Creating slides	Chapter 41
Working with graphics boxes	Chapter 9
Creating TextArt	Chapter 8
Understanding bitmaps and vectors	Chapter 9
Converting a vector image to a bitmap	Presentations' online Help
Converting a bitmap to a vector image	Presentations' online Help

✦   ✦   ✦

Charting Data

Charts and graphs are effective tools for making a point. Suppose you are reporting the five-year growth in earnings at Cyclops Software, or writing about the relationship between smoking and heart disease. A strategically placed chart or two can give your words clarity and impact.

This chapter is based on the Presentations Chart Editor, which WordPerfect also uses. Quattro Pro's charting variations, including analytical charts, are shown in Chapter 36, "Creating Charts, Maps, and Shows."

Understanding Data Charts

The terms *chart* and *graph* are used interchangeably to mean the graphical representation of data. This chapter, following the WordPerfect Office convention, uses the term chart throughout. It covers only data charts — for organization charts and bulleted lists, see "For More Information..." at the end of this chapter.

The chart itself can be boiled down into the following two elements:

♦ The *chart data*, either entered directly or taken from an existing table or spreadsheet

♦ The *style of the chart* (such as bar, pie, or line), plus variations and perspectives

The term style sometimes refers to the entire range of formatting options, which you can save as a custom style to apply to charts. At other times, the suite uses "style" in the narrow sense of the three or four variations of a particular chart type.

The instructions that follow use the charting terms summarized in Table 56-1, most of which are illustrated in Figure 56-1.

Table 56-1 Charting Terms	
Term	**Description**
Title	The title and subtitle describing the chart. You can also assign titles to the X and Y axes.
Axes	The horizontal (X) and vertical (Y) dimensions of a chart, usually scaled with tick marks, much like a ruler. The independent variable (such as "time") is displayed along the X axis, with the various series being tracked (such as "temperature" or "snowfall") scaled to the primary Y axis on the left or the secondary Y axis on the right.
Grid and Tick	The lines and marks used as visual guides.
Series	A row of the data you're charting, graphically represented by a bar, line, pie segment, or other means.
Legend	The visual key to the chart's series.
Framef	The 3-D box that lets you view the chart from various perspectives.
Labels	Values displayed on the scales and data items.
Layout	The arrangement and shape of bars, lines, and other chart elements.
Perspective	The angle from which the chart is viewed.

Creating a Chart

You have two ways to create a chart in WordPerfect:

✦ To create a chart starting with sample data, click Insert ➪ Chart.

✦ To create a chart with data from a WordPerfect table, click the table and click Insert ➪ Chart.

By working from a WordPerfect table, you can update your chart simply by updating the table in WordPerfect — you'll only have to return to the Chart Editor if you want to edit the chart's appearance. See "Creating a chart from a WordPerfect table" later in this chapter for details.

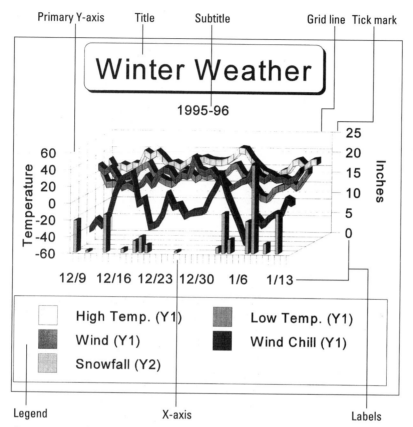

Figure 56-1: Charting terms on display.

To create a chart from sample data in Presentations:

1. Click the Chart button (or click Insert ➪ Data Chart).
2. Drag to create your chart.
3. Select a chart from the gallery (see "Touring the Chart Gallery" later in this chapter).

A look at the Chart Editor tools

A chart appears in your document or presentation (see Figure 56-2), with various elements to customize your chart:

✦ The spreadsheet-like *datasheet* containing the chart data (if you didn't start from a table)

✦ The Presentations menus, toolbar, property bar, and tool palette, from which you can change the perspective, layout, and other elements of your chart's appearance

✦ A *range highlighter* (normally not displayed) that lets you apply distinguishing colors to various parts of the datasheet (the chart itself is not affected)

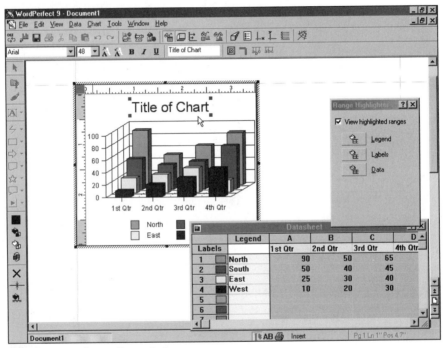

Figure 56-2: Chart Editor window.

Click the View Datasheet button to alternately hide and display the datasheet, and View ➪ Highlighter to toggle the highlighter display.

Click the Close button or click outside the chart to return to your document or presentation. Double-click the chart to go back to the Chart Editor.

Touring the Chart Gallery

When you're creating or editing a chart, click Chart ➪ Gallery for a tour of the available chart types (see Figure 56-3). (Click the Data Chart Gallery button to select a type from the palette.) Table 56-2 describes the various chart types and their uses.

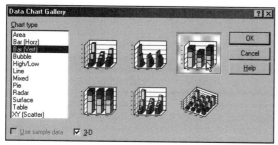

Figure 56-3: Touring the Chart Gallery.

Table 56-2		
Chart Types		
Chart	**What It Does**	**Use It To**
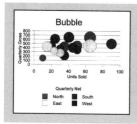	Connects data for each series in a continuous solid area.	Show the trend for each series and, when stacked, the contribution of each series to the whole.
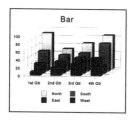	Presents data as vertical or horizontal bars of varying height.	Show comparative amounts or trends, and, when stacked, the contribution of each series to the whole.
	Displays three types of data in two dimensions.	Show comparative amounts, but not trends.

Continued

Table 56-2 (*continued*)

Chart	What It Does	Use It To
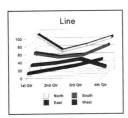	Displays connected high and low values, and one or two values in between.	For example, show daily high and low values for stocks, as well as the opening and close.
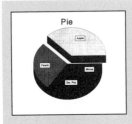	Connects data for each series in a continuous line.	Show the trend for each series, but normally not its contribution to the whole.
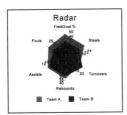	Serves each item as a slice of a circle. Individual slices can be exploded for emphasis. You can have up to nine pie graphs in one chart.	Show the comparative amount of various items, as well as each item's contribution to the whole.
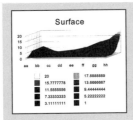	Displays series of data on a circular grid, with a central X point and Y axes radiating from the center.	Bring out comparative strengths and weaknesses of various related groups.
(Surface chart)	Represents data as a contoured landscape with shaded valleys and peaks.	Display continuous trends in financial, scientific, and other data.

Chart	What It Does	Use It To
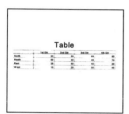	Plots data as the interception points between two values on the X and Y axes.	Show the relationship between two variables (such as age and income).
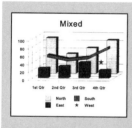	Displays the data as a two-dimensional table, minus the chart. You have the option of displaying the table along with any other style of chart.	Display the data on its own.
	Employs different styles of series in one chart.	Separate different types of data into visual categories.

Tip You need not specify a mixed chart from the start. You can start with the basic type you want, and then change the type for a particular series.

In the gallery, you can choose from six varieties for each type of chart. The differences are more than cosmetic. For example, the stacked 100 percent bar chart shown in Figure 56-4 emphasizes Cyclops Software's increasing market share, rather than its absolute increase or decrease in sales.

As the 3-D check box in the gallery indicates, all types of charts (other than bubble and radar) can be displayed in either two or three dimensions.

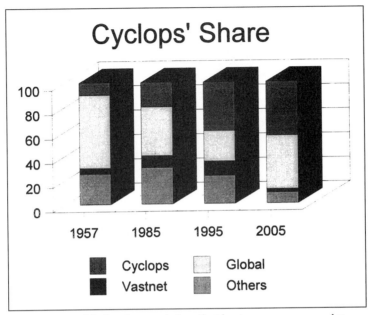

Figure 56-4: Pick the chart variation that best conveys your point.

Editing a Chart

To edit a chart, double-click the chart, or right-click the chart and click Edit Chart (Presentations) or Chart Object ⇨ Edit (WP). Your basic Chart Gallery operations are described in Table 56-3.

Table 56-3 Basic Chart Gallery Operations	
Do This	*In Order To*
Edit the datasheet	Specify the legends, labels, and data values for your chart.
Click Chart ⇨ Layout Type	Change the chart type, style, and other display properties.
Double-click or right-click a chart item	Edit or specify options for the item.
Select menu, toolbar, and bar items	Switch the perspective, change the layout, edit the property appearance of a series, and perform other operations.

Entering, editing, and selecting data

The data for your chart (including labels and legends) can be entered in the datasheet. (When creating pie charts, each pair of columns describes an additional pie in the group.) You can resize the datasheet with the mouse, or drag it by the title bar out of the way of your chart.

You edit the datasheet much as you do a WordPerfect table or Quattro Pro spreadsheet. You can click (or double-click) cells to revise their contents, and move from cell to cell by using the arrow keys or tab.

 Caution There's no undo when editing a chart's data in the datasheet. Before you start, you may want to save your document with the chart to another name, so you can recover if things go wrong.

You can click or drag to select cells (see Figure 56-5) and employ any of the standard editing tools (such as cut, copy, paste, and delete). For example, you can select a column or row, and then cut and paste to move it to another location. Use any of the selection tricks listed in Table 56-4.

	Legend	A	B	C	D	
Labels		1st Qtr	2nd Qtr	3rd Qtr	4th Qtr	
1	North	90	50	65	85	
2	South	50	40	45	70	
3	East	25	30	40	20	
4	West	10	20	30	45	
5						

Figure 56-5: Drag to select a group of datasheet cells.

 Caution Be careful when right-clicking to cut or copy selected information. If you right-click a cell outside of your selection, you'll cut or copy that cell instead.

Table 56-4
Datasheet Selection Tricks

To Select	Do This
A group of cells	Drag from one corner to the other.
Columns or rows	Click or drag the column or row labels.
The entire datasheet (including empty cells)	Click the upper-left label.
Only the cells with data	Right-click the datasheet and click Select All.

Clearing or deleting data

You can clear entries in the datasheet, leaving the columns and rows intact, or you can delete entire columns or rows. To clear the sample data to start from a clean slate, click the datasheet, and then click Edit ⇨ Clear All.

To clear a cell or selected cells:

1. Select the cell or group of cells you want to clear.

2. Right-click the selection and click Clear. You can also press Delete, or click Edit ⇨ Clear.

3. Click one of the following (see Figure 56-6):

   • *Data,* to clear the data but leave the format intact.

   • *Format,* to return to the general numeric format, leaving the data intact. (See "Changing the data format" later in this chapter.)

   • *Both,* to clear both the data and the format.

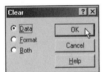

Figure 56-6: Clearing data.

To delete rows or columns:

1. Click a cell in the first column or row you want to delete.

2. Click Edit ⇨ Delete.

3. Click Row(s) or Column(s), and then specify the number of rows or columns to delete (see Figure 56-7).

Figure 56-7: Deleting rows or columns.

Changing how the datasheet is displayed

To change the width of datasheet columns, do either of the following: (1) click Data ⇨ Column Width, and then specify the number of digits to display; or (2) drag the lines between the columns in the top (Legend) row of the datasheet. (Select multiple columns to adjust them all at once.) Adjusting datasheet columns affects the table (if displayed) accompanying the chart, but not the chart itself.

You can enter as much information as you want in a cell, regardless of the column width. Numbers too large to display will appear in scientific notation, or with a greater than sign (>), depending on the number format. For example, the number 5,500,000,000 displays as 5.5E +9. Text that's too long to display scrolls in the cell.

Displaying a data table with the chart

To display the tabular data from the datasheet along with the chart, click the data chart Show Table button (or click Chart ⇨ Layout/Type ⇨ Table, and then check "Display table").

Tip   If the chart gets squished by the table, you can drag the bottom of the chart box to stretch it.

Redrawing the chart

When View ⇨ Auto Redraw is checked, your chart is automatically redrawn after every change. If not, you can click View ⇨ Redraw (Ctrl+F3) to update your chart.

Inserting rows or columns in the datasheet

To insert rows or columns in the datasheet:

1. Click where you want to insert rows or columns (existing data shifts down or to the right).
2. Click Edit ⇨ Insert.
3. Click Row(s) or Column(s), and then specify the number to insert (see Figure 56-8).

Figure 56-8: Inserting rows or columns in the datasheet.

Changing the data format

To specify a variety of numeric and date formats for the data in your chart:

1. Select the datasheet cells you want to change.

2. Click the Number Format button on the property bar. (You can also right-click the datasheet and click Format, or click Data ⇨ Format.)

3. Select Numeric, Date, or General from the "Format type" drop-down list.

4. Select the format you want from the list (see Figure 56-9), and then select particular display options.

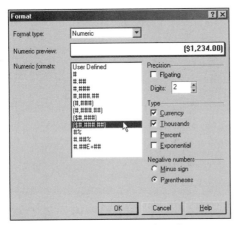

Figure 56-9: Changing the data format.

 Cross-Reference   For an in-depth discussion of numeric and date formats (including custom formats), see Chapter 32, "Entering Data and Formulas."

Editing the chart title or subtitle

The default chart has a title but no subtitle. You have many ways to customize the title or subtitle—you can even add fill to the text. To edit the title or create and edit a subtitle:

1. When creating or editing the chart, click Chart, and then click Title or Subtitle. You can also double-click a title or subtitle.

2. Check "Display chart title" or "Display chart subtitle," if necessary, edit the text, and specify the font face, style, size, color, and appearance (see Figure 56-10).

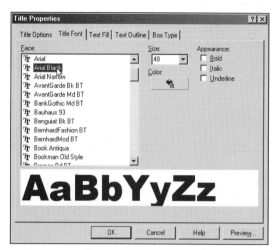

Figure 56-10: Editing a title or subtitle.

Tip

Edit the text and appearance of a selected title or subtitle directly in the property bar.

3. Click the tabs (see Figure 56-11) to specify the title font, text fill, text outline, box type, box fill, and title options (position left, right, or center).

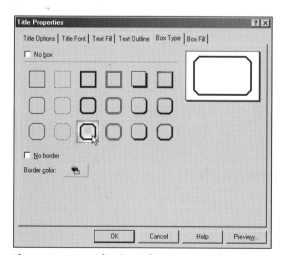

Figure 56-11: Selecting a box type for the title or subtitle.

Tip

Drag a selected title or subtitle to any location. Right-click a title or subtitle to position it left, right, center, or back (Reset Text) to its original location.

See Chapter 54, "Adding Graphic Lines, Borders, and Fills," for more on box borders and fills.

Adding axis titles

You can add descriptive titles to the axes, such as "$ millions," "Temperature," "Region," or "Year" (see Figure 56-12).

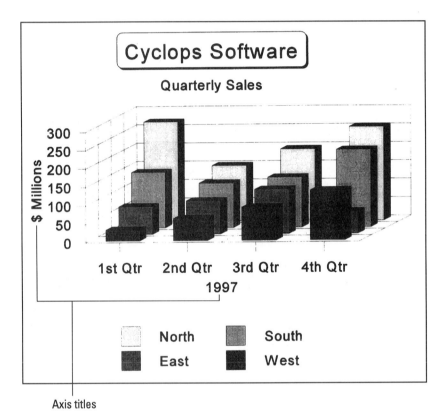

Figure 56-12: Descriptive axis titles.

To add axis titles:

1. Click the data chart X-Axis button or the data chart Y-Axis button to edit the X or Y axis. (You can also click Chart ⇨ Axis, or double-click an axis.)

 To edit the secondary Y axis, you must first click Chart ⇨ Series and assign a data series to it.

2. Click the Title Options tab to enter the title and select a vertical or horizontal orientation (see Figure 56-13).

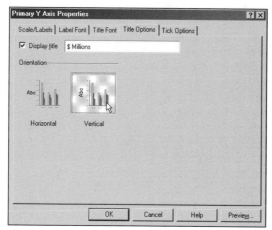

Figure 56-13: Adding an axis title.

3. Click the Title Font tab, enter the title, and then specify the font face, style, size, color, and appearance (refer to Figure 56-13).

Changing the legend display

The legend provides a visual key to the colors and lines used in your chart. A legend is automatically created when you create a chart; the legend items are displayed in the Legend column on the datasheet. But you can customize how the legend looks, or even delete it. To change the legend display:

1. Click the data chart Legend button. (You can also click Chart ⇨ Legend or double-click the legend.)

2. Click Vertical or Horizontal display, select from eight possible positions, and check if you want to display the legend inside the chart (see Figure 56-14).

Tip   Click the Preview button to see the effects of your selections before you accept them.

3. Click the Text Font tab to change the font for the legend items. (Edit the legend names in the datasheet.)

4. Click the Title Font tab to add a legend title and specify its font.

5. Click the other tabs to change the legend box type and fill.

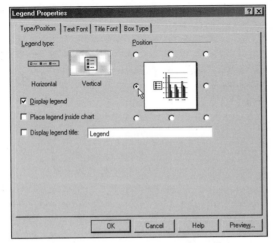

Figure 56-14: Changing the legend display.

Tip Select and drag the legend to any location (hold the Shift key down to snap it left, right, or center).

Displaying and editing descriptive labels

Labels from your datasheet are normally displayed along the X and Y axes. You can also specify data labels for particular values displayed in the chart (see Figure 56-15). (Pie charts have unique label features explained in the next section.)

To display and edit a chart's descriptive labels:

1. Click the data chart X-Axis button or the data chart Y-Axis button to edit the X or Y axis. (You can also click Chart ➪ Axis, or double-click an axis.)

2. Specify the font face, style, size, color, and appearance. To turn off labels for the axis, click the Labels tab and uncheck "Display labels."

3. To display data labels, click Chart ➪ Data Labels. Check "Display data labels," click the inside or outside display, and then click the various tabs to specify the font, box type and border, and box fill (see Figure 56-16).

To display and edit a chart's descriptive labels:

1. Click the data chart X-Axis button or the data chart Y-Axis button to edit the X or Y axis. (You can also click Chart ➪ Axis, or double-click an axis.)

2. Specify the font face, style, size, color, and appearance. To turn off labels for the axis, click the Labels tab and uncheck "Display labels."

3. To display data labels, click Chart ➪ Data Labels. Check "Display data labels," click the inside or outside display, and then click the various tabs to specify the font, box type and border, and box fill (see Figure 56-16).

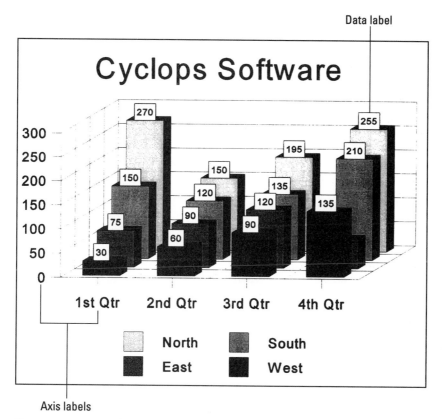

Figure 56-15: Descriptive chart labels.

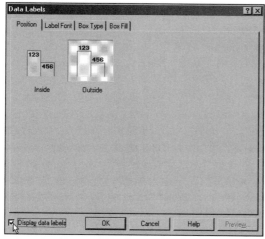

Figure 56-16: Displaying data labels.

> **Tip**   Click data chart Display Labels button to toggle the display of all the labels in your chart.

You can also specify how frequently the descriptive labels appear. See "Changing the X-axis label and tick display," later in this chapter.

Changing a pie chart's data labels

Pie charts are a different species when it comes to labels. Because they have no axes, they display segment labels instead (see Figure 56-17). The following three items can be displayed in the pie chart labels:

✦ The descriptive text from the data sheet

✦ The absolute value of the segment

✦ The percent of the segment in relation to the whole

Only the descriptive text displays by default.

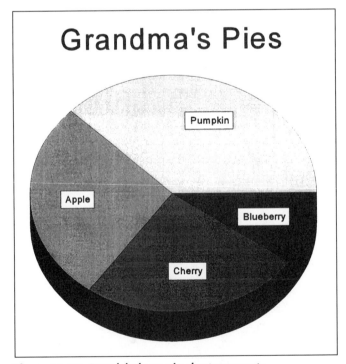

Figure 56-17: Data labels on pie chart segments.

To change a pie chart's label display:

1. Click Chart ⇨ Data Labels in the Chart Editor, or double-click a label.

2. Click the Value, Percent, and Label pop-up lists to display these items either inside of or outside of the pie (see Figure 56-18).

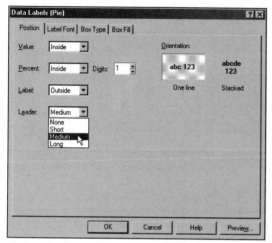

Figure 56-18: Specifying pie chart data labels.

3. Change the number of digits after the decimal point, if necessary.

4. If two or three items are displayed together, click the "One line" or "Stacked" button to select their orientation.

5. If items are displayed outside of the pie, you can click to connect them to the segments with short, medium, or long leaders (see Figure 56-19).

Changing a Chart's Appearance

So far, you have learned how to enter data in your chart, and define titles and labels. This section explores the various ways to change the appearance of a chart. (Click View ⇨ Datasheet to remove the datasheet from view when editing a chart's appearance.)

Changing the type or style of a chart

From the Chart Editor you can click Chart ⇨ Gallery to select a different chart type or style. You can also click the data chart Gallery button for a real-time preview of possible selections (see Figure 56-20).

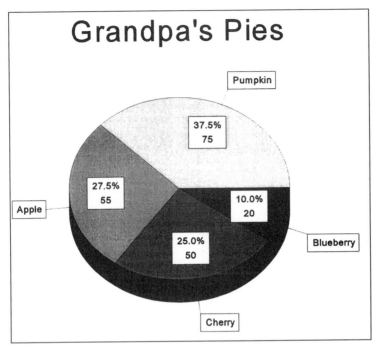

Figure 56-19: Pie chart with stacked inside labels and medium leaders.

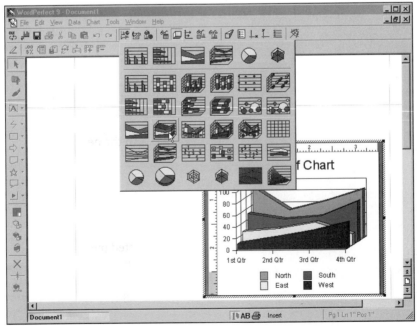

Figure 56-20: Use the Gallery for real-time preview and selection of chart types.

The best way to change a chart's type or style, however, is with the versatile Layout/Type Properties dialog box (see Figure 56-21). Access the dialog box in any of the following ways:

✦ Click the data chart Layout button.

✦ Click Chart ⇨ Layout/Type.

✦ Right-click a blank area in the chart and click Layout/Type Properties.

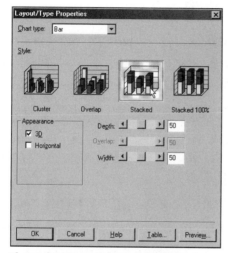

Figure 56-21: Select a variety of appearance options from the Layout/ Type Properties dialog box.

In addition to changing a chart's type or style, the Layout/Type Properties dialog box lets you specify layout properties that change the shape of bars, lines, and other chart elements, as described in Table 56-5. (Note that pie, high/low, radar, and surface charts have unique layout features, described in the next sections.

Changing a pie chart's layout

A pie chart has unique layout features. To change a pie chart's layout:

1. In the Chart Editor, click Chart ⇨ Layout/Type.

2. A number from 1 to 9 indicates the currently selected pie (see Figure 56-24). If there are two or more pies, you can click the "Current pie" drop-down list to switch among them.

3. Specify any of the layout options shown in Table 56-7.

Table 56-5	
Chart Layout/Type Options	
Option	**Lets You**
Style	Select a style displayed in Figure 56-22 and described in Table 56-6. You can show pie charts as columns instead of pies. High/low charts have styles particular to that type.
3D	Display the chart in 3-D.
Horizontal	Switch from vertical to horizontal display.
Table	Display an accompanying table with the chart and specify other table display options.
Misc.	Adjust the width, depth, overlap, and other aspects of the series on display (see Figure 56-23).

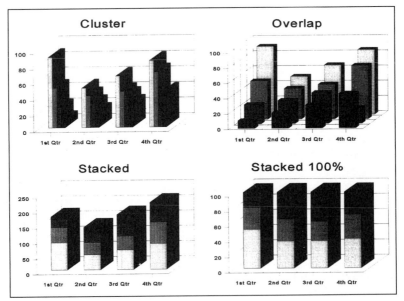

Figure 56-22: Style options for bar charts.

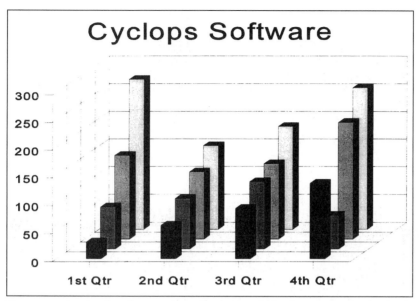

Figure 56-23: Overlapping 3-D bars sized to a width of 20 and a depth of 40.

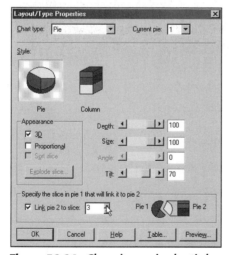

Figure 56-24: Changing a pie chart's layout.

Table 56-6
Chart Layout Styles

Style	What It Does
Cluster	Clusters bars by column (bar charts only).
Overlap	Overlaps bars, lines, or areas.
Stacked	Stacks bars, lines, or areas vertically.
Stacked 100%	Stacks bars, lines, or areas vertically to show relative, rather than absolute, values.

Table 56-7
Pie Chart Layout Options

Option	Lets You
Style	Select pie or column display.
3D	Switch between two- and three-dimensional display.
Proportional	Check to display two or more pies as different sizes, based on their absolute values.
Sort slice	Sort the slices by size (going counterclockwise).
Explode slice	Move the slice (numbered counterclockwise) the distance you specify. You can also drag the slices to explode them.
Depth	Change the 3-D height from 1 to 100.
Size	Change the size of the pie from 10 to 100.
Angle	Change the counterclockwise rotation from 0 to 359 degrees.
Tilt	Change the frontal view from 10 to 90 degrees (flat).
Link pie 2 to slice:	Link pie 2 to the slice you specify in pie 1.

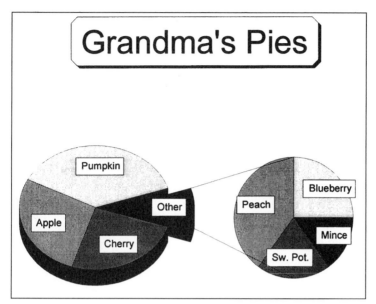

Figure 56-25: Pie chart with exploded slice, linked pies, and other options.

Changing the layout for high/low, radar, and surface charts

High/low, radar, and surface charts have various custom layout features (some peculiar to individual styles):

Chart Type	Custom Layout Features
High/low	Styles of line, bar/error, error bar, and area.
Radar	Appearance of line or area. Styles of overlapped, stacked, and stacked 100 percent. The scale for the stacked 100 percent radar chart can be shown as a series of concentric circles (radial), or as lines radiating out from the center (linear). You can also select to display a separate Y axis.
Surface	Surface color range and blend, plus outline contours and colors.

Switching between two and three dimensions

For most types of charts, you can click the data chart 3D button to toggle between two- or three-dimensional display. You can also switch dimensions in the Chart Gallery or Layout/Type Properties dialog box.

Switching between vertical and horizontal display

For most types of charts, you can click the data chart Horizontal button to toggle between vertical and horizontal display. You can also switch the orientation in the Chart Gallery or Layout/Type Properties dialog box.

Taking a different perspective

You can change the perspective of a 3-D chart to view it from various angles.

To understand perspective, think of a downtown city block as a vertical bar chart. Then imagine that you are a passenger in a helicopter flying over and around this block. From high overhead, the buildings look like two-dimensional figures. From outside of the block, you can see both the tops of the buildings and their sides. When you land and get out of the helicopter, you see one or two vertical sides from ground level. The buildings don't change, only your perspective did. In changing your chart's perspective, the chart moves while the data remain the same.

To change the perspective of a 3-D chart:

1. Click the data chart Perspective button (or click Chart ➪ Perspective), and then specify one of the following Angle options:

   • *Right-angle axes*, when checked, provides the conventional display of the X and Y axes at right angles (see Figure 56-26). Remove the check to allow the X axis to follow the horizontal rotation.

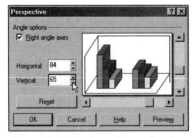

Figure 56-26: Changing a chart's perspective.

   • *Horizontal* changes the angle from which you view the X axis, from 0 (sideways) to 100 (straight on). Figure 56-27 shows the X axis at a perspective of 70.

Tip Use the scroll bars next to the preview window to quickly adjust the horizontal and vertical perspectives.

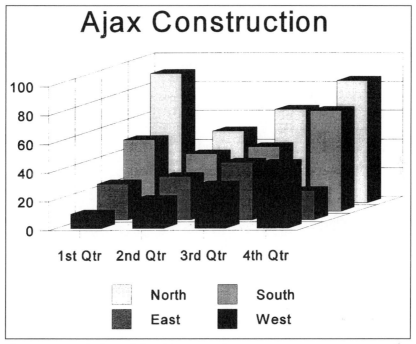

Figure 56-27: Horizontal (X axis) perspective at 70.

> • Vertical changes the angle from which you view the Y axis, from 0 (directly above) to 100 (directly in front). Figure 56-28 shows the Y axis at a perspective of 50.

2. Click Preview to test your selections on the chart.

3. Click Reset to return to your original perspective.

To change the perspective of a pie chart, see "Changing a pie chart's layout," earlier in this chapter.

Changing the properties of a series

You can specify how each row of data displays as a series on the chart. You can change the type (as from bar to line), color, width, and a number of other display properties. (However, you should keep such mixing to a minimum or you'll confuse the viewer.) Figure 56-29 shows a mixed chart composed of different types of series.

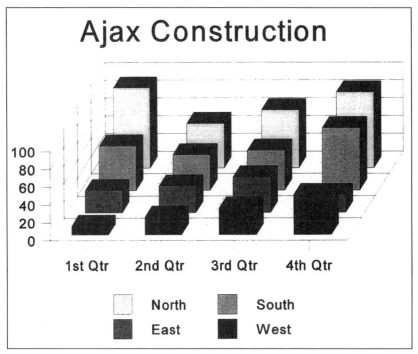

Figure 56-28: Vertical (Y axis) perspective at 50.

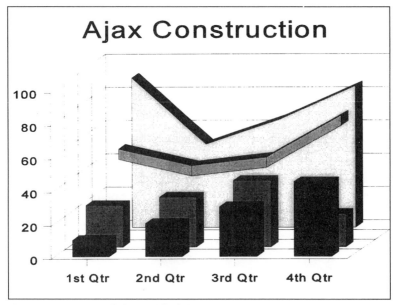

Figure 56-29: Mixed chart with different types of series.

To change the properties of a series:

1. Click the data chart Series button (you can also click Chart ⇨ Series, or double-click the series you want to change on the datasheet label, legend, or chart).

2. Select from the series types (see Figure 56-30). The available series types, displayed in Figure 56-31, depend on the chart's type and number of dimensions.

Click to edit a different series

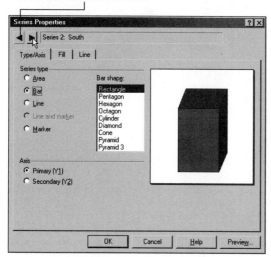

Figure 56-30: Changing the properties of a series.

3. Specify the color, pattern, fill, width, or style attributes, depending on the type of series you selected.

4. For a bar series, select from the available shapes.

5. For a series with markers, select from the available marker shapes, and then specify a marker size from 1 to 15.

6. Select the Y axis to which you want the series to be scaled (see "Changing Y-axes scales, values, and ticks" later in this chapter).

7. Click the arrows at the upper-left to edit a different series.

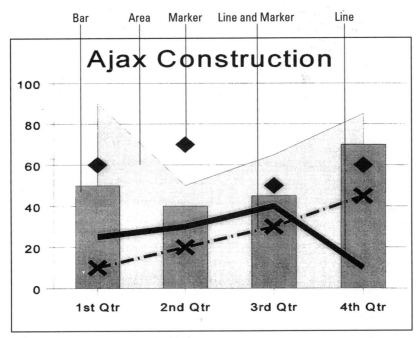

Figure 56-31: Series types on display.

Changing the X-axis label and tick display

To clean up your X-axis display (with fewer labels and other options):

1. Click Chart ⇨ Axis ⇨ X, and then select from the following (see Figure 56-32):

Select	In Order to
Display labels	Display the axis labels.
Show ticks on labels only	Remove the ticks not attached to labels.
Stagger	Display the labels with alternating long and short tick marks (see Figure 56-33).
Skip labels	Specify the number of ticks to skip between labels.

2. Click the Tick Options tab to specify the display of ticks on major and minor vertical grids. (Grids are explained in "Changing the grid display," later in this chapter.)

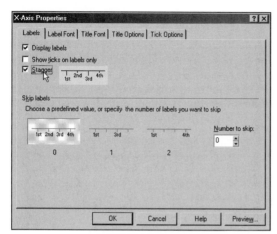

Figure 56-32: Changing the X-axis label and tick display.

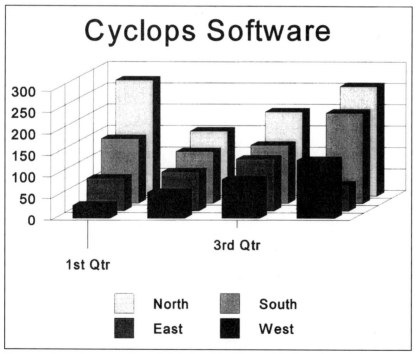

Figure 56-33: Staggered X-axis labels with ticks on labels only and skip of one.

Changing Y-axis ranges, values, and ticks

The Y axes display ranges of values, with ticks, by which the series are measured. For example, the primary Y axis in the chart shown in Figure 56-34 has a range from $0 to $300 million. If you're displaying two different types of series on the same chart, you can use the secondary Y axis on the right to display a second range of values (the market share in this case). The chart legend indicates the Y-series for each item.

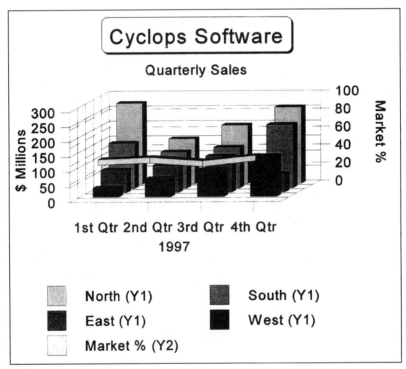

Figure 56-34: Axes ranges, values, and ticks.

To change Y-axis ranges, values, and ticks:

1. Click Chart ⇨ Axis in the Chart Editor, click the Y axis you want to change, and then specify any of the items in Table 56-8 (see Figure 56-35).

2. Click the Tick Options tab to specify the display of ticks on major and minor vertical grids (see "Changing the grid display").

Table 56-8
Y-Axis Range, Value, and Tick Options

Option	Lets You
Minimum value/ Maximum value	Specify the starting and ending values for the range, or check Automatic to let the program calculate the values for you.
Major grid value	Specify the interval between major (usually numbered) grid lines, or check Automatic.
Label scale factor	Divide the range of values by a number, to make the scales easier to read. If the range is from 0 to 50,000, for example, a scale factor of 1,000 changes the range to 0–50. (Tip: Put the "Thousands" in the Y-axis title instead.)
Linear	Displays the scale in uniform increments (such as 20, 40, 60, and so on).
Logarithmic	Displays a logarithmic scale with increments (such as 10, 100, 1,000, and so on).

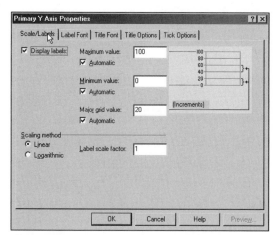

Figure 56-35: Changing Y-axis ranges, values, and ticks.

Changing the grid display

Horizontal grid lines extend the visual scale of the Y axes across the chart. Normally, you do not need vertical grid lines, although they, too, can be specified.

Grid and tick lines are either major or minor. Major lines usually have long ticks with labels. Minor lines usually have short ticks (if any) and no labels. Click the data chart Grids button (or click Chart ➪ Grids in the Chart Editor) to change the style and color of major and minor grid lines (see Figure 56-36). Click the Line Ratio tab to specify the number of major grid lines, and the number of minor grid lines between each pair of major ones.

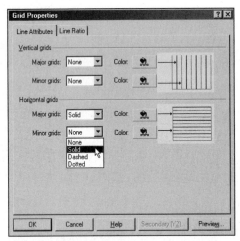

Figure 56-36: Changing the grid display.

When a series is assigned to the secondary Y axis, you can define its grid lines as well. Figure 56-37 shows a chart of quarterly sales, and the same chart after changing the minimum value and displaying minor grid lines.

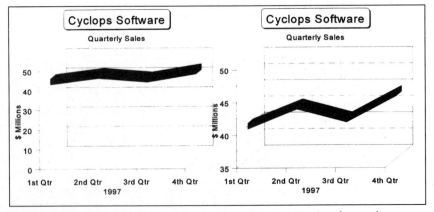

Figure 56-37: Before and after changing the minimum Y-axis value and displaying minor grid lines.

Changing the chart frame display

The chart frame consists of the lines and fills around the various sides of the chart. These are used to aid the eye in gauging the values of the elements within. Figure 56-38 shows the chart of quarterly sales with a frame around all sides, including the top and bottom.

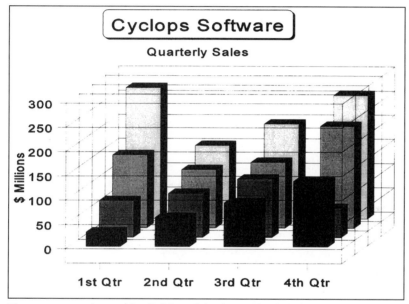

Figure 56-38: Chart with all sides of the frame displayed and a base height of 10.

Tip A frame can interfere with the general picture, so you might want to hit the Preview button before you apply it.

Click Chart ⇨ Frame in the Chart Editor to select the sides of the frame to display, and then specify the line color, fill, and other options.

Customizing the chart's graphics box

When you create a chart, it is placed in a graphics box that can be edited like any other to change its border, fill, size, position, and so on. See Chapter 54, "Adding Graphic Lines, Borders, and Fills," for information on customizing graphics boxes.

Chart Tips and Techniques

This section discusses some special techniques for creating, displaying, and manipulating your charts. You'll also learn how to save a customized style and apply it to other charts.

Creating a pictograph

Ever wonder how newspapers and magazines create those fancy pictographs? It's time to stop wondering and create your own.

To create a pictograph similar to the one shown in Figure 56-39:

1. Create a cluster bar chart, in 2-D.

2. Click Chart ⇨ Layout Type and widen the bars, if necessary.

3. Click Chart ⇨ Series ⇨ Fill, and click the arrows to select the series you want to fill with pictures.

4. Click the data chart Picture Fill button and select a picture from one of the categories (see Figure 56-40), or click Browse to locate another bitmap image.

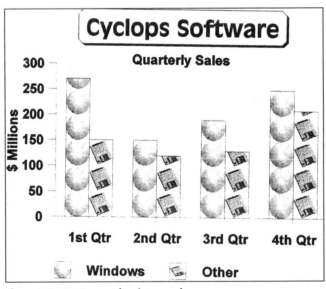

Figure 56-39: A sample pictograph.

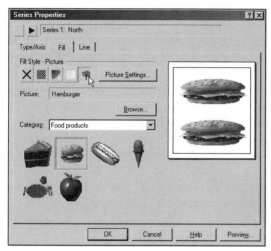

Figure 56-40: Selecting a picture fill.

5. Click Picture Settings to specify how the pictures display on the bar (see Figure 56-41). (The normal display is Stack.) Experiment with the Preview button until you are satisfied with the display.

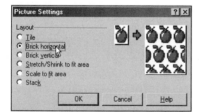

Figure 56-41: Specifying how the picture fill displays.

6. To fill other series, click the arrows and repeat Steps 4 and 5.

7. If you don't want grid lines showing through the bars, click Chart ➪ Grids, and set both horizontal grids to None.

Creating a chart from a WordPerfect table

You can create a chart directly from a WordPerfect table. You can also copy a table's data to the Clipboard and paste it into the Chart Editor.

To create a chart directly from a WordPerfect table, click the table, and then click Insert ⇨ Chart. A default bar chart is created from your table's contents, using the first column and row for the chart's labels and legends. To update your chart, all you have to do is update the table in WordPerfect—you'll only have to return to the Chart Editor if you want to edit the chart's appearance.

To create a chart by copying table information:

1. Select the table cells that you want to chart (including row and column labels, if desired).

2. Click the Copy button on the toolbar, and then click OK.

3. Place the insertion point where you want to create the chart, outside of the table, either in the same or another document.

4. Click (in WP) Insert ⇨ Chart.

5. Click the upper-left corner of the datasheet to select all the cells, and then click Edit ⇨ Paste. (Click Edit ⇨ Paste Transpose if you must reorient the data, as explained in the next section, "Transposing columns and rows.")

6. The sample data in the datasheet is overwritten by the information you copied. (Be sure to delete any remaining sample data.)

Since you have copied the table information into the Chart Editor, you can now edit the chart's data as well as its appearance.

Transposing columns and rows

To transpose rows into columns, or columns into rows, in the datasheet:

1. Select the datasheet columns or rows you want to transpose.

2. Click Cut or Copy from the Edit menu.

3. Select the columns or rows where you want the transposed data to be placed, or click the upper-left cell at the new location. (The transposed data will be placed in the selected cell, as well as in those cells below it or to the right.) Transposed data replaces any existing data.

4. Click Edit ⇨ Paste Transposed.

Sorting chart data

To sort chart data in a datasheet:

1. When creating or editing your chart, select the datasheet column(s), row(s), or cells you want to sort.

2. Click the Sort button, or click Data ⇨ Sort.

3. Select sorting by rows (top to bottom) or columns (left to right) and whether to sort in ascending or descending order (see Figure 56-42).

Figure 56-42: Sorting chart data.

4. Specify the key row or column by which to sort, while keeping the remainder of the cell entries in place.

Tip

To sort the legends by row, specify the Legend column (0) as the sort key. To sort the labels by column, specify the Labels row (0) as the sort key.

Numeric values are sorted first, text values second, and empty cells last.

Excluding columns and rows

You can exclude datasheet rows or columns that you don't want to appear in your chart.

To exclude columns or rows in the datasheet:

1. Select any cells with data in the rows or columns you want to exclude.

2. Click the data chart Exclude Row/Column button (or click Data ➪ Exclude Row/Col), and then click Row(s) or Column(s).

The excluded columns or rows appear dim and don't display on the chart. To restore any or all of the excluded columns or rows, select the cells as before, and click the data chart Include Row/Column button (or click Data ➪ Include Row/Col).

This feature is particularly useful when you want to chart only a portion of an imported spreadsheet.

Saving and applying custom chart styles

To save the layout of a customized chart as a style that you can apply to new charts you create:

1. Click Chart ⇨ Save Style in the Chart Editor.

2. Give your custom style a name (WordPerfect will use the default extension of .CHS), and specify its folder and path.

To apply your custom style to a new chart, click Chart ⇨ Retrieve Style, and select the style.

For More Information . . .

On	See
Creating charts in Quattro Pro	Chapter 36
Creating organization charts	Chapter 41
Creating bulleted lists	Chapter 23
Changing numeric and date formats	Chapter 32
Applying graphic box borders and fills	Chapter 54
Working with custom styles	Chapter 28

✦   ✦   ✦

Customizing Toolbars, Menus, and Keyboards

Thanks to usability tests and an enhanced graphical interface, WordPerfect Office is easier than ever to use. Still, your needs are unique, and you have a particular way of getting things done.

What You Can Customize

You can think of the toolbars, application bar, menus, and keyboards as alternative paths to getting things done. *Toolbars* include two specialized variants, the context-sensitive *property bar* and the informative *application bar*. All three can be customized to activate a feature, run a macro, play keystrokes, or launch a program. You can also customize the WordPerfect application bar (see Chapter 29, "Customizing WordPerfect").

WordPerfect toolbars, menus, and keyboards can also be customized for a particular template. For example, you can create a special toolbar for a specific publishing project, without having it appear among the selections when you create a standard document.

Displaying and Removing Toolbars

By default, WordPerfect, Presentations, and Quattro Pro display one toolbar, plus the property bar and application bar. To display an additional toolbar, right-click the toolbar and select from those available.

Corel-wide toolbars, menus, and keyboards

WordPerfect Office is in transition to the new, Corel-wide toolbars, menus, and keyboards that can be found in Quattro Pro and Paradox. This chapter shows you how to customize the current toolbars, menus, and keyboards in WordPerfect and Presentations. When performing similar operations in Quattro Pro and Paradox (only toolbars can be customized in Paradox), refer to the online Help in those programs.

You'll also notice that if you right-click your application bar in Quattro Pro or Paradox, you can customize its features as with any toolbar, position it at the top or bottom of your screen, and switch between one- and two-line display.

The easiest way to switch, add, or remove toolbars is to click View ⇨ Toolbars, and then check or uncheck the various toolbars (see Figure 57-1).

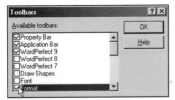

Figure 57-1: Check the toolbars you want to display; uncheck those you want to remove.

To remove a toolbar, you can also right-click the toolbar and remove the check mark.

To remove the property bar or application bar, right-click the bar and click Hide Property Bar or Hide Application Bar. Click View ⇨ Toolbars to restore the property bar, and View ⇨ Application Bar to restore the application bar.

Changing Your Toolbar Display

To change several toolbar display options for WordPerfect or Presentations:

1. Right-click the toolbar, and then click Settings (or click Tools ⇨ Settings ⇨ Customize ⇨ Toolbars).

2. Click Options, and then select any of the options shown in Figure 57-2 and described in Table 57-1.

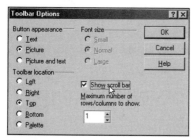

Figure 57-2: Changing your toolbar display.

Table 57-1
Toolbar Display Options

Option	Lets You
Toolbar location	Change the location of the toolbar on the screen (instead of dragging it with the mouse).
Button appearance	Choose whether to display as text only, picture only, or picture and text. (Picture only gives you many more buttons in a row, and you can always point to a button to see its QuickTip text.)
Font size (WP only)	Change the font size if you're displaying text buttons. A larger font results in wider buttons.
Maximum number of rows/ columns to show	Display two or three rows of buttons if they can't all fit on a single row. (Leave this at 1 to preserve screen space, and check "Show scroll bar" instead.)
Show scroll bar (WP only)	Display a scroll bar to the right of a toolbar when there are more buttons than can be displayed.

Quick Toolbar Editing

To quickly edit the toolbars on display:

✦ Hold down the Alt key to drag a button or separator (the bars between groups of buttons) to another location, including another toolbar. Delete buttons by dragging them off the toolbar. (If you mess up a system toolbar and want to restore it to its original state, right-click the toolbar, click Settings, and then highlight that and click Reset.)

✦ Hold Ctrl+Alt and drag to copy a button or separator.

Customizing Toolbars

You can create your own toolbars. You can also modify existing toolbars, including property bars and the Presentations toolbox.

To create a custom toolbar, either from scratch or from a copy of an original:

1. Click Tools ➪ Settings ➪ Customize ➪ Toolbars.

2. Select a toolbar (see Figure 57-3), and then click

   - *Create,* to start a new toolbar from scratch

   - *Edit,* to modify a toolbar, as described in "Editing a toolbar," later in this chapter (only custom toolbars can be edited in Presentations)

   - *Copy,* to create a custom duplicate under a new name

   - *Rename,* to change the name of a custom toolbar (you can't rename a system toolbar)

   - *Reset,* to return to its factory settings a system toolbar you edited (WP only)

   - *Delete,* to remove a custom toolbar (you can't delete a system toolbar)

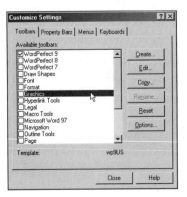

Figure 57-3: Selecting a toolbar to customize.

Because property bars and tool palettes are specific to various program features, you can't change how they're invoked and you can't create a custom one. You can only edit or reset them.

Copying a toolbar in WordPerfect

When copying a toolbar in WordPerfect, you'll be asked to select the template you're copying from and to, as well as the toolbar(s) you want to copy (see Figure 57-4). If you're copying a toolbar within the same template, you'll be asked to give the copy a new name.

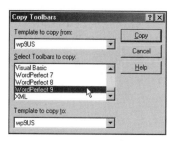

Figure 57-4: Copying a toolbar in WordPerfect.

Tip

To keep the new toolbar near the old one in the toolbar list, make the new name similar to the original name, such as Oldbar2 instead of Oldbar.

See Chapter 28, "Working Quickly with Templates, Projects, and Styles," for more information on using WordPerfect templates.

Editing a toolbar

To edit a toolbar, tool palette, or property bar:

1. Right-click the toolbar or property bar, and then click Edit. (You can also click Settings, pick another toolbar, tool palette, or property bar, and click Edit.)

Tip

To customize a toolbar that takes up more than one row, click Options and set your display to two or three rows, so you can rearrange and edit all the buttons.

2. You're now in the Toolbar or Property Bar Editor (see Figure 57-5), where you can perform any of the following:

   • Click the Features tab to select a feature from any of the categories, and then click Add Button, or drag it directly to the location you want. (Select features from the menus at the top of the screen.)

   • Click the Keystrokes tab, type in the keystrokes you want the button to play, and then click Add Keystrokes. Keyboard scripts are unformatted, although you can use curly brackets for function and formatting keys, such as {Alt+F7}, or {Tab}Sincerely yours,.

Tip

QuickCorrect abbreviations are generally handier than toolbar buttons for inserting unformatted script. Use QuickWords for formatted text (see Chapter 52, "Writers' Lib").

   • Click the Programs tab, click Add Program, select an executable ".EXE," ".COM," ".BAT," or ".PIF" file, and then click Open. (Try adding the Windows calculator, CALC.EXE, which is in your Windows folder.)

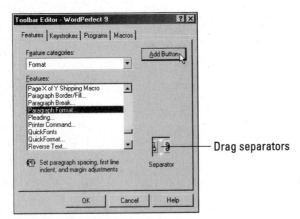

Figure 57-5: Editing a toolbar.

- Click the Macros tab, click Add Macro (or Template Macro), select the macro you want to run, and then click Select.

Note When you add a macro to a toolbar, menu, or keyboard, you'll be asked if you want to save the macro with its full path. If you click Yes, the program first looks in that folder to find the macro. If it doesn't find it there, it then looks in your default macro folder and finally in your supplemental macro folder. If you click No, the program looks only in your default and supplemental macro folders.

3. Move a button by dragging it to a new location. (You can even drag it to another toolbar.)

4. Delete a button by dragging it off the toolbar (or right-click the button and click Delete).

5. Drag a separator to where you want to put a space between two groups of buttons.

Customizing a button's text and QuickTip

You can customize the text that appears on a button and the QuickTip that displays when you point to it:

1. Right-click the toolbar, click Edit, and then double-click the button you want to customize.

2. Type the button text and QuickTip for the button (see Figure 57-6).

With the default picture button display, the button text appears as the first part of the QuickTip.

Figure 57-6: Customizing a button's text and QuickTip.

Editing a button's graphic

To edit the graphics that appear on buttons:

1. Right-click the toolbar, and then click Edit.

2. Double-click the button you want to customize.

3. Click Edit to call up the Image Editor (see Figure 57-7). You can edit the existing image or click Clear to create a new image.

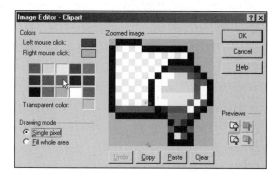

Figure 57-7: Editing a button's graphic.

4. Click the left and right mouse buttons on the palette colors to select the colors you want to apply. The transparent color on the right allows the toolbar background color to show through.

5. Click or drag the left and right mouse buttons in the image area to draw the image one bit at a time, or click "Fill whole area" to change the color of groups of adjacent pixels of the same color.

You can also use the Image Editor to copy images from one button to another, by way of the Windows Clipboard. Copy the first button's image to the Clipboard, use the Image Editor to clear the second button's image, and paste the first button's image onto the second button's.

Customizing Menus

The cascading structure of menus provides access to an unlimited depth of features, without putting everything on display at once. As with toolbars and keyboards, you can assign anything you want to menus (including macros, scripts, and other programs). Presentations won't allow you to edit its original menus, but you can copy and edit them to suit the way you work.

This section describes how to customize menus. You also have various menu display options (Tools ⇨ Settings ⇨ Environment ⇨ Interface in WordPerfect; Tools ⇨ Settings ⇨ Display in Presentations).

You can modify WordPerfect's system menus. You can also create custom menus in WordPerfect or Presentations, either from scratch or from a copy of an original. To modify a system menu or create a custom menu:

1. Click Tools ⇨ Settings ⇨ Customize ⇨ Menus.

2. Select a menu (see Figure 57-8), and then click

   - *Create,* to start a new menu from scratch

   - *Edit,* to modify a menu (only custom menus in Presentations)

   - *Copy,* to create a custom duplicate under a new name

   - *Rename,* to change the name of a custom menu (you can't rename a system menu)

   - *Reset,* to return to its factory settings a system menu you edited (WP only)

   - *Delete,* to remove a custom menu (you can't delete a system menu)

Figure 57-8: Selecting a menu to customize.

Copying a menu bar in WordPerfect

When copying a menu bar (set of menus) in WordPerfect, you'll be asked to select the template you're copying from and to, as well as the menu bar(s) you want to copy (see Figure 57-9). As was the case with toolbars, if you're copying a menu bar within the same template, you'll be asked to give the copy a new name.

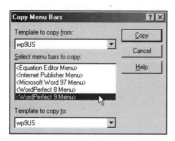

Figure 57-9: Copying a WordPerfect menu bar.

Editing a menu bar

To edit a menu bar:

1. Right-click the menu bar, click Settings, and then pick a menu bar and click Edit.

2. You're now in the Menu Bar Editor (see Figure 57-10), where you can perform any of the following:

   • Click the Features tab to select a feature from any of the categories, and then click Add Menu Item, or drag it directly to the location you want. For example, you might want to add the "Close the document window without saving changes" feature to the File menu.

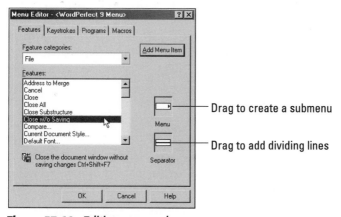

Figure 57-10: Editing a menu bar.

- Click the Keystrokes tab to type the keystrokes you want the button to play, and then click Add Keystrokes. Keyboard scripts are unformatted, although you can use curly brackets for function and formatting keys, such as {Alt+F7}, or {Tab}Sincerely yours,.

- Click the Programs tab, click Add Program, select an executable ".EXE," ".COM," ".BAT," or ".PIF" file, and then click Open.

- Click the Macros tab, click Add Macro (or Template Macro), select the macro you want to run, and then click Select. (See the note on macro paths in "Editing a toolbar," earlier in this chapter.)

3. Drag the item to the menu location you want. Drag items off menus to delete them.

4. Add a cascading submenu by dragging the Menu icon to the location you want.

5. Drag a separator to place a dividing line between groups of menu items.

Editing a menu item's text and QuickTip

You can customize the text that appears on menu items (including the submenu indicators), and the QuickTips that accompany them. To do so:

1. Right-click the menu bar, click Settings, and then click the menu and click Edit.

2. Double-click the menu item, and then type its text and QuickTip, as shown in Figure 57-11. (To edit a submenu item, drag it to the main menu bar before you double-click it.)

Put an ampersand before the shortcut letter

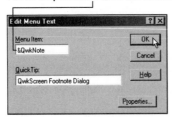

Figure 57-11: Editing a menu item's text and QuickTip.

Tip

Put an ampersand (&) in front of a letter to make it a mnemonic (shortcut) that you can activate with the letter key when the menu is displayed. Just be sure that the letter isn't already used by another item on the menu.

Customizing Keyboard Shortcuts

For all the glamour of the WordPerfect screen, the keyboard is still the most flexible and responsive input device. Keyboards are a great place to incorporate your own favorite shortcuts. You can also create a custom keyboard in Presentations (not to be confused with slide show QuickKey assignments).

Windows keyboards follow the conventional assignments found in other Windows programs. If you're more comfortable with the WordPerfect DOS keyboard, however, there's no need to apologize. Function keys aren't used that much in Windows, and the PgUp and PgDn keys actually work by the page in DOS, not by the screen. You can even create a hybrid DOS-Windows keyboard combining the best of both, using the comparative tables in Chapter 16, "Mastering the WordPerfect Interface." Anyway, it's your keyboard.

You can modify WordPerfect's system keyboards. You can also create custom keyboards in WordPerfect or Presentations, either from scratch or from a copy of an original. To modify a system keyboard or create a custom one:

1. Click Tools ⇨ Settings ⇨ Customize ⇨ Keyboards.

2. Click a keyboard in the list (see Figure 57-12), and then click

   - *Create,* to start a new keyboard from scratch

   - *Edit,* to modify a keyboard (only custom keyboards can be modified in Presentations)

   - *Copy,* to create a custom duplicate under a new name (a wise precaution when modifying the standard keyboards)

Figure 57-12: Selecting a keyboard to customize.

- *Rename,* to change the name of a custom keyboard (you can't rename a system keyboard)
- *Reset,* to return to its factory settings a system keyboard you edited (WP only)
- *Delete,* to remove a custom keyboard (you can't delete a system keyboard)

Copying a keyboard in WordPerfect

When copying a keyboard in WordPerfect, you'll be asked to select the template you're copying from and to, as well as the keyboard(s) you want to copy (see Figure 57-13). If you're copying a keyboard within the same template, you'll be asked to give the copy a new name.

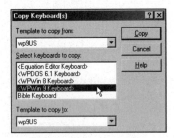

Figure 57-13: Copying a WordPerfect keyboard.

Editing keyboard shortcuts

To edit keyboard shortcuts:

1. Click Tools ➪ Settings ➪ Customize ➪ Keyboards, pick a keyboard, and click Edit.

2. You're now in the Keyboard Shortcuts Editor (see Figure 57-14). Highlight the key you want to change by scrolling the list or pressing the keystrokes, and then do any of the following:

   - Click the Features tab to select a feature from any of the categories, and then click Assign Feature to Key.

   - Click the Keystrokes tab to type the keystrokes you want the shortcut key to play, and then click Assign Keystrokes to Key. Keyboard scripts are unformatted, although you can use curly brackets for function and formatting keys, such as {Alt+F7}, or {Tab}Sincerely yours,.

   - Click the Programs tab, click Assign Program to Key, select an executable ".EXE," ".COM," ".BAT," or ".PIF" file, and then click Open.

   - Click the Macros tab, click Assign Macro (or Template Macro) to Key, select the macro you want to run, and then click Select. (See the note on macro paths in "Editing a toolbar," earlier in this chapter.)

Tip

Instead of assigning a macro to a keystroke, you can name a macro for a Ctrl or Ctrl+Shift keystroke so that you can play it no matter what keyboard you use (see Chapter 58, "Automating with Macros").

3. Click Remove Assignment to remove the assignment from the selected keystroke.

4. To display the keystroke feature on the corresponding menu item, check "Shortcut key appears on menu."

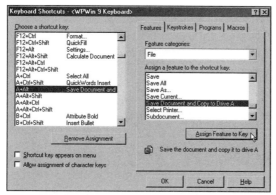

Figure 57-14: Editing keyboard shortcuts.

Caution

You can map plain keys (not in combination with Ctrl, Alt, or Shift) by checking "Allow assignment of character keys." However, if you assign Date Text to the letter "d," for example, you will no longer be able to type the letter "d"! That's __umb.

For More Information . . .

On	See
Customizing WordPerfect's application bar	Chapter 29
Positioning toolbars with the mouse	Chapter 3
Using WordPerfect templates	Chapter 28
Creating QuickWord abbreviations	Chapter 52
Using WordPerfect's shortcut keys	Chapter 16
Creating control key macros	Chapter 58

✦ ✦ ✦

Automating with Macros

Tired of performing the same series of actions over and over? Capture them as a macro file that you can play back at the click of a button or the press of a key. A macro file can contain

✦ A recording of the results of your actions, including keystrokes, mouse selections, and text you typed

✦ Nonrecordable macro *programming commands*, such as those to check your system or present a dialog box with custom selections

This chapter shows you how to record and play back WordPerfect macros, add smarts to your macros with programming commands, and even create custom user dialog boxes. The examples you'll create in this chapter are for WordPerfect, but the PerfectScript commands apply to Presentations and Quattro Pro as well.

Why Macros?

Just as a QuickCorrect abbreviation is handy for words or phrases you regularly type, a macro can make quick work of any repetitive task.

Suppose that you frequently have to create a pointing finger bulleted list, set in from the left margin with a custom indent that puts the bullet and text closer together. Instead of reinventing your custom bullets each time, you can record them once as a macro and then play them back whenever you need such a list.

The macro programming language offers especially powerful custom solutions that can accept user input and respond according to tested conditions. Many of the PerfectExpert projects employ built-in macros.

Note   Check the QwkScreen Web site (http://www.qwkscreen.com) for such great macros as English-Metric conversions, perfectly formatted footnotes and end-notes, and enhanced move, copy, insert, and delete.

Alternatives to macros

Even though it's easier than ever to record a macro, you may now have less occasion to do so because of WordPerfect improvements. For example, it took four clicks to display the ruler in WordPerfect 7, but now two clicks do the trick.

With Spell-As-You-Go, Grammar-As-You-Go, QuickCorrect, Format-As-You-Go, SmartQuotes, and other tools, there's less need for custom macros to do everyday tasks. Formatted text (such as the closing of a letter) is easily handled with QuickWords. PerfectExpert now handles many complicated tasks (such as creating a term paper or résumé).

The power of macros

So, who needs macros? Well, maybe you don't need one now. But, as the examples in this chapter illustrate, when you're looking for a solution to a particular need, macros are a powerful and flexible instrument.

Recording a Macro

So much for the theory. To record a macro:

1. Click the New Blank Document icon to open a blank document (unless you want to record steps you're doing in the current one).

2. Click Tools ⇨ Macro ⇨ Record (or press Ctrl+F10).

3. Type a name for the macro, then click Record (see Figure 58-1). WordPerfect automatically gives your macro an extension of .WCM (it won't play without it). Note that the words "Macro Record" appear in the status bar.

4. Perform the keystrokes and mouse selections you want to record. (The mouse won't work in the document area.)

5. To end the recording, click the Macro toolbar Stop icon (Tools ⇨ Macro ⇨ Record).

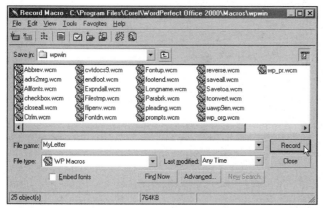

Figure 58-1: Give your macro a name, and then click Record.

Playing a Macro

To play a macro:

1. Click Tools ➪ Macro ➪ Play (Alt+F10).

2. Specify the macro and then click Play.

To pause a macro that's playing, click Tools ➪ Macro ➪ Pause. To cancel a macro that's playing, press Esc.

Creating Some Macro Examples

Following are three macro examples you can record and play.

Custom bullet macro

To create a macro for the custom bulleted list described previously:

1. Open a blank document and click View ➪ Ruler to display the ruler.

2. Make sure QuickBullets is on (Tools ➪ QuickCorrect ➪ Format-As-You-Go ➪ QuickBullets).

3. Click Tools ➪ Macro ➪ Record (Ctrl+F10), give your macro a name (such as "BulletPoint"), and then click Record.

4. Drag the tab markers on the ruler to adjust the first two tabs to your liking (for example, move the marker at 2" to 1.75").

5. Press Tab, click Insert ⇨ Symbol, and select the pointing finger (WP character [5,43] or another bullet). Click Insert & Close, and then press Tab again.

6. Click Macro toolbar Stop icon on the Macro toolbar (Tools ⇨ Macro ⇨ Record) to stop recording and save the macro (see Figure 58-2).

Figure 58-2: Stopping your macro recording.

Tip   By displaying the ruler *before* you start recording, it won't display when you play the macro.

QuickBullets must be on when you play the macro for it to work. You normally leave QuickBullets off? No problem. Turn QuickBullets on when you start recording the macro, and then turn them off just before you stop.

But wait . . . QuickBullets will always be turned *off* by the macro, even when you want them on! Later in this chapter (under "Waving a flag"), you'll see how programming commands can get you out of this dilemma.

Creating a letter opening macro

Suppose you want to create an informal letter opening, with your address and date at the top, followed by "Dear . . .." You might use QuickWords, but a macro has the following three advantages:

✦ It can open a blank document to begin your letter. (You'll add the command later, instead of recording it.)

✦ It can insert the current date, without using a code that changes the date every time you look at it.

✦ It can pause for you to type the recipient's name, and then continue.

To record your letter opening macro:

1. Open a blank document, click Tools ⇨ Macro ⇨ Record, and give your macro a name (such as "MyLetter").

2. Put your name, address, and anything else at the top, with whatever formatting you normally use.

3. Press Enter a couple of times, and then click Insert ⇨ Date/Time ⇨ Insert.

4. Press Enter a couple of times more, type Dear plus a space, and click the Macro toolbar Pause icon (Tools ➪ Macro ➪ Pause) to pause the macro when you play it back.

5. Click the Macro toolbar Pause icon again to remove the pause, type a comma, and press Enter twice.

6. Click Macro toolbar Stop icon on the Macro toolbar to stop recording and save the macro.

Now open a blank document and play your letter macro. Type the recipient's name when the macro pauses, and then press Enter. The result should resemble the opening shown in Figure 58-3.

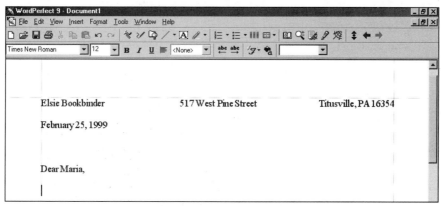

Figure 58-3: You type the name . . . and the letter macro does the rest.

Creating a macro to transpose two paragraphs

Now create a macro to transpose two paragraphs when you press Ctrl+Shift+T:

1. Create some text with a few paragraphs, and place the insertion point in any paragraph other than the first.

2. Click Tools ➪ Macro ➪ Record, and give the macro the precise name of "CtrlsftT."

3. Click Edit ➪ Select ➪ Paragraph.

4. Click @cut (Cut) ➪ Ctrl+@ua (up one paragraph) ➪ @paste (Paste).

5. Click Macro toolbar Stop icon (Tools ➪ Macro ➪ Record) to stop the recording.

Now, every time you press Ctrl+Shift+T, you'll transpose the paragraph at the insertion point with the one above it!

Naming keystroke macros

The macro to transform two paragraphs is an example of a *keystroke macro* in the form of "Ctrl*x*" (Ctrl and a letter) or "Ctrlsft*x*" (Ctrl+Shift and a letter) that plays without being assigned to a keyboard.

Actual keyboard assignments take precedence, so you must name the macros for vacant keystrokes. Look at the tables for control-alpha shortcut keys in Chapter 16, "Mastering the WordPerfect Interface," and you'll see such vacant keys as Ctrl+H (name your macro "Ctrlh") and Ctrl+Shift+E (name your macro "Ctrlsfte").

Using Shortcuts to Play Macros

When you play macros over and over (that's what they're for), you may get tired of typing their names (unless they're Ctrl+key macros). Try either of the following shortcuts instead:

✦ Assign macros to keyboards, menus, and toolbars (see Chapter 57, "Customizing Toolbars, Menus, and Keyboards").

✦ Click Tools ➪ Macro, and then select any of the last nine macros you played from the Macro submenu.

Managing Your Macro Collection

Macros are stored in folders, like any other files. When you install WordPerfect, the program sets up a default macro folder, where it places ready-made macros you install. (There are separate subfolders for WP, QP, and Presentations macros. If you didn't install all the macros, you'll also find shortcuts in the subfolders to macros on your WordPerfect Office CD.)

If you create numerous macros, you should set up a separate folder for them. In that case, be sure to designate the folder as your default or supplemental macro folder (Tools ➪ Settings ➪ Files ➪ Merge/Macro). That way, you'll always be able to play your macros by name alone, without designating the path.

Recording and Playing Template Macros

WordPerfect comes with a ton of macros, but you won't find them in the macro folder. Why? Because they're stored out of the way in various PerfectExpert templates for creating letters, reports, memos, and so on. Template storage is efficient for large complex macros that are used only with that template. You can also package any number of macros in a custom template, and then distribute the template to others, instead of distributing the individual macros.

Recording a template macro

To record a template macro:

1. Open a blank document and click Tools ⇨ Template Macro ⇨ Record.

2. Give the macro a name and click record (see Figure 58-4).

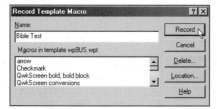

Figure 58-4: Recording a template macro.

3. Follow the steps you want to record. When you are finished, click Macro toolbar Stop icon, or Tools ⇨ Template Macro ⇨ Record.

If the current template differs from the default, you can click Location to select the template you're recording to or playing from. (For more on templates, see Chapter 28, "Working Quickly with Templates, Projects, and Styles.")

Playing a template macro

To play a template macro:

1. Click Tools ⇨ Template Macro ⇨ Play.

2. Select a macro and click Play (see Figure 58-5).

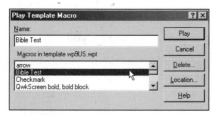

Figure 58-5: Playing a template macro.

You can select recently played template macros from the Template Macro submenu.

Editing or deleting a template macro

To edit or delete a template macro, click Tools ➪ Template Macro ➪ Edit, select the macro, and click Edit or Delete.

Tip When using a PerfectExpert project that employs a template macro, you can copy the macro as a separate macro file that you can browse or experiment with. Bring the macro into the template macro editor (don't change it), click Options ➪ Save As Macro, and save it to your personal macro folder or another location.

Cross-Application Macro Recording

WordPerfect's PerfectScript macro language is used with Presentations and Quattro Pro as well. This means that you can record and program cross-application macros — individually, or as part of a template. For example, you can have a macro describe a table in WordPerfect, switch to Quattro Pro, select and copy spreadsheet data, and then return to WordPerfect and paste it into your document. Because you record the macro yourself, it does precisely what you want.

To record a cross-application macro:

1. Start recording the macro in WordPerfect.

2. Switch among the applications, performing whatever steps you need.

3. When you're finished, return to WordPerfect and stop the recording.

You can play the cross-application macro in the usual manner.

Adding a Macro to the PerfectExpert Projects

You can add a macro (cross-application or not) to the PerfectExpert projects, to make them readily accessible from anywhere in the WordPerfect Office. To add a macro to the PerfectExpert projects:

1. Click the PerfectExpert icon on the Windows taskbar (or click File ➪ New from Project in an application), and select the category to which you want to add your macro.

2. Click Options ➪ Add Project ➪ "I want to add another document" (see Figure 58-6).

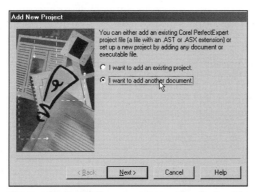

Figure 58-6: Adding a macro to the PerfectExpert projects.

3. Click Next and follow the steps to give your project a name and description, and to specify the macro's location.

Cross-Reference

For more information on using PerfectExpert, see Chapter 5, "How to Get Help."

Playing the Shipped Macros

WordPerfect comes with several ready-made macros you can play, described in Table 58-1. Those not in your default macro folder can be found on the WordPerfect Office CD. Presentations ships with the macros described in Table 58-2.

	Table 58-1
	Macros That Ship with WordPerfect 9

Macro	*What It Does*
Abbrev	Allows you to manipulate multiple abbreviations
Adrs2mrg	Copies the Address Book into a merge data file
Allfonts	Creates a document containing a sample of all your installed fonts, which you can then print
Checkbox	Adds to a document boxes that you can click to check
Closeall	Closes all open documents, prompting you to save changes
Ctrlm	Activates the Macro Command Inserter
Cvtdocs9	Converts a document or entire folder to the WordPerfect format
Endfoot	Converts endnotes into footnotes

Continued

Table 58-1 *(continued)*

Macro	What It Does
Expndall	Expands all QuickWord abbreviations in the current document
Filestmp	Displays the document's filename and path in the header or footer
Flipenv	Creates an envelope rotated 180 degrees
Fontdn	Decreases the font size by 2 points
Fontup	Increases the font size by 2 points
Footend	Converts footnotes into endnotes
Longname	Converts DOS (8.3) filenames to long filenames based on the Description field in the document summary
Parabrk	Inserts graphical breaks between paragraphs
Pleading	Creates lines and numbers for a legal pleading statement
Prompts	Creates and edits the prompts in an automated template
Reverse	Reverses background and foreground colors in selected text or table cells
Saveall	Prompts you to save all open documents
SavetoA	Saves the current document and copies it to drive A
Tconvert	Converts templates created under WP 6.0a/6.1 that used the _Autofil macro
Uawp9en	A "system macro" used by PerfectExpert. Do not edit or delete!
Wp_org	Creates an organization chart in WordPerfect
Wp_pr	Sends a WordPerfect outline to Presentations

Table 58-2
Macros That Ship with Presentations 9

Macro	What It Does
Chngfnt	Changes the font throughout a slide show, with the exception of data and organizational charts, bulleted lists, and any other graphical text objects
Headfoot	Creates a header and/or footer in a slide show
Imgemap	Creates an HTML image map code on a bitmap image
Macedit	Edits a macro in Presentations
Mastconv	Converts older Presentations masters to the current version

Macro	What It Does
Obj2back	Sends selected objects to the background layer
Shw2wpg	Saves each slide in a slide show as a WordPerfect graphic file
Textanim	Converts text to curves and animates each character
Textbttn	Creates a text button

Adding Macro Programming Commands

Previously, you learned how to create macro recordings of your actions, which you can play back again and again. Now you'll learn how to enhance your macros with nonrecordable macro programming commands, using the examples created previously.

Macro programming opens up possibilities way beyond simple macro recording. For example, you can prompt the user for input, evaluate expressions, perform calculations, and make a decision about what happens next in a macro, depending on various input or results.

Understanding macro commands

To get an idea of what macro commands look like, click Tools ➪ Macro ➪ Edit and open the letter-opening macro you created previously (probably MYLETTER.WCM), just as you would open a document (see Figure 58-7).

Your macro will differ, depending on your text and formatting. If you look at line 6 in the example:

```
Type (Text: "Titusville, PA  16354")
```

you'll see that it has

   ✦ A *command name* of "Type," and

   ✦ A *parameter*, in parentheses, of the particular characters to type

The parameter names, such as "Text:," are helpful, but optional. The following also works:

```
Type ("Titusville, PA  16354")
```

Some commands can have multiple parameters:

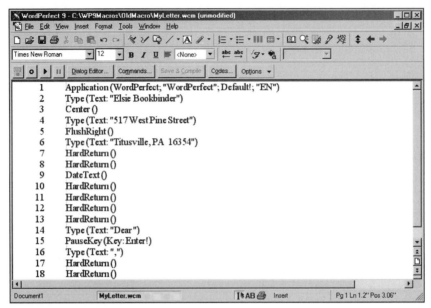

Figure 58-7: Looking at your letter opening macro.

Prompt (Title: string; [Prompt: string]; [Style: enumeration]; [HorizontalPosition: numeric]; [VerticalPosition: numeric])

In such cases, semicolon (;) *separators* are placed between parameters. Parameters in square brackets are optional. An *enumeration* parameter lets you specify two or more options, separated with |, such as "StopSign! | Beep!" for the Prompt parameter.

Sometimes, as with the TabSet parameter in your custom bullet macro, you can have a series of repeating parameters enclosed in braces ({}).

Note   Every PerfectScript macro should start with an Application command, to identify the application and version for which it's written. This command is automatically inserted when you record a macro.

What's in a macro?

A macro contains various types of *statements* (instructions to the computer to perform specific actions) and *expressions* (groups of symbols that represent values), including the following:

✦ *PerfectScript Programming Commands* direct the execution of the macro and can be used with any product. For example, you can use the Label command to identify a location in your macro, then use a Go command in another place to jump to the label.

✦ *Product Commands* are specific to WordPerfect, Quattro Pro, or Presentations (such as a TabSet command in WordPerfect).

✦ *System Variables* can be queried to find out the current state of the environment. For example, ?MarginLeft returns the width of the left margin. Presentations system variables begin with Env, as with EnvBackgroundTitle.

Using the PerfectScript Command Inserter

You can type commands in your macros, just as you do in an ordinary document. Commands are not case-sensitive, but their wording must be precise. That's one of the reasons why QuickCorrect is suspended (in all your open documents) while you're editing a macro.

You can also use the *PerfectScript Command Inserter* to insert or edit commands in their precise syntax. Let's use it to add some macro commands to the letter-heading macro you created earlier:

1. Place the insertion point at the beginning of line 2 of your letter-heading macro.

2. Click "Commands..." on the Macro toolbar, and select the WordPerfect commands from the "Command type" list (see Figure 58-8).

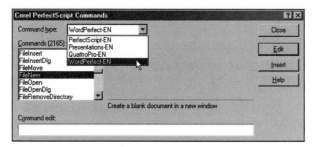

Figure 58-8: Displaying the WordPerfect commands.

3. Type filen to select the FileNew command, click Insert (see Figure 58-9), and then click Close.

4. Click "Save & Compile" to record your changes.

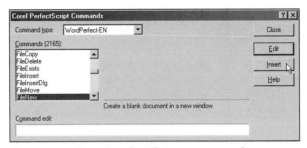

Figure 58-9: Inserting the FileNew command.

The FileNew command has the macro open a blank new document as soon as it starts, so it won't mess up an existing document on the screen. The *compile* part of the "Save & Compile" command is what puts your text commands into a language the machine can understand. (The text and machine code are in the same macro file—you read one part, your computer reads the other.)

When using the Command Inserter, you can right-click on a command in the listing to pop-up a detailed description of the command, including helpful examples.

Executing a command if a condition is met

To get an idea of how clever and flexible macros can be, use the If and EndIf programming commands to execute a command only if the conditional statement's test is true. (Other conditional statements are described in "Testing for conditions," later in this chapter.)

You just added the FileNew command to your MyLetter macro to automatically open a new blank document. But suppose the screen is blank already? To avoid opening another blank screen in that case:

1. Click Tools ➪ Macro ➪ Edit and open your letter-opening macro again.

2. Type the following three lines between lines 1 and 2, so that the new lines 2–4 read as follows (type the number 0 in the first line):

```
2       If (?DocBlank () = 0)
3           FileNew ()
4       EndIf
```

3. Click "Save & Compile" to record your changes.

Tip You can format your macros with tabs, indents, blank lines, and so on, to make them easier to read. Except in very specific instances, the formatting won't affect the execution of the macro.

Now your macro asks "Is it not true that the document is blank?" If it is not blank (0), a new blank document is opened. If it is blank (1), the "If" test is not met, so line 3 is skipped.

You can add to the fun with an If-Else-EndIf command sequence, in which everything between the If and the Else is run if the test is met, and everything between the Else and the EndIf is run if the test is *not* met.

Waving a flag

If your head isn't spinning from the previous example, perhaps you're ready for more. (Again, these are just examples of what macros can do, not systematic programming instructions.)

Returning to the custom bullets macro you created earlier, recall how you can record the macro one way if you normally keep QuickBullets on, and another if you normally keep them off. But you can't have it both ways. Well, you *can* with programming commands:

1. Click Tools ⇨ Macro ⇨ Edit and open your custom bullet macro (see Figure 58-10). Don't be shocked ("Did I write all that?") by lines 2–20. That's one TabSet command—when you change one tab you reset them all.

2. Edit the macro so lines 2–5 read as follows:

```
2       QBFlag:= QuickCorrectQuickBulletsQry ()
3       If(QBFlag = 0)
4             QuickCorrectQuickBulletsSet (State:On!)
5       EndIf
```

3. At the very end of the macro, add these lines:

```
If(QBFlag = 0)
     QuickCorrectQuickBulletsSet (State:Off!)
EndIf
```

Line 2 defines a *flag* (an on/off switch to signal a particular condition or status) "QBFlag." It then sets the flag to the result of the QuickBullets query command ("0" if off; "1" if on). The If-EndIf instructions in lines 3–5 turn on QuickBullets if they are currently off.

This ensures that QuickBullets will always be on while the macro runs. But when the macro gets to the end, how does it know whether QuickBullets was on or off at the start? That's where your flag comes in. The last three lines are identical to lines 3–5, only this time, if QuickBullets was off before you played the macro (QBFlag = 0), the macro turns QuickBullets back off when it's done.

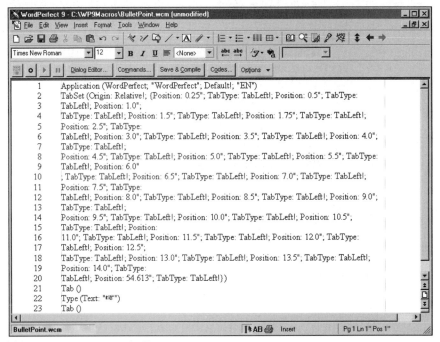

Figure 58-10: Custom bullet macro.

Try out these changes, both with QuickBullets on and off before you play the macro, and see what happens. (Exit the macro editor first; otherwise, QuickBullets will automatically be off.)

Programming on Your Own

As you can see from the examples so far, the PerfectScript macro language lets you extend control and flexibility to your recorded macros to suit your particular needs. This powerful, robust facility lets you create your own WordPerfect environment, complete with menus and dialog boxes.

While no prior programming experience is required to create and edit macros, the remainder of this chapter covers the basic concepts and commands, with examples to get you started.

Sketching out your macro

You may find it helpful to draw a programming *flowchart* using boxes for the macro steps, connected with arrows to indicate the flow. Flowcharts are particularly handy when creating chained and nested macros with many self-contained routines.

Your flowchart will provide a visual template for programming the variables, expressions, conditional statements, and other commands to control the flow of the macro itself.

Using Variables

A *variable* is one of the key tools for performing calculations and controlling the flow of your macro. A variable is nothing more than a place in memory in which to put things, as with the system variables described earlier. When you define a variable you give it a name, and often specify its initial contents, or *value*, which can change during macro execution. This information is used elsewhere in the macro, or even in another macro.

Types of user-defined variables

You can define three types of variables:

- ✦ *Local variables* (the default) that don't hang around after a macro is done
- ✦ *Global variables* that can be passed to other macros named in a Chain or Run command (see "Subroutines and calls," later in this chapter)
- ✦ *Persistent variables* that can be used by any PerfectScript macro or merge any time during the current WordPerfect session

Defining variables

You can define local variables in either of two ways. You can use the Declare command:

```
Declare (VariableName; value)
```

or you can simply use the assignment operator :=, as follows:

```
VariableName := value
```

If the value of a variable is a character expression, you need to enclose the value in quotation marks.

It's good practice to place all your variables at the beginning of your macro. And while not required, it's also a good idea to give them an initial value, even if 0 or blank:

```
MyNumericVar :=0
MyStringVar :=""
```

When defining a global or persistent variable, use Global or Persist in place of Declare.

There's also an Indirect command that creates a variable out of a combination of character strings and numbers: Indirect("var"+x):=x

Using arrays

An *array* is a variable that stores multiple values under one name, like a row of mailboxes:

```
Declare(KidNames[10])
KidNames[4] := "Seth"
```

These statements create an array called KidNames with 10 values, and then assign "Seth" to the fourth element.

You can declare arrays with as many as 10 dimensions (directions):

```
Declare(KidNamesBirthdays[30;2]
KidNamesBirthdays[4;2] := "March 29"
```

These statements create a two-dimensional array with 30 rows and 2 columns named KidNamesBirthdays, and then assign "September 23" to the second column in the fourth row.

Strings and numbers

Variables can contain either of the following:

✦ *Strings*, or sequences of characters or numbers

✦ *Numerical values*, with up to 300 digits with an accuracy of up to 25 decimals

With either a string or number variable, you can

✦ Assign it a value

✦ Display or write its value

✦ Assign its value to another variable of the same type

✦ Check whether it is equal to another text string or number

With a number variable, you can also

✦ Use its value in a mathematical calculation

✦ Compare its value to that of another variable or a number constant

Note that a number in quotes is just another string, so it can't be used in calculations.

Expressions and operators

An *expression* is a statement that uses variables to calculate values or perform comparisons. You can output the results or use them as a basis for further macro decisions.

You can use logical operators or functions (such as AND or OR) and mathematical operators (such as < and =) to build your expressions. Logical expressions are expressions, mathematical or otherwise, that can be evaluated as true or false. Table 58-3 describes various operators and their order of precedence.

Table 58-3	
PerfectScript Operators and Their Order of Precedence	
Order of Precedence	*Operators*
1	(), - (unary minus), + (unary plus), ~ (bitwise not), NOT (logical not)
2	* (multiply), / (divide), % (mod), DIV (integer divide), ** (raise number to power)
3	+ (add), - (subtract)
4	<< (shift bits left), > (shift bits right)
5	< (less than), <= (less than or equal to), > (greater than), >= (greater than or equal to), <> or ! (not equal), = (equal)
6	& (bitwise and), | (bitwise or), ^ (bitwise xor)
7	AND (logical and), XOR (logical xor)
8	OR (logical or)

Cross-Reference More details on operators and their order of precedence can be found in Chapter 32, "Entering Data and Formulas."

Numeric expressions can also employ the following units of measure:

Unit of Measure	Measurement Type
"	Inches
i	Inches
c	Centimeters
m	Millimeters
p	Points (72 per inch)
w	WP unit (1,200 per inch)

Using snips of a string

To use only part of a character string in an expression (such as just the area code for a phone number), use the SubStr command:

```
SubStr (String: string; Beginning: numeric; [NumberOfChars:
numeric])
```

String is the name of the variable; Beginning is the first character you're selecting; and NumberOf Chars is how many characters you want. Thus:

```
AreaCode := SubStr (PhoneNumber;2;3)
```

creates a new string variable, AreaCode, from characters 2–4 of the PhoneNumber string.

Subroutines and calls

To simplify and shorten complex macros, create subroutines (reusable segments of code) out of any repetitive instructions. Much of the art of programming goes into creating a logical arrangement of such bite-sized routines. Your macro will be easier to code, and much easier to maintain. Subroutines come in three flavors:

✦ *Labels* have one parameter, which is the name of the subroutine. The Label command is followed by one or more statements, followed by Return or Quit. (Labels don't have to be called for their subroutines to execute.)

✦ *Functions* must be called to execute and return a value. The calling statement passes any parameters required by the function. They begin with the word FUNCTION and end with ENDFUNC, and can be placed anywhere in a macro, or in another macro that serves as a *macro library* file.

✦ *Procedures* begin with the word PROCEDURE and end with ENDPROC. They are similar to functions, but they cannot return a value.

Subroutines play when they're *called* by the following statements:

Calling Statement	What It Does
Go (label)	Unconditionally jumps to the Label it names. Macro execution does not return when the subroutine is done.
Call (label)	Executes the subroutine whose name is label. When Return is encountered, execution resumes with the statement immediately after the call.
Call FuncOrProc({<Parameter>})	Executes a function or procedure, passing any necessary parameters, and then resumes with the next statement when the called subroutine is done.
Subroutine Name({<Parameter>})	Executes a named function or procedure, without the Call statement.

Custom functions and procedures you put in a macro library can be used in any of your macros. Include a Use statement in the calling macro to identify the path and name of your macro library:

```
Use ("C:\...\Library.wcm")
```

Execute a nested macro with the Run command, passing any parameters, if necessary:

```
Run (MacroFile: string; {[Parameter: any]})
```

Control returns after the nested macro is done, unless the nested macro ends with Quit.

The Chain command is similar to Run, except the called macro is not executed until the calling macro is done.

Controlling the flow of your macro

A statement to call a subroutine is one example of a macro control statement, which alters the sequential play of macro commands. Two other types of control statements are conditional statements and loop statements.

Testing for conditions

A conditional statement is a fork in the road of macro execution. A conditional statement can perform a test and then send the macro in one direction if the condition tests true, or in another if it tests false. (See "Executing a command if a condition is met," earlier in this chapter.) It can also test the contents of a variable and then head in various directions depending on what it finds. You can use four sets of conditional statements:

Conditional Statement	What It Does
If (<Test> boolean)	Performs a test using Boolean algebra in which every statement is either true (1) or false (0). Executes the statements between If and Endif when the test result is true. When optional Else is included, executes statements between If and Else when the test result is true; executes the statements between Else and Endif when the test result is false.
Case (<Test> any; {<Case> any; <Label> label}; [<DefaultLabel> label])	Compares <Test> to a set of <Cases> (values). If the first match is true, the Label following <Case> is called. If the comparison is false, the next <Case> is evaluated, and so forth. If no comparison is true, DefaultLabel is called.
Case Call (<Test> any; {<Case> any; <Label> label}; [<DefaultLabel> label])	Similar to Case, with execution continuing with the statement that follows Case Call when Return is encountered.
Switch (<Test> any {<CaseOF> any; statements}; [<Default> statements)	Tests for matching expressions, executing statements when a match is found. If no test is met, optional Default statements are executed.

Using Loop Statements

Loop statements execute statements a specified number of times until an expression is true, or as long as an expression is true (see Table 58-4).

Table 58-4 Loop Statements		
Statement	What It Does	Example
For (<ControlVariable> variable; <InitialValue> any; <TerminateExp> boolean; <IncrementExp> any)	Executes statements until the terminate value is reached, incrementing the initial value by the specified amount with each execution.	`For (x; 1; x < 5; x + 1)` `    Statements...` `EndFor` Initializes x to 1, and then executes the statements while x is less than 5, incrementing by 1 with each execution.

Statement	What It Does	Example
For Repeat	Repeats execution until the expression at the bottom of the loop is true.	```
Repeat
     Statements...
x := x + 1
Until (x >= 5)
```
Repeats the statements until x is equal to or greater than 5. (The x must change to make the expression true or the loop will never end.) |
| **While** | Repeats execution as long as the expression is true. | ```
While (x <= 5)
     Statements...
x := x + 1
EndWhile
```
Repeats the statements as long as x is less than or equal to 5. |

Variations of For are ForEach, which executes a number of times equal to the number of specified expressions; and ForNext, which executes a specified number of times.

Note that Repeat statements always execute at least once, because the test is at the bottom of the loop. The While statement tests the condition at the beginning, so it never has to execute.

Communicating with the user

PerfectScript provides several commands to communicate with the user, both to display information and to receive input (see Table 58-5).

Table 58-5
PerfectScript Commands to Communicate with the User

Command	What It Does	Example
Beep ([BeepType: enumeration])	Sounds a beep, either the default sound or another type from the Windows Control Panel.	Beep(Question!)

Continued

Table 58-5 *(continued)*

Command	What It Does	Example
Prompt *(Title: string; [Prompt: string]; [Style: enumeration]; [HorizontalPosition: numeric]; [VerticalPosition: numeric])*	*Displays a message box with an OK button to dismiss the prompt, and a Cancel button to remove the prompt and create a Cancel condition (see Figure 58-11). Normally followed by Pause, so it waits for user input. If not, the prompt displays until the macro ends or an EndPrompt is encountered.*	*Prompt (Title:"Do You Want to Procede?"; Prompt:"Click OK to procede or Cancel to terrminate" Style:WarningIcon!) Pause ()*
GetNumber *(VariableName: variable; [Prompt: string];)*	Prompts the user to enter a number (see Figure 58-12).	GetNumber(MyNum; "Enter a number from 1 to 10"; [Title: string] " Take a Guess!")
GetUnits (VariableName: variable; [Prompt: string]; [Title: string])	Prompts for the user for a number and the default units of measure (normally WP units).	DEFAULTUNITS(Inches!) GETUNITS(vUnit; "Enter units to advance down"; "GETUNITS Example") ADVANCE (AdvanceDown!; vUnit)
Menu (<MenuPick> variable; <MnemonicType> enumeration; [<HorizontalPosition> numeric]; [<VerticalPosition> numeric]; <MenuChoice> {string})	Displays a menu of options for a calling statement (see Figure 58-13). The Mnemonic Type is Digits! for numbers, or Letters! for alpha characters.	Menu (MyVar; Letter!;;; {"Apples"; "Oranges"; "Bananas"; "Quit"})

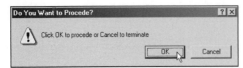

Figure 58-11: Prompting the user.

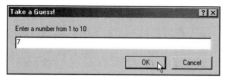

Figure 58-12: Prompting for a number.

 Figure 58-13: Displaying a menu of options.

 Note that the "Getnumber" example can be written as follows: GetNumber (VariableName: MyNum; Prompt: "Enter a number from 1 to 10"; Title: "Take a Guess!"). The inclusion of parameter names is optional when writing command statements, but they do make the commands easier to understand.

Creating your own dialog boxes

To add a professional-looking interface to your macros, create your own dialog boxes with multiple options for user input to several variables at once. The task may appear daunting at first, but after copying some examples and doing a little experimentation, you may find that they're a lot of fun to create. Dialog boxes can be either of the following:

✦ *Modal* (the default), which require a user action, such as clicking OK or Cancel before control is returned to the application

✦ *Modeless*, which lets the user input to the application without taking a dialog box action (such as Find and Replace Text in WordPerfect). They can also verify user input or even call up another dialog box (such as Help) while the dialog box remains on the screen.

When employing a modeless dialog box in a WP macro, add the following two lines to the beginning of your macro to ensure that you can write to the screen:

```
InhibitInput(Off!)
Display(On!)
```

Using dialog boxes in macros involves several statements in which you

✦ Define the dialog box.

✦ Define the dialog box controls.

✦ Display and dismiss the dialog box.

Defining a dialog box

You define a dialog with the DialogDefine command:

DialogDefine (Dialog: string; Left: numeric; Top: numeric; Width: numeric; Height: numeric; Style: enumeration; Caption: string)

The parameters are straightforward:

✦ *Dialog* is a name (up to 25 characters) or a number (larger than 10) that identifies the dialog box.

✦ *Left/Top* is the number of dialog units (see "Width/Height" below) from the left side/top of the screen to the left side/top of the dialog box. When using the Percent! Style parameter, the number is a percentage of the screen width/height minus the width/height of the dialog box.

✦ *Width/Height* is the width or height of the dialog box in dialog units that allow the dialog to display on different screens and at different resolutions. A vertical unit equals 1/8 of the font height, and a horizontal unit equals 1/4 of the font width.

✦ *Style* is any of the styles described in Table 58-6. Type | between enumerations (not all combinations are possible.)

✦ *Caption* is the text displayed in the title bar.

	Table 58-6 Dialog Box Styles
Style	**What It Does**
OK!	Creates an OK button.
Cancel!	Creates a Cancel button.
Percent!	Sets Top and Left parameters to a percentage of the screen width or height minus the width or height of the dialog box. (When you use Percent!, set the Top and Left parameters to 50 to display the dialog box in the center of the screen.)
NoFrame!	Creates a dialog box without a frame. (No effect in Windows 95.)
Sizeable!	Allows resizing of the dialog box.
NoTitle!	Removes the title (caption) bar.
Modeless!	Allows input to the application without taking action in the dialog box or closing it (as with the Find and Replace dialog box in WordPerfect). The Corel WordPerfect command InhibitInput must be Off!. Unless otherwise specified, a dialog box will be modal.
Enter2HRtn!	Lets the user press Enter in a multiline edit control to move the insertion point to the next line.
NoCloseBox!	Keeps the dialog box open.

Adding controls

The real fun in creating a dialog box is in adding controls — the input or output windows through which the user interacts with the parent application. You can add a whole slew of controls, as described in Table 58-7. For further details and examples, right-click the commands in the PerfectScript Command Inserter.

Table 58-7
Macro Dialog Box Controls

Control Command	What It Does
DialogAddBitmap	Displays a bitmap. Doesn't accept input unless used in a callback (described in "Displaying a dialog box," later in this chapter) with Hot Spot (DialogAddHotSpot).
DialogAddCheckBox	Lets the user check off options.
DialogAddColorWheel	Lets the user select a color.
DialogAddComboBox	Displays an edit box and a list box, so the user can either type text or double-click a list item.
DialogAddControl	Adds a custom control to a dialog box.
DialogAddCounter	Displays an edit box and a counter button, so the user can either type a number or click the counter.
DialogAddDate	Displays the current date or another defined date. (Doesn't accept input.)
DialogAddEditBox	Displays a single or multiline edit box for text input.
DialogAddFileNameBox	Displays an edit box and a button, so the user can either type a filename or click the button to select a file.
DialogAddFrame	Visually groups items in the dialog box.
DialogAddGroupBox	Groups items in the dialog box with a titled frame.
DialogAddHLine	Visually separates sections of the dialog box.
DialogAddHotSpot	Adds an invisible control to close the dialog box when the user clicks a defined area, such as a graphic or icon.
DialogAddIcon	Displays an icon. (Doesn't accept input unless associated with a Hot Spot.)
DialogAddListBox	Displays a list of options to choose from.
DialogAddListItem	Adds an item to a List control or combo box.
DialogAddProgress	Displays a progress indicator.
DialogAddPushButton	Displays a push button the user can activate.

Continued

Table 58-7 *(continued)*	
Control Command	**What It Does**
DialogAddRadioButton	Lets the user select one of the available responses in a callback.
DialogAddScrollBar	Adds a vertical or horizontal scroll bar.
DialogAddText	Adds descriptive text to the dialog box. (Doesn't accept input).
DialogAddViewer	Lets the user view a text file.
DialogAddVLine	Visually separates sections of the dialog box.

Take a look at one of the control commands:

```
DialogAddPushButton (Dialog: string; Control: string; [Left:
numeric]; [Top: numeric]; [Width: numeric]; [Height: numeric];
[Style: enumeration]; ButtonText: string)
```

You'll notice that the Dialog Control statement is similar to the Dialog Define command.

✦ *Dialog* is the name of the dialog (in DialogDefine) to which you're adding the control.

✦ *Control* is the name or number that identifies the control.

✦ *Left/Top* is the number of dialog units from the left side/top of the dialog to the left side/top of the control.

✦ Width/Height is the width/height of the control in dialog units.

✦ *Style* is the style of the push button (see Table 58-8) or other control.

✦ *ButtonText* is the text displayed on the push button.

Table 58-8 Push Button Control Styles	
Style	**What It Does**
NonDefaultBttn!	Creates a push button.
DefaultBttn!	Creates a default push button, with a heavy black border, that dismisses the dialog box. Press Enter to choose the default button. If the Enter2HRtn! style is specified in DialogDefine, pressing Enter in a multiline edit control produces a hard return rather than the default button action.
OKBttn!	Creates an OK button.

Style	What It Does
CancelBttn!	Creates a Cancel button.
HelpBttn!	Creates a Help button.

When a push button or QuickSpot is activated, the Control parameter value of the button or QuickSpot is returned in the implicit variable MacroDialogResult. Other controls return the following Control parameter values: 1 for OK, 2 for Cancel, 2 for Close (system menu box), 2 if you press Alt+F4 or Esc.

Displaying a dialog box

Display a dialog box with the DialogShow command:

```
DialogShow (Dialog: string; [Parent: string]; [Callback:
label]; [Focus: string]
```

✦ Dialog is the name of the dialog box you're displaying.

✦ Parent (normally optional) is the name of the parent window, such as "WordPerfect."

✦ Callback identifies a callback function (see below).

✦ Focus specifies the control initially selected (the control name or 1 for the OK button; 2 for the Cancel button).

A *callback function* permits modeless operation in which the user can input to the application while it's on display (without dismissing the dialog box and resuming macro execution). For example:

```
DialogShow ("Dialog1"; "PerfectScript"; CallMe)
DialogDismiss ("Dialog1"; "OKBttn")
DialogDestroy ("Dialog1")
Quit
Label (CallMe)
...other statements...
```

Return displays the dialog box, continuously executes the "CallMe" callback instructions, dismisses (hides) the dialog box, and then destroys it.

The Return command at the end ensures that no instructions outside of the callback execute as the dialog box is displayed.

Dismissing a dialog box

Dismiss (hide) a dialog box with the following command:

DialogDismiss (Dialog: *string*; Control: *string*)

For example:

```
DialogDismiss ("1000"; "OKBttn")
```

dismisses dialog box 1000, and clears the value of the implicit variable MacroDialogResult.

Tip If you need to keep the MacroDialogResult value for later use in your macro, assign it to another variable before executing DialogDismiss.

Remove a dialog box without a callback with DialogDestroy. For example:

DialogDestroy ("1000")

dismisses dialog box 1000, and clears the value of the implicit variable MacroDialogResult.

You should destroy all dialog boxes when the macro ends, to avoid possible memory conflicts.

Using the Macro Dialog Editor

The easiest way to create a dialog box is usually to modify a copy from another macro. However, if you're creating a dialog box from scratch, you should know about the visual palette provided by the built-in Macro Dialog Editor:

1. Open a blank document, press Ctrl+F10, give the macro a name, such as "DialogTest," and then click Record.

2. Type //, click @mcrstp, and then close the document without saving it.

3. Click Tools ➪ Macro ➪ Edit, select DialogTest, and click Edit.

4. Click Dialog Editor to display the blank listing of PerfectScript dialog boxes stored with the macro (see Figure 58-14).

5. Click File ➪ New from the dialog box menu, and type the name of the dialog box you're creating, such as "Dialog1."

6. Double-click the dialog box name to open the Dialog Editor work area and palette.

7. To line up dialog box controls, you can click the Dialog Editor Grid Display icon to display the grid, and then click the Dialog Editor Snap to Grid icon to turn on Snap to Grid. (Click View ➪ Grid Options to change the size of the intervals.)

8. Click the various control buttons in the middle row of the palette, and then click the work area and drag the controls to position them (see Figure 58-15).

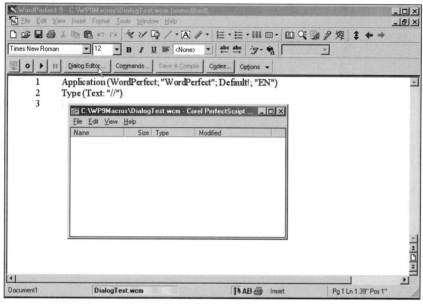

Figure 58-14: Blank PerfectScript dialog box listing for your macro.

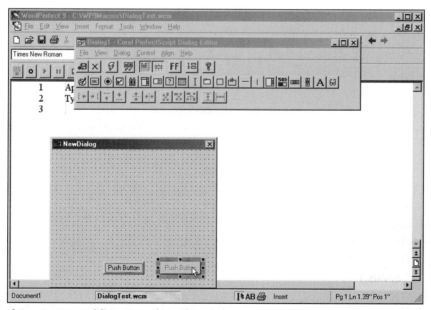

Figure 58-15: Adding controls to the work area.

9. Drag the edges of the work area to adjust the size of the dialog box. Double-click the background to specify the caption for the title bar and other properties.

10. Drag the handles of a selected control to change its size. Double-click a control to specify its properties, such as items for a list box or the type of push button (see Figure 58-16).

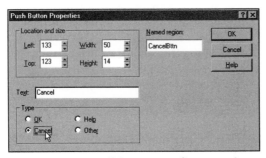

Figure 58-16: Specifying a control's properties.

11. Once the dialog box is designed to your satisfaction, click File ⇨ Save from the Dialog Editor menu to save the dialog box, and then click File ⇨ Close to close the Dialog Editor.

12. The dialog box code is now saved with the macro you created it in and can be called by name.

13. If you want to use and edit the raw dialog box code in another macro, select the dialog box from the listing, click Edit ⇨ Copy to copy it to the Windows Clipboard, and then click Edit ⇨ Paste to paste it in the other macro.

See online PerfectScript Help for more information on using the Dialog Editor, including how to create, copy, edit, and test dialog boxes, and how to link dialog boxes to macros.

Formatting and commenting your macros

Note how you can format and comment your macros to make them easier for you and others to read and maintain. Type // anywhere in a line and everything to the right will be treated as a comment.

Testing and debugging macros

When you save changes to your macro code, the compiler stops at any syntax error and displays its best guess as to the error and its location (see Figure 58-17). Click Cancel Compilation and correct the error, or click Continue Compilation to test for other errors. Only an error-free macro can compile.

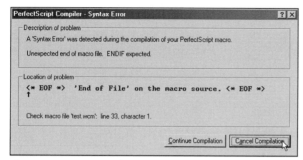

Figure 58-17: Compiler error message.

Converting Macros

Macros created in WordPerfect 6, 7, and 8 don't have to be converted to run in WordPerfect 9, although some complex statements, such as DLLCall, may have to be changed (see online Help). To optimize their performance in WordPerfect 9, however, it helps to recompile them by making a minor editing change (even to add and remove a space) and then saving your change. You may also find that dialog box sizing needs adjusting.

Note Many WP 5.1 for DOS keystroke-based macros can be converted to work with later versions of WordPerfect for Windows. You can download a macro converter from Corel at `ftp://ftp.corel.com/pub/Suites/coreloffice/mc5x6x.zip`.

More Macros You Can Create

It's time to put this dialog box theory to practical use by creating a character-selection dialog box, and an all-in-one macro to repeat a selected block, a line of text, or a table row.

Character-selection dialog box

In this exercise, you'll create the Currency Symbol macro displayed in Figure 58-18, which makes it easy to select from any of the currency symbols in your WordPerfect documents.

Figure 58-18: Creating a handy Currency Symbol macro.

To create the Currency Symbol macro:

1. Open a blank document, press Ctrl+F10, give the macro a name of "Currency," and then click Record.

2. Type //, click Macro toolbar Stop icon, and then close the document without saving it.

3. Click Tools ⇨ Macro ⇨ Edit, select Currency and click Edit, and then create the following code as it appears partially in Figure 58-19 (don't type the line numbers):

```
 1  Application (WordPerfect; "WordPerfect"; Default!; "EN")
 2  //Currency.wcm
 3  //Description: Menu to select currency symbols.
 4
 5  If(Exists(CurrencySymbol)=0)
 6       Persist(CurrencySymbol)
 7       CurrencySymbol:="Cent"
 8  Endif
 9
10  DialogDefine(100; 50; 50; 120; 105; OK!|Cancel!;
    "Insert Currency Symbol")
11  DialogAddListBox(100; 1000; 13; 10; 91; 75; 0;
    CurrencySymbol)
12  DialogAddListItem(100;1000; "Cent")
13  DialogAddListItem(100;1000; "Pound/Sterling")
14  DialogAddListItem(100;1000; "Yen")
15  DialogAddListItem(100;1000; "Pesetas")
16  DialogAddListItem(100;1000; "Francs")
17  DialogAddListItem(100;1000; "Florin/Guilder")
18  DialogAddListItem(100;1000; "Cruzado")
19  DialogAddListItem(100;1000; "Lire (Italian)")
20  DialogAddListItem(100;1000; "Won (Korean)")
21  DialogAddListItem(100;1000; "Naira (Nigerian)")
22  DialogAddListItem(100;1000; "Rupee (India)")
23  DialogAddListItem(100;1000; "Euro")
24  DialogAddListItem(100;1000; "General Currency")
25
26  DialogShow(100;1000)
27  Button:=MacroDialogResult
28  DialogDestroy(100)
```

```
29
30  If(Button=2)
31       Go(End)
32  Endif
33
34  Switch(CurrencySymbol)
35  CaseOf "Cent": TypeChar(4; 19)
36  CaseOf "Pound/Sterling": TypeChar(4; 11)
37  CaseOf "Yen": TypeChar(4; 12)
38  CaseOf "Pesetas": TypeChar(4; 13)
39  CaseOf "Francs": TypeChar(4; 58)
40  CaseOf "Florin/Guilder": TypeChar(4; 14)
41  CaseOf "Cruzado": TypeChar(4; 59)
42  CaseOf "Lire (Italian)": TypeChar(4; 61)
43  CaseOf "Won (Korean)": TypeChar(4; 86)
44  CaseOf "Naira (Nigerian)": TypeChar(4; 87)
45  CaseOf "Rupee (India)": TypeChar(4; 88)
46  CaseOf "Euro": TypeChar(4; 72)
47  CaseOf "General Currency": TypeChar(4; 24)
48  EndSwitch
49
50  Label(End)
```

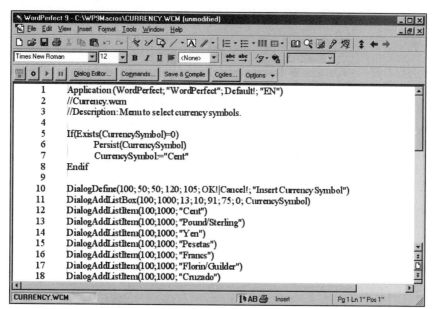

Figure 58-19: Creating the Currency Symbol macro.

 Tip This may seem like a lot of coding, but don't forget that you can cut, copy, and paste in a macro just like in any other document!

Here's how the macro works:

✦ Lines 5–8 create a persistent variable CurrencySymbol for the last symbol you used, so that symbol is displayed the next time you run the macro during the current session. If CurrencySymbol doesn't already exist, it's created and initialized to "Cent."

✦ Lines 10–24 define the dialog box, the list box, and the list items for the various symbols.

✦ Lines 26–28 display the dialog box for the user to make a selection, save the MacroDialogResult to a Button variable, and then dismiss the dialog box.

✦ Lines 30–32 direct execution to the end of the macro if the user cancels or dismisses the dialog box.

✦ Lines 34–48 test the CurrencySymbol for a number of Switch conditions, and type out the appropriate symbol.

Note The Currency Symbol macro, and all the other macros in this chapter, can be downloaded from the QwkScreen Web site at `http://www.qwkscreen.com`.

Repeating a block, line, column, or row

Ready for another way to extend the power of WordPerfect? Try out this all-in-one macro to repeat a selected block, a line of text, or a table row. When you're in a table, you can either insert blank rows or repeat the current row a specified number of times (see Figure 58-20). You can then assign this or any other macro to a convenient toolbar button or keystroke, such as Ctrl+R (see Chapter 59).

Figure 58-20: Using your all-in-one Repeat macro in a table.

To create the all-in-one Repeat macro:

1. Open a blank document, press Ctrl+F10, give the macro a name of "Repeat," and then click Record.

2. Type //, click Macro toolbar Stop icon, and then close the document without saving it.

3. Click Tools ➪ Macro ➪ Edit, select Repeat, click Edit, and then create the following code (don't type the line numbers):

```
1 Application (WordPerfect; "WordPerfect"; Default!; "EN")
2 //Repeat.wcm
3 //Description: repeat block, line, or row
```

```
 4
 5  OnCancel (End)
 6
 7  InsertB:=1
 8  InsertA:=0
 9  Repeater:=1
10
11  If (?BlockActive)
12      EditCopy ()
13      SelectMode(Off!)
14      EditPaste()
15      Go (End)
16  EndIf
17
18  If (?Row>0)
19      Go (Table)
20  Else
21      PosScreenLeft ()
22      If (?RightCode=135)        // If dormant HRt
23          PosCharNext
24      EndIf
25      SelectMode (On!)
26      PosScreenRight
27      PosCharNext
28      If (?RightChar=" ")
29          PosCharNext
30      Endif
31      CopyAndPaste
32      MoveModeEnd
33      Go (End)
34  Endif
35
36  Label (Table)
37  DialogDefine(100; 50; 50; 188; 70; Cancel!;
    "Insert or Repeat Table Row")
38  DialogAddText(100; 1000; 13; 10; 190; 13; 0;
    "Insert blank row or repeat current row:")
39  DialogAddRadioButton(100; 1001; 145; 9; 35; 12;
    "&Before"; InsertB)
40  DialogAddRadioButton(100; 1002; 145; 20; 35; 12;
    "&After"; InsertA)
41  DialogAddText(100; 1003; 13; 31; 30; 13; 0;
    "Row(s):")
42  DialogAddCounter(100; 1004; 43; 28; 27; 15; 0;
    Repeater; 1; 20; 1 )
43  DialogAddPushbutton(100; 1005; 65; 51; 32; 13;
    1; "&Insert")
44  DialogAddPushbutton(100; 1006; 103; 51; 32; 13;
    0; "&Repeat")
45
46  DialogShow (100;1005)
47  Button:=MacroDialogResult
48  DialogDestroy(100)
49
```

```
50  Switch (Button)
51  Caseof "1005":
52      If (InsertB=1)
53          TableInsertRow(Repeater; Before!)
54      Else
55          TableInsertRow(Repeater; After!)
56      Endif
57  Caseof "1006":
58      ForNext (Xrows; Repeater; 1; -1)
59          TableEdit
60          TableCopy(Row!)
61          TableMoveModeEnd
62      EndFor
63  Endswitch
64  Label (End)
```

Here's how the macro works:

✦ Line 5 allows for a graceful exit when there's a cancel condition.

✦ Lines 7–9 define and initialize the local variables used in the macro.

✦ Lines 11–16 check if you've selected a block. If so, the macro repeats the block and goes to the end of the macro.

✦ Lines 18–34 send you to the Table subroutine if you're in a table. If not, they select and repeat the current line of text. They account for certain characters and codes to make a neater job of it.

✦ Lines 37–44 define the table row dialog box, including descriptive text and various types of controls. The InsertB variable equal to one selects the Before radio button. The ampersands (&) before the descriptive names define underlined hot keys.

✦ Lines 46–48 display the dialog box, with default focus on the Insert button; save the MacroDialogResult to a Button variable; and then dismiss the dialog box.

✦ Lines 50–63 check your dialog box selections, and then insert the Repeater number of rows before or after the current row, or repeat the current row the Repeater number of times.

Macros to delete extra spaces and hard returns

For this exercise, you'll create macros to delete those pesky leading spaces and extra hard returns you often get when you copy and paste from Web documents or e-mail to WordPerfect. Then you'll create a third macro that executes the first two, to accomplish both tasks at once.

Deleting leading spaces

To create a macro to delete leading spaces:

1. Open a blank document, press Ctrl+F10, give the macro a name of "DelSpace," and then click Record.

2. Type //, click Macro toolbar Stop icon, and then close the document without saving it.

3. Click Tools ⇨ Macro ⇨ Edit, select DelSpace and click Edit, and then create the following code (don't type the line numbers):

```
Application (WordPerfect; "WordPerfect"; Default!; "EN")
//DelSpace.wcm: Delete spaces when pasting from e-mail to WP

OnError (End)
OnNotFound (End)

PosDocTop ()

Label (Top)
SearchString (" ") //Type a single space between the quotes.
MatchPositionAfter ()
SearchNext ()
While (?RightChar = " ") //Type a single space between the
quotes.
        DeleteCharNext ()
EndWhile
Go (Top)

Label (End)
```

Deleting extra hard returns

To create a macro to delete extra hard returns:

1. Open a blank document, press Ctrl+F10, give the macro a name of "DelHR," and then click Record.

2. Type //, click Macro toolbar Stop icon, and then close the document without saving it.

3. Click Tools ⇨ Macro ⇨ Edit, select DelHR and click Edit, and then create the following code (don't type the line numbers):

```
Application (WordPerfect; "WordPerfect"; Default!; "EN")
//DelHR.wcm: Delete hard returns when pasting from e-mail to
WP

OnError (End)
OnNotFound(End)

PosDocTop ()

Label (DelHRt)
SearchString ("[HRt]") //Click the Codes button, then type
"hrt" to select
```

```
MatchPositionAfter () //and insert the [HRt] code — don't
type the code.
SearchNext ()

If (?RightCode = 204)
      PosCharNext ()
      While (?RightCode = 204)
            DeleteCharNext ()
      EndWhile
Else
      DeleteCharPrevious ()
      Type (Text: " ") //Type a single space between the
quotes.
EndIf
Go (DelHRt)

Label (End)
```

Playing your macros

Now create a macro to play the first two macros:

1. Open a blank document, press Ctrl+F10, give the macro a name of "CleanPaste," and then click Record.

2. Type //, click Macro toolbar Stop icon, and then close the document without saving it.

3. Click Tools ⇨ Macro ⇨ Edit, select CleanPaste and click Edit, and then create the following code (don't type the line numbers):

```
Application (WordPerfect; "WordPerfect"; Default!; "EN")
//CleanPaste.wcm: Delete spaces and hard returns when pasting
from e-mail to WP

Display (Off!)
OnError (End)

Run (?PathMacros + "DelSpace.wcm")
Run (?PathMacros + "DelHR.wcm")

Label (End)
```

More Help on Writing Macros

There's much, much more you can do with macro programming. You'll find more information and examples within the WordPerfect Office Help facilities. From WordPerfect, click Help ⇨ Help Topics ⇨ Contents, and then do either of the following:

✦ Double-click the "Recordings, macros, and automation features" book for detailed information on writing and editing macros (see Figure 58-21).

Figure 58-21: Getting online Help about writing and editing macros.

✦ Double-click the "Reference information" book, double-click the "WordPerfect macros help" book, and then double click the "Lists of commands" book (see Figure 58-22) for detailed lists of system variables, product commands, and programming commands (see Figure 58-23).

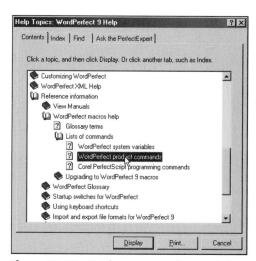

Figure 58-22: Getting macro reference information.

Figure 58-23: Browsing the list of
WordPerfect product commands.

Note   If various components of a macro's online Help are not installed, you can follow
the installation instructions that appear.

If you're heavily involved in programming, you can install the Software Developer's
Kit (SDK) on your WP Office CD. Among the things you'll find are a Macro Code
Wizard, a Dialog Callback Wizard, detailed file descriptions, a WP Document Viewer,
and tools for integrating with Delphi or Visual Basic programming languages (see
Figure 58-24).

Figure 58-24: WordPerfect Office Software Developer's Kit.

For More Information . . .

On	See
Using default keyboard assignments	Chapter 16
Assigning macros to keyboards, menus, and toolbars	Chapter 57
Using templates	Chapter 28
Using the PerfectExperts	Chapter 5
Understanding operators and their order of precedence	Chapter 32

✦   ✦   ✦

Setting Up WordPerfect Office 2000

As you saw in Chapter 1, the various editions of WordPerfect Office 2000 offer a huge variety of applications and options. This appendix provides a road map to what you can install and how to install them.

Sizing Up Your Installation Options

During the installation, you're offered the following three setup choices:

+ *Typical* — what the average user needs, minus the extra bells and whistles.

+ *Compact* — to trim the components down to their essentials. (You won't have the writing tools and other secondary features.)

+ *Custom* — to have complete control over which applications and features are installed.

New Feature Thanks to the Install-As-You-Go feature, you can save disk space by selecting the typical or compact setup, and then letting the program automatically install additional features as you use them.

You can also add applications and components at any time by running a general office update (see "Adding WordPerfect Office Components," later in this appendix).

If you're hard-pressed for disk space, you can check the CD-ROM Based option with any of the setups to run a number of essential files from the CD. While this saves disk space, you'll take a major performance hit because CD access is much slower. You'll also have to leave the CD in the drive whenever you run WordPerfect Office 2000.

The typical Office setup for the Professional version, including Paradox 9, costs you 289MB of disk space. An exorbitant amount, you say? Not when you consider that hard disks are now going for less than three cents a megabyte. At that price, the disk space for a typical setup of the Standard Office runs around $5 — not much consolation, perhaps, if you bought your machine a couple of years ago and you're short on disk space.

Table A-1 shows the core WordPerfect Office 2000 applications, along with the optional components you can select.

Table A-1
Core Applications and Their Optional Components

Core Application	Optional Components
WordPerfect 9	Program Files, Help Files, Macros, Equation Editor, Java Applet Support, PerfectExpert Project Files (Common, Business, Personal, PaperDirect), Borders, Trellix 2.1 (Document Designs, Program Files, Samples)
Quattro Pro 9	Program Files, @functions, Database Imports/Filters, Help Files, PerfectExpert Project Files (Business, Personal), Samples, Database Desktop, Mapping, Drag and Drop Image from Browser, OLAP
Corel Presentations 9	Program Files, Help Files, Sample Slide Show, Masters (selectable), Import Filters (selectable), Sound Files (Sound Effects, MIDI music, WAV music (all selectable)), Movie Clips, Macros, Macro Help Files, PerfectExpert Project Files (Business, Personal, Teaching and Training), CorelMEMO, Show on the Go, Graphicsland
CorelCENTRAL 9	Program Files, Help Files, Address Book Files, Card File Files, Nexal NexCard SQL Service Provider
Paradox 9	Program Files, Help Files, Delphi Add-In Kit, Experts (selectable), PerfectExpert Project Files (selectable), Samples (Paradox Samples, Framework Samples, Tutorial), Web Utilities (Publish to HTML, Corel Web Server, Corel Web Server Samples), Paradox ODBC Files

Table A-2 shows the bonus applications and utilities in WordPerfect Office 2000, plus other optional components used by more than one core application.

Table A-2	
Bonus Applications and Shared Options	
Bonus Application or Option	**Description**
Reference Center	Program documentation viewed in the Acrobat Reader
Graphics	Additional backgrounds, textures, clip art and photos
XML 9 Authoring Tools	Program and tools for creating XML Web documents
Utilities	Bitstream Font Navigator, DAD 9, Scrapbook, QuickFinder, Corel Versions, TextArt, Customer Support, VBA 6 Scripting Support, Borland Database Engine Version 5.01, SQL Link Drivers
Conversion File Types	Various import and export conversions for text and graphics
Writing Tools	Spelling and grammar tools in various languages
Trellix 2.1	Structured web publishing from WordPerfect
Dragon NaturallySpeaking 3.0	Files and utilities to speech-enable core applications
NetPerfect	Corporate Web server
Corel Print Office	Design layout and image editing
Adobe Acrobat Reader	View portable document files including Reference Center documents
Paradox Web Form Designer	Create platform-independent Web forms
SDK	Tools for software developers (separate setup in SDK folder on the CD)

Reviewing Your Requirements

Now that you know what's in WordPerfect Office 2000, you can tailor your setup to your particular needs. You can start with a typical or custom setup, then add bonus applications (such as Corel Print House, NetPerfect, or Corel Versions) if and when you need them.

What kind of machine do you need? In addition to the necessary hard disk space, Corel recommends the following minimum specifications:

✦ Personal computer with a 80486, 66MHz processor (Dragon Systems recommends a 150MHz processor for speech)

✦ Microsoft Windows 95/98/NT

✦ 16MB RAM (64MB recommended for Dragon speech)

✦ VGA graphics adapter and monitor

✦ CD-ROM drive

✦ Mouse or other pointing device

If your machine is at the low end of these specifications, it will be slow, indeed. Basically, if you're running Windows 95/98/NT, you should have no problem with the WordPerfect Office 2000, aside from the additional speech requirements.

Setting Up WordPerfect Office 2000

Now that you know what you need, you can set up WordPerfect Office 2000. There are three types of installation: on a stand-alone machine, to a network (if you're a systems administrator), or to a network location.

You don't need to delete earlier versions of WordPerfect applications before installing WordPerfect Office 2000, unless you need to free up the disk space. The new files will not overwrite the old. Settings and QuickCorrect entries from WordPerfect 7/8 will be incorporated into WordPerfect 9.

Installing on your machine

To install WordPerfect Office 2000 on your machine:

1. Close any open applications and virus protection.

2. Insert the WordPerfect Office 2000 CD-ROM. to display the WordPerfect Office 2000 Setup screen in Figure A-1. (Click Release Notes if you want to read any last-minute product information.)

Note   If the setup screen doesn't appear, click the Start button on the Windows taskbar, click Run, then type **D:\Setup** (where D is the letter of your CD-ROM drive).

3. Click Corel WordPerfect Office Setup, then follow the prompts to:

• Accept the license agreement

• Enter your name and company (if it exists)

• Enter your serial number from the WordPerfect Office 2000 Product Authenticity Card

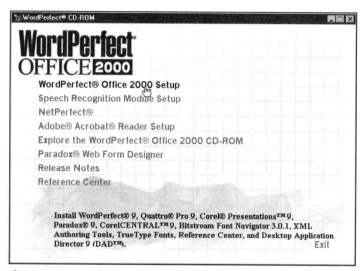

Figure A-1: WordPerfect Office 2000 setup screen.

4. Select the type of setup you want (Figure A-2).

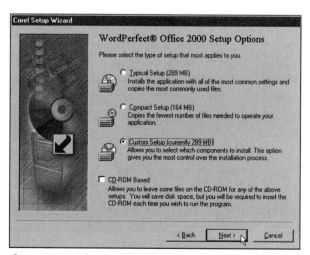

Figure A-2: Selecting the setup type you want.

5. If you selected a custom setup, you can select or deselect several levels of individual components (Figure A-3).

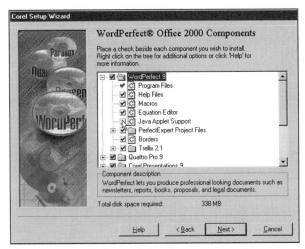

Figure A-3: Selecting individual components for a custom setup.

6. Select the conversion filters you want to install (Figure A-4). Normally the defaults will suffice.

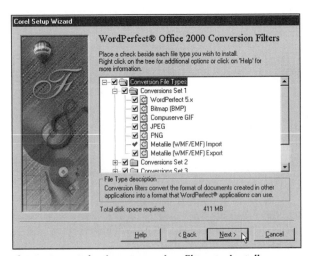

Figure A-4: Selecting conversion filters to install.

7. Select writing tools for the additional languages you want to install (Figure A-5). You can also change the default language from the drop-down list.

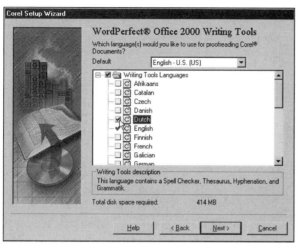

Figure A-5: Selecting writing tools for additional languages.

8. Select any fonts you want to install (Figure A-6). The installation defaults to a representative selection, including the special symbol fonts.

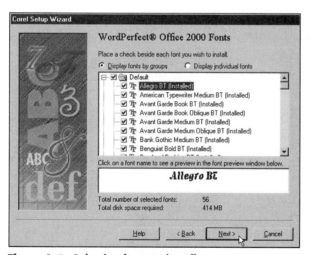

Figure A-6: Selecting fonts to install.

9. Make any changes to the destination folder and short folder, if necessary, and then review your selections and click Install (Figure A-7).

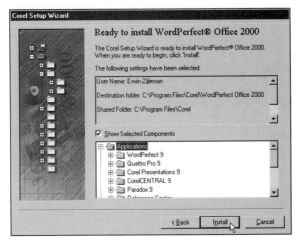

Figure A-7: Final review before the installation.

10. If you want the CorelCENTRAL Day Planner to be loaded whenever you start Windows, answer Yes when prompted (Figure A-8).

Figure A-8: Choosing whether the CorelCENTRAL Day Planner automatically loads when you start Windows.

Registering WordPerfect Office 2000

At the end of the installation process, you are prompted to register WordPerfect Office 2000 online (Figure A-9) for product updates and support (Internet access is required). If you don't register online, you can fill out the WordPerfect Office 2000 Product Authenticity Card and return it to Corel, or fill in the Web registration form at `www.corel.com/support/onlineregistration.htm`.

Installing the speech recognition module

To install the speech recognition module for WordPerfect Office 2000:

1. Insert the WordPerfect Office 2000 CD-ROM.

2. Click Speech Recognition Module Setup, and then follow the prompts to install and register Dragon NaturallySpeaking (Figure A-10).

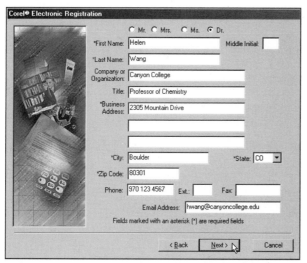

Figure A-9: Registering WordPerfect Office 2000 over the Internet.

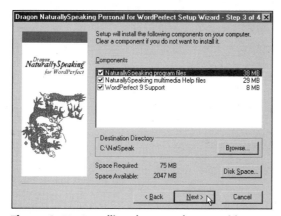

Figure A-10: Installing the speech recognition module.

Installing to a network server or location

For complete information on network installation and administration for WordPerfect Office 2000:

1. Insert the WordPerfect Office 2000 CD-ROM.

2. Click Reference Center, and then click the Network Administrator reference icon.

Adding WordPerfect Office Components

After you've been using WordPerfect Office 2000 for a time, you may decide that you want to add certain components that aren't automatically handled by Install-As-You-Go, such as additional export filters or graphics:

1. On the Windows taskbar, click Start ⇨ Programs ⇨ WordPerfect Office 2000 ⇨ Setup and Notes ⇨ Corel Setup Program.

2. Select Add New Components (Figure A-11), and then follow the prompts and select the additional components you want.

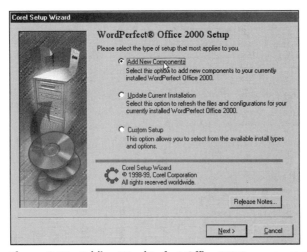

Figure A-11: Adding WordPerfect Office 2000 components.

Removing WordPerfect Office Components

If you aren't using some WordPerfect Office components, you can remove them in order to free up disk space:

1. On the Windows taskbar, click Start ⇨ Programs ⇨ WordPerfect Office 2000 ⇨ Setup and Notes ⇨ Corel Remove Program.

2. Follow the prompts, selecting the components you want to remove.

Refreshing Your WordPerfect Office Installation

You can refresh your WordPerfect Office installation in the event that something isn't working right or you accidentally delete an application file:

1. On the Windows taskbar, click Start ➪ Programs ➪ WordPerfect Office 2000 ➪ Setup and Notes ➪ Corel Setup Program.

2. Select Update Current Installation and follow the prompts.

Customizing Your DAD Display

To customize your DAD display, right-click among the Office icons, click Properties, then do any of the following (see Figure A-12):

✦ Click Add, select a program to add, such as a dictionary or calculator not part of WordPerfect Office, and then click Open.

✦ Click Delete to remove the highlighted icon.

✦ Click Properties to change the icon or its properties.

✦ Check or uncheck "Include DAD in Startup folder," depending on whether you want DAD to automatically appear when you start Windows.

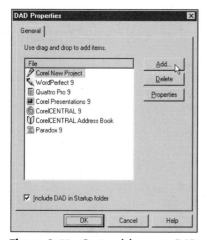

Figure A-12: Customizing your DAD display.

Installing Bitstream Font Navigator

WordPerfect Office 2000 comes with the Bitstream Font navigator—a powerful utility that lets you view, organize, install, and remove the fonts on your system. To install the Bitstream Font Navigation select it during a custom setup, or add it to your current installation (see the section "Adding WordPerfect Office Components" earlier in this appendix.)

For information on using Bitstream Font Navigator see Chapter 8, "Fonts Fantastic."

✦   ✦   ✦

WordPerfect Settings Quick Reference

A *setting* is any element in your working environment that stays put from session to session. Thus, a change to the Current Document Style is not a setting, but a change to the Default Document Style is a setting that affects future documents. A change of keyboards or a customized shortcut key is also a setting, as it stays put until you change it again. A custom style or macro is not a setting, as it is only applied when called upon. A custom page or envelope size could become the new default.

Several Windows settings that have a major impact on the suite's working environment are shown in Table B-1.

Table B-1
Some Windows Settings That Affect
the WordPerfect Office Environment

Setting	Chapter	How to Access It	Recommended Setting
Screen fonts	None	Right-click Windows desktop, click Properties ⇨ Settings	Small Fonts
Screen font smoothing	None	Right-click Windows desktop and click Properties. Click the Effects tab in Windows 98, or the Plus! tab (if installed) in Windows 95	Smooth edges of screen fonts.
Screen resolution	3	Right-click Windows desktop, click Properties ⇨ Settings	800 x 600
Show filename extensions in file dialog boxes	7	Right-click the Taskbar Start button, and click Explore ⇨ View ⇨ Options	Leave "Hide MS-DOS file extensions..." unchecked
Show path in file dialog boxes	7	Right-click the Taskbar Start button, and click Explore ⇨ View ⇨ Options	Check "Display the full MS-DOS path in the title bar"
Taskbar display	3	Right-click Taskbar click Properties	"Always on top" and "Auto hide"

WordPerfect has the most user settings of any of the WP Office applications, although some user settings in previous versions, such as the document view and zoom, are now "sticky" settings that automatically default to your last selection. While most of the user settings discussed in this book are found among WordPerfect's Settings dialog boxes, many are not. Table B-2 shows user settings, the chapter in which they are discussed, how to access them, and, where applicable, the author's recommended settings.

Table B-2
WordPerfect User Settings Quick Reference

Setting	Chapter	How to Access It	Recommended Setting
Application bar, customizing	29	Right-click application bar, click Settings	
Backup folder	6, 29	Tools ➪ Settings ➪ Files	
Bar display	3, 57	View ➪ Toolbars	
Beeps, program	29	Tools ➪ Settings ➪ Environment ➪ Prompts	
Border, fancy, folder	29, 57	Tools ➪ Settings ➪ Files ➪ Graphic	
Code pages, changing	29	Tools ➪ Settings ➪ Environment ➪ General, Code Page	
Codes, deleting the old DOS way	29	Tools ➪ Settings ➪ Environment ➪ Prompts ➪ "Confirm deletion of codes..."	Leave unchecked
Comment display	18	Tools ➪ Settings ➪ Display	Check Margin Icons to see comments
Comment and summary user information	18, 29	Tools ➪ Settings ➪ Environment	
Document backup	6	Tools ➪ Settings ➪ Files ➪ Document	Timed every 10 minutes; no original backup
Document, default extension	29	Tools ➪ Settings ➪ Files ➪ Document	Leave default .wpd
Document, default save format	29	Tools ➪ Settings ➪ Files ➪ Document	WordPerfect 6/7/8/9
Document defaults, setting	21	File ➪ Document ➪ Current Document Style ➪ check "Use as default"	
Document folder, default	29	Tools ➪ Settings ➪ Files ➪ Document	The one you use the most

Continued

Table B-2 (*continued*)

Setting	Chapter	How to Access It	Recommended Setting
Document summary configuration	7	File ⇨ Properties ⇨ Setup ⇨ Use as Default	
Document summary (automatic) settings	7, 29	Tools ⇨ Settings ⇨ Summary	Normally leave options unchecked
Drag to create graphics	29	Tools ⇨ Settings ⇨ Environment ⇨ Graphics	Leave unchecked, use shadow cursor instead
Equation Editor, default	29	Tools ⇨ Settings ⇨ Environment ⇨ Graphics	
Endnote options	24	Insert ⇨ Footnote/ Endnote ⇨ Options	
Envelopes, custom sizes	19	File ⇨ Page Setup ⇨ Size ⇨ Options ⇨ New	
Envelope options	19	Format ⇨ Envelope, then click the Bar Code and Envelope Positions buttons on the property bar	
Favorites, update with changes option	29	Tools ⇨ Settings ⇨ Files	Leave unchecked
File-management display	7	File ⇨ Open ⇨ View	Check Toolbar and Status Bar; leave menu bar for Favorites; No Preview
Fast Search indexes (configuring)	7	File ⇨ Open ⇨ Advanced ⇨ Index Manager ⇨ Quick Finder Configuration	
Fast Search indexes (enable/disable timed updates)	7	Double-click Scheduler icon on Taskbar	
Fast Search settings	7	File ⇨ Open ⇨ Advanced ⇨ Index Manager ⇨ Fast Search Setup (Standard/ Custom) ⇨ Settings	See Table 7-4

Setting	Chapter	How to Access It	Recommended Setting
Favorites folder, adding to	7	File ⇨ Open ⇨ Favorites	
File dialogs, enhanced	29	Tools ⇨ Settings ⇨ Files	Leave checked
Find and Replace options	18	Edit ⇨ Find and Replace ⇨ Options	
Folder, default document	29	Tools ⇨ Settings ⇨ Files ⇨ Document	
Font, document and printer default	21	File ⇨ Document ⇨ Default Font	
Footnote options	24	Insert ⇨ Footnote/ Endnote ⇨ Options	
Format-As-You-Go options	17	Tools ⇨ QuickCorrect ⇨ Format-As-You-Go	
Grammatik, customizing checking styles	52	Tools ⇨ Grammatik ⇨ Options ⇨ Checking Styles	
Grammatik options	52	Tools ⇨ Grammatik ⇨ Options	
Graphics display	29	Tools ⇨ Settings ⇨ Display	
Graphics folders, default	29	Tools ⇨ Settings ⇨ Files ⇨ Graphic	
Guideline display	16	View ⇨ Guidelines	
Hidden text display	18	Tools ⇨ Settings ⇨ Display ⇨ Document	Leave unchecked (hidden) and turn on from View menu when you need to see it
Hyperlink activate option	29	Tools ⇨ Settings ⇨ Environment	Check
Hyphenation prompt option	20	Tools ⇨ Settings ⇨ Environment ⇨ Prompts	When Required
Hyphenation zone, setting	20	Tools ⇨ Language ⇨ Hyphenation	

Continued

Table B-2 (*continued*)

Setting	Chapter	How to Access It	Recommended Setting
Keyboard, creating and customizing	57	Tools ⇨ Settings ⇨ Customize ⇨ Keyboards	
Keyboard, selecting	1, 29	Tools ⇨ Settings ⇨ Customize ⇨ Keyboards	
Label file and default labels display	27	Tools ⇨ Settings ⇨ Files ⇨ Labels	Set default labels display to your type of printer
Language tools, selecting	52	Tools ⇨ Language ⇨ Settings	
Language Resource Database, editing	52	Tools ⇨ Language ⇨ Settings ⇨ Edit LRS	
Menus, creating and customizing	57	Tools ⇨ Customize ⇨ Menus	
Menu display options	29	Tools ⇨ Settings ⇨ Environment ⇨ Interface	Display Last opened documents and QuickTips (When "Shortcut keys" is unchecked, the shortcut keys still appear in the QuickTips)
Menu, selecting	29	Right-click menu	
Merge codes display options	29	Tools ⇨ Settings ⇨ Display ⇨ Merge	Display merge codes (setting can be changed during merge)
Merge/Macro file settings	29	Tools ⇨ Settings ⇨ Files ⇨ Merge/Macro	
Mouse, select words with	2, 29	Tools ⇨ Settings ⇨ Environment ⇨ General	Check "Automatically select whole words when dragging..."
Page, custom definition	21	File ⇨ Page Setup ⇨ Options ⇨ New	

Setting	Chapter	How to Access It	Recommended Setting
Page size and orientation	13	File ⇨ Page Setup ⇨ Size	
Print, custom settings	13	File ⇨ Print ⇨ Settings	
Print resolution and color	13	File ⇨ Print ⇨ Details	
Prompt-As-You-Go	2	Tools ⇨ Proofread	Check unless it slows your computer
Printer, adding	13	File ⇨ Print ⇨ Details ⇨ System Printers	
Printer, selecting and configuring	13	File ⇨ Print ⇨ Details	
Property bars, customizing	57	Tools ⇨ Settings ⇨ Customize ⇨ Property Bars	
Property bar display	3, 29	Right-click property bar, click Settings ⇨ Options	
Proofreading-As-You-Go	2, 52	Tools ⇨ Proofread	Grammar-As-You-Go
QuickCorrect formatting options	17	Tools ⇨ QuickCorrect ⇨ Format-As-You-Go	
QuickCorrect replacement (on/off)	17	Tools ⇨ QuickCorrect, "Replace words as you type"	
QuickFinder Fast Search Indexing Settings	7	File ⇨ Open ⇨ Advanced ⇨ Index Manager ⇨ Fast Search Setup ⇨ Settings	See Table 7-4
QuickMark, set on save/go to on open	17	Tools ⇨ Bookmark	
QuickWords, expanding as formatted or plain text	52	Tools ⇨ QuickWords ⇨ Options	Check Expand as text with formatting
RealTime Preview (using)	16	Tools ⇨ Settings ⇨ Display	Leave checked

Continued

Table B-2 (continued)

Setting	Chapter	How to Access It	Recommended Setting
Redline method, changing	18	File ⇨ Document ⇨ Redline Method	
Reformat document for default printer option	29	Tools ⇨ Settings ⇨ Environment ⇨ General	Leave checked
Reveal Codes display options	29	Tools ⇨ Settings ⇨ Display ⇨ Reveal Codes	Wrap lines, show spaces as bullets, show codes in detail
Ruler options	29	Tools ⇨ Settings ⇨ Display ⇨ Ruler	Check both options
Save workspace options	29	Tools ⇨ Settings ⇨ Environment ⇨ Interface	
Scroll bar display	16, 29	Tools ⇨ Settings ⇨ Display	Vertical
Sentence correction options	17	Tools ⇨ QuickCorrect ⇨ Format-As-You-Go	
Shadow cursor display	16, 29	Tools ⇨ Settings ⇨ Display	Snap to Margins, Active in Both
SmartQuotes (on/off)	17	Tools ⇨ QuickCorrect ⇨ SmartQuotes	
Sort options	53	Tools ⇨ Sort ⇨ Options	Allow Undo after sorting
SpeedLinks	14	Tools ⇨ QuickCorrect ⇨ SpeedLinks	
Spell Check options	52	Tools ⇨ Spell Check ⇨ Options	
Spreadsheet/ Database folders	29	Tools ⇨ Settings ⇨ Files ⇨ Spreadsheet/ Database	
Symbol display options	29	Tools ⇨ Settings ⇨ Display ⇨ Symbols	
Tab Bar icon display	29	Tools ⇨ Settings ⇨ Display ⇨ Document	Check "Margin icons"

Setting	Chapter	How to Access It	Recommended Setting
Table formulas, confirm deletion of	29	Tools ⇨ Settings ⇨ Environment ⇨ Prompts	Leave checked
Table gridline display	29	Tools ⇨ Settings ⇨ Display	Leave unchecked, turn on and off from View menu
Table position, default	22	Table ⇨ Format ⇨ Table ⇨ Table position on page	
Table, auto calculation	26	Table ⇨ Calculate	Calculate tables in doc; update associated charts
Template, default	29	Tools ⇨ Settings ⇨ Files ⇨ Template	
Template, updating default option	29	Tools ⇨ Settings ⇨ Files ⇨ Template	
Thesaurus options	52	Tools ⇨ Thesaurus ⇨ Options	
Toolbars, creating and customizing	57	Tools ⇨ Settings ⇨ Customize ⇨ Toolbars	
Toolbar display	29, 57	Right-click toolbar, click Settings ⇨ Options	"Show scroll bar"
Toolbar, selecting	57	Right-click toolbar	
Typos, automatically correcting	52	Tools ⇨ QuickCorrect	Check "Correct other mistyped words when possible" (except for scientific writing)
Undo/Redo options	6	Edit ⇨ Undo/Redo History ⇨ Options	
Units of measure	29	Tools ⇨ Settings ⇨ Display ⇨ Document	

Continued

Table B-2 (*continued*)

Setting	Chapter	How to Access It	Recommended Setting
Viewer setup	7	File ⇨ Open ⇨ View ⇨ Preview	
View/Zoom, default	16	View menu selections	Experiment to find the view and zoom you're comfortable with
Warning beep options	29	Tools ⇨ Settings ⇨ Environment ⇨ Prompts	
Windows metafile options	29	Tools ⇨ Settings ⇨ Convert ⇨ Convert	
Windows system colors (using)	29	Tools ⇨ Settings ⇨ Display	Leave checked unless you have a custom color scheme
Word lists, creating	52	Tools ⇨ Spell Checker ⇨ Options	
Word lists, specifying	52	Tools ⇨ Spell Checker ⇨ Options ⇨ User word lists	
Writing tools, disabling	52	Tools ⇨ Language ⇨ Settings	

✦   ✦   ✦

Dragon Naturally-Speaking Quick Reference

This quick reference lists the commands you can say with the WordPerfect Special Edition of Dragon NaturallySpeaking. Pause briefly before and after saying commands (or hold down the Ctrl key) so they'll be recognized as commands, rather than as text. Many commands have optional parameters you can speak.

Pausing the Microphone

To . . .	Say . . .
Pause the microphone	Go to Sleep
Release the pause	Wake Up

Dictating Numbers

To Enter . . .	Say . . .
Numeral 1–9	Numeral one–nine
4	Four
No. 4	Number four
46	Forty-six
253	Two fifty-three

Continued

	(continued)
To Enter . . .	Say . . .
13,684	Thirteen thousand six hundred eighty-four, or thirteen comma six eight four
VI	Roman six
XIX	Roman nineteen
XLII	Roman forty-two
June 21, 1999	June twenty-one comma nineteen ninety-nine
August 19, 2004	August nineteen comma two thousand four
April 3, 2006	April three comma twenty oh six
876_5432	Eight seven six five four three two
404-876-5432	Four oh four eight seven six five four three two
$63.29	Sixty-three dollars and twenty-nine cents, or dollar sign sixty-three point twenty-nine
10:00	Ten o'clock
10 P.M.	Ten p m
4:30 P.M.	Four thirty p m

Entering Punctuation and Symbols

To Enter . . .	Say . . .
&	Ampersand
'	Apostrophe
's	Apostrophe s
*	Asterisk
@	At sign
`	Backquote
\	Backslash
^	Caret
>	Close angle bracket
}	Close brace
]	Close bracket

To Enter . . .	Say . . .
"	Close quote
'	Close single quote
)	Close paren/parenthesis
:	Colon
,	Comma
—	Dash
$	Dollar sign
.	Dot
...	Ellipsis
=	Equal sign
!	Exclamation point/mark
/	Forward slash
:-(	Frowny face
>	Greater than
-	Hyphen
{	Left brace
[	Left bracket
(	Left paren/parenthesis
<	Less than
_	Minus sign
#	Number sign
,	Numeric comma
-	Numeric hyphen
‹	Open angle bracket
{	Open brace
[	Open bracket
(	Open paren/parenthesis
"	Open quote
'	Open single quote
.	Period
#	Pound sign

Continued

To Enter . . .	Say . . .
?	Question mark
}	Right brace
]	Right bracket
)	Right paren/parenthesis
;	Semicolon
/	Slash
: -)	Smiley face
a space	Space bar
a tab	Tab key
~	Tilde
_	Underscore
		Vertical bar
; -)	Winky face

Correcting mistakes

To correct the last phrase, say **Correct That;** then, to select a replacement phrase, say **Select** and the number from 1–10 (or say **Choose**, the number, and Click OK).

To spell out your correction, say **Spell That**, followed quickly and continuously by the first four to six correct letters of the word or words.

To correct a previous passage, say **Correct** and then the word or words you want to change.

Asking for Help

To ask for help say **What Can I Say?**, and then say the following:

Say . . .	To . . .
Click button	Navigate in Help via the buttons
Click Help Topics ⇨ Contents	Open the Help contents
Move Up/Down 1–10	Move up or down in the Help contents

Say . . .	To . . .
Open/Close	Open and close Help topics
Switch to Previous/Next Window	Switch among Help, WordPerfect, and other applications

WordPerfect Speech Commands

From within WordPerfect, you can issue any of the speech commands described in this section.

Starting a New Line or Paragraph

To Start a New . . .	Say . . .
Line	New line
Paragraph	New paragraph

Specifying Caps and Spaces

Say . . .	To . . .
Caps word	Capitalize the first letter of a word
All Caps word	Capitalize all the letters in the word
Caps On/Off	Start/stop initial capitalization of all words
All Caps On/Off	Start/stop capitalizing all letters of all words
No Caps On/Off	Start/stop dictating words with no capitalization
Space bar	Enter a space
No Space word	Prevent a space before the word
No Space On/Off	Start/stop no spacing between a series of words

Selecting and revising text

Say **Select**, and the word or phrase you want to change. Then edit your selection with the keyboard or say any of the following:

Say . . .	To . . .
Delete/Scratch That	Delete your selection
Spell That	Spell out your revision by saying the letters, numbers, and punctuation
Correct That	Call up the Correction dialog box
Bold That	Bold your selection
Italicize That	Italicize your selection
Cap That	Make your selection initial caps
All Caps/No Caps That	Make your selection all/no caps
Center That	Center your selection
Left/Right Align That	Left/right align your selection

Setting font attributes

To make a limited number of font changes, say **Set Font** (for the word at the insertion point or from the insertion point on), or **Format That** (for selected text), followed by any combination of the following:

	Face	Size	Style
Set Font/Format That	Arial	4–120	Bold
	Courier		Italics
	Courier New		Plain
	Times		Plain Text
	Times New Roman		Regular
			Underline

You can also say **Set Size** or **Format That Size**.

Deleting text

To delete a selection, say **Scratch That** or **Delete That**.

To delete the last phrase, say **Scratch That**. You can repeat Scratch That up to 10 times.

When no text is selected, saying **Delete That** is the same as pressing the Delete key in WordPerfect.

Cutting, copying, and pasting

To cut, copy, and paste your selections, say **Cut That**, **Copy That**, and **Paste That**.

To copy your entire document to the clipboard, say **Copy All to Clipboard**.

Undoing editing actions

Say **Undo That** to undo your editing actions.

Moving the Insertion Point

Say . . .	Then . . .	Then . . . (if needed)	Then . . . (if needed)
Move to Go to	Top/Bottom		
Move to Go to	Top Start Beginning Bottom End	of	Selection Line Paragraph Document
Move	Left/Right Up/Down	1–20	
Move	Left/Back Right/Forward	1–20	Character(s)
Move	Left/Back Right/Forward	a	Word
Move	Left/Back Right/Forward	1–20	Word(s)
Move	Up/Back Down/Forward	1–20	Line(s)

Continued

		(continued)	
Say . . .	*Then . . .*	*Then . . . (if needed)*	*Then . . . (if needed)*
Move	Up/Back Down/Forward	a	Paragraph
Move	Up/Back Down/Forward	1–20	Paragraph(s)

Quattro Pro Speech Commands

In Quattro Pro, you can use Dragon to enter, select, and edit data, apply numeric formats, navigate your notebook, and much more. One especially nice feature is the ability to say menu commands, such "File New," "File Close," or "Go to Draft View."

To start Dragon in Quattro Pro, click Tools ➪ Dragon.

Issuing Menu Commands

To . . .	Say . . .
Open a new notebook	File New
Open a new project template	File New Project
Open a file	File Open
Close the current file	File Close
Save the current file	File Save
Save the file with a new name	File Save As
Print the current file	File Print
Open the Styles dialog box	Format Style
Open the Active Cells dialog box	Format Selection
Open the Active Sheet dialog box	Format Sheet
Open the Active Notebook dialog box	Format Notebook
Open the Settings dialog box	Application Settings
Go into edit mode (double-click)	Edit Cell
Calculate a formula	Calculate

Applying Styles

To Set Numbers to Show . . .	Say . . .
Commas and decimals	Format Comma
Commas and no decimals	Format Comma Zero
Currency and two decimals	Format Currency
Currency and no decimals	Format Currency Zero
The default date format	Format Date
A fixed numeric format, no decimals	Format Fixed
Percent	Format Percent
Totals (a double line above a cell)	Format Total

To Set Text to Show . . .	Say . . .
Arial font, 18-pt. bold	Format Heading One
Arial font, 12-pt. bold	Format Heading Two
Default styles for text	Format Normal

Changing Your View

To . . .	Say . . .
Go to Draft view	View Draft
Go to Page view	View Page
Go to Page Breaks view	View Page Breaks
Go to the Objects sheet	View Objects
Define locked titles	View Locked Titles
Go to Print Preview	View Print Preview
View all comments on a spreadsheet	View Comments
View all formulas on a spreadsheet	View Formulas

Editing Spreadsheets

To . . .	Say . . .
Enter data in a cell	Enter
To delete the last command	Undo That
To cut selected cells	Cut That
To copy selected cells	Copy That
To paste selected cells	Paste That
Delete cell contents	Delete Cells
Delete cell contents and formatting	Clear Cells
Delete cell values only	Clear Values
Delete cell formats only	Clear Formats
Delete cell comments	Clear Comments
Edit cell comments	Edit Comment

Formatting Data

To . . .	Say . . .
Bold the selected data	Format Bold
Italicize the selected data	Format Italic
Underline the selected data	Format Underline
Make the selected data superscript	Format Superscript
Make the selected data subscript	Format Subscript
Put a strikeout line through data	Format Strikeout
Display the SpeedFormat dialog box	Speed Format
Display text vertically	Format Vertical
Wrap the text within the cell	Format Word Wrap
Join cells together	Format Join Cells
Align cell content on the left of cell	Align Left
Center cell content	Align Center
Align cell content on the right of cell	Align Right

To . . .	Say . . .
Align content over several cells	Align Across
Indent cell content	Align Indent
Align content with the top of cell	Align Top
Align content with the bottom of cell	Align Bottom

Inserting Spreadsheet Components

To Insert A . . .	Say . . .
Cell	Insert Cell
Column	Insert Column
Row	Insert Row
Spreadsheet	Insert Sheet
Chart	Insert Chart
Comment	Insert Comment
Formula	Insert Formula

Navigating Your Notebook

To . . .	Say . . .
Move to a new line to enter data	New Line
Click the Cancel button	Cancel
Escape from a dialog box	Escape
Move across cells to the right	Tab
Move across cells to the left	Back Tab
Move to start of spreadsheet	Go to Home, Go to Sheet Start
Move to end of spreadsheet	Go to End
Move to start of document	Go to Document Start
Move to the end of the spreadsheet	Go to Sheet End
Move to the beginning of a column	Go to Column Start
Move to the end of a column	Go to Column End

Continued

(continued)	
To . . .	*Say . . .*
Move to the beginning of row	Go to Row Start
Move to the end of a row	Go to Row End
Access the Go To dialog box	Go To Dialog
Move up one cell	Move Up
Move down one cell	Move Down
Move left one cell	Move Left
Move right one cell	Move Right
Move the selected word to the left	Move Word Left
Move the selected word to the right	Move Word Right

Selecting Data

To . . .	*Say . . .*
Select the cell above	Select Up
Select the cell below	Select Down
Select the cell to the left	Select Left
Select the cell to the right	Select Right
Select the word on the left	Select Word Left
Select the word on the right	Select Word Right
Select the first cell with data	Select Home
Select the last cell with data	Select End
Select the first cell on the sheet	Select Sheet Start
Select the last cell on the sheet	Select Sheet End
Select the first cell in the column	Select Column Start
Select the last cell in the column	Select Column End
Select the first cell in the row	Select Row Start
Select the last cell in the row	Select Row End

Using Functions

To Use the Spreadsheet Function . . .	Say . . .
SUM	Speed Sum
MIN	Speed Minimum
MAX	Speed Maximum
AVG	Speed Average
PUREAVG	Speed Pure Average
COUNT	Speed Count
PURECOUNT	Speed Pure Count
MULT	Speed Multiply
PAYMT	Speed Payment
RATE	Speed Rate
IRATE	Speed Irate
TERM	Speed Term
PV	Speed Present Value
FV	Speed Future Value

Zooming Your Display

To Zoom . . .	Say . . .
25%	Zoom 25
50%	Zoom 50
75%	Zoom 75
100%	Zoom 100
125%	Zoom 125
150%	Zoom 150
200%	Zoom 200
A selection of cells	Zoom Selection

Paradox Speech Commands

Use Dragon in Paradox to navigate tables, records, and cells; enter and edit data; and more.

To start Dragon in Paradox, click Tools ➪ Dragon NaturallySpeaking.

Changing Your View

To . . .	Say . . .
Go to Edit mode	Edit Data
Go to View mode	View Data

Editing Data and Records

To . . .	Say . . .
Copy the selected data	Copy That
Cut the selected data	Cut That
Paste the selected data	Paste That
Delete the selected data	Delete That
Undo the last voice command	Undo, Undo That
Insert a record	Insert Record
Delete a record	Delete Record

Deleting Table Data

To Delete . . .	Say . . .
Words in a field	Delete Previous Word
	Delete Back Word
	Delete Next Word
	Delete Forward Word
	Delete Previous [#] Words
	Delete Back [#] Words
	Delete Next [#] Words
	Delete Forward [#] Words

To Delete . . .	Say . . .
A line	Delete Line
Characters in a field	Delete Next Character
	Delete Forward Character
	Delete Previous Character
	Delete Back Character
	Delete Next [#] Characters
	Delete Forward [#] Characters
	Delete Previous [#] Characters
	Delete Back [#] Characters
A record	Delete Record

Moving Around Cell Entries and Memo Fields

To Navigate . . .	Say . . .
Documents (Memo text)	Tab Key
	New Paragraph
	Go To Top
	Go To Top of Document
	Go To Start of Document
	Go To Beginning of Document
	Go To Bottom
	Go To Bottom of Document
	Go To End
	Go To End of Document
Lines	New Line
	Go To Top of Line
	Go To Start of Line
	Go To Beginning of Line
	Go To End of Line
	Go To Bottom of Line
	Move Up One Line
	Move Back One Line
	Move Down One Line
	Move Forward One Line
	Move Up [#] Lines
	Move Back [#] Lines
	Move Down [#] Lines
	Move Forward [#] Lines

Continued

	(continued)
To Navigate . . .	Say . . .
Words	Move Left One Word
	Move Back One Word
	Move Right One Word
	Move Forward One Word
	Move Left [#] Words
	Move Back [#] Words
	Move Right [#] Words
	Move Forward [#} Words

Moving Around Cells and Fields

To Navigate . . .	Say . . .
Cells	Next Cell
	Previous Cell
	Move Right [1–20] Cells
	Move Forward [1–20] Cells
	Move Left [1–20] Cells
	Move Back [1–20] Cells
Fields	Next Field
	Previous Field
	Move Right [1–20] Fields
	Move Forward [1–20] Fields
	Move Left [1–20] Fields
	Move Back [1–20] Fields

Moving Around Records and Tables

To Navigate . . .	Say . . .
Records	Go to Next Record
	Go to Start of Record
	Go to Previous Record
	Go to Beginning of Record
	Go to Top of Record
	Go to End of Record
	Go to Bottom of Record
	Move Down [1–20] Records
	Move Forward [1–20] Records

To Navigate . . .	Say . . .
	Move Up [1–20] Records
	Move Back [1–20] Records
Tables	Go to End of Table
	Go to Bottom of Table
	Go to Top of Table
	Go to Start of Table
	Go to Beginning of Table
Columns	Next Column
	Previous Column
	Move Right [1–20] Columns
	Move Forward [1–20] Columns
	Move Left [1–20] Columns
	Move Back [1–20] Columns
Rows	Next Row
	Previous Row
	Go to Beginning of Row
	Go to Start of Row
	Go to Top of Row
	Go to End of Row
	Go to Bottom of Row
	Move Down [1–20] Rows
	Move Forward [1–20] Rows
	Move Up [1–20] Rows
	Move Back [1–20] Rows

Selecting Items in Fields

To Select . . .	Say . . .
Words	Select Previous Word
	Select Back Word
	Select Next Word
	Select Forward Word
	Select Previous [#] Words
	Select Back [#] Words
	Select Next [#] Words
	Select Forward [#] Words
A Line	Select Line

Continued

(continued)	
To select . . .	_Say . . ._
Characters	Select Next Character
	Select Forward Character
	Select Previous Character
	Select Back Character
	Select Next [#] Characters
	Select Forward [#] Characters
	Select Previous [#] Characters
	Select Back [#] Characters

✦   ✦   ✦

Index

continued

continued

G

continued

H

continued

continued

continued

continued

continued

continued

continued

continued

continued

my2cents.idgbooks.com